ALDER

Theatre

Who pulls the st₁

THE ULTIMATE CONSPIRACY!

Volume I

About The World Order, bloodlines, Atlantis,
The World Grid, Magnetic Reversals, Global Weather, Magicians,
Cosmic Powers, Secret Lodges, Secret Codes, Phi, Pi, Occult, Scientologists
UFOs, European Union, Extra-terrestrials, Cosmic Computing Intelligence,
Apocalypse, Iraq, Genetic Engineering, DNA, Atoms, Standing Waves,
The Hidden Science, God Genes, The Minoans, The Holy Grail, Druids,
Re-incarnation, September 11, Galactic Confederations, Crop Circles,
Rosicrucians, Mind Control, a Conspiracy against Planet Earth
and a plan that has never ceased to exist.

For book orders including other books written by the Author (referenced)
please address to:
Alpha Education Ltd
P.O. Box 2
Rottingdean
Brighton
BN2 8JW
U.K.

ISBN 0-9529567-1-3
First printing 2001-05-27
Printed & bound by Antony Rowe Ltd, Eastbourne

THE PLATONIC MAXIM IS 'BEFORE YOU CAN CURE A MAN 'S
BODY YOU MUST CURE HIS MIND AND BEFORE THAT HIS SOUL '
–THE QUESTION BECOMES HOW DO YOU CURE A

MANS 'S <u>SOUL</u>?

THIS BOOK IS ABOUT THE BATTLE FOR MAN 'S <u>SPIRIT</u>

This book is available in four volumes and can be ordered from all good
bookshops as well as Amazon. It may also be purchased directly from the
publisher through the internet *www.alpha-education.co.uk* The contents of
the volumes are listed in the frontice pages.

THIS BOOK IS DEDICATED TO THOSE IN ALLAGES
WHO HAD THE COURAGE TO FACE THE TRUTH
AND SPEAK OUT

CONTENTS AND ORDERING DETAILS
OF FOUR VOLUMES OF THEATRE EARTH

Volume I   ISBN 0-9529567-1-3

The Hidden Science; In the Beginning was the MRC (Magnetically Reversed) Case; The World Grid; The Keys to the New World Order; UFO's; Domes and Pies in London and New York; Order in the asylum; Dome Theatre; Prehistoric Atomic Wars; Transgenerational Collective Intelligence; Cabalistic origins of the Hidden Science; The Rosicrucians; The One Dollar Note of America; Spiritual Seership Manipulation of the Grid; A Coded Secret Doctrine; Cyclical Cosmology and Atomic Theory; Cabalistic Symbology; Who Killed the Minoans? Acting on Orders no Questions Asked; Hidden Masters; The Holy Land of Scotland; A Matter of Genealogies; Egypt; The Vine Man that Draws Together; The Celts and Druids; The Essenes; The Bible; The Celtic Commonwealth; Esoteric Theology; Gnosticism; The Knights Templar; The World Order of the Rose; Crete as Atlantis? Cretan Zeus and a Theocracy; The All-Seeing Eye; The Vacuum Pattern; Hidden Archaeology; A Stone-Age World Order; Climatic Mysteries; Hydrophobia; Free Energy; anti-Gravity Propulsion; Hitler and Occult Science; Spirals; Spirit and Anti-Worlds; Mind Energy Grid Interface; Thought Imprints or Implants? One-ness; The Universal Mind; Ron Hubbard's Space Opera; Xenu; Incident One; Yatrus.568 pages with 43 Figures.

Volume II   ISBN 0-9529567-2-1

Hill Figures; Gogmagog; The Lost Thirteenth Tribe of Israel; The Secret War Against Beliefs (Re-incarnation); Scientology – A Secret Group? The Great White Lodge and Brotherhood; Britain a Tribal Battlefield; The Hidden Agenda; Existing Policy; Changing the Script and Policy; God Genes; The One Slit World; Bohemian Grove and 'Shape Shifting Reptiles'; Two Jerusalems; Actual Incident One; September 11. 602 pages and 14 Figures with Plates 1-28, which cover volumes I & II.

Volume III ISBN 0-9529567-3-X (NEW)

The Hidden Christian Card; Dan; Y Chromosome; Evolution of the Y Chromosome; DNA Music; DNA Phantom Biowave Computer; Quantum DNA; Virtual Reality; La Place's Demon; Schwarzschild Geometry; Quantum Postulate versus Egg Timer; The Geometric Construction and Administration Point; TheGE Survival Trap; Synchronization of Prophecy to Galactic Clock; The 4-D rhombus Computer; Close Packing of Atoms to create the Rhombus Computer; Trapped in the geometry of the Rose; How Long is a Piece of String? Von Neumann Architecture and the Self-Replicating System; Fibonacci

Bees and Numbers; Games for Atoms – End Day Game Cycle; Kelley's Heroes and Iraq; Root Race Embryology and Metapsychosis; Inside the Mind of the GE and World Order; Borromean Rings; Federation of Faith's or World Order Religion?; The Reshel Grid; The Master Magician's Final Trick at the End of Days; The Möbius Net; Building the Temple of Solomon; Decoding 9/11 and the Judgement Card. 602 pages and 161 Figures.

Volume IV ISBN 0-9529567-4-8 (NEW)

Atomic World War and the Battle for the Mind of Europe; The Noble Lie of Blood and Soil and Neoconservatives; Secrets of the Sphinx and Merovingian Line; A Mad Hatter's Tea Party in Europe and Washington; Muscle-Bound Minoans and European Union; Visions of Hell? Occult background to the Iraq War; The Hidden Energy Recycling Programme; Genesis to Revelations according to Standing Waves; The Cosmic Mind; Euro 2004 – Football and Atoms; Weapons of Maths Destruction; The Mirror Maze of Mind Control; A Personal Note. 696 pages and 71 Figures with 11 Plates (9 in colour).

I very gratefully acknowledge the contribution of all quoted authors cited in reference and in acknowledged diagrams. I am particularly indebted to B. Dunford who wrote *The Holy Land of Scotland* and Comyns Beaumont who wrote *Britain The Key to World History* . I also very gratefully acknowledge the 'saplings 'Ru-Barn who had the courage to stand with the author. I also acknowledge Heraklion MuseumCrete, for iconography and sealings;The Ashmolean Museum for sealings; The Bibliotheque Nationale Paris; The Archives Nationale Paris; The British Library London; Cardiff Castle Wales.

"Actuality means 'What is '...Are you facing in yourself what actually is going on...You don 't take actuality and look at it ".

"Man has been concerned throughout the ages to discover or live in 'Truth '."

(Taken from a series of discussions between Krishnamurti and David Bohm, Professor of Theoretical Physics at London University.In Truth and Actuality by J.Krishnamurti –London Victor Gollancz Ltd.–1986)

TABLE OF CONTENTS

Volume 1 **Page**

TABLE OF FIGURES AND PLATES

PLATES

INTRODUCTION

In 1986 the author as a Biochemist, set out to resolve the mechanism of cancer outside of the orthodox establishment. No funding or grants were made available to the author for this research, despite the numerous attempts and requests from grant funding bodies and Trusts for a slice of the solid gold 'gravy train' of funding that is available for cancer research: the eventual bill was to cover 15 years of intensive research. Utilising the methods of Dr. Max Gerson M.D. (1881 –1959) the author was soon to recognise that orthodox medical research had dismissed this genius, who initially applied his nutritional therapy to patients with "incurable" Lupus in the 1920's and obtained a 99% success rate in 450 cases. In 1928 he healed his first three "incurable" cancer cases: one advanced, inoperable bile duct cancer and two advanced inoperable stomach cancers. Gerson went on to cure many so-called "incurables" with terminal cancer and Dr. Albert Schweitzer the Nobel Prize humanitarian and physician and one of the 20th Century's most honoured men was treated successfully by Dr. Gerson at the age of 75, for advanced diabetes. After treatment by Dr. Gerson, Dr. Schweitzer returned to Africa and won the Nobel Prize and worked past the age of 90. Dr. Schweitzer was to later write of Dr. Gerson: "I see in Dr. Gerson one of the most eminent geniuses of medical history".

Dr. Gerson in the 1940's appeared before a Senate hearing in America to present the medical histories of some of his cured cancer patients, in attempts to gain a slice of the multi-billion pound 'gravy train' of research funding and grants. The Editorial in the AMA (*American Medical Journal of Nov. 16 1946*) mentioned Dr. Gerson's appearance before the Senate sub committee that year. The hearings also covered "A Bill to authorise and request the President, to undertake to mobilize at some convenient place in the United States, an adequate number of the world's outstanding experts, and co-ordinate and utilize their services in a supreme endeavour to discover means of curing and preventing cancer". Don C. Matcham wrote in *Herald of Health* magazine: "The Committee report of 227 pages, Document No. 89471, gathers dust in the archives of the Government Printing Office". Dr. Gerson was to die a discredited man professionally, despite the brilliance of his work and presumably not fully understanding the role of The Syndicate and goals of a World Order, who had not intention (or policy) of resolving the first part of the Platonic Maxim – the cure of the body.

Whilst the author recognised the importance of Dr. Gerson's work in healing the body, it was evident from the author's own research that there was a mental component working in cancer and that cancer was a psychosomatic condition of *mind and body*. In 1989 the author published a scientific paper on cancer, utilising the Gerson Therapy with counselling, in order to resolve two parts of the Platonic Maxim – mind and body (*R. Henry, S.McLean "A Theory for Cancer based on a Study of Cancer Patients Using The Gerson Cancer Therapy in Conjunction with Psychological Counselling": Complementary Medical Research Spring 1989 Vol. 3 No. 2 –British Library Medical Information Service, Document Supply Centre, Boston Spa, Wetherby, west York's LS23 7BQ United Kingdom*). *The Second Millennium Working Report into Cancer*, by the author, outlining fully the mechanism proposed, subsequently supported the paper. The mechanism lies, after many years of attempting to gain professional support and evaluation in the U.K., collecting dust in the archives of the British Museum Library (*Appendix I and II*).

The author has always retained a scientific and open viewpoint in her quest for truth and thus after reviewing many psychological models and theories, the only model that meshed with the biochemical (body) mechanism of cancer as outlined in *The Second Millennium Working Report into Cancer*, was the mechanism of the mind forwarded as a thesis by Ron Hubbard in *Dianetics – The Modern Science of Mental Health*. Ron Hubbard was the founder of the Church of Scientology and from the moment that the author placed her scientific foot into this field – all hell let loose! It became apparent to the author that not only was there a hidden barrier to the freedom of science in the field of the body, orchestrated by the pharmaceutical industry and what can only be termed the chemical Syndicate (*Appendix I*), but that there was a virtually identical battle and hidden agenda, being played out in the field of the mind between The Syndicate or psychiatry and Scientology. If the field of the body was a battlefield of conflicting orthodox and alternative viewpoints, then the field of the mind was another virtually identical battlefield of conflicting interests. If Dr. Gerson failed in his radical new dietary approach to cancer, to gain financial and professional backing, manpower and research facilities to further his research and clinical testing, then one could only view the battle to gain acceptance for *Dianetics* as the same battle game, of orthodox and alternative viewpoints. The author was willing to accept the story and this background to Scientology promoted by The Church of Scientology, until she herself was to astoundingly become a victim of Scientology. After a horrendous series of events, depicted on the front cover of *The Second Millennium working Report into Cancer*, it very soon became apparent to the author that the barrier to the freedom of science and the resolution of the Platonic Maxim, was not only inclusive of the profits to the pharmaceutical and psychiatric medical Syndicate that would be threatened by a resolution of the Platonic Maxim and healing of mind and body by alternative methods, but a deeper barrier existed in the resolution of the final part of the

Platonic Maxim – the soul.
The cancer research like an errant child, led the author through the mined battle fields of history, religion, politics, psychology, biochemistry, archaeology and anthropology and finally into the forbidden no-man's land of metapolitics - or the politics of the soul. The author on instinctive intuition returned to Greece in 1993, on one level to escape the vicious attacks shown on the front cover of *The Second Millennium Working Report* into cancer, but on another level not quite clear to the author at that time, it was a Cycle of Eternal Return. The result of the research in Greece was the author's first book, *The Battle of The Trees*. The book was produced in a 'T-Shirt' factory in Crete over the period of 1994/5 against appalling odds. A band of spiritually aware people from around the world responded to that book and the author's second book *Alternative 4 – UFO's Mind and Body Control*, with a positive spiritual understanding, despite the lack of editing. There were some however who appeared not to grasp the research at all. I acknowledge that a student only understands as well as his teacher explains it, however as I hope this book will explain, this was no ordinary story or research/book. I hope that in this book, it will be understood that the author was grappling not only with attempts to regain her own memory, but whatever the Grid and Masters might throw to prevent that! The barriers to freedom were *formidable* and at each turn there was no assurance that the author would survive to tell the tale, thus the decision to print regardless of editing or aesthetics of printing. This was always a far more serious battle than the majority realised and in the author's loneliest moments, there was always the thought that if something was published, some may remember that truth – the alternative was to wait until the author discovered the whole truth and the entire track of time, but then this story is not about publishing books, **it is about the battle for man's soul.** This thesis reveals the entire conspiracy from the beginning to the present day and is crucial in understanding the mind and goals of The World Order.

Given optimal circumstances one could produce a product, even research that is perfect, which seems to be the requirement in this age of spin and gloss, however this is not a story about perfection, it is a story about *imperfection* and the highly uncertain and improbable attempt by the author to place an alternative viewpoint on the last 10 000 years, which contradicts most of what mankind has been led to believe in. I thank Dagmar in Canada who wrote after reading the first two books: "Do not ever give up writing, our children are depending on you" – a message that appeared at a particularly low ebb. The author also thanks others that wrote to her and passed on support, which gave the author the impetus for this book, believing that there were still a few out there, who were earnestly searching for the truth. This was far from an easy book to write, it has taxed the author to present it to you the reader, in some form that may indeed warn you of the crisis that humanity now faces, whilst unravelling the great misunderstandings in occult science and the hidden science that have led man into this predicament: Indeed I doubt whether those who are manipulating this science, unknown to humanity understand or know of what I have written here and yet the unknown manipulation of this science stands to destroy humanity. These misunderstandings on the nature of the past and space-time have remained within hidden initiation levels, which drive the World Order and secret groups. If man thought that he would reach the end of the cycle, without any trouble or soul searching, he was only a fool unto himself. This crisis is of an individual nature, there will be no safety in numbers, and it is for each man and woman to search their own soul on what I say here.

This story is really about the hiding away of certain natural laws of science and physics within the secret groups, however I was once told that if you put one scientific equation into a book, your reader numbers are immediately halved! I have tried to keep the science to a minimum, so that anyone without a background in science can understand. It would be helpful if the reader had some background into the World Order, which can be gained from back editions of *On Target* magazine (cited in reference), along with authors such as Mullins (cited) and Professor Noam Chomsky (cited): also *Tragedy and Hope – A History of The World in Our Time* by Professor Carroll Quigley (*GSG and Associates P.O. Box 6448 Rancho Palos Verdes California 90734)* is another source of excellent background material. Whilst the author's first two books provide important background and research material to this book, I hope that this work will clear up misunderstandings that readers may have had. No man or woman however owes man a complete story, for it is eternal spiritual struggle that provides one with the keys to freedom. Further you must accept that there are some things that cannot be said, for there are always forces that would use that information against mankind and it is not my intention to hold secrets, but one must be cognisant that there are some things which must remain unsaid and only you the reader will find those unsaid things, by eternal struggle and searching – It is the route and search for the Philosopher's Stone. I first advertised *The Battle of The Trees* in Athens in March 1995 and on returning to the U.K. the author carried on her research and published *Alternative 4 – UFO's Mind and Body Control,* which provided further insight into the hidden science and the World Order. Although the research seemed very far removed from the cancer research and the final attempt to resolve the third part of the Platonic Maxim – the soul, it was in fact another convoluted turn in the hidden agenda of the World Order and the battle for mans'soul. The first two books provide important insight into the scientific research process and illustrate just how one arrives at the final conclusion. One should not discount that process as it evolves, for it is a testimony to never using the Grid and its memory, but your own. This point is crucial to this thesis and the search for truth. In fact I could have in the production of my books omitted my past life memories or the one that I recount in *Chapter I of The Battle of The Trees* and the statement in this book that I was a witness at the events of Golgotha and the alleged Crucifixion of Jesus; however to do so would be to negate or omit the message of The Holy Grail. The message is one of recognition of the continuous immortality of the soul. This message finds expression in the resolution of the Platonic Maxim: **'before you can cure a man's body, you must first cure his mind and before that his soul'**; and the healing of the soul further finds a mechanism that was outlined in the cancer research.

In 1996 the author felt that she had enough evidence to challenge the World Order, including the vast cover up on the treatment of cancer and approached her local MP Tim Rathbone, then Conservative MP for Lewes, with a Petition to Parliament (*Appendix II*). Despite the support of the Rt. Hon Tim Rathbone MP who agreed to table the Petition in The House of Commons in the U.K., the Petition was predictably scuttled and the author was referred to the procedures of Open Government, where supposedly the various organisations and body's that the author's questions were presented to, were obliged by law to answer. As one eventually comes to realise in World Order politics and policies, those policies and the World Order are not only above the law, but also above the democratic process. In effect the Petition as part of the law and democratic process, was 'lost' down the avenues and cul-de-sacs of labyrinthine and secret government policies and hidden agendas. The Power of the private banking system was such that governments lacked the will and were increasingly unable, to issue their own money at low interest into the economy to finance public expenditure, instead borrowing their own money, from private banks, such that the compounded geometric rise in the national debt and the interest needed to serve that debt, led to the practice of selling off national assets. In the United Kingdom in the 1980's during the regime of Margaret Thatcher as Prime Minister, privatisation of public sector services and academic activity occurred. The freedom of science to search for truth, declined in proportion to subservience of academics to private sector research funding. The big pharmaceutical and emerging 'Life Science' companies were mainly those who paid the grants in research establishments and thus science no longer became impartial, but merely a tool in the hands of the multinational companies associated and interlocked through directorships and consultancies. It became impossible for the individual scientist to engage in true research or in fact any research that threatened private sector profit and monopolistic control (*Appendix I*). Any scientist that approached the truth or questioned current methods, would be excommunicated as a 'heretic' by the 'Inquisitional Church' of a secret hierarchy with tentacles that reach out and control every aspect of politics, religion, commerce and industry, research, publishing and media, banking, insurance, the drug trade, the petroleum industry – a group that is answerable to no one, but its members. With the increasing debt and globalisation of the economy it has been argued that the private sector has been driven in turn to ever expanding growth, as the debt inherited from privatisation continues to "chase its own tail", as part of the overall corporate debt. The greater the commercial operation in the global markets, the greater are the stakes and the greater the concentration of Power at governmental levels.

The Chairman of Biotechnology Investments is the powerful establishment figure of Rothschild director and former Cabinet Secretary Lord Armstrong of Illminster. His deputy is former Cambridge University don, Dr John Bradfield. Another university don, Sir Brian Richards, co-founded British Biotech., linked through its directorships to the Daily Mail (newspaper in the U.K.), Glaxo-Wellcome and Royal Dutch Shell. The Oxford Molecular Group is linked to Pfizer, manufactuerer of Viagra. Sir Brian Richards also sits on the board of Peptide Therapeutics, linked to N.M. Rothschild, Aventis Pasteur and Smith Kline and Beecham Pharmaceuticals. International Biotechnology Trust, in 1997, listed Professor Sir Keith Peters and Sir Mark Richmond amongst eight academic and scientific advisers. This is just the tip of the networking process that occurs worldwide and provides a safe inner sanctum of power, which is impenetrable to questions from alternative and independent viewpoints, particularly when those viewpoints seek to question policy. Virtually, if not all official advisory and regulatory bodies are disproportionately populated by individuals beholden to the multinational conglomnerates, through investments, consultancies or directorships. The same situation prevails in the United States where the term "revolving door" is openly applied to the relationship between the biotechnology Corporation of Monsanto and the Food and Drug Administration (F.D.A.). The F.D.A and Medical bodies such as the American Cancer Society have been instigators (along with the FBI as enforcers), in blocking alternative cancer therapies in America.

Alternative therapist Jimmy Keller was kidnapped by the FBI in 1991 after he fell foul of The National Council Against Health Fraud (NCAHF) and alleged front organisation for the AMA (American Medical Association). The FDA (who are not a law enforcement agency) with the help of police stormed a natural Health Clinic in Washington, where guns were used to terorrise the doctor, staff and patients. Dr Jonathon Wright a renowned doctor along with the community was absolutely and rightly outraged that this incident could occur in the Capital of Americ in 1992. People are not afraid of alternative medicine, so *who* is exactly afraid? Illness is BIG BUSINESS and profits to the multinational companies and the vice-like grip on monopoly can only be maintained, through a hidden agenda or policy *acting through governments*. The Senate Bill 3642 and the NLEA (Nutrition Labelling Education Act) in America which was claimed by Dr Wright as seriously bias against natural health products, mirrors the bully-boy tactics in Britain orchestrated by the Medicines Control Agency (proposal MLX 249) and backed by forthcoming European legislation (*Appendix I*). The reach of the tentacles of an Elite hierarchy into governments and subsequent determination of policy is not as has been suspected, merely driven by power, profit and money. The World Order Elite have continuoulsy throughout millennia existed through and within secret groups, where the actual policies and hidden agendas of national governments originate, thus stripping the electorate of any meaningful control over their own destinies and the environment. It has been the aim of the author to discover what drives the mind of the World Order, where and why this Order evolved and the true nature of their identity, along with their hidden agenda and goal. Secret levels of initiation are revealed in this book, which furthers research and the cracking of various secret codes, which as 'keys' have unlocked many of the inner sanctum mysteries that surround the World Order and the variously associated secret groups. The conclusions are astounding even to the author, who has long since passed the stage of being surprised by the World Order. The author asks whether a case of treason can be brought, on the basis that this is a significant and all encompassing treachery against humanity and in the case of The United Kingdom the conclusions are pivotal to that question.

I trust the Scientologists will not view what I say here as an attack, but rather they will view it as reasonable scientific valid critique and evaluation. In some respects what the author states on the basis of her research, is validation of the secret initiation levels in Scientology, however the author as with Christianity and other religions, offers a varying scientific viewpoint, opinion and belief. The philosopher Alfred North Whitehead stated: "The worst homage we can pay to genius is to accept uncritically formulations of truths which we owe to it". Whilst Alfred North Whitehead was speaking of Einstein, I could equally apply this statement to Ron Hubbard. The question arises in this book, whether or not Hubbard was a genius or whether Scientology is a secret group, with an inevitable higher Order behind it. The same question could be applied to Christianity at the time of its inception, which includes the very secret events of Golgotha covered here. All human knowledge should be preceded by a disclaimer, such as the referral in my own research to "Working Report", signifying that the research is ongoing, however this book is meant as a final personal statement, as I intend to resign my post. Man should accept that he does not know very much at all and knows even less, when he places barriers to truth. The search for truth requires that man does not accept dogma or wrote word of law: an open mind and acceptance that at any one given time – this is the way it appears now, would invite improvements and open discussion. Religion and the World Order invite dogmatism and stuck viewpoints, purely for the purpose of control or power and financial gain. The truth however, is the evolving front of spiritual and scientific research that has every barrier to freedom placed in its path - such is the author's story and the barriers placed to her research, even sadly by those who claim truth or the freedom of humanity as their goal. If there were nothing to hide, then those barriers would not exist, since the truth would pose no threat. The fact that the author's research has taken 15 years (at least!) to evolve, whilst jumping barriers on a daily basis, with a trail of secrecy and lies, emphasises that there are many groups on this Earth, who have great fear of telling the truth. Truth is the ultimate reality and only from that reality will mankind ever achieve understanding, it is for those few who have no fear of reality and wish to understand and confront that reality or ultimate truth, that this book is written It may spoil your day, but far better than to destroy your eternity! I am afraid there was never any safe group ticket out, or assurance of safety or salvation in numbers, this is the story of **the individual** and the ability of that individual to think, reason and on balance decide the fate of his own soul: that is a horrible thing to face, but then the problem here on Earth was always viewed as *a desperate case and the fate uncertain* – "They don't stand a chance unless...". All religions however have warned man to nurture and keep his soul clean from wrong-doing and one can see much truth in that, for it will not be so much the "books" (the account of the individual) that are opened at the end according to the book of *Revelations*, but the anti-matter holographic electro-magnetic imprint or **soul recording**. Man's **conscience** will become his own judge. The World Order misunderstood the **HIDDEN SCIENCE** from the very beginning in their rush to utilise the power, control and wealth to be made from it; and just how that misunderstanding has weaved its way into occultism, occult science, certain New Age therapies, politics, metapolitics, religion, archaeology, history and current biotechnology creating the insanity we are now witnessing on Earth is taken up in this thesis. The Dunces of the World Order might even cause one to roar with laughter, if this was not a very Greek Tragedy for Mankind, as humanity stands on the precipice of disaster. Now that you have opened 'Pandora's box', read on!

THE HIDDEN SCIENCE

The world energy grid explains much in terms of The New World Order, UFO'S, Crop Circles, Mythology, Pre-History, Secret politics and religion and secret weapons technology. If you are asking what is the world energy grid? Then let me outline here a whole science, that has been withdrawn from mankind, a science that used correctly would have enormous beneficial potential in the field of healing and cancer, used incorrectly it has become the basis of a **hidden science** held within the secret groups for thousands of years and at detriment to humanity.

It was not always safe to write the truth, just as it is so today, therefore those 'in the know' often encrypted their work, or used symbolisation, which I discussed at length in my first book *The Battle of The Trees*. Symbolisation also became a method used by secret groups, to retain knowledge within a secret hierarchy, not accessible to the masses. Much of what is left of the truth in The Bible is retained in symbolic form only and cannot be fully understood by the masses unless the keys to the symbols are known. Further thousands of years of 'the wrong end of the stick' have led to variations of the truth. Since The Hidden Science has been a source of global power for thousands of years, you will find elements of this science referred to in veiled terms and cryptic myths and further in iconographic symbology. **To find the truth one has to know the codes.** As any good spy knows, in order to break a group, even The One World Order, you have to know 'what makes it tick'. Consider the problems or the **Questions:**
a) What is their plan?
b) How do they hope to achieve that plan? .
c) What is their philosophy?
d) What are their methods?
e) Which is (are) the main Controlling Secret Group(s) and what is its (their) Philosophy?
f) Is that plan rational? Does it serve the higher ideals of man such as Freedom, Democracy, Truth, and Ethics? Choice? Or The Right To Know? Or is it self-serving for a few - the Elite?
g) What is the **Psychological and Spiritual Case** of the Controllers?

As a Biochemist with some 15 years experience in Scientific Research I, approached these questions through the mind of a Scientist In my first two books *'The Battle of The Trees'* and *'Alternative 4 - UFO's Mind and Body Control'* I was able to answer some of these questions but never reached the great overview I reach here. Finally one has to conclude that there is a plan, there is a goal, there is a philosophy, there is a psychological and spiritual case and there is a

19

controlling group, which can be identified by that Philosophy; spiritual and psychological case. Certainly it would have been impossible to deduce these things, if I had not returned to the beginning, the Alpha and Greece, where I found the "KEYS", to decode the myths, icons and the Philosophy using the ancient alphabets.

The use of such alphabets to decode iconography, mythology and legends associated with The Holy Grail, led me to concluded in *The Battle of The Trees*, that not only was their one controlling group but that an important split in that group had occurred in the 12 th Century in a curious ceremony of The Cutting of the Elm at Gisors in France. The possibility then existed that there were two controlling groups, with quite different philosophies but possibly a common goal of world domination. The decipherment of The Grail legends appeared to confirm such a suggestion. The second book *Alternative 4* revealed some of the hidden science in the mechanism of the UFO phenomenon (*'The Onion Ring Model'*) but it seemed that a third book was necessary, to completely clarify the nature of the two groups and help those readers who had followed the mind blowing horrendous task of regaining my memory of events dating back thousands of years, covered in my first two books. For those who could not easily grasp where my memory was leading me, then I hope to rectify matters here. I may be forgiven for having to jog my own memory by writing the complex web that has been woven into two books, before I could finally confront my own psychological and spiritual case, in the story. The willingness to confront a large chunk of one's time track (past lives) and the horror of this story, is decreased proportionately by the number of times that you were defeated, murdered, betrayed, interrogated, chased, tortured, subjected to black propaganda, lied to, tricked, cheated and the rest of the tricks that the ruling elite and even man utilised to stop you ever getting this particular story and truth into print – anywhere: A 'civilized' Planet - Earth.

IN THE BEGINNING THERE WAS THE MRC
(MAGNETICALLY REVERSED CASE)

What drives man to produce World Orders and ultimate control of humanity? Well I am sure if you scan the voluminous and confusing myths and legends, you will come up with that old word Evil, some bogey-man but nothing based in the hard facts of science. I have preferred to base my explanation on the facts that can at least be proven in terms of scientific understanding of world events. Such events are not openly in the public domain, although scientific references do exist, I have used mythology in decoded form, to support such science and from that comes a reasonable **scientific hypothesis** that covers point g above. Any hypothesis is only as good as it is able to tie up as much hitherto unexplained data as possible. A hypothesis in science only becomes a **law**, if the hypothesis can be used to **predict accurately future events**. The Prophetic Apocalypse or Revelations in The Bible predicts future events and one has to ask, whether it is merely a hypothesis or whether in fact it rests upon some knowledge and laws of science that man has lost from the public domain. Further any hypothesis is only as good as it touches down with reality - pre-history (mythology and legends), geological world events, history, psychology, science including cosmology and archaeology, politics and religion. The problem becomes in verifying a psychological (mind) and spiritual case of certain men that were on earth from the beginning, as opposed to the majority of mankind. Could it be that certain men were different in some way from the majority and that their whole presence and goals on Earth could be an extension or indeed a manifestation of their psychological and spiritual case? Thus the only evidence for identifying such a case, comes from archaeology, pre-history and therefore myths, legends and early religious texts. This is satisfactory up to a point, for there is ample evidence from such sources of a ruling elite who ruled as despots and arch-manipulators of humanity. However there has always been a lack of understanding of the origins and source of this ruling elite and the history of the psychological and spiritual case for the 'evil ones'.

It was once said that there are no demons except in a man's mind. That is very true. One might conceivably try to find a psychological case for those who currently dominate, control and instigate Globalisation plans by looking into their childhood and concluding, that such men have existed throughout time. This as we know does not answer the question of recorded history, which I have shown in *The Battle of The Trees*, is a record of control, secrecy and manipulation dating back at least to 1,400 BC where it appears the World Globalisation plan really took off. Neither does it answer the question why such a plan has exhibited such continuity and apical direction, throughout Millennia, being the cause of both The French and Russian Revolutions and the majority of wars on this planet. One might consider that tyrants come and go randomly, but throughout the millennia there has existed a tightly knit hierarchy who constantly worked towards world domination through a world globalisation plan. Such a plan has been enigmatically referred to and historically recorded as being perpetuated through the secret societies, particularly Freemasonry and the infamous group the Illuminati. The Jews historically have also been frequently associated with the world revolutionary plan, a plan that is coming to fruition in our times as European Union (The Federal European Super state) and The New World Order. Why has this plan persisted? Time and time again, one comes back to a certain controlling **influence,** men and women who display a unique psychological and spiritual case, together with **predictable social and behavioural characteristics**. I have labelled this case as **The Magnetically Reversed Case** or **MRC**. It is this case who has retained a hierarchal position on the realisation of a plan for world domination, which dates back millions and probably billions of years on this Planet at least. This case I fully describe in *Alternative 4* and in *The Second Millennium Working Report into Cancer*.

I have given previously in those publications (particularly the Cancer report), the background to **Magnetic reversals** occurring on Earth, where the north and south **magnetic** poles have periodically reversed, causing great climatic disasters and species extinction, which although are recorded in the **scientific literature,** are not generally known about or understood by lay men. This knowledge has I conclude definitely been suppressed. Further I have suggested that some beings or individuals, who were on Earth from the beginning, were subject to this reversal (perhaps numerous times, which has fully defined their psychological and spiritual case in terms of social/behavioural traits and goals. One could simply leave it at that, which would be sufficient to describe the hypothesis for the case of evil in Psychological and Scientific terms. Thus it would have a base in scientific and psychological reality. However, there is always the nagging question that pops up, like – yes, but why were they here from the beginning? Whilst Science can provide by analysis, the conclusion that there have been magnetic reversals in the past and can date those periods millions of years ago, material scientific research cannot answer the pre-history of man, or the time when recordings were not made and archaeological evidence is not available. Thus to answer what happened in the beginning one must rely on world myths and legends and religious texts. However here in this book I have utilised a method of cross-weaving evidence from a large number of sources, with the unique utilisation of mans own memory of pre-history – his continual spiritual presence as observer of his own history on the track of time. I have produced a brief breakdown of early Creation myths and legends in the *Cancer Report (Section: The Road To Truth Has Many Turns)*, which identify common agreement on:

a) **A global catastrophe** (recorded as The Flood in the *Genesis* account and as a climatic catastrophe in virtually all world myths and legends.

b) *Evil was lurking on Earth from the beginning* - Contrary to *Genesis* and The Garden of
Eden story.

c) **An Elite group** with attempts to **enslave man**.

With regard to point c, I have traced this back in *The Battle of The Trees* via iconography and archaeology to 1,400BC by utilising the Knossos site in Crete and other sites in Greece. Point (a) can be verified to some extent from scientific data proving magnetic reversals, with the possibility of a major reversal recorded as The Flood, which occurs in virtually all recorded world myths and legends: Point (b) and the case of what I proposed as the MRC (Magnetically Reversed Case) is much more difficult, since one cannot prove from current data, events at the beginning in terms of Man. I sought to prove it via a round-about route, by looking at the behaviour, thinking and **THE MIND** that would be attracted to tight control, secrecy, domination, surveillance, manipulation and lies, **which is the world globalisation plan**. Such a case I have hypothesised, might have arisen as a direct result of being subject to a magnetic reversal, which occluded the spiritual memory of the individual and the tremendous wrongs they have committed over many millennia. Here we start to enter the field of psychology and the mind and that illusive field of the soul. For the moment, let us just consider the analogy that a man committed evil acts and then was hit by a car and totally forgot what he had done, but somewhere back of his mind and in his soul, he knew he had to hide something, but could not remember what it was. Thus we have a man who obsessively hides everything, is attracted to the secret groups, supports tight control and surveillance (stops others from finding out) and becomes the head of some secret group, government or the FBI or CIA! Whilst in *Alternative 4*, I believed that only this case (the MRC), had suffered a magnetic reversal, I would revise that conclusion here, to only this case had serious crimes to hide on the track of time *and* experienced a serious magnetic reversal. Whilst mankind may have suffered minor pole shifts on the track of time in magnetic reversals, his crimes were not comparable to those of the MRC case, thus his psychology was not obsessive on the subject of control and secrecy. It seems to me, that the MRC case has suffered very many or one terrific reversal which had catastrophic consequences for his psychology. To answer the question of how evil was lurking here from the beginning was sought again from world myths and legends and religious texts, which I hypothesised might cover the so-called ' "Fallen Angel", or the Lucifer in religious texts, a case I prefer to identify as the MRC case. The hypothesis went something like this:

A group outside of Earth sought to manipulate the indigenous population of Earth via the Energy Grid (an electro-magnetic energy field rather like a net in space that surrounds Earth) and the DNA (De-oxy Nucleic Acid) or hereditary material, which exists as a **master blueprint in space.** This master DNA reflects the physical DNA in our cells which carries the hereditary genes, but it is a master pattern **for the species** e.g. man, dog, amphibia, reptiles etc. The master blueprint is if you like the 'Head Office', where the master plans, which govern the survival of the species, are kept. The Physical DNA in our bodies is the equivalent of 'the sub office', which receives plans from 'Head Office'. Whilst it has been previously assumed that the physical DNA in our cells, which comprise our bodies, is the only master blueprint; I would maintain that there is a *higher* master pattern and blueprint, which exists as an *electromagnetic pattern and field* in space. I covered some aspects of this in the cancer document and *Alternative 4*, where the remarkable DNA shaped crop circle patterns were referred to, as if some master field pattern from space had been imprinted on Earth.

There is known to be a non-specific field in space, which governs e.g. the shape of the young animal as it develops. Such a field also seems important in transmitting un-learned or innate behaviour between individuals within species. I suggested that the 'Fallen Angel ' or The Lucifer, is in fact a group originally exterior to Earth, who tried to manipulate man and his Genetics through this field and on entry to Earth suffered a magnetic reversal through the continual obsess ional misuse and manipulation of this field Such an obsession would arise from unconscious and irrational attempts to control this field in an attempt to once again be free of Earth and the trap they fell into, through their own wrong doings. After being 'scrambled' in a magnetic reversal , they subsequently **became the effect of what they had caused,** in other words they were destined to become fixated with The   Energy Grid and Genetic manipulation, manifesting today as the psychological and spiritual case of those who promote GM technology (Genetically Modified species and Food) and cloning . Cloning incidentally is a present time or current manifestation of the psychological and spiritual case of those who sought enslavement of humanity in the long past through genetic tampering. Once again they have some idea that the answer to their case, lies somewhere in this murky field, but merely re-enact their whole case by repeating such prior actions – justified naturally under the heading of progress! Further by hiding the science of the Grid in the past, it became a method of control, man had no idea of the wonders of the Grid, but the Masters did! The obsession with secrecy and elitism today is merely a manifestation of the psychological and spiritual case of the MRC, a case that has governed planet Earth for millennia. The worst nightmare of the MRC is to be found out for his crimes.

24

Let us assume for one moment that this case - the MRC, has suffered the same cycle many times, each time committing the same sequence of events on Earth i.e. control of the Grid, secrecy, confusion, attempts to regain control, use of the Grid for weapons, development of weaponry associated with the physics of Grid energies, followed by disruption of the equilibrium of the Grid and subsequently causing another cyclical magnetic reversal as recorded presumably in The Apocalypse of the future and perhaps in the past as the Flood in Genesis. Let us further assume this cycle has continued to turn many times in many Apocalypses, which would thus enable an Initiate into these Grid Energies to predict future events, which may account for The Apocalyptic Prophecy. The possibility exists, that on at least one of these cycles, the resultant geological and climatic disaster was so great, causing vast species extinctions, that only a semi-water world remained and where only Amphibians could survive. Let us further assume that these beings (MRC case) rather than remaining in the etheric layer of Earth as souls, waiting for the geological disaster to subside, **took over the bodies** of amphibians in order to have some 'game' (and all beings even now, seek a 'game ' rather than no game - and some 'games' are just bigger than others). It may be that those beings had to Re-incarnate into an Amphibian body for quite some time, perhaps millions of years, before they could Re-incarnate into the genetic evolutionary line of a mammal, since the process of evolution is very slow for bodies and species. I put forward this suggestion to decode the referral to "out of the mouths of frogs come blasphemies" in the apocalyptic account of *Revelations*. There is now a current line of research and support for the evolution of man from fish through amphibia with branches to the reptiles, which I discussed in *Alternative 4*. In tht book I also discussed the curious orange-eyed reptilian like creatures observed in some UFO accounts, which suggested that man (or some men) may have occupied some branch or line of the reptiles. Such a scientific theory was truly hampered by David Icke and there is certainly no connection between my *scientific* theories and those of Mr. Icke, which appeared after publication of *Alternative 4*. I did give another interpretation of the apocalyptic account of frogs in the event, that some would prefer a less dramatic solution, which was the use of a psychedelic substance obtained from certain frogs skins and toads, which created hallucinations, or more correctly gave the power of prophesy by enhancing a psychic state and presumably connection to the Grid. Ancient man has long used such substances to empower him with prophecy. But what is prophecy, other than in the case of my theory here, a restatement of past events, which will be re-enacted in the future as one performs the lines of a play by memory and habit, after so many performances!

I did suggest that the Genetic Codon Project, which is a worldwide scientific collaboration seeking to unravel the secrets of the DNA code, might productively look at the DNA of the amphibian, since the DNA strip is extremely long and much more so than Man, which is unexpected and one might reasonably ask what exactly is encoded on that extra length? I did ask whether such a strip with its encoded information on survival, conferred upon the amphibia the ability to live and survive (which is the purpose of DNA), under **both** electro-magnetic polarities, i.e. pre and post-magnetic reversals. The long history of the amphibia who would have been the only species apart from fish, that could have survived the post climatic and watery world of a magnetic reversal, would certainly be encoded as survival data on the DNA and perhaps accounts for the extra-ordinary length of this DNA. The curious accounts of bulbous-like eyes of aliens in UFO reports, covered more fully in *Alternative 4*, reflect ancient iconography where rock sketching portray beings with bulbous eyes. There appears to be some memory and record of such beings, which must have been considered different from the normal, in order to be sketched onto rocks. I further discussed the hormonal changes that might ensue following a magnetic reversal and medical states of hyperthyroidism, which confers a bulbous eyed appearance.

Certain characteristic traits of the MRC personality define his psychological and spiritual case:

a) The need for **secrecy** (no-one should find out what he did)

b) The MRC case **never goes for Counselling** (his own abberative mind and black soul steers clear unconsciously of any procedure, which might reveal to his conscious mind the way he acts as he does). The MRC case never questions the fact whether he is sane or not, he simply would not question it.

c) The MRC case **fights any Purpose including Religion which seeks to make others more able**, he would fight Re-incarnation as a belief, since it aims at restoring memory (of the past) and would threaten secrecy in point a above. Here also is the curious fact that many secret groups have a belief in Re-incarnation, but the members never seek to know or **rectify** past lives.

d) **Tight Control.** He has an unconscious memory of loosing control before in a magnetic reversal and whilst he probably has no rational explanation for why others must be organised like ants and bees, he has this unconscious need for Order, with himself in control at the apex of any organisation. In fact he seeks a position of leadership in order to control and communism with an elite at the top is a political system, which appeals to him or complete fascism.

e) **Surveillance methods** at a high pitch for reasons above.

f) **Belief in his own superiority and infallibility** and there are many abberative outcomes of this thinking including the idea of "Hidden Masters"; "Spirit Guides"; "The Chosen Ones"; Elitism; "Super-Races"; Man as God or Superman; "One World Order".

g) Sadistic nature when repressed appears as **cold hard and calculating**, with no emotion-inability to contact pure love or compassion. Love experienced sexually only and in perverted form. War-like.

h) Forms **Power Political and Religious Pyramids** as a necessity of Control -usually Elitist Right running a Communistic State for the masses, which supports a belief in his own superiority. Neglects ethics, democracy, freedom of the individual and rights of the individual and removes law and justice together with superior education from the masses. Deals in lies, gossip: leads by authoritarian arrogance and revels in red tape and laws that will stranglehold freedom. Talks apparent good, but actions do not tally with words and his rule is marked by a reduction in freedom.

j) **Cannot finish a cycle of action**. This is most prominent in so far as the end of the cycle to the MRC case is a magnetic reversal with total chaos and whilst seeking to avoid his prior experience at all costs, unconsciously re-enacts the entire cycle repeatedly, thus creating another magnetic reversal. This point is strongly indicated from pre-history, myths and legends. The MRC continually brings in new projects, which continually fail and which he fails to finish. He will then introduce another project, thus creating confusion.

k) **Magnetic quality.** Hitler has this quality very strongly in the latter part of his career.

l) **Upsets and confuses others**, never passes a complementary remark **on the ability** of another, unless it furthers his own ends. Continually suppresses others by derogatory remarks.

m) **Poor sense of justice**, seeks to remove justice - no right and wrong.

n) **Poor sense of property and ownership** (usually a **parasite** on others hard work or ideas giving them no credit) - lacks inherent creativity supports **cunning methods of destruction** of beauty e.g. art

o) **Supports monopolistic politics and religion**. Sense of survival only for self (can be very cunning in distraction by utilising false words and actions feigning survival of others and humanity)

p) **No sense of direct causation** - unable to apologise or conduct reparation projects. Continually expresses **what was done to him**, but never considers his own case to any degree, which would require confronting what he has done to others or indeed the **truth of events**. Since the MRC case has no perception of space or time, where yesterday is today, then he views things from odd angles and cannot string together causation leading from a logical and true sequence of events, thus if he has to blame someone, he will often hit the wrong target .He has a low concept of truth simply because he cannot string together direct causation, he lies as a matter of course.

q) **Destruction of Reality** - changes historical data, alters time place and event, also supports art that destroys reality. Lies and cunning methods to support this destruction, uses law to **prevent** justice; law becomes a tool for his own methods.

r) The worst nightmare of the MRC case is being found out and for this reason he operates in **secrecy**.

Of all these points, the last point q. represents the most serious barrier to ever exposing the MRC case and waking man to the reality of what has occurred on Earth. I do not know, whether it has gone to far and whether we will reclaim the soul of man before it is too late and another magnetic reversal ensues. There are other traits that identify the MRC and usually chaos surrounds these individuals, or those people who are under their control. In fact any long association with the MRC case would find a person affected by illness and/or mental instability, since there may be a dual effect caused by an electro-magnetic quality in these individuals, coupled with appalling behaviour that often defies any rational explanation. Certainly these types or the MRC Case carries out terrible crimes without even acknowledging the faintest responsibility for them. People, who surrounded Hitler at Berchtasgaden, were often relieved to get away from the stifling atmosphere and certainly Hitler's magnetic quality was discussed in *Alternative 4*. Hitler may have been under the power of Higher Initiates as MRC cases or an MRC case himself. Hitler was however, a very disturbed man and crippled the World with chaos and let us not forget, an Atomic War followed. This in itself may be merely a repeat of the cycle that has gone before and European Union will end in the same chaos, since the MRC case lies behind it. One may accept the behavioural characteristics outlined above, and recognise those behavioural characteristics in world politics and yet reserve judgement on whether those characteristics are the result of a Psychological case merely dependent on a childhood this lifetime, or dating back millions of years to the beginning. However those behavioural traits **are Psychotic behaviour** and that Psychotic behaviour is in control of world politics .It would certainly be interesting to look at the electro-magnetic field of The MRC case (if you could get him into the chair!). I think you could even probably help him, for no man is truly evil there is always **a point** at which his soul descended into aberration.

To accept the possibility of this hypothesis and the question - Why evil was lurking here from the beginning, one would have to ask why a plan for the enslavement of humanity has persisted through the millennia? If one was going to conclude that a certain group has relentlessly pursued such a plan, it would require one to assume either such a plan was passed to the hereditary successors of secret groups, or that individuals return in many life-times, to complete their

obsess ional plan. To accept the latter answer would require two assumptions:
a) **Re-incarnation**
b) **The Hidden Science** that has been secreted away from humanity, so that he might never understand the MRC case in our midst, or utilise such understanding to facilitate mankind's release from the trap. The hidden science would reveal much in the understanding of pre-history, religious texts, mythology and archaeology let alone religion and politics. Once man understands the method of control, the possibility of his becoming an enslaved species vanishes.

THE WORLD GRID

The Earth and its energies are arranged into an intelligent geometric pattern, termed the world grid. According to Webster's dictionary, a grid is: "a network of uniformly spaced horizontal and perpendicular lines, specifically one used for locating points (as on a map, chart or aerial photograph) by means of a system of co-ordinates". If one could consider the earth enveloped in a lace doily of electromagnetic fields and pulsing points of light, the intricate lace pattern consisting of glowing energy lines, one would have a perception of what is otherwise invisible to the naked eye, since it is incapable of registering the energy or wavelengths which are a part of the field.

In *Alternative 4,* I proposed a mechanism for the **natural UFO Phenomenon**, as a magnetic-vortex of   **information** relating to two distinct types a) the pre-history of man as an evolutionary line and b) spiritual memories recorded as archetypal symbols, mainly if not entirely dating to ancient Greece circa 2-3,000 BC. The historical significance of these symbols relating to a battle between Patriarchal and Matriarchal religion was covered in *The Battle of The Trees.* The disturbance of this energy field or vortex e.g. by solar flux, results in the natural phenomenon of the UFO. This is entirely different from the **manipulated UFO phenomenon**, which has been orchestrated by secret groups to cover up the hidden science of which the natural UFO phenomenon is a part. The energy field that I postulated must exist and which is responsible for storing these genetic or morphogenetic memories and spiritual memories in what I termed **morphogenetic and spiritual bioplasmas** *(fig.1)* is I would consider from later research to be the Earth's energy Grid, i.e. the two may well be synonymous. Thus memories both spiritual and evolutionary are stored within the energy field of the Grid, or in my own terminology the double Diablo of the bioplasma. From my own research, I perceive that the pattern created by the Grid is probably a composite and three-dimensional pattern, composed of many diablo type organisations as in *fig.1.* Each mini Diablo would contain information relating to the evolutionary line of the species, together with a spiritual memory thus each species e.g. amphibian, reptile man etc. Would have an individual Diablo of information containing both the evolutionary line and spiritual memory of that particular species. Some of the shuffling animal-man like creatures recorded in natural UFO accounts, would appear to indicate that man or his soul, has in some very distant past occupied bodies other than the form of today – Homo sapiens. It was these sorts of accounts that lead me to hypothesise that the soul of some men had occupied bodies from the animal kingdom in the past. The disturbance of these information fields in space e.g. by atomic explosions or secret weaponry, cause such information to become available to the mind of man, where the brain acting as dipole radio-receiver picks up the information. This in essence is the basis of the natural UFO phenomenon and witness accounts. Thus the UFO incident often involves a curious 'not now' or metaphysical quality, which is experienced as a religious initiation. In fact it is a glimpse into the long and distant past of man's history, which includes alien beings and space ships.

It is interesting that I postulated two separate bioplasmas for genetic and spiritual memories, since in the 1960's, three Russian scientists examined the globe, to see if any pattern should emerge linking significant places in history with the pattern of the world grid and published their findings in a paper entitled *'Is the Earth a Large Crystal?'* These Scientists proposed that a "matrix of cosmic energy" was built into the structure of Earth at the time of formation as a crystal and only eventually became the globe we know today as a solid structure[1]. According to this hypothesis, the crystal can still be observed as twelve pentagonal slabs covering the globe's surface (*fig.2*) - as a dodecahedron. Socrates remarked as much to his pupil Simmias: "My dear boy, the real earth viewed from above is supposed to look like one of those balls made out of twelve pieces of skin sewn together". Evidently then, Socrates and the early Greek Philosophers including Pythagoras who were generally members of secret groups (in the case of Pythagoras - The Pythagoreans) were quite conversant with the Earth Grid. According to the Russians, overlaid on these slabs are 20 equilateral triangles and the overall geometric structure they claim can be seen in the siting of ancient civilizations, being placed at either the intersections of the Grid, or its energetic lines.

Fig.1 **Proposed model of Bioplasma vortex organisation Of morphogenetic and spiritual memory/experience**

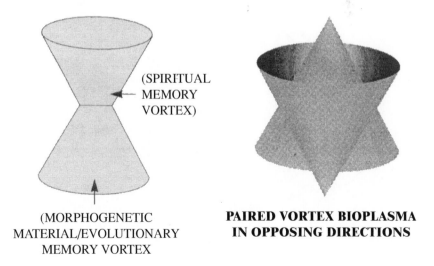

(SPIRITUAL MEMORY VORTEX)

(MORPHOGENETIC MATERIAL/EVOLUTIONARY MEMORY VORTEX

PAIRED VORTEX BIOPLASMA IN OPPOSING DIRECTIONS

All life on earth is based on the carbon atom *(Fig. 3)* and the geometric model proposed by the Russians had a definite similarity to the model of a carbon molecule. Further the remarkable co-incidence of the world's megalithic monuments and ancient civilizations which were sited along the grid geometry, has led to speculation that ancient civilizations were aware of this energy grid, which may have been more visible in the past, or man was able to consciously discern this geometric energy via magnetic senses that we have lost or that have become vestigial e.g. the pineal gland in the brain has been proposed as a rudimentary or vestigial magnetic sensor organ, which may still function in the natural UFO phenomenon and the way information from the energy field is picked up, rendering the brain with radio-receiver properties.

Whilst I had concluded from my own archaeological research in Greece (*The Battle of The Trees*) that a Religious Revolution had occurred in Greece (Crete), circa 1400BC which was directed by a secret cabal who had sought to eradicate not only a belief in Re-incarnation, which I conclude was the **first**
Belief held in the West, but there was an indication, that knowledge on what later was to be described by Einstein as **curved space-time**, had also been lost or withdrawn into the secret group or cabal behind the Revolution. The identity of the secret cabal was not clear, however The Druids with their University in Britain at the time, must surely be a contender as one group with the power to instigate this Religious Revolution, over the powerful but peaceful Minoan civilization. Thus I concluded that not only was a belief in Re-incarnation lost to the West during this period, but a whole Cosmology also.

Fig.2   **Earth cystaline energy grid**

The so-called Russian Grid,
Treating the earth as if it were a gigantic crystal.

Fig.3   **Computer simulation of molecule C60   - a hollow sphere, it can hold other atoms.**

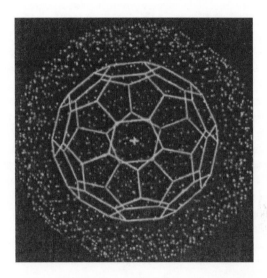

Note: similarities in grid concepts with this computer model of a carbon molecule (*from*: *Anti-Gravity and the World Grid Ed. David Hatcher Childress*)

In the Ashmolean Museum in Oxford, England, are several hand-sized stones, with true geometric proportion and a precise carving which Keith Critchou[2] links to Neolithic Britain, with a conservative construction date circa 1400 BC This was precisely the date of the Religious Revolution in Crete. The stones are an octahedron, icosahedron, dodecahedron, tetrahedron and cube. Whilst the stones have been given an earliest construction date of 20,000 BC, the main point to notice is that knowledge of geometry existed some 1000 years at least, before Plato described his five solids in Timaeus. Some researchers have proposed that knowledge of these geometric solids existed in Pre-Egyptian civilizations (2,500 BC) and further similar finds have been discovered in Scotland. The link between Scotland in the U.K. and Crete, will form a large part of the thesis of this book, building on the thesis of *The Battle of The Trees*, where I proposed a secret group engineered the events or plans of Golgotha which sought to eradicate once again the belief in Re-incarnation and which I concluded was directed by a secret group in Scotland. It should come as no surprise that stones portraying the Earth Grid and the hidden science, should be found there. Without stretching the point too far beyond what can be proven at this point, is it possible that wherever knowledge surrounding the belief in Re-incarnation and its associated Cosmology of Curved Space Time has tried to surface in a message to the people, a message that I have stated is a part of **The Holy Grail**, there has

33

been a concerted attempt by a secret group/s to push that knowledge back underground, where it became known as the **Underground stream** (of wisdom). I hope to provide persuasive evidence here, to prove that this has been the case from the very beginning. If the belief in Re-incarnation carried with it, knowledge of curved space-time and the trap that holds man, it becomes apparent why such knowledge should have been sequestered very early on in man's history, since such knowledge would require recognition of the intimate effect of

Earth's energies and the Grid upon our own mental, emotional and physical functions and without such knowledge, the possibility of the manipulation of those functions by secret groups became possible – **manipulation by the Earth energy Grid.** Knowledge of the Grid and control over it provided a source of power and wealth to the Elite. However it appears to me from my own research, that the MRC case knew very well what wealth and power was to be had by manipulation of the Grid, but his understanding of the Grid as an energy field of information has been little. The covert attempts today to veil the natural UFO phenomenon is merely the MRC case doing what he has always done, suppress any area of the hidden science, which threatens to enlighten man as to his past. More specifically the past of the MRC case our Fallen Angel, or Lucifer.

The ancient stones which are wrapped in thongs (*fig.4*) define a particular geometry and which Becker and Bethe Hagens 3 postulate reveals their use as planning models for a single sphere (the globe), upon which would be combined all the (thong) wrappings and points of all five solids, perhaps creating the model of a polyhedron, with fifteen great circles or "equators" of leather thong thus creating a 120 (triangles) polyhedron, with intersections at 62 predicted common points. The 120 polyhedron could be used for mapping, dowsing or geometry (earth measure) and the armillary sphere or "celestial basket", discovered in Crete although not explained or catalogued as such, used as an astronomical device to measure time via the solstices and daily sunrises.

Fig.4a **Ancient leather thong-wrapped stones from Minoan Crete**
(Ashmolean Museum Oxford U.K.)

I have pointed out in my own research that many icons from the Knossos archaeological site in Crete, do not in current catalogue description, reflect scholarly knowledge and I have re-interpreted the icons based on my thesis. The Cycle of Eternal Return as a religious belief of The Minoans is not referred to in museum literature, which means that millions of visitors to the site of Knossos in Crete Greece are deprived of the true meaning behind it. I have re-interpreted in *The Battle of The Trees,* The Cycle of Eternal Return based on the icons, mythology and folklore as a belief in Re-incarnation, which was held by the Early Minoans. Sir Arthur Evans from Oxford the prime archaeologist and excavator of the site, appears to have set the impetus for viewing the site of Knossos as a palace of kings, rather than what it was - a religious building for the burial of the dead in honour of the Great Goddess in her death aspect - the White Goddess. There is no doubt that royal and kingly dynasties existed at Knossos and one such famous King is recorded in myth as King Minos. However from my own research of the site and its iconography, I conclude that such a dynasty toppled a peace loving and artistic civilization, which believed in Re-incarnation (The Cycle of Eternal Return). The Minoan civilization was subjected to a religious revolution, whereby The Holy Grail and cosmological knowledge of great importance was stolen. This was certainly catastrophic, since the secret cabal and power who stole that knowledge thereafter hid it from humanity and it would take many thousands of years and numerous attempts to wrestle this stolen knowledge back into the hands of the people, for whom it was meant. Neither is there any certainty that despite this book, it will ever again reach the people, who have so far and so long been manipulated in their thinking, that it might be impossible for them ever to grasp the enormity of this story. A few might recognise the truth however and this book, is written for those few.

Fig. 4b **R. Buckminster Fuller's configuration of electro-magnetic band widths** *(small sphere) is a hidden master pattern in the UVG 120 sphere. The similarity to hand-held decorative reed spheres from Southeast Asia is further evidence that such "planning models" have been in common use throughout history. A.M. Davie has used bandwidths to forecast an event in Catastrophe Theory: "I have done experiments (with band widths of frequency turnability) in the lab and found the same experiences as reported in the Bermuda Triangle and UFO incidents. This experiment is too dangerous to repeat, and*

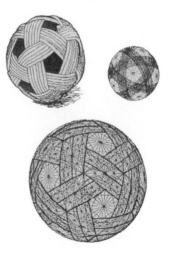

Edinburgh University has agreed to a ban on all attempts to re-enact the experiments. It is potentially lethal. The theory of this phenomenon was known to Aristotle ... It is definitely TIME-SPACE -COLOUR HARMONY syndrome in content, and therefore obeys a numerical law of nature to allow forecasting the event" (*From: Anti-Gravity and The World Grid Ed: David Hatcher Childress*)

Fig: 4c **Pages from Fuller's U.S. patent covering the Dymaxion map**
Science referred to this as "the first cartographic patent to issue from the U.S. Patent Office".

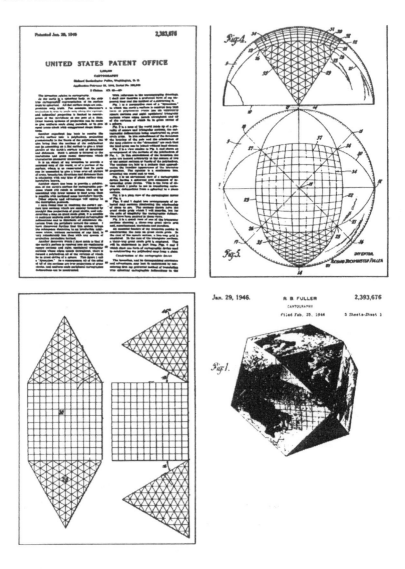

Author's note: Compare these lines of force and the ball of string appearance to Fig. 27b and Ariadne's ball of golden string, which in myth she gave to Theseus to get in and out of the maze to kill the Bull-Minotaur of Knossos. Also compare to Plate 10 and the early Kamares incised (zig-zag) pottery of Minoan Crete (prior to the Religious Revolution).Compare to zig-zag pattern (falling leaf tradjectory) of UFOs in Alternative 4. Did spiritual intervention c. 10 000 B.C try to teach man how to exit the trap of the Grid and control of humanity by the MRC case? Further did the MRC case or earthly Masters take over that knowledge and misuse it, which caused the Masters, initiates or magicians (Black Cabalists), to become trapped in another dimension, accounting for Masters in the Great White Lodge on Sirius? Does the Brotherhood communicate with them through the Crystal and does that Brotherhood hope to see their return to Earth at the end of things in the Catastrophe (for man)?

Fig.5 "**Ritual Swinging**"
A figure in terracotta swings between two upright supports Palms or Tree of Life? Or Twin Kings? With the epiphany (bird) of the Goddess at the top of each pillar:and may represent the philosophy of Rhea "as I go away, so must I return" (Re-incarnation) Note either head deliberately missing or lost on excavation. (Heraklion Museum Crete)

37

The suppression of the truth of the Knossos site cannot merely be laid at the door of ignorance or disagreement, for the omissions are so startling that I must conclude that there has been a concerted attempt to veil the truth here. To answer the question as to why such knowledge has been suppressed, the circle turns once again to the control of Orthodox Religion welded to politics and the enormous cover up of past religious history and the hidden science, which has enabled the secret global elite to fix an unreality and lie upon world history. If the swinging icon (*fig.5*) from Crete is merely labelled as "figure swinging" in museum literature, then such a description ignores the ancient Philosophy of Cretan Goddess Rhea: "As I go, so shall I return", which I equate with Re-incarnation. The museum catalogue of icons for Knossos in Crete refers to the carved granite figure (in which an armillary sphere rests) as an "unknown object", or possibly a barbeque device! However, curiously these objects were of such apparent significance, that archaeologists have cast concrete replicas for restorations. The armillary sphere (*fig.6*) casts a shadow on the captured stone within its framework, which parallels Hermetic philosophy: "As above so below". This perhaps refers to a greater pattern in space that is replicated below as I have proposed is the case for DNA. I have mystically proposed that the god Hermes was the first downgrade of the Matriarchal religion of Re-incarnation, which sought to introduce Solar Kingship - Apollo. The armillary sphere may have been introduced into Crete after the Religious Revolution (1,400BC), possibly by The Druids or a secret cabal, utilising certain knowledge taken from the Teacher of the Early Minoan civilization.

Fig.6 **Carved granite figure** "unknown object" in *Heraklion Museum* archives of Crete – possible rest for armillary sphere (*From: Anti-Gravity and World grid Ed: David Hatcher Childress*)

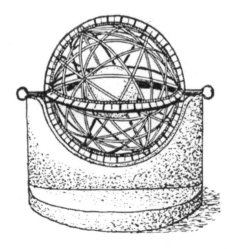

If the five solids (the geometries of the stones) are overlapped upon one another, a polyhedron with 121` great circles is produced with 4,862 points which represents the ultimate single sphere pattern housing all five Platonic solids, which Becker and Hagen's term **The Unified Vector Geometry (UVG) 120 sphere.**

This geometry defines the crystal-like lattice pattern of energy, which surrounds the earth, which is commonly referred to as the Earth Grid. Donald Cyr and Sir. J. Norman Lockyer 4 as experts in archaeoastronomy has noted angles of 22, 11, 46, 90, 120 and 180 degrees, for site layouts of ancient stone circles and cities. Further such sites show the circular plan of radiating lines diverging from sacred centres. Such angles also link with other sacred sites and interestingly the basic triangle of the UVG 120 sphere is represented in such geometry.

Richard Benson[5] proposed Cairo as an ancient surviving example of a precise geometric plan with angles similar to the UVG 120 sphere, radiating from a central point of the pyramids of Gizah. The Piri Reis Map found in Istanbul in 1929 and said to be a copy of a map from the library of ancient Alexandria, and the Buache map of 1737, are unique documents which show Antarctica correctly positioned, despite the fact that Antarctica was not known before the International Geophysical Year of 1958. In the Buache map, Antarctica is shown without ice cover, which indicates not only a dramatically different climate from today, but also begs the question whether a change in the Earth Grid was responsible for such climactic alteration of geophysical conditions and which I have discussed under magnetic reversals (*Alternative 4 and Part II of the Cancer Document*).

Interestingly the centres of all 10/12 Pentagons which form part of the geometry of the 120 sphere, fall at the edges of land continents or in oceans, indicating that any changes in the grid would dramatically re-define "what is below", "as above" (Hermetic philosophy) and equally land masses could have been predicted and mapped through a knowledge of the Grid and indeed it is thought that navigation and the discovery of various continents portrayed in ancient maps reflect this knowledge. Researchers in the 60's and 70's correlated ship and plane disappearances worldwide to magnetic phenomena at twelve equally spaced areas of the globe; the Bermuda Triangle was one such area: These same areas in the pattern of an icosahedron were mapped out by J.J. Hurtak[6] where he proposed time warp areas, where objects and even ships could pass into another dimension. Despite the apparent science fiction, the physics of the Earth Grid and Einstein's theories, were looking towards a fourth dimension in that era. Although we know now, that teleportation is not considered immediately possible for large objects.[7]

The research of Ivan Sanderson and Christopher Bird[8] initiated a worldwide research effort to understand the World Grid, an effort you will note that came not from orthodox science, but the Alternative Field. The idea of **morphogenetic fields** were introduced by British biologist Rupert Sheldrake[9] before whom there was little comprehension of this complex concept, which Sheldrake explained in terms of once something comes into existence e.g. an idea, a gene code or even a chemical or crystalline structure or a process that has not been achieved before, it exclusively fills a cosmic niche and sends a kind of formative energy through Gaia (Earth) and makes its appearance quickly and with increasing ease throughout the world. Harold Burr was the originator of such thought although his work was little if at all known outside the scientific community. Burr proposed "jelly moulds" which governed the formative shape of animals as a non specific field in space, thus laying the groundwork for my own theory that there is a master pattern in space, which may not only govern the formative shape of the young embryo, but may include the genetic blueprint of DNA itself, on the Hermetic and esoteric principle of: "as above so below". Dr. R. Becker, who has twice been nominated for a Nobel prize and has recently drawn the attention of the scientific community to the prospect of magnetic reversals, for which labour of conscience and courage I believe he has been severely repressed in his academic career, was later to take up this idea of a non specific field governing the formative shape of the young animal in his research and which I discuss in *Part II of The Second Millennium Working Report into Cancer.*

If one was going to perceive Hermetic philosophy: "As above, so below" as a greater truth, then one might expect an etheric or electromagnetic form of the hereditary material - DNA in space, which acts as the master blue-print upon which the physical DNA in the cells is formed. In other words the morphogenetic blueprint of body shape, which appears to exist as a non-specific field in space, may be etherically coded information on the genetic line of a species. I have questioned in my own research, whether the DNA shaped crop circles re-produced in *Alternative 4,* were evidence of that natural field and pattern in space, or whether there has not been a manipulative experiment to simulate that pattern in order to observe the effects (of control) on man, either way the fact that this pattern is being observed in crop circles warrants interest/concern. The mystic always sees the Universe, as the Cosmogony of one cell and all that exists in the universe, or macrocosm is really just a replica of the smallest cell in our bodies and the microcosm. Indeed as I pointed out in the decoding of the floor of the summer smoking room at Cardiff castle in Wales (UK) in *The Battle of The Trees,* secret groups appear to have understood this point very well. The mystic would find no objection to the postulated existence of a master DNA thread of living vibratory energy in space, which acts as a master blue-print for the DNA that occurs on the physical level in the cells of our bodies. **All is vibration**, which is a periodic impulsation or wavelike oscillation of forces. Vibrations occur in solids, liquids, air, and in electromagnetic phenomena. If the master DNA blueprint exists in the etheric layer of space, then it would simply replicate the vibratory pattern but possess a higher vibratory resonant rate, than the physical DNA in the cell. Further the postulation of this master DNA resonant pattern, would explain the research of Burr, Becker and Sheldrake and the control of the body-shape of the young animal or plant by a non-specific field in space. It is but one step further to postulate that a master blueprint of DNA governs the entire genetic line of a particular species and all species. The UFO field and Crop Circles have become another area of confusion where agents? Have been employed to confuse and alter natural phenomena, which might have lead to an understanding of the Earth Grid and its energies, such energies relate to the hidden science. Deliberate and manipulated confusion and the attachment of the label 'lunacy' to any scientist who attempted to look at these fields, has meant that a scientist would not risk his or her credibility by venturing into these areas of research. Undoubtedly my own research into these fields has cost me my orthodox scientific career - how do you add UFO research to your curriculum vitae! However, I have managed in *Alternative 4*, to propose a mechanism *The Onion-Ring Model*, which describes how the natural UFO phenomenon works, based on the existence of the bioplasma organisation of electro-magnetic energy within the ether. The fact that such a mechanism depends on a realisation of the hidden science, accounts for the deliberate attempts to add significances to the natural phenomena, creating what I called the unnatural or manipulated UFO phenomena. Three men in black, messages that drop in bottles, agents from the intelligence services with Mongolian-type eyes, are all part of the UFO confusion and the willingness to go to great lengths, in order to cover up an energy phenomenon which is natural and associated with the Earth Grid. Obviously to keep a cover up of this magnitude in place and the suppression of a whole science, required complete control over publishing, media, education, research and grants, the intellectual community and many other spheres, which has proven itself an effective force, in preventing the true background to world politics and religion currently being known by the majority of people. These forms of suppression in order to create "Monster Government", which many perceive as the world globalisation plan with a Federal European Super state, were referred to in the notorious *Protocols of Zion*, a document that purported to emanate from Jewish sources, as a plan for world domination. The source of the document has been disputed and whilst such a plan could be seen at the top of virtually all secret societies in the past, the fact remains that virtually all the goals in the document whether Jewish or not, have come to fruition.

Apart from the possibility of the control of the mental and physical functions of man (after all the Grid can govern the shape of continents), the Grid has another possibility, which was later to be proven by the independent researcher and

Cardiff Castle

genius Nikola Tesla - **FREE ENERGY**. The Global Elite have evolved into a position of immense power and wealth by controlling and profiting from world resources, particularly those resources concerned with energy (coal, oil, petroleum etc,). Free energy would have posed a severe threat to the globalisation plan and the Chemical Syndicate who control not only resources but retain a monopoly of healing via the pharmaceutical industry, any understanding of the Grid or the hidden science would have mortally threatened profits to be milked from humanity. As has been noted, there are a few extremely rich people on this planet who control virtually all resources and through vast profits and wealth – politics and religion.

Whilst man was unaware of a whole **information system** that existed in what was formerly known as the ether or space, this was not so for secret groups or occultists. Rudolph Steiner the founder of Anthroposophy, referred to this information system as the **"Akashic Record"**. Scientists have long known of such an information system, when it was observed that learning behaviour could be transferred within social groups of the same species, but separated physically at different locations. The learning behaviour could only have been transferred by a non specific species field, the field that Dr. Becker was subsequently to work on and previously described by Harold S. Burr and developed as a theory by Sheldrake i.e. the master blue-print in space, which I associate with the morphogenetic bioplasma and which must form the structure or overall geometry of the Earth Grid.

The Russians were actively engaged in electro-magnetic research in the 20's and 30's and numerous scientific papers emerged and a great deal of this research was included in *Part I of The Second Millennium Working Report into Cancer*. Photographic imaging techniques had allowed the Russian researcher Kirlean to photograph the **biofield** of plants and leaves and later photographic imaging of the human biofield or **aura**[10] or the electro-magnetic field that surrounds all living things including man. This field is part of the hidden science and although the aura and biofield have been extensively reported in Eastern medicine and literature, giving the impression that such knowledge is not hidden or repressed, how many cancer sufferers or sick people know that their illness is a result of a disturbed energy field, with its corresponding effect on the glandular and hormonal system? In fact there is an energy field that surrounds all living organisms and man, which operates at an overall vibratory rate that determines health or sickness. Man has a seven-layered energy field that surrounds him, which has an overall egg-shape, which I more fully discuss in the *Cancer report and Alternative4,* along with the iconographic significance of the egg-shape. The natural scientific progression of this research was to apply these techniques and develop them, to look at healthy and diseased tissues including cancer cells and further apply electro-magnetic wavelengths to determine whether the field could be reverted from a diseased to a healthy state. Such research never occurred officially and any researcher or scientist who subsequently applied this knowledge to healing, became subject to the familiar forms of suppressive attack outlined in *Appendix I*. Lieutenant Commander T.E. Bearden[11] in a paper he published, claimed that electro-magnetic research into disease control by the Russians had been ongoing since the 1950's and indeed there has been a well documented case of the use of such research, in illicit application to staff at the American Embassy in Moscow (The Woodpecker signal); which it has been alleged caused a number of staff to subsequently become very ill. Whilst their illness has never been related to this claim, Bearden maintains that if the Americans had questioned it, it would have meant admitting that they had advanced enough in this field, to understand what The Russians were doing. The application of electro-magnetic research to secret weaponry had not surpassed the Russians or the Americans. Cancer patients and the sick are merely sacrificed to the cause of total control of the Grid together with the profits and power to be had.

Bearden further claimed that: "in the 1960's in Siberia, Vlail Kaz Nacheyev and his researchers accomplished enormous experimentation **proving that cellular death and disease of any type whatsoever could be transmitted electro-magnetically**". This team went on secretly to phase conjugate (time reverse) the "death photon" signals, to show that "**any cellular death and disease can be reversed or "cured" electro-magnetically as well**" (my emphasis). This is an extremely important point which if proven correct and I have no doubt that it is, since research tables exist that I have seen, which give a resonant vibration for various bacterial and viral infections, including the common cold. A bacterium or virus may be viewed as an overall resonance, which can be simulated as a particular vibratory frequency. Every living thing has an overall vibratory resonance and obviously a diseased cancer cell will show a different type of resonance to a healthy one, with the possibility of rectifying the field, electro-magnetically and thus bringing about a cure. Thus Bearden if correct, is maintaining that the research existed as far back as 1960, for looking at disease in a completely different way than drug orientated approaches which bear no known resemblance to the natural process of healing and sympathetic vibratory resonance of the body's energy field. What greater condemnation can one bring against those who have hypocritically stated that they were looking for a cure, whilst covering up the hidden science and using that for purposes of control, power and wealth; further condemning out of hand those alternative practises which sought by natural means to rectify that imbalanced energy field.

Whilst it is obvious from a Scientific standpoint, that such research must have been carried out, since disease as a battle of electro-magnetic vibrations had been recognised for quite some time, at least since the 30's by men such as

George Lakhovsky[12] and Paracelsus had said as much, long before the early pioneers went on to prove this was so. Despite the obvious potential in healing Bearden remarked that such research was never published, since he claims the Soviet Union had become the only nation in the 1960's, who had developed an electro-magnetic antidote to new lethal bacteriological weapons such as viruses, which gave the Russians the advantage of mass electro-magnetic treatment, as an antidote to such weapons. Cancer patients were simply expendable in the face of gains in biological warfare, defence and the possibility of control of humanity. Scientists like Upton Knuth and Armstrong, De La Warr and Wilhelm Reich who I referred to in *Alternative4* as having embarked on this field of research   in the 30's - 50's, were suppressed and in the case of Reich who had tried to apply his research to the field of healing, he had his research taken by the FBI. This occurred in the case of the research of the future genius Nikola Tesla. Bearden pointed out that:" in the late 1960's and early 1970's a French inventor - Antoine Priore built and tested several large electro-magnetic devices that cured thousand of cases of terminal cancers and leukaemia's in laboratory animals. He worked with members of the prestigious French Academy of Sciences. His work was funded by the French Government and was presented to The French Academy by Robert Courrir, head of the biology section". Evidently such research was not applied to humans, or if it was, it was never published, despite the promising nature of the animal study.

If electro-magnetic research was not applied to saving human life, then the failure to explain the workings of the UVG 120 Earth Grid to those engaged in navigation was also a serious omission in the saving of human life. According to Becker and Hagens the overall organisation of the planetary Grid is anchored in the north and south axial poles and the area where the great pyramid at Gizeh sits. The Grid which has 121 great circles or 120 identical triangles running through 4,862 points also contains 10/12 polyhedrons within its geometry or ten basic triangles all approximately 30, 60 and 90 degrees in composition, which create a **pentagon** and thereby producing **12** large pentagons in the entire structure. For those who have followed my previous books, the symbolic numbers will be evident. The Grid for this reason is also described as the **UVG** (Unified Vector Geometry) **10/12**.Becker and Hagens have suggested that the flight KAL 007, a jumbo jet lost in an explosion on September 1st 1983 and KAL 902 from Paris on April 20th 1978. Which also crashed, may be due to untimely crossings of major grid points, in the former case grid 6 and the latter grid 11.Both incidents were caused it is argued, as they crossed specific grid points at pre-dawn times and when the grid was at its most active. Importantly both aircraft were dependent upon computerised navigational system, which could have been severely affected by changes in Grid energies. KAL 007 left Anchorage on an intended flight to Seoul, South Korea, but was diverted down a minor grid line to a crash site near Sakhalin Island. KAL 902 left Paris bound for Anchorage and was diverted down a minor grid line and was shot down by the Soviets, near Murmansk in the Soviet Union.

If science has been held back in the field of healing, by unpublished research on the Grid, then that is also the case with archaeology, meteorology and anthropology. The curious lines of the Nazca area in Peru, with an elaborate pattern of lines produced by stones placed at intervals for many miles, has been portrayed by media as a curiosity and yet clearly here are the **ley or energy lines** of the corresponding Earth Grid ;on the Hermetic principle of: "as above, so below". In *Alternative 4* I remarked that a spider when given the psychotropic drug LSD weaves a perfect web of concentric circles, which is more perfect than it would weave under normal circumstances i.e. without the drug. Has no Scientist wondered how and why the spider weaves its web that way? Well certainly this is a reflection of Grid energy patterns and specifically the concentric circles one would expect from a concentric bioplasma of electro-magnetic energy. A pattern of concentric energy has also been reported in UFO incidents and manifests in tornados. I also suggested that the interest the CIA took in occultists and mediums in the 60's, who tramped through their offices in mysterious numbers, was an attempt to use these psychics to pull information down from the Grid.The inexplicable and rapid advancement of technology after this point may prove that the method of pulling down information from what Rudolph Steiner referred to as the "Akashic Record" or what is really just a rather large library in the sky, was effective. The interest of the CIA in the drug LSD, with the well documented abuses by the agency in illicit testing in the 60's and 70's, may well have been based on the question as to whether LSD enhances perceptions of Grid memories and specifically **past technology**, by tuning the mind to this harmonic band on the Grid. The spider certainly can tune to the geomagnetic energies of the Grid far more accurately under this drug. The Nazca lines in Peru, quite clearly show certain animals attached to the positions of the electro-magnetic ley lines, one of those animals is curiously enough the spider.

Was it really co-incidental that Nostradamus the prophet, should predict that 1997 was the year of the Spider? - Certainly within these predictions as with the prophetic Apocalypse - The Book of *Revelations*, one has the feeling that such predictions are based on a cyclical repeated experience, and that the whole sequence has **turned in entirety before**, in a prior era. Imagine that one could use a psychic or seer to pull information of past events from the Grid. One could create a new war based upon an old battle and predict the outcome on the basis of the past, provided that one utilised enough elements of the past. The prophesies of Nostradamus often mention a Third Reich vision, which may have represented some past battle. Hitler was indeed obsessed, as were most of the hierarchy of the Nazi party with astrology and perhaps the reason becomes clear. The persistent site line ups of ancient megaliths and sacred constructions e.g.

Stonehenge and Glastonbury Tor including Cathedrals and Churches, which are for the main built on prior sacred sites and electro-magnetic ley lines, indicates that ancient man was quite aware of the Earth Grid. However it is questionable whether he understood the Etheric Grid as an **information system**, or UVG120 sphere, before such knowledge was obtained from Crete at the time of the Religious Revolution 1 400 BC. And where significant knowledge was stolen.

The Sefirotic Tree of Life of the **Kabbalah** (Kabala or Cabbala) may not only be related to the energy centres within the human body, through which energy flows and which are known as the **chakras**, but can be applied to the great intersections of the earth and energy Grid, as the body of Universal Man, giving rise to a number of connected 'trees' over the surface of the globe, corresponding to major intersections or pentagrams (12) indicating either root races and sub root races or indeed the 12 tribes of Israel. The Kabala is a word taken from the ancient Hebrew and, literally translated means: "Doctrines received by ancient traditions". The written teachings of the kabala go back perhaps no later than the Eleventh Century. There is evidence however, that the oral teachings were in existence at a far earlier date. Traditionally they are said to date back to the time of the Secret Wisdom related by Moses. There is no doubt that such doctrines referred to the rituals and knowledge pertaining to the hidden science and the Grid, with its energies. Moses himself utilised it in the energies he conjured on Mt. Sinai and the production of the Ten Commandments, where there was "thundering and lightening" and Moses descended the mountain with a horribly burnt face that one might expect of radiation burns. Similarly Joshua utilised the hidden science when he used vibratory resonance knowledge to destroy the walls of Jericho.

Bruce Cathie[13] has theorized over a pulsating Grid and how that might relate to the UFO phenomenon and it is curious how in my own research I found the UFO phenomenon to be linked to an energy field, which I termed a **Bioplasma Vortex.** Whilst the genetic and evolutionary line memories appear to be stored within the information energy field, I further proposed that spiritual memories were recorded as archetypal symbols as evidence of the mythological mind of man, before the use of language to portray complex religious beliefs and such symbols were *purposely* imprinted into the vibratory electro-magnetic pattern of the Grid at a higher frequency period of activation of the Grid. Such periods of high activity of the Grid were recognised as the spring and autumn, which were then made to co-incide with with the religious festivals. The fact that I noted in my own research, that many of these archetypal symbols of the UFO phenomenon related to Greece, is further evidence that true religion or its philosophical beginnings were found in ancient Greece. Such early religion would appear to centre in my own research on the early tribes of the Peloponnese and subsequently the Early Minoans of Crete, where a secret cabal stole that belief system of Re-incarnation along with knowledge of curved space-time and the Grid, hiding such knowledge from humanity. Whilst it seems probable that the cabal who conducted the Religious Revolution in Crete had their own knowledge of the Grid, they did not have any concept of space- time. Virtually all world religions later utilised that stolen knowledge to form their own religious festivals at the same periods, particularly the spring associated with re-birth (Re-incarnation). Christianity borrowed a great deal from *the* Teacher. The KAL 007 and KAL 902 tragedies occurred during significant holiday periods (007 during the major Hindu feast for Vishnu and 902 during Good Friday/Passover). One suspects at these times of high solar flux, there was the possibility of witnessing a natural UFO phenomenon, which must have appeared to man as visits from the gods or some supernatural happening of great import. In fact the UFO phenomenon occurs mainly at significant calendar cycle dates, particularly in the spring and autumn.

Credible researchers like Moray B. King[14] a PhD graduate in systems engineering, noted that anti-gravity (artificial gravity propulsion) was the only possible method to describe the reliable witness accounts of reported UFO's. As King noted in the way I had done, reliable witnesses such as airline pilots and police officers, could not easily be discounted. The question became how far research into the Grid had advanced and whether that research had produced hard sightings of UFO's (as opposed to the metaphysical), where witnesses reported silver discs. In *Alternative 4* I preferred to separate the natural UFO phenomenon from the manipulated kind, set up to confuse. Whilst crop circles are undoubtedly part of the manifestation of the hidden science how far secret research has now utilised the Grid and imprinted symbols on that Grid with a view to changing the information system is unsure. Some of the more spectacular crop circles with their intricate patterns may well derive from this route. If we remember that the MRC case fell to Earth after manipulating the genetic master blueprint as I proposed was the case, it seems entirely likely that such men would be found repeating that action. Wheeler[15] who is probably today's foremost Physicist and authority on gravitation, proposed that in quantum mechanics there existed an all-pervading energy embedded in the fabric of space consisting of fluctuations of electricity. It was called the **zero point energy**. Quantum mechanics showed that this energy was constantly interacting with matter and the elementary particles in what is called vacuum polarization. King proposed that if only a small amount of this energy could be made available, then not only could artificial gravity be induced, but the energy could be tapped as an energy source, and certainly Nikola Tesla was working in this field. Hitler himself appeared to have some idea of the fact that space was not empty when he stated, "space is not a vacuum"[16]. This is certainly an odd statement unless Hitler's scientists were already researching the Grid and Space, which was the case and which I will cover later. Thus hard sightings of UFO's may represent on-going research into the Grid and the zero point energy, with anti gravity effects.

The alleged Philadelphia Experiment[17] where a United States Navy vessel the destroyer escort U.S.S. Eldridge, was supposed to have been made invisible and then made to appear at another shipyard only to appear back at the original dockyard some minutes later, has been deemed too fantastic to be true and has ended up with Morris Jessup an astronomy and mathematics Professor who investigated the incident, in the annals of UFO's for the year of 1943. Did it happen? Could it have happened? Has always been the question. In fact teleportation of large objects is not considered possible and thus whilst some unusual experiment may have occurred, it could not have been teleportation7. The fact that the Eldridge had been outfitted with several tons of specialised electronics equipment, capable of creating a tremendous pulsating force or field around itself, has never been explained; or the eye witness accounts of some bar maids who said that the crew from the Eldridge after the experiment, whilst on shore leave, had suddenly walked through doors and become invisible, which as a reminder of the Gospel account of Paul on the appearance of Jesus after The Resurrection is curious. The United States Government has for the last 43 years officially denied that the experiment ever took place and whilst many claim that Jessup was murdered and did not commit suicide, the fact that many of the Eldridge's crew subsequently became ill has never been explained. I have no doubt that some experiment had been undertaken utilising the Earth Grid energies and quite possibly some facet of Einstein's theories of relativity. The whole experiment may have gone horribly wrong and a different outcome to the expected one may have occurred. Alternatively it may have been an elaborate piece of disinformation (brown propaganda) to force the Russians into believing that the US had advanced in research on the Grid.

Morris Jessup wrote a book *The Case for the UFO,* a copy of which was forwarded to The Office of Naval Research, presumably by the mysterious figure of Carlos Allende or Carl Allen (whom plagued Jessup) and who had added some notes to the book. Key words that Allende had used in footnotes were "mother ship", "great arc", " great war", "little man", "force fields", "magnetic fields", "gravity fields", "*vortices*", "*magnetic net*" etc. The words and phrases indicate some knowledge of the structure of space and the Grid. The Navy naturally took a great interest in these notes and not long after Jessup's contact with The Navy, Jessup allegedly committed suicide. Jessup related to his friend Dr. Valentine that the alleged incidents of the Philadelphia experiment, in his view were accomplished by using magnetic field generators called degausses, which were "pulsed" at resonant frequencies to create a huge magnetic field around the ship. Jessup according to Dr. Valentine was on the verge of discovering what was happening in the experiment, which evidently was based on magnetic resonance, Jessup explained: "An electric field created in a coil induces a magnetic field at right angles to the first and each of these fields represents one plane of space, but since there are three planes of space, there must be a third field, perhaps a gravitational one - by hooking up electromagnetic generators so as to produce this third field through the principle of resonance ". Jessup believed that the Navy had discovered this by accident .In asking whether the Philadelphia Experiment actually occurred, one has to ask why Albert Einstein as noted in naval employment records, was employed as a Scientist for the Office of Naval Research from May 31st 1943, until June 30th 1944. Further he was recorded as having met with naval officers in his Princeton Study, three months prior to the Philadelphia Experiment. Charles Berlitz and William Moore, who wrote an account of the Philadelphia Experiment, came across a Navy source which remains anonymous and whose verbatim statement of the event runs:

> "I think that the conversation at this point had turned to the principles of resonance and how the intense fields which would be required for such an experiment might be achieved using this principle...I do remember being at least one other conference where the matter was a topic on the agenda. During this one we were trying to bring out some of the more obvious-to-us side effects that would be created by such an experiment. Among these would be a 'boiling ' of the water, ionisation of the surrounding air, and even 'Zeemanising' of the atoms, all of which would tend to create extremely unsettled conditions. No one at this point had ever considered the possibility of inter-dimensional effects or mass displacement... We also felt that with proper effort some of these problems could be overcome... and that a resonant frequency could probably be found that would possibly control the visual apparent internal oscillation so that the shimmering would be at a much slower rate.
>
> I recall strongly that for a few weeks after the meeting in Albrecht's office (Albrecht is a fictitious name for the actual officer), we kept getting requests for tables having to do with resonant frequencies of light in optical ranges. These were frequently without explanation attached, but it seems likely that there was some connection here."

Not only during the period of this alleged experiment was Nikola Tesla working on resonant energies and very nearly brought a high rise New York building down with his experiments, but he was also in contact with Einstein, just what the connection was to the ultimate famous equation linking matter or mass with Energy may never be fully known, however $E = MC^2$ proved that the value for M or Mass can be replaced by a wave-form which is matter. According to Bruce

Cathie, the substituted term is a function of the velocity of light: Thus energy or E can be expressed in terms of pure electro-magnetic energy and is interchangeable with matter. The equation involves the speed of light and there is thus a consideration of what happens to matter as the harmonic of light decreases and increases when matter and energy in the equation at some point become interchangeable. The concept that Einstein proposed with gravity as a product of curved space- time, begs the question of how far experiments went to try to change the fabric of space-time by playing around with the geometric matrix of space and its inherent energy – the zero point energy. Was it possible that such experiments sought to modify frequencies which controlled matter and anti matter cycles? In theory at least this would allow traversal of tremendous distances in space by altering the structure of space itself. Zero time in Physics was always inherent within Einstein's theories and laws of relativity. Bruce Cathie, who studied the latitudes and longitudes of the Philadelphia and Norfolk Navy Dock Yards involved in the Philadelphia experiment, discovered that the latitude of the Philadelphia Naval Base set up a prime harmonic of the speed of light, which was 143,795.77 seconds of the Arc. *Also the college of Science was established at this latitude.*

In assessing whether the Philadelphia experiment ever took place and whether there was an attempt to look at the geometric of space time, it should be asked whether it is significant that the latitude of the Norfolk Naval Docks (36 55 08.634 North and 76 19 45 West longitude), and the Penn's Landing Area Philadelphia (75 08 55.8 West Longitude and 39 56 35.77 North latitude), coincide with the Earth Planetary Grid line[18] on the Becker-Hagen's World Grid system. Is it also significant that this grid line connects with the Bermuda Triangle, a place associated with the mysterious disappearance of boats?

Unfortunately little explanation of the geometric of space has been available for those who do not possess advanced degrees in the subject of physics, but to obtain a clearer grasp of what Physicists were hoping to gain from experimentation, it might be useful to cover briefly some of the main ideas that surfaced at the time. In 1980 the expanding view of space was expressed as, empty space, is not empty at all, its full, an immense sea of energy on top of which matter, as we know it is only a small quantal wave-like excitation. Rather like a tiny ripple. The entire Universe of matter is to be treated as a comparatively small pattern of excitation on the energy sea. This was an advance on the Bohm-Attaromov effect[19] and underlines the work of Moray B. King[14], who took up Tesla's research in postulating how free energy and antigravity might be possible with today's physics. Briggs and Peat[20] in discussing Bohm's work stated: "In one cubic centimetre of empty space the amount of energy is much greater than the total amount of energy of all matter in the known Universe".

Thus the first point to be noted is that there is an awful lot of free energy out there in space, if only it could be trapped! However Einstein transformed the three- dimensional world into a four- dimensional world, based on curved space-time, (although the Early Minoans I would maintain knew all about this with their curved-rim sarcophagi, in which the dead were laid to rest in a Cycle of Eternal Return). Today physicists see The First Order of Reality that is observable, emerging from the vector interactions of electro-magnetic energy with matter. There is however also a more fundamental Second Order of Reality, which is unobservable and which consists of virtual (subquantal) vectors and conditions and this is the Second Order which Nikola Tesla discovered in his sympathetic vibration energy experiments. Thus physicists today, see more than four dimensions explaining theoretical physics and models of 8, 11, 32 and more dimensions have been proposed. In *Alternative4* I suggested that advances in theories of the zero-point energy and non-linear thermodynamics, had opened up the possibility of trapping or cohering this energy and the production of ball lightning in the laboratory may have been behind the UFO witness accounts of public near to sensitive research facilities, who had reported coloured balls of lights. There is no doubt that research and experimentation with the fabric of space, has been going on at least since the 40's and the rapid rise of UFO sightings in the 60's and 70's are I conclude the result of dislodging information from the energy matrix or vortices, which I term bioplasmas. Further the enormous number of atomic bombs detonated since Hiroshima and Nagasaki must have added to this instability of what Rudolph Steiner called the Akashic Record, or that great library of information in the sky. A memory that I have proposed is composed of both genetic or evolutionary line memories (the master blueprint) *and* spiritual memories retained as archetypal symbols, mainly connected to Greece.

Wheeler who is the foremost authority on Gravity and space geometrics had derived a view of the fabric of space in which the large energy densities of the zero-point fluctuations caused space to pinch in a manner similar to the formation of black holes. Wheeler's view was that the vacuum of space was in fact a fluctuating sea of mini-black holes and mini-white holes with electric flux passing through channels in hyperspace, which he called **wormholes**. The fluctuating 'sea' was called the **quantum foam**, which allowed connectiveness between distant objects in space instantaneously, with the idea of many universes parallel to our own.

Moray king stated that by introducing a slight coherence in the action of the zero-point energy this may curve the space-time metric yielding artificial gravity and I proposed in *Alternative4* that whilst solar flux may have caused warps in space time resulting in the natural UFO phenomenon in the past, one could not discount that Atomic explosions and the possible 'tinkering' with space in Grid or zero-point energy cohesion experiments, would have disturbed the intelligence or information carried or imprinted on these energies which I termed **hyper spatial Bioplasmas**, which are electro-magnetic in nature. This would account for the steep rise in the number of UFO incidents reported since the 60's with the parallel rise of Atomic tests. The model I proposed for this mechanism was 'The onion Ring Model' described in *'Alternative 4'*.

Richard Lefors Clark PhD[22] gives a method of conducting **human levitation using** the gravity magnetic anomalies on the Earth Grid, which are covered by the underlying principle of diamagnetism. This is certainly an exceptional 'party trick' and has been used in the past to impress the ignorant of supernatural powers. The famous Bermuda Triangle exists at a gravitational anomaly point on the grid and is renown as an area where sea and aircraft are periodically 'lost'. The earth itself may be considered as a huge magnet and the earth's magnetic field creates the electro-magnetic Grid, which surrounds the earth. New concepts of the laws of magnetism show that a point exists on the North South pole axis, where there is a neutral centre -The **Bloch Wall**, which is the junction between the two magnetic poles *(fig. 7)*. The Bloch wall has interested me from several points of view. Firstly I am intrigued as to why I intuitively in my own research, separated morphogenetic and spiritual memories of the natural UFO experience as **two opposing bioplasma fields** *(fig. 1)* which roughly in 3 dimensions looked like a **DIABLO** *(fig. 8)* a model generally associated with balance; and secondly since the Bloch Wall is the point of division of the circling vortex or spin, of the electro-magnetic energies of the North and South poles, what part is played by the Bloch Wall in maintaining balance within the Grid? Thirdly the negative energy pole and North pole magnetism spins to the LEFT, the positive energy pole and South pole magnetism spins to the RIGHT. The point of zero magnetism and no-spin and also the point of a magnetic reversal is where these two spin fields join - the Bloch Wall, which is the weak pressure (gravity) generator.

The archetypal pattern of the figure-of-8 is seen in this balanced spin diagram, a pattern that is repeated at the atomic level in the pattern of spin of electrons around a nucleus. Thus the Diablo of energy appears to reflect the Hermetic principle, "as above, so below" and the materialisation of a pattern on the material plane as a reflection of a master pattern in space. In *Alternative4* I noted that the balanced Diablo of the opposing 3D pyramidal bioplasmas for the morphogenetic and spiritual memory or information system, were in fact an archetypal sign, that may be represented by the Star of David. If the spiritual bioplasma as I have noted from own research carries mainly, if not entirely archetypal symbols and thoughts dating back to the earliest times of religious initiation, then the morphogenetic Bioplasma contains the genetic or evolutionary history of man, which relates to **survival of the species and**

matter. It is interesting to pose the question as to whether the Teacher had the forethought to place the truth of The Holy Grail within a higher more finely graded level of energy, which I term the spiritual bioplasma. I did propose in *Alternative 4,* that the point of exit of the spirit in The Near Death Experience (NDE) where people report travelling through a tunnel towards a bright white light, was through the morphogenetic vortex, an experience associated with matter where an after **life review** of all their life's actions, good and bad occurs. People often report meeting with their dead relatives and in those that survive the NDE, which has recently been proven as a time of clinical death, where the heart stops beating and to all intent and purposes the body at the time is clinically dead; there often occurs a requirement to return and finish some cycle that has not been completed. It is interesting that most witnesses speak of an **"intense white light"**, which must be the perception in some form, of the zero point energy embodied within the matrix of space. As an icon, the figure-of- 8 shield appeared in Minoan iconography after the Religious Revolution circa 1, 400 BC, after a secret cabal I proposed had entered Crete in order to eradicate the belief in Re-incarnation, sequestering at the same time, substantial knowledge on curved space and other aspects of Cosmology.

Fig.7a **Bloch Wall as Neutral Zone in Earth's Dipolar Magnetic Field**

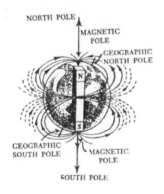

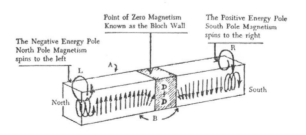

Fig.7b **Bloch Wall illustrated in a Magnet**

Fig.7c **The "Broken 8" Wave Zone in the Bloch Wall**
(Richard Lefors Clark, Ph.D in Anti-Gravity and the World Grid)

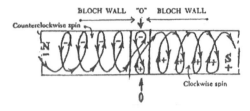

It has to be noted here, that the success of The Gerson Therapy which I utilised in my own research on cancer and which is more fully covered in *The Second Millennium Working Report on Cancer* depended on applying active enzymes which Dr. Gerson deemed necessary for the success of the therapy and which were supplied through the preparation of juices using a juicer which employed a grinder with a *counter-clockwise* spin (centripetal). This action may hold more significance than has previously been recognised. One might theorise that the bio chemicals in the cells require a certain polarity in enzymes to retain the activity of the active sites necessary for their function. *I* have no idea now, why I chose in my research to assign the centripetal movement or anti-clockwise direction for the *spiritual* bioplasma flow. The 'suck up' or exit effect of the bioplasma flow *(Alternative4)* which I intuitively applied to the **spiritual** bioplasma, has a motion that is replicated in the preparation of the juices. I cannot comment any more upon this intuitive application other than the observation, that every Cancer patient has suffered extensive and accumulative loss in the material world (jobs, relationships, bereavement etc) which is dependent on an initial loss in childhood and further from my own research can be further regressed into significant loss in a prior existence (past life). We simply do not understand fully the relationship of the atoms and molecules, to the vacuum or space energy, but I would tentatively suggest that the centripetal movement is perhaps a reflection of a higher graded energy mirrored by the larger spiritual bioplasma in space. Loss in cancer patients results in a severe reduction in available energy within the body chakra system, thus the centripetal movement or spin, may well allow a higher graded energy to enter through the chakra system, or the biochemicals exhibit more activity in certain spin forms.

***Fig.*8 Proposed Model of exit and Tunnel of the Near Death Experience**
(Bioplasma field of energy organisation in hyperbolic diablo model of space)

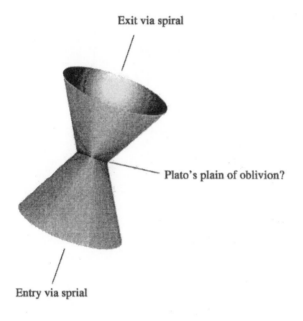

Exit via spiral

Plato's plain of oblivion?

Entry via sprial

Every electrified body has its aura (*Fig.9*), and when that aura is active it constitutes a magnetic field and the aura is sometimes called magnetism. Magnetism from an electrical point of view is described differently. Some minerals are naturally magnetic, such as iron of a certain nature, while others can be made magnetic, which indicates that magnetism is not a result of the atomic or molecular structure of matter, but rather of an electrical action that is taking place within the substance or which can be set up in the substance. One can induce magnetism in a metallic body by surrounding it with an electrical charge; but this further illustrates the law that magnetism results from action in the aura that surrounds all matter. Electrons can have auras; some auras are positive and some negative or repulsive and thus have either attractive or repulsive properties. It may be that the aura of the sick cell is merely a disconnection of the aura from its fundamental particles, which in turn rely on space energy for their integrity. The cells of the human body are surrounded by an aura and the whole body of man also has an electro-magnetic aura. This aura has some connection through the chakras, or energy points within its field, to the main flux of energy in the bioplasma. The human mind, which is able to control electrical energy in the body, is the prime activator of the aura, which through the chakras controls physical processes through the glandular and hormonal system. The mind is used in the psychic sense and not in the physical sense of a brain. These points are more fully covered in *Alternative 4*.

I will follow Everett's interpretation of many worlds shortly, but here it is interesting to quote Moray King[14] in the view that the zero-point energy or the higher graded system of energy that is in the matrix of space, is not separate from matter (our bodies) but forms a connectiveness. The Gerson Therapy in supplying a great deal of electro-magnetic energy in the form of the raw prepared juices from vegetables and fruit, may simply in the quantum system that is man, raise the energy within that system to a point, where it has access to the Many Worlds of Everett, which is the basis it has been suggested for **positive thinking** and perhaps underlines the observation in my own research, that after approximately 3 months on The Gerson Therapy, patients experience extreme negative (paradoxically) emotions, which represent an unconscious (not recognised by the conscious mind) confront of past life experiences (Other or Many Worlds in Everett's interpretation): "However, there is evidence that the zero-point energy is not a passive system but actually is a manifestation of an energy flux passing through our space orthogonal from higher dimensions. Wheeler derives such hyperspace channels (wormholes) in his geometrodynamics. Also, a picture of nonlocal connections is implied by quantum physics EPR paradox, Bell's Theorem, and hidden variable concepts. In addition, Sarfatti, Fenyman, and Dirac describe quantum mechanical propagators summing across the higher dimensions of super space, a picture that Everett similarly derives in his Many Worlds Interpretation of Quantum Mechanics". Quite a mouthful for the non-scientist, but simply no man or his energy field is an island; there is only a greater pattern of connectedness, even with the energy patterns within space. I perceive in the Gerson Therapy for cancer an attempt to connect the sick person once again to the greater pattern of which they are a part. When a man disconnects from the pattern, he is merely turning off his systems in an effort to no longer be a part of that pattern. However the soul and life is eternal a man can no more jump off life, than he can ignore the entirety of his being, which includes past lives. The man who says he has never lived before and "ashes to ashes", is merely disconnecting from the greater pattern.

Fig.9 **The seven layered Auric and Chakra system of man**
(see also Plate 2 for photograph of the biofield or aura)

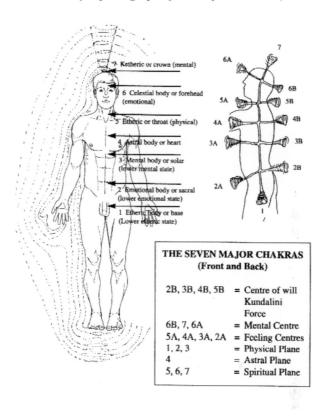

THE SEVEN MAJOR CHAKRAS
(Front and Back)

2B, 3B, 4B, 5B	= Centre of will Kundalini Force
6B, 7, 6A	= Mental Centre
5A, 4A, 3A, 2A	= Feeling Centres
1, 2, 3	= Physical Plane
4	= Astral Plane
5, 6, 7	= Spiritual Plane

The early Minoan Bronze Age Civilization along with certain early Matriarchal tribes in the Peloponnese Greece, principally I considered the Tuatha de Danaan who were driven out of Greece in the early invasions and which I covered in *The Battle of The Trees,* and whom went to Denmark giving that country its name, whilst some continued to Ireland; had I maintain, substantial knowledge of a certain Cosmology connected to a belief in Re-incarnation. The appearance of the figure-of-8 shield in Minoan iconography, after the Religious Revolution and which appears as a fresco painted on the walls of The Queens Chamber, at the Knossos site in Crete, remarkably may represent The Bloch Wall figure-of-8, the two- dimensional concept of a quadropole pattern. The Minoan seals which portrayed The Cycle of Eternal Return and which I equated with Re-incarnation, providing substantial evidence for that view in *The Battle of The Trees*, included one particularly interesting seal - A late (post Religious Revolution circa 1,400BC) Minoan gem from the Psychro Cave. In Myth the cave is where Zeus The Captain of The Twelve Olympian gods was reported to have been born and

57

which I equate in a broad sense, with the birth of materialism and "666", the origin of Power Politics and Religion in a **POWER PYRAMIDAL STRUCTURE** which has dominated world politics and religion ever since. The seal plainly shows The Bull Minotaur as a *single* Calendar Beast in the arched position indicating a downgrade of the original concept of the cycle, which involved *the woman*. One cannot dismiss the conclusion that birth of Solar Kingship (and the removal of the woman) saw its origins in this downgrade. Interestingly in this icon (*fig.10*) there is a triangle impaled, which may represent the cross as the four quadrants of the solar year and Calendar watched over by the four Calendar beasts. The structure may also be a representation of the pyramid, the significance of which was given in *'The Battle of The Trees* and certainly Hermes was associated with the 'T' shaped or Taur cross on which Jesus was apparently crucified as a Solar Hermetic King. Unusually though there is also present an odd 'dumbbell' structure and whilst no interpretation whatsoever for this seal is given in the museum literature, the 'dumbbell ', may well represent the Earth Grid field with The Bloch Wall clearly shown. How much did the Patriarchs know of atomic fusion or atoms? An interesting question that I will come to later.

I concluded in *The Battle of The Trees*, that a "gigantic plan" for world domination which can be traced back to The French Revolution of the 18th Century on the basis of historical reference and quotes, which have also been suppressed, went back further still to 1,400 BC and the Religious Revolution in Minoan Crete. The success of such a plan required a manipulation and control of the Earth Grid and the withholding of significant knowledge relating to Earth Grid energies together with any true Cosmology, which also included a belief in Re-incarnation. Such a belief always stood to be dangerous to the Global Elite, since a recognition of past memories and lives might uncover this plan completely - hence my story for a few thousand years at least in my commitment to what I consider to be the true word of a Higher Spiritual Source. Whilst many people may, if they have never accessed past lives, have difficulty with my account of the Crucifixion and the events of Golgotha, one has to be reminded that an infinite number of parallel Universes or what Everett describes as ' Many Worlds' answers more questions in theoretical physics, than could be answered otherwise. In short I doubt whether a Physicist would have any trouble at all with the concept of Re-incarnation, or a parallel universe but those religions steeped in dogma and edited versions of the truth would and will no doubt denounce my truth of the crucifixion.

Fig.10 **Late Minoan gem from Psychro cave**. (A.M. 1938.1071.) Man-bull in circle of eternal return with figure of eight shiled and impaled triangle (Ashmolean museum)

The intriguing question of which hierarchal group/s or Cabal were behind this plan of the crucifixion continually evaded me as did the question of which cabal conducted the Religious Revolution in Crete 1400BC which was really the start of the world Globalisation plan that we see today. I certainly will not allow that beautiful 'Moon' in the orbit of Greece - Crete, to be sacrificed to the manipulation of The Prophetic Apocalypse - The Book of *Revelations*, which appears to be the script or format of the World Order plan which I have covered in my two previous books. World events manipulated to parallel the prophecy undoubtedly authenticate such prophesy, -"you see it is all happening according to the prophecy", they cry as Christians await the coming of Jesus to sort out the mess. This is not to say that the prophesy is not founded on secret knowledge including the archetypes decoded in *The Battle of The Trees*, however "**The Great City**", which is identified with "666"in the Biblical account, suffers a large and devastating earthquake. One might conceivably conclude that perhaps Crete would be nominated or pre-determined for such an event, using secret Tesla vibration technology, which could then be slotted nicely into the scheme or plan for the supposed "Paradise on Earth", which is inevitably translated by the Global Elite as a Communistic 'Hive' controlled by the ultra rich extreme right. This is really all the plan for European Union or the Federal Super State as it is now acknowledged in all but name is, together with the extension of that, in the world Globalisation plan. The plan was referred to as a "United States of the West", at the time of the French Revolution, which was carried out by the secret group the Illuminati acting under the cloak of Freemasonry. Not that such a truth would appear in the school curriculum. The New World Order is merely what the MRC case or Magnetically Reversed Case perceives as **his** paradise.

There are of course other contenders for "The Great City" of the Revelations account, Rothschild a major player in the world Globalisation plan, was the first to name London "The City", and according to the Biblical account "The Great City", sits on "seven mountain tops". Knossos in Crete is surrounded and 'sits on' seven equilateral triangles drawn up using Pythagorean geometry from the peaks of the mountain ranges that surround the site. Equally I suppose at a pinch one could say that London sits on the Seven Sisters a cliff range on the south coast of England. So which site will the World Order sacrifice to their cause in fulfilling the prophetic Revelations account – London or Crete? It seemed essential therefore to discover which group has been behind world Revolution and to discover the nature of the two opposing groups I had essentially uncovered by decoding iconography in The Battle of The Trees. One strong contender for the cabal who conducted both the Religious Revolution in Crete and the plan of the Crucifixion were the Druids of Britain. Equally neither can one dismiss the Egyptians or a particular sect or ruler from Egypt, who had trading links with The Minoans. Both of these contenders possessed knowledge of the Earth Grid presumably utilising that knowledge and anti gravity anomalies of the grid to erect monolithic structures, henges and the Pyramids. The pre-determined contender for the "The Great City" in the Apocalyptic account would certainly identify the second group on the world's stage, the first group supporting the religious goals of the Twelve Tribes of **Israel for whom the Bible is written** .If the plan or prophesy of the Apocalypse is being followed, then there has to be another group, whom the prophesy is aimed at, together with the destruction of the "Great City". **The only communication line that has the power to harm is a secret communication line** and in having said this much, I trust that all contenders will be spared the prophetic manipulative and pre-determined plan.

Central to this plan is an understanding of the Earth Grid, its energies and imprinted information. The Bloch Wall is the neutral centre gravity wave source and in terms of the Electromagnetic Spectrum, the point of 10^{12} Hertz is marked as gravity, while below this is radar, radio and standard Electromagnetic frequencies, the very frequencies that according to *Part 1 of the Cancer document* have effects on biological systems. Above 10^{12} Hertz are infrared and optical energy frequencies. In terms of the Earth Grid, where the Bloch Wall of gravity wave field source exists is the place where physically anomalous events can take place e.g. spontaneous levitation. The magnetic reversal areas of South to North magnetism flow are not located at the geographical equator but near the tropics of Capricorn and Cancer. Richard Lefors Clark [20], calculated a total of 20 magnetic reversal points within the Earth Grid (*fig.11*) This provides a 'zigzag' pattern within the geometry of the UVG 120 sphere. Such a pattern I noted has been observed in the natural UFO phenomenon e.g. "the falling leaf trajectory", as the manifestation of matter I concluded along the successive windings of the torroidal vortex bioplasma. Such a bioplasma may be nothing more than a pattern of the triangles (or the centripetal and centrifugal windings of energy bioplasmas in 3D) of the UVG 120 sphere, inclusive of the pattern of the 20 magnetic reversal points. The female apparition (**not** the Virgin Mary) in The Fatima Prophecy recounted in *Alternative 4,* which some 70,000 people witnessed, appeared headless on one occasion, as a reflection of the previous events of The French Revolution? The apparition also warned of another Revolution - The Russian (or World War 1). Further it appears that the woman tried to give some indication of a world tragedy with a graphic display of the falling leaf trajectory, which might be concluded was to provide some understanding of the Earth Grid and a future Magnetic Reversal. Unfortunately The Vatican has in the past always declined to reveal the last prophecy, even though a Cardinal turned white and was shaken after he left the presence of the Pope who read it. Recently the Catholic Church has claimed the prophesy for their own faith, but uniquely and predictably never mentioned the entire witness accounts of 70,000 people with the obvious Grid symbology.

Fig.11 **Earth's 20 Magnetic Reversal Areas**
   (*Richard Lefors Clark, PhD*)

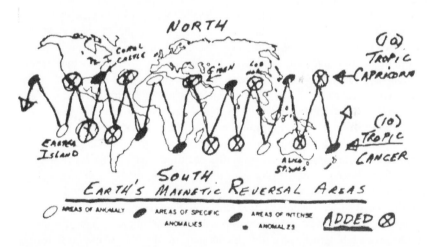

Richard Lefors Clark asked: "why haven't we known about the existence of these 20 magnetic gravity anomaly points on the Earth Grid before?" and answers the question by saying that: "A compass points North-South anywhere, and so hiding facts and using the myth of the Equators magnetic polarity was expedient for our cunning "masters"..."the power elite", who control this planet. The reason for hiding the truth is obvious: "If you knew this truth you would know that...Giza, Alice Springs etc. were Bloch Wall or Diamagnetic Vortex points. Extra-ordinary things can be done at these diamagnetic...reversal points,

61

such as levitating extremely heavy objects (building ...the Great Pyramid of Giza) and launching (secretly) the real, massive space ships and probes (as at Alice Springs, Australia and Lop Nor, China, for example)". I suspect that if you rounded up the top research establishments for defence over the Globe, you might find some rather co-incidental positions with these important Grid points. The truth is that a whole hidden science exists which has not been explained to man.

Archaeology and mythic Anthropology have not addressed myths of giants once existing on Earth and the appearance in virtually all religious world myths, of a final last battle before some cataclysm. Neither has the great size of the dinosaurs ever been explained, when under today's gravitational field such a size would be impossible. I have proposed in my own research, that these so-called myths, are in fact accounts recorded verbally from memory, covering a time when the last so-called Apocalypse occurred in the form of a Magnetic Reversal of the Bloch Wall points. These verbal accounts were not written down until much later and certainly elements may have been lost together with the source, since it would seem that there has never been a time, when those accounts were not controlled by an elite (media) for public consumption. The appearance of giant human footsteps alongside, or in the same geophysical strata as Dinosaur tracks in the Paluxy river bed *(Plate I)*, implies man was co-existent with the Dinosaurs and thus this cuts the evolutionary time scale of man to shreds. Certainly it might also lead to the conclusion that certain men (mirroring the world myths that evil was here from the beginning, contrary to the *Genesis* account of The Bible), were present from the beginning and those men existed under a different gravitational field, which led to growth differences, thus giving some credibility to the myths of giants. I will return to Apocalyptic myths later, but it is certainly interesting to note, that despite the global elite's knowledge and research on the Earth Grid, that the public are still being duped by propaganda articles such as the one that occurred in *The Express* newspaper *(Nov 18th 1999)*, *'Did Dinosaurs roast to death along with the veg?'* - whereupon that good old standby of the meteor was used to explain the geophysical disaster. Dear me, rather similar to the tidal wave that was supposed to have wiped out Knossos! Where exactly did this piece of dis-information come from? Dr. Burton Hurdle mentioned in the newspaper article, co-incidentally works at the Naval Research Laboratory in Washington D.C. Washington DC; is incidentally where all the dis-information on The Church of Scientology arose, I will come to the case of Scientology later, but here let me ask Dr. Burton Hurdle how in fact a Dinosaur could manage to live under the gravitational field of today? If he works the maths, it is not possible.

I did proffer the view in *Alternative 4,* that the global elite or more specifically the MRC case, is evidently aware of a past Cataclysm and the probability of a future cataclysm and had developed a space programme, to find a safe haven from a Magnetic Reversal, "the chosen ones" who would survive presumably. There can be no other rational explanation for the immense money that is being pumped into space research projects (at cost to the tax payer!) The book *Alternative 3*[21] which formed a basis for that conclusion, reported that a secret base on Mars had been founded, employing slave labour and key scientists, who had mysteriously disappeared from homes and jobs and whilst the author later stated that it was not true, there were certain accounts and figures in that book, which gave it a ring of truth, in so far as there were predictions for the future demise of the geophysical climate. Those predictions were fairly accurate in terms of today's so-called global warming and one can only consider that the author was *manipulated* to retract. Whilst such a base may have never been formed, there is a certain silence that always emanates from the Space Programme and NASA and whilst conspiracy theorists have read into the current and ongoing failures of the Mars Mission a conspiratorial silent role which belies the truth, it is difficult to determine whether the Missions have been failures, or whether such failures ensure more funding to continue with a prior goal - a safe haven? Billions of dollars of public money go missing in the U.S every year, money paid by taxpayers and unaccounted for, where does it go? into black ops. research?

A recent book, *Dark Moon - Apollo and the Whistle-Blowers,* have asked whether the Apollo moon landings were the greatest sting in history. Discrepancies between the stills and the film images of the landings together with the evident slip-up of a flag blowing in the wind in an anti-gravity environment! Are discussed by the authors together with the link of World War II, or NAZI rocket scientists who went to Russia and America after the war. According to the authors NASA have questions to answer and I would certainly from my own research agree. Further I would pose the question as to whether they have been directed by Rosicrucian philosophy and knowledge and have known for some time, that a cataclysm will wreak havoc on earth and have sought a safe base for the elite survivors? Funding that on taxpayers' money. Certainly it would not surprise me to know that "144 000" had been chosen, which would parallel the Apocalyptic prophesy, despite the fact that it was written for the 12 Tribes of Israel.

The Daily Telegraph (*23 Nov. 1999*) reported '*Planet Found 50 Light Years Away*'. The research reported the search for planets outside our solar system, with British astronomers observing the first "exo-planet". Despite the team from St. Andrews University in Fife having made the discovery at about the same time as an alleged rival team from Harvard University in The United States, neither will talk about the research. Why the secrecy? - And surely if they are public grant maintained, they have a duty to report and explain that research to those who pay their salaries! Certainly the sparse pictures and scant information that has come from successive Mars Missions warrants concern by the American public, on how the enormous amount of money concerned is being spent.

It is questionable whether research and scientists are manipulated in their thinking by the 'guide - lines' set by the global elite, who have taken control of just about every facet of research, which means that scientists like myself have to operate outside of that system, unable to obtain grants or funding. This is very observable in the political support of the theory for the Universal Mind. Research that fits with the political philosophy of the global elite is supported and a concept of a Universal Mind fits admirably with Communism, although it is doubtful whether the elite believe that! Such research tones man up for a belief that his mind is controlled and we are all just part of one big happy oneness! The Universal Mind however is an important and valid concept that does have some association with my own research. Thomas[22] proposed that a group organization and a "Universal Mind" existed throughout biology. Sheldrake went on to suggest that there is in existence a hyper spatial morphogenetic field which guides the hierarchal organization of matter and Dr. Becker[23] researched such a field in the formative stages of the development or shape of an animal. Whilst in my own research I see this field as important in the mechanism of Cancer as a growth mechanism (*Part II Cancer Document*), there is certainly a danger in guiding research towards a belief in any **"Universal Mind"** with the implications obvious to those who perceive the goal of current secret research into alleged defence weaponry as part of A **MIND CONTROL PROGRAMME.** If scientists have been persuaded to work for the global elite, they have truly mistaken the goals of that elite and even the assumption that a cataclysm is inevitable.

Whenever I hear these terms such as "Universal Mind", alarm bells immediately ring which may not be apparent to scientists who are not aware of the One World Order programme and its religious and political history. The problem is that I am sure that Scientists brought up on a diet of atheism never consider the spiritual possibilities or the existence of an immortal soul. Being practical individuals they generally think in terms of reality and if a politician was to explain that research towards 'healing' humanity via coded signals utilising the Earth Grid, was necessary to control Homo-Sapiens as his mental faculties decline (for the good of others naturally) a scientist might take a good look at the real world and see that this might be a good solution, given the alternative of the violent world in which we live. Scientists can either be brought or they can be sold moral issues, as was the case with the Atomic Bomb, which I discussed in the Appendix to *Alternative4 -In Search of The Philosopher's Stone* I have no doubt, that as I write this, scientists are engaged in research on the energy Grid, the UFO phenomenon and the secret knowledge of the Rosicrucian's, apart from the space programme and an eventual cataclysm. I believe many of them have been sold a package on the survival of humanity, a package that represents just one side of the spiritual story.

Many of the migratory patterns of animals e.g. birds and butterflies are governed by the Earth Grid.The Monarch butterfly was reported in *The Daily Telegraph* (23 Nov 1999) as using a magnetic compass to navigate. Professor Orley Taylor and colleagues at the University of Kansas published the research in the *Proceedings of the National Academy of Sciences*. However none of this research actually identifies The Grid or the electro-magnetic energy patterns, which govern such migration. Professor Orley Taylor may be ignorant of the overall pattern, but there is no doubt, that scientists are restricted in what and how much of the Grid secret they can publish. Scientific papers are inexplicably turned down, when they contain too much information, after all one might apply the fact that butterflies use a magnetic compass to the early archaeology. e.g. of the Nazca lines in Peru, which appear to track magnetic ley lines and ask whether or not man had a more developed magnetic sensory system then and why it has become vestigial, which might reflect on the question whether man's input to the environment and the electro-magnetic spectrum has altered this ability, or whether his awareness of the system decreased in the proportion to the knowledge which was repressed. One question leads to another and hence the Global Elite have had to exert tight control on Scientific thinking and research apart from publication.

If a scientific conference had been organised regularly, drawing together alternative and orthodox, independent and non independent scientists, as I suggested in my Petition *(Appendix 2)*, then certainly new fronts of science could have been discussed in relation to world politics and scientists would have at least had some idea of both sides of the argument. The problem has been that only one side has ever been allowed a forum to speak and publish. Hardly a choice! Recently (1997), the ground breaking work of the chemist Peter Plitchta[24] has appeared, this research underlines the significance of **prime numbers** in the organisation of matter including the atomic nuclei. These numbers are not imaginary but appear to have some basis as a coded signal I would conclude. Remarkably following his pattern of organisation for matter one comes across the **Pascal's Triangle**, which was known as an archetypal design amongst the Moors many Centuries previously *(fig.12)*. This of course not only ties in with the World Energy Grid and the UVG 120 sphere with its equilateral triangles, but also provides corroborative evidence for my own model of organisation of the Ether or vortex, which I based on a 3D torroidal vortex Bioplasma - in 2D it would become a triangle.

Fig.12 **Pascal's Triangle** This pattern was kown to the Moors many centuries ago. Today, mathematicians generally consider it nothing but an interesting curiosity with no relevance to the present. The special knowledge of prime number coding should also have become common knowledge ever since it was formulated by E Kummer in the 19 th Century (From: God's Secret Formula by Dr. P. Plitchta)

This obviously is of interest to science - free science not controlled by the World Order. Further if the triangle or vortex, is coded in Prime numbers and is organised into a 65 line series of Pascal's Triangles forming what is termed a **Sierspinski Triangle,** then a more noticeable geometric pattern evolves consisting of 36 (or 6 X 6) hexagons, which is once again part of the fundamental pattern of the UVG 120 sphere and the Earth Grid Geometrics. Mirroring also the fundamental pattern of the Carbon molecule, which is basic to life on earth. The Methane molecule is pyramidal and certainly in Hermetic Philosophy 'as above so below', the Earth Grid geometry would appear as the geometry of mass and its composition from atoms and molecules. Man's body composed of atoms and molecules with a large percentage of the Carbon atom, is not disconnected from the intricate patterns of energy and the Earth Grid geometry. Once again man is an intricate part of the pattern, with his body composed on such a composite pattern and perhaps too his mind.

The implications of Plitchta's work hit me straight away, in so far as what will be the effect, on the earth Grid and organised matter, if digital TV signals are transmitted through The Grid! To underline the point, Plitchta's organisation of matter and the atomic nucleus, rests on a code of *prime numbers*, however Digital TV is based on a *binary system*. Will these transmissions act to destabilise what is otherwise a perfectly ordered geometric structure and pattern of energies and matter based on a harmonic signal? If politicians and media moguls such as Rupert Murdoch, have found no reason for alarm in digital TV transmission, then surely scientists must raise some objection, until more detailed research can be undertaken. Finally with regard to Plitchta's research is it not curious that the organisation of the atomic model he gives - The Prime Number Cross -describing the arrangement of electrons in the nuclei of atoms, as a geometric figure, resembles accurately the Pate Cross of The Knights Templar. Further the appearance of the number 3, which codes as a significant geometric signal, in not only the body shape (head, thorax and abdomen), but appears in many fundamental building blocks in biochemistry e.g. the triplet base sequence of DNA and also makes its appearance in the early Minoan religion. Archetypal, the old Trinity, shown as one born only to die to be reborn through Her - The Great Goddess, whose gift to man was Immortality. This is beautifully shown in the so-called 'Bull-vaulting' Fresco from Knossos (*The Battle of The Trees).

Richard Lefors Clark located special vortex-gravity regions in the Earth Grid, which he proposes makes them appropriate sites for specialised research pointing to Brookhaven Long Island and Los Alamos New Mexico where Atomic Bomb research was carried out, as sites connected to vortex-gravity regions of the Grid. He stated that: "International governmental vortex-gravity research would have to be at Alice Springs/Pine Gap in Central Australia", further Lefors Clark maintains that the geopolitical importance of certain diamagnetic Earth Grid points introduces the subject of Earth Grid wars, where he claims: "The Three Florida's (Florida, Korea and Vietnam) are still critical Earth Grid points after two bloody wars; and further the "boost-point" to this triangle is Libya". As with my 'Colombo ' detective tendency to write things down in my note pad that don't add up, I was talking with a Shepard in a rural district of Crete (not far off Libya), when he complained that the young of animals were being born deformed, which was unheard of. Why that should have been so was curious to me, since there was no apparent visible pollution when I thoroughly checked the area. There was however an American Military base on Crete, which the Cretans for the main objected to. I would not like to add two and two and make five, however there is some ring of truth I feel in Lefors Clark's claim. Certainly Electro-magnetic pollution can cause abnormal births, through DNA mutation and replication, but can also alter the geometric of space, to interfere with the morphogenetic field, which according to the research of Dr. Becker, Harold Burr and Sheldrake, may correspond to the non-specific field, which governs the initial shape of the animal. Apart from other recent apparent political wars, Lefors Clark mentions Afghanistan, which he states was secured by The Russians as a significant Earth Grid point.

THE KEYS TO THE NEW WORLD ORDER

Is it not remarkable that in 1776 at the time of The French Revolution, Eliphas Levi a member of the secret societies, claimed that a "**Universal Kingdom**"(both religious and political) would come into being and that those with "the keys to the East" would have it. Was this a reference to Hermes who as the ancient magus, Hermes Trismegistos, Thrice-Great Master and Geomancer of Earth, with his Smagdarine Emerald Tablets, the keys to Gaia's Earth energy? This implies that at the time of The French Revolution, which was not the will of the people but a planned Masonic affair, the secret group who orchestrated this Revolution, were aware of the power of the Earth Grid and followed Hermetic Philosophy. Hermes as the Master Grid engineer and the gods messenger to Earth, who in the tired old story (no apologies for my yawn here), then passed the flame of **his** mastery for our time allegedly to the Archangel Michael with his solar initiatory sword. The sword of course pops up in all sorts of myths, legends and iconography including Arthur and the Knights of the Round Table and even in the book of *Revelations*! As an archetypal symbol of Hermes as Master of Grid knowledge. Well it's a fairly well worn story with lots of myth and legends along this path, but it isn't true I'm afraid. Michael according to the Hebrews is the keeper of the secrets of the relations between Hermes and Earth. Geomancy in fact means "divination of the earth's secrets" (from the Greek, Gaia - mantos) .It is blatantly apparent, that the earth Grid and its energies has been intricately tied to myth, prophecy and the final goals of a One World Order.

Without wishing to derail what little sanity there is left in the precarious psychological case of the MRC, the New World Order and those Europhiles, by making their Hero Hermes touch down on reality, but Hermetic Philosophy was not I am afraid the first word, it was a downgrade of an original truth in Crete. A fusion of the Twin Kings in death with The Great Goddess, which was an attempt to wipe out the Matriarchal religion and principally the belief in Re-incarnation, along with the substantial knowledge of a certain Cosmology. Hermes was no part of the Philosopher's Stone and as such carried no word of God. He simply was not the Alpha, but a mere invention to rid Patriarchal religion of the woman and therefore finds no part at the Omega - a wasted Philosophy I might add, since the Grid is not the paramount spiritual phenomenon on Earth. Hermes I might add as an invention of fusion of male and female to rid the priests of the power of the woman, was often described as bi-sexual, which has lead to all sorts of legacies on Earth!

The Hermetic keys to the Planetary Grid were apparently inscribed on Hermes mythical Emerald Tablets, which I am afraid again is a piece of mistaken identity, in so far as it was evidently believed that this was the Philosophers

Stone (in myth made from Lapis Lazuli). The Philosopher's Stone, which "fell from the heavens". Evidently Moses re-enacted the Hermetic underlying philosophy of the secret group that he was initiated by, when he wrote his Ten Commandments on stone. The Stone or tablet was a **Semitic** symbol and Moses was supposed to have received God's word on stone tablets on Mount Sinai. There is a very large untruth here in that Hermes is given as the originator and keeper of the keys. The truth which I will come to in greater detail, is that Hermes as god of vagabonds and *thieves* stole the secrets of the Grid together with a whole Cosmology and belief system (Re-incarnation) from The Teacher, in Minoan Crete in the period that I have designated The Religious Revolution - 1400 B.C. The *seven* (an archetypal number *originally* associated with the woman) keys of Hermes Geomancy and the Earth Grid also utilise the Semitic significant number "seven, a number that appears frequently in the Apocalyptic Revelation. Reminding us, that the One World Order (Semitic) plan, which IS the script of *Revelations*, is further based on control and knowledge of the Grid.

The seven keys of Hermes were known esoterically as:
The Principle of Mentakim - The Universe is mental; the All is infinite Mind, which is the fundamental reality.
The Principle of Correspondence - ' As above so below' which accomplishes the miracles of the one.
The Principle of Vibration - Nothing is still - all moves and vibrates
The Principle of Polarity - Everything is dual, has poles and pairs of opposites. (Hence the idea within secret groups of philosophical dualism i.e. good and evil and Satan/ Lucifer and the idea that god is composed of those two opposites which again is a fault in the philosophy)
The Principle of Rhythm - Everything has its tides, peaks and troughs, left and right of the pendulum
The Principle of Causation - every effect has a Cause and every Cause has an effect- all events are by law, never chance. (As Einstein noted "God does not play dice")
The Principle of Gender - everything has its "masculine " and "feminine" parts.

There is nothing wrong with these principles per se, however to assign to them the word of God, which is implied by the cross reference of tablet to the Philosophers Stone, is to omit a greater truth and to assign control to The Earth Grid. Principle number one can be adapted to the Universal Mind concept which like the virus of Communism I note later in this book, is being slowly filtered down from some hierarchal source into scientific thought and healing today. Principle two (Correspondence), can be linked to control via the Grid, and the concern today of mind and body control of a populous which I elaborated in greater detail in *Alternative 4*. Thus alone and without implied connection, the

Principles are true in some respects, but if they are part of some form of dogma within a secret philosophy and group which requires ultimate control, then the Principles can very easily become a justification for that control, on the basis that it was God's will. Whilst this might sound crazy to you or I, you have no idea,' how far South ' a secret group can go, when imbibed on a daily diet of these half spun truths. The principles as expressed here, are the very basic principles of a whole science that has been hidden and developed to fantastic degrees over thousands of years. The important point, is that the knowledge and source was NOT Hermes or the Semitic source that stole the basis of this science. I will by degrees come to unfold the story of Hermes god of thieves.

UFO's

The hidden science has caused major tracts of Eastern medicine and teachings relating to the human biofield, to remain unknown to the majority of people, this has been catastrophic in terms of understanding the hidden science and its application to the body with its electro-magnetic energies and the role of those energies in healing. Knowledge of this science has been incorporated into my own theory of cancer *(Appendix 1)*. I have already given some account of the human biofield and these energies in *Alternative 4* and the Cancer report. Briefly, the body is surrounded by an electro-magnetic biofield, said to be *seven* layered, which controls emotional or mental and physical well-being. In my last book, I looked at the possibility that this field had been manipulated in the case of UFO witnesses and as such were illicit experimentation on mind and body control on unwitting 'guinea pigs'. As I reported in that book, there was a *Jewish group* or interests tied up in the UFO unnatural or manipulated phenomenon. One might speculate that since the Patriarchs had used such knowledge of the Grid energies, then it would be expedient to confuse the UFO phenomenon, thus deterring any serious scientist from researching the phenomenon. Whilst knowledge of the hidden science has existed, there has bee no major attempts by any Government to undertake a major and public research effort to identify the basic science that underlies the UFO phenomenon or the underlying science of Eastern medicine and its unique approach to the healing of the human biofield. In *Appendix 1* the reasons why that has not occurred in the latter case are very well illustrated. Such reticence must depend on the fact that the Grid not only has application to free energy and warfare, but also has foreseeable application to mind and body control of a populous. Dr. Becker, who was twice nominated for a Nobel Prize, but now I believe is threatened in his research position, over his outspoken stance, has referred to the latter point in no uncertain terms. The HAARP and GWEN systems are more fully discussed as potential systems of mind control in *Alternative 4*.

Eastern medicine has long known that in addition to nerves and blood circulation, many subtle energy pathways exist in the body and Chinese medicine describes 72,000 main paths - the acupuncture meridians and nadis. The spine is considered the main axis around which the electro-magnetic energy field forms. The North Pole of the human energy field is located in the brain and the South Pole at the base of the spine, which is referred to in energetic terms as the Kundalini. Magnetism develops at a right angle to the flow of the electrical impulses producing an overall **egg shape** for the human biofield; the field is recognised in the mapping of this energy and in photo aura imaging where the aura and its colours can be clearly seen on photographic emulsion *(Plate II)*. The chakras are the main power points in this energy system *(fig. 13)* having endocrinal functions associated with them. The endocrine glands produce hormones, which regulate all body functions including emotional functions and behaviour. On the Hermetic Principle ('as above, so below'), the biofield pattern or egg-shape is immediately recognised as comparable to the Grid, with the North and South Pole axis around which an electromagnetic current flows. The implication of course, is that the two are connected in some fashion through energy patterning and what happens in one will be registered and monitored in the other and one might conceive of total harmony and balance, unless one was immediately aware of the implications, for control of a populous, by an elite who hold the 'keys' to such knowledge.

Having looked at the possibility of altering chakra vibrating energy and harmony in *manipulated* UFO incidents. e.g. **UFO abductions**, there was the possibility that such abductions were the result of illicit testing of electromagnetic weapons on mental functioning. These incidents were for the main, so far removed from the *natural* UFO phenomenon, which consists of certain identifiable metaphysical phenomena, that it could only be concluded that such people had had their human rights violated. One of the groups who were manipulating the UFP phenomenon also appeared to be Apocalyptic and certainly at least one group was Jewish in nature, deduced merely from the content of the abducted person's experience. It is difficult to determine any other purpose for these manipulated incidents other than (a.) the confusion of the UFO phenomenon and a purpose of veiling the hidden science (b.) research on the manipulation of the human biofield and mental functioning with either a goal of a psycho civilised society (mind controlled) or data for biological or electromagnetic war.

Fig.13 **The reverse side of the Great Seal of the United States**
Illustrating the Illuminatus Eye and the power pyramidal political system
as on the reverse side of the one-dollar note.

If there was a further reason for withholding research into the human biofield, with its obvious application to healing, apart from the previous explanations, it was because much of the terminology and ancient history of this science would automatically reveal the truth of certain religious mysteries, including so-called miracles. The Bible most certainly would come under scientific scrutiny. Whilst this science of medicine known to the East for thousands of years has only recently in the last 20 years or so become more recognised in the West, secret groups have for thousands of years held on to this knowledge and the mysteries connected to it. The art of healing was to utilise such knowledge and inevitably certain powers became attached to it and thus the Patriarchal Priesthood sought to retain not only the mysteries for themselves, but also the power that was inherent within the application of this science. The Greek methods of healing and the lost records of Hippocrates and Asklepios meant that it was impossible to retain such methods and knowledge in public view. It might be argued, that it has been in view for quite some time, but then it was viewed as an Eastern oddity and certainly would make no impact on a pre-conditioned public brought up on a daily diet of the wonders of pharmaceutical drugs.

Chinese geomancers who practised Feng Shui, described the electro-magnetic ley lines as "dragon paths" and the Apocalyptic Revelation certainly refers to a " dragon": "and I saw three unclean spirits like frogs come out of the mouth of the dragon, and out of the mouth of the beast, and out of the mouth of the false prophet. For they are the spirits of devils, working *miracles*." (*Revelations17, v.13*). Thus what we have here is either a referral to the use of drugs - hallucinogenic chemicals from the skins of toads and certain Amphibians, or the MRC case and the use of the Grid to obtain information, which can then be placed as a prophecy. This method of obtaining information is called channelling which I will return to later.

In my own research I have stated that the "bulbous eyes", which are a prominent feature of the morphogenetic memory of the natural UFO experience, represent some feature of the pre-history of man. It is interesting that ancient icons from South America show these bulbous eyes and I further suggested that this might be worship associated with elite who utilised drugs to enable them to use the power of prophecy e.g. as in the pre-Columbian Toadstool cult, who idolised Tlaloc, who was represented as a toad with a serpent headdress. Tlaloc presided for thousands of years over the communal eating of the hallucinogenic toadstool psilocybe, a feast that gives visions similar to those when LSD is taken. A similar cult existed in Greece, where the spotted toadstool called 'flycap' was eaten. Evidently this gave the imbiber the gift of prophecy and as with the hallucinogenic drug LSD, must facilitate a connection with the Earth Grid to utilise past knowledge. In other words any cult of this nature would simply apply a control mechanism from the Grid and repeat in cyclical fashion all past cycles, it is in this manner that a book such as Revelations can prophecy future outcomes, simply by assuming a powerful authority that is itself controlled by The Grid. Unfortunately *Revelations* and all these types of religious writing, were written from the Patriarchal point of view and the Jews even today in Israel start off the day by citing the traditional morning blessing in which all Jewish men thank God for not making them women! (*International Herald Tribune: Nov.23 1999*). Not surprisingly women are getting a little fed up with the Serpent routine, which was a re-positioning of the archetypal symbols during the period when the cult of Jehoweh took over the brand leader religion of the time - Matriarchal, the boys couldn't confront what they had done (removed the truth) so used a justifier mechanism of damning the woman ever-after. It's an abberrative mechanism of the mind! And how that abberration has through the millennia affected women is one example of the damage to society, by secret group abberrative religion and politics.

The other interpretation of the use of "frog" was I suggested previously some obscure form of early evolution from the time of a magnetic reversal, where possibly those who were here from the beginning, had evolved slowly (in body form *not* spiritual) from Amphibian or reptilian forms and where this information will still be retained on the Grid, giving some further explanation as to why the MRC case would wish to control all information on The Grid. From a scientific point of view, the fact that the chromosomes of the Frog are so long, much longer than man, it would be interesting if the Genetic Codon project was to discover why there is such a lot of information recorded on the Amphibian chromosomes and the nature of that information.

Although there is a secret edition of the prophetic Apocalypse by John, which differs from the vulgate version and is held in some ascendant secret group, presumably from The Knights Templar, the standard version - *Revelations*, has all the re-positioning 'tricks' of the Religious Revolution era, note the damning of the archetypal number three, since it relates to a former truth that was hidden from humanity, and refers to Re-incarnation (based on The Cycle of Eternal Return). The obvious conclusion from *Revelations* is that there is another secret group, which has not been identified and with whom the Twelve Tribes of Israel are in conflict with.

DOMES AND PIES IN LONDON AND NEW YORK

Prince Charles was so vehement on not attending the Millennium Dome building in London (built to celebrate the Millennium) on the alleged grounds of his dislike of its architecture that there seemed to be more to that pie than meets the eye. (To pie: used by Robert Graves in The White Goddess - referring to poetry that was in coded form so as to **deceive the uninformed** reader of the real meaning. Subsequently used by myself as 'pied' to encompass the idea of a secret hidden from man coupled in rhyming slang with 'porky pie '- lie: or to make a pie and put a pastry crust on top to bury a secret – also related to the Greek letter Pi). The question becomes **IS THE DOME A PIE?** Quite co-incidentally I am afraid to say the architectural design resembles one!

Attached to the secret mysteries surrounding the Earth Grid is one particular branch of esoteric doctrine called **Dome Centres**. According to this doctrine there are Dome centres or etheric energy canopies occupying the space over sacred enclosures and in a sense creating those centres. From there, Dome energy lines radiate spiralling out. There are a number of Dome centres linked by Dome lines and therefore connected to each other in a subtle communications grid. These Domes of energy were apparently brought here in response from the **Architect of the Cosmos** (a term frequently used in Freemasonry). Such accounts of Domes exist in various ancient mythologies notably Irish and Sumerian, where the Domes were portrayed as the house of the sky gods. Clairvoyants affirm such Domes over places like Stonehenge, Machu Picchu, Palenque, Mt.Shasta etc. Although the Domes have in a sense left, the energy imprints remain and such imprints as a pattern are fixed according to star formations. The Domes according to this theory were originally the home of **ley lines (Dome lines)** .As we look more into this theory and the co-joined two-toned (gold and silver) colour of the Millennium icon, a semi-male and female figure designed ostensibly to become the archetypal symbol of the millennium in Britain, looking remarkably like a Prince or Solar King of the Knossos Fresco and Early Minoans! It is hard not to believe that a secret enclave, who held a particular philosophy – perhaps of Hermes the bisexual, oversaw the millennium festival in Britain? We know from mythical tale or legend, that Domes were apparently linked by way of interwoven **gold and silver lines**, which joined together at one specific planetary node, which is the Grid's umbilicus and **Master Dome**. Gold was traditionally the colour attached to the Sun King in ancient Greece and silver was a colour traditionally associated with the woman, or Moon Goddess. Such colours also symbolised in the Sun and Moon, also reflected deeper mysteries in the ancient Calendar alphabets and mysteries. Dome theory makes no note of this more ancient and *first* route of knowledge and history. Neither is there any mention of The Cycle of Eternal Return, where the original idea of as one dies, then in death he is united with her, The Great Goddess and then is reborn again through her and the womb, very well portrayed in ancient Greek iconography, together with its archetypal symbolisation - the labyrinth, as it appeared in Minoan iconography *(The Battle of The Trees)*. Thus already in this Dome theory we see considerable co-incidences and hidden archetypal symbols intentional or not. Further the semi-male and female figure is an obvious reminder of Hermes, who in myth was the bisexual god. However this was meant to cover an original and deeper secret of Hermes, who was the first attempt to downgrade the truth in Crete at the time of The Religious Revolution. Originally the gift of Immortality and the belief in Re-incarnation was HER gift to humanity, but man disliked the idea and stole not only the apples of Immortality, but also the Grid knowledge and a whole cosmology and thereafter justified his actions by blaming the woman! The original intent of the male and female joining in a transcendent third stage beyond death in the earliest Minoan belief has been overlaid with other significances that are not correct in Dome theory, since the gold and silver cords are supposed to represent the balanced energy inputs of positive and negative, female and male energy entering the Dome: co-incidentally paralleling the hermaphroditic quality of the Millennium icon *(Plate 3)*

The Domes were part of the old Paradise on Earth theory and were seen as high consciousness meditation halls, where human awareness could be healed and uplifted and perhaps connecting with Rudolf Steiner's so-called Akashic Record or the great library in the sky, which is an entire history of man and events recorded or imprinted on the Grid energies. This then is all part of assigning control to The Grid, since the Domes were supposed to facilitate meditatively acquired insight into the planetary thought matrix, in other words Domes were places like caves, where John allegedly wrote Revelations and where a connection with the Grid could be facilitated. Since the Grid contains a record of the past, then the prophecy of revelations becomes merely recognition of that past, which is then presented as a prophecy of the future!

Mt. Sinai where Moses allegedly acquired his own 'Hermitic Tablets'-The Ten Commandments, and the alleged word of God, was apparently a Dome centre and this certainly ties in with esoteric knowledge, that Moses was an initiate of The Rite Of Memphis or a high Initiate in cabalistic or hidden science. Thunder and rumblings on Mt. Sinai indicated that some form of Cabalistic knowledge of vibratory resonance was being used. Such knowledge of Cabalistic science has been used from very early times and the so-called Palaeolithic cave painting from Africa - *Lightening Man (Plate 4)* is evidence that shamans, magi and even demi-gods such as Moses, utilised this secret science to gain power and control as Moses did with the "children of Israel". Also Moses face was horribly burnt when he descended the Mount, indicating that he had some form of radiation burns. As I pointed out in *The Battle of The Trees,* the fact that Moses was born in a basket, indicates he was part of the re-positioning era, where Matriarchal belief and knowledge was suppressed and withdrawn into the secret groups. Ancient iconography showing the chequered basket design has conveniently not been covered in explanation in Museum accounts of the icons although I have explained this archetypal sign in *The Battle of The Trees.* The under utilisation of Museums and miss-representation of icons is a great crime against the next generation.

In *Alternative 4,* I put forward the 'worst case scenario', of one controlling signal passed through the energy network, or broadcasted to control humanity. The fact that ley lines and the Grid can be utilised for such signals makes the scenario more plausible in the light of the frightening degree of globalisation, which is becoming apparent in nearly every facet of life. The pre-occupation with a Universal Mind in Science; with its potential to soothe man into the belief that he should be connected (to the signal) and Philosophy together with New Age propaganda, coupled with the parallel construction of a power political pyramid in Europe as it heads rapidly towards a New World Order can only be viewed in the light of the Philosophy BEHIND THE POLITICS and inevitably the esoteric background I produce in my research. Did you really believe that those in charge of it all were sane! Whilst I have given a broad definition to cover the **Biblical "666",** as 'pied' religion and politics, dating back to the introduction of Solar Kingship and Apollo, whom is condemned interestingly enough in The Revelations account, it has not been generally recognised that Hermetic Philosophy is also a false downgrade of the original truth. In the mystical science of the **Cabala** (also spelt Quabala and Cabalah) the primary solar numbers are (666) and the lunar numbers are (1080). The archetypal numbers tied to the esoteric mysteries, also related to religious festivals, alphabetic mysteries, archetypal Calenderism and the iconography, but also these archetypal numbers appear connected to the energy fields. For example in *Alternative 4* I pointed out that 7 was a mystery number, it was also designated as female and 7 is mentioned many times in the book of *Revelations* in coded reference; 7 however relates to the number of chakras in the human body (Sanskrit - 'Spinning wheels'). Under Matriarchal knowledge the chakras were to become the forces of healing, however under a Patriarchal Priesthood and the cult of Jehoweh, they were to become controlled just as the 7 days of the week, were assigned to various so-called angels under the control of The Patriarchal God of The Hebrews.

The Tree of Life, so well represented I concluded in iconographic finds, after The Religious Revolution in Crete, where a secret Cabal entered Knossos and took over The Matriarchal knowledge and belief, relates to the Quabala and to the **7 Key Dome Centres** according to Dome theory. The Great Pyramid at Giza not only exists along a vortex Grid and anti gravity anomaly, but also it was considered a Dome Centre. The Earth was considered as a chakra system itself and I am afraid as we get more into this esoteric doctrine of Hermetic Philosophy, the plot thickens, the Earth is visualized as **a mighty wheel with many spokes**, co-incidentally mirroring *that* wheel (Millennium Eye) in London, which ostensibly as a large fair ground type structure dominates the London sky-line alongside the Dome. In Dome theory, which is now becoming somewhat indistinguishable from the London skyline, there is at each spoke a point of light. "The wheel has a hub and each spoke has two ends, as the wheel turns it is the earth." 25 Is it also co-incidence, that the wheel originally referred to as a large Ferris wheel was later for some un-explained reason being muted as the "London Eye" (*The Independent 10 Dec. 1999*), which presumably has nothing to do with The Illuminati Eye, the all-seeing eye of Jehoweh. The Sun wheel once again has an earlier origin and dates back to iconography of ancient Greece post Religious Revolution, and again we see a re-positioning of the icons. However the sun wheel does imply Sovereignty, be that through Solar Kingship which developed into hereditary Monarchy, which was better suited to combination with a secret Priesthood as a method of control and unequal distribution of wealth and power; or whether it is now implied through the final machinations of globalisation and centralisation of power, where Europe would have its own federal "head of state" and central government as part of the New World Order plan. Thus Prince Charles who refused to visit the Dome for the Millennium celebrations, may be more quietly versed in such background than Londoners? A touch arrogant, even by secret group standards to invite half of London to a party and not let them in on the secret.

A French government think-tank has recently proposed (The *Express Nov. 17 1999*) a new-style **President of Europe**, who would act like the head of a Federal state. Whilst media questions the position of European monarchies in countries such as Holland and Spain, the globalisation plan that I claim originated at Knossos 1,400BC and was fully recorded as such during The French Revolution, only used hereditary Monarchy as a means towards achieving power. As The French and Russian Revolutions illustrated, Monarchy was superfluous to that plan by the 18th and 19th centuries, as many of Europe's Monarchies were systematically eliminated. The Revolutions were orchestrated by Masonic societies - the people were once again duped. I cover The French Revolution quite fully in *The Battle of The Trees*, since it is a lesson in the art of Revolution (how they did it). It would be fair to comment that the very same plan is now being applied in Europe and once financial control is complete with the Euro, you will see the true colours of the **COMMUNISTIC HIVE**. It is deceitful and ridiculous for politicians to have claimed that a Federal Europe was never the goal and then feign surprise in the media at so-called new advancements (*The Daily Telegraph Tuesday May 30*) where it was reported that German plans to prepare for a European super state were being endorsed by Romano Prodi. The European Commission President, had already had his knuckles wrapped once, for premature disclosures on the push for a Federal European super state, with its own army! Now Prodi is endorsing a two-tier Europe, with some nations forging ahead to build a Federation. The German proposals for a small group of committed EU states to press on with a "federalist agenda", gives the impression of the will of their peoples, but I suspect that if you allowed those people to speak, they would voice as many concerns as the British. NO this is not about the will of the people; it is the realisation of a plan, set thousands of years previously and which many men and women in history have warned about. Such warnings however have been meticulously edited out of any media publication, subservient as they are to the global elite (God help their souls). God knows I have tried to stop it here in Britain, by hunting through Parliamentary procedure (which took many hours in the library), the results of that can be viewed in Appendix 1, where my Petition to The House of Commons was turned down and I failed to find one independent publication who was willing to print the Petition questions.

The plans for the French Revolution, initiated in a Lodge of German Freemasons, must have come full circle now that German ambitions for a full-blown European super state have been laid bare. What a sick joke that Joschka Fischer should urge the creation of a Federation, with its own government, parliament and directly-elected president as the final stage of European integration, launched it is claimed 50 years ago! Mr Fischer urged the "transition from a union of states to full parliamentarisation as a European Federation". The "introduction of the euro was not only the crowning point of economic integration, it was also a profoundly political act". Quite! Control of the money system, was always a major consideration and goal for the elite and do not feign surprise when an army is formed and WORLD WAR III results, since there are two groups on this planet in opposition. As I edit this book (a rare treat for my readers!), I note that a European army is now a foregone conclusion! The fact that Britain has held back from full integration implies that she is part of the ideology of that second group, a group that was evident when I decoded certain iconography in *The Battle of The Trees* and which I pinpointed at that curious ceremony of The Cutting of the Elm at Gisors in France in the 12th Century. It has emerged that Chancellor Gerhard Schroeder has already drawn up a secret plan to create a "hard core" of EU states, and has discussed the proposal with French leaders. Britain is evidently not in the secret discussions and this further implies a dichotomy of secret group interests, which may rest on the dichotomy of goals and interests of the Gisors ceremony between French and British Kings.

Whilst The British Government has assured America that the proposed increase in European Union's military capability would not harm NATO, Washington has every right to be concerned that any increase in Europe's military ambitions would come at the expense of the alliance *(The Daily Telegraph 23 Nov 1999)* Again Britain promised no hidden agenda to replace NATO and further, no hidden plans to create a European standing army, a point since disproved as a lie, with proposals for a European army supported by the British government in 2001. All this, despite a short while ago Romano Prodi from Italy, calling for such an army whilst being denounced by the British! Do they take us for fools! It is blatantly obvious that Europe will not only have its own army, but when after signing **irrevocable** legislation of Maastricht and every country is irretrievably tied into one financial and controlled bag, there **WILL BE A THIRD WORLD WAR**. "666" just can't visualise a quiet Planet or finish a cycle of action, since the end of the cycle to him is a magnetic reversal, which he tries to avoid at all costs, whilst enforcing that conclusion on the planet by his repeated actions - in a repeat of the cycle. The great words that fall from the mouths of politicians bear no resemblance to the actual reality and goals that are not Freedom or Democracy or Choice, these ideals are not part of The New World Order Plan. The MRC case commits the most appalling crimes against his fellow man without a shadow of conscience. In Britain we find that the cross-party, pro-European campaign group is secretly buying up shares of companies with Euro-sceptic bosses, so that it can sabotage their annual meetings, this is a predictable methodology of secret groups and the One World Order. This organisation is backed by Tony Blair and is investing in dozens of businesses whose chairmen or chief executives oppose the single currency (The *Daily*

Telegraph Nov. 23 1999). Where is the "choice", "Freedom"; "Democracy" and come to that where is the promised **REFERENDUM?** far from the claims that there was a Referendum on joining the EEC, I am afraid it was null and void.[26]

IS MAN BLIND? IS MAN PARALYSED? Are The British going to sit back in apathy, whilst their democratic freedoms are re-defined for them, without one voice of anger, to be told that as a little bit more freedom and choice slips down the drain into a Federal Super state, that millions are helpless in the face of a few? How can it be that man remains in such apathy when it was announced that all Councils in England and Wales will be forced to adopt directly elected mayors or cabinet-style management, under **more plans** announced by the Government (*The Independent Nov 27 1999*) This Local Government Bill which is criticised as "diktat" gives local authorities and residents **little freedom** to decide for themselves how they want to run their own affairs. It has also been warned that more **decisions will be taken in secret** Inevitably as has been claimed, the Bill will ensure that Labour "cronies" will be given highly paid posts and greater power (bigger fleas have lesser fleas). We note then the slow and gradual erosion of democracy coupled with a deterioration of liberty and freedom in the west, particularly the right to free speech and an opinion or even the right to ask questions regardless of that piece of rhetoric entitled the Bill of Human Rights. Whilst I had thought of running an advertisement carrying the Petition questions (*Appendix II*) - with the headline "Honourable Gentlemen I have waited long enough" (for an answer), I am afraid that such actions require backing.

Unfortunately European Union is built as is The New World Order Plan on thousands of years of lies and secrecy ('pies') and the **arrogant** assumption that a few knew better how to run billions of peoples lives than those people have a right to do so for themselves through the process of democracy not secrecy. It is also built on a religious lie and numerous philosophical faults coupled with the wrong assumption that the Grid held the spiritual word (of God or as I prefer a Spiritual hierarchy). The importance of this point I cannot stress too strongly, there is absolutely no spiritual freedom or possibility of exit from the eternal trap created by the grid, if you support this philosophy in any way - the message did not come from the grid. The grid is solely concerned with the physical laws that govern matter, as a quantum mechanical system. Provided that the elite can stop you using your own mind and thinking then you become merely a body or matter and just another cog in the quantum mechanical system, subject to a past pattern, and events in that past patter; in this way the cycle turns repeatedly and periodically corrects the imbalance via a magnetic reversal, where the Bloch Wall shifts which creates a cataclysm with vast species extinctions including man.

Would it surprise you to know that when I started to push out and make waves to break the silence of media, publishing and education, which are the lower grades of manipulative mind control and as such are merely a part of the trap and pattern which prevents exit, that an attempt was made to impinge an emotion and thought upon me that I immediately recognised was not my own? Part of **Psychic defence** involves recognising your *own* mind and thoughts. Does the cover of *The Second Millennium Working Report Cancer,* which depicts in cartoon form some of the Grid reactions exerted against me, surprise you? I am afraid that if there is one thing that drives the MRC case crazy, it is **disorder.** The MRC case also hates the prospect of being found out and thus represses all forms of free speech. Further, the MRC case dislikes anything, which reminds him of the magnetic reversal he endured and the inherent chaos or disorder, which is the key to his psychological case in so far as **ORDER** is, required which extends even to people having opinions, dissidents and free speech. It is being asked here in Britain, whether new anti-terrorist laws will apply to those who took part in the anti-capitalist demonstrations and indeed whether it will refer to those who have taken part in animal rights activist activities and most certainly those who try to destroy genetically modified crops. Such activities, which seem perfectly right to those who fight the One World Order plans, are viewed as intolerable to the MRC case. Democracy would represent too much disorder for the MRC case and a feeling of loss of superiority and control. Referendums do not have an assured outcome, again disorder. Freedom to the MRC case is far too much disorder for him; things must be kept still, quiet - **CONTROLLED.** The MRC case cannot stand random motion, which once again reminds him of the excess of motion in the past event during a magnetic reversal. The Grid is a highly ordered structure and therefore this would appeal to the MRC case as a method of controlling a PAST EVENT, in PRESENT TIME, moreover it is doubtful whether he even recognises that the Grid controls him. This might be difficult for the sane person to understand, but the MRC case is **stuck in a past event** and quite possibly has suffered many Magnetic Reversals, which have driven him slowly insane, however he never appears insane unless you study him closely and that is why the MRC case has remained undetected – he is a clever boy. The curious aspect of his case is that he actually cannot recognise right from wrong and his behaviour seems perfectly right to him, even though it requires his constant attempts at justification, by downgrading the person or persons who have he imagines damaged him. His own superiority and arrogance is his greatest psychological defence. Quite possibly he has become the effect of the Grid in the same way as he has become the effect of the past, with the two now so closely defined in his psychology, that they are inseparable and he functions on Genetic line survival and correspondingly shows no morals or ethics, since the Grid or morphogenetic bioplasma is merely a master pattern for survival of the species. **Animal-like** behaviour where another is happily sacrificed to the cause of survival for the

83

MRC would be considered normal for the MRC case. The MRC case plays out his case in present time, a mechanism of the mind that is called DRAMATIZATION. These dramatizations define his case and the previous defining traits of his case. A One World Order of total control is a manifestation of his case, as is a Federal Europe. The asylum he controls is merely a product of his psychological and spiritual case.

The mechanism of dramatization will be referred to many times in this book and thus it is important to understand that this a psychological definition which describes the repeat in present time (the now) of an action that happened in experience (or back then – on the track of time). It is something that is being replayed out of context of its time and period. A man's thinking and actions can become totally dictated by past events, traumas and cycles of action in the past. He can bring forward into present time the same thinking, actions or cycles of action playing them out inappropriately in present time. The MRC case (the elite of the World Order) is actually a dramatizing psychotic since he is fixed in one cycle or incident of the past and lives mainly in the illusion of his own past and not in his actual surroundings or reality (the now). The problem with the MRC case is that he is often in a position of power and always in a secret group wielding that power unseen to Homo sapiens. His obvious menace to Homo sapiens is not recognised and therefore he is not deemed insane, but this fellow is at the back of virtually all wars and revolutions on this planet and is insane, however his ideas and his secret group philosophy based on the past is never recognised, since he has surrounded himself by other secret initiates who re-inforce each other's out-reality and dramatizations. The case of the MRC will become increasingly clear as the book unfolds, but it is sad that the majority of people (as high as 99%) dramatize some aspect of their past (lives) on a regular basis. The majority however do not dramatize all the time and occasionally wake up to reality or the now. The MRC case however is not in present time (the now) at any time and his danger lies in his attraction to power and control and secret groups, where he can act out his dramatizations, since the majority of secret groups are power based and hold significant data on the past. This environment merely re-stimulates him - the case of a sick man becoming sicker.

It is impossible to say whether the MRC case actually has any perception of time, or whether he is conscious of this mechanism, other than he might occasionally catch himself doing odd things that are considered 'animal-like' (Grid mechanism with no social/educational/moral modifications e.g. complete selfish and self centred behaviour concerned only with survival of self), but he would never question the morals of this. The MRC case supports the Darwinian principle of survival of the fittest and despises the weak sick or helpless. What's in it for me? Is his main concern, he therefore has no conception of unconditional love, indeed love would probably be degraded to sexual gratification. The MRC case does little if anything to truly help his fellow man and uses charitable status for tax purposes only and apparent increase in self worth, although it is another hiding defence mechanism, which he advertises as his great humanity - cunning fellow our "666".

DOME THEATRE

The Millennium Dome building in London has an infrastructure that is remarkable for its **spiders web** appearance, co-incidentally paralleling the Earth Grid energies. What another co-incidence too! That the significant numbers of **12** rays are present and **5** concentric circles, the significance of which is the former number is a Patriarchal number and the latter a Matriarchal number. According to *The Sunday Telegraph (5th Dec. 1999 - 'Dome Wars - 'The Theatre of the Age')*, rather than being a monument to "urban generation" The Dome has become the focus of fierce political conflict (naturally). Originally apparently shaped by the ambition of Simon Jenkins, a former editor of The Times (Rupert Murdoch naturally) and Millennium Commissioner. The Dome was to provide a great celebratory gathering along the lines of the Festival of Britain. However it is evident that **what** exactly happened in The Dome was never the primary issue, whereas the **building itself was.** "The Dome, conceived of as a great political gesture, shaped by politicians, eventually owned by politicians, spoken up for by both governments, denigrated by both oppositions, floating as a big vulnerable target through which first Michael Heseltine and then Peter Mandelson could be attacked, was **political at its core**" (my emphasis) Thus The Dome was first conceived under a Conservative government and where exactly the architectural plan originated is lost in the 15 architectural/design practises who worked on The Dome. By the time that Chris Smith as Secretary of State at the Department of National Heritage took it over in 1997, it seems that those obsessed with the building, had rather over looked *what* exactly should go in it - "the experience". As Smith noted "At that stage it looked like a building in search of something to put inside, rather than a cluster of activities that were looking for a suitable building". However did not Mr. Reddy who produced the design for The Millennium icon say that it was supposed to represent "the spirituality that we have lost"? Did The Dome represent this too? What spirituality was he referring to, if not Hermes the bisexual god of thieves, who was the first downgrade of the belief in The Cycle of Eternal Return (Re-incarnation) held by the Early Bronze Age Minoans, before a secret cabal entered Crete and destroyed the Minoan civilization, withdrawing the hidden science and the cosmological knowledge from the people. Perhaps Mr. Reddy who after all designed the Millennium icon with its bisexual quality could enlighten us as to what spirituality he was referring to, if not Hermes.

The Story of The Dome[27] on which *The Sunday Telegraph* article was based, is a complex one and there was a lot of legal manoeuvring to allow Millennium Central Ltd (MLC) a public sector company in charge of The Dome to receive a public funded lottery grant, without violating the specific rules governing the allocation of lottery money. The **public in fact will have contributed £600 million** to the exhibition, either through buying Lottery tickets or by paying at the door. As the author of the article notes: "But what was its point? What was the significance of this *strange enterprise*? The Dome has struggled with that question throughout its life" (my emphasis). Well lets see if we can't pull any more significances out of the occult Magician's Black Cabalistic hat, by returning to Dome theory. The Domes although energy imprints of a past presence are also explained as similar to specially set tuning forks, which when struck by an incoming beam, resonate this tone throughout the local Grid system. Who? One might reasonably ask was activating these Domes and beaming signals on an unsuspecting populous using presumably vibratory resonance, which Nikola Tesla used in his research in the 1930's. Well in the past apparently it was the Elohim who originally engineered and installed the system in accordance with HERMES PRINCIPLES (What a surprise!) Evidently then, Hermes is looking more and more like the god of Britain, with his hermetic keys to the World Grid.

"Curiouser and Curiouser" said Alice and as we proceed through the Mad Hatter's tea party and run into Advertising. Surely here one might expect to find a reason for it or "the point". Simon Dicketts drafted the original script at M&C Saatchi Company for advertising The Dome. Did not Mr. Saatchi say once in The Guardian newspaper, that there was "nothing left to hide" and if there was "no-one would care anyway". Well I don't know £600 million of public money for no apparent worth, is either an expensive dramatization and mad hatter's folly, or there was a symbolic and Millennial point to the Dome only meant for the few in the know, whilst the rest of Britain scratched their heads in wonder and picked up the bill (for arrogance?). The brief that Dicketts received included "people's expectations about the Millennium itself". Was it not odd, that of all the places where one might have sought to portray that "expectation", if not in Britain itself, Dicketts chose Easter Island! "...The sheer antiquity of those stone heads, their easy reach into the distant past, would bring poetry and depth to the idea of the Millennium ...allied to a sense of the future and to the idea of personal involvement in what it might be, the advertisement would be a way of setting the Millennium on track". (Sic.) Well as hard as I try to see the connection or any link to a Festival for Britain, I can't quite grasp Dickett's connection or should I say Mr. Saatchi who previously covered advertising for the Conservative party in Britain. Although **those heads** do certainly have a history! A Polynesian elder from Easter Island told a folk tale from his own people, of their being a red rock in Antarctica, which was found several hundred miles inland and not observable from the coast. It would have been impossible for a Polynesian in very early times to traverse Antarctica in its present frozen state to see the rock and live to tell the tale. If the legend is true then Antarctica must have experienced very different weather patterns than today. Indeed at one time geologists believe that Antarctica was not frozen.

Hitler was very well versed in pre-history and the secret group connections of Hitler were discussed in *Alternative 4* along with the Third Reich. Amongst secret groups including the Nazis, there was always knowledge of a cataclysm, before which a super-race had existed. Hitler believed that The Atlanteans were the forerunners of the Nordic people and various expeditions to Thule in Greenland were organised to take up these theories. Various ancient Renaissance maps such as the Zeno brothers Map of 1380, and the Piri Reis Map, show Greenland free of ice and the maps show the actual coastline, which would have been impossible to define at that time without current technology, unless the land was ice-free. The maps were believed to have been drawn up not via navigation, but by using predictions of landmasses and coastal lines, which are a direct result of the Grid pattern. Thus knowing the pattern above on the Hermetic principle of "As above, so below", one could predict very accurately the coastline.

The Norse legend of Fimbelvetr the 'Terrible Winter', that launched the epic disasters of Raynaruk and the destruction of the gods of Valhalla, may reflect a true historical event - the obliteration of a pre-historic Civilization in the boreal regions, by the Ice Age Catastrophe, which may be the shifting of The Bloch Wall and a Magnetic Reversal. The old mythical legends of giants, which once existed are also I feel, a very true historical fact based on a reversal and a change in the gravitational field. Even *Genesis* in The Bible speaks of "giants in those days". Those heads on Easter Island, which are enormous and weigh many tons, are thought to be deity figures. Certainly there is some question of whether this civilization was subservient to a master, giant or god like race, which the heads depict.

The Norwegian explorer Thor Heyerdahl set out in 1956 to prove that only manpower, ropes and a workforce of some 500 men could have moved the stone heads on Easter Island into place, however he took 18 days to move a head that was one of the smallest (10-15 tons). He ignored those heads of 35 and 50 tons and the fact that he had utilised wooden poles, when trees on the Island were sparse. He also ignored the fact that to import the trees would require a trip to a forest 2500 miles away. Further he ignored the fact that stone heads sitting on ledges in the cliff of Ahu-Ririki   precariously reside over a rock face that plunges 1000 feet straight into the sea. Gusty winds make the cliff face a rather dangerous place and yet here at an elevation of 600 feet on the cliff wall stands a platform that bears the marks of a number of 25 ton statues, the remains of which lie on the ocean floor. At the quarry of Rano-Raraku, 20-ton statues were carved near the top of the crater, then lowered 300 feet, over the heads of other statues. This was accomplished without leaving a mark. The obvious inference is that like other great monuments that have been inexplicably erected why should those giants, be indirectly connected to The Millennium Dome in London?

Few researchers have noted the group of stone buildings, 39 in number located on the Island in Orongo. Each structure is **oval** in shape reminding one of the electro-magnetic biofield shape and the structures are topped with a low **circular** ceiling, reminding one of the wheel (in the Heavens) and the Earth Grid energy chakra system, with its gravitational anomalies and further reminding one of the Millennium Eye in the sky in London. The foundation stones were laid beneath the surface and were followed by rings of stone blocks, with each ring narrowing towards the centre until the sides converged in a rounded roof. This remarkably reminds one of the connections between the ley lines and the Grid. There is one more feature that links these structures with the Megalithic structures in Europe such as Stonehenge on Salisbury plain in Wiltshire England, the presence of the ruins of a small solar observatory, so necessary to calculate times of activity in the Grid, with gravitational anomalies. Stonehenge reputedly built by the Druids in England also shows megalithic stones, which would have created the same problems of transport. Stonehenge too, was thought to be a solar observatory. Perhaps now we are getting to the bottom of Mr. Reddy's lost spirituality, when we ask whether it was the Druids of Britain, who stole the cosmological knowledge from the Early Minoans whilst setting up a Solar Kingship, which would define the political system in Europe for thousands of years. Indeed the Millennium icon looked remarkably similar to the Minoan Fresco entitled "Prince" (*The Battle of The Trees*).

If Mr. Dickett's use of the stone heads was to give "a sense of the future "and "what it might be", then surely the heads hark back to the Druids and the Third Reich, the idea of a "Super-race", Atlantis and a giant people, who may well be the old Atlanteans before the flood, when gravity prior to a Magnetic Reversal was at a different level. Unfortunately perhaps Mr. Dickett's forgot or failed to recognise that they also encompass the idea of *a cataclysm* – happy New Year folks!

PREHISTORIC ATOMIC WARS

The Hindu literary work, the *Mahabharata* is an epic poem of 200 000 lines, sating back in its present form to 500 B.C Textual evidence, however, indicates that the events depicted in the *Mahabharata* took place 1000 to 2000 years earlier. European scholars had access to these ancient scriptures during the British Imperial rule of India. *The Mahabharata* is an epic poem of 200,000 lines dating back in its present form to 500 BC however; textual evidence in *The Mahabharata* indicates that the events took place much earlier. Repeated references are made to great god-kings riding about in "Vimanas" or "celestial cars", described as "aerial chariots with sides of iron clad with wings". In a time of a great war, the Vimanas were used to launch a terrible weapon of great and terrible destructive power. The accounts of the devastation caused by this weapon are remarkable for their comparable effects to Atomic destruction. *The Mahabharata* relates:

> "The valiant Adwattan, remaining steadfast in his Vimana, landed upon the water and from there unleashed the Agneya weapon, incapable of being resisted by the very gods. Taking careful aim against his foes, the preceptor's son let loose the blazing missile of smokeless fire with tremendous force. Dense arrows of flame, like a great shower, issued forth upon creation, encompassing the enemy. Meteors flashed down from the sky. A thick gloom swiftly settled upon the Pandava hosts. All points of the compass were lost in darkness. Fierce winds began to blow. Clouds roared upward, showering dust and gravel.
>
> Birds croaked madly, and beasts shuddered from the destruction. The very elements seemed disturbed. The sun seemed to waver in the heavens. The earth shook, scorched by the terrible violent heat of this weapon. Elephants burst into flame and ran to and fro in frenzy, seeking protection from the terror. Over a vast area, other animals crumpled to the ground and died. The waters boiled, and the creatures residing therein also died. From all points of the compass the arrows of flame rained continuously and fiercely. The missile of Adwattan burst with the power of thunder, and the hostile warriors collapsed like trees burnt in a raging fire. Thousands of war vehicles fell down on all sides."

The description of the second battle is as frightening as that of the first:

> Gurkha, flying in his swift and powerful Vimana, hurled against the three cities of the Vrishnis and Andhakas a single projectile charged with all the power of the Universe. An incandescent column of smoke and fire, as

brilliant as ten thousand suns, rose in all its splendour. It was the unknown weapon, the iron thunderbolt, a gigantic messenger of death, which reduced to ashes the entire race of the Vrishnis and Handshakes. The corpses were so burnt that they were no longer recognizable. Hair and nails fell out. Pottery broke without cause. Birds disturbed, circled in the air and were turned white, foodstuffs were poisoned. To escape, the warriors threw themselves in streams to wash themselves and their equipment.[28]

Whilst many have attributed these descriptions to the overactive imagination, there are too many details, which make this a parallel description to eyewitness reports of an atomic bomb explosion, followed by the effects of radiation poisoning. Whilst it has been assumed that the primitive tools of early man and his societies were the evolutionary foundations of modern man, the equally plausible theory is that these finds related to a remnant of mankind that had survived from a cataclysm - they may be degenerate remnants of higher cultures that decayed when a conflagration occurred, following the use of knowledge relating to the Grid and Atomic Physics. Perhaps the 'flying chariots', were aircraft or even craft that utilised Grid energies. However the use of atomic weapons in India 4400 years ago presupposes knowledge of nuclear physics rivalling our own. The Physicist Frederick Soddy, in his *Interpretation of Radium*, published in 1909, remarked concerning the ancient accounts: "Can we not read in them some justification for the belief that some former forgotten race of men attained not only to the knowledge we have recently won, but also to the power that is not yet ours... I believe that there have been civilizations in the past that were familiar with atomic energy, and that by misusing it they were totally destroyed".

This was a very odd thing for Soddy to say, given that he was a Physicist working on research that would lead to the splitting of the atom and eventually that research would culminate in the Atomic bomb developed in America at Los Alamos. Scientists generally do not stray much outside their own field in my experience, thus it was unusual in my opinion, that Soddy should have had access to these translations, unless they had been passed to Rutherford and Soddy by those (Intelligence Services?), who thought that these accounts were not mere imaginings, which was the black propaganda line that has been asserted to the public, but were in fact weapons of Atomic or Grid warfare.

Several Sanskrit books contain references to divisions of time that cover a very wide range. At one extreme, according to Hindu texts dealing with cosmology are the Kalpa or 'Day of Brahma', a period of 4.32 billion years. At the other, as described in the Bihath Sathaka, we find reference to the kashata, equivalent to three one hundred millionths (0.00000003) of a second. Modern Sanskrit scholars have no idea why such large and such miniscule time divisions were necessary in antiquity. All they know is that they were used in the past, and they are obliged to preserve the tradition. The only phenomena in nature that can be measured in billions of years or in millionths of a second are the disintegration rates of radioisotopes. These rates range from those of elements like uranium 238, with a half-life of 4.51 billion years, to subatomic particles such as K mesons and hyperons, with mean half-lives measured in the hundred-millionths, billionths, trillionths, and even smaller fractions of a second. Thus one cannot discount a civilization that could study and measure nuclear and sub nuclear matter.

Another curiosity at Easter Island apart from those heads is a unique form of woodcarving called moaikavakava. The carving is of a shrunken man, with certain grotesque anatomical features depicted in remarkable detail. Today the miniature men are regarded by the Easter Islanders as fearful and alien - a reminder of something that was not of their experience. Native legend attributes these statues to King Tu'ukoiho. One night the King caught a glimpse of two misshapen dwarfish beings, which he believed were the spirits of the last members of a race that had inhabited the Island, before the present native population. Even though they were never seen again, the King made a replica of these beings, carved in wood. The style of these carvings is not in the least Polynesian, and the sculpted facial features - hooked nose, staring eyes and small squared beard - appear to be very similar to some of the early Semitic Pharaoh's mummy's preserved in Egypt. The most interesting peculiarity is the appearance of the body; it is emaciated, showing goitres, tumours, clenched mouth, collapsed cervical vertebrae, and a distinct break between the lumbar and the dorsal vertebrae, which are medical indications of exposure to a severe dose of radiation.

The Stanzas of Dzyan from Tibet like *The Mahabharata*, depict a holocaust engulfing **two warring nations** who utilize flying vehicles and fiery weapons .If my thesis that I have developed here of two secret and opposing groups with their plans for a One World Order is correct, then it would also provide evidence for my conclusion, that we repeat past cycles (with their cataclysms), since the MRC case merely repeats those cycles continually. The Stanzas translated within the past century, are believed to date back originally several millennia and according to the Stanzas:

> "The great King of the Dazzling Face, the chief of all the Yellow-faced was sad, seeing the evil intentions of the Dark-faced. He sent his air vehicles to all his brother chiefs with pious men within, saying, prepare, arise, men of the good law, and escape while the waters have not yet overwhelmed the land.

The Lords of the Storm are also approaching; their war vehicles are nearing the land. One night and two days only shall the Lords of the Dark-faced arrive on this patient land. She is doomed when the waters descend on her. The Lords of the Dark-eyed have prepared their magic Agneyastra (the Hindu "Agneya weapon" - nuclear missile)... They are also versed in Ashtar (the highest magical knowledge). Come, and use yours.... When the kings were assembled, the waters of the earth had already been disturbed. The nations crossed the dry lands. They went beyond the watermark. The kings reached then the safe lands in their air vehicles, and arrived in the lands of fire and metal...Stars (nuclear missiles?) showered on the lands of the Dark-faced while they slept.The speaking beasts (radios?) remained quiet. The Lords waited for orders, but they came not, for their masters slept. The waters rose and covered the valleys...In the high lands there dwelt those who escaped, the men of the yellow faces and of the straight eye."

Is it not significant that apart from weapons of great destruction associated with "magic" and what must be the Grid energies or atomic physics, there is also a cataclysmic movement of ocean waters, reminiscent of the Flood, which is not unique to Biblical accounts but appears in the majority of world religious myths. Curiously I reported in *Alternative4*, the appearance of male Mongolian types in UFO incidents and since they had a physical presence, I concluded that this was part of the manipulated UFO phenomenon and that there was an attempt to connect the UFO experience with Mongolians for some reason. Was this not yet again an attempt to prove a superior race that had survived some cataclysm, in the way that Biblical texts claim such superiority for the Jews and the Biblical Patriarch Noah? If the "Lords of the Yellow-faced" were the Mongolian inhabitants of the ancient Gobi high civilization centre, the flooding may have been the great tidal wave that swept across eastern Asia and into Siberia at the end of the Ice Age. This may have been a Bloch Wall shift - magnetic reversal, which was precipitated by manipulating the Grid for weaponry purposes, coupled with atomic warfare.

This is beginning to look familiar is it not? In *Alternative 4,* I discussed the development of secret strategic defence weapons, which are utilising Nikola Tesla technology and are interfering with the ionosphere - I will return to this in a moment, but the text does not indicate who the 'Dark-faced' are, other than a comparable high civilization; what it does mention, is that amongst the survivors of the cataclysm are 'the straight-eye' suggesting peoples of Europe and the Middle East, and that they were a part of the conflict. Well this is looking remarkably like a World War, followed by a cataclysm due to the manipulation of the Grid? I hope as I weave my evidence here, that you are beginning to get the picture loud and clear of the cycle of events that **PREDICTABALY** follow when the Cabalistic use of knowledge and manipulation of the Grid goes unnoticed and unchallenged, whilst the majority 'sleep' on, following the pattern of the Grid as a past pattern of **EVENTS** recorded as a memory and intelligence within the electro-magnetic fields of the Grid – or in my terminology the bioplasma, that big library in the sky. UFO incidents not co-incidentally warned many times of the miss-use of Atomic weapons.

On the basis of curved space-time and the cyclical repeat of events, is it not significant that China has invaded Tibet? - Ransacking her monasteries causing monks to flee. Is it significant that the 'straight-eye', the Americans this time dropped a bomb on Japan? Is it not significant that as Europe builds its power it will inevitably form its own army, which will in time mean that Europe and America will become world powers, with the inevitable squabbles over trade and supremacy by the ego boys, with I have no doubt will be promoted to the level of conflict by the MRC case, one destabilised leader (and I can spot a few in the world today), is all it takes and remarkably no-one has suggested that Power Pyramids and One World Orders controlled by the mentally insane and ill, should be banned. One should NEVER centralise power into the hands of a few. If there were **15 stars** in the original design for the flag of Europe, then co-incidentally again the Earth Grid has **15 Earth traversing "Dragon Lines"** that "like the mythic **Oroboros Serpent,** link their tails with their mouths, making a complete energy circuit". Thus the cosmic circle so well represented in iconography and archaeology such as the Tholos in the Temple of Asklepios at Epidaurus in Greece, which I discussed in my first book and the concentric closing in of knowledge in one sense and the Earth Grid in another, is also shown at Cardiff Castle UK Wales on The Summer Smoking Room Floor. In Nordic mythology, the massive World Serpent envelops the World. This is no more than a coded term for the energy Grid. Interestingly the Serpent occurs frequently in Biblical texts, although there are several interpretations of this and the original serpent represented wisdom and knowledge. The fact that Patriarchal religion utilised that knowledge for bad purposes and control, does not signify that the knowledge was bad, only those who misused it would qualify. Knowledge is never bad, it is simply knowledge, however how that knowledge is used or applied defines wrongness.

The Yggdrasil world tree, which was the Cosmic Ash tree, which lie at the heart of the Universe, is another veiled reference to Grid chakras, the Sefiritic Tree of Life and Cabala knowledge. The Jormungund snake was one of the evils threatening the survival of the Norse World, along with its siblings it epitomised darkness and destruction. The massive serpent lurked in the ocean depths circling the world in a stranglehold, ready to burst forth at Ragnarok home of the Aesir gods and spew venom in all directions. Thor the Nordic god had many life and death battles with serpents and dragons and numerous mythological figures in

Nordic legends have fought the evil Dragons. It is a well known fact in Viking and Nordic mythology that women were regarded as man's equal and perhaps even more so, since they were highly thought of and valued for their intuitive insights and psychic abilities. We find in the legend of Idun, Idunnor or Iduna, who was in Germanic mythology the goddess who guarded the apples of youth, a reflection of The Grail Romances discussed in *The Battle of The Trees*, and the Apples of Immortality - **Re-incarnation**. The woman carried the Holy Grail openly and the man in secret. Since the Grid knowledge was held for thousands of years in male only secret groups, there was an implicit understanding that woman would threaten that secrecy and you certainly won't find any women at the top of Freemasonry or powerful; secret groups.

The Frost giant captured "Loki -fire god", and he had to promise to steal the "apples" from Idun (Eden - "My thoughts") to secure his release. On his return to "Asgard - a stronghold of younger gods", Loki told Idun that he had discovered the "apples" of much better quality when growing nearby and so the goddess trustingly accompanied him to the forest where "Thiassi -Frost giant", in the shape of an Eagle waited for his prey. He took "Idun" and her "Apples" in his claws and flew to "Jotunheim - land of Frost giants". The loss of the apples at first caused the gods to become weak and old with bleary eyes and loose skin. Their minds began to weaken - as a general **"Fear" of "Death"** settled on Asgard (all signs of the loss of Immortality and a belief in Re-incarnation). At last Odin gathered his remaining strength and found 'Loki'. By threat of magic (presumably as a last resort - Atomic war? or as was more usual the **curse** or threat of **ill-fated luck eternally** for those who damage the Holy Grail message) he compelled Loki to bring back "Idun" and her "Apples". Loki flew to Jotunheim as a falcon and changed Idun into a "Nut" (Wisdom) and carried her home. The Frost giant gave chase as an Eagle, but was burned to death by fires placed along the tops of Asgard's mighty walls. Loki then restored Idun to her true shape and she gave the "Magic Apples" to the ailing gods. Idun's "Golden Apples" kept the gods "eternally young". The fabulous "fruit Tree" (comparable to a later Garden of Eden Story), was tended and guarded by the three wise Norns (Fate, Present and Future). The Mountain of Nuremberg in Germany was where they resided and interestingly this location was chosen for the Nuremberg Trials, which if it had hoped to divulge the real truth behind World War II and the facts in *Alternative 4,* hardly revealed the story of either "the apples" or the occult group behind Hitler. The three wise Norns allowed only Idun, the "deity of spring" to pick the magic fruit. The giants who sought to strip the gods of their vigour, youth and Eternal Life and Thiassi disguised as a bird makes off with the gods "Elixir of Life". Here then, you have a myth often repeated of a Sovereign power (The Eagle), who makes off with the knowledge of Re-incarnation, taking it from the woman who is rightful owner of the knowledge and thereafter retaining the knowledge to *empower himself.* A story that I concluded occurred at Knossos 1,400BC and at the Crucifixion, having also occurred prior to the Bronze Age and is occurring now, as man descends that fatal spiral downward into The Second Millennium. It was never a sexist issue there was simply a greater truth that was never known.

The Dragon Lines intersect with Dome Lines or the ley lines and certainly the prophetic Apocalypse mentions "The Dragon"- also the Cabalistic magician Alistair Crowley utilised the sign of the Dragon in his rituals. The Michael/Solar and Oroboros/Lunar lines actually touch down beginning and ending their planetary circuit and consequently activating the 12 Zodiacal Ororobos lines at the site of the Master Dome, the original Round Table of King Arthur and Camelot, the Zodiacal court of the Sun - which is at Avebury Circle. Interestingly enough "The **Solar** Oroboros comes in as a burst of pure spirit, fiery, almost deadly, carrying absolute, eternal consciousness; it is assigned the Gematria **666** by the Cabals. The Lunar Oroboros is cool, moist, refreshing, like a revivifying draught, carrying incarnate consciousness subject to temporal **cycles of birth and death, time and space**, it is assigned the Gematria 1080" [29] (my emphasis).

TRANSGENERATIONAL COLLECTIVE INTELLIGENCE

Throughout my own research, there has always been the concern that Science is being manipulated towards an acceptance of the Holodynamic psychology and The Universal Mind. In *The Battle of The Trees* historical research into the background Philosophy of secret groups revealed a pre-occupation with **ant-heaps and beehives**. The idea of **self-organisation** as a **social model** not only appeared in reference to secret groups, but also curiously arose in iconography from Knossos Crete. A beehive with the Goddess at the top may have been transferred as an archetypal symbol during the re-positioning era post Religious Revolution circa 1,400BC. The idea of a spiritual figurehead may have been substituted for the idea of a power pyramidal system of control, with that one controlling signal from the top. Further the model of a beehive is interesting, since the Grid in 3-D would resemble the cells of a hive. The **step pyramid**, which is seen in Russian Communistic architecture in Red Square in Moscow, relates to a power pyramid of social and political organisation. Such a pyramid can be seen on the reverse side of the American One Dollar note, where the Illuminati Eye is seen at the top.

Adam Weishaupt as the founder of **Illuminism** (a secret group that has played a notorious role in world history and the revolutionary scene), in his doctrines referred to this requirement for Order as a principle of absolute power. That such an organisation is now being completed in Europe, as a Federal Super state is no more of a surprise than the goals of Weishaupt, on which one would conclude European Union is based. As Weishaupt stated: "Do you realise sufficiently what it means to rule - to rule in a secret society? Not only over the lesser or more important of the populace, but over the best of men, over men of all ranks, nations and religions, to rule without external force, to unite them indissolubly to breathe ones spirit and soul into them, do you know what secret societies are? What place they occupy in the great kingdom of the world's events? Do you really think they are unimportant transitory appearances? (*'The Battle of The Trees)*

Within the secret societies there was always the desire to replace the network of Freemasonry with a more effective system, such a system may have presented itself with completion of scientific research into the Grid. Certainly the thought was always there in the secret societies that the Grid could offer the opportunity to control via one signal from the apex of the power pyramid, to cohere behaviour into a socially acceptable form, without choice but through compliance to a cohesive signal - **mind control.** Whilst co-operation by choice infers spiritual evolution and awareness incorporating integrity, morals and self-control in bringing about socially acceptable behaviour in terms of the group, the world experience is not quite this paradise, in fact quite the reverse. Crime and violent behaviour is on the increase and compliance to a cohesive signal may have been seen as the solution. The fact that secret groups and Patriarchal religion have removed from a very early date the choice of belief (Re-incarnation), thus removing the possibility to contact past lives or Everett's "other worlds", means that as these lives and the holographic experience impinge in current time, without conscious knowledge, they have the power to drive a person into an irrational course of action. The **choice** becomes whether a person chooses to access those **past lives** in order to erase the possibility of their acting or impinging unknowingly on the mind of the individual in present time driving him into irrational courses of action.

Communistic doctrine which is supported by virtually all secret groups *and* the rich right wing elite as a method of controlling a populous is based on the ant-heap and Beehive philosophy of ORDER and CONTROL incorporating the idea of "co-operative" and **"collective group mind"** - where there is **no choice**. It really does not matter which system of politics the MRC uses whether it is fascism or communism, the overall result is always loss of freedom and democracy. It did not surpass my notice in researching *Alternative 4,* that the idea of "spirit guides" ('Voices in your head') whom one is being advised to consult before making decisions by the New Age healers, was a dangerous route against the background of "The Universal Mind" and the possibility of control via broadcasted signals. 'The Guardian Angel' (some spirit more enlightened than yourself) brigade and the ignorant people who promote this type of advice to an unsuspecting public, giving them no possibility of 'psychic defence' or indeed the process of their own thinking, are typical of the New Age rubbish that magazines pump out from people who would be better off under-going therapy themselves, rather than tramping their ignorant ideas around so-called 'workshops', disseminating ideas that would only aid mind control - and unbelievably advising people to walk round **"cosmic circles"** meditating, which is the pattern and memory of the Grid! My advice to anyone has always been, you have a mind so USE IT! - Otherwise it becomes vestigial and through its capacity as a dipole radio-receiver picks up everything from the Grid, including any message that may be broadcast from 'Big Brother'! The anthroposophist irritates me intensely with their "Guardian Angels" - and as we shall see their guru Rudolph Steiner was locked into the secret groups. Worse still with his Akashic Record he was locked into the Grid!

Whilst order and social or psycho civilised behaviour may be one goal of ant-heap and bee hive philosophy, with the one controlling signal from the top, I further speculated in my UFO research, that the elite hoped to initiate man on mass, by exposing him to certain symbols through the Grid, which hold significance to the past and man's mythopoeic mind. I was uncertain whether the justification for such actions by the Elite would be sought in the idea that **Initiation** by opening the mind to a new set of symbols or even the old archetypes would be a desirable psychic evolution. Certainly in *Alternative4* I gave evidence for the conclusion that symbols were being used on members of an un-suspecting public. There was also evidence to show that resonant and artificial external frequencies may have been applied in some cases to open the chakras, which would then promote a form of initiation, aimed at opening the corresponding chakras, with a corresponding change in mental state.

The idea of **Transgenerational collective intelligence** is a major impetus I believe behind The New World Order and the promotion of The Universal Mind. An example of this collective intelligence occurs in the insect world with Bees and ants and termites. In the latter their pattern of building or moving pellets is random and meaningless when there are only a few termites, but when more termites are added a threshold phenomenon occurs where their behaviour radically changes and they begin to co-operatively create the multi-arch structures of their nest. It is entirely possible given what I have said previously of the insistence of science in using animal experiments to portray a parallel system in man, as is the case with cancer research, that the elite and their scientists who lack any spiritual dimension, are applying a scenario of collective animal survival intelligence to man, as guinea pig to their great experiment for man, utilising Grid knowledge and energies of the hidden science. If that is so, is it not also a repeat of the scenario that I gave on just how the MRC case or "fallen angel" came to be trapped in the first place, by manipulating Homo Sapiens through his energy fields? Thus once again we observe a cyclical repeat of the past and more evidence for the thesis of the MRC case. Animals utilise Grid mechanisms for survival in the absence of higher moral faculties, but man by way of education and moral tuition has the choice to override the Grid. However it never ceases to amaze me how many individuals operate on Grid survival mentality, despite their avowed religion or morals. I am afraid that politicians just don't get it, as they struggle with Grid survival mentality and crime. They prevent man from thinking or using his moral judgements, thus connecting him up nicely as a mind controlled slave of their own politics and the Grid! They could give man back his mind, but no the MRC conjures up the idea of signals from the Grid or mind control and a psycho civilized society of zombies, which is where the MRC case came in as the "Fallen Angel", probably billions of years ago.

With one or just a few squid gathered, there is no awareness of direction in which to swim, but with a sufficient number, new group intelligence occurs and the collective acts as a single organism, which is able to migrate across the ocean. This may be so in birds. All these animals however, use the electro-magnetic vectors of the Grid. These animals must as is the case with the

Monarch butterfly, have a magnetic organ that can only weakly pick up the Grid vectors individually, but which must be enhanced with the presence of more individuals and magnetic organs. One might theorise, that as man collects in cities and crowding occurs, then Grid survivalist or animal-like behaviour would occur. Since the 19th Century a particular species of mice has been used in psychological experiments, where the mice have been taught to run mazes. Later generations of mice (with no physical contact) are able to learn to run the maze faster. Monkeys on a Pacific Island taught to wash sweet potatoes free from sand ate them, whereas previously they had been discarded because the monkeys did not like the sand. Other members of the same species on other Islands soon learnt this behaviour, despite the fact that they had no contact with the first group. The only way the learning behaviour could have been transferred is via a non-specific field - a field I have termed a morphogenetic field for the species. This may simply be the etheric field of master DNA. Such a field is manifested on the physical level as the DNA in our own bodies. The DNA very probably has conductance and capacitance properties, which confer radio-receiver properties. The religious idea of not cutting ones hair and conserving the strength as in the Biblical story of Sampson may merely be a desire to retain as much DNA (in the hair) on the head, which is the position of the crown chakra, in order to maximise the radio-receiver properties and connection with the Grid.

Behaviour then can be encoded into a species where it exhibits collective intelligence as part of the collective group mind. This really does not apply to man in his more highly evolved state, who is not a mere animal operating as a machine or quantum mechanical system purely on the basis of matter, which is controlled by the Grid. Woolf[30] describes a connection with the Universal Mind as increasing Psychic, extrasensory perception, telepathy, psycho kinesis, cognition of former lives etc. However one's past lives are not known immediately to others, thus one cannot include such information in with any Universal Mind. There is an **INDIVIDULALISTIC ELEMENT**, and this does not allow for the concept of a Universal Mind to be applied to the soul. This is a serious fault in the path Science is taking, or is being forced to take in compliance with the goals of The One World Order. Scientists have always been vulnerable to the promoted view of man as a quantum machine, which is the thinking behind the One World Order, simply because they have been trained or educated along strict orthodox lines and as I have stated anything of value has purposefully been left out of the educative process- **brainwashing.** I would say the majority of scientists would wince at the word God - a higher Spiritual Order. The Universal Mind based on the Grid or energy system, would however appeal to them, I have no doubt.

In *The Battle of The Trees* I noted that members of secret societies in the 18th and 19th centuries had constantly referred to a "hidden hand", a society more powerful than all the rest, which indeed may have controlled the rest. The identity of that higher echelon was not known, however it was the moving hand behind the French Revolution and was probably the moving hand behind the Russian Revolution, which sought to eradicate Monarchy as a step closer towards a "United States of The West" - European Union. Indeed in East West politics over many years a number of observers have noticed that there appears to be some form of co-operation, even during the so-called cold war. The highest and most secret order, the order that I have proposed carries a document covering the true events of the Crucifixion, may well be the Illuminati in the form of the Rosicrucian's and the highest degrees - The Rose Croix. There is a basis for my assertion that such a group has not only withheld significant knowledge of The Grid, but since this group had access to the Cabala they have not only used the knowledge themselves, but have carried out significant research over a long period, thus advancing their knowledge to include powerful psychology, which may have been developed by various psychologists and scientists in their employ over the years. Thecollectiveunconscious may represent such an advance towards the idea of a Universal Mind.

CABALISTIC ORIGINS OF THE HIDDEN SCIENCE

The Cabalistic Jew Dr. Falk, who certainly possessed Cabalistic knowledge of Grid energies, used that knowledge to gain for himself a reputation as a sorcerer in the 18th Century. On his arrival in London in 1742 he was already noted in some circles as an important figure in Germany. Falk stood alone in his generation for his knowledge of the mysteries connected to manipulation of Grid energies. Neither did Falk impart such knowledge since the Jewish Encyclopaedia states that a Royal Prince applied to Falk for this knowledge in search of the Philosophers Stone. Whilst Saint Germain and Cagliostro figure in every account of 18th Century magicians, it is only exclusively in Judaic or Masonic works that you will find any reference to Falk, re-iterating M.Andre Baron's dictum: **"Remember that the constant rule of the secret societies is that the real authors never show themselves".**

Whilst no reference has ever stated that Dr. Falk was a leading member of Freemasonry, he is shown in *The Jewish Encyclopaedia* holding in his hand a pair of compasses, which archetypally suggests the double triangle or Seal of Solomon, known amongst the Jews as "the Shield of David", which is an important emblem in Masonry. Further the two opposing triangles indicate the idea that was held in secret groups, that God is both good and evil (Satan) and further the extension can be made of dualistic philosophy and the Principles of Hermes, which undoubtedly refer to the Grid energies. The Rosicrucian Kenneth Mackenzie wrote a detailed article in The Royal Masonic Encyclopaedia on Dr. Falk, but again no mention is made of any link with Freemasonry, which leads one to conclude that in Masonic circles, the importance of Falk is recognised but must not be divulged. The **black cabala** is involved here and obviously Grid energies - on no account was the connection to be made. Mr. Gordon Hills contributor to *Ars Quatuor Coronatorum* observed: "If Jewish Brethren did introduce Cabalistic learning into the so-called High Degrees (of Freemasonry) here we have one, who if a Mason, would have been eminently qualified to do so." Falk was more than a Mason he was a high initiate "the supreme oracle in which the Secret Societies applied for guidance".

Salvalette de Langes when providing dossiers of all the secret societies referred to Falk: "Some believe him to be the Chief of all Jews and attribute to purely political schemes, all that is marvellous and singular in his life and conduct. He is referred to in a very curious manner, and as a **Rose -Croix** in the Memoirs of the Chevalier de Rampsow..."(my emphasis). Falk was recorded as having a light that burnt constantly without any means of doing so, which is a 'trick' that Nikola Tesla demonstrated in the 20's when he was conducting experiments on Grid energies - free energy. Once when a wheel came off Falk's carriage on the way to mysterious meetings in Epping Forest, it followed on its own after the carriage, which remained in motion. It is believed that Cagliostro the Jew who more than anyone achieved the downfall of Maria Antoinette over the manipulated affair of the necklace, where Maria was implicated in a love affair, was the pupil of Falk. As poor young and naive Maria Antoinette struggled with her efforts to find out who was behind The French Revolution, it would seem that she discovered too late that the Masons were behind it. Whilst Cagliostro was reported to have devised the Egyptian rite in Freemasonry, many believe he was under the direction of Falk, who was described as "almost inaccessible" by Savalette de Langes.

In *The Battle of The Trees* I noted a cruel ceremony that Falk had carried out on a he-goat and almost certainly the archetypal use of the he-goat and apples identified Falk as using a perverted form of the Matriarchal religion, dating back to Knossos. If Falk was a member of The Rose- Croix, the highest and select degree of Freemasonry, then the Matriarchal knowledge can also be seen in perverted form in the design of The Summer Smoking room floor at Cardiff Castle Wales, UK., which I deciphered in *The Battle of The Trees*. Lord Bute whom I assumed was a member of **Scottish Rite Freemasonry** laid the floor. In the final enclosing circle (Cosmic circle and Earth Grid?) of the floor which was laid before The French Revolution, there is a design showing the archetypal use of petals, which I not only related to the Knossos double axe, symbolising the Cycle of Eternal Return (which I equated with Re-incarnation), but also with **The Rose-Croix degree** of Freemasonry. It is certainly curious, that the rose design is one that occurred at the Temple of Asklepios in Epidaurus in The Peloponnese Greece, which was not only a place of healing but political power. I doubt whether Lord Bute would have entertained even as a member of the Aristocracy, any manipulation of the Grid energies for control of a populous, however he might have been fed a false line by the secret societies that The Grid or the hidden science was to be used for healing in the future goal of "Paradise on Earth", which is the promise of the Prophetic Apocalypse or The Book of *Revelations*, by John. Certainly Jesus does not figure anywhere in Lord Bute's castle, however John does, giving some validation for my claim in *The Battle of The Trees*, that the Book of Revelations, is the plan of the One World Order. John himself was probably a high initiate of a descendent form of Scottish rite Freemasonry.

The Crab mural on the wall of The Summer Smoking Room, at Cardiff Castle, actually portrays not only the true events of The Crucifixion and the **SECOND CUT**, but it also portrays **WRONGFUL** information on the **FIRST CUT**. The cut in one sense, refers to a ceremony conducted at Gisors in the 12th Century, whereby according to my decoding of the names of the secret groups involved in that ceremony (CAPUT and ORMUS), two groups separated and forged completely different goals for a World Order; one group wishing to release the mysteries and the other group wishing to keep them hidden from man. The fact that Lord Bute as a sexist member of the Aristocracy and a member of the sexist organisation of Freemasonry, displayed a black Madonna on the roof of Cardiff Castle and a wrongful portrayal of the first cut, is in my conclusion an indication that Lord Bute was fed the wrong information as regards the Crucifixion details. Magdalena or The Mary Magdalene fled Jerusalem with John within an inch of her life. She had a bad cut to the left upper arm, which had nearly severed it. She had her genealogies stolen (as a Princess) and with one child (a boy) from a union with Jesus, she fled with the few possessions, which had not been stolen. Her wealth in the form of precious oils taken along with the important genealogies, she fled to a region north of Marseilles in France, where a Greek colony existed and where legend states that she took the Holy Grail, which was knowledge attached to Re-incarnation, the Grid and curved space time i.e. a whole Cosmology. She was healing people in this area with John, who subsequently wrote Revelations. She was pregnant with John's child, even though he was much older than her, having turned to him for shelter and support after the events of Jerusalem. Magdalena was subsequently betrayed and she was mown down by a horse and killed with the unborn child, during a raid on the settlement. She died with her unborn child trying to save the few remaining truths left and the Jesus child. The archetypal messages coded into Poussin's paintings related in *The Battle of The Trees*, are a reference to her death and the disappearance of the knowledge underground - **The Underground Stream**. The Jesus child I assumed was used to propagate the Merovingian dynasty, which is said to be a dynastic line emanating from Jesus and the Mary Magdalene. There is no assurance here, that John who subsequently utilised the truth to benefit the Global Elite along with her son did, not also betray the Mary Magdalene. The Holy Grail was to remain underground until the Renaissance and Joan of Arc was to secretly embody this knowledge, but unfortunately she was also betrayed.

The final and enclosing ring of the design at Cardiff Castle shows a plan for a Universal Kingdom - both political and religious. The kingdom that Eliphas Levi a member of the secret societies at the time of the French Revolution spoke of, as being had by those: "with the keys to the East" - the keys of Hermes and the secrets of The Earth Grid. The German poet Gotthold Ephraim Lessing published a series of dialogues in which Lessing claimed Falk was initiated into the highest degrees of Freemasonary, whilst the Duke of Brunswick, a high ranking Freemason at the time of The French Revolution, forbade publication, the series did get into print however. Falk is named in a dialogue with Lessing under the name of Ernst. Falk explains that Freemasonry has always existed, but not always under that name and later in this book I will give the names, which I believe it has worked under. Its real purposes have never been revealed, although I hope to shed some new light on these goals later in the book. On the surface an apparent philanthropic organization, but in reality, philanthropy formed not part of its scheme, its object being to bring about a state of things, which will render philanthropy unnecessary. Importantly we arrive in this dialogue at the idea of self-organization and "The Universal Mind", once again, with Earth Grid energy implications, encompassing the whole of the current Holodynamic Psychology, which was incorporated into physics and scientific research in the 80's, which is curious enough in itself, to warrant the question of who is the guiding hand behind the pre-determined conclusions and path of science?!

Falk illustrating his point to Ernst (Lessing), points predictably to an ant-heap at the foot of a tree: "Why", he asks. "Should not human beings exist without Government like the ants or bees?" Falk then goes on to describe his ideas of a Universal State, or rather a **"FEDERATION OF STATES"**, in which men will **no longer be divided by national, social or religious prejudices and where greater equality will exist.** In this statement, you have the World Revolution plan in its entirety, which has given us European Union, orchestrated by those Freemasonry groups who in ascendancy have never cease to exist. You will note that there was always a plan to introduce a religion which would unify the world's religions and the only religion capable of that would be a religion, dating back to Greece which forms a common basis for all religions, which Falk I believe followed in its Pagan mysteries. However I noted in *The Battle of The Trees*, that the elite presumably a conjoined group with both political and religious goals, appeared to have undergone another schism in the 80's which lead to a priority of goals and where the religious plan was thrown out in favour of a more immediate political goal and European Union or the "Federation of States", plan. The fact that the Millennium Dome has appeared in London **may** signify that the religious goal was held in Britain or more principally with Scottish Rite Freemasonry and the Rose-Croix of that degree. The fact that Britain is the last to hold out on the final stages of European Union to me, signifies that perhaps the original dual purpose of "The Universal Kingdom", i.e. religious and political goal is still being sought by the secret Order in the UK: However there is no indication from the recent State visit by China's President to London last year (2 000), that there is any intention to reveal the whole truth of the Matriarchal history and The Holy Grail - Re-incarnation. There is however every reason to believe that the current moves to restrict freedom and choice, mean that there is every intention to realise a more controlled and directed society where freedom of belief and choice will be a thing of the past.

In Lessing's dialogues, Falk states that although the great secrets of Freemasonry cannot be revealed by any man, even if he wished it, that one thing that had been kept dark which should now be made known was the relationship between the Freemasons and the *** "The *** were in fact the Freemasons of

105

their time". The asterisks I believe relate to the Rosicrucian's and the forerunners of their group, which I intend to cover later. In the same dialogue, it is interesting that Falk stated that the real and concealed superiors never attend Freemasonry. Certainly one group today that appears to act on such a 'freelance' basis, is the Bilderberger's, a group that has been coined the "Secret Government of the World".

All anarchists from Proudhom onwards have placed schemes for re-organising human life into the context of some form of the holodynamic, self-organising structure: The "World State"; "The Universal Republic"; have been the war cry of the |Internationalist Socialists, the Grand Orient Masons, the Theosophists and all anarchist groups. The two worst 'run-ins' that I ever had, were with the Scientologists and Rudolf Steiner's Anthroposophist movement, both groups expected some miraculous self-organising structure of ethics to appear in the "ant-heap", which never happens, despite the claims of spiritual supremacy and high levels of initiation and ethics. This may be unfair to the original goals of Hubbard who founded Scientology, but I will return to this later. The fact is, unless you have a system of justice and which operates in the absence of *any* control via morphogenetic Grid mechanisms i.e. survival of the group or species and purely concentrates on the survival of the **individual**, then you cannot expect any organisation or humanity to operate with any sense of morality and justice, on the basis of a self-organising system - it is just not going to happen. Unless there is justice and law for the individual, you merely subscribe to the One World Communistic thinking where the individual is expendable if they are perceived as not powerful and that was my entire experience with Scientology and Anthroposophy, which as you will come to see, may not be entirely co-incidental. Thus the goals of secret societies were a prescription for **anarchy**. A case of 'Do what thou wilt, is the whole of the law'. The law today has been removed from the people, where a lawyer will not pick up a pen for under a hundred pounds. The New World Order plan for anarchy under the guise of "self-organisation" and transgenerational collective intelligence is in direct opposition to order through access to law and justice. Whilst the Grid controls man and his past lives I am afraid, that law is the only deterrent to anarchy. Why should anyone remain true to higher principles, when those principles are not rewarded by society? A man, who is struggling with the hard economics imposed by the One World Order thinking, is hardly likely to view the salvation of his own soul at some future date as a priority. Thus you see the great thoughts and words, simply do not tie up, man knows, that ethical behaviour and self-organisation does not work in the absence of true justice, for all individuals. Individualism however, is not part of One World Order thinking, where the individual is sacrificed to a cause - the survival of the parasite, The One World Order Elite. All secret groups have this mentality of sacrificing individuals to their cause, whilst feting those who can benefit them, all secret groups are usurious and capable of trampling individuals in their cause of saving the world – and there you have their insanity.

Falk was implicated very strongly in The French Revolution, he gave the Duke d'Orleans who was the chief instigator of the black propaganda against Maria Antoinette, a talisman of lapis-lazuli (The Philosopher's Stone - that fell from the Heavens), implying that the succession to throne of France was his and ordained by God. The Masons duped him and betrayed him, a point he may have realised when he went to the guillotine, after he had performed his use. The Masons in conjunction with Falk were in all probability behind the so-called bread riots at the time of The French Revolution, which lead ultimately to the murder of Maria Antoinette on the guillotine, for a crime she did not commit and her individual case for justice, has never been heard, despite my efforts to place her story and case. What does it matter now the brainwashed will cry - she is dead. The reality however is that she has Re-incarnated and must be somewhere, carrying the deepest grief of her experience and injustice. We see at work behind the French Revolution and the events of Golgotha a plan at work, both political and religious with definite Masonic if not Jewish influences. Those influences can be further defined.

Given that I thought Lord Bute who had The Summer Smoking Room Floor laid at Cardiff Castle, was a Scottish Rite Freemason, what is the link between that order, the highest degree of the Rose-Croix and the group to which Dr. Falk apparently belonged - The Rosicrucian's? Robert Bruce is said to have instituted the **Royal Order of H.R.M. (Heredom)** and the **knights of the R.S.Y.C.S. (Rosy Cross)**.[31] These two degrees constitute the **Royal Order of Scotland** and it is thought that they were brought to Scotland by **The Templars**, who it will be remembered *(The Battle of The Trees)* held some information that inevitably denied the Crucifixion, since they spat on the cross and referred to Jesus as "the thief on the cross". Thus since an early date, there has always been a recognition that Jesus and the background to Jerusalem and the Crucifixion, was not entirely known and a secret alternative account existed. This is the account that I have asked to be made known in the hope it will corroborate my version of events, as a witness of the time.

According to early writers on Freemasonry, the degree of the Rose-Croix originated with the Templars in Palestine as early as 1188.[32] In 1314 Robert Bruce is said to have united The Templars and The Royal Order of H.R.M., such an order being constituted at the Lodge of Kilwinning in Scotland in 1286:[33] thus the head Lodge for this Order was in Scotland, co-incidentally Heredom Kilwinning means 'The Holy House of Masonry' and it has been designated as the first Lodge of Freemasonry. It is implied from this, that the religious aspirations of Freemasonry were centred in this Lodge and that Lodge contained

The Johannite heresy and a body of evidence that had descended from The Templars, which questioned The Crucifixion. The two pronged goal of "The Universal Kingdom "as a political and religious goal, was presumably either held jointly in the Lodge, or at a later date there was a joining with another group with a political goal, which then formed the two-pronged goal behind The French and Russian Revolutions, which paved the way for "A Federal United States of The West". (*The Battle of The Trees*)."Mother Kilwinning", was also a term applied to the Lodge, which implies a Matriarchal belief, which co-incidentally is coded into the Floor of The Summer Smoking Room at Cardiff. A floor I associate with Scottish Rite Freemasonry and the Rose-Croix degree.

The union of The Templars and The Royal Order of H.R.M. was also described as a "fruitful" union between the professional guild of mediaeval masons and a secret group of "**Philosophical Adepts**" (my emphasis). The Philosophy was in all probability Hermetic, based on The Principles of Hermes and the hidden science, the adepts presumably carrying substantial Cabalistic knowledge on the Grid. **The Rose-Croix degree** was the most important degree in what was later called **Scottish Rite** (Ancient and Accepted Rite). Importantly the doctrine in the degree according to Dr. Oliver[32-34] was known much sooner, although probably not as a degree in Masonry: "for it existed as a **Cabalistic science** from the earliest times in Egypt, Greece and Rome as well as amongst the Jews and Moors in times more recent and in our own country the names of Roger Bacon and Robert Fludd, Ashmole and many others are found in its list of adepts". This is very important, since the chemist Plitchta in his research, which has previously been discussed, found in the pattern of the Sierspnski Triangle a pattern for the organisation of matter based on the prime number cross, which co-incidentally I remarked, was the Pate Cross of The Knights Templar. The fact that the Sierspinski Triangle was seen in designs from the ancient Moors, led me to speculate, that the order of atomic matter was known very early on in man's history. Further I have proposed earlier in this book, that there existed significant knowledge on the atomic nucleus and the splitting of the atom, which may have caused Atomic warfare at a very early date. Certainly from Dr. Oliver's statement we know that the hidden science that had developed in the growing subject of Cabalistic science, was known amongst the Greeks and Egyptians and the Romans.

The mention of Robert Fludd as a secret "adept" of this science is interesting and also important, since I traced Fludd *(The Battle of The Trees)* as a Grand Master of a secret group - The Prieuré de Sion, in the period 1595-1637. This group appeared to support The Merovingian Royal Dynastic line, a line that dated back to a possible union between Mary Magdalene and Jesus. In my own account, I have stated there was a child, but he was taken after Magdalene's murder in France and in all probability, was used to propagate that royal line. I concluded in my first book, that perhaps it was hoped that descendents from this line, would act as spiritual heads in Europe (Sun Kings), thus fulfilling a religious goal. A past Grand Master of The Prieuré de Sion in the 80's, acknowledged there had been a split in the group into **two factions** and there appeared to have been another significant 'Cutting of The Elm Ceremony', which signified to me after decoding that ceremony in *The Battle of The Trees,* that International financiers had taken over the political goal of a "Federal United States of The West, or European Union as more expedient, than continuing with both a religious and political goal. In short, the religious goal was turned out in the 80's, which is not to say that the group, who supported it, did not try to continue with that goal. Further a past Master of The Prieuré de Sion, had been responsible in his earlier days for the illustration in *Vaincre*[35] magazine (*Fig.48*), which showed a Hermetic Knight riding down a road, towards a "United States of The West". The illustration showed in archetypal illustrative form, not only symbolism dating back to the archetypal symbols of ancient Greece and The Matriarchal religion and mysteries surrounding what I have proposed was a Religious Revolution in Crete, where the Minoan symbols are quite clearly shown; but also the mention of "Bavaria" in the illustration on one side of the road on which the knight travels, undoubtedly cross-connects the formation of European Union with Adam Weishaupt, the founder of Illuminism who was born in Bavaria and the Power Pyramid of Communism - the ant heap or bee hive. The other side of the road, which the knight rides down, is labelled "Brittany", which relates to the Merovingians and what must be a religious goal. Quite plainly in this illustration, there are two goals in a Federal Europe, one political and one religious. The illustration was produced before World War II reducing to farcical proportions the lie, that European Union was the outcome of democratic discussion and vote. In fact I have suggested elsewhere, that World War II may have been a plan to finally manipulate Europeans to accept European Union, following a climate of devastation through war. It is probably only under such conditions that Europeans could have been duped into this plan, beaten into apathy as they were.

One can assume that The Prieuré de Sion was a group that represented The Rose-Croix degree of Freemasonry, holding both political and religious goals within a European Super State; and evidently this group must have been connected to The Royal Order of Scotland. However one thing is certain from the Hermetic knight image of the *Vaincre* illustration produced in both my prior books, Hermetic Philosophy was involved and The Principles of Hermes and vibratory Cabalistic knowledge. Interestingly as I discussed in *Alternative4*, the end of the road is marked by a blazing sun, which I have previously connected to the Gematria "666" and Solar Kingship, further the date of 1937 at the end of the road on which the Hermetic knight travels is significant, as Hitler was to initiate a Second World War, in conjunction with initiates of the secret societies

- a war that would only aid the future formation of European Union. The implication is that World War II was planned and Hitler was the mere dupe of an occult power. If the Jews had truly wanted justice for their Holocaust, then it is a mystery why they have not utilised this knowledge and Hollywood, unless the Cabalistic science stood to be revealed and the whole history of War and Revolution, which undoubtedly involves a great deal of lies and ultimately must question their own elders. The Jews were never persecuted because they were Jews; it was the persistence of their elders in the role of World Revolution and the world globalisation plan through Masonry that caused their suffering. Freemasonry which is Jewish in all its higher degrees, including the Rose-Croix was the reason.

The futures Grand Masters of The Prieuré de Sion not co-incidentally, were the famous *scientists* Robert Boyle (1654-91) and Isaac Newton (1691-1727). Newton of course was famous for his laws on gravity and Einstein was to follow some time later in the 30's with his Laws of Relativity, which linked gravity to curved space- time. I should not think for one minute, the story of the apple falling on Newton's head was true. The apple co-incidentally was the sign of immortality and was discussed in *The Battle of The Trees*. The apple falling on Newton's head, sounds to me, more like an initiation into what increasingly looks like Cabalistic Rosicrucian knowledge of Grid energies and the hidden science. The iconographic distortion in the *Genesis* account of The Bible and the fact that woman (Eve), gave Adam an apple to eat, which was a forbidden fruit in "The Garden of Eden", is merely a switching and re-positioning of the archetypal symbols by the Cult of Jehoweh, where Matriarchal knowledge and specifically knowledge of Space time and Re-incarnation was labelled as forbidden knowledge, simply because that would keep man ignorant and further allowed abuse of such knowledge by the Patriarchs. The point that was always missed by the Jews was it was **they,** and not the woman who misused such knowledge and further without that knowledge man would *never* find his way out of the trap. Billions of souls trapped for all eternity in never ending cycles under the control of the MRC case. What was meant as an *open* message and cosmology for humanity, became the hidden science that was sequestered by the MRC case utilised for their own purposes of power and wealth coming to fruition as a goal of a One World Order controlled by the MRC case. The Serpent is also positioned in the *Genesis* account with evil and yet nowhere in ancient mythological accounts is the Serpent described as anything but good and wise. The fact that the curse in Genesis is on the woman is part of the attempts to obliterate Matriarchal knowledge and specifically so that secret groups could retain the knowledge of the Cabalistic science utilising it in methods of war and control. The woman in myth and legend carried the Holy Grail openly as a gift to humanity, whilst the man held it in secret. The Masters considered the laying of such knowledge before mankind as akin to laying "pearls before swine", to quote.

The fact that Dr. Falk sacrificed a he-goat in a horrible fashion, relates to the ritual of the kid or goat being sacrificed in ancient Greece to Dionysus (the god of wine) a remnant of which is retained in Holy Communion. Dionysus and Apollo the Sun King were combined as Hercules, and significantly in Greek the words for goat, sheep and apple are identical (melon). Hercules was called Melon, because apples were offered to him in worship. Thus he would become immortal. Only male Messiahs and Sun Kings were to become immortal in an attempt to obliterate the former truth that as one died, one was united with Her, The Great Goddess, whose gift to man was Immortality, to be reborn. The *crab* apple was the true apple and the story of that and the first cut, was even wrongly portrayed at Cardiff Castle! It appears that the truth on that particular story has been lost. Further discussion of the mythic importance of the apple is recounted in *The Battle of The Trees.*

The degree of the Rose-Croix was founded circa 1741 and after the period of Grand Mastership of Robert Boyle, who was yet another famous *scientist* who was nominated as Grand Master of The Prieuré de Sion. It might be concluded that these famous scientists had added to Cabalistic science and the theories of curved space time, long before Einstein came up with the magical formula connecting gravity to curved space time. It may have been deemed expedient to form higher degrees to retain such knowledge in secrecy for the elite few, who would then have control over the science and could use that science for their own ends. The Rose-Croix degree and 33rd degree and above Masons, were however the highest initiates and this was the most secret of degrees. The ritual of "the eminent Order of The Knights of The Black Eagle or Sovereigns of the Rose-Croix", is a secret and unpublished document of the eighteenth century, which differs entirely from the published rituals, and which explains that no one can attain to knowledge of the **"higher sciences"** without the **"clavicles of Solomon"**, of which the real secrets were never committed to print and which is said to contain the whole of Cabalistic Science.[36] It is this Cabalistic science I maintain, that has been mixed by the secret groups particularly Rosicrucianism, with the Holy Grail message (Re-incarnation) and the Cosmology that was stolen from the Early Minoans and prior The Tuatha dan Danan, the early tribes of the Peloponnese in Greece.

The research that the genius Nikola Tesla was to conduct in the 1920's and which was based on sympathetic vibration, was already known in the Cabalistic science and had been stated as such in the Principles of Hermes and this is the probably the reason why the public for the main, have never heard of Tesla and the reason why his research was sequestered by the FBI after his death. The Rite of Perfection maintained this Cabalistic influence and the "Ineffable Degrees"

111

derived from the Jewish belief in the mystery that surrounds the Ineffable name of God, centred on the custom of the Jews to accord the sacred name of Jehovah as composed of four letters Yod, he, vau, he; forming the Tetragrammaton, which was only uttered once a year on The Day of Atonement, by the Priest in the Holy of Holies amidst *trumpets* and cymbals (which is a *dramatization* of Incident I, which I will come to later). The Jews believed "He who pronounces it shakes heaven and earth and inspires the very angels with astonishment and terror". This undoubtedly represented Cabalistic science and knowledge relating to vibration and such knowledge is more fully recounted in *Alternative4*, where in antiquity it was used as a source of power and wealth. Moses as a high initiate of the secret Rite of Memphis undoubtedly also used this knowledge, conferring on him when engraved on his famous rod (or *rood* the significance of which I will come to), an ability to perform wonders. This ability and same powers according to The Toldot Yeshu was conferred to Christ, indicating that he was an initiate of Cabalistic science and used it to perform alleged miracles. Certainly as I recount in *The Battle of The Trees,* Jesus was versed in the secret alphabets, which indicated his initiation into a secret society. The nature and name of that group will finally unlock the mystery of Golgotha, as I will cover.

The cabalist Dr. Falk utilised a *three-fold* circle, where he wrote the names of all the angels in one circle, the God in Hebrew in the second and in the third the first chapter of the *Gospel of St. John*. Such a three-fold circle becomes a triangle and reminiscent of the UVG 120 sphere with its triangles, which is the Earth Grid geometry. The three-pointed triangle was one, which L. Ron Hubbard who founded The Church of Scientology used and remarked it was related to the foremost signs of the Universe, although he declined to elaborate and evidently Hubbard was well versed in secret group knowledge. The tri-syllable "schem-hamm-phorasch" was another term for the Tetra-grammaton (the Holy unspeakable name of God), which forms the sacred word of the Scots degree. The importance of the archetypal number three was explained in the work of Plitchata and the fundamental geometry of matter based on the prime number sequence. The non-specific code or blueprint that also determines body shape (head thorax and abdomen) is also reflected in the 3 base sequence of the hereditary material DNA. However in the ancient Minoan religion the archetypal number three revolved around a religious mystery or more specifically a belief (as one died, one was united with Her, The Great Goddess and through Her was reborn - The Cycle of Eternal Return, which I equated with Immortality and Re-incarnation) This archetypal number three, was used again in the re-positioning era and became incorporated into the idea of 'Father, son and Holy Ghost' in Christianity, which Robert Graves the poet pointed out, was the product of Latin grammar! (For which reason he never obtained the Poet Laureateship!)

The pentagonal geometry of the UVG 120 sphere of the Earth Grid is obliquely perhaps mentioned at the head of the instructions for the "third degree of the knight of the Black Eagle", called the Rose-Croix.

Q. What is the most powerful name of God on the penataculum?
A. Adonai
Q. What is this power?
A. To move the Universe"

The **Rose-Croix degree was purely Jewish in origin,** where in the address to the candidate for initiation at the Lodge of the "Contrat Social" it stated:

"This degree, which includes the order of Perfect Masons, was brought to light by Brother R., (Christian Rosen Kreutz) " who took it from Cabbalistic treasure of the Doctor and Rabbi Neamuth, chief of the Synagogue of Leyden in Holland, who had preserved its precious Secrets And its costume, both of which we shall see in the same order in which he placed them in his mysterious Talmud".[37]

According to Fabre d'Olivet, Moses who: "was learned in all the wisdom of the Egyptians", drew from the Egyptian Mysteries a part of the oral tradition which was handed down through the leaders of the ISRAELITES.[38] That such an oral tradition, distinct from the written word embodied in the Pentateuch, did descend from Moses and that it was later committed to writing in the Talmud and the Cabala is the opinion of many Jewish writers:[39] whilst the Talmud relates to the affairs of everyday life outlining in meticulous detail laws covering how many white hairs a red cow must have (Somewhat similar to European Law!), the Cabala a Hebrew word signifying "reception" or "a doctrine orally received" contained the speculative and philosophical or the Theosophical doctrines of Israel. The Cabala almost certainly in the arrangement of the Divine Emanations under the name of the Ten Sephiroths, and in the permutation of numerals and of the letters of the Hebrew alphabet, is a coded form of initiation and ritual into the mysteries of Grid Energies.

The Cabala is contained in two books the Sepher Yetzirah and the Zohar. The former is a book of extraordinary obscurity and almost certainly of extreme antiquity. One date has placed it as early as the sixth century before Christ and another as late as the tenth century A.D. It is certainly older than the Talmud as a reference in the Talmud shows that the Rabbis are described as studying it for *magical purposes.*[40] The Sepher Yetzirah is also said to be the work referred to in the Koran under the name of the "Book of Abraham."[41] The large compilation known as the Sepher-Ha -Zohar, or Book of Light, is, however, of greater importance to the study of Cabalistic philosophy (and science?).

According to the Zohar itself God imparted the "Mysteries of Wisdom" to Adam whilst he was still in the Garden of Eden, in the form of a book delivered by the angel Razael. This is an important point, which I wish you to take note of, the fact that **Cabalistic science was imparted to Adam**. From Adam the book passed on to Seth, then to Enoch, to Noah, to Abraham, and later to Moses one of its principle exponents.[42] What we do know is that Noah survived the Flood and if that was the result of a Magnetic Reversal, Noah according to Biblical accounts had some forewarning and certainly the Ark may have been a high technology affair, rather than a simple wooden structure. We begin to see why the pre-history of man has been covered up in Archaeology and Anthropology and why it becomes impossible to mount the barrier of State Religions in order to get a mechanism for cancer evaluated (*Appendix 1*), and indeed why my Petition was quietly ignored. The hidden science has remained in the possession of the Patriarchs since antiquity and utilised by them. It is certainly curious that long before I had managed to sort out this entire tale and when I regressed and contacted a past life, recounted in *The Battle of The Trees (chapter 1)*, I had remembered that there was a reference: "Shem son of Noah" in the secret document I carried for safe keeping in that life.

The mysteries of the Zohar as part of Cabalistic science were alleged to have first been written down by the disciples of Simon ben Jochai. The Talmud relates that the Rabbi Simon and his son Eliezer concealed themselves in a cavern (which incidentally was the repeated significance of John, when he wrote Revelations in a cave on Patmos); where, sitting in the sand up to their necks, they meditated on the sacred law and were frequently visited by the *prophet Elias*.[43] This sounds remarkably like channelling information off the Grid - that great Library in the sky, using a black occult method that Crowley the black magician utilised, by seeking information from an *elemental spirit*. Further sand is mainly composed of Silicon, which acts as a transistor, which may have aiding channelling. Just how much of religious texts have been reported as the word of God, but were in fact channelled information from the Grid is a question that begs an answer. It was then in this manner that the Zohar was composed. If it was channelled straight off the Grid or Akashic Record, then it was bound to be channelled thoughts of past Masters. Theodore Reinach declares the Cabala to be: "a subtle poison which enters into the veins of Judaism and wholly infests it"; Salomon Reinach calls it: "one of the worst aberrations of the human mind.[44] What is certain is that a mystical tradition existed amongst the Jews, from remote antiquity and as M. Vulliaud stated: "it is only a matter of knowing at what moment Jewish mysticism took the name of Cabala."[45]
Edersheim46 stated that:

It is undeniable that, already at the time of Jesus Christ, there existed an assemblage of doctrines and speculations that were carefully concealed from the multitude. They were not even   revealed to ordinary scholars, for fear of leading them towards heretical ideas. This bore the   name of Kabbalah, and as the term (of Kabbalah, to receive, transmit) indicates, it represented the spiritual traditions *transmitted from the earliest ages* although mingled in the course of time with impure or foreign elements *(author's emphasis)*.

If the assertion of Gougenot des Mousseaux[47] is correct, that the Cabala is older than the Jewish race, a *legacy handed down from the first Patriarchs of the world*, then one must consider that Cabalistic science was known from the beginning and The Jewish Cabala itself supports this by tracing its descent from the Patriarchs - Adam, Noah, Enoch, and Abraham - who lived before the Jews as a separate race came into existence. The important point to note, is that there has existed a secret body of knowledge which was handed to Adam, supposedly by God, but what has been lost or omitted, is that the knowledge was substantially added to, by the raid and stolen knowledge from Crete, which did originate from a very high and Holy source, not on Earth. Eliphas Levi a member of the secret societies at the time of the French Revolution, who notoriously spoke of a "universal Kingdom" and seemed to be well versed in the coming New World Order stated that:" the Holy Cabala" was the "tradition of the children of Seth carried out of Chaldea by *Abraham*", who was "the inheritor of the secrets of Enoch and the *father of initiation in Israel*."[48] *(author's emphasis)*. What is evident then, is that there was a secret body of wisdom and knowledge that was handed down orally from the very first patriarchs and through Abraham, this became available to Israelites. There is no doubt that this knowledge contained some aspects of the hidden science, which was used by those patriarchs for their own purposes.

According to this theory, the American Freemason Dr. Mackey[49], stated there was besides the Divine Cabala of the children of Seth, the magical Cabala of the children of Cain, which descended to the Sabeists, or star-worshippers of Chaldea, adepts of astrology and necromancy. Sorcery and presumably so-called miracles attached to Earth Grid energies were practised by the Canaanites before the occupation of Palestine by the Israelites. Despite the imprecations against sorcery contained in the Law of Moses, the Jews disregarded such warnings and mixed the sacred tradition with magical ideas, borrowing from the Persian Magi, the Neo-Platonists and the Neo-Pythagoreans. Whilst there can be little doubt that there were two Cabalas one which was of great antiquity dating back to the first Patriarchs and the other although still representing basic truths had been mixed with speculations. The modern Jewish Cabala presents a dual aspect both theoretical and practical; the former concerned with theosophical speculations, the latter with magical practises. When I speak of magical practise I am of course referring to resonant energies and the use of the Grid for channelling information. According to the Cabala, every letter in the Scriptures contains a mystery only to be solved by the initiated. By this method whole passages of the Old Testament are shown to bear meanings totally unapparent to the ordinary reader (as I once commented do those who so avidly support The Bible know exactly what they are supporting?) The Zohar explains that Noah was lamed for life by the bite of a lion whilst he was in the ark[50] and I did question whether this related to the Minoan background, in that a lion or more precisely two lions were the gate of the New Year as shown in Mycaenae at the famous *gate of the lions*. The fact that he was lamed and a *similar* account occurs for Jesus is a secret code presumably to cover the fact that lameness is transposed for Twin King or Solar King. In *The Battle of The Trees,* I showed a Minoan Seal where he Twin Kings each had one heal lifted from the ground to indicate Twin-Kingship. Since The Ark, was an event that happened before the time of the Early Minoans (1400 B.C.), then it can only be assumed that the account of the Flood was written later and re-positioned alongside Solar Kingship created after the Religious Revolution in Crete 1400BC The fact that secret groups borrowed from Matriarchal religion and superimposed ideas on patriarchal religion means that it becomes a horrendous detective journey! However the Indian Epics refer to Princes before the Flood or cataclysm and thus it may be that kingship was a method of control of the populous before the Flood and such a system was superimposed onto the Matriarchal religion of the Early Minoans at the time of the Religious Revolution. The original belief system did not contain kingship only a spiritual leadership that was educative rather than controlling.

In the practical Cabala this method of "decoding" is reduced to a theurgic or magical system, in which the healing of diseases plays an important part and is effected by means of the mystical arrangement of numbers and letters, by the pronunciation of the Ineffable Name and by the use of amulets and talismans, or by compounds supposed to contain certain occult properties. Undoubtedly the sounds or pronunciation and the vibration of those sounds, perhaps with musical instruments would create sympathetic resonance, which may well have been used to initiate chakra opening and thus alter the course of a disease by opening metabolic functions or mental processes, which are associated with the various chakras. The chakras themselves open according to certain scales of vibratory resonance and the various colours shown in the aura surrounding living things are dependent on a spectrum of energies in much the way white light can be separated into a colour spectrum with a scale of resonant energies. The power to heal in antiquity would have undoubtedly conferred upon the healer god-like qualities by an appreciative patient. Thus in this manner, the Patriarchal Priests became not only wealthy, but also powerful.

If the Elohim were supposed to have been behind the Domes in Britain, then it is interesting that the Zohar explains that words of the Scripture: "Jehovah Elohim made man", means that He made Israel. Whilst you may assume that

Israel is being referred to, there is some question, whether in fact what is being implied is another' Israel' - Scotland in the U.K. I will return to this point later, but the Messianic hope which forms the dominating theme of the Cabala is made to serve purely **Jewish interests**. However this idea of a Redeemer who would save the world is common to other traditions besides the Jewish one. The tradition of a Man-God, who should present Himself as the teacher and liberator of the fallen human race, was constantly taught amongst all the enlightened nations of the Globe (after Patriarchal priests ousted a former truth). Five hundred years before Christ, the leader of the Zoroastrians predicted the coming of the Messiah, at whose birth a star would appear. He also told his disciples that the Messiah would be born of a virgin and that they would be the first to hear of Him, and they should bring him gifts. Drach believes that this tradition was taught in the ancient synagogue.[51] The Foundation of the whole system and the oral doctrine was the belief in a Redeemer. Whilst some sources claim that the path of Freemasonry is sourced from Adam, Noah, Enoch and Abraham through Moses, David, and Solomon, this is precisely the path of the Cabala and modern Freemasonry is entirely built up on the Solomonic rather than the Hiramic legend. It is believed that at the time of the Crusades the Masonic guilds became linked with Cabalistic teaching, whereas before that, the traditions of Masonry are traced from Adam, Jabal, Tubal Cain, from Nimrod and the Tower of Babel. They also had links with Hermes and Pythagoras through the exoteric doctrines of Egypt and Greece. Thus it was not apparently until after the Crusades that Judeo-Christian mysteries and the Cabala were introduced into Freemasonry.

The fact that the outer circle of The Floor of The Summer Smoking Room at Cardiff Castle illustrated the archetypal Essene hedges, which were placed around all Essene Communities to keep prying eyes out, indicates that this particular branch of Freemasonry presumably Scottish Rite and the higher degrees i.e. The Rose-Croix held a particular version of the Cabala. In my own account Jesus was the initiate of the higher degrees of a secret Brotherhood, which many have believed was the Essenes, although I will cover this point more carefully shortly. The crab mural at Cardiff Castle indicated that the secret of The Crucifixion and the cut arm of the Magdalene were at least known to the Scottish Rite Freemasons at the Rose-Croix level I concluded. Further that group in the past had some descecendancy from the Knights Templar. In fact I was fairly flabbergasted to see that mural as confirmation of my own witness account. Thus throughout the story of Jesus there is some connection to Scotland and a secret group that eventually took the name of Rose-Croix Masons and Scottish Rite Freemasonry, but with some connection in the past to the Essenes.

By the time of The Crusades, no less than three Cabalas appear to have existed; firstly, the ancient secret tradition of the Patriarchs handed down from the Egyptians through the Greeks and Romans; secondly the Jewish version of this

117

tradition, the first Cabala of the Jews, which is not compatible with Christianity, descending from Moses, David and Solomon to the Essenes and the more enlightened Jews. It is the ancient and secret tradition form of the Cabala that I believe has ascended with the truth of the Crucifixion into Scottish Rite Freemasonry and the Order of the Rosicrucian's. Certainly the fact that the Matriarchal knowledge and the Knossos archetypal images are seen, together with a final enclosing ring of petals which cross -connect with the Knossos Double Axe of the Minoans, in the Summer Smoking Room Floor at Cardiff Castle, indicates that the whole background of Twin Kingship, Solar Kingship etc. is known in this particular branch of Freemasonry, presumably with the whole secret doctrine and hidden science. The fact that these archetypal symbols from Knossos not only turn up in Scottish Rite Freemasonry and the Rose-Croix degree, but in the Vaincre magazine article attributed to a future Grand Master of the secret group the Priure de Sion, leads me to believe that this group too is Rosicrucian in nature or Scottish Rite Freemasonry. It was the group behind the *Vaincre* magazine article that showed they to be the impetus behind European Union. However I did refer to a schism in the secret groups in the 80's, when I believe that the religious aim originally intended to combine with a political aim for Europe, was thrown out. Thus I conclude that Scottish Rite Freemasonry and the Rose Croix level, together with the Prieure de Sion were Rosicrucian's who carried a religious purpose that had some connection to Jesus and the events of Golgotha. Such conclusions are also supported by the wealth of iconography I decoded in *The Battle of The Trees*, related to the Holy Grail. Did The Knights Templar contribute this knowledge of the crucifixion to Scottish Rite? Or was it already existent in The Royal Order of Scotland, when the two combined knowledge? Thus the Templars may have had their own version of events, which The Royal Order of Scotland sought to keep quiet by combining with the Templars. If the Crucifixion was planned as I proposed, then was such a plan instigated via a secret Order in Scotland?

The third Cabala was the perverted one containing magic and appears to have contained secret rituals utilising Earth Grid Energies, for the purpose of obtaining information and contacting past thought of the Masters, it may be this Cabala that has been developed through thousands of years of research into understanding how the Grid energies worked and that knowledge retained in the secret groups, particularly one suspects Rosicrucian higher Orders. This Cabala also contained anti-Christian legends. Thus it may be that whilst the second Cabala was retained for some initiates, those in the higher orders were allowed access to the developed knowledge based on the third Cabala. As I noted in *The Battle of The Trees* the design on the Summer Smoking Room floor, at Cardiff Castle contains a plan for a World Order, with a map presumably of that Order at its centre. The fact that the higher degrees of the Rose-Croix are entirely Jewish indicates that the highest secrets handed down presumably from Adam, are purely for the Jews, or those loyal to the goals of the One World Order. I was told privately that Lord Bute's heart was buried in Sion.

There are striking resemblances between Freemasonry and Essenism - degrees of initiation, oaths of secrecy, the wearing of the apron, and a certain Masonic sign. Thus the joining of the two degrees of the Royal Order of H.R.M. (Heredom) and Knights of the R.S.Y.C.S. (Rosy Cross), which constituted the Royal Order of Scotland in 1307 and with the first Lodge held on St. John the Baptist's Day (June 24); may well have presented a combined knowledge. It seems probable that The Templars brought the two degrees to Scotland after originating the degree of the Rose-Croix in Palestine as early as 1188. Robert Bruce is said to have united the Templars and the Royal Order of H.R.M. with the guilds of working masons, who had with the Templars fought in his army at Bannockburn against Edward II, who had suppressed the Templars in England. The first Lodge at **Kilwinning** was founded in 1286. It appears then at this Lodge a speculative element of a fresh kind may have found its way into the lodges. A: "fruitful union between the professional guild of mediaeval masons and a **secret group of philosophical adepts"**. This was a very strange liaison as Mr. Waite stated[52]: "The mystery of the building guilds-whatever it may be held to have been - was that of a simple, unpolished, pious, and utilitarian device; and this daughter of Nature, in the absence of all intention on her own part, underwent, or was coerced into one of the strangest marriages which has been celebrated in occult history. It so happened that her particular form and figure lent itself to such a union".

The alliance between the Templars and Scottish guilds of working masons, the Templars being peculiarly fitted by their initiation into the legend concerning the building of the Temple of Solomon to co-operate with the Masons, and the Masons being prepared by their partial initiation into ancient mysteries to receive fresh influx of Eastern tradition from the Templars. Dr. Bussell[53] notes that: "No doubt together with some knowledge of geometry regarded as an esoteric trade secret, many symbols to-day current did pass down from very primitive times". Was it more that many Earth Grid energy secrets were portrayed in architecture and to utilise this knowledge which the building Masons may have possessed, an alliance of mutual benefit i.e. the "marriage" of the Grid energy mysteries to Grid architecture, produced the Kilwinning Lodge?

It appears then at some point Cabalistic and Grid knowledge was aligned with architecture, probably with the aim of understanding the esoteric mysteries of Grid energies, which were used in the erection of large megalithic monuments such as steles and presumably in the building of the pyramids. Weishupt the founder of Illuminism, whose goal was always rule of power and the Power Pyramid held nothing but contempt for the Rose-Croix masons who were bracketed with the Jesuits as necessary to outwit at every turn. Whatever controversy rages within Europe is probably nothing more than a power play by the ascendants of these secret alliances as they split into their respective groups. The Illuminati with their obsession of self-regulation and ant heaps and beehives may have ascended into the group today who envisage a far from self-regulatory society, but one with strict control and presumably where Grid energies will be utilised as a method of creating a psycho civilised society. Robert Fludd the Rosicrucian in classifying magic termed "Natural Magic" the most occult and secret department of Physics. Dr. Falk possessed the secret of perpetually burning lamps and Eliphas Levi stated that the Rabbi Jechal a Cabalistic Jew also possessed this secret. The Rosicrucian's, who appear to have been the outcome of Cabalistic teaching, mingled with the teachings of Paracelsus, who maintained that all matter was vibrational energies, another reflection of Hermetic Principles

THE ROSICRUCIANS

The founder of the Order of Rosicrucian's was supposedly a mysterious character called Christian Rosenkreutz (C.R.), a German born in 1378. Some believe that he did not exist but the story of C.R. as with the story of the origins of all secret groups is clouded in mystery. Brother C.R. was to meet some wise men in Damascus Arabia as the story goes, where he studied Physics and Mathematics, proving that very early on there was indeed a secret science open to initiates, which required higher study. C.R. obtained more information in Fez and Spain from learned men. On returning to Germany he took two initiates and formed a *circle of three*, which indicates the mysteries of Knossos and The Cycle of Eternal Return. The three became the Fraternity of the Rosy Cross. The Rosicrucian manifesto claimed information, which was a combination of ancient secret tradition, handed down from **Adam** and the Patriarchs, through the philosophers of Greece including Plato, Aristotle and Pythagoras, together with the Cabala of the Jews. However this grand legend of Rosicrucianism did not rest on historical evidence and there was no real proof that C.R. had ever existed. This sort of set up is usually a more powerful secret group finding it expedient to 'float' another society for their own purposes. Thus it was probably the case that Rosicrucianism was set up, by a more powerful group, who remained hidden. Exactly what the goal of Rosicruciansism was and why the Masters set it up, will emerge later in this thesis.

Where did the term Rosy-Cross come from? According to one Rosicrucian tradition the word "Rose" did not derive from the flower depicted as the Rosicrucian Cross, but from the Latin word 'ROS', signifying "dew". However the rose design is a prominent architectural feature, which I noted on my trip to the Peloponnese in Greece, at The Temple of Asklepios in Epidaurus. I noted in the *Introduction to Part II of The Second Millennium Working Report into Cancer*, that the initiates of Asklepios were probably using resonant vibratory knowledge, which rested upon secret knowledge dating back thousands of years, and only known to an initiated secret Priesthood. However I would claim that such healing knowledge was also stolen and originally the healing knowledge was not attached to priesthood or the quest for power through the act of healing. Healing utilised the knowledge of the hidden science and sympathetic vibration. It seems curious that of all emblems that the Labour Party in the UK could have chosen, it was the *red rose* together with New Labour, implying a New Dawn? - "Dew"? Notably since I questioned the significance officially, there is to be a new Labour emblem, which figures the heart! (in red). The Rosicrucian's further claimed that Crux, the Cross, was the chemical hieroglyphic for "light" and light was associated in Dome theory with the Gematria "666" - The Sun and of course in resonant vibratory knowledge with the Electro-magnetic spectrum, which

121

would be absent without the sun. This has further connotations to Solar Kingship and the sequestering of knowledge from Crete, after which Solar Kingship was implemented.

The words "Rosie Cross" appeared in 1614 following co-incidentally the publication of a Cabalistic treatise by the Rabbi of Prague in 1612 entitled *The Effusion of Dew.* Unfortunately no copies of the latter exist in The British Museum and thus other explanations of the Rosy Cross as being derived from the Red Cross of the Templars provide an alternative source. Mirabeau asserted that the Rose-Croix Masons of the seventeenth century were only the ancient Order of the Templars secretly perpetuated and the story of R.C. may well be just another group of the Templars in connection with the Kilnwilling Lodge.

The Millennium icon (*Plate 3*) of a bisexual character portrayed in gold and silver (Sun King and Moon Goddess archetypal colours), produced in conjunction with the millennium celebrations in Britain and previously discussed under the Dome, was portrayed as: "holding the hand out to the stars". This is curious in so far as Lecouteulx Canteteleu[54] stated: "In France the Knights (Templar) who left the Order, henceforth hidden, and so to speak unknown, formed the Order of the Flaming Star and of the Rose-Croix, which in the fifteenth century spread itself in Bohemia and Silesia. Every Grand officer of these orders had all his life to wear the Red Cross. Was there some hidden symbolism in both the Millennium Dome and icon, which symbolised the goals of the Rose-Croix Freemasons, for the British Millennium? A goal that I associate with a religious and political "Universal Kingdom"; which was the original goal for European Union, before a schism occurred in the secret groups in the 80's: A goal that was documented at least at the time of the French Revolution and muted as a "United States of the West". Eckert stated that the rituals and symbols and names of the Rose-Croix were borrowed from the Templars and that the Order was divided into **seven** degrees, according to the seven days of Creation, at the same time signifying that their "principle aim was that of the mysterious, the investigation of Being and of the **forces of nature**" (*author's emphasis*). 55 This undoubtedly reminds one of the Seven Principles of Hermes and Hermetic magic, which I have identified as Cabalistic research on Grid energies. If I am correct over the hidden symbolism of the Dome in London, then we can assume, that there is a Rose-Croix degree in Britain, which either has power over Governments or is the driving philosophy behind them! What is more, this probably supplies the reason why my Petition remains unanswered. The fact that people die of Cancer is presumably of no importance to them, they have no concern for individuals, only their eternal sacrifice to their greater cause!

Kenneth Mackenzie in his Masonic Cyclopaedia claimed the Rosicrucian's had a Templar origin and had existed from very ancient times, with a legend preserved by the Royal Order of Scotland. He further claimed that the Rosy Cross had been instituted by that Order in conjunction with the Templars in 1314.This is interesting in so far as there was obviously significant knowledge of the Grid in the Order and given that on the floor of The Summer Smoking Room at Cardiff Castle was a map at the centre of the enclosing concentric circles, which in one sense depicted the closing in of knowledge and in another sense the Cosmic Circle and further still levels of initiation into the religious mysteries and perhaps Grid energies it also implied the stages of history passed in order to reach a goal of a New World Order. The Royal Order of Scotland in combination with the building crafts joining to perhaps understand the Grid mysteries and yet in the higher echelons, (symbolised in the innermost enclosing circle of the Smoking Room floor with petals) which Lord Bute belonged to, presumably the Rose-Croix degree, we have a map indicating a "Universal Kingdom", which covers "Europe, Greenland, Africa and Asia as well as Jerusalem and Australia". The map on the floor was laid prior to the discovery of Australia by explorers in the late eighteenth century, a point that is inexplicable unless we realise that land masses were in all probability predicted from the geometric pattern of the Grid even in ancient times, illustrated previously with the Piri Reis map." The Universal Kingdom", I believed referred to both a political and religious aim. Thus the Rosicrucian's and Scottish Rite Freemasonry appear to have a two-pronged goal in any Federal Super state.

The Templars did not have scientific pretensions, but I did conclude that they held a religious secret of an anti-Christian kind; presumably I concluded the true events of Golgotha. The Rosicrucian's however were a pre-eminently learned society and outwardly Christian, although in the higher degrees did not appear to be so. Mr. Waite throws more light on The Rosicrucian's from the manifesto and *The Fama, the Confession Fraternitalis of the Order of Rosicrucianism*[56]: "We are accustomed to regard the adepts of the Rosy Cross as beings of sublime elevation and preternatural physical powers, **masters of nature** and **masters of the intellectual world** (*author's emphasis*). There is every reason to believe then, that if there were a group who had developed the hidden science and had considerable knowledge of the Grid energies the Rosicrucian's would be a prime candidate. Cabalistic knowledge undoubtedly was involved, since the Order claimed certain knowledge had passed through a few hands since Adam, who was the first Rosicrucian of the Old Testament. Waite also claimed that Christ established a new "college of magic" among his disciples and the greater mysteries were revealed to St. John and St. Paul. I would slightly disagree with this in the light of my own account, in so far as John was with Magdalene just before her death, he may have taken what few remaining truths she had, together with the Jesus child and returned to a secret Order (in Scotland?).

123

Thus there exists it would seem in Rosicrucian knowledge, some evidence that Jesus was a magical initiate of the Cabala. Jesus was outwardly utilising this knowledge for healing and this would be the correct use. The Templars perhaps knew his subsequent deflection or duplicity, since they openly spat on the cross and referred to Jesus as a "thief". It is also curious that St. Paul chose to describe Jesus after The Crucifixion in terms of what can only be described as a physical manifestation, matter as being interchangeable with energy. Jesus apparently was seen to walk through walls and his body existed in a semi-permanent or transparent state, which uncannily parallels the witness accounts of crew on the SS Eldridge, the US Navy boat that was allegedly made to disappear and then re-appear using vibratory resonant knowledge in the so called Philadelphia experiment. One cannot be sure of the account of St. Paul since my recollections of the event are somewhat different. The laws of physics tell you, that you can't just dematerialise matter, without creating an atomic explosion. A pint size mug of material wiped out 100 000 people at Nagasaki and the same number at Hiroshima thus if a body dematerialised one might expect an atomic explosion that would have wiped out the entire Middle East! Since no Atomic explosion was recorded after the events of Golgotha, one might suppose that St. Paul as an initiate was not being exactly liberal with the truth here. Indeed according to my own witness account, the character of Jesus was more in line with the accounts given in *The Nag Haamidi Scrolls*, which I covered in *The Battle of The Trees*. I am afraid the event of Golgotha was **planned**. No matter the story, you can't evade the Laws of Physics; naive man could have been duped then, but with the advancement and understanding of science, despite the barriers to that understanding, the gullible have moved on. The problem with Christianity is that at no time does it touch down with reality. The Crucifixion and the events of Golgotha as given in The Bible could *not* have happened. Indeed The Archbishop of Canterbury has recently stated in the UK with regard to the resurrection: "we cannot be sure". Full marks to the Archbishop for touching down with reality and his conscience. The Templars and in fact all secret groups up to the present day as John Yarker[57] points out, regard Jesus as an "initiate". Certainly in *The Battle of The Trees*, I gave evidence based on historical quotation, to show that Jesus was versed in the secret alphabets particularly the Tree alphabet and further pointed to the *Gospels of The Nag Haamidi scrolls (Dead Sea Scrolls)*, which show a completely different personality for Jesus, than the accounts of The Gospels in the *The Bible*. Despite their comparable antiquity to Biblical Gospels, not only have they been ignored but also they were suppressed for a long time and still have not been fully released. Certainly my own memory of Jesus (past life) supports the accounts of his personality as given in The Nag Haamidi scrolls. I could say more but will refrain.

The goal of world domination which was alluded to by Eliphas Levi in 1879 when he referred to a "Universal Kingdom", as being had by those with "the keys to the East" was followed by the setting up of Socialist organisations and in 1880 Leopold Engel re-organised Weishaupt's Order of Illuminati, which according to M. Guenon played thenceforth "an extremely suspect political role". Bearing in mind that one explanation of the word Rosi (Rosy Cross), was "dew" is it not curious that in 1884 the Reverend A.I. Woodford allegedly came across an old manuscript in a bookshop in Farringdon Street London, which advised the finder to make contact with Sapiens Dominabatur C/o Fraulein Anna Sprengel in Germany. This tale is the often-told story of how the secret group **The Golden Dawn**, was set up. "Dew" finds a connection to dawn. It has to be asked importantly whether The Golden Dawn was not an offshoot of Rosicrucianism, set up for a pre-determined purpose and shortly I will follow that purpose as I see it, but to continue presently with the story of The Golden Dawn, the Reverend just happened to take the manuscript to two members of the Societas Rosicruciana in Anglia (S.R.I.A.), a Dr. Wynn Westcott and Dr. Woodman and by another fortunate co-incidence, one of them was the person to whom Eliphas Levi's property had been sent after his death. These men with a *third,* Mac Gregor Mathers, then founded The Golden Dawn secret society. Whilst there was a vague connection in "dew" and "Dawn", the fact that "golden" is used as part of the name indicates significance. If as I proposed, Lord Bute who had The Summer Smoking Room Floor laid at Cardiff Castle, was a Rose-Croix Mason of Scottish Rite Freemasonry, with substantial knowledge of the Greek background to The Holy Grail, then "golden" may well bear the significance of Sun King. The New Dawn was just another branch of Rosicrucianism, set up by The Rose-Croix Order of Scotland. The hidden and Secret Chiefs behind the Golden Dawn, referred to as "The Third Order", were never revealed, but the use of the archetypal three surely at least signifies the Rosicrucian's and Cabalistic knowledge. Dr. R. Felkin M.D., an active member of The Golden Dawn, stated that he had been unable to find out any more about the hidden Chiefs, other than the original document that the Reverend found. Included were notes of ceremonies made by a man who had been initiated into a Lodge in Germany and stated that the temple from which the notes had originated was "a special temple", *working on the Cabala tree*. This almost certainly identifies the Grid and the earth chakras, which formed the Seforitic Tree. Thus one assumes that the purpose of The Golden Dawn was to draw in persons, who would be useful in developing research on an occult level into Grid energies. Such a personage did appear in the form of Aleister Crowley.

"Most people who enter secret societies are adventurers, who want somehow to make their way in life, and who are not seriously minded. With such people it will be easy for us to pursue our object, and we will make them set our machinery in motion".
(*Protocols of Zion p.52*)

125

"The Masonic lodge throughout the world unconsciously acts as a mask for our purpose".

(Protocols of Zion p.16)

Aleister Crowley the occult Cabalist magician who famously coined the name "the beast" or "666", may have utilised this name to signify the Gematria of the Sun energy "666", which is connected to the Cabala and Dome theory. Crowley joined the Golden Dawn in 1898, after which he started on his magical rites using powerful psychic mediums - Madame Horus, aiding contact with the Earth Grid, that library of **information** in the sky, or what Rudolf Steiner the founder of Anthroposophy called - The Akashic Record. Crowley was himself in no doubt that there was a secret powerful Order in the background, which many people have referred to throughout history. Many believed that the hierarchical and hidden Chiefs were the Illuminati, who despised the Cabalistic Rosicrucian's, and sought to destroy other groups, presumably in order to retain power for themselves. It should be remembered however, that Weishaupt the founder of the Illuminati was not interested in healing; he was interested in self-organizing states (ant-heaps and beehives and total control), which is really just a method of anarchy. I suspect personally, that the Higher Order was in fact a Rosicrucian Order, since the ultimate trail of this group (The Golden Dawn) leads to the personages of Jack Parson's a rocket scientist and Ron Hubbard (the founder of The Church of Scientology). Crowley even came to view Madame Horus as an emissary of this very powerful Order.

Crowley was a shady character and it is impossible to know the full extent of his activities, although he did go to The United States in 1914 and was in close relations with pro-German propagandists editing The New York International and German propagandist papers. In *Alternative 4* I questioned whether it was Aleister Crowley who influenced Henry Ford to accept the notorious *Protocols of Zion* purportedly emanating from the secret societies, which were allegedly written by *The Learned Elders of Zion,* outlining a plan for Jewish World Domination. Henry Ford was to go on to have an enormous influence over Hitler, mainly in his anti-Semitic policies and Ford always claimed that his anti-Semitic policy had come from two **Jews** who had convinced him of the authenticity of *The Protocols.* Whatever the case, it seems that the cauldron was already being stirred for a Second World War and the formation of The State of Israel. Why the Jews kept so quiet about this episode of history is any-ones guess, but evidently there is a lot here on the basis of Hitler's anti-Semitic policy that the Jews themselves do not want known. I would not like to suggest that The Holocaust was the result of the desire to fulfil The Messianic prophecy of the Cabala, with a State of Israel as a necessary part of that, but it may be somewhere near the truth, otherwise the fact that Israel has stayed very quiet about this murky background to Hitler, becomes inexplicable. The fact that the lies of history have been allowed to remain despite Nuremberg, to me is a great crime against the younger generations of Germany and Israel. Alisteir Crowley certainly worked with the secret Revolutionary Committee, which was a body working for the establishment of an Irish Republic. Aleister Crowley was a very able magician and I suspect that The Golden Dawn group was set up to attract people like Crowley who would channel information from the Grid or morphogenetic bioplasma on the past. Such past would include the history of man and more importantly technology and past events.

Pope John XXIII attended a secret ceremony in an Illuminatus Temple in New York in the 70's, where a woman tapped an **egg** with a **wand**, thus I concluded from my own deciphering of those symbols in *The Battle of The Trees,* displayed symbols relating to Solar Kingship. The egg and penetrating member of phallus (or wand) was displayed in seals from Knossos post the Religious Revolution c. 1 400 BC. This is somewhat significant, since I did propose that the group, who could have conducted the Religious Revolution in Crete, was the Druids and the wand or rood, was a symbol that they used. Thus a connection appears hear between Knossos, Druids, Illuminati, and Rosicrucian's, could they all be part and parcel of one group directed by a higher Order The Rose-Croix? He also displayed the Illuminatus sun sign on his Papal glove and the symbolisation of the Gematria "666", and further archetypal symbols relating to The Holy Grail in Ireland.[58] The Pope had been initiated into the secret group of Illuminati, and that Illuminatus group had a "special Temple", which The Pope attended in New York. Can we connect Crowley much earlier to the forerunner of that secret group in New York? If one could, it would identify Crowley as being connected to the Illuminati, the Rosicrucians and The Golden Dawn: Certainly this Pope visited Ireland. One might conceivably conclude that the Rosicrucian's (religious aim) in tandem with the political group the Illuminati (political aim) intended to set up a "Universal Kingdom". Indeed since the mysterious "Third" order behind The Golden Dawn was never identified, with only a loose trail connected to the mysterious Anna Sprengel in Germany; then it is not inconceivable that the "Third Order", was actually placed in New York and not Germany and was Illuminatus. Equally the Third Order could have been the Rosicrucian's and Scottish Rite Freemasonry. The third alternative and one I suspect is nearer the truth may have been a Third Order who controlled both Illuminati and Rosicrucian's i.e. both political and religious aims for a World Order. Since Crowley was British but evidently involved himself in political matters in America it is questionable whether Crowley was in contact with this Third Order or whether he was under the direction of the Rosicrucian's .You may think I am 'nit-picking' here, but this connection is very important, since this may form the background to Anthroposophy and Rudolf Steiner and L Ron Hubbard who founded The Church of Scientology. If the "Third Order", which set up The Golden Dawn was none other than the Illuminati in New York, whom it might be assumed held the old Weishaupt goal of one controlling signal for self-organisation in man, which had been developed over the years to incorporate new Grid research, that goal could have been viewed as being possible via advanced so-called defence technology, which today has appeared as The Strategic Defence Initiative (SDI), or Star Wars, incorporating HAARP (High Active Auroral Research Programme) and GWEN (Ground Wave Emergency Network) systems which scientists have warned have a mind control capability. However, if the group behind the Golden Dawn were a higher Order of the Rosicrucian's, then the ultimate goal would have been a "Universal Religion". Is this really the background to The Church of Scientology? Rosicrucianism? I will return to the case of Scientology later.

THE ONE DOLLAR NOTE OF AMERICA

The One Dollar bill from The United States of America on the reverse side shows various symbols, which I have decoded and represent quite clearly it would seem, both a religious and political goal. On the left side of the note is shown the Illuminatus Power Pyramid and at the bottom of the pyramid are the numerals MDLCLXXVI or 1776, the year of the Revolution and The Declaration of American Independence, drawn up by Thomas Jefferson. That year was also the year that the infamous Adam Weishaupt founded the secret group of the Illuminati, which in its conception, provided the Communistic political structure, or power pyramid, which would become the political model for the New World Order and is indeed the model for Europe as power is centralised. Indeed on the One dollar note is the inscription "Annuit Coeptis, Novus Ordo Sectorum" -New Order of the Ages. The motto was borrowed by the colonists from the works of the Roman Philosopher Virgil and on an occult level, from the Freemasons and Roman Catholics. Further, the Latin motto "Epuribus unum", which also appears, is translated as "One out of many" and identifies not only the structure of Freemasonry, but also identifies once again the Power Pyramid.

On the right of the one dollar note are displayed the archetypal symbols which relate to knowledge and symbols connected to the story of The Holy Grail, with their corresponding significances. Notably the *eagle* appears, which is a sign of sovereignty and it was the eagle in myth that carried off the nymph Thalia from Crete (and the Hidden Science). There are *nine* tail feathers for the eagle, which portrays the original length of time in years that a Sun-King or Twin King reigned. The eagle carries what looks like an *olive* branch in its right claw and the branch significantly has *thirteen* leaves. Thirteen is a number that has great archetypal significance that I fully discussed in The Battle of The Trees signifying at least one secret group the Prieuré de Sion who I have concluded was probably Rosicrucian or Scottish Rite Freemasonry. Thus the symbolisation on the right side of the note probably depicts Rosicrucianism or Scottish Rite Freemasonry; particularly since there is a *rose*tte above the eagle's head, also carrying thirteen *stars*. The rosette also has the *sun symbol rays*, once again indicating Solar Kingship and the whole sorry tale dating back to Greece. The olive branch has connotations of Noah and thus from previous connections made in this book, connects with "the secret doctrine" that was handed down from the Patriarchs to Noah from Adam. Thus we might conclude that the religious aim is a Jewish one, even though the Jews have constantly denied a plan for world domination and the Protocols of Zion as their own authorship. However as I suggested in The Battle of The Trees this religion and belief system is based on the combination of the secret doctrine handed down from the patriarchs, together with significant knowledge taken from the Early Minoans or earlier from the Tuatha Dan Danaan the matriarchal tribes of the Peloponnese in Greece. The eagle significantly holds in its left claw *twelve arrows*. This would certainly indicate the Twelve Tribes of Israel. If thirteen represents a secret group, presumably the Rosicrucian's, or some Hierarchal Order such as Scottish Rite or the Rose-Croix, then it appears from the symbology here, that the religious goal is held by both groups, who are *both* Jewish! It has always been recognised, that the Hierarchal degrees of Freemasonry, which in the main are closed to all but the Elite, are Jewish, but here we appear to have two distinct groups who are both Jewish. I will return to this significant point later. Further both the left hand side of the note, with political goal as the Great Seal of America, and the right side as religious goal, are heavily ornate in scrollwork, which is portrayed in Cretan iconography to represent The Cycle of Eternal Return - which I equate with Re-incarnation. If we are going to look for a One World Order Religion, should we be looking for a group, who believe in Re-incarnation? Well certainly Scientology holds that belief and is probably the only Church in the West that does so, which is significant in itself. If the olive branch is being held as a peace offering to the woman in the story, who has been conveniently dispatched, then I am afraid it won't after thousands of years of deceit, treachery, battle and USARY do, I'm afraid.

SPIRITUAL SEERSHIP MANIPULATION OF THE GRID

Rudolf Steiner in the 19th Century belonged to the Theosophical Society and it has been suggested that at some period he may have been connected with the revived Illuminati of Leopold Engel. A few years before the First World War Steiner started his own Anthroposophical Society a name borrowed from the work of the XVIIth Century Rosicrucian Thomas Vaughan -"Anthroposophica Magica". The leader of Rosicrucianism in Germany was Dr. Franz Hartmann, founder of the "order of the Esoteric Rose-Croix". He was connected in some way with the Illuminati and *also* with the Theosophical society. One cannot discount amongst this, that the Illuminati group in New York, was the powerful "hand that moves" and that The Golden Dawn, The Anthroposophical Society and Rosicrucian's were part and parcel of the same group and its ramifications in world politics and religion. Certainly this Order may as depicted on The One Dollar Bill, have possessed not only a dual goal for a "Universal Kingdom", obliquely referred to by Eliphas Levi, but like Levi they may have been Rosicrucian's. Rudolf Steiner reserved *Rosicrucianism* for his higher initiates, although he never referred to it as such, instead calling it **"occult science"**. Science or the hidden science however is increasingly a word we are coming to associate with Rosicrucianism. Unfortunately, Steiner's higher grades of initiation were never made public, however in my association with them, which was before I had ever conceived of embarking on this life's journey (at least consciously!), I remember being highly irritated with their loose terminology: "Etheric" and *"Two* Jesus figures" and "Akashic Record". The Scientist or was it the truth in me? Baulked at the whole gibberish. Deep within me, I recognised that there was something here, or I would not have become associated, but the terms did not satisfy the clarity or indeed the truth that I sought. The terms however did portray not only knowledge of the Earth Grid, but also of Twin Solar Kingship ("two Jesus figures") and the role of John The Evangelist, although there was severe confusion in this group, which represented the double-speak and tiered hierarchy of initiates of the founder, Rudolf Steiner. No doubt higher initiates knew very well about "two Jesus figures". The idea of "guardian angels", was I am afraid far too much of an imposition on my Scientifically trained mind, however subsequently I realise this is just Cabalistic knowledge and the whole of Cabalistic science. Indeed Steiner once edited a magazine entitled *"The Lucifer"*, according to Nester Webster. The idea of "Guardian Angels" I feel is somewhat of a precedent to the idea of that one controlling signal, and the idea that someone else is looking after you, other than the stark cold reality, that only *you* are responsible for what happens to you and only *you* should and must be in control of your own mind and soul. Neither can it be dismissed that there is not something more sinister in New Age groups, that recommend that you trust a "Guardian Angel", for guidance on decisions in your life. I perceive that this New Age cult of the "Guardians" is none other than the One World Order propaganda conditioning, to accept controlling signals from Big Brother. Further is it not curious that in the region of Forest Row, I was to experience the attempt to impose a thought that was not my own into my mind? This was after my experiences in both Scientology and Anthroposophy, after which, I left rapidly for Greece. There is no implication here other than that event did happen and I have no idea of the source, other than the event occurred in Forest Row U.K. and curiously accounts that I came across many years later of people who felt they had been psychically attacked followed the exact course of events I experienced. I think there is always that quiet karmic crossroads in everyone's life, where they could have gone one of two ways and if I had not gone to Greece, this research would never have been written. One of the loneliest moments I experienced in my long journey, was standing on Heraklion docks in Crete at two in the morning, with my passport, car and suitcase, with nowhere to live and with one goal to solve the Platonic Maxim: 'Before you can cure a man's body, you must cure his mind and before that his soul'. When your karmic call comes, take it with both hands and with courage.

An initiate of the Stella Matutina another secret society, maintained that the dynamic Life Force which is present at the base of the spine, known as **"kundalini"** and which is symbolically portrayed as the coiled serpents, in reality is a force associated with the electro-magnetic energy. It rises from the first or basal chakra at the base of the spine, typically associated with the sexual driving force and the **ego** and is a force awakened by all secret groups (until you meet secret groups you have never really met the ego!) It is often wrongly assumed that all initiates are arrogant, whilst undoubtedly many are; there are those who simply appear different from the average man, by way of their knowledge, which many mistake for arrogance. The *manner*, in which knowledge is used, depends on the soul of the individual. The initiate went on to say, that the aim of the Stella Matutina like that of all subversive esoteric orders, is by means of such processes as eurhythmics, meditation, symbols, ceremonies and formulas to **awaken this force and produce false illumination.** The degree of ego in these groups held by individuals is phenomenal, many of whom are so poorly read in any other philosophies that they become slaves to their guru, whether he be Steiner or Hubbard - the Male Messiah syndrome. It is traditionally accepted in Eastern teachings, that the awakening of the Kundalini force is the initiatory procedure, which allows sequential opening of the other chakras thus allowing supposedly on the opening of the crown chakra, a sense of total illumination. One might reasonably ask what that initiation is geared to; does initiation lead to an awareness of the Grid? Certainly if Rudolf Steiner represented the Akashic Record as the super library in the sky and a bountiful source of wisdom and knowledge, then it might be easy to convince people that tuning into the Grid or Guardian Angels and a higher source of wisdom and knowledge other than you yourself, is a good thing. The assumption here is that the Grid or Akashic Record contained **higher spiritual** knowledge and wisdom, which I have categorically stated it does not. What it does contain, is a record of the *past* and any *attention placed* on the Grid, will merely enforce *all that has gone before.*

One saving grace in Rudolf Steiner's Anthroposophy was the acceptance of past lives, thus one cannot say that the knowledge and the experience does not have some remnant of a former truth. Neither can one say that the educational system that Steiner evolved, does not provide a better system for the provoking of imagination in the young, although ultimately my children's experience was a Grid mentality that caused a tremendous trauma. The initiate of the Stella Matutina stated:[59]

"I have been convinced that we, as an order have **come under the power** of some very evil occult Order, **profoundly versed in science**, both occult and otherwise, though not infallible, their methods being **black magic**, that is to say **electro-magnetic power**, hypnotism and powerful suggestion.

We are convinced that the Order is being controlled by some **Sun order** after the nature of the **Illuminati**, if not by that order itself.... We are told that all that has taken place in Russia and elsewhere is due to these International Occult Forces set in motion by Subversive Esoteric Lodges.... England as well as Europe seems to be drifting along in a hypnotic sleep, and even our soundest politicians seem paralysed and all they attempt is turned to foolishness. Is there no authority who understands these things and realizes the danger both to country and to individuals from these forces working for disruption and world revolution?" (My emphasis)

Given that this statement occurred just after the Russian Revolution in the early 19th Century, it is remarkably prophetic and somewhat accurate. It identifies secret electro-magnetic research (into the Grid), it also identifies Cabalistic science and further identifies Solar Kingship and presumably from my own research the entire background to that, dating back to Greece. This leads us back to two possible contenders for the ultimate secret group, The Illinunatus Lodge that I thought was in New York, or the Order of Scottish Rite Freemasonry, in Britain. The third alternative is that there is a Third Order, who controls both groups and seeks to combine religious and political goals. The one-dollar note is confirmation of that alternative.

I have long since felt, that the New Age movement has been hijacked by the

World Order and is being infiltrated, with agents who are dispersing their own active propaganda and manipulating views through the media and magazines. You will remember that from the beginning of this book, I emphasised that no group of any threat to the One World Order, would remain without control from that Order. I note so-called healers are recommending attention to be placed on the Grid. Listening for those "voices in your head" (*Alternative 4)* or much more psychologically subtle mechanisms, such as those noted by the Stella Matutina initiate, where arrogance and the awakening of Kundalini and ego is encouraged, the rights of man carried to its ultimate conclusion, where every man has the right to **be** God or a holy Messiah, it is a recipe for anarchy in any group. Exercises and training and the form of language and knowledge within a group, instil the idea of superman qualities, unchallengeable by authority or process of law or ethics requiring no consideration other than the survival of the group or hive. Such training, which has become the current scene not only in secret groups, but also in Medicine and Politics, merely produces false "Illumination" and promotes "spiritual seership". In other words, the Initiate becomes tuned into the Grid! And with it, the morphogenetic memory of **survival** of the *individual, group,* species and ultimately translates into **Darwinian theory**, which covers the survival of species as **the fittest survive**! This invariably leads to cold hard thinking, where the Initiate can look quite discompassionately upon what he has caused and dismiss it, with the justification that he did it to help his hive survive, but is that hive a pre-determined goal of the One World Order? There goes my Petition and there unfortunately goes my experience of secret groups. I believe the problem with secret groups is the development of mental processes, which disregard the heart. Emotion is frowned upon and robotic un-emotion is rewarded. Robotic action and the removal of emotion and the heart and compassion however merely favour a condition in the individual where he would pick up Grid animal-pack mentality. After all the Grid or morphogenetic bioplasma is a **blueprint for survival** of the group or species and the individual. Thus the other individual is dispensable if he is perceived as a threat to the survival of group individuals or the group itself. Scientology has an actual policy of setting out to destroy the individual who threatens even in the mildest form (a difference in opinion or free speech) the group (Scientology). I have always considered this very Grid! And have fought constantly for free speech and the freedom of belief.

When *The Bible* recommended, "Blessed are the meek" (those without ego), it was a wonderful piece of advice, which kept you off Grid lines! Staying off Grid lines is to use your *own* mind, to have your *own* opinions and to use your *own* conscience, remaining compassionate and nurturing a love of living things and beauty in the environment, whilst actively helping others to live and keeping a higher spiritual source other than yourself within your humble sight. Importantly never sacrifice any individual to any cause, self or other (usury). The emphasis that some groups place on group and survival claiming exclusive and encompassing knowledge which requires total commitment and absorbance, whilst drawing attention to the Grid memory, coupled in some cases with battle-like mentality of siege, merely connects the individual to animal-pack survival mentality where the individual becomes dispensable in the cause of survival of the group. I perceive in my own experience of Anthroposophy and Scientology Communistic thinking! The all encompassing State which with its diktat decides individualism is not survival and yet the history of mankind shows that it is individuals who have used their own minds, who have contributed more to the survival of humanity than any one group. I believe it was Ghandi who said: "Even if you are in a minority of one, the truth is still the truth". Woe betide the individual who travels the path of truth for he will find he may barely survive morphogenetic Grid actions of groups and can anyone be sure of the goal of those groups. But there lies a conundrum, for secret groups do have vital information.

One must ask, what is the real motive power behind such societies as the Stella Matutina and again behind Rudolf Steiner in the past? In the case of Steiner, the quest of the Hidden Chiefs, undertaken by one intrepid pilgrim after another, seems to have ended only in further meetings with Steiner. Astral messages spurred the pilgrims after occult knowledge onward and one of these exhorted: "Go on with Steiner, which is not the ultimate end of search, and we will come into contact with many serious students who will lead us to the real master of the Order, who will be so overpoweringly impressive as to leave no room for doubt". One in some cases is constantly reminded of the story of Mary Shelley's Prometheus and Frankenstein, where the fatherless and motherless child continually seeks its parent. Further there is often a link between secret groups, in terms of phraseology e.g. between Co-Masonry and the Stella Matutina, the idea of the "Astral light", "The Great White Lodge" and "The Great Work", by which both Orders denote the supreme object of their aspirations - "the union of the East and the West". The curious thing is, that these groups or Orders believe themselves to be entirely un-connected. My experience of Anthroposophy, saw them in abject hysterics over Scientology - would it be surprising, to find that the Rosicrucian's, had played a part in the founding of *both* groups, for different purposes on the track of time? Or are we to assume that despite the curious parallels of thought, and the curious fact that the Headquarters of Scientology are based at East Grinstead in the U.K., a few miles from Forest Row, the main location of Anthroposophy and Rudolf Steiner's group, that there is nothing beyond co-incidence and the groups are to all intent and purposes separate?

Hitler of course directed by a higher occult group, utilised his rallies to awaken the kundalini force of a whole Nation. The best way to awaken that force and connect a person to the Grid and its survival morphogenetic data and control, is to awaken a **battle mentality** and thus the desire to kill or destroy anyone who threatens the **perceived** survival of the individual, group or Nation. Clever fellows are the Puppet Masters on Theatre Earth, for they have even stopped people asking questions, which might not only require answers, but might disconnect people momentarily from the Grid, to **stop and think of what they are doing and why?** A point that the physicist Fennyman made when questioned over the ultimate use of the Los Alamos research, which resulted in Hiroshima and Nagasaki (*Appendix Alternative 4*). Returning for one moment to Steiner's occult science, let us consider one of his own passages:

> "This is the change which the occult student observes coming over himself - that there is no longer a connection between a thought and a feeling or a feeling and a volition, except when he creates the connection himself. No impulse drives him from thought to action if he does not voluntarily harbour it. He can now stand completely without feeling before an object which, before his training would have filled him with glowing love or violent hatred. He can likewise remain action less before a thought which heretofore would have spurred him to action by itself, etc."[60]

Having some knowledge of secret occult knowledge, I can see where Steiner is going with this. If The Grid is a pattern of behaviour and a mechanism of control, it would be considered an advantage if one recognised this and resisted behaviour that is automatically dictated by the **Grid or the irrational mind**. As previously discussed there is within *both* an animal pack mentality based on survival. The irrational mind may even be just memories of times when Grid behaviour occurred. You have all experienced it, where some minion at work or in a position over you makes your life a misery, because they have some small fraction of miniscule power (ego) and you pose some perceived threat to them and their survival, or they dislike your ability which is another perceived threat to their survival and make it their life's work, to reduce *your* survival. Even the psychotic who kills believes his survival is increased by such action. On a spiritual level it would be morally right to resist reacting irrationally to that behaviour, however such resistance can only come if one recognised that this behaviour was part of the Grid mechanism or the person's irrational mind. Without such knowledge could one resist it? One might be able to resist, if one held **any** spiritual knowledge that indicated such behaviour was highly abberative and therefore refrain from placing your hands around their mindless throats! Thus one might perceive that such information and exercises, DO HELP and I can assure you having undergone these exercises, it has saved many a throat! However as I have already pointed out, there is an element in all secret society doctrine and illumination that elevates man to an ego-conscious state by the awakening of Kundlini, coupled with a closing of the heart.

136

The initiate of the Stella Matutina claimed that a secret and powerful "Sun Order", possibly the Illuminati had taken over their group in the 20's, but these initiates have not considered the possibility that initiatory groups are often set up, with a *pre-determined outcome*. Just as the apical point of Anthroposophy was questionable together with its goals in the same era, the leading edge has moved on and one must look to the more current scene. It is certainly interesting that in the 80's a group broke away from The Church of Scientology unable to come to terms, with the high powered marketing of the Church of Scientology, the cost of services and an increasing alienation from the Church Hierarchy. Certainly by the time Ron Hubbard the founder of The Church of Scientology was dying from Cancer in the 80's he had lost control of the Church, to those who exist in senior management today. In Hubbard's time ethics in a last resort could always be applied by Hubbard and there was a feeling in those who left the Church, that ethics were not being applied and further, many good Scientologists who were actually positively helping the cause of humanity, were rapidly being declared "suppressives " (enemies of the Church) and being thrown out of the Church. A "suppressive", is a perceived enemy of the Church of Scientology, who in horrendous policy that I have seen becomes "fair game" and are harassed, prosecuted, investigated and subjected to all manner of pressures from the Church. The lingering question in the case of Scientology, which is fast becoming an extremely powerful Organisation, is whether Hubbard acted independently of secret groups, in conjunction with them, or was set up for a pre-determined outcome from the start and played like a puppet, with money and power as bait.

On the 1 st April in 1984, the protest group who left The Church of Scientology staged a demonstration and termed themselves "Independent Scientologists". They resigned from the Church on the point of principle at some of its practices. They believed that "there is a great deal of wisdom in the works of L. Ron Hubbard and that it should be made freely available to everyone to use, or not use, as they see fit to assist themselves, their family and their friends to greater happiness". The protest centred of "the Church of Scientology's actions of barring this wisdom from the ordinary man by charging very high prices and attempting to maintain a monopoly on the use of this wisdom for reasons of their own". Whilst there is no doubt in my own mind, that there is extremely valuable data in the Church my own (horrendous) experience was based on these grievances and Grid mentality. However that experience was underlined by my attempts to discuss this experience with David Miscavige – the current public Head of the Church. What a surprise (or not) when nobody recognised the difference between right (survival of the individual) and wrong (survival of the group) at *any* cost. My questions (in 1992) curiously followed those of the protest group in their demands, which are worth quoting here:

"We demand the following reforms:

1. Since L Ron Hubbard resigned as Executive Director of the Church of Scientology in 1966, we demand that the Church of Scientology makes known exactly **who** is in charge of the Church.

2. That the Church of Scientology allows open communication to and from that person without censorship or perversions of the truth.

3. That the Church refuses to: issue works bearing the name L Ron Hubbard which were not written by him issue tape recordings of persons impersonating L Ron Hubbard under the name of L Ron Hubbard issue compilations of past L Ron Hubbard works as if they were written now.

4. That the Church of Scientology refuses to interfere in the sexual, marital and family affairs of its members.

5. That the Church of Scientology refuses to use trademarks and copyright as an excuse to prevent the free and widespread use of the wisdom contained in L Ron Hubbard's works.

6. That the Church of Scientology refuses to bar ordinary people from the benefits of this wisdom by the maintenance of exorbitant prices or unreasonable conditions for its use

7. That the Church of Scientology refuses to operate as a jealous monopoly seeking the exclusive use of L. Ron Hubbard's discoveries. That it encourages it's use by anyone who will use it to help his fellow man, and that it refuses to be tempted to do otherwise for financial gain.

8. That the Church ends once and for all the immoral practice of Disconnection and encourages "coming together" rather than splitting up of friends and family.

9. That the Church makes known, truthfully, what happens to the considerable amounts of money that are paid for counselling. Which domestic and foreign corporations, trusts or individuals benefit and to what purposes are the large sums put?

10. That the Church of Scientology refuses to allow fees paid in by its parishioners to be issued to: hire private investigators to harass ex-members of the Church fight expensive legal cases designed to protect the monopoly of the Church or penalise ex-members of the church.

11. That the Church refuses to be an exclusive, mysterious and antagonistic group. That rather, it aligns itself with other groups who wish to help mankind so that together we can create a better world.

12. That the Church refuses to stray from it's own creed, including
"All men have inalienable rights to think freely, to talk freely, to write freely their own opinions and to counter or utter or write upon the opinions of others".

The first point, **who** exactly is in charge of the Church is a question I will return to, but my own experience was one of astonishment when after requesting help for the dissemination of my cancer research and/or the funds to set up a cancer centre in which a clinical trial to test the model could be carried out was ignored at the very highest level. My suggestion to print text re-produced here in the *Appendix 1* as a charitable gesture was ignored. A booklet I produced independently of the Church to test Hubbard's assertion of the dangers of ECT despite its "Research only" label was used by the Church (with no contribution!). Further despite their brave words, I was unceremoniously dumped by the Church to fight a court hearing in London on the issue of The Declaration of Human Rights (the right to one's own belief) which I did win and I believe it set a legal precedent and has been used by the Jehovah's witnesses. Further after a horrific experience I began to ask questions of the Church and became I believe a declared enemy (an official Church term) of them! All this is curious enough in itself, but it was not until many years later that I perceived all of this was a covert effort to stop me regaining my memory or accessing the OT (Operating Thetan –spirit- Levels), which are classed as secret. If this book is of any help to humanity, then it should be realised that it was only through the courageous individuals of conscience, who could still think standing on their feet, who broke away from Scientology who supplied a crucial piece of the jigsaw, which I will come to. As a point of personal comment and record, what a pity this group did not wrestle control of the Church, I believe you would see a very high order of win on this planet.

Crowley is shown in one particular photograph, wearing a hat with an emblem of the power Illuminatus pyramid surrounded by 'Sun Rays' of the all-seeing **Illuminatus Eye.** It is not known whether Crowley's group was under a higher Order e.g. The Illuminati in New York? Although in all probability from the evidence it was. Although I will cover the case of Scientology in more detail later, Ron Hubbard did have connections to Aleister Crowley, indirectly through the secret group of the O.T.O (Order Templis Orientis). Phoenix the breakaway group from The Church of Scientology in the 80's, claimed that a take over of the Church of Scientology was instigated by MI5, the secret British Intelligence Service, this is probably far too simplistic with regard to the World Order scene, but what is absolutely certain, is that given the Church of Scientology has some of the foremost psychology and initiatory knowledge on the planet, it is hardly likely that the Church would be allowed by the One World Order to remain independent or uncontrolled, this is simply not the policy of the World Order and any Scientologist who believes their Church has beaten the system is deluding themselves. NOTHING, which promises freedom for humanity, exists on this planet, without the all-seeing Eye of control or subversion. If the Church survives, it is because a powerful group on this planet want it to survive; if the Church of Scientology has been viciously fought, which it has, then there are two possible reasons for that: Either a powerful antagonistic group and perhaps the second group in this battle - Orthodox religion (and the Twelve Tribes of

Israel?), wish to wipe out Scientology since Hubbard released the mysteries whilst the other group in the battle supported the survival of Scientology; or Scientology fought both powerful groups and won; or the final alternative is that both secret groups at the highest level *orchestrated* a battle to ensure *unquestioning* loyalty from Church members. With the final alternative do not underestimate the methods of the elite Masters, for it is only the first or third alternatives that answer so many questions even regarding my own experience. Whilst I am sure Scientologists would like to believe the second alternative, it will not be the case – the MRC case is far too cunning! Hubbard was viciously fought that is historical fact, but was it with the pre-determined outcome of building up a zealous following, who are prepared to 'walk on hot coals', in order to build The Church of Scientology into a Universal Religion and Kingdom? Thus paralleling One World Order plans? Thus Hubbard was either independent, set up by one group to fight the other group in this story, or Scientology is the pre-determined Universal Religion of the One World Order. If I had to stab a guess at this point, I would take the first alternative – Scientology as one half of the battle. Further where did the technology of Scientology come from? Is it the culmination of Rosicrucian research dating back to that which was stolen from the Early Bronze Age Minoans and added to over the thousands of years, with many more significances than were ever dreamed of added including excessive payment! The first thing that hit me, when I came across Scientology was the thought I had seen it before, but not exactly in that form. Now let me think where exactly was it? At which point I was unceremoniously thrown out to undertake the long journey back to Greece in pursuit of a cure for my amnesia!

A CODED SECRET DOCTRINE

Unfortunately symbols and knowledge have been manipulated for thousands of years, during which the truth has been almost lost even within the secret societies. Significances have been added and various groups hold some part of the truth in their secret document archives. Roerich who claimed Jesus had studied in Tibet, did not mention that he himself was a Rosicrucian and that The Rosicrucian's had a centre in Tibet in ancient times. Further The Rosicrucian's in their secret degrees at the top, claim that **Jesus and his disciples followed and believed in Re-incarnation!** Which verifies my own witness account. I will tell you that secret groups do not claim anything as bold as this statement, unless they have documentary evidence, which in the case of the events of the Crucifixion and Golgotha I believe that Scottish Rite Freemasonry, which, is probably a higher Order of Rosicrucianism have the necessary documentary proof. Such evidence however does not become open to humanity, but is retained in the secret groups, wielded like the sword of Damocles over Churches. Let us ignore for a moment the veracity of whether Jesus was a Rosicrucian or its founding group in earlier times, let us ignore whether he obtained the obvious Buddhist elements in his doctrine from that group and whether he duped the Magdalene as I have claimed. Let us consider the broader implications - if Jesus evolved the doctrine of Heaven's Kingdom a spiritual Heaven, is this not similar to the beliefs of The Rosicrucian's and hidden Masters, claiming spiritual identities who exist in the etheric? Further if documentary evidence does exist that Jesus believed in Re-incarnation then why one may ask, are Christians being allowed to believe otherwise?

There has always been an incompatible" secret doctrine" within certain secret groups, which poses a threat to Orthodox Christianity. Such knowledge rests upon secret documents and sometimes comes into public view obliquely through e.g. artist's work. The Work of Leonardo da Vinci portrays a secret regarding Jesus just as the paintings of Poussin and Guercino, which I covered in *The Battle of The Trees,* are coded. The idea of two Jesus figures, which was to surface in Anthroposophy, and the teachings of Rudolf Steiner, undoubtedly rests on Twin-Kingship and the mysteries of Crete. Leonardo da Vinci was a Rosicrucian and the mathematical form he brought to his works was based on Rosicrucian teachings. The woman who posed for the Mona Lisa was a member of the Rosicrucian fraternity, and he spent four years in trying to bring the spiritual beauty of her soul to the canvas. `Da Vinci's manuscripts were written with the left hand, back-handed and from right to left, a method typical of Rosicrucian manuscripts of that day.

Salvador Dali may have been a later member of the Rosicrucian's. In *The Battle of The Trees*, I produced a painting by Dali *Le Persistance du Memoir*, which showed many of the Matriarchal symbols produced in my first book. The perfume bottle associated with Magdalene, the Seforitic Tree of Life (Cabala), the Pyramid, and the Mother Goddess connected to the sea ('As I go so shall I return'). However the presence of a clock and a saddle type structure over the pyramid, portrays in coded form I would conclude, in one sense the white Mare of Irish legend in The Holy Grail and in another sense the dolphin portrays the totem beast of Early Minoan Crete and the idea of The Cycle of Eternal Return and Re-incarnation - which finds some connection with the title of the painting. Further the use of the clock (time) and the saddle may represent new archetypal symbolism again of a whole Cosmology held by the group to which Dali may have belonged - if not the Rosicrucian's? Co-incidentally both Leonardo Da Vinci and Dali were homosexual, which leads me to believe that Hermetic teaching may tend towards a fusion of positive and negative, female and male, unfortunately a miss-belief that leads to Homosexual practise. Certainly the ancient schools of mystics in line with hermetic teachings taught that in his psychic state or nature, man is both male and female. This is certainly a miss-conception, based on a loss of the ancient knowledge of The Cycle Of Eternal Return, which was replaced with Hermes by the Cabal who conducted the Religious Revolution in Crete in 1 400 BC. Hermes as the transcendent third state beyond death hoped to combine male and female principles. In terms of historical truth, the Patriarchal group, who conducted the religious Revolution in Crete, removed the significance and role of the woman, whose gift was Immortality, where one died to be reborn through Her, the Great Goddess. The belief in Re-incarnation was cleverly being veiled and super-imposed by Hermes. The new belief injected Solar Kingship initially as Twin Kings to retain some elements of the former belief system and later as a sole Sun King, which became a political system of control. Thus a belief in the ability of *all* to Re-incarnate became the belief, as one Twin *King* died, he was reborn through Her. This was perfected as a distortion in the Second coming, where only a Sun King (Jesus) could return. Hermes who combined Twin Kings and Goddess in one personage became the conductor of souls to the underworld, to return. Hermes then, developed bisexual significance. Obviously we lead incarnations as both sexes at different times or in **different lives**. However if one re-incarnates as a man then there is something one must learn from that state and likewise for a woman.

Jesus expressed some of this doctrine in a text by *Clement of Alexandria* (*Stromata iii*): When in *The Gospel according to the Egyptians*, Shalom asked the Lord: "How long shall death prevail?" He answered: "So long as you women bear children." And when she asked again: "I have done well then in not bearing children?" He answered: "Eat every plant but that which is bitter." And when she inquired at what time the things concerning which she had questioned Him should be known, He answered: "When you women have trampled on the garment of shame and when the two become one, and when the male with the female is neither male nor female." And the Saviour said in the same Gospel: "I have come to destroy the works of the Female". Re-incarnation. There is also the question here of whether Jesus was referring to a new religious World Order, based on Hermeticism and Solar Kingship as a political system also.

And of course the planned events of Golgotha, did exactly that, they destroyed the hope of the millennium and the matriarchal belief of Re-incarnation, which was the Holy Grail message. Only holy Messiah's would be able to return, and significantly The Bible has nothing much to say about the soul after death, other than the belief that somehow we are all stored somewhere until the last day of Judgement. The text importantly, as with the Nag Haamidi Scrolls, shows a completely different character for Jesus, than Biblical Gospel accounts and contains a subtle reference to the future victory of a Hermetic group; a group that hold the Hermetic keys of the Hidden Science. As I have proven above, this group also held the background to the Religious Revolution in Crete and have gone by at least one name - Rosicrucianism. The events of Golgotha paved the way for a Universal Religion of the time - Christianity, which effectively removed the religious mysteries from man in the West. One cannot dismiss that it was pre-determined that the mysteries would one day "be known" or given back to man, when the Masters had decided man had evolved sufficiently. What surprise and elation would follow that release, when a whole science would suddenly descend upon man with another holy Messiah! Whether that was Ron Hubbard, I don't know, but his story has all the hallmarks of muddy waters.

The Christian religion must be applauded in many respects, since it does allow its members questions and doubts. The Jewish, Moslem and Hindu religions have no modernistic developments or questionings on the part of those who have practised it all their lives. The many changes that have been made by the various Christian sects during the past several hundred years indicate that the present-day Christian religion is something still in the creative process and does God give not a spiritual creation to man. There is a considerable difference between Christianity and the present day Churchianity of the Christian religion. The doctrine of Re-incarnation is typical of the great changes in the Christian teachings. It was in the third or fourth century after the events of Golgotha that the founders of the Christian church began to eliminate this doctrine of Re-incarnation along with several other doctrines. The ancient methodologies and laws which enabled a man to work out the key to his past incarnations and the moment and hour of birth, has been lost. In my own journey I tried to illustrate through my own experiences, some of which I have re-counted, how such a methodology works, based on holographics and the Hidden Science. You have only to look at your present life to see a reconstituted hologram combining many elements of the past. Every man is your teacher of the past and if you miss his "knock", the possibility to rectify or change the outcome, whereupon the new "door" that was "opened" to you, has gone The person you fight today, the person who seeks your destruction finds no rational excuse in the present, you must look to the past. Ultimately it does not matter whether my account of The Crucifixion is accepted or even discussed, since this is really personal Karma, it is only essential that we discuss Re-incarnation. As God said, "there will be death no more"..."I will wipe away every tear from their eye" *(Revelations)*.

Peter Plitchata (cited) the chemist whose work I have referred to, as a child was fascinated by the fact he was a Twin and with the symbol of the St. John's ambulance cross. I am sure that you can remember something that affected you, a book, and a film - something that strangely held your attention. There is a difference between actuality and reality. Actuality is those things, which conform to rational observation by the objective mind. On the other hand, realities are real things to the subconscious mind or psychic consciousness, regardless of the lack of actuality. Actuality does not create realization of our consciousness. Mystics are affected by both actualities and realities. As far as our consciousness is concerned, it is our realities that affect us - our realization of things - whether actual or not. Mystically if you live in the world of realities or realization, where any stimulus or impulse or urge or inspiration can cause a realization in our consciousness, then whilst you may not understand the path you choose at the time, the reality will eventually make itself known as actuality. I will give the example of my own experience - in the crisis following my experience with Scientology and Anthroposophy, I had a reality that I had seen this information before - where? After a spontaneous holiday in Crete, I knew it was vital that I return to look for something on one plane, to avoid personal danger on another. The actuality was that there was no apparent danger in the environment other than a massive dose of chaos produced by dead life forms (illustration on the cover of the Cancer Report), a curious incident of a thought that was not my own with some alteration of the magnetic field in my immediate environment and several other curious incidents. The trip to Crete produced ultimately my three books and an actuality.

A symbol is a device or object such as a sign to represent an idea. A symbol is the embodiment of a thought, which it concisely suggests. Symbols may be of two kinds, natural and man-made. Natural symbols are for example a dark sky representing a storm. However in *The Battle of The Trees*, I gave the painting by Guercino (1618) as an example of how this natural symbol had been used to overlay man-made symbolism. A dark sky has come to mean in symbolisation, fore-boding and applied by secret group initiates in the case of Guercino, to the events of Golgotha and the burial of the Matriarchal wisdom. I shall cover some symbolisation in more depth later, but secret groups have utilised symbols to

144

depict some idea for a particular class of people for universal acceptance. The Pope (Angelo Roncalli), as I have mentioned utilised the significant egg and wand symbols in a secret Illuminati ceremony. Thus the decoding of the symbols of secret group iconography, has led me to a number of conclusions that would otherwise have been impossible. Numbers are also symbols and may have more meaning in terms of the Ether energy as harmonics or signals. For instance sound the word "ONE" and you end up with the sound of humming bee! And perhaps the goal of secret groups as witnessed by the One Dollar note of America, to control via that one signal and harmonic of the Universe - "ONE" - "One out of many". The harmonious hive of Communism, very quiet, controlled and ORDERED. The asylum will only be peaceful when the chief inmate that controls it, perceives when nothing moves he is safe! He will churn out red tape, laws, rules, and regulations, withdraw money and any other process of creating stillness. Movement reminds him of a period of chaos –a magnetic reversal that he seeks to avoid at all costs.

The Rosicrucian's developed the cross within the triangle as a sacred symbol, and Pythagoras who was initiated by The Idian Dactyls in Crete who had some connection to Abaris the Chief Druid, signifying that he usurped matriarchal knowledge, also used this symbol of the upward pointing triangle, signifying the material creation and the secret Pythagorean Brotherhood swore oaths on the 'Holy Tetracys' a figure of 10 dots representing the upward pointed triangle (material). Pythagoras presumably developed his laws of geometry to resolve the material world of matter and the UVG 120 sphere. Pythagoras as did many other ancient Philosophers, believed in Re-incarnation although more specifically Transmigration of Souls; a belief which Hitler subscribed to. The pyramid, whose symbol was "P", was the first letter of the word Pyramid in the pre-classical linear alphabet, which was archetypally shown as a Triangle around the letter "T". The pyramid was known to embody truths of sacred geometry and the symbol embodied the idea of the spread of rays from above. The Greek word Pyramid stands for "fire" ('Pyr'), at the point, or top, "concentrated fire", or "constant Light", which finds some connection to the Illuminatus symbol of the Power Pyramid and the step pyramid of Freemasonry arriving at the apical point and Illumination. The association of Hermes as the god who discovered fire, is perhaps the story of the withdrawal of the Holy Grail Knowledge into a secret initiated priesthood, who utilised such knowledge for global control (*Fig. 13, Fig. 14*).

Fig.14 **The two interlaced triangles**
  explain Lantoine's remarks that Satan is an equal
and indispensable part of God, as seen when the
picture is reversed. Simply translated,
the motto means: 'What is above equals what is below',
which is Hermetic and illustrates that the Masters run man from above
(Sirius and Great White Lodge?).

The knowledge that was stolen from Crete, contained a whole cosmology including the concept of curved space- time, which was incorporated into the design of the curved rim of the burial sarcophagi, where the dead were laid to rest among sea shells (with archetypal significance of the Goddess connected to the sea 'as I go, so shall I return'). If that knowledge and the hidden science had been developed by successive scientists who were drawn into the secret groups who held this knowledge, then it might be that the saddle in Salvador Dali's painting recounted previously, was a concept of space-time (*fig. 15*). The scientist John Dalton, who worked on the atom, was a Rosicrucian. Dalton who lived in the 18th Century produced Atomic Theory which is the foundation of modern chemistry, based on the conclusion that elements and indeed all matter is made up of atoms. Given that Boyle and Newton were also members of secret societies, possibly some ancient order of the Rosicrucian's, then it is conceivable that the great turning points in science were really based on occult knowledge and the basis of which was stolen from a Bronze Age group. One cannot say whether the saddle in Dali's painting is really an archetypal symbol for the shape of space or just an archetypal symbol relating to the white Mare and the story of The Holy Grail in Ireland. However there is in ancient doctrine, an archetypal symbol that is a circle with a triangle in it. Hubbard in his lectures referred to this symbol and whilst refraining from giving the background, reminded his students that it was one of the most ancient signs in the Universe, stating that if they knew fully about this sign, they would know everything there is to know. I wonder whether he was referring to the law of three!

CYCLICAL COSMOLOGY AND ATOMIC THEORY

There was a whole Cosmology taken from Crete during the Religious Revolution and it seems to have surfaced occasionally within the secret groups. Several theories exist for the shape of space (*fig.15*) - Riemanian, Euclidian or hyperbolic, described as closed, flat or open respectively. **Open space is curved** but curved oppositely, in orthogonal directions **like a saddle** (compare Salvador Dali's painting of *Le Persistance du Memoire* in *The Battle of The Trees*) so that it never closes back upon itself. In an open Universe, a spaceship travelling in a straight line would never return to its departure point. A flat Universe would be basically smooth, but with scattered warps caused by local concentrations of mass (the Earth, Moon and Sun for example); like the surface of a sheet covered with marbles. This flat, nearly Euclidean Universe is the Einstein de Sitter model formulated in 1932. The fate of the Universe or final Omega is the ratio of the actual density to the critical density of mass in the Universe. If there is sufficient mass in the Universe, gravitational forces will be strong enough one day to bring the alleged (it is not fully agreed), post Big Bang explosion to a halt and even reverse it, so that it recedes back into the original point of causation or what the physicists call a singularity. Thus there would be a catastrophic 'Big Crunch'. If however there is insufficient mass to cause this to happen, expansion will continue forever. The temperature of the Universe will slowly fall and 'the Big Chill' would result. Those who would like to believe in the comforting thought that the Universe expansion will halt, but never 'recede, find solace in the hope that the density of mass in the Universe, is poised precisely at the boundary between the diverging paths to ultimate collapse and indefinite expansion, in this way the Hubble expansion may be slowed perhaps coming to a halt, but never receding, into the Big Crunch.

Einstein constructed the first general relativistic cosmological model in 1917; His goal was to prove a static universe. His general relativity equations would not allow a static universe, so he added the cosmological constant. In his model, space had the geometry of a three-dimensional sphere -finite but with no border. In other words, if you flew a spaceship in a straight line for billions of years, you'd never come to the edge of the Cosmos but would eventually return to the starting point. The general theory of relativity stated that gravity is caused by the curvature of space-time. Thus Einstein believed that the Universe is so massive, that it gravitationally curves space back on itself, rather like a balloon or sphere. When Einstein described his revolutionary cosmological model before a gathering of the Berlin Academy of Sciences in 1917, he explained his rationale for adding the cosmological constant to the equations." That term is necessary only for the purpose of making possible a quasi-static distribution of matter, as required by the fact of the small velocities of the stars". The mathematical device expunged the implications of an expanding universe from the equations of general relativity, and left intact the old notion of a static universe. Unlike today there was no strong observational evidence of an expanding universe at the time, and there was philosophical comfort in believing in a static universe, thus one did not have to question **what happened in the beginning** - the singularity. So Einstein for some curious reason despite his genius, clung to the static universe, even though his equations predicted a dynamic one as future empirical evidence would demonstrate. It was certainly uncharacteristic for Einstein to fail to trust his equations, something he would later describe as "the biggest blunder of my life".

It is difficult to know why Einstein despite his theory of general relativity was struggling to avoid its implications, of a nonstatic (probably expanding) universe, when Alexander Friedmann and Willem de Sitter were interpreting Einstein's equations and accepted their implications of a nonstatic universe; despite the official view that Einstein could not accept a singularity, or a point in time at the Big Bang, when the Universe exploded out from a single point. It has to be asked whether Einstein's involvement with the Navy (prior to the alleged Philadelphia experiment) did not imply that Einstein had access to certain secret and ancient documents concerning Cosmology - or the Hidden Science. He would not have been alone, for many great scientists did have access to secret doctrine and perhaps the implications of his calculations, did not sit easily with that doctrine.

Strangely whilst it is assumed that Einstein was deeply involved in the Manhattan Project, he was at Princeton and was suddenly seconded into the US Navy in June 1943. Einstein was intermittently employed in the Special Service Contract of the Dept. of the Navy, Washington DC as a Scientist from 31st May 1943 to 30th June 1944. According to several biographers not only were the Navy interested in the shipboard use of strong magnetic fields in the early forties, but also certain witnesses recall having seen "a relatively large ship carrying a strong magnet weighing many tons." [61] According to Ronald Clark's biography of Einstein, he mentions George a colleague of Einstein, and ideas that included using convergent detonation waves formed by combining two explosives with different propagation velocities. The Bureau of Ordnance publication, later confirmed that Einstein's work concerned: "The theory of explosion, seeking to determine what laws govern the more obscure waves of detonation, why certain explosives have marked directional effect, etc". Further a conversation alleged by 'Albrecht' (an identity cover) discussed how it might be possible, using resonance, to achieve the high electromagnetic field required for optical *invisibility*. Such conversations and record of employment are given, along with Einstein's association with Nikola Tesla, as proof that Einstein had worked on secret research that involved the Philadelphia experiment. There are several curious connections that come to my mind: One is that The Rosicrucian's left England to colonise the New World and landed at Philadelphia: Second, is that The Rosicrucian's held substantial knowledge of the atom and vibrational energy research along with certain Cosmological theories: Thirdly and I am only speculating here, did Einstein refuse his equations and an expanding universe, in favour of some secret doctrine to which he had an allegiance?

Is it not a strange co-incidence that whilst Einstein was working for the US Navy on new kinds of naval mines, Francis Crick obtained the Nobel prize with Watson for the discovery of DNA structure, (incidentally a woman who did the hard grinding work of X-ray crystallography was never acknowledged and was to later die of Cancer not long after the research was utilized –cancer is loss). Watson and Crick were working for the Admiralty in London on exactly the same subject as Einstein. In a letter to Otto Stern, in December 1944, Einstein seemed to dwell on the consequences of his work and whilst it has been assumed he was talking about the atomic bomb, he could have been talking about the implications of advanced research into magnetic fields, which may have been a methodology for accessing Grid information on past technology:
.

> "I can report no more on the matter than that **we are not the first who have faced similar things.** I have .the impression that one must strive strenuously to be responsible. One does best not to speak about the matter for the time being, and that it would in no way help, at the present moment, to bring it to public notice. It is difficult for me to speak in such a nebulous way, but for the moment I cannot do anything else (*author's emphasis*).

What exactly did Einstein mean by this statement? Since whether it referred to the atomic bomb or magnetic field research, both were apparently the result of recent scientific breakthroughs in knowledge and therefore the implication is that some men had faced such dilemmas before, brings into question whether or not the hidden science containing Archetypal Cosmological knowledge, was being used. Certainly as I have explained previously, certain ancient Indian and Tibetan texts recall a battle that appeared to utilise fierce weapons with the possibility of atomic warfare.

Fig.15 **The Geometry of Space**

How is space shaped? That depends on how much matter there is. Space is Riemannian, Euclidian, or hyperbolic –closed, flat, or open, respectively – depending on whether its density is greaterthan, equal to, or less t han the critical density (*Christopher Slye*)

Geometry of Space

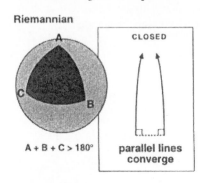

Riemannian

CLOSED

A + B + C > 180°

parallel lines
converge

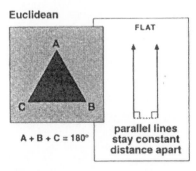

Euclidean

FLAT

A + B + C = 180°

parallel lines
stay constant
distance apart

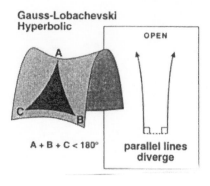

Gauss-Lobachevski
Hyperbolic

OPEN

A + B + C < 180°

parallel lines
diverge

151

In trying to decide what happened to a whole Cosmology which was withdrawn and whether a conflagration occurred in the past, which utilised a secret Cabalistic science that included knowledge of atomic structure and atomic fission which had application to nuclear warfare, it is difficult to obtain direct documentary proof, other than in epic accounts such as *The Mahabharata* and Tibetan ancient texts. There is a record of a great battle and "four Kings with five" recorded in *Genesis* (*Chapter 14,v 1-10*) And the "vale of Siddim" as "the salt sea" given as the location (Dead Sea?) and this battle evidently used unusual weapons since the soil was reduced to "slimepits". This may appear differently in other translations other than the authorised version, which is highly censored with approximately 57,000 mistranslations!

The mention of "chariots" of "gods" in the Indian *Mahabharata* text and in Tibetan texts is a reminder of the ancient Tarot pack based on Cabalistic knowledge. The Seventh key of the Tarot pack *(fig.16)* shows Hermes in a chariot with two sphinxs' (light and dark tones - signifying combined Goddess and Twin Kings combined as Hermes and thus a religious mystery) drawing the chariot. This tarot card corresponds to the 7th Hebrew letter Zain. Hieroglyphically the Zain expresses an arrow (compare to symbolisation of the 12 Cabalistic arrows held in the left claw of the eagle on the One Dollar note) and therefore it suggests the idea of a **weapon**, of the instrument which man uses to rule and conquer and obtain victory. The development of the HAARP and GWEN programmes today, which Dr. Becker and others, have warned have a mind control capability are without independent scientific or governmental control and ultimately as I have pointed out in *Alternative 4*, derive from the research and patents of Nikola Tesla, whose work was taken by the FBI after his death. Einstein was also associated with Tesla, which might account for Einstein's reticence recounted above. The Zain expresses **victory in all the worlds**. As a simple letter it corresponds with the astronomic sign of the *Twins* in the Zodiac (Gemini). The symbolism of this card corresponds in all points with the ideas, which it expresses. I hope by now the reader is becoming acquainted with the symbolism and obviously here, Twin refers to the religious mystery secret of Hermes who was introduced to remove the woman and the belief in Re-incarnation, substituting that belief with the figure of Hermes who combined the role of the woman and Twin Kings into one personage as a method of political and religious control by the elite. This was the first downgrade of the truth following the Religious Revolution in Crete 1400BC. Thus one might conclude behind the World Order with their Hermetic philosophy is the threat of an all powerful weapon which will indeed give "victory in all the worlds": If not atomic warfare, then some use of Grid technology.

Hermes a *Conqueror* (World Order) crowned with a *coronet* (Sun King*)*, upon which rise *three* (Twin Kings and Goddess incorporated) shining *Pentagrams* *(*UVG 120 sphere and female number*)* of *gol*d (male colour of sun King), advances in a *cubical* (4 corners of the earth) chariot surmounted by an *azure* (Philosopher's Stone, the stone that fell from the heavens) star-decked canopy supported by four columns. According to esoteric Cabalistic doctrine the four columns represent symbolic quaternary in all its ramifications. The Conqueror is the one who occupies the centre of the four elements and it is he who has vanquished and **directed the elementary forces;** this victory is confirmed by the cubical form of the chariot, and by the Pentagrams, which crown the **Initiate.** On his shoulders he carries the Urim and Thummim of the sovereign sacrificant, represented by the two crescents of the moon on the right and left; in his hand is a sceptre surmounted by a globe, a square and a triangle. Upon the square, which forms the front of the chariot, we see the **Indian lingam**, surmounted by the flying sphere of Egypt. Whether this a symbolic representation of Egyptian pre-history and Semitic race I will cover later. The word Yod-he-vau-he (the patriarchal God) is portrayed upon the front of the chariot by the winged globe, to indicate that the septenary or 7th Tarot card gives the **key** to the whole Tarot. This certainly reminds us of that curious prophecy by Eliphas Levi, the Magi who stated that **"those with the keys to the East"** would have **"A Universal Kingdom"**. In *Alternative 4*, I concluded that this referred to secret weaponry and specifically the HAARP and GWEN systems, which could be used to control the masses as man slowly descends into insanity. The blue azure sky may indicate this, with connotations to The Philosophers Stone, which in myth was "Lapis Lazuli" in colour. Significantly the Conqueror corresponds especially with the Sword and the Vau of the sacred name. The card also represents the Yod or the God of the 2nd septenary, which is **Man performing the function ofGod the Creator!** The arrogant assumption of those who havehidden significant knowledge of the hidden science and the Grid, together with Cosmological knowledge is that **they** and not God should control this knowledge and its uses. Thus rests the condemnation of Man, which I referred to in my previous work. Further the law of the 2nd Septenary was Realization and The Man of the 2nd septenary was Nature performing the function of **Adam!** Surely this goes back to the whole history of the secret doctrine and Cabalistic Science descending from the Patriarchs through Adam and thus we come up against that mysterious group of thirteen again, which was evident on the One Dollar note. Here the implication is that **Nature is subservient to Adam** and the Tribes of Israel! But surely also we are not referring to the *12* tribes of Israel, since this number *13* arises again. What is this 13 that crops up in symbols and throughout the One World Order archetypes? Slowly we will come to this number and its significance. This is certainly a reflection of the whole of Scientific thinking in the last 3 centuries, which did not seek to **understand** Nature, but sought a **CONQUEST** (as in "Conqueror") of **NATURE** as I described in the *Appendix* of *Alternative 4*, as a parallel to a sexually aggressive conquest, so aptly described in the Space programme and Atomic Bomb research. Man, who sought to dominate The Grid, merely became the effect of it and the downward pointing triangle of material morphogenetic matter, containing the evolutionary survival history of the species, which is dependent on sexually dominant behaviour by the male of the species. Control and Conquer is a part of that Nature as Grid survivalist mechanisms of the master blueprint. Nature will never be controlled though, since Nature is not woman as secret groups view her, but physical laws that *no man* can baulk. 'She' will assert 'Her' own balance in 'Her' own time - a Magnetic Reversal, where 'She' will ruthlessly wipe man from the face of 'Her' Earth, for not obeying

'Her' laws. The MRC case in his own superiority and ideas of superman capabilities could never accept that he was subject to 'Her' laws. Surely too, just karma in so far as he originally used those laws to control man and became a Fallen Angel, trapped by his wrongdoing!

Why should the 7th Card of The Tarot be related to The Twins *and* the Month of May? Here perhaps we have the clue to the "battle of Kings" in the *Genesis* account and the frequent mention of great "god-kings", riding about in their "Vimanas" or "celestial cars", described as "aerial chariots with sides of iron clad with wings". It seems ordinary folk in the past, deprived of knowledge of the hidden science and the Grid, were as much dumbfounded in ways to explain the technology as perhaps UFO'ologists are today. However one cannot dismiss the possibility that at some level, there was in *The Mahabharata* recognition of the history of the Philosophy and the knowledge of the "chariot" as related to Hermes and the Conqueror of the Tarot pack. As I have been at pains to point out in my research, there was a point in history, when the truth of the Cosmology and laws relating to the Grid, were withdrawn from the masses and retained within the secret Priesthoods. However, importantly you should recognise that certain Cabalistic knowledge was already known and understood from the beginning by the Patriarchs and was always held in secret and may have survived a Magnetic Reversal through Noah. However approx. 10 000 BC, there was a spiritual message that arrived on Earth, which sought to explain a Cosmology and Grid laws together with a belief (Re-incarnation) to man, to release him from the trap. The wars then may indicate that after such knowledge was sequestered there was a battle for supremacy of he Grid, in much the same way, as it appears that Grid wars are secretly fought today. Neither can one discount that the old Matriarchal team were not a part of this, to gain back control of the knowledge. In other words the ancient battles may or may not be true, there is the possibility that they are written in code to be handed down as a secret oral tradition to avoid censorship.

Fig.16 **Seventh Card of the Tarot**
    The Chariot of Hermes

THE CHARIOT.

THE CHARIOT.

155

The Conquerer, who occupies the centre of the four elements, is the man who has vanquished and directed the elementary forces: this victory is confirmed by the cubical (compare 4 pillars of equal height of Beth-Luis Nion alphabe and Druid (13 th tribe) form of the chariot. The Conqueror has three right angles upon his curass, and he bears upon his shoulders the Urim and Thurimim of the sovereign sacrificant, represented by the two crescents of the moon on the right and left; in his hand is a sceptre surmounted by a globe (World Order), a square and a triangle (significant symbols of Freemasonry). Upon the square, which forms the front ofthe chariot, is the Indian lingam, surmounted by the flying sphere of Egypt. Two sphinxes, one white, the other black (Hermes and Sirius or World Order) are harnessed to the chariot. The word Yod-hevau-he is portrayed upon the front of the chariot by the winged globe, to indicate that the septenary gives the key to the whole Tarot. The two sphinxes correspond to the two principoles, active and passive or Sirius A and B. The Conqueror corresponds to the Sword and the Vau of the sacred name. Signifies Man performing the function of God the creator (Tribes of Israel). Astronomically related to The Twins (or 12th and 13 th tribes of Israel). The primitive sign or hieroglyphic symbol of The Chariot is the arrow, which is displayed on the right hand side of the one-dollar note of America. Symbolically related to the month of May and signifies the Law of Realization or completion of a plan (World Order). The nature performing this function is the Astral Light of Adam.

If the realization of the 7th Tarot is equilibrium or mediation, then it is strange that the 8th Tarot card (*Fig. 17a*) which follows, is the Hebrew Letter Heth. Hieroglyphically the Heth expresses the field. From it springs the idea of anything that requires labour, trouble, and effort, which may elude to the release of the mysteries which in study to require *effort* (how many pick up a book today!) Continued effort results in the establishment of equilibrium, hence the idea of **balancing power**, and consequently of **JUSTICE** attributed to this letter. Truth and Justice were co-incidentally a part of the prophetic Revelation of John._Astronomically the Heth corresponds to the sign of **Cancer** in the zodiac. Thus the ideas expressed by this symbol are of equilibrium in all its forms. A woman is seen full face, and wearing an iron coronet, and she is seated on the throne. She is placed between the *two columns* (Twin Kings) of the temple. The solar cross is traced upon her breast. She holds a sword pointed upwards in her right hand and a balance in her left, which incidentally reminds one of certain iconography at Courts of Justice in London. Significantly justice is in the form of woman and this relates to the events of Crete and earlier Palaeolithic times and returns I would conclude to the first cut. As the Mary Magdalene stated: "There will be no peace on this Earth until the cut is healed". Occult science at first theoretical has become practical and has been taught verbally, the secrets never being committed to print. Now it appears in all the pitilessness of consequences, terrible for the false Magi - the Sword or wand, but just toward the *true* initiates (Balance). In esoteric law the woman fulfils all the functions of God the Son, she does so on the basis of the first cut. The card represents the Mother as Preserver of God the Son in Humanity. As Justice it is a part of the 7th Tarot, realization and authority. As woman it is Nature fulfilling the function of Eve. It also signifies the preservation of Nature in the World. The 7th and 8th Tarot, in *The Battle of The Trees,* was a battle of 7 versus 8; Male and Female; Jesus and Magdalene; Holly (The Holy One) versus Oak (Royal); truth versus lies; justice versus injustice and destruction versus conservation; Democracy versus The New World Order, secrecy versus openness and orthodox versus alternative: However only one side has been given the opportunity to speak.

Fig.17a **Eighth Card of the Tarot – Justice**

JUSTICE.   JUSTICE.

Corresponds to 8th Hebrew letter (Heth) and expresses a field. From it springs the idea of anything that requires labour, trouble, and effort. The idea of a balancing power (12 and 13?) Equilibrium in all its forms. The woman with a coronet is seated upon a throne. She is placed between the two columns of the temple (Twin Kings – 12 and 13, or Hermes and Bull-Minos cult – Rosicrucian's) the solar cross is traced on her breast (woman locked up with Hermes and Rosicrucian's) She holds a sword pointed upwards in her right hand, and a balance in her left. Occult science, at first theoretical has become practical and has been taught verbally. Now it appears in all the pitilessness of consequences, terrible for the false Magi –the sword, but just toward the true Initiates (Balance). Expresses nature performing the function of Eve and woman fulfilling the functions of God the Son as Mother.

157

Fig.17b **Tenth Card of the Tarot – The wheel of Fortune**

THE WHEEL OF FORTUNE.

THE WHEEL OF FORTUNE.

Corresponds to 10th Hebrew letter (Yod) and the hieroglyphic symbolism is the finger (fore-finger? – "fool" or psychic finger of Druid?) extended as a command. The eternity of time and all ideas (secret group continuity?) relating to it, together with the idea of supremacy (World Order?) refer to Ezekiel wheel of fortune Signifies magic power, fortune – the whell is a line without beginning or end, the symbol of eternity. The whell of furtune is suspended upon its axis. To the right Anubis,the genius of good ascending; to the left typhoon, the genius of evil descending. The Sphinx is balanced on the centre of the wheel and ruler between positive and negative (12 and 13?).

According to Diodorus Siculus[62] the Cretans professed that they gave their mysteries to Greece and that they were performed openly on their Island and were **communicated to everyone.** Thus prior to an invasion by an occult influence in Crete, there was an open sharing of the knowledge, which is characteristic of a Matriarchal society. In trying to identify the origins of the group that overtook Knossos and I concluded re-positioned the archetypal symbols, concealing a prior Cosmological knowledge and belief system, there were a number of contenders including the Egyptians and Druids. I was looking for a group, who possibly held links in ascendancy, with the Rosicrucian's. The Egyptians certainly had trading links with Knossos, but the same writer says that the Cretans received the mysteries from Egypt, the mysteries of Isis being the same as those of Demeter and the Mysteries of Osiris the same as those of Dionysus. Certainly this ties with the evolution of the archetypal symbol of the

158

cross in its Egyptian form as the **Crux Ansata or Cross-of Life, which** symbolised **Immortality** or the continuity of Life. (*Fig.18*). It is often found in iconography in the hands of Kings and Queen, gods and goddesses as the *"key of Life"*. This implies though Immortality for Son's of God, gods and Kings and Queens, the idea of the "chosen ones" and that the knowledge of Immortality was only preserved for Royalty, thus implying that Re-incarnation or Immortality as a belief, was withdrawn from man: Whereas we are specifically told by Diodurus Siculus that the Cretan Mysteries were **open to all**. Thus the idea of the "chosen ones" and Immortality of Kings is a post Religious Revolution idea I conclude, signifying the time when the open mysteries were withdrawn into a secret group who then through ascendancy passed that knowledge on, deeming as 'gods' themselves or God, when and where to release those mysteries - a case of misuse of power or no power!

Whilst the Crux Ansata has been associated with fertility, this is a miss-interpretation of the mystery ofreproduction. The seed and its potential to provide continuity, demonstrated to the Egyptians as it did to the Greeks, the principle of Immortality, through birth, transition and rebirth. The doctrine of Re-incarnation had to be taught to man, since the MRC case had so long removed any spiritual awareness from man, that man had forgotten. The Crux Ansata became the symbol of that belief with the Egyptians. The oval or lozenge shape of the Crux Ansata, is a referral back to the ancient Goddess and Immortality as Her gift, she gave birth to the truth. That lozenge shape has been maintained as having survived in the current group of Freemasonry, by the placing of the square and the compass.

The Evolution of the Primitive Cross

Fig.18 **Evolution of the cross and Egyptian Crux Ansata**

159

Martin Short[63] maintained that in Latin vesica piscis means 'bladder fish', and in Architecture it means pointed oval shape, whose sides are formed by the intersection of two equal circles, which pass through each other's centres. Medieval artists used it to enclose religious portraits. In medieval heraldry it became an acute diamond, which co-incidentally parallels the upward and downward pointing triangles. J.S. M. Ward[64] stated that in Freemasonry the lozenge is easily represented by the square and compass, into which the nose of the initiate is so abruptly thrust in a Masonic Initiation ceremony. In Masonic ceremonies the masculine tools, the level and gavel complement the square-and-compass's femininity. This of course may merely represent a religious mystery that was inherent in Freemasonry from early times, covered with the outward show of the building guilds. Ward explains that alongside the square and compass in the Masonic lodge "lies the gavel or Tau, and so the cross and the vesica piscis are brought together in conjunction with the third great light in Masonry (The Bible) at the very moment the candidate takes his oath". This symbolises perhaps, that ancient Christianity incorporated the religious secret and mysteries, which involved Matriarchal knowledge and Re-incarnation. Ward explains that the candidate makes his first step in Freemasonry through these symbols: "obligated in the vesica piscis" and **"ruled by the Tau Cross"**. I will come to the Tau Cross presently, but in passing note that the Tau Cross specifically links to the group who revere the number thirteen. Out of this he concludes that the newcomer 'thereby publicly declares his intention of trampling underfoot those primitive and animal passions which war against the soul'. Thus he is reminded that:

"As he must enter this material world through the vesica piscis, so he must enter the life of initiation by the same road, and only after he has done so can he see the Light.... This vesica piscis is the female or preservative principle of God, without which we could not exist for a single day, nor without it could we hope to be preserved from the powers of darkness and evil, which threaten us on our spiritual journey. The 7th Tarot comes into play as Ward explains that the Master of the lodge represents the male aspect of the deity, as is shown by the Tau crosses, called levels, on his **apron,** and by his use of the gavel, which represents the Taur.

WHO KILLED THE MINOANS?

In my research at the Knossos site in Crete, I had struggled to find the significance of the stilted figures, almost mechanical, who with the stone pillars appeared after the Religious Revolution and which seemed totally out of keeping with the liberty and freedom and colour expressed in the brightly coloured and natural wall-painted frescoes of the Early Minoan period. The appearance of Goddesses with hands raised to Ra (the Sun god) and the probable introduction of the drug Opium into the culture (the Poppy goddesses) (*Plate5*); along with finds from the Psychro cave of Zeus (who in myth was born in the cave not far from the site of Knossos), such as boats which indicated the belief in the passage to a spiritual after-world by boat, all led me to conclude that a Religious Revolution had occurred which had irradiated The Cycle of Eternal Return and Re-incarnation. The stiff formality of later iconographic finds particularly the icon with four figures worshiping? *Pillars (Plate 6)* seemed to provide the clue to the group that had overtaken Knossos and removed the mysteries from open view.

Sir Arthur Evans who first researched the site threw light on the significance of the pillar and other symbols of Crete by stating his belief that tree and pillar worship in Palestine and Anatolia was: "taken over from the older stock" by Semites and Hittites: "The undoubted parallelism observable between the tree and pillar cult of the Mycenaean (Aegean) and that of the Semitic world" wrote Evans, "should be always regarded from this broad aspect...The co-incidences that we find, so far as they are to be explained by the general resemblance presented by a parallel survivals due to ethnic elements with European affinities which on the east Mediterranean shores largely underlay the Semitic.....The **worship of the sacred stone or pillar .. is very characteristic of Semitic religion**" (*Author's emphasis*).65

The appearance in Cretan iconography (post Religious Revolution), of a tree with **seven** spiralling branches, which I produced in *Alternative 4* and which is curiously described as "a vase in the shape of a tree with birds in its branches" cannot surely have surpassed Greek Museum collators and Archaeologists, that it is possible given the appearance of stone pillars, that this icon demonstrates a Semitic influence of the Cabala - the *Tree of Life*, with Matriarchal symbol of the dove in its branches. This is a classic example of re-positioning of the matriarchal symbols and the fusion of Cabalistic archetypal symbols with the matriarchal religion and knowledge, symbolised by the dove that was also to become in Grail legend the symbol of the Mary Magdalene. Thus it appears that tree and pillar worship related to a **Semitic group** which must have contained Cabalistic science, since one icon which I produced in *Alternative 4,* shows a figure with the right hand raised to the position of the fore-head (the position of the third-eye and the seat of intuitive power related to Cabalistic doctrine). The fact that the *New Scientist* magazine chose to produce this icon when trying to convince its readers of a tidal wave at the Knossos site accounting for the destruction of the Early Minoan Civilization, must then be interpreted I assume as 'woe is me, here comes a tidal wave'! Since no other explanation is given. As a point this raises the question of isolation of various branches of science with other academic fields and the failure of Editor's to allow both sides of an augment to speak, such isolationist thinking prevents full evaluation of all aspects of history, conspiratorial or not. Whilst the article in *New Scientist*, followed a suggestion of covering my own research, entitled *who killed the Minoans*? My research was ignored, but the magazine in its next issue produced an article on clever wave action research, accompanied by the icon - with no apparent explanation for its inclusion. As I pointed out in a letter to the Editor, if the researchers had actually vacated the laboratory and visited the site, they would have observed the obvious fact that the whole site is covered in gypsum, which dissolves in running water- whoops! I thought the researchers might like to explain, how the gypsum survived a tidal wave. The letter was not printed naturally even in a footnote somewhere, which I suspect is all the space and justice matriarchal science can expect However the one-sided views (not altogether co-incidental) that exist in publishing and academic research demonstrate, that only one side of the story has ever been told, or allowed to surface in what is now effectively controlled media and publishing.

The origins of the secret alphabets, which I discussed in *The Battle of The Trees*, did not discount an origin in The Middle East pointing to Semitic origins. Graves[66] asked whether it was The Boibel-Loth Alphabet, which held many of the religious mysteries that contained and composed the life and death story of the Essene's god - Moses. The vowel names of the alphabet, when preceded by the letter **J**, Yod-He-Vau-He became the quadrants of King, Knight, Knave and Queen of the Tarot pack and ultimately **J**ehovah - The Patriarchal God of the Jews. The Boibel-Loth alphabet, which I have used to decode many of the religious mysteries in my first book, was laid out in **four pillars** of equal height (*fig. 19*). Such pillars are found at the Knossos site as religious icons, dating I conclude from a Religious Revolution c. 1400 B.C. when secrecy entered a once open society and the Cosmological knowledge and belief in Re-incarnation was sequestered, by what increasingly in evidence looks to be a **Semitic group following Mosaic Law**. The case of who killed the Minoans, stole the hidden science and buried Re-incarnation, whilst working towards a World Order, is beginning to unravel!

Jesus was evidently tutored in The Tree alphabet and the associated alphabets, the evidence for which I gave in *The Battle of The Trees*. Thus was Jesus an

Initiate of the ascendant group who killed the Minoans, with access to their stolen science and Re-incarnation? The Tree Alphabet or Beth-Luis-Nion alphabet, which relates its letters to specific trees, which carry religious mysteries and significance, is said to be an ancient **IRISH** Alphabet, although Graves states that it originated in the Black Sea region. It is found in Roderick O' Flaherty's Ogygia where he interestingly states that with the Boibel-Loth it is a genuine relic of **DRUIDISM,** orally transmitted down through the centuries. Thus could it be that the Druids were responsible for the Religious Revolution in Crete? What is more are the Druids Semitic?! In Crete and the Eastern Mediterranean in general, sacred trees are formalised as pillars. Certainly The Druids in their megalithic Henge constructions were aware of the Grid knowledge. The appearance of the alleged Armillary in Cretan Archaeological find discussed earlier, may have been another relic from such a change in beliefs and the re-instatement of a Cosmology based on observation of Solar -Lunar cycles which were then incorporated into the calendars and alphabets.

Fig.19 **Beth-Luis-Nion alphabet and calendar**
   (*Robert Graves – White Goddess*)

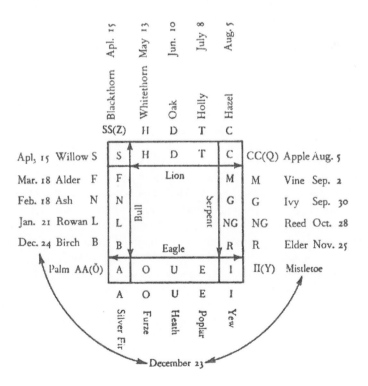

I have already discussed in my first book, the symbolisation of the tomb at Golgotha with its upright pillars and lintel across, as relating to the secret Alphabets The Boibel -Loth represented as four pillars of equal height, containing the four totem beasts of the Knossos calendar i.e. Lion, Bull, Eagle and Serpent, with the four upright pillars of Bull and Serpent holding the lintel across, as the Lion, which is seen in The Lion's Gate at Mycenae in Greece (*Plate 7*); where entry is over the portal as Eagle and thus it was a King's gateway and the Mycenaean Kings e.g. Agamemnon were Sun-Kings buried with Gold death masks. The Lion's Gate also has a single upright pillar or 'Herm' between the Lions over the lintel, which depicts hermetic philosophy. The tomb of Jesus was a dolmen burial chamber, which if it had meant to signify the joining of the 7th and 8th Tarot of Male and Female and Balance, together with Justice would have represented a 'womb of Earth', consisting of a cap-stone or lintel supported on two upright pillars, in which the dead hero is buried in a crouched position like a foetus in the womb, awaiting rebirth, which was a burial practise I equate with Re-incarnation. However Jesus was laid on the unexpected flat or horizontal pillar - the baetyllic pillar, at the last moment of **a plan that was not adhered to** (in my own account). The symbolisation of His tomb depicted **Hermetic Philosophy** and as such indicated there was to be no joining (in a truce) of Matriarchal and Patriarchal, King and Queen for the benefit of humanity. This message would have been clearly understood by the people who had not yet then, lost the symbolisation entirely, thus the lost hope of Jerusalem in bringing back the Hidden Science and belief in Re-incarnation was dashed. Further in the quote of Alexandria given earlier Jesus implied that he was a follower of hermetic philosophy.

The rose emblem on the ceiling architraves at the Epidaurus site in the Peloponnese Greece, at The Temple of Asklepios, where an initiated Priesthood carried out healing, is used in the emblem of the Rose and the Cross by The Rosicrucian's, which had a double meaning. **The Rose** is an ancient symbol in Greece of **healing**. The rose, the perfume of the Magdalene, the cycle of budding into life, maturing to full bloom and potential beauty, followed by decay and returning to dust in the earth to be reborn represents the cycle of Life. The Cycle of Eternal Return of the Early Minoans: Start - change - finish, start etc: The opportunity on incarnation to do nothing at all, or many things, with potential for the spirit to learn and develop. The sense of panic that sometimes grips people in middle age is the recognition of incarnation goals not being met or fulfilled. However within the seed (or spirit) is the opportunity for rebirth and the mystical use of the emblem of the Rose as an archetypal symbol indicates **Re-incarnation** although the Labour party in Britain and Tony Blair appeared to use it as a symbol of rebirth of their own particular phoenix in politics! But was it a Rosicrucian emblem to the few in the know!

The official Rosicrucian cross bears a single rose at the centre of the cross and the derivation of the cross is inextricably linked to the secrets of the alphabets. This starts with the ancient **Tau Cross** of Greece, although maintained also by the Phoenicians. The appearance of this cross in Greek iconography is striking. Certain symbols denoted a Sun-King and in a red-figured kylix from Vulci (*Fig.20*). The bull-Minotaur is spotted with eyes like Argos. Argos was a Sun-king like the Cretan Minotaur and his **eyes were Sun symbols**. The spots on the Minotaur bull represent Sun symbols. Further an early sixth Century B.C. ceramic piece from Corinth shows a Minotaur surrounded by four eight-rayed Sun Symbols (*Fig.21*). The Sun -King ruled for nine years according to the calendar, but eight was also an important number in both calendric symbolism and has previously been alluded to in the form of the figure-of-eight shield. Thus the eight stars in fig. *21* depict a Sun-King.

Fig.20 **A red-figured kylix from Vulci**. The Minotaur is spotted with eyes like Argos (*The British Museum*).

165

Fig.21 **A Corinthian pinax from Pente Skouphia**. Early sixth century B.C.
The Minotaur surrounded by four eight-rayed sun symbols (*Berlin Museum*).

In another variation of archetypal symbolism portraying a Sun -King in (*fig.22*)
a black-figured vase with Minotaur is marked with eight T's which are shaped
like the Greek letter 'T', pronounced in Greek as Tau - hence the derivation of
the word Tauros meaning bull. In *figure 22,* again there are 8 T's on the
Minotaurs body, which is part of the 8 year cycle of calendric symbolism
depicting the number of years of a Sun-King's rule, as a waning King of the pair
(Twin Kings) he would be sacrificed to make way for his Twin and the waxing
or New Year King. The Solar-Lunar calendars carried religious mysteries also
myths and legends often referred in veiled terms to these mysteries, some of
which I produce in *The Battle of The Trees*. It is possible that a further
significance was attached to the letter 'T'. Lucian in his Trial in the Court of
Vowels circa 160 AD writes:

"Men weep and bewail their lot and curse Cadmus with many curses
for introducing Tau into the family of letters, they say it was his body
that tyrants took for a model, his shape that they imitated, when they
set up the erections, on which men are crucified. Stauros the vile engine
is called, and it derives its vile name from him". [67]

Fig.22 **A black-figured vase**. A Minotaur marked with eight T's.

'T' as Holly or Holy one in the ancient Tree alphabet, signified Holy Messiah, crucified on the cross and the usurpation of an earlier knowledge where D and T as Twins ('D' is Duir for Oak (Royal) and 'T' for Tinne or Holly (Holy one) in the Tree Alphabet) meant that as I reported in *The Battle of The Trees,* Jesus tried to combine both in one personage i.e. Royal as King of the Jews and Holy one, thus removing a former truth of the Twin Kings and the Goddess as the first downgrade of the Matriarchal Religion and Re-incarnation, which in its purity did not involve Kings in any way, one simply died to be re-born. This is a reflection of the curse in Revelations on Apollo The Sun -King, who fused the male and female roles into one personage - Solar Kingship, which became hereditary Monarchy. The two syllables of the word Tauros or "bull" derive perhaps from Stauros and Tau, which leaves the "S" a mystery. What is clear is that the ritually sacrificed Minotaur, the mythical Bull-Man of the labyrinth of Crete, was associated with the T-shaped Cross, upon which human sacrificial victims were crucified. Thus there is a mystery wrapped up in this myth, which connects the emergence of a Bull cult at Knossos, after the Religious Revolution, with a Semitic group and the practice of Crucifixion, which also provides the clue to the origins of Solar Kingship and hereditary Monarchy. Thus the group that we are seeking, who sequestered the hidden science and killed the Early Minoans, destroying a great Civilization, must show all these

167

connections. Further I used the Nag Hamaadi Scrolls in *The Battle of The Trees*, to show that Jesus and the Mary Magdalene re-enacted the Cretan mysteries. The goal of the Magdalene was to bring back the mysteries and a belief in Re-incarnation, but the duplicity of Jesus prevented that. As he stated in the Egyptian Alexandria text, he came "to destroy the works of the Female" (Re-incarnation) and by inference sought victory for a Hermetic group, that had no intention of acknowledging the great wrong committed to humanity at Knossos, when The Holy Grail, was stolen by Hermes god of thieves. This is not mythical, these events really **did happen.**

Ron Hubbard in his works wrote only one poem that mysteriously referred to a "rose". The poetic in Hubbard seemed odd to me given the nature of the man, however certain symbols that Hubbard used apart from the" Law of Three", in his Communication triangle, were the lozenge shape containing a T, which he denotes as a symbol for the Scientology grades of OT (Operating Thetan), which is a spirit. Hubbard also used two upright (point facing upwards), triangles interlaced with S for Scientology as another symbol. Aleister Crowley as you will recall became head of the secret group the Ordo Templi Orientis (OTO), a neo-Masonic Order, which was assumed to be of German origin, but which I have posed the possibility of American origin in New York as Illuminati or British as Rosicrucian? Ron Hubbard was to become connected with Crowley's OTO group in Pasadena California and whilst The Church of Scientology, has always maintained that Hubbard broke up black magic in America, it is certainly odd that Hubbard should have designated a spirit (Thetan) as Operating Thetan, shortened to OT, when clearly it would, if the Church is telling the truth provide an unwanted and undesirable link to Crowley and the OTO. I will return to this whole scene later but Crowley's views on the devil were astonishingly similar to those attributed to the giant American Freemason, Albert Pike.

Crowley was also associated with The Golden Dawn, which had been organized in 1887, and in 1987 a conference was held in London to mark the centenary of the Golden Dawn's conception. The Hermetic Research Trust, whose trustees included the Marques of Northampton, a prominent Royal Arch Freemason, who organized it Crowley, was directly linked with Grand Lodge through a man who was one of England's leading Masonic scholars John Yarker. Yarker admitted Crowley as a 33rd degree Freemason in his own version of the **Rose Croix**, or Ancient and Accepted Rite. Despite that Grand Lodge had always denied that Crowley was ever a member United Grand Lodge they never expelled Yarker from Craft Freemasonry. J. Ward states that in the "Christian" Masonic order known as the Rose Croix, the 'cross' and the 'rose' are again 'only another name for the phallus and the vesica piscis'. He then depicts the symbols united as a lozenge shape with cross in the centre and the Crux-Ansata, which in Egypt depicted Immortality. Whilst Hubbard's lozenge shape is not strictly oval but close to and curiously more egg-shaped, given that Scientology deals with past lives then the implication of symbols based on Rosicrucian and Rose-Croix symbolism is possible. George Draffen who asserted in 1986 that the "hoodwink" or blindfold in the first-degree ritual reminds the candidate that he is "**undergoing a birth process**", just as "conception and fertilisation take place in the darkness of the **womb**". Here then we have symbolism relating back to Knossos. Even the cable-tow round his neck is "a symbolical umbilical cord" which, when cut, symbolizes "**birth and new life.**" [68] There is no doubt, that the belief of Re-incarnation is held at the top of Freemasonry, which is Jewish in its degrees! Thus not only have I assumed that the highest aspirations of the Jews, embodied a return of the belief of Re-incarnation to humanity (as their gift naturally!), but they had no intention of acknowledging the great wrong committed and the stolen apples of Immortality from Crete, which was **her** gift. This is not simply a case of bruised apples, since the question becomes, how will anyone ever pass the Grid, if they can't duplicate reality?

The obsession with birth and women's organs in Freemasonry, dates back to Crete and the hidden symbology of e.g. labyrinth as womb where the Bull Minotaur was held; together with the story of The Holy Grail and the withdrawal of the former belief in Re-incarnation and the role of the woman. In 1933 W. L. Wilmshurst delivered a lecture to the Leeds research lodge (*Living Stones -no. 4957*), of which he was the founding Master. His subject was the new Freemason's Hall in London, then known as the Peace Memorial Temple. He explained that it was "deeply and designedly symbolic", and launched into this eulogy:

Every Masonic Lodge is impliedly... a secret place of birth, and is known to those initiated in it as the 'Mother' from whom they received their Masonic life. It is fitting, therefore, that the inmost sanctuary of the Mother Grand Lodge of the worldwide Craft should be located as to be a symbolic place of birth and be in structural correspondence with the human female organism. The Grand Temple is literally a symbolic womb, centrally placed within, but isolated from, the body of the edifice. In this respect it follows the oldest known symbolic place of Initiation, the Great Pyramid, whose central chamber of rebirth and resurrection is similarly constructed and with the same mystical intention". As Martin Short 63 pointed out " It seems some 6 million men alive today have been conceived and incubated in a Masonic womb, then 'born again' through 'mother lodges' consisting entirely of men. No wonder they do not let women join!" If Freemasonry hopes to unite the 7th and 8th Tarot The King and Queen or male and female as bisexual Hermes symbolically without for one minute re-tracing the injustice that has been committed, their cause at once becomes not only a quest for power and control, but shows so little spiritual understanding or what was intended in the Holy Grail message, that it would be extremely funny, if not for the fact that such a wrong will see them trapped for all eternity unless they could square their compass and conscience!

There is no doubt that in the highest levels of Freemasonry, which the average man will never reach they possess much of the background to the true history of The Holy Grail and the Hidden religious mysteries and in the very highest levels of certain branches, almost certainly at least in The Rose-Croix degree and in associated branches of Rosicrucian's the knowledge of the hidden science. The womb is acknowledged and certainly underlines the hidden symbolism of **The Knossos labyrinth** as womb, maze, re-birth and the emblematic under world of the dead in one sense, but it also was a place of re-birth. The Great Goddess is an Earth Goddess and the dead are laid to rest in the Earth: But it is also from the womb of the Earth-Goddess that Sacred Kings are reborn. The labyrinth was thus an emblem of the womb. The floor design of The Temple of Freemasons Hall in London is I would conclude a symbolic womb, with phallic member entering, as an indication of combined male and female principles, with the arrogant assumption that hope for mankind presumably lay in the Male Demi-urgus or impregnating principle. This floor archetypally parallels Minoan Seals showing egg, with phallic member and thus harks back to the Religious Revolution in Crete, where they came by their stolen apples of Immortality (*Fig. 23 and 24*)

I discussed in *Alternative 4* Hitler's association with secret groups and his belief in Re-incarnation. The symbol of the swastika is another symbolic representation of the derivation of the labyrinth as womb. The memory of the original significance of the labyrinth, which I cover more fully in *The Battle of The Trees*, remained with its connection to the calendar at Knossos, well into the Classical period. Coins of Knossos from circa 500 B.C. Represent the labyrinth as a maze-like Swastika *(fig. 25)* Two coins in particular show identical maze-like Swastikas, one with an eight rayed Sun-disc and the other with a crescent moon at the centre of the maze. The placement of these two symbols in the centre of a labyrinth points to a traditional association of the labyrinth, with an eight-year solar lunar Calendar cycle, in the city where both the labyrinth and the Calendar originated.

Thus it appears that a Semitic group overran Knossos and that group appeared to have been a Bull-Minos cult, which through their calendar mysteries appear to have some connections to the Druids and later Rosicrucian's and Freemasonry itself which is Jewish in the higher degrees, but we must assume a rather un-orthodox form, which relies on the mysteries and symbolism of Crete and the post Revolution era, when the apples of Immortality along with the hidden science were stolen. The question becomes, whether it ended up in Scientology!

170

Fig.23 **Late Minoan Talismanic gem from East Crete**
(*Ashmolean Museum. 1938.984*).
Two serpents surmounting rustic shrine of two
pillars with pierced egg within.

Fig.24 **The Grand Temple within Freemasons' Hall, London**:
a symbolic womb, according to the Masonic author W.L. Wilmhurst
(*From: Martin Short – Inside the Brotherhood*)

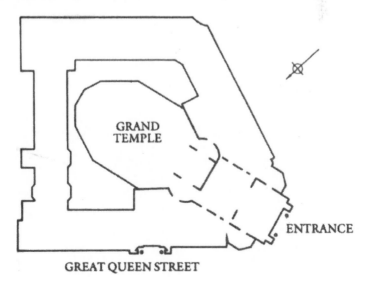

Fig.25 **Four coins from Knossos of the fifth century B.C.**
Above, the labyrinth as a swastika with symbols of the sun and the moon in the centre; below the labyrinth as a maze. This maze, which takes eight turns to reach the centre, is structurally the same as the maze on the Tragliatella oinochoe (*The Battle of The Trees*).

ACTING ON ORDERS - NO QUESTIONS ASKED

It is rather difficult to determine whether high earthly Initiates are utilising information from The Grid and channelling that in a conscious form and representing that as a higher knowledge, or whether they are merely dupes to some earthly higher power and become manipulated via **suggestion** whilst in meditation or sleep, believing that their "Orders" come from a higher source. Certainly it is highly suspect when anyone receives anything in sleep and then takes no steps to check the veracity of the knowledge, without posing questions. However the only men to make it to the top of these secret Orders are those who show unswerving devotion and comply with the policy of "no questions asked". Thus there are two possibilities here:
a) Orders and knowledge received directly from The Grid and then presented as a higher source: Such knowledge then, coming from PAST EVENTS AND MASTERS. Thus by a repetition of such events, the past events are likely to re-occur - Cyclical Apocalypse?
b) High Initiates receive Orders from some Hierarchal earthly group either directly, or indirectly in the setting up of pre-determined groups or whilst asleep or in meditation and believe that to come from a higher source - Hidden Masters. The goals then are only known to those Hidden Masters and whilst high Initiates often do not fully understand the implications of the tasks set for them, they do it believing that the Order comes from a more knowledgeable being than themselves whose true purpose will be revealed to them. Either way this is a very dangerous and naive state of affairs and the simple question that has to be asked, is why release knowledge of The Grid in 'dribs' and 'drabs'? Why not release all the extremely advanced knowledge that MUST AND DOES EXIST in the field of sympathetic vibration? The answer of course is that whilst someone still holds the documents, the ancient texts, the ancient books, THE TONIC MUSICAL SCALES, SOUND SCALES, CELLULAR VIBRATIONAL SCALES, EMOTIONAL RESONANT BEHAVIOURAL SCALES ETC. there is still POWER to be had. When Ron Hubbard released *The Chart of Human Evaluation*, explained in his book *Survival*, he was applauded for a marvellous almost astounding discovery, but was the research his own? One cannot easily dismiss Hubbard's connections to the OTO secret group and its connections to the Rosicrucian's. The Church of Scientology was attacked viciously for 25 years, which saw just about every American Government agency in an all out attempt to destroy Scientolgy. It is extremely unlikely that the battle would have escalated to such proportions, if Hubbard had not either released some aspect of the hidden science independently, which no doubt the Church would claim, *or* he may have released the highest echelons of knowledge of The Rosicrucian's? And thus precipitated the wrath of The Illuminati or the Rosicrucian's? Or was it all just set up? By those hidden

Masters who never reveal themselves. Certainly all attacks on Scientology were traced back to one location - Washington D.C.

Hubbard's chart, predicts behaviour, emotions attitudes and physical changes in hearing, sight etc. as the energy of the biofield, or Life Force increases or decreases. The predictions are made into a scale and indeed, the Chart is highly workable and one of the most useful pieces of information, that you could ever hope to come across. However the basic and underlying principles of this chart exist in secret groups, where the Life Force, or energy, which emanates from the Source of all Life, possessing positive and negative polarity, manifests in vibrations of various rates of speed, which then follow natural laws. The vibratory character of the Life Force means that the opening and closing of the chakras, which govern mental, emotional and physical parameters, are entirely dependent on the rate of vibration of the Life Force. It operates through a system of harmonics by means of a Cosmic Keyboard of eighty octaves. Each octave represents a definite number of vibrations of Life Force, beginning with two vibrations per second for the first octave, and ending with trillions of vibrations per second for the last one.

Octaves constitute not only groups of notes, but also groups of manifestations, thus the behaviour and mental attitudes change accordingly. Thus the first ten octaves produce the sensation of feeling and hearing. The next octaves give different manifestations, and so on throughout the eighty octaves of the Cosmic Keyboard. Theoretically as I discussed in *Alternative 4,* by beaming a resonant wave at a body, you could open or close the corresponding chakras of the body and create different sensations, emotions or actions and mental attitudes. This I proposed would form the basis of any mind control programme and may have already been tested in illicit research, where it was passed off, as an alleged UFO experience. Pythagoras was initiated in Crete, after the Religious Revolution by the Idian Dactyls a group I associate with the priestly and Semitic cabal that stole significant knowledge including a cosmology and sympathetic vibratory knowledge whilst suppressing the belief in Re-incarnation. Pythagoras knew of this scale perhaps in more rudimentary form, however he noticed that certain pieces of music and harmonies had the ability to change behaviour. If you listen to some pieces of music they make you sad, others create elation; it is a matter of the effect of vibration on the Life Force resonant vibration. Diodorus quotes Cretan historians to the effect that the Dactyls made magical incantations that caused a great stir in Samothrace. They were also associated with the mysteries of smith-craft, and Diodorus identifies them with the Curetes, tutors of the infant Zeus and founders of Knossos. Thus was Hubbard's chart the results of his own research, or did he use secret group knowledge that had been researched over thousand of years? This is a very important question, however there is a policy of no questions asked (or tolerated) in Scientology, which in itself is symptomatic of Secret group policy. The fact that Hubbard's chart rests on prior knowledge, which has been suppressed and then utilised by a secret priesthood to impress man, seems to be an ongoing scenario.

The Great White Brotherhood is the school or Fraternity of the Great White Lodge and into theseINIVISIBLE Brotherhood of VISIBLE members the dedicated student of Rosicrucianism hopes to pass. Initiation then by Spiritual Masters whilst described as Cosmic Illumination or Cosmic Consciousness, is aimed at giving the Initiate HIGHER KNOWLEDGE USUALLY WHILST ASLEEP OR IN MEDITATION. Warning bells seem to go off, when I recall warning in *Alternative4*, of so-called healers who are currently advising people to listen! For their "Spiritual Guides" or those who are advanced in knowledge greater than themselves (*voices in your head*). Further these healers admit that they use a higher Intelligence in the process of their healing and "He" guides them (I am surprised women fall for this lark, but they do). It could be just another piece of substantial New Age insanity on planet Earth at best and at worst, one could say that healers are being churned out by a secret group who themselves are merely the dupes of a still higher power - possibly Illuminati whose true goal is not recognised; utilising secret knowledge on the hidden Science, in order to impress their devotees, whilst at the same time 'plugging ' them into the Grid, under the misconception that they are receiving information from a higher source. Further the High Initiates of these Orders could be nothing but dupes themselves to a goal of the so-called Invisible Masters, who in REALITY are nothing more than Initiates in the Secret group Hierarchy, who planned this scenario way down the line a couple of hundred or thousand years ago, to cue man up for those inevitable electronic signals (aimed at control or slavery). Alternatively and what I feel is more plausible, one could conclude that those who set this up (MRC case), **are the effect of the Grid** and seek subconsciously to make others the effect of it too. Either way anyone in his or her right mind would realise that you do not defer your own decision-making and thought process to something or someone else!

The last three degrees in Rosicrucianism and initiation into The Great White Brotherhood does prepare the Initiate, for the ultimate goal, which is not exoterically known. Madame Helena P. Blavatsky was evidently under a Master of The Great White Brotherhood and was guided by "HIM". As higher Initiates of the Rosicrucian Order admit, the great goal of the Great White Brotherhood is not known and they follow orders and methods as directed (no questions asked). Blavatsky was to form the Theosophical Society **in** New York in 1875.I have already alluded to the mysterious manner in which the secret group 'The Golden Dawn' was set up by Messrs Woodman, Westcott and Mathers who sought the mysterious Anna Sprengel. The founders of the group were advised to set up their own magical link with the Secret Chiefs, the mysterious "Third

Order", which was thought to be German, but may well have been a group in New York, the very group perhaps that Blavatsky was under. Secret Chiefs or Masters were typically described as those who watch over the affairs of men from their Caves in Tibet. The concept of Secret Chiefs or Mahatmas is of ancient Indian tradition. In recent times it was popularised under the name of Hidden Masters by Helena Petrovna Blavatsky and her Theosophical Society. These Hidden Masters (two of them are called Koot-Hoomi and Morya) are at the centre of her doctrine.

In the secret societies the lower orders were engaged on esoteric study, but it was only in the higher Orders or The Second Order and the Order of the Rosy Cross, where magical rites were conducted utilising the hidden science and Cabalistic ritual. The Second Order could not be created until contact was made with the Secret Chiefs. Blavatsky with Colonel Olcott set up a society to study magic and the evocation of spirits using certain geometrical formulae, which sounds very much like vibrating resonance of Grid information. Blavatsky wrote in 1875:"Olcott is now organizing the Theosophical Society in New York. It will be composed of learned occultists and cabbalists, of *hermetic* philosophers of the 19th Century, and of passionate antiquaries and Egyptologists generally. We want to make an experimental comparison between spiritualism and the magic of the ancients by following literally the instructions of the old Cabbalahs, both Jewish and Egyptian. I have for many years been studying Hermetic philosophy in theory and practice, an am every day coming to the conclusion that spiritualism in its physical manifestations is nothing but the Python of the ancients, or the astral, or starry, light of Paracelsus, i.e. the intangible ether which Reichenbach calls Od..."

Certainly here Blavatsky was referring to Grid Energies. The nature of the Theosophical Society's attempts to "make an experimental comparison between spiritualism and the magic of the ancients" is well conveyed by its member's endeavours to reproduce the **phenomenon of levitation.** If there was an attempt to study the electro-magnetic qualities of anti-gravity and the Grid properties, then clearly Blavatsky was considering such an inter-relation when she caused the unfortunate demise of a cat through electrocution, declaring that levitation was an electrical phenomenon. Blavatsky's book *Isis Unveiled*, which Olcott described as written on the basis of "visions seen in the astral light". Was channelled information from The Grid? I will cover channelling later, but briefly here, it is the pulling down of information imprinted on the Grid or Akashic Record, with events or thoughts of the past. "Her pen would be flying over the page, *when* she would suddenly stop, look into space with the vacant eye of the clairvoyant seer, shorten her vision so as to look at something held invisibly in the air before her, and begin copying on her paper what she saw. The quotation finished her eyes would resume their natural expression..." This is the exact description that a scientologist gave for the manner in which Ron Hubbard wrote his bulletins!

Isis Unveiled gave an impression of a secret knowledge previously available only to a few, but now about to be revealed to the world: The impression of timeless wisdom, of learning beyond the powers of ordinary men. Blavatsky described The Hidden Masters:

> "A lone handful of primitive men - in whom the spark of Divine Wisdom burnt bright, and only strengthened in its intensity as it got dimmer and dimmer with every age in those who turned to bad purposes- remained the elect custodians of the Mysteries revealed to mankind by the Divine Teachers. There were those among them who remained in their Kumaric (divine purity) conditions from the beginning; and tradition whispers, what the secret teachings affirm, **that these elect were the germ of Hierarchy, which has never died since that period**" [69] (*author's emphasis*).

This **undying Hierarchy, the Masters** - was to assume a considerable importance in Blavatsky's system, and it is interesting to note that it derives from the traditions of Western occultism, rather than from any Oriental source; for **the ancestors of the Theosophical Mahatmas were the 'Unknown Superiors' of eighteenth-century Templarism.** Blavatsky made it clear to her followers that she was only "a mere instrument of the Masters" whose chela (pupil) she had become on a visit to **Tibet.** Tibet of course was to be the place where it was claimed that the Rosicrucian Masters existed and initiated Jesus. A.P. Sinnett, who apparently received the answers to many questions from Blavatsky's so-called superiors, went on to write *Esoteric Buddhism, which* provided the first draft of the racist evolutionary system given a full exposition in Blavatsky's own *Secret Doctrine* (1888). This reminds one fully of the stated source of the so-called secret doctrine, which had descended it is claimed from the Patriarchs and **ADAM** through a successive line.

Even today in the field of the manipulated UFO phenomenon, I noted that there are attempts to try and connect UFO wisdom and messages, with racial Mongolian-types or the three men in black, who are described as having, slant Mongolian-type eyes. One UFO witness after having experienced a natural UFO phenomenon described how these three men came to her house in a rented car! The obvious inference is that unlike the natural UFO phenomenon, which is metaphysical, this was a blatant attempt to re-position the experience with higher wisdom, or the Masters. Such an action would not only confuse anyone who tried to seriously investigate UFO phenomena, but would also confuse the underlying science of the Grid, which is responsible for the phenomenon and which I described in *Alternative 4,* as *The Onion-Ring Model.* The important point is there has been a persistent attempt by these Masters to link higher knowledge with Tibet in Pre-history. There is also a racialist element, the old Aryan idea of a 'Super-Race' and the whole of racialist theory. This theory was strongly evident behind the events of World War II. The important point is that Theosophy had at its base a racialist-evolutionary system as outlined in *Esoteric Buddhism,* the *Secret Doctrine* and other Theosophical writings and importantly it is not recognised that Theosophy popularised the idea of a secret wisdom, available only to a few with its belief in a divine hierarchy, THE SECRET GOVERNMENT OF THE WORLD, AND ITS DOCTRINE THAT INDIVIDUAL HUMAN BEINGS ARE CAPABLE OF DEVELOPING INTO SUPERMEN. On the basis that the One World Order and Masters pre-determine the outcome of any group set up, Blavatsky obviously served her purpose.

The notion of super human powers, is a persuasive idea that runs through many secret groups, coupled with the promotion of will and ego, which as I have pointed out awakens Kundalini power, which leads to egotistical individuals whose belief generally centres on them being able to do no wrong. Secret groups are invariably arrogant in their belief of their own superiority and infallibility and thus the idea of 'supermen' is a limiting thought in many ways. The Theosophical version of evolutionary theory, on which was based its racial doctrines, was derived Blavatsky maintained, from the "oldest book in the world", *The Stanzas of Dzyan.* It was supplied to her by her Masters and while no-one but they and she have ever actually seen this volume, we know a little of what it looks like from her description of it:" An Archaic Manuscript - a collection of palm leaves made impermeable to water, fire, and air, by some specific unknown process - is before the writer's eye. On the first page is an immaculate white disk within a dull background. On the following page, that same disk, but with a central point...." This sounds very much like the most secret sign of the Illuminati, which was a circle, with a dot in it.

The back-ground to Blavatsky's root race system was given in *Alternative 4,* it is not a system that can be fitted with Science and was behind one of the tragedies of our times - The Holocaust.

What madness do I have to relate to you next? - You may quiver in horror of expectation! However it was reported in *The Daily Mail (Dec. 24th 1999)* - *Genetic horror of the glowing monkey*; that the world's first monkey to be given genes from another species has been born. George the monkey may look like any other rhesus monkey, but his DNA has been fused with a gene taken from a **jellyfish**, which gives it a fluorescent glow. George was born at Oregon Health Sciences University, where scientists want to create genetically modified strains of monkeys and apes for research into diseases such as Alzheimer's, cystic fibrosis, diabetes and muscular dystrophy. Although it is explained that the gene, which makes jellyfish fluorescent, was used because it provides dramatic visible proof (presumably poor George will glow), if successfully transferred to another species. The tired old cliché for inflicting this horror on experimental animals, is given by Dr. Schatten who published his findings in the *Journal of Molecular Human Reproduction*: "When you think of their value as a disease model or for understanding mental disorders or all sorts of diseases, that appear in people, this is a very small but significant step". Professor Steve Jones, of University College London, said the possibility of genetically engineering humans had been growing since the early 1980's.Significantly the role of the mind in psychosomatic illness and cancer has yet to be revealed (although known) and the fact that all diseased tissues and cells show irregular resonance when compared to their healthy controls, means that you could theoretically alter the resonance to the healthy state. This however would mean revealing the hidden science. Meanwhile poor old George is just another casualty to the Chemical Syndicate (Appendix 1), at best and at worst he is the victim of someone's dramatization.

As I read this new horror, I ask myself whether this is not more research engineered by that ever present secret Hierarchy, that utilise academia for questions they wish to pursue on their eternal secret doctrines, in the same way that Nazi scientists used concentration camp victims to test their Aryan Super-Race theories. According to Blavatsky's Root Race doctrine, the third Root Race were the inhabitants of Lemuria, a "gigantic Continent, which stretched from the Indian ocean to Australia", but which has now "Wholly disappeared beneath the waters of the Pacific, leaving here and there some of its highland tops which are now islands". The original Lemurians were a sort of **ape-like jellyfish**, later sub-races evolved into vaguely human giants - brown-skinned, fifteen feet tall, eyes so far apart that their owners could see side-ways as well as forwards, and with contorted limbs that could not be completely straightened. The mention of giants' leads us back to the proposal that I made of some form of Magnetic Reversal, where-bye the MRC case had to occupy an Amphibian body. However

Blavatsky makes no attempt to explain such theory in terms of science or geological world events. Further since Blavatsky obviously channelled her information from the Grid, it is likely that if such creatures did exist, that it may have been in a period prior to a magnetic reversal, when gravity was at a different level. Without dwelling too much on this doctrine of Blavatsky's apparently the Lemurians bred Monsters "going on all fours". This is given by Blavatsky to explain the existence of inferior races, not truly human, which was to rise as a doctrine in the events surrounding The Holocaust. This "monster" on all fours seriously reminds one, of the Palaeolithic cave paintings of Tres-Freres, in France where a shaman being, has a similar quality *(Plate 8)*.

The Lemurians in the procreation of semi-animals was to illicit "the fall" - the entry of sin and violence into the world. The Lemurians then appealed for aid to those whom Blavatsky called "the higher gods"; and "the wise Serpents and Dragons of Light came, and the precursors of the Enlightened. Divine Kings descended and taught men sciences and arts, for man could live no longer in the first land which had turned into a white frozen corps"'. Evidently then this was in some ice age. These divine Kings were natives of the planet Venus - or perhaps of an astral planet of which the physical Venus of the astronomers is a mere reflection- and are usually referred to as 'the Lords of Flame'; it was they who made the Lemurians capable of **individual reincarnation and immortality (previously they had only a collective survival after bodily death)** and taught mankind agriculture, the use of metals and weaving.

Before I give you an anchor into reality here, let us complete this story by mentioning that according to Blavatsky's theories at the end of the Age of Reptiles - that is about 70 000 000 years ago - the Lemurian continent began to break up and a fourth Root race, **the Atlanteans**, came into existence on a Lemurian peninsula situated at a point which is now the middle of the Atlantic. This peninsula became the nucleus of a new continent "formed by the coalescence of many islands and peninsulas which were up heaved in the ordinary course of time". Blavatsky goes into the sub-races of the Atlanteans and introduces the Toltecs, who were a civilized people according to her doctrines. They were the discoverers of the principle of hereditary rule and their Kings - guided by superhuman Masters - ruled as enlightened despots. After 100 000 years or so of this happy existence, some Toltecs began to misuse the occult sciences in order to gain personal power and wealth, and sex-worship became widespread. Under the leadership of a brotherhood of black magicians a section of the population overthrew the rule of the initiate King, replacing them with demon monarchs who created elemental spirits whom they and their followers worshipped with orgasmic and blood rites. Somewhere about 800 000 BC most of that part of Atlantis ruled by the Toltec sorcerer kings sank beneath the waves, destroyed by the angry gods, thus reducing the former continent to no more than a large island.

As the result of another great inrush of the sea, roughly 200 000 years ago, Atlantis was split into two islands, both ruled by dynasties of black magicians. Before this catastrophe however, white priest-magicians had led the most virtuous section of the people to Egypt, where they built pyramids. Meanwhile the more cultured of the cruel Turanians had immigrated to Asia where they evolved into the seventh sub-race, the Mongolians, represented by the present-day Chinese. The fifth sub-race, the Semites - who are not to be confused with the Semitic peoples of modern times, came into existence. They engaged in warfare with the Akkadians (Arcadians?), the sixth sub-race - a cultured people whose main activities were trading and colonizing. Great sailors, the Akkadians settled most of the Mediterranean lands, their remote descendents being the Basques. In spite of their unpleasantly quarrelsome natures, the Semites were possessed of remarkable intellectual powers and sensing the importance of these, the Divine Teachers of humanity led the most spiritually advanced of the Semites into Asia where they developed into the fifth Root Race, the Aryans, who so far Blavatsky maintained were the summit of evolution. As for the Jews, they too are descended from the Semites, but there is "something sinister about them"; they "constitute an abnormal and unnatural link between the Fourth and Fifth Root races".

These Theosophical and racial doctrines have been absorbed into the general body of western occultism, they are to be found in the writings of such magicians as Dion Fortune and Aleister Crowley, in the lectures of Rudolf Steiner, who developed them to more extra-ordinary lengths and in the supposedly scientific theories of Edgar Daque, which is where Hitler contacted them, if not through the secret Orders who initiated him into secret doctrine. Such doctrine was behind the extinction of the Tasmanian aborigines, and Otto Ohlendorf the Theosophist commanded one of the extermination squads of the SS and in just six months allegedly murdered 92 000 people. The fact that the Jews, who despite their power in Hollywood have never chosen to tell the full story, is really a reflection of the Cabalistic knowledge that exists at the top of all secret societies and whilst one perceives that the inevitable introduction of 'Holocaust Day' will seek to make people remember what was done to the Jews, there will be no attempt made to outline what the Cabalistic doctrine has done to humanity including the Jewish people themselves.

The fact that Blavatsky and the Theosophical Society were really dealing in Grid information in their treatise on the pre-history of man, was emphasised by Blavastky when she stated: "An impenetrable veil of secrecy, was thrown over the occult and religious mysteries... lest they should be shared by the unworthy and so desecrated". This in itself is a highly arrogant statement. Elsewhere she stated that the knowledge of practical occultism must be kept secret from the crowd because it may be used to control others. However not only did she have a distorted view of pre-history, but in the act of secrecy, it would inevitably be used by those so-called Hidden Masters, that she willingly admitted was the source of her information. A point echoed by Darre, Hitler's Agricultural Minister and an advocate of a blood and -soil peasant mysticism, "It is not ", he said "until knowledge recovers its character of **secret science** and is again **no longer available to all,** that it can again exercise its normal function, the means of **ruling** human and non-human nature" (*Author's emphasis*). In that statement you have the very essence of what we fight as moral human beings.

Whilst Blavatsky professed to have been initiated into certain esoteric doctrines in Tibet, she arrived in New York to set up The Theosophical Society after being directed by her Hidden Masters or concealed superiors on the Continent of **Europe** and one suspects that the Hidden Masters were really that group who had sequestered the mysteries from Crete, where they were given openly. The Masters in actuality who held the Secret Doctrine, descended from the Patriarchs and Adam. Monsieur Guenon stated:
"What is very significant...is that Madame Blavatsky in 1875 wrote this: I have been sent from Paris to America in order to verify phenomena and their reality and to show the deception of the Spiritualist theory". Sent by whom? Later she will say: by the 'Mahatmas'; but it was in **Paris** that she received **her mission**, and not in India or in Tibet" (*Author's emphasis*). In *The Battle of The Trees*, I described a group The Prieuré de Sion, which held the number thirteen in high esteem, which I associate here with Rosicrucianism and the hidden science and it could well be the group, which initiated Madame Blavatsky, a group that held Secret Doctrine which had originated with Adam.

Monsieur Guenon concluded that in the background of Theosophy there existed a mysterious centre of direction, that Madame Blavatsky was simply "an instrument in the hands of individuals or occult groups sheltering behind her personality" and that "those who believe **she invented everything by herself and on her own initiative, are as much mistaken** as those who, on the contrary, believe her affirmations concerning her relations with the pretended Mahatmas". In deciding who exactly was behind Blavatsky one must look at her account of Christ: "For me, Jesus Christ, that is to say the Man-God of the Christians, copy of the Avatars of all countries, of the Hindu Krishna as of the Egyptian Horus, was never a historical personage. Hence the story of His life was merely an allegory founded on the existence of a personage named Jehoshua born at Lud. But elsewhere she asserted that Jesus might have lived during the Christian era or a century earlier "as the Sepher Toldoth Jehoshua indicates". Thus there is every indication that Madame Blavatsky's Masters were Cabalists and she has been given the Toldot Yeshu story of Jesus. To support this legend she stated:" It is our Masters who affirm it". Thus her Masters were not some Trans-Himalayan Brotherhood, but a strong Judaic influence which appears more strongly in a book published by the Theosophical Society in 1903; where the Talmud and the Toledot Yeshu are quoted at great length and the Christians are derided for resenting the attacks on their faith contained in these books, whilst the Jews are presented as innocent, persecuted victims. "The Christ (said the mystics) was born "of a virgin" the unwitting believer in Jesus as the historical Messiah in the exclusive Jewish sense, and in his being the Son of God, nay God Himself, in course of time asserted that Mary was that virgin; whereupon Rabbinical logic, which in this case was simple and common logic, met this extravagance by the natural retort that, seeing that his paternity was unacknowledged, Jesus was therefore, illegitimate, a bastard". I am afraid that Blavatsky's Masters were economical with the truth that they gave her, for Jesus did exist and he was not a "bastard", but fostered which I will cover later.

This story derives from Jewish Cabalists, thus not only did the inner circles of Theosophy contain Cabalistic magical practise utilising the hidden science, but there was also significant doctrine on The Toledot Yeshu story of Jesus. Mrs. Annie Besant another hierarchal Theosophist endorsed the Toledot Yeshu story and in her book *Esoteric Christianity she* related that Jesus was brought up amongst the Essenes, and that later He went to Egypt, where He became an initiate of the great esoteric lodge - that is to say, the Great White Lodge - *from which all great religions derive*. This then was the old story of the Talmudists and Cabalists, perpetuated by the Gnostics, the Rosicrucian's, and the nineteenth-century Ordre du Temple. When The Theosophists spoke of the coming of Christ, they did not mean the Christ of the Gospels, since they claim that the Christ of the Gospels never existed, but was an invention of the monks of the second century. The Theosophists believed that Jesus and "the Christ" are two separate and distinct individualities, and when they spoke of "the Christ" they referred to someone living in a bungalow in the Himalayas with whom Mr. Leadbeater a prominent Theosophist had arranged interviews concerning his approaching event. Towards this end Mr. Leadbeater and J. Krishnamurti in 1911 founded "The Star in the East" Order to prepare the world for the coming of the Great Teacher. Well one important fact emerges from this discourse, which is that Jesus allegedly had links to the Great White Brotherhood and Lodge, who are directly linked to the Rosicrucian's, the group not only linked indirectly to Ron Hubbard, but to the Religious Revolution in Crete!

In fact Theosophy was a secret Order in so far as it was composed of inner and outer circles, the former being controlled absolutely by supreme directors. The inner circle, known as the Esoteric Section, or rather the Eastern School of Theosophy, also consisted of three inner circles, the innermost composed of the

183

Mahatmas or Masters of the White Lodge, the second of the Accepted Pupil or Initiates, and the third of the Learners or ordinary members. There is no doubt in my mind, that whilst even Madame Blavatsky as an inner Initiate was given The Toledot Yeshu story of Jesus, the highest Hidden Masters, the Supreme Directors had an entirely different story of Jesus, one comparable to my own witness account. Thus even higher initiates like Leadbeater, Blavatsky and Besant, did not have access to the true secrets. Dr. Weller van Hook who is said to have been a Rosicrucian and an important member of the Grand Orient (who played an infamous role in The French Revolution) once cryptically observed that "**Theosophy is not the hierarchy**", implying that it was only" **part of a world-organization"**, darkly hinting that if it did not carry the work *allotted* to it, the "**Rosicrucian's would take control"**. Thus the Hidden Chiefs appear to be not the Masters in Tibet, but the Rosicrucian's, the only group with sufficient knowledge in the hidden science, to set up these groups and the group to which Theosophists, Anthroposophists, Jesus and Ron Hubbard were directly or indirectly attached. It is interesting to reflect on the ideas that Theosophy imparted, the idea of superhuman abilities and observance of instructions and masters. Scientology of course promotes the former idea and has a great many red tape rules and regulations and is run along naval or military style. It may well have been the case then, that not only was Rosicrucianism the controlling group of Theosophy, but that group may have also controlled Anthroposophy (Rudolf Steiner's group) certainly as I have pointed out "The Akashic Record" is proof of knowledge of the hidden science and one cannot be sure but perhaps Ron Hubbard either based his work on Rosicrucian knowledge and was then fought or he worked for a higher Order for the purpose of creating a Universal Religion. Which is it to be? Or are the Scientologists still going to persist in the view that Hubbard was a Messiah- genius? Because from where I sit I have to say I have seen it all before on the track of time.

Let me clear up one miss-understanding here, there has been a virtual identity of outlook between the radical Right and the occult counter-culture. Extreme right-wing politicians and esoteric occultists share both a profound hostility to the Christian ethic and a conviction that human beings are essentially unequal in value to one another. The deep hatred of esoteric doctrine for all churches whether Protestant, Catholic or Orthodox, which includes the historical person of Jesus, whom the Templars reviled, by spitting on the Cross and calling Him "The thief on the Cross", rests upon an esoteric doctrine and *proof* via historical record that Jesus had an entirely different background to the one proposed in the Gospels. A secret body of knowledge exists (whose proof is verified by historical documentation) comparable to that given in the Nag Haamadi Scrolls (Dead Sea Scrolls), for the life and times of Jesus. Until the entire truth of The Crucifixion is known, there will be, as the Magdalene prophesied "no peace on Earth". If I have stated that Jesus stole her secret doctrine, then it is **not** comparable with Blavatsky's doctrine and the Jewish legends of the Middle Ages (Toledot Yeshu) according to which the Virgin Mary was a loose woman, Jesus her bastard child by an unknown father, and the New Testament miracles achieved as the result of magical powers Jesus had acquired by stealing a scroll from the Temple, which may form the Secret Doctrine. More is it that there is a whole story here given in part by The Dead Sea Scrolls that has not been told, despite the fact that the scrolls are of comparable antiquity to the Gospels. Why include the Gospels and not the Dead Sea Scrolls? In Biblical texts and why were The Dead Sea Scrolls withheld from the public for so long with many scrolls not yet divulged? It is not as some supposed that there could be no acceptance of a great spiritual leader and teacher who was to be a Jewish Redeemer, and not the fair-haired and blue-eyed Redeemer of the Super-Race, more was it a continuing battle of man versus woman, Holly and Oak and the secret doctrine of Reincarnation. However there are subsequent attempts to link Jesus with Hidden Masters, Tibet and the Aryan super-race, which only seeks to confuse the true story of The Holy Grail and Reincarnation dating back to Bronze-age Greece and the mysteries I revealed surrounding Reincarnation.

THE HOLY LAND OF SCOTLAND

I have queried whether the Druids were behind the events of the Religious Revolution in Crete 1 400 BC as descendents of a higher Rosicrucian Order today, presumably the Rose-Croix level of Freemasonry or The Great White Brotherhood. Assuming that the Druids were a descendent group of the Rosicrucian's, then were the Druids in fact behind the events and plan of Golgotha? Barry Dunford who wrote an exceptional but slim volume, which I have credited at the beginning of this book as one of the most important books I have read[71] and in his book he maintained that Scotland in the U.K., was the real Holy Land and drew attention to the following: "In many respects Scotland is a chosen land; there is a Greek tradition that Abaris was a Caledonian, and visited Greece in the days of her early mysteries, and brought to the Druids and others some knowledge of the Ancient Wisdom.... Furthermore, many of the traditions are steeped in ancient lore, derived from the dim past, and even from Atlantean days. Some of the sacred spots seem still to be alive with the spirit of the old gods and initiates.... let Scotland prepare the way of the Lords of wisdom" (*Theosophy in Scotland -August 1910*).

Barry states: "This story revolves around the coming to the British Isles of Joseph of Arimathea and Lazarus (John) on a secret Essene mission after the crucifixion and escape of the historical figure known as Jesus, the Nazarite. With them was a small band of relatives including several women initiates. It is possible this small group came to Scotland, to a place now known as Fortingall where is to be found a very ancient yew tree. Here, a monastic settlement may have been established for the dissemination of an ancient mystery tradition centred on the Christ teaching. This could have formed the basis of a Johannine Grail Church which incorporated the mystery teaching of St. John the Evangelist, in the guise of Lazarus and who may also have previously been 'John the Baptist'...".

In my own witness account (taken from past life regression), I stated that John the Evangelist, was with the Mary Magdalene before she was murdered by a raiding party in France with her unborn child from John (The Evangelist) and her other child from Jesus, who was taken presumably after the raid of her settlement; where she was teaching the Holy Grail Wisdom in Healing – Reincarnation and utilising what became known as secret doctrine. What happened to John and the Jesus child after the raid? Did they return to Scotland and what part did John play in this raid? Thus there is certain corroborative evidence here. The need to define clearly the events of Golgotha where I claim a **whole Cosmology as well as a belief in Re-incarnation was lost to a Patriarchal group** echoes the need to define clearly the group who was behind the Religious Revolution in Crete 1400 BC where once again a whole Cosmology and the belief in Reincarnation was lost to a Patriarchal group, and thus the two events have similarities. I have previously alluded to the *Semitic* group who introduced pillar worship in Crete after the Religious Revolution and the Dactyls who may be synonymous with that group who caused a stir by using vibratory knowledge and are intimately tied in myth with the birth of Zeus and power in the Western world. Icons of the Serofitic Tree of Life and Cabalistic doctrine also accompanied pillar worship. Icons of boats were found in the Pschro cave, the mythical birthplace of Zeus not far from the Knossos site, along with cauldron icons. The boat indicates that belief in an after life, but not on Earth was part of the Cabal's belief system, thus replacing The Cycle of Eternal Return and Re-incarnation. Sacred trees were introduced, as can be deduced from Archaeological finds, which parallel the use of the Tree Alphabet, which I used to decode many mysteries surrounding the Holy Grail in *The Battle of The Trees*. There was also the question of the Armillary a device for accurately measuring the Solar-Lunar Cycles, which must have been required to construct the Solar-Lunar Calendar of Knossos. The Druids certainly paid great attention to the Solar-Lunar cycles in the construction of their Henges, the most important one being at Stonehenge on the plain of Salisbury in the U.K. The introduction of opium (the Poppy Goddesses), begs the question whether the Cabal used that drug to promote sleep, whilst laying in their suggestions to initiates who would then become slaves to their masters, imposing their will on the people. Certainly there is a great deal of difference between Early and Late Minoan times (post Religious Revolution), where the joy of life and colours of the frescoes depicting the Cycle of Eternal Return, were replaced by stilted figures and where art declined and war-like instruments evolved, marking the decline of a peace loving and great civilization. This led me to formulate an important datum: 'Before the decline in any civilization can occur, an occult and secret presence is working within that society'. I see this process in Britain, America and many other countries. The MRC case not only works to destroy countries but groups – *from within*!

Barry Dunford cites numerous references to support the conclusion that a mission involving Joseph of Arimathea and John The Evangelist came to Britain *after* the events at Golgotha. I posed the question in my own witness account, of whether John the Evangelist betrayed the Mary Magdalene. Freculphus[72] stated certain friends and disciples of: "our Lord, in the persecution that followed his Ascension, found refuge in Britain in A.D. 37." He further states that Joseph of Arimathea and his company, including Lazarus (John The Evangelist), Mary, Martha, Marcella and Maximin came to Britain at the **invitation of certain Druids of high rank**. According to Eusebius of Ceasarea (c. A.D. 264-340), an ecclesiastical historian: "The Apostles passed beyond the ocean to the isles called the Britannic Isles". Further, Thomas Innes in his Civil and Ecclesiastical

187

History of Scotland quotes the Scots historian, George Buchanan, as saying: "the ancient Britons received Christianity from St. John's disciples by learned and pious monks of that age". Innes further quotes David Buchanan, another Scots writer, who remarks that: "those who came into our northern parts," i.e. Scotland, "and *first made known unto our fathers the mysteries* of heaven, were the disciples of St. John the Apostle" (My emphasis). Which reflects my own assertion that the knowledge did not belong to St. John or the Druids who were probably the descendants of the Rosicrucian's. David Buchanan states further that the Scots received "their tenets and rites", that is the doctrine and discipline of Christianity, "from their first apostles, disciples to St. John."[73]

Barry Dunford asserts through accumulative historical evidence that the Culdee's were the remnant Druids who had received their doctrine from St. John. Certainly in the Biblical story of Jesus being visited by "wise men from the east", in the *St. Matthew* text, is rendered in the |Irish version of the gospel as: "the Druids came from the east". Thus can we assume as I stated that from the very beginning, Jesus was chosen for a mission, which eventually saw a whole Cosmology and belief in Reincarnation dashed in the immense betrayal of the Mary Magdalene in the events of Golgotha which was **planned**, and further the Holy Grail was once again withdrawn, along with the truth, into a secret Patriarchal Priesthood: In the Old Testament, *Exodus vii. II* the "magicians of Egypt" are made "Druids of Egypt".

The Bethany group, who landed in Britain, was never referred to by the British priesthood as Christians, nor even later when the name was in common usage. They were called 'Culdees', as were the other disciples who later followed the Josephian mission into Britain. Thus they were in fact on Barry Dunford's evidence, non other than Druids. In the ancient British Triads, Joseph and his twelve companions are all referred to as Culdees, as also are Paul, Peter, Lazarus (St.John), Simon Zelotes, Aristobulus and aothers. As Barry points out this is important since the name was not known outside Britain and therefore could only have been assigned to those who actually had **dwelt among** the British. Cymri.George F. Jowett[74] stated:" The astounding fact is that whereas the Sadducean Judeans were never familiar with the name of the Messiah, His name was known to the British long before the memorable event transpired in Golgotha's Hill. It was a name familiar on the lips of every Briton. The indisputable fact is that the Druids proclaimed the name first to the world. How the Druidic Priesthood knew the consecrated name so long beforehand is indeed a mystery in itself. The name 'Yesu' was incorporated in the Druidic Trinity as the Godhead. In Britain the name Jesus never assumed its Greek or Latin form, I was always the pure Celtic 'Yesu'. It never changed". One can conclude the reason why the name was known in Britain, is that the events of Jerusalem was planned from there.

188

With regard to the stone pillars that occurred in Cretan iconography after I would propose the Religious Revolution circa 1400BC it is interesting to note that whilst pillar worship was of Semitic origin, Brigadier George Wilson in *Co-incidences -Pointers to our Heritage* makes the observation: "Contrary to the propaganda assiduously perpetuated by the Church of Rome and others, there is very strong evidence that the Druids were highly cultured and were of **Israelite** origin. Their language had a basic similarity to Hebrew (syntax as well as vocabulary) and they NEVER opposed Christianity when it was brought to them. Caswell's History of England states: "Druidical rites and ceremonies were almost identical with **Mosaic** ritual", also: "the Chief (Arch) Druid and the Israelite High Priest were similarly arrayed - even to the Breast Plate of Judgement with the twelve stones representing the Tribes of Israel and the Holy Name on the headgear". Charles Hulbert (AD 1825) in his *Religions of Britain* writes: "so near is the resemblance between the Druidical religion in Britain and the Patriarchal religion of the Hebrews that we would hesitate not to pronounce their origin the **SAME** " (*emphasis supplied*). Thus the Druids were not only Israelites, but had some connection not only to the Religious Revolution in Crete, but the events of Golgotha and in both cases Re-incarnation as a belief was buried in the Grail Underground Stream (of wisdom). As Jesus said he had come: "to destroy the works of the female" (Re-incarnation). Further in his quote from the Alexandrian text, Jesus appeared to hold hermetic philosophy dating back to Crete at the time of the Religious Revolution.

From The British Isles then according to Isabel Hill Elder, the author of *Celt, Druid and Culdee*, the mission that arrived in Scotland set into motion a plan to **Christianise the whole world**: "They acquired great missionary zeal and great numbers of them went forth as missionaries and Christianised the whole of Europe from Iceland to the Danube. This is a fact of history, which has been **diligently suppressed**, but it is a fact, which cannot be denied. The plan of Golgotha was a Universal Religious Kingdom based on Christianity, whilst retaining the true secret doctrine (Re-incarnation) for the elite who utilised it symbolically in their Freemasonry rites. It is remarkable that while the Church of Rome was sending her Emissaries to 'Christianise' the Saxon, the Celtic Church was sending her missionaries to convey the Gospel of salvation to France". Here then you have the entire goal of the plan of Golgotha, a Universal Religious Kingdom, which as a plan, always existed as part of the One World Order goal, the other goal was a Communistic Political Kingdom, run by a Theocratic initiated Priesthood descended from Adam, who held the Cabalistic Science. They took the Holy Grail message and Cosmology from Crete and from this date of the Religious Revolution withheld the Holy Grail from humanity. That such an aproned priesthood is behind European Union I have no doubt.

Not only was Jesus initiated into the secret Alphabets, but also he had knowledge of the Grid and healing methodology. Evidently whilst the mysteries had been openly given to all on the Island of Crete prior to The Religious Revolution, afterwards the Semitic or Druidical Priesthood that organised and executed a plan I would maintain for secreting away the mysteries hid them. The Cosmology and ancient belief in Reincarnation was not to be shared with the "ignorant" or the "profane" a point verified by Blavatsky, who founded Theosophy and was one their emissaries. The mysteries were to be only open to high Initiates and USED AS A SOURCE OF POWER. Christianity was to become the World Religion, jealously stamping out any dissident views and indeed sequestering all final documents on the truth, which was the basis of the mystery of Rennes le-Château and my own past life recounted in the first chapter of *The Battle of The* Trees.

According to the Rev. W. Morgan in *St Paul in Britain*: "Lazarus is asserted to have accompanied Joseph, the only record we possess of him beyond the Scripture narrative is in a very ancient British Triad. It is difficult to explain how the name and counsel of Lazarus could find their way into these peculiarly British memorials except by his presence and teaching in Britain." [75] According to Barry Dunford: "As for the possible connection between John the Baptist, Lazarus and John the Evangelist, it appears that these three key historical figures may relate to the same soul channel in order to secure the continuity of the purity of the Christos Gospel Teaching. Lazarus being 'raised up' in the cave suggests an esoteric mystery initiation. However it sound remarkably like a Freemasonry ritual and the symbolic raising up as Re-incarnation, or re-birth which as I have recounted is very much still a part of Masonic ritual today and refers back to Crete. According to Rudolf Steiner (1861-1925), when Jesus raised up Lazarus, John the Baptist returned to dwell in the body of Lazarus and subsequently he became known as St. John the Divine, author of the Fourth Gospel and the Revelation. The implication is that "he whom the Lord loved" was both Lazarus and John. The dual identity of Lazarus and St. John is confirmed by the researches of Robert Eisler: "The whole story is told in the Fourth Gospel as clearly as it could be done without immodesty by him 'who wrote that', i.e. by Lazarus himself whose account the Evangelist professes to 'know to be true'. Lazarus is dead, but John is very much alive. It is he who adds his witness to the testimony of the dead man, whose witness 'he knows to be true".

When I stated in my research that the elite to enter significant bodylines, thus perpetuating the plan that had been instigated at Knossos for World Power, was USING Re-incarnation here we have some corroboration of that. Today Freemasons know this and concern themselves over Reincarnation. One could leave a life with a purpose and Reincarnate specifically into a genetic line that would further that purpose (good or bad). Further whilst some may have thought the idea of the MRC case commanding the body of an Amphibian after a geological disaster (Magnetic Reversal) far fetched, this is no more strange than the soul of St. John commanding the body of Lazarus. As Barry Dunford points out:" the 'John' entity later incarnated as Taliesin, the sixth century Bardic teacher and poet and may have incarnated as Merlin the magician of Arthurian fame". Interestingly, in her work entitled *Merlin*, Professor Norma Lorre Goodrich finds distinct parallels between the lives of the Arthurian Merlin and John the Baptist, Professor Goodrich further connects the Arthurian Merlin with the Isle of Whithorn in South West Scotland.

In her classic study on Celtic mythology and folklore, *The Flaming Door*, Eleanor C. Merry states: "The number Three is continually met with in Druidism and especially in the whole theology of the Bards." Whilst this has been interpreted as the Trinitarian conception of Divine rulership, with the word 'Druid' also derived from 'three', it may have also referred to the basic unit triangle and the 'Law of Three' relating to the UVG 120 Grid structure. It may be that lower initiates were tutored in the Trinity, whilst higher initiates were tutored in Cabalistic knowledge relating to the Grid. Certainly the Culdees, who were the last remains of the Druids, were Pythagorean Druidical monks. The Law of Three also incorporates Hermes, who evolved after the Religious Revolution, as a method of combining the Goddess (whose gift was Immortality), to the Twin Kings whose Immortality was through her. This is not merely a mythical point it is a point of truth and the *origin* of a gift and mission that has not been recognised. The moral of the story is that you cannot steal a gift and present it as your own. Neither could one pass the Grid (the trap) unless one could as-is (as it is) the truth, but I will return to this point later.

E. Graham Howe, the author of *The Mind of the Druid*, stated that the Druids were known as the "men of the threes". Three men in black was a feature of the manipulated UFO phenomenon recounted in *Alternative 4*. Was this some in-the-know game by the elite? A bit of fun whilst the Masters amused themselves with man's ignorance or was it was an effort to relate the UFO phenomenon back to the Druids and some ancient knowledge that the Druids perceived to be from a higher spiritual source or those Hidden Mongolian Masters of Blavatsky. This is curious in so far as at least one group who were manipulating the phenomenon were Jewish and perhaps now we can conclude were also Druids and Israelites! Fortingall, which was considered a special site by the ancient British Druid Magi, has three stone circles sighted below the 'crags'; the area at Fortingall which geographically is located at the centre of the Scottish mainland, may be the focus for a central 'Ley' energy vortex system, possibly indicating a planetary Chakra centre marked by a very ancient yew tree, which is considered to be the oldest in Europe, and which may be the oldest tree on the planet itself according to Barry Dunford. Certainly this indicates the whole of the Sefiritic Tree of Life, Cabala knowledge and since the yew tree is significantly split into two sections, has implications of Twin Kingship, dating back to the Religious Revolution in Crete c. 1`400 B.C.

J. Foster Forbes[76] stated: "They (the Druids) erected magnetic centres and constructed Pits known as Vortices in which they induced magnetism through their Auras (biofields): The influence so induced went deep down into the ground even to the Inner Magnetic Poles thereby making a fusion and thus veered the Earth round so that it came much nearer to the correct North as it is to-day; but still with this slight magnetic variation. By this connection the Druids were able to cast their observatories much more truly and from then onwards things went forward and ushered in the later Monastic Communities... which in themselves were meant originally to be Spiritual Vortices for the purification of the Earth's Aura, so that when the time was ripe the true Spiritual Powers should gain in volume and true impetus".

Eleanor Merry in *The Flaming Door* [77] gives another insight into the Brotherhood of the Rosy Cross and the mysterious figure of Christian Rosenkreuz by stating that Lazarus or St. John passed the mysteries into the Cymric race and the old Celtic mysteries were concealed and later through the missionary work of the Irish monks in middle Europe they met with the Johannine 'Gnostic' Christianity and gave rise in the fourteenth century, to the foundation of the secret school of Christian Rosenkreuz, the Brotherhood of the Rosy Cross, also called 'John Christians'. This Brotherhood adopted a certain symbol, a black cross, encircled by **seven red roses**. In its outer form it is similar to the encircled cross of Celtic origin. Merry maintains that cosmologically the roses represent the seven stages of the evolution, purification and ultimate resurrection of the Earth itself. Out of this there arose what became known in the ninth century as the Wisdom of the Grail, whose knights had the emblem of the Dove on their armour. To quote Merry:" And so there came about, in the fourteenth century, not only the ripe fruit of the meeting of these two aspects of the old Mysteries as the esoteric teaching of the Rose and the Cross, but in this secret Brotherhood all other aspects as well were drawn together to form **a nucleus of teaching which has survived beneath the surface of civilisation into our own time, and will be able to make itself known little by little**"(*Author's emphasis*). Here again then the Secret Doctrine of Adam supposedly but from Crete, which evidently was mixed with a secret doctrine from Adam and passed as Cabalistic science into the Druids and later presumably to the Rosicrucian's. The Masters exercising monopolistic control of the Grid, deeming what should and should not be made known to "the cattle" and at what price! Had the Holy Grail remained open in Crete and not sequestered by this group, I can assure you, that the world would have been a very different place than it is today, where despite their Cabalistic efforts, Dr. Becker twice nominated for a Nobel Prize, has stated that another Magnetic

Reversal has already started, which accounts for the loss of defined climatic seasons. Further not too shortly, I can also assure you that you will see many colours flickering in the sky, which as "a great sign", will herald the beginning of chaos and not I am afraid to say "Paradise".

There can be no greater sin or objection to the USE of this wisdom, which was once free and given openly to all in the beginning as a gift. The knowledge and truth was secreted away into these Patriarchal groups, who then decided how much and when such knowledge was to be released to humanity, however it was her gift to humanity and until that lesson is learnt and the humility to thank the Higher source that sent it, then man will consign himself to perpetual chaos.

A MATTER OF GAENOLOGIES

Why is it so important to identify what happened at Golgotha 2000 years ago? Why is it so important to identify what happened in Minoan Crete 1 400BC? As I pointed out in the initial pages of this document, it is essential to untangle completely the past in order to gain any control over the present and in order to control the future one must certainly control the present. Thus it is essential to know in detail not just how a whole philosophy and belief system in Minoan Crete was eradicated, but it is essential to form some idea of why a whole Cosmology and Science was hidden from man and withdrawn into secret groups. It is also essential to know the identity of the secret groups behind such covert behaviour and whether even in The Bronze Age such hidden science, cosmology and esoteric theology were removed for a political purpose by a Global Elite.

In my own account of the events at Golgotha as a witness of the time accessed through my **own** (Scientific) methods, being unable to trust anyone, or any group with my past time track (somewhat of a condemnation wouldn't you say?) I stated that as part of those events Jesus took the genealogies of the Magdalene. At the time this made no sense, since I personally was only aware (consciously or in actuality), of the Orthodox Christian account in The Bible. I took the courage to check the details of one past life, recounted in the first chapter of *The Battle of The Trees,* by returning to the location, which was not too distant from the place I was living in at the time in Britain. When the location turned out to be just as I had given in my past life memory, I recognised that at some unconscious level I had, for quite some time, been drawing closer to the location and furthermore my life from a very early age, was pulling me closer to resolving something I should have had the courage to face a long time before. In the attempt to act on my intuition (often guided by one's subconscious memory or past lives) I returned to Greece and the Alpha - the beginning, to draw back the dusty veil of time. I consciously invited the "Other World's" of Everett, I was finally ready to experience once again in a Cycle of Eternal Return, past lives which I had tried hard to forget! With my first book published in 1994 in Crete, I returned to England to write my second book and it was then, that I came across the work of Barry Dunford and his book[71], which was published in 1996 and in it, he gives a startling account of the **genealogies of the Jesus family**, deriving from Anna a member of the ancient **British Celtic Royal Household**. For the spiritual among you, you will realise that answers only come, when you have shown yourself worthy and in my own case not before I had suffered the traumas of a return to Crete. You will also remember, that I had in my own witness account in *The Battle of The Trees*, stated that Jesus had stolen the **genealogies** of the Magdalene. The Virgin Mary, St. John the Divine, John the

Baptist and Joseph of Arimathea, were all inter-related! *(Fig.26)*. Further they were linked through Anna to Caractacus who inherited the British Throne and thus the family was linked to the ancient British Royal Family. The current Royal Family - The Windsor's of course came from German ancestry and is not related to the ancient Royal British Dynasty, which may be significant, given that the "Third Order", was considered German. Certainly there were successful attempts to wipe out certain hereditary lines in Britain.

Fig.26 **The Pedigree of the Jesus Family** –Roll 33, Box 26 in The English College of Arms, the Herald's Office U.K. (B. Dunford –The Holy land of Scotland)

```
(Celtic Princess) ANNA married Joachim - brother of (Lord) Joseph of Arimathea
              |                    \                    |            |
Metallanus - sister  married  Bran      MARY        daughter Anna    son
(King at              (the Blessed)       |           married       married
Fortingall)              |             JESUS          brother of    British
   |              CARACTACUS           (Isa)          Caractacus     Princess
PONTIUS          (through his mother
PILATE?         inherited British Throne from Metallanus his uncle)
```

NB: According to ancient tradition, Bianca, the sister of Anna, was the grandmother of John the Baptist who later may have been St. John in the guise of "Lazarus".

Barry Dunford states that:" According to Cornish and Breton legend, Anna, a member of the ancient British Celtic Royal Household, was married to Joachim, the brother of Joseph of Arimathea and further, that she was the mother of the 'Virgin' Mary, mother of Jesus who therefore on his mother's side would have been Celt of British Royal descent and not 'Jewish' as is popularly surmised. This is confirmed by the Rev. Lionel S. Lewis in his book, *St. Joseph of Arimathea at Glastonbury* who states: "It will surprise most people to know that in the English College of Arms, the Heralds' Office, there is a pedigree of Christ and His relatives from **Adam** downwards. It is both in chart and narrative form. The pedigree of Our Lord's immediate family is startling. It is strange to find it there, it is Roll 33, Box 26" *(Author's emphasis)*. Thus are we to assume that Christ or Jesus was a Druid and that he belonged to a group, who had conducted the Religious Revolution in Crete, who now held the Cosmological secrets, along with the Holy Grail message of Re-incarnation, together with a plan to introduce a World Religion? If so, what can be surmised from my own witness account, that Jesus had stolen the *Magdalene's genealogies*? What was so important, about those genealogies?

If my account is to be believed, then it would require the acceptance that a plan emanated from Scotland under the control of the Essene/Druidic priests and this entire family, who betrayed the purpose of the Magdalene, removing her genealogies (which I suspect had a connection to Greece), without which she would be unable to fulfil her mission of attaining a position of power, in order to bring back truth to the people. Even if you were not prepared to accept my account, is it no evidential that the importance of the genealogies was stressed, when I contacted this past life *before* I went to Greece and *before* Barry Dunford had written his book. However what is certain is that a whole story behind Golgotha has been omitted **purposefully**. Since I perceive at least the **second** 'cut' (The Cutting of The Elm/ [arm] ceremony - *The Battle of The Trees)* is portrayed in the Crab Mural at Cardiff Castle Wales U.K. which signifies, the cutting of Magdalene's arm by Jesus at Golgotha which I witnessed, then this group whom I possibly identified as Rosicrucian's or Scottish Rite Freemasonry, must have further documentation (proof) of the events surrounding Golgotha, together with the story of the Jesus child I claimed was brought from France by St. John The Evangelist. This child may have been used to continue a dynastic line presumably from Adam on Jesus' side, but perhaps Greek on his mother's side (Magdalene). It is probably significant that legend has it that Magdalene went to Marseilles in France after the Crucifixion, which was a Greek colony. It is my contention that St. John was with her. (Incidentally the story for the **first** 'cut' is wrongly portrayed in the Crab Mural).

In all probability Jesus was a Druid, who sought to supplant a Jewish priesthood, that of Aaron with the Gentile priesthood of "Melchizedec"; and represented by the east station of the circle, the position occupied by Judah. When I decoded iconography including *The Grail Romances* connected to the history of The Holy Grail in *The Battle of The Trees*, using ancient alphabets, there was obviously an on-going propaganda battle between two opposing sides or secret groups, who were claiming rightful ownership of The Grail. In real terms one was a Cabalistic secret group claiming a 'holy lineage' from Joseph of Aramathea and specifically Judaic, indicating that this group was obsessed with blood lines and hereditary dating back one assumes, to a significant personage, if not Adam himself through Noah. This group was evident in Robert de Boron's *Grail Romance*: whilst the other secret group were not concerned with blood lines, but more at pains to point out that the means whereby one proves oneself worthy to carry The Grail, is more important than hereditary, which was evident in Wolfram's *Parzifal.* The World's stage and 'theatre' of political events, including wars, may yet prove to be the warring factions of two opposing ideologies. It is not hard to determine which country was the seat of power for the group, who believed WHO you are, is more important than WHAT you are, I live in this country and witness that every day, despite the grand words of politicians the philosophy is perpetuated by aristocracy and monarchy and an elite public school system based on an entrenched ideology dating back to the earliest times.

Hitler's loathing of Jews was very much tied up in this secret knowledge, with Hitler appearing as a Grail Knight (Parzifal's team), in one poster issued in 1936,which I reproduced in *The Battle of The Trees,* but which was withdrawn shortly afterwards. The Grail Romance – *Parzifal* spoke of knights in castles and is it not curious that the Headquarters of The Church of Scientology is a castle; was Ron Hubbard on Parzifal's team? - Having built that curious archetypal symbol of the womb – a Castle, at East Grinstead in the U.K. Curiously and co-incidentally? Utilising an Illuminatus-type Power Pyramidal Organisational system of management developed by Adam Weishaupt the founder of Illuminism, with the 'Knights' co-incidentally? In their sea/naval type uniforms, which is the standard dress for Scientology staff. Illuminism I have suggested was the political goal of a Universal Kingdom as Communism in tandem with the Rosicrucian goal of a Universal Religion. You might remember that my entire experience of Scientology was the sacrifice of the individual to the cause of group in what I considered a Communistic action, despite the apparent paradox of catering for those who have substantial funds to pay Scientology costs and therefore politically elitist and far right. If Hubbard had wanted to distance himself from secret group symbolism, then the architectural design of a castle for his UK headquarters was somewhat curious if not blatant. If Ron Hubbard experienced a great backlash organised from New York? Or at least by the proven source of Washington D.C. manifesting as a concerted effort by just about every American Government agency, was that attack orchestrated by those who clung to hereditary bloodlines and resented a release of the mysteries to the masses? Or was it from the 12 Tribes of Israel that other group in this cat and mouse game of 12 versus 13? Or is it just really the lame excuse that the Church of Scientology would maintain, the battle with psychiatry and vested interests in the battle for the mind? If Scientology really is Rosicrucian, then is it really such a wild claim by Phoenix, the breakaway Scientology group of the 80's after Hubbard lost control of The Church of Scientology, that M15 (British Intelligence) were responsible.

"Why?" asks Barry Dunford: "was the B'nai B'rith, a Zionist International Masonic Order, apparently weeding out from libraries in the USA, two books by Comyns Beaumont, a Scot, who wrote that Scotland was the true "Holy Land". As Barry points out: "the *New York Herald Tribune (January 14, 1947*), reported that: "an independent Jewish state in Palestine was the only certain method by which Zionists could acquire complete control and outright ownership of the proven Five Trillion Dollar (85,000,000,000,000) chemical and mineral wealth of the Dead Sea". Evidently though there is no wish for the hidden story of the events of Golgotha to be told, since the State of Israel has been claimed on

Biblical grounds, which would be negated if the truth came out. In the Old Testament Israel is often called 'the house of Joseph', in pointed distinction from 'the house of Judah'. The Jewish Encyclopaedia says, 'Joseph and Judah typify **two distinct lines of descent'** (*Author's emphasis*). Perhaps now, we are coming to the bottom of the Magdalene's genealogies and a marriage of Jesus and Magdalene would have united in one goal the house of Judah and Joseph, in what the Magdalene believed would be a return of the ancient mysteries to the people. Certainly this line of Judah appeared in iconography I decoded in *The Battle of The Trees*. Somewhere however in those genealogies, I strongly suspect a Greek influence. The Encyclopaedia Britannica says that Judaism developed long after the Israelites had merged themselves with mankind, and that the true relationship of the two peoples is best expressed in the phrase, "The Israelites **were not** Jews" (*Author's emphasis*). Thus we conclude that the Druids, who had connections to both Crete and Golgotha and the historical family of Jesus, practised Mosiac law, were probably hermetic philosophers after the Religious Revolution, were Semitic and derived a secret doctrine from Adam, which was mixed with the stolen knowledge from Crete, which ultimately conferred upon them power, which they sought to utilise in a plan for a World Order, both religious and political and which incorporated Christianity for the masses, whilst retaining a secret doctrine for the elite.

Douglas Reed in *The Controversy of Zion* stated:" The Chief Rabbi of the British Empire in 1918, the very Rev. J.H. Hertz, in answer to an enquiry...said explicitly, 'The people known at present as Jews are descendents of the tribes of Judah and Benjamin with a certain number of descendents of the tribe of Levi'. This statement makes perfectly clear that 'Israel' had no part in what has become Judaism...Therefore the use of the name 'Israel' by the Zionist state which was created in Palestine in this century is in the nature of a forgery". [78]

The Druids then I would propose may have been and probably were, behind the grand betrayal at Golgotha. Whether they were behind the Religious Revolution at Knossos in Crete can only be concluded on iconographic evidence, myth and legend and the historical reference quoted previously of their receipt of a secret doctrine from Greece. We know that Druidical rites and ceremonies were almost identical with Mosiac ritual and the Chief (Arch) Druid and the Israelite High Priest were similarly arrayed, even where the Breast Plate of Judgement with the twelve stones representing the Tribes of Israel was worn. Also, as I stated earlier the Druidical religion in Britain and the Patriarchal religion of the Hebrews had the same origins. We know that Pillar worship, which is typical of Semitic beliefs, was found in Knossos after the date 1 400BC and the date I propose a Religious Revolution occurred. We also know that the title and role of Messiah was specifically Druidical in origin. It is certainly curious that an icon of the classical period

(*Fig. 27*), a red-figured kylix, shows Pasiphae with the Minotaur as a child on her lap in Mother and Child pose. Pasiphae was the Mother of the Bull- Minotaur in myth of Cretan labyrinth fame. That the child was born in a symbolic sense from the labyrinth as womb is depicted by the hanging basket decorated with a *chequer pattern*, which is an archetypal variant motif for the maze or labyrinthine womb archetype. Moses was born in a basket, which archetypally depicted he was a Sun-King and the absence of a mother conveys that this is the first downgrade of the Early Minoan religion, the removal of the significance of the Mother goddess and **her gift to man** of the 'apples' of Immortality. The fact that Moses was found among *Reeds* signifies the archetypal symbol of Sovereignty. Co-incidentally at Knossos we find in later archaeological finds the 'Reed Vase' as further evidence of the influence of a Semitic group. Slowly then we see a penetrating Semitic influence at Knossos, corresponding to The Religious Revolution era circa 1 400 B.C. Icons displaying a Semitic Patriarchal belief system appear, whereby Semitic and Mosaic Law are displayed in archetypal symbolic form. Such religious significances, laws and archetypes were absent in earlier archaeological finds corresponding to the Early Minoan period. Further it was from the Teacher in Crete, that the invading Semitic group stole the idea of portraying a complex philosophical belief system, through these archetypes. Originally the idea of the swing, the tides and agriculture were used as archetypes for the philosophy of Rhea and: 'as I go, so must I return' (Re-incarnation). The idea of the dead buried on sea shell shells and in sand, representative of tides, in ellipsoid sarcophagi reminiscent of baths to convey the complex idea of curved space-time was all part of the open learning process of the Minoan people who had a very nice civilization going until the Semitic group invaded and stole the lot! The archetypes, which were part of the educational system for a whole philosophy and belief system including a cosmology, became the secret games for the elite and those in- the- know, to appear in the works of painters initiated into the secret doctrine. I noted recently (*Sunday Telegraph magazine 16 Sept. 2000*), that Anthony de Rothschild has found a young painter (Guy Hindley), who has left Lancashire for New York and who now uses Greek mythology, particularly fine linear drawings of the Labyrinth of King Minos (surprise, surprise!). Not only the Labyrinth, but pyramids and the Cabalistic Tree of Life are symbolically represented.

Co-incidentally at the time of The Religious Revolution, the Minoan Sea-Power was lost, the quality of art declined, drugs (opium) entered the society exemplified by the so-called *Poppy-goddesses* (in museum literature) and artefacts of war such as swords and helmets, which were hitherto not present, indicating a more aggressive and war-like attitude had become prevalent, in what had previously been a very peace-loving and open society. Were these parallel co-incidences merely the outward signs of decay of a society, which had become decadent? Or was this decline a planned result of removing a whole belief system and cosmological viewpoint from a Society, which Greek Historians acknowledge, was at one time open with its mysteries? So what happened here? Can it be just co-incidence too, that icons taken from the Psychro Cave on Crete and supposedly in myth the birth-place of Zeus (materialism), show boats indicating a belief in a life here-after but not on earth (as Re-incarnation teaches). Further some of the trappings of Cabalistic knowledge in the form of cauldrons and tripods were found. It is my considered opinion that the whole of the Knossos archaeological site must be re-evaluated, since there are far too many co-incidences of proof that a Religious Revolution occurred at this site. Further it would be justice to the Early Minoans who were subjected at the site of Latrus to the most horrible of deaths.

It is important to recognise what happened in Crete 1400BC, since a whole cosmology I know was lost, together with a whole belief system (Re-incarnation) and this I conclude happened **again** at Golgotha. Both events are clouded in historical and archaeological secrecy. Why for instance did the Cretan sarcophagus (burial urn) shape change? From an ellipsoid rim and flat-bottomed trapezoid, which may indicate curved space-time and the manner of Cyclical events (The Cycle of Eternal Return) where the dead were buried in the foetal position among sea-shells, awaiting rebirth, with goddess connected to the sea as tides and the Philosophy of Rhea 'as I go, so must I return'. The sarcophagus became the square shaped coffin we know today with its pillar like quality, indicative of Semitic origins and the square of the Beth-Luis Nion Alphabet, with celebrated the life and death of the demi-god Moses *(Plate 9)*. The Druids of course revered Mosaic Law

The myth of Theseus slaying the Bull-Minotaur in the Labyrinth, with the help of Ariadne, who gives him a ball of thread to find his way in and out again from the maze, is certainly a good story for students of Classical mythology to read, providing they understand the archetypes that are being used. Was it really a ball of thread? Or was it the umbilical cord of the new-born Sun-King in one sense, who is born from the Labyrinth which is both womb of the goddess and her Solar-Lunar Calendar, or is it that only with the use of the missing Cosmological link or thread to the Minoan Great Goddess that had been taken from the Minoans by a Semitic Patriarchal Religion, was it possible to defeat that group and their Solar King? (as Minotaur). Are the Cretan stones mentioned earlier, somewhat similar to the 'ball of thread'? The stones perhaps representing knowledge of a Cosmology and the geometry of the electro-magnetic Grid. Only perhaps through the golden Theseus thread, would it be possible to return to Knossos where a Patriarchal religion installed a Solar King and hereditary monarchy on Crete, with the introduction of stiff taxation laws, indicated by Linear A and B tablets found in Knossos where lists of goods indicate the second Plank of **Marxism** - taxation had been introduced. The Semitic source, which we have already defined as having a predilection towards hereditary monarchy, could well be the Druids.

The story told in the recovered iconography from the Knossos site in Crete, when placed in position with mythology, tells a completely different tale of events circa 1 400 B.C. than has been told before and compliments the history of the early Greek invasions. Robert Graves in *The White Goddess* stated that the first Greeks to invade Greece (prior to which there were only the true 'Greeks' or Pre-Hellenic Matriarchal tribes) were the Achaeans who broke into Thessaly about 1900 BC. They were patriarchal herdsmen and worshipped an Indo-European male trinity of gods, originally perhaps Mithra, Varuna and Indra, subsequently called Zeus, Poseidon and Hades. Little by little they conquered the whole of Greece and tried to destroy the semi-matriarchal Bronze Age civilization that they found there, but later compromised with it, accepted matrilineal succession (succession through the female line) and became devotees of the goddesses. However the Knossos site in Crete shows a very definite presence of INITIATED ADEPTS IN THE CABALA, which cannot be equated with a general patriarchal invasion. The re-positioning of the archetypes, so evident at the site is major evidence for such manipulation by a Cabal.

It is interesting that the Pelasgians or seafarers a mixed population on the mainland of Greece, claimed to be born from the teeth of the cosmic snake Orphion, whom the Great Goddess in her character of Eurynome had taken as her lover, thereby initiating the material Creation. This may have been a veiled truth of the Grid energies in the Matriarchal mysteries being taken over by a male Cabal. However the Achaeans who had occupied Argolis also took the name Danaans mimicking another group and also became seafarers, whilst those north of the Isthmus of Corinth were known as Ionians, children of the Cow-goddess Io. It is interesting that a Templar Church in Galway Scotland Great Britain, shows graffiti of a Trinity (pre Moses and Ezekiel) of Q're (Sun) Ashima (Moon) and Anatha (Ishtar) or the Cow-goddess, which is shown as a winged pyramid (*The Battle of The Trees*). The invasions of Greece certainly led to some of The Matriarchal tribes leaving and making their way to other lands.

In Keating's *History of Ireland*, he gives a very interesting story of **Feniusa Farsa** a grandson of **Magog** whose grandfather was **Noah**, who established a university near Athens. He was desirous of mastering the seventy-two languages created at the confusion of Babel and sent seventy-two persons to learn them. It seems that a tiered alphabet was created, which retained the secret mysteries in the higher tiers or initiated alphabets for the Priesthood, whilst creating 'lower' alphabets for soldiers and the "vulgar". Feniusa Farsa was also termed the "**vine-man who joins together**". It seems that under Foenius (Feniusa Farsa) were the Canaanites who are referred to in Greek myth as Agenor, who invaded Greece and drove the Tuatha de Danaan out of Greece. These were the old Matriarchal tribes. In

201

Genesis the original Canaanite empire is described as extending to Sodom and Gomorrah and in *Genesis XIV* the Canaanites were expelled in 2300B.C. The invasions of Greece are quite complicated, but it seems that very early on in the history of Greece, the Semitic invasions drove the Matriarchal Tribes or original Greeks, out of Greece and overran it, setting up a position of power in Athens. These invaders it would seem were the Canaanites.

Fig.27a **A red-figured kylix**. Pasiphae with the Minotaur as a child on her lap Compare with the Christian Madonna and a child. To the right, a basket and a goose (*Bibliotheque Nationale, Paris*).

Fig.27b **A red-figured vase from Nola**. Zeus as a vulture abducts the mountain-nymph Thalia. At the right, a basket with a checker-pattern and four spirals and above it, a ball of thread (Ariadne's golden ball of string given to Theseus in myth to find his way out of the maze after killing the bull-Minotaur). (*Formerly in the Hamilton collection*). Compair with Fig 4b.

The Canaanites were part of a Semitic invasion worshipping the Great Goddess under such titles as Belili or Danae and part of these invasions of Semitic origin, was a group whose chief religious emblem was the vine and these men invaded the Argos in the Peloponnese. I have already produced an icon (*Fig. 20*) showing that the archetypal symbol of the eye was depicted on the Minotaur in Argos, as the sign of a Sun-King. The eye today is an archetypal symbol used by the infamous group The Illuminati, who may well be the prominent group behind the One World Order and the eye appears on the One Dollar Bank note from America. Taking the alphabetic mystery above, which refers to the *number 72* in conjunction with the Canaanite invasion, it seems that Boibel-Loth and Beth-Luis Nion alphabets are indicated here and that 72 referred to the total composition number of letters in the alphabets. These alphabets were not only Semitic but when applied, as the Tree alphabet was Druidic! It might be inferred, that the Canaanites introduced Solar Kingship and the idea of a Messiah-like role for the Sun King: The icon, which showed the Minotaur in a Mother and Child like attitude on Pasiphae's lap (*Fig. 27*) is the classical prelude to the Nativity story of Jesus. What we do know, is that a dynasty of Solar Kings were introduced into the Peloponnese in Greece at Mycenae and Solar Kingship in the form of King Minos was introduced into Crete. It would be wrong to assume that no directing power lay behind this move to political power through solar-Kingship. That political power I assume is non other that Feniusa Farsa, the grandson of Magog, who was the grandson of Noah, who presumably in surviving the Flood, not only represented the descendent Adam, but also held the whole of Cabalistic science and the "Secret Doctrine" and further can be connected to the Druids in Britain who were Semitic Israelites but not apparently Jews i.e. the "Masters". Whilst it has been assumed that the Achaeans who broke into Thessaly about 1900 B.C. were part of two groups who sacked Knossos circa 1400BC, the iconography and mythical memory indicates that it was no rough herdsmen who overran Knossos, but a group of high Semitic initiates, who covertly changed a whole belief system and substituted quite cleverly, a whole new set of archetypal symbols overlaid onto prior Matriarchal symbols, thus removing the entire meaning. Alphabetic changes then locked these religious mysteries into the alphabets and in *The Battle of The Trees;* I spent quite some time, decoding the icons connected to The Holy Grail and this whole story of duplicity and deceit over the original Holy Grail message. The archetypal symbols were cleverly altered positioning them with the patriarchal religion and removing any meaning by stylising them, just as Picasso stated of his own art, where he sought the same process of "destroying reality". One should remember that people in the Bronze Age were not as sophisticated in language and concepts as they are now and the archetypes such as the swing icon (*Fig. 5*) easily portrayed as a concept Re-incarnation ('As I go so must I return'). By overlaying the archetypes with other significances and stylising them, the whole meaning was lost to man.

Thus whilst the History of invasions in Greece is complicated, one cannot discount the similaritybetween Druid beliefs and Semitic origins and a line of descent from Adam. Certainly there is no reason to suppose that there was no contact between

Druid Universities and the University set up at Athens to study and re-arrange the Alphabets, sea-faring was already of a high standard and certainly continents were being mapped on the basis of the Grid as I discussed previously. Whilst the overthrow of Crete has been conveniently 'lost' in the complexity of invasions, the fact remains that the iconography of archaeological remains and myth have not been closely analysed for a more secret quest. It seems probable that the Israelites or Druids had embarked on a goal of world conquest and through this came across the Early Minoan civilization, studying their open mysteries and cosmological system, with its knowledge of sympathetic vibration before overthrowing it. Greece was the centre of the world and it seems natural that the Druids or Israelites would seek to dominate the intellectuals by setting up their own University, which evidently occurred with Feniusa Farsa, the great grandson of Noah: Noah being the descendent of the Israelites and Druids.

During the Third Semitic migration referred to as the Aramaean, when Syria was sustaining the first shocks of Aramaean invasion, the last wave of Achaeans, "the tamers of Horses" and "shepherds of the people", had achieved the conquest of Greece and contributed to the overthrow of the dynasty of King Minos of Crete. Interestingly Professor Ridgeway identifies this stock, which had been filtering southward for several centuries, with the tall, fair-haired and grey-eyed **"Keltoi" (Celts)**.[79] Dr.Haddon believes they were representatives of "the mixed peoples of Northern and Alpine descent.[80] Mr.Hawes, following Professor Sergi, concludes that the Achaeans were "fair" in comparison with the native Pelasgian-Mediterranean Stock, but not necessarily blonde. Since Priesthood of Druids governed the Celts, the conquest of Greece, looks remarkably like a quest for a **One World Order**, where the Celts followed in the footsteps of their Masters.

It is certainly interesting that in the archives of Rome, there is a physical description of Jesus, apparently written during his lifetime by a Roman Publius Lentulus, to the Emperor Tiberias. It states: " He is a tall, well-proportioned man, ...His hair is the colour of *new wine*...upon the forehead, it parts in two after the manner of Nazarenes. His forehead is flat and *fair*. His face without blemish or defect. His nose and mouth are well proportioned. His beard is thick and the colour of His hair. His eyes are grey and extremely lively. He is very straight in stature." [81-82] The "grey eyes" and the colour of the hair as "new wine" or orange/red certainly indicate a non-Mediterranean stock, which could be Celtic and this would align with the genealogy of Jesus as coming from Celtic stock in Britain. However Rome was certainly a plotting partner in the events of the Golgotha.

EGYPT

The early Cretans were known to the Egyptians as the "Keftiu" and traded on the Mediterranean Black Sea. It is significant however, that no mention is made of them in the inscriptions of the Pharaohs after the reign of Amenhotep III. There is some enigma relating to the Egyptian Dynasty in this period which coincides with the Religious Revolution era of Crete circa 1400BC. The rise of Amenhotep's son also called Amenhotep who chose to worship a new god Aten, identified with Re-Horakhte, shown as a falcon with a sun-disc on his head, has certain parallels to the Cretan Religious Revolution in so far as Aten in falcon form was depicted alongside the archetypal symbols of old, traditional Egyptian gods, there appears to be a pre-eminence of the sun god Ra, a god that overtook Matriarchal symbolism in Crete to become the major divinity and evidently some parallel religious Revolution occurred in Egypt.

Two of the finest surviving mummies of commoners found in Egypt were Yuya who was master of the King's chariots and Thuya his *blonde-haired* wife. Why should his wife have had blonde or fair hair?

Is it that she was of Celtic origins? Certainly their racial stock origins were clearly different, Yuya showing the broad-face Armenoid-racial type and Thuya a long face Aryan type. Yuya and Thuya were the parents of Queen Tiy, the wife of Amenhotep III and thus the grandparents of Akhenaten and possibly great-grandparents of Tutankhamun. There has been much debate as to what happened to Tutankhamun and the exact dates of his period of kingship. However it is clear that Amenhotep his father in his fourth or fifth year of rule changed his name to Akhenaten and appears to have openly expressed his dissatisfaction with Egyptian traditions. His artists depicted him and his wife in a distorted artistic form, with swollen thighs, pendulous breasts and large bellies, which were the archetypal symbols relating to the earliest Palaeolithic representations of the Mother Goddess belief - the Earth Mother. I will return to Queen Tiy later, but she too was surrounded in a conspiracy of silence and one must conclude that there was a battle between the Priesthoods for control -the two groups and Priesthoods, who have sought for thousands of years to cast a veil of silence over their aims, beliefs and origins.

It could be concluded that Akhenaten had discovered some science or knowledge connected to the Earth Grid, since he ordered that the new image of his god would be the sun with rays radiating from it, terminating in hands holding the hieroglyphic symbols for life and power, with himself, his wife and two daughters receiving benefit. Whilst this image is frequently described as being the Sun-disc, inscriptions in the tomb of Ramose (No. 55), on the west bank of Luxor, make it clear that the Aten was regarded by the King as being the creative force of the universe that was manifested by the sun. The god itself had no image. This all indicates some physical laws relating to the Earth Grid and Electromagnetic spectrum as the actual "creative force", rather than the god himself who had no image.

The parallel to the Druid Temple and astronomical observatory of Salisbury Plain in the UK is given by reports that the young King Akhenaten sailed north in his sixth year from Luxor and 370Km away on the east bank of the Nile, near modern Ashmunein, found a cliff-encircled plain that belonged to no man and owed allegiance to no god. This sounds remarkably like certain grid geometry with no gravitational anomalies. The following morning he rode around the cliffs of the west bank and the east bank and ordered 14-boundary stele erected to show the limits of his new city. He called it Akhetaten- 'The Horizon of the Aten'.

The excellent preservation of mummies from Egyptian tombs also gives some idea of the racial characteristics of the various dynasties. The face of Ramesses II shows a large hooked nose typical of all the Rameside Kings of the Nineteenth Dynasty, however the third Amenhotep had a distinctly non-Semitic and non Egyptian face, but of somewhat different type to that of his father; the cheeks are long, the nose curves upwards, and he has the pointed chin and slim neck which distinguished his favourite wife Queen Tiy, who may have come from Celtic stock and their son Akenaton. Much controversy has been waged over the racial origin of Queen Tiy, who was one of Egypt's most notable women. There is a persistent legend that she was fair-haired, rosy-cheeked and blue-eyed beauty and evidently must have carried the Celtic? Racial characteristics of her alleged mother Thuya. If a Celtic Royal Bloodline had been intermarried with the Egyptian Dynasty of Kings at the time of King Amenhotep's marriage to Queen Tiy, the change in religious practise of Akenation (their son) is a reflection of Druid beliefs and knowledge of the Energy Grid. Thus once again in Egyptian history and Archaeology we meet the secrecy over Racial types, religious beliefs and Royal dynastic bloodlines, but evidently here at approximately the parallel and somewhat co-incidental time of the Cretan Religious Revolution and the introduction of a Royal Minos Dynasty into Crete, along with the worship of the god Ra - a sun god, we have a somewhat identical series of events occurring in Egypt, with what looks very much like the attempt to introduce a Celtic Royal Dynasty and Priesthood (Druids), presumably the tribe of Judah dating back to Noah and Adam, onto the throne of Egypt, with the consequent elimination of another Semitic power and Priesthood presumably that of Joseph, that had long existed behind the throne of Egypt since early Biblical and Old Testament times. I will pursue the Old Testament and the Patriarchs of the tribes of Israel shortly, but importantly at this point, we might tentatively conclude, that **two power brokers** existed on Earth at this time, one of which was **The Druids who were Semitic and the Patriarchs of the Tribes of Israel descended from Noah,** both groups had significant knowledge of the Energy Grid and Cabalistic magical ritual, both groups sought a hierarchal control of such knowledge and the fact that Crete openly communicated the mysteries was a threat to that world or global monopoly of power and control exercised through the Thrones of Royal Dynasty's. However it appears that the Druids or descendents of Noah were to incorporate in their highest levels certain knowledge they obtained from Crete and I have questioned whether this knowledge finally ended up in Rosicrucianism.

We know that Amenhotep's reign of thirty-six years from circa 1411 to 1375 B.C. was relatively peaceful however his son Amenhotep IV or Akhenaton is associated with the religious revolt that followed the death of his father. This may not be entirely true, since the last half-dozen years of the life of Amenhotep III were clouded in gloom. He had some disease or paralysis and Queen Tiy may have governed in his absence and it is possible that it was she and not her fourteen-year-old son who initiated the religious revolt, which may have been directed by Druids, if indeed Queen Tiy was Celtic. The Queen was very progressive and certainly displayed artistic persuasions parallel to the early Minoan Dynasty culture, encouraging art and observational drawing. The Queen may have sought to counteract no only the retrogressive tendencies of the priesthood of Amon, but also perhaps to curb their political power. Whilst she may have sought to do this alone, it is more probable that some other powerful priesthood sought to challenge the existing power.

There is no doubt that the Egyptians held a belief in Re-incarnation, since Herodotus was informed by the sages of Egypt that the souls of the dead passed through "every species of terrestrial, aquatic, and winged creatures", and after a lapse of about three thousand years, "entered a second time into human bodies". The Celts and Druids co-incidentally held this belief. This sounds very much like channelled information from the Grid and you will remember that I posed a similar theory, when I stated that after a magnetic reversal the MRC case had no other option but to Re-incarnate into t he amphibian line, since no other body forms apart from fish were available. One must assume then, that this information of genetic evolutionary history had come from channelling Grid information from the morphogenetic bioplasma through presumably cabalistic methods. There is every indication that Akhenaton appears to have resolved while yet still a boy, to fight against a patriarchal Priesthood of Amon, for these were prone indeed to "tyrannize without reproach and check". He began to "Heap knowledge from forbidden mines of lore", and "from that secret store wrought linked armour for his soul"; he embraced and developed the theological beliefs of the obscure Aton cult, and set forth to convince Egypt that: "The One remains, the many change and pass, Heaven's light forever shines, Earth's shadows fly..." These words together with what sounds like today, Socialist doctrine, in his noble desire to make all men: "wise and just and free and mild", could hardly have appealed to the Egyptian Imperialists and the Patriarchal Cabalists who had since Old Testament times wielded their power behind and through the throne of Egypt. However according to historical documents, Crete had been invaded during the reign of Amenhotep III; the "sack of Knossos" was already a thing of the past indicating that the power and knowledge behind Akhenaton, was the very power that had sequestered the secrets of Cosmology held by the Minoans. Amom's high priests had been wont to occupy high and influential positions at Court under Amenhotep III, where one had been chief treasurer and another grand vizier. Akhenaton was threatening the cult with complete political extinction. Akhenaton declared himself to be "the spirit of Aton" - the human incarnation of the "strange god". He deserted the priesthood at Thebes, an at Tell-el-Amarna, about 300 miles south, built his "garden city", with a somewhat familiar Biblical "Garden of Eden", parallel to "Paradise".

Thus whilst Akhenaton sat in his paradise invaders had wasted his lands "The whole territory of my lord, the king, is going to ruin". There is no doubt that Akhenaton's pacifist views were ancient Matriarchalism, (which was to bring about the downfall of Queen Tiy's rule and also was inherent in the downfall of the Minoans), in so far as he regarded it sinful to shed blood or to take away the life which Aton gave. No sacrifices were offered up in his temple; the fruits of the earth alone were laid on the altars. When his allies and his garrison commanders in Syria appealed for troops, he had little else to send them but a religious poem or a prayer addressed to Aton. Interestingly he preached the gospel of culture and *universalbrotherhood*, and his message to mankind is the only vital thing, which survives to us in Egypt amidst the relics of the past.

> 'T'is naught
> That ages, empires, and religions there
> Lie buried in the ravage they have wrought;
> For such as he can lend, - they borrow not
> Glory from those who made the world their prey;
> And he is gathered to the Kings of thought
> Who waged contention with their time's decay,
> And of the past are all that cannot pass away.
>
> He remains to us as one of: "the inheritors of unfulfilled renown":
> Whose names on earth are dark
> But whose transmitted effluence cannot die
> So long as fire outlives the parent spark.

He believed in the "one and only god", Aton, whose power was manifested in the sun. No statues of Aton were ever made and Akhenaton forbade idolatrous customs. Although Aton was a sun god, he was not the material sun; he was the First Cause manifested by the sun: "from which all things came, and from which ever issued forth the life-giving and life-sustaining influence symbolized by rays ending in hands that support and nourish human beings". "No such grand theology had ever appeared in the world before, so far as we know", stated Professor Flinders Petrie, "and it is the forerunner of the later monotheist religions, whilst it is even more abstract and impersonal, and may well rank as scientific atheism,"[83] Interestingly Professor Flinders Petrie stated: "If this were a new religion, invented to satisfy our modern scientific conceptions, we could not find a flaw in the correctness of its view of the energy of the solar system. How much Akhenaton understood we cannot say, but he had certainly bounded forward in his views and symbolism to a position, which we cannot logically improve upon at the present day. No rag of superstition or of falsity can be found clinging to this new worship evolved out of the old Aton of Heliopolis, the sole lord or **Adon** of the Universe" (*Author's emphasis*-ADAM?). One descendent, One God, One Tribe, One descent, One Religion, One World Order, a position that has not changed for thousands of years. However such great thoughts were derived from the Teacher and muse of Crete, but originated in quite a different form. However it presumably even in this altered form had some beneficial impact. The chief source of our knowledge of Akhenaton's religion is his great hymn, the finest surviving version of which has been found in the tomb of a royal official at Tell-el-Amarna. It was first published by Bouriant, and has since been edited by Breasted, whose version is the recognized standard for all translations. In Vaville's *The Old Egyptian Faith* (*English translation by Rev. C. Campbell*) the view is maintained that Akhenaton's religious revolt was *political* in origin. It seems the groups of 12 versus 13 was making themselves known in Egypt!

The development of Aton (Ad-om/ Adam?) religion may have been an adaptation of Minoan beliefs and Cosmology, since it appears that it was introduced into Court circles in the time of Amenhotep III, but was not widely available outside of those court circles. Thus the philosophy of the early matriarchal Minoan beliefs and Cosmology may have been adapted to suit a Patriarchal dynasty such as existed in Egypt. There indeed lies the entire problem, since one cannot take TRUTH and mix and marry it to suit one's own Matriarchal or Patriarchal inclinations. Truth has a requirement to be seen and told **as it was and is. The important and overwhelming fact remains that the causation of the message was not patriarchal and did not originate with Adam.** The conception of the life and the universe as male in origin can be traced back to the ancient conception of the soul of the world-shaping giant as in the chaos *egg*. The egg as infinite potential requiring the male demi-urgus principle to cleave it, such a concept was noted in symbolic iconography which occurred in the later Minoan period in Crete after the Religious Revolution. That principle can also be seen in the design of the floor of the Temple for Freemason in London. In the Theban recension of *The Book of the Dead* Ra is addressed:

O thou art in thine Egg, who shinest from thy Aton.
O thou beautiful being, thou dost renew thyself, and make thyself young again under the form of Aton....
Hail Aton, thou lord of beams of light; thou shinest and all faces (i.e. everybody) live.[84]

There was an Aton cult at Heliopolis, which taught that the creator Ra was "Shu in his Aton". Some authorities identify Aton with the old Syrian god Adon. The root "ad" or "dad" signifies "father" and I suspect is the root of Adam. The marked difference between the various Egyptian and Asiatic "Great Fathers" and the god of Akhenation, consists in this - Aton was not the chief of a Pantheon: he was the one and *only* god. "The Aton", says Professor Petrie, "was the only instance of a "jealous god" in Egypt, and this worship "was exclusive of all others and claims universality". The Patriarchal God of The Hebrews Jehoveh was to become the same "jealous god" - there was to be no sharing with the woman. However if Akhenation's religion had been the same as that of the Aton cult at Heliopolis, one might expect that he would have received support from the priest of the sun god Ra, however to them, he was as much a "heretic" as he was to the priests of Amon, or Amon-Ra, at Thebes. What is clear however is that the development of the idea of *One God* greatly improved the goal of a Universal Religion and a monopolistic dynastic *One World Order* run by a select few- a "Universal Kingdom". Thus the story of Egypt appears to be very closely tied into this story of the quest for a Universal Kingdom with political and religious goals.

Whilst there is no indication from the hymn of any clear idea of Akhenation's conception of evil, there is some concept of the difference between light and dark or philosophical dualism, which I will cover later in connection to the Early Minoan pottery commonly called the Kamares ware, which I propose is an indication of a certain early philosophy. It appears that to Akhenation as it appeared to the Early Minoans, light was associated with life, goodness and beauty, darkness was similarly filled with death and evil, although there is an implication of Illumination, whilst that Illumination is thought to have come from Patriarchalism, the first sign of light on dark, was in the Kamares pottery ware of *Crete.* Interestingly such pottery shows the zig-zag pattern that was a prominent feature of UFO witness accounts and which I have previously explained in terms of the helical windings of the bioplasma with its stored information which is electro-magnetic in nature and therefore derives from the sun and the electro-magnetic spectrum – light. "Let there be light" in Biblical texts", appears to concern Initiate illumination of this knowledge (*Plate 10*).

As with the Early Minoan Civilisation the revolution in art, which was inaugurated under Amenhotep III, is a marked feature of Akhenation's reign. Similarly poses of the King are natural showing him leaning on his staff with crossed legs or accompanied by his Queen and children. The Early Minoans also showed a natural quality in their art, which after the Religious Revolution became formal and stylised and suffered a marked decline. Thus in the two cultures there was some philosophical or theological thought which gave rise to higher concepts of beauty and art and in *The Battle of The Trees*, I concluded that a belief in the idea of Re-incarnation and the concept that through all difficulties and pain and suffering, that life would go on and mans soul would remain Immortal, was the thought that civilized Greece, when the majority of Europe at that time was in the Dark Ages. Whether the same thought of Re-incarnation was responsible for the artistic and aesthetic feeling which marked Akhenation's reign is not known, since the records which survive of the period like those of the Religious Revolution era of Crete are very scanty, for when the priests of the old faith again came to power they were at pains to obliterate them.

It is stated that Akhenation died while still a young man, and left no son to succeed him. Semenkh-ka-ra, who had married a princess, became the next Pharaoh, but he appears to have been deposed by another son-in-law of the "heretic", named Tutenk-aton, who returned to Thebes, allied himself with the priests, and called himself Tutenkamon, "Image of Amon": Thus for a brief period in Egyptian history there appears to have been a parallel series of events to Minoan Crete, with a political and religious upheaval. More importantly there may have been an Egyptian Celtic Dynasty, which would have repercussions some years later in the events of Golgotha.

The land raiders that Rameses III of Egypt (II98-II67 B.C.) fought off were said to be the Philistines of Crete. The date of Rameses reign indicates that the Philistines were the product of the Religious Revolution in Crete and were not the original stock of Early Minoans or Eteo Cretans who had always traded peacefully with Egypt. The conflicts of these Philistines with the Hebrews is familiar in The Old Testament and must surely represent conflict between the two Semitic groups and Priesthoods. This leads one to assume that the overthrow of the Minoans was principally by a European people probably the blonde blue-eyed Celts and Priesthood descended from Adom - the Druids. The conflict of Druid as Celtic Priest with Hebrew Priests or Sanhedrin would make sense. When the Philistines overran the coastline of Canaan, the country they occupied became known as Palestine. -" The land of the Philistines".

It is curious that the Philistines in the History of Civilization in Palestine are referred to as the "*Fen*ish". This is odd since King *Fen*iusa Farsa, the grandson of Magog, whose grandfather was Noah, established a University at Athens in

Greece (Achaea); which established a tiered system for the Ogham Alphabet, the upper or top secret tier of which was to appear as a Druidic finger signalling alphabet in so many mysteries connected to The Holy Grail and which I used in *The Battle of The Trees*. The common dialect of the alphabet spoken by the soldiers was referred to as "*Fen*ian". Feniusa Farsa was also an ancestor of the Irish (Celtic) Milesians. Whether or not this common root for the name Fenish, provides the link between the people who overthrew the Minoans and attempted to conquer Egypt in the reign of Rameses III, as the Celts or more specifically The Druids who organised the Religious Revolution in Crete is not certain, however in *Genesis X, 2* Magog (grandfather of Feniusa Farsa) is described as a son of Japhet and Feniusa Farsa as Foeneus ho Farsa "the vine-man who joins together". This vine-man that joins together, I maintained in *The Battle of The Trees*, was some form of early pre-Masonic Brotherhood, which presumably later formed the system of Masonry and which even in its early conception of joining together inferred a religious and political system or One World Order, which in all probability has materialised as a "United States of The West" or Federal Europe. This Super State finds its greatest supporter in Germany and Germany of course has a history of belief in the Aryan Super-Race, with its inference of White rule. We know that the Druids and the Celts were blonde-haired and blue-eyed and that Magog was in fact the grandson of Noah. Thus we might assume that Noah and the Israelites and this clan of Celtic Freemasonry in its descendent form of Druids had already embarked on a plan of globalisation with a "joining together". Thus as early as 1400 B.C. and the overthrow of the Minoan Civilization, there appears to have been a far reaching European domination goal exercised by a particular Brotherhood descended presumably from the Patriarch Noah who survived the so-called Biblical Flood, a point which takes on further significance later when I review the beliefs of the Druids. However here it is interesting to theorise that the **true and early origins of Freemasonry or at least the Rosicrucian's and Scottish Freemasonry in Britain are the Druids and prior to that the vine-men.**

THE VINE MAN THAT JOINS TOGETHER

Once again it is interesting to return to myth where Foeneus according to Greek legend, was the first man to plant a vineyard in Greece, with its implications of a pre-Masonic Brotherhood. As a legend it may cover the much wider truth that a secret Brotherhood was first introduced into Greece by the Druids or at least King Foeneus, who through manipulation of a tiered system of secret alphabets particularly The Ogham Script, brought the world the art of secrecy and covert religion and politics. However once again confusion enters the scene as Foeneus was reported as deriving from Arabia, probably Southern Judaea and the Irish bards who were the Celtic Druids, reported that Feniusa Farsa was turned out of Egypt "for refusing to persecute the children of Israel", understandable if they both represented Semitic groups and members of Israel's tribes. Presumably this group under Feniusa Farsa then wandered into Southern Judaea.

The history of Foeneus is concerned with mass emigrations from Canaan and the Canaanites are referred to in the Greek myth of Agenor, where they invaded Greece and set up a King in Argos. This in all probability was the invasion, which drove the Tuatha de Danaan out of Greece. This tribe passed by way of Denmark giving that country its name and some appeared in Ireland and to the Celts they were considered gods and were I have concluded instigative in producing a Royal dynastic bloodline, which it is claimed that Jesus was descended from. The question of the stolen genealogies has not yet been resolved and since I thought the Magdalene had Greek connections through hereditary her descent may have been through this tribe. I suspect there was something special with the bloodline of this tribe, relating to the 'first cut' and the crab (which was part of the story that Scottish Rite Freemasonry, or Rose-Croix, managed to get wrong at Cardiff Castle or perhaps they never knew the real story). In Genesis the original Canaanite empire is described as extending as far south as Sodom and Gomorrah at the extreme end of the Dead Sea. The Canaanites were then expelled around 2 300 B.C. and invaded Greece.

The connections between Israelites, Celts, Cretans and Egyptians are curiously clouded. Barry Dunford pointed out that there are a number of place names in Scotland closely connected to the Hebrew, "when, historically speaking, circa 700 B.C. 'Israel' was captured by Assyria the 'Israelites' appear eventually to have developed into the 'Scythians', some eventually travelling westwards not back to Palestine, their earlier homeland, but further west to the British Isles". Whilst we know that the Druids practised Mosaic Law displaying some connection to the Patriarchs of the Israelites why? It might be asked, would they travel to Scotland, unless there was an earlier descendent link. The Declaration of Arbroath, a historic document that can be seen at the Register House in

Edinburgh, supports the Scythian connection. The Declaration was drawn up under King Robert the Bruce and was signed and attested by the Seals, not only of King Robert himself, but also by all the Scottish Chiefs and Nobles. It records the known origin and previous migrations of the Scots, declaring that they came from Greater Scythia, passing through the Pillars of Hercules, sojourned a while in Spain, and thence to Scotland **"one thousand two hundred years after the outgoing of the people of Israel from Egypt"**.

It is interesting that Barry Dunford provides evidence that Jerusalem was in fact Scotland, and Professor Thomas Thompson in 1992 as a leading authority on biblical archaeology published *The Early History of The Israelite People*, in which he concluded that many of the events portrayed in The Old Testament, were not supported by archaeological evidence. For this conclusion he suffered the all too familiar attack by those vested interests that have no wish for this story to be known and the Professor lost his job at Marquette University, Milwaukee USA. However there is another important link that I have found here and that is, Feniusa Farsa grandson of Magog, who was grandson of Noah, was King of Scythia, this King was evidently a part of some Brotherhood if not the instigator and further as "the vine-man", that "binds together" I proposed was instigator of a plan for a political and religious unity under a World Order within Europe. Further I have previously concluded that the Celts or perhaps the particular descendents of the Scythians - Israelites, may well have organised the Religious Revolution in Crete. Further still Foeneus ho Farsus according to legend was a son of Aegyptus who came from Arabia. The pattern of the Pascal Triangle I produced earlier shows the spatial geometric pattern for the bioplasma or UVG 120 sphere, which in the case of the Pascal Triangle indicates the order of atomic matter. The Pascal Triangle is thought to originate in Arabia among the Moors, but equally one cannot deny that The Israelites have a link to Arabia.

Dr. R.S. Macalister in his *Ancient Ireland* (1935) states that New Grange is a flat-topped barrow built of heaped stones in Ireland and was built by the Milesians and Feniusa Farsa, who was in legend an ancestor of the Irish Milesians and was also described as a Scythian and founder of the Milesian race. Dr. Maclister dates the Milesians at 1000B.C.Thus once again we return to the Celts, Druids and through Feniusa Farsa great grandson of Noah to Adam and the Israelites. The fact that New Grange is generally believed to be a Bronze Age sepulchre in honour of the White Goddess obviously implies the Scythians (descendents of the Scots - who are Israelites) held a Matriarchal belief. New Grange was originally covered in white quartz pebbles, which may account for the legends of Kings housed after death in glass castles, quartz being a major constituent of glass manufacture. Ten enormous stone herms, weighing eight or ten tons apiece at New Grange are arranged in a semi-circle around the southern base of the barrow and one formerly stood at the summit. A 'hedge' of about a

214

hundred long flat stones, is set edge to edge surround the base. This 'hedge' is reminiscent of the outer hedge design and concentric circle of Cardiff Castle Summer Smoking Room Floor, in Wales UK. The 'hedge' is shown in the outer and final ring of the design and I maintained that this design carried in archetypal form knowledge of Scottish Rite Freemasonry at presumably Rose-Croix level. Further given that the Druids had some connection to the Essenes, presumably a pre-determined outcome group, who played a part in the events of Golgotha, under the direction of their Masters; then there is a double archetypal significance here, in so far as the Essenes formed communities surrounded by high hedges, to keep prying eyes out. Is this intimation that the Druids/Scythians held such knowledge in descendent form? Interestingly the ground plan of New Grange is in the shape of a Celtic cross. The shaft consists of a narrow passage, sixty feet long through which one must crawl on one's hands and knees. This is no doubt the birth passage in one sense and the umbilical cord in another, the barrow the archetypal womb which connects with the Cretan maze or cnothic underground world of the dead; but it is also a place of re-birth and in Early Minoan times in Crete, was a place of re-birth for ALL, but here at New Grange it has become a place of re-birth of Sacred Kings The structural design of New Grange is therefore in archetypal form, a reflection of the Cosmology and beliefs held by the Early Minoans. The passage or birth canal leads to a small circular chamber (the womb), with a *beehive* or corbelled vault roof twenty feet high, with *3* recesses, which make the arms of the Celtic cross. It seems that the Roman occupation may have interfered with the interior remains, apart from 3 large empty boat-shaped stone basins, perhaps reflecting the after-life, the sides of which are engraved with stripes and some stag antlers (as totem beast). The Danes also presumably sacked the chamber.

The spiral motif patterns, which adorn the doorway, are reminiscent of the Knossos spirals and the Cycle of Eternal Return was discussed in more detail in *The Battle of The Trees,* with the spirals as archetypal symbols of immortality (the pattern when traced with the finger implies into a life and out of a life and so on). There is also unusually at New Grange a pattern of forked lightening, or perhaps the chevron pattern of the Knossos design, it is difficult to say. The Chevron pattern was seen on the Early Kamares pottery of Crete as light on dark with the concept of "let there be light"; and the zigzag pattern occurs in the UFO phenomenon and may well indicate the successive coils of the morphogenetic bioplasma as an electro-magnetic phenomenon. The bioplasma organisation, which I described in diablo form, may provide a composite 3D geometric structure that forms the Grid itself. Thus giving it an overall honeycomb appearance, which might also account for the beehive dome shape of the roof of New Grange. It is not inconceivable that the Cabalistic priests or magicians including the Druids channelled information from the Grid and knew of its structure (from the Minoans). The zigzag pattern or chevron may have held double significance. The Minoans very early on through their Teacher, recognized the significance of the migration and return of Cranes flying in a V formation pattern and utilised this in their seal designs encouraged by their Teacher, in order to impress the idea of the cyclical return of the seasons and of life which helped to convey the concept of Immortality to the people and certainly as the majority of Europe struggled in the Dark Age of ignorance, this was a highly difficult concept of Theology and Philosophy for the Teacher to convey to mankind.

In my research at the Knossos site, I remarked that the alphabetic script that was introduced and appeared on tablets in the later Minoan period, looked remarkably like some figures in Ogham Script and at New Grange there appears the Ogham letters B and I, which are the first and last letters of the Ogham Alphabet and presumably in a parallel way to Biblical texts, convey the idea of a Patriarchal god as Alpha and Omega, the beginning and the end. The Sacred Kings or Solar Kings of Bronze Age Ireland were buried in the barrows, the King's spirit at New Grange in legend went to "Caer Sidi", the castle of Ariadne and the pagan Irish called New Grange 'Spiral Castle'. Castles became a necessary part of legend relating to the underground stream of knowledge and the Holy Grail. The Grail Romances related in *The Battle of The Trees*, were really propaganda stories by two opposing teams (Celtic/ Druid and the Twelve Tribes of Israel?) where stories of Knights and Castles were veiled references to this hidden story dating back to Bronze Age Greece. Inevitably once again there is confusion in the mists of time, as to who built New Grange. Graves85 maintains that the Danaans took over the shrine from the previous occupants, who in Irish history are the tribes of Partholan and Nemed that invaded the country in 2048 B.C. coming from Greece, which would verify that Greece was Matriarchal at this time. The arrival of the Danaans (Tuatha de Danaan) in *The Book of Invasions,* is dated the middle of the fifteenth Century B.C. a time associated with the Religious Revolution in Crete, although it is thought that the Matriarchal tribe of The Tuatha de Danaan fled from the Peloponnese in Greece c.1 900 B.C., although it is conceivable that they did not appear in Ireland until the fifteenth Century B.C. Dr. Macalister states that New Grange was built by the Milesians (circa 1000 B.C.) thus disagreeing with Graves, but all evidence points to the date Graves gives. What seems more probable is that the Tuatha de Danaan as a Matriarchal tribe from Greece built the barrow in honour of The White Goddess (in her death aspect). The Milesians, who were associated if not led by the Scythian Feniusa Farsa a descendent of Noah, overtook the shrine.

The three basins found at New Grange certainly indicate Mosaic Law, *Exodus XXIV, verse 4-8*; states that Moses, having set up twelve stone herms, or posts, at the foot of a sacred hill, offered bull-sacrifices and sprinkled half the blood on a **thirteenth** herm in the middle of the circle, or semi-circle, the rest of the blood he put into basins. Interestingly the blood in the basins was sprinkled on the people as a charm of sanctification, but its use was also to feed the ghost of the dead hero and to encourage (him) returning from Caer Sidi to answer questions of importance. The Druid finger- signalling keyboard of the Ogham Script, was used also to decode the mysteries of Poussin's paintings in *The Battle of The Trees*, where the forefinger I proposed was the requirement to return to answer difficult questions. Such questions relate in Poussin's paintings to the events of the Crucifixion at Golgotha. The number thirteen arises again and in association with Mosaic Law and thus Druids and Israelites and in some way signifies the group.

The Druids I have intimated may have been behind the events of Golgotha, but it seems that the Druids in their observance of Mosaic Law as priests to the Celts, that they may have derived such law from the Milesians or Feniusa Farsa and therefore from the Patriarch Noah. Feniusa Farsa also perhaps as a reigning sovereign of the Minoans or Cretans after the Religious Revolution, may have led them into Palestine and certainly as I discussed previously, the Philistines or Cretans had also been called" Fenish". The important point is that much later the drama of Jesus would be enacted in Palestine and would have enormous influence on the next millennium. If Jesus and Magdalene sought to become King and Queen and depose the priesthood of Aaron or effectively the Twelve Tribes of Israel under the direction of another supposedly non-Jewish (Celtic/ Druidic) priesthood - the priesthood of Melchizedec, who although a priest of the Most High God (Patriarchal) was not a son of Abraham, then in the Epistle to the Hebrews, the superiority of the priesthood of Melchizedec is acknowledged over the tribe of Levi and the purely Jewish priesthood. Melchizedec was a contemporary of Abraham, but not a son and existed before the priesthood of Levi, he was a *Gentile* and head of a Gentile priesthood, which was **Druidic and represented by Judah.**

Is it any wonder that the Dead Sea Scrolls and particularly the document of 'Levi' have been withheld from professional and public scrutiny? Undoubtedly also as I deciphered in *The Battle of The Trees*, the Grail Romances also covered this augment over the rightful "root and branch", of the Grail Family, which brings into question the genealogies that were stolen from the Mary Magdalene. Thus hereditary origins were considered by one group as the necessary requirement in order to be able to carry The Grail, whilst
another group considered one's actions as more important than any hereditary or blood-line link, however in those days, the only way to regain power and in the case of the Magdalene to bring back the truth as her goal, was by the possession of genealogies. This hereditary versus non-hereditary conflict in ideological thinking between the two secret groups who dominated The Grail and The Grid, was to play out on the world's battle fields and within political ideologies and

217

religion, which underpinned those battles for many thousands of years. Neither could one assume that the two priesthoods did not always work together to cause conflict towards their greater goal of a One World Order. Hitler's Supreme Race project and his hatred of the Jews, centres upon this very issue and it would seem that the secret groups who surrounded Hitler must have been the Celtic or Aryan priesthood, who became in his time The Third Reich (The Black Order). Personally I always thought it odd that Rudolph Hess chose to fly to Scotland to speak with the Duke of Hamilton, believing that there had been a misunderstanding between Hitler's Germany and Britain, whom Hitler viewed as a friend. Why should he believe that, unless they were both under the direction of the same priesthood? Which suggests that Hitler was duped and the point of World War 2 was not to set up a German Super Race, but to devastate Europe and dupe Europeans into accepting European Union on the grounds of peace! Further after the Holocaust, which appears to be one secret (Gentile) priesthood versus another (Jews), a State of Israel was possible. I would hate to suggest that the Jews were sacrificed to that cause, but one should never underestimate the MRC case for his lack of any conscience as he moves the pawns around his chessboard.

In The Holy Trinity based on Ezekiel's vision, The First person was the true Creator, the All-Father, 'Let there be Light', represented by Acacia which was the wood of Noah's Ark, the tree of Sunday and the Patriarchal God of the Jews and the tree of Levi. The question becomes whether Feniusa Farsa, descended from Noah was a progenitor of the Druids and presumably the Royal Celtic Bloodline, which it is alleged produced Jesus. I myself have thrown one more question into this pot, by stating that Jesus stole the genealogies of the Magdalene and it may well have been her and not Him, who was a descendent from this bloodline, with its Greek connections through the Danaans. The Templars appear to have known something about this, when they spat on the cross and referred to Jesus as: "the thief on the cross". The Second Person of The Trinity in Ezekiel's vision was enthroned man, spiritual man in God's image, who was represented by 'F', the fire-garnet, the pomegranate, and the tree of the Sabbath and of Judah. The Apocalyptics identified him with the Son of Man in Daniel's vision. The upper half was amber, the royal part, linking him with the Third Person: and the Third Person comprised the remaining six letters of the name, six being the number of life in Pythagorean philosophy; The letters were the original White-Goddess vowels AOUEI that represented the Spirit that moved on the face of the waters in the Genesis account.

Jesus was also held to have fulfilled the prophecy in the *110th Psalm*: "Jehovah has sworn and will not repent, thou art a priest forever after the order of Melchizedek". This is enlarged upon in St. Paul's Epistle to the Hebrews. Melchizedek (*Genesis XIV, 18-20*) the Sacred King of Salem who welcomed

Abraham to Canaan (Abraham in this sense the wandering tribe that come down into Palestine from Armenia at the close of the third Millennium B.C.) 'had neither father nor mother'. 'Salem' is generally taken to mean Jerusalem. The original base of the high priesthood was Hebron, but David moved his capital to Jerusalem ('Holy Salem') or 'The New Jerusalem'. Further The Talmud records a heretical sect of Jews, called **Melchizedekians**, who frequented Hebron to worship the body of **Adam**, who was buried in the cave of Machpelah. Now the only character in the Bible with no father or mother was Adam, thus if the Melchizedekians worshipped Adam, they were identifying a racial and priesthood bloodline from Adam, which included Melchizedek's kingship in an unbroken line. Adam has been described as 'the red man' (either on account of his hair in much the same way that Jesus was described as having hair of "new wine" i.e. red colour which was typical of the Celts or red would typify a Sun King) and in the Druidic mysteries eggs were always coloured scarlet in the Sun's honour (which became the custom of Easter eggs) and took the place of snakes, which had an ancient connection to the belief of Immortality even in Early Minoan Crete, where the so-called snake Goddesses would display the snakes on their arms. Presumably then, the curse on Adam in Genesis (which blamed Eve) and the eating of "the tree of knowledge", referred to Cabalistic and Grid science. The distortion is obvious in so far as woman did not utilised the science for control and power, but man having stolen it, could not help himself. The Grid is a terrible trap, as we shall come to see.

Healing was also related to snakes and Asklepios the Greek healer held a staff with snakes entwined around it, which became the symbol of the medical profession in Greece. Thus at some stage the maleprinciple and power of a Sacred or Solar (Sun) King overtook and replaced a belief system. This was very important and catastrophic for humanity, since the Holy Message that came to earth circa 10,000 B.C. was replaced by Solar Kingship (Divine Kingship) and an initiated secret priesthood; consequently the message of Immortality was replaced by the abberative message of Kingly and Divine power maintained through a priesthood descended in an unbroken line from the earliest Patriarchs, where presumably the secret knowledge was passed on, with the priests re-incarnating into that line and thus maintaining their power over humanity. The Late Minoan period shows Cretan "Princes" in Frescoes at Knossos as "red men" and this certainly relates them to Adam, thus giving further evidence for my proposal that a priesthood of Celtic/Druidic origins had instigated a religious revolution in Crete. If Jesus hoped to fulfil the world's male potential as a Solar (Sun) King, the egg symbolising birth, but only as a potential until split by the male demurgus principle, the phallus which is architecturally recorded on the floor of the Freemasons Temple in London and appears on a Late Minoan seal in Crete. The Demiurge was Helios the sun, with whom the Orphics identified their god Apollo. The transition from snake to egg, which was all part of the re-positioning of the archetypal symbols which expressed various aspects of this knowledge also involved a transfer of power from Matriarchal to Patriarchal and from God to man. The message and its source were now to be hidden perhaps forever and The Lucifer principal took control. No doubt the warped logic that was fed to an ignorant populous, was that the sun hatched the snakes eggs, the fact that the snake sheds its skin periodically to be reborn as a memory of the Teachers words, was probably long since forgotten. The alphabets retained the religious mysteries (which was the reason why the alphabets had to be tiered, so the profane would not discover any secrets) where the glain or 'red egg of the sea serpent', which figured in Druidical mysteries may be identified as the World Orphic Egg. The Greek alphabetic Omega and great Capital O seemed to signify the world egg or potential and as Jehovah stated as a jealous and Patriarchal god, where there was to be no sharing with the woman, or revealing of the truth of what had happened: "**I** am the alpha and the Omega", the beginning and the end. This of course was a lie, because the message came to earth c. 10 000 B.C. However the cult of Jehovah was non existent at that point and appeared later only through manipulation the mysteries removing and utilising a great deal in terms of Matriarchal ideas. The truth and the reality was **in the beginning there was only a message from a Higher Source**, such a source did not encompass any vengeful and wrathful God of the Jews or any other group. Neither was that message here from the beginning with the Patriarchs, the true Alpha and the true beginning did not occur until circa 10,000 BC. The Story of how that message became tied to the UFO story was wrongly portrayed in the Crab mural at Cardiff Castle Wales UK.

THE CELTS AND DRUIDS

The most remarkable social custom of Celtic society was the equal role of the woman parallel to some Asiatic societies particularly Thailand and Tibet. Men and women shared manual labour and women under Celtic law were guaranteed property even in marriage and could choose their own husbands, divorce and were even entitled to substantial damages at law if deserted or molested. Women also played an important part in political life and fought on the battlefield and could even ascend to the chieftaincy. However apart from this, Celtic religion was as Caesar declared the province of the Druids and males.

How far Druidism remained as an ancient institution was remarked on by Diogenes Laetius (AD 200 -250) who made it clear that even in the time of Aristotle in the 4th Century B.C. it was regarded as a very ancient institution. Even at the time of the Religious Revolution in Crete circa 1400B.C. it is not improbable that the Druids were a powerful priesthood with International influence through their Universities. Interestingly enough with regards to Patriarchal origins in the post Deluge era the Druids themselves had but one fear, which was recorded about the 5th Century B.C. as a meeting between Alexander the Great and a Celt, possibly a Druid. Alexander asked his visitor what it was his people most feared? Instead of the expected answer of Alexander himself, he was told nothing: "so long as the sky does not fall or the sea burst its limits". Thus there was within Druid memory or teaching a legend, myth or physical memory of presumably some Apocalyptic Deluge or the biblical Flood: Hardly surprising if they were descended from Feniusa Farsa through Magog and Noah back to Adam.

In an Irish legend *The Cattle Raid of Cooley*, once when things were going amiss, Sualdaen seeks to put new heart into the Ulstermen (in Ireland): "Are the heavens rent?", he asks; "Is the sea bursting its bounds? Is the end of the world upon us?" Later, the warriors of Conchobhar assure him:" We will hold out until the earth gives under us, or until the heavens fall on us and make us give way". In the 5th Century A.D. it was employed in slightly altered form by the bards Taliesman and Myrddin, Thus Myrddin (later translated as Merlin) says: "Since the Battle of Arderydd, nothing can touch me - even if the sky falls and the sea overflows". The bards were synonymous with the Druids and often Druids wrote their secrets in poetic form in coded manner, such that it would not be understood by anyone other than another bard or Druid. In fact the problem with discovering the beliefs and teachings of Druidism, is that they never committed anything to writing. The nineteen years tutorage it took to become a Druid, was spent in learning poetic secrets passed down orally and it might be construed that there was an awful lot of secrets to learn or exercises to be undertaken. What we can say is that they definitely did know of an earlier time of a cataclysmic climatic disaster, presumably the biblical Flood.

Whilst there is no systematic account of the Druid religion and their teachings, we do know that they studied the alphabets including the Ogham keyboard finger signalling alphabet (which I suspect is the basis of the Masonic handshake), which Jesus was evidently well versed in as I recounted in *The Battle of The Trees* and they attached particular significance to the Oak (Royal) tree. The implication that Jesus, John the Evangelist and Baptist (who may have been synonymous) were Druid priests and tutored in the religious mysteries, is furthered when we realise that each of these men preached the eminent approach of The Kingdom of Heaven and St. John in The Apocalyptic Revelation spoke at length of the end of times. Both the Druids and the Essenes who may well have been a pre-determined group set up by the Druids for a purpose at the time of Jesus, were both groups who were violently Apocalyptic.

Druidic practises were associated with water as the entrance to Other World's and in Poussin's famous painting *Et in Arcadia Ego*, which I deciphered in *The Battle of The Trees*, there is a water-deity as the River god Alpheus (the Alpha or beginning), Lord (Hidden Master) of the Underground Stream (the Secret Doctrine as it is used here, but in Matriarchal belief The Holy Grail). This painting shows some mystery over the events at Golgotha and the presence of the water deity with what looks to be a crown of Laurel? On his head, signifies not only Divinity but also some Druidic presence, particularly as in Poussin's paintings he used in archetypal form the fore-finger of the Druidic signalling keyboard of the Ogham alphabet, which in code means the requirement to return and answer difficult questions, implying that some Druidic mystery is entangled in the events of Golgotha. If as I stated the events of Golgotha were the second time that the Holy Grail Message and knowledge had gone underground, the first being in Early Minoan times at the time of the Religious Revolution, then it is curious that in the Psychro Cave, reportedly the birthplace of Zeus in myth and perhaps historically the cave where a secret Cabal directed the Religious Revolution there were cauldrons and tripods, the trappings of Cabalistic science. In the Welsh *Mabinogi of Branmen Daughter of Llyr*, a huge man emerges from a lake with a cauldron on his back and similar archetypes occur in Arthurian legend, where a woman's **arm** emerges from the lake bearing Arthur's sword - EXCALIBUR. Merlin who was supposedly the magician at King Arthur's court in legend in England, was thought to be a Druid, thus the lake from which the woman's arm emerged becomes significant as the Underground Stream. The appearance of the arm which is usually shown emerged from the upper arm only and thus in one sense 'cut' by the water's surface, gives more significant credence to my witness account, that the Magdalene's arm was cut by Jesus with his sword on the upper left arm as he betrayed her and after she had requested that he return the genealogies. 'The Cutting of the Elm' ceremony which I recounted in *The Battle of The Trees,* related to a curious ceremony at Gisors in the 12th Century, where I concluded a cutting of the ties between two groups occurred resulting in a divergence of aims into Matriarchal and Patriarchal goals, one group willing to release the mysteries and one group wishing to keep the mysteries hidden. The fact that Jesus cut the Magdalene's arm with his sword really conveys or re-enacts his promise as stated in the Clement of Alexandria text that He had come: "to destroy the works of the Female" and part ways with the Matriarchal goal (truth). The Arthurian legends were written from ancient Druidic sources in coded form and thus it is curious that they should retain this secret relating to The Crucifixion and events of Golgotha, which even more curiously appears on the Crab Mural at Cardiff Castle Summer Smoking Room, although the mural is meant to convey the Magdalene's cut together with an underlying and much deeper secret, I note to my own amusement from the mural, that there happens to be one last and somewhat crucial secret in the world, which the secret Masonic groups failed to find out.

Nuada's sword was one of the most treasured possessions of the Tuatha de Danaan, the people of Dana who came to be revered as gods by the Celts. Lugh's Spear, which also belonged to the Tuatha, was such that the woman or man, who held it, could not be conquered in battle. St. John was often shown with a sword emanating from his mouth and the spear or sword mentioned in the Grail Legend had similar properties and no doubt bears an archetypal background to the alleged piercing of Jesus on the Cross-, by a *Roman* soldier. The sword then becomes another archetypal symbol containing a secret only understood by those in the know. The fact that the woman delivered the sword to Arthur implies she *gave* him the secrets of the hidden science and the Holy Grail! The fact that Hitler dressed as a Grail knight in a poster in 1936 (*TheBattle of The Trees*) implies that he also knew all about the Grid and the hidden science, which I will discuss later. Arthur's *right to the throne* was determined by the drawing of the sword from the *stone* (Semitic), which implies that Arthur depended on the Druid priesthood for his right to rule and Arthur later received the magical Excalibur from Merlin (a Druid magician). Thus if the Druids are a descendent group of the Rosicrucian's, then one might expect the whole of the hidden science in much researched form today to rest with them, a point I will take up later in the case of Scientology. It is certainly curious that I specifically remember Ron Hubbard somewhat tantalizingly referring to a book that he might publish entitled *Excalibur.* If Ron Hubbard took the apples of Immortality from a secret group, then surely the sword did not belong to him. However let us not split mythological hairs, but if Hubbard's Alma Mater was Druidic (Rose-Croix) or Rosicrucian, then certainly Scientology still carries that definable Druidic trait of Sacrifice to a Cause and salvation for the "chosen ones" (with enough money to pay for it!). This would certainly answer the question as to why Hubbard chose a castle for his headquarters in the UK. Druids also chose a hierarchial structure with an Arch Druid in much the same way as Freemasonry organises itself today with its Arch Degree and Mason of that degree.

Caesar, who invaded Britain it would seem to disband the Druids, spoke of the Druids as a potent force in Celtic Unification. They were organised under a powerful leadership according to Caesar and such organisation shows remarkable similarity to Essene organisation and Freemasonry. Ammianus Marcellinus referred to the Druids as being: "bound together in a fraternal organization" and interestingly he also claimed that the fraternity had been instituted by Pythagoras. However it may have been forgotten or not known that prior to the Pythagorean Brotherhood a rather sexist organisation, there was Feniusa Farsa or "the vine man that draws together", who was the grandson of Magog and great grandson of Noah. Pomponius Mela circa AD 43 also corroborated the central organisation of the Druids although the date might be inaccurate. Given that I had proposed that the secret Cabal that had directed the Religious Revolution in Crete had done so from the Psychro Cave, Pomponius tells us that much of the training of Druidic initiates was done in secret caves (also woods and valleys). The fact that St. John allegedly wrote the biblical book of *Revelations* from a Cave on the Greek Island of Patmos, certainly indicates that John was also a Druidic priest which was confirmed the genealogical tree. Whilst it has been assumed that Caesar and the Roman occupation of Britain terminated the Druids, Geoffrey of Monmouth, writing in the 12th Century AD referred to a: "College of two hundred learned men", at Caerleon-on-Usk (Wales UK) in Arthur's time circa 6th Century AD. These men were skilled in "astronomy and other arts". This may indicate that the Druids did survive in some form after the invasion by Caesar.

The word "bard" was virtually synonymous with Druid and the bardic colleges in Ireland existed until the 17th Century and in Scotland until the 18th Century. It is intriguing to theorise that whatever knowledge the Druids had was finally incorporated into the first lodge of Freemasonry set up at Kilwinning in Scotland "Mother Kilwinning" as it is still known to Freemasons. As I previously noted, this was one of the strangest 'marriages ' of secret groups where there was a: "fruitful union between the professional guild of mediaeval masons and a secret group of philosophical adepts". This alliance between the Templars and the Royal Order of H.R.M. with the Scottish guilds of working Masons under Robert Bruce in 1286, constituted the Royal Order of H.R.M. (Heredom) and knights of the R.S.Y.C.S. (Rosy Cross) into one order: The two degrees constituting the Royal Order of Scotland. It is stated that the Rose-Croix originated with the Templars in Palestine as early as 1188, whilst the origin of the word Heredom is derived from a mythical mountain on an island south of the Hebrides, where the Culdees practised their rites and further this can be traced to a Jewish source.

In 1784 some French Freemasons wrote to their English brethren saying:" It concerns us to know if there really exists in the island of Mull, formerly Melrose...in the north of Scotland, a Mount Heredom, or if it does not exist". In reply a leading Freemason, General Rainsford, referred them to the word 'Har Adonai' in Hebrew i.e. Mount of God. A more probable explanation appears to be that Heredom is a corruption of the Hebrew word "Harodine", signifying Princes or rulers. Whether this is a direct referral to the Celtic dynasty of the Jesus family and the Druids are not apparent. What is known is that the Druids were considered magicians and therefore had some form of magical knowledge, which may well have been and probably was Cabalistic knowledge relating to the energy Grid. The Norse Odin, who appeared to convey in mythology some knowledge of the Grid, allegedly had correspondence with two Celtic gods, Zugh and Esus. Gods may have been merely those men who held knowledge of the Grid and used it to impress an ignorant populace. The bards or Druids were also Shamans or the "memory of the people" and certainly that memory included the event, which had caused terror to the Druids - some Apocalyptic or geological event that had caused massive tidal waves; "the sky falling and the sea bursting its bounds". The "sky falling" is something that arose as part of a warning in the early part of the 20th Century AD, in The Fatima Miracle and which I covered as part of the UFO phenomenon in *Alternative 4*. When Posidonius asked the Druids how the world would end, they told him it would come by fire and water and some part of this end was to be repeated in the prophetic Apocalypse of St. John in the book of *Revelations* in The Bible.

There is no doubt that the Druids held great power and in Gaul an area of land that covered part of France and Europe Caesar stated that only the Druids and the knights had any socially accountable position, whilst in Ireland the Druids stood just below the nobility. Druids became chieftains e.g. Conchobhar, the Ukter Chieftain was the son of the Druid Cathbadh and since the chieftaincy was restricted to members of a "royal family" this would mean that the Druids might themselves be part of a Royal blood line, perhaps dating back to Adam through Noah. Thus if there were kings in the beginning as the Indian Epics imply, before a Flood or some cataclysm, then it is not recorded in *Genesis*!

A secret oral tradition has existed through the ages and John the Evangelist was associated with this tradition in some form. This Secret Doctrine is given as the history of the Primitive Church and further it has been claimed that Moses and Jesus had access to this tradition. Dr. Ranking an eminent Masonic authority stated:" that from the very commencement of Christianity there has been transmitted through the centuries a body of doctrine which is incompatible with Christianity in the various official churches. That the bodies teaching these doctrines professed to do so on the authority of St. John to whom they claimed, the true secrets had been committed by the Founder of Christianity. That during the middle Ages the main support of the Gnostic bodies and the main repository of this knowledge was the society of the Templars". 86 Was this secret and oral tradition none other than the oral tradition and the 19 years of tuition that Druids underwent? Knowledge that ultimately turned up in The Summer Smoking Room of Cardiff Castle Wales UK as the secret levels of knowledge in the Rose-Croix degree or at least the highest level of Scottish Rite Freemasonry. In my own observations of Cardiff Castle I could find no representation of Jesus and only John the Evangelist was represented.

Ragon another eminent Masonic source, claimed that Weishaupt, the founder of political Illuminism in the 18th Century, was initiated by a Jewish Cabalist Kolmer, who may have been one of the actual hidden Masters. Ragon claimed that the Templars learned from the "Initiates of the East" a certain Judaic doctrine attributed to St. John the Apostle. Thus and this is a most important point, the Illuminati who in all probability stood behind the French and Russian Revolutions, to pave the way for a Federal European Super state, were initiates into a secret doctrine descending from John the Evangelist and The Templars. Why should this point be so utterly important? That such doctrine was non other than Druidic knowledge dating back to the very earliest times, the "Secret Doctrine" of Adam and further as we shall shortly see the **Druid goal was always a Federal Super state**, a goal that had been initiated from the time of the Religious Revolution in Crete; circa 1400B.C.This being so, there must be a religious goal and that goal must require a Universal Religion. There seems to me, to be two contenders Christianity or Scientology, which may or may not define the two opposing groups,

The magical tales of weapons such as swords in the story of *Excalibur* may be archetypal glosses for weapons and knowledge relating to the earth's Energy Grid, which the Druids manipulated. Given the ancient Indian legends, which spoke of terrible weapons and flying machines, it is not improbable that even the magical sword that in legend Merlin gave to Arthur was a gloss for secret knowledge on Grid energies. Such knowledge could have included advanced Cosmology and nuclear physics, which may have been part of the knowledge that was taken and hidden at Knossos circa 1400B.C. In *The Battle of The Trees*, I produced a painting *The Son of Man in the midst of candlesticks* by Albrecht Durer (1948), which shows a sword emanating from a man's mouth, with the archetypal 4th Candlestick and fourth light in prominence. The man I assume is St. John the Evangelist. If John was a Druid tutored in the oral tradition of the Druids, then in archetypal form the painting shows such tradition portrayed by a sword. Thus Arthur's magical sword given to him by the Druid Merlin is none other than the Hidden Science that includes knowledge of Grid Energies. The sword in one sense is the magic wand and rood of the Druid.

If Nuada's sword was the most treasured possession of the Tuatha de Danaan, it is curious that in Celtic legend the Tuatha de Danaan were regarded as gods. Naturally any manipulation of the Grid would appear to the uninformed as god-like powers. The Tuatha de Danaan the Bronze Age Pelasgains who were expelled from Greece in the middle of the Second Millennium definitely had contact with the early Minoan Civilization and it is extremely probable that they possessed Grid energy knowledge together with the Cosmology and beliefs of the early Minoans. Thus some repository of Greek knowledge ended up in the hands of the Celts. The "cauldron" that so often appeared in Celtic legend and myth was an archetypal symbol of rebirth or Re-incarnation for sacred Kings, where the remains of the sacrificial victim, the totem beast representing waning Twin King would be placed with his successor the waxing Twin into the cauldron to be 'reborn': where he would swim and partake Eucharistically of the remains of the totem beast e.g. a white horse or bull. Such is the background to the Christian Eucharist and the symbolic partaking of the flesh (bread) and blood (wine) of Christ, so that He may be **reborn again in the receiver.** The Christian Eucharist signifies how far the original truth of Re-incarnation and the original beliefs held by the Early Minoans had been lost. The history of which was also noted on the floor of The Summer Smoking Room at Cardiff Castle, signifying that at the top level of Scottish Rite Freemasonry and presumably other higher degrees such as the Rose-Croix, this Theological background for the origins of Christianity is known. In *The Battle of The Trees*, I proposed that any plan for a unified political and religious Universal Kingdom, as a final goal of a Federal Europe, would involve a religion based on the unifying history of all religions, which really dates back to Minoan Greece and further still, to a message that came to earth circa 10 000 B.C. However there certainly seems no intention of revealing the final roots by uncovering The Cycle of Eternal Return and the original invasions of Greece and much of what I have revealed in my books and research.

The power of the Pre- Achaean Goddess Danae of Argos expelled with the Tuatha de Danaan extended to Thessaly and her earthly representative mothered the early Achaean dynasty called the House of Perseus, but by Homers time Danae was masculinised into Danaus son of Belus. However when the Indo European hordes swept into Greece around 1,900B.C. Certain tribes including the Tuatha de Danaan left Greece and migrated to other lands including Ireland and then into Scotland. The Tuatha De Danaan worshipped a Mother Goddess figure named Danu or Dana and it may be that the name Ana or Anu derived from this source. The genealogical tree of the Celtic royal dynasty, which Jesus is said to derive from, gave Anna as his grandmother. It might be that the royal lineage was derived from the Tuatha De Danaan, who were considered gods by the Celts. Ana or Anu is perpetuated in the St. Anne's Wells, to be found all all over Britain and Ireland, but also in Brittany, (which was once part of Gaul and therefore Celtic), which has St. Anne as patron saint. The Celtic Royal Bloodline from which Jesus was allegedly descended (and perhaps Mary Magdalene?) was in all probability from a Greek source. As I recount later and in *The Battle of The Trees*, Mary Magdalene and Jesus in the events of Golgotha, re-enacted the Greek religious mysteries of their Matriarchal ancestors (The Tuatha De Danaan) and the Druids would have held those mysteries. Stories of the marvels achieved by the Tuatha are told in myth in Ireland, but also in Scotland and Wales.

The association between Celtic Gods and wells, which implies the Underground Stream (of wisdom and knowledge) of The Holy Grail, is one found repeatedly; many are either curative or wishing wells, both aspects being related to the Mary Magdalene. The connection of healing to The Underground Stream is also an important part of Grail myth and recurs constantly in The Grail Romances, where the ultimate healing is perceived as never growing old (Re-incarnation). From the Romances the implication is there, that a knowledge or belief in Re-incarnation and man's Immortality has a curative property, in the sense that it can cure a man's soul, which was the question that lead me to research *Part II of The Second Millennium Working Report into Cancer*, apart from the books I have also written. In Brittany one of the most renounced healing wells is that of St. Anna d'Auray.

It is difficult to know without records whether the Druids were already present in Britain at the time when the Tuatha de Danaan arrived or whether The Druids represented the upper caste system that the Tuatha de Danaan created in their attempts to retain a tight control and secrecy of their knowledge of the Grid Energies. There are accounts that The Druids were existent in Britain as far back as 1800 B.C. and thus were present when the Tuatha de Danaan were expelled from Greece arriving in Britain circa 1472 B.C. - a time curiously that parallels the date I gave for the Religious Revolution in Crete. In the *Book of Invasions,* according to Irish tradition, the so-called Indo-Europeans had driven the Tuatha de Danaan northward from Greece as a result of an invasion from Syria, presumably. Herodotus in his book *History* relates the capture by "Phoenicians" of the Danaan shrine of the White Goddess Io at Argos in the Peloponnese in Greece, which was then the religious Capital of the Peloponnese. The Cretans (Early Minoans) had colonized it about the year 1750 B.C. Thus the Tuatha de Danaan must have been fully aware of the Cosmology and belief system of the Minoans, since the religious mysteries were given openly and freely during this period. It might be assumed that when the Tuatha de Danaan were driven from Greece and subsequently came into contact with the Celts and Druids in Britain, that the knowledge they possessed was taken over by the Druids, who conducted

228

a Religious Revolution in Crete, in order to retain total control of the knowledge, which added to their "Secret Doctrine", presumably Cabalistic science already in their possession, handed down from Adam and the Patriarchs, through Noah and Moses.

The Tuatha de Danaan as Pelasgains who honoured the Goddess Dana or Danu (Anna), sister of Belus and regarded by some as the Moon goddess Minerva and by others as Io of Argos, definitely has some historical importance to the Freemasons in Scotland, since in *The Battle of The Trees*, I produced Masonic graffiti at a church in Galway Scotland, which refers in symbolic form to the Goddess Io (the horned or Cow Goddess). It may well be then, that the Royal Celtic Dynastic line of Jesus' grandmother Anna was an unbroken line deriving from ancient Greek sources and the Tuatha de Danaan. The festival, which celebrates the Goddess Dana/Danu? Or Anna occurs on March 15th, which is a significant date in the Beth-Luis Nion Calendar/Alphabet. Anna probably also means 'Queen', 'Goddess' or Mother', she appears in Irish mythology as the Dannaan Goddess Ana or Anan; Ana was the mother of the three original Danaan gods Brian, Iuchuba and Iuchar. Ana was later depicted as a nun. The name Anna confers divinity and it is odd that Ar-ri-an (Aryan?) means 'High fruitful Mother' who turns the wheel of Heaven. Her Cretan counterpart was Aria (d) ne i.e. Ariadne (Arian?), who helped Theseus overthrow the Bull-Minotaur Cult (Solar Kingship) at Knossos. As I will cover later Hitler was very well read in this particular story. Further as the Germans push ahead with a Federal Europe, is it not their long awaited goal?

Anna to the Christian mystics was 'God's grandmother'. It is certain that at some point a certain Anna did propagate a Royal dynastic line of the Celts and also by intermarriage with the ancient British Royal Family (not the current House of Windsor, who were imported from Germany) According to a manuscript in Jesus College MS. 20, Anna was mother of Penardin who married King Lear, and was therefore mother of Bran the Blessed and grandmother of Caractacus, thus linking the Celtic Royal Family with the Ancient British Royal Family. Also Anna daughter of St. Joseph of Arimathea is said to have married King Beli and there is a claim that King Beli's grandson, King Lear, married Penardin daughter of St. Anna. Thus in this MS there are claims that members of the Celtic Royal Family married two British Kings, Beli Mawr the Great and King Lear.[71] Thus Anna it seems was vital as a link between British and Celtic Royal Families and as the descendent of a hereditary line that allegedly bore Jesus and probably the Mary Magdalene.

The Druids had some race memory of a cataclysm or Deluge and it seems that they may have existed in Britain and adapted their beliefs to those held by the god-like Tuatha de Danaan. The reliance upon myth for historical truth is dependent upon interpretation. There is a myth for instance, which records the emasculation of Uranus by his son Cronos (time) and the vengeance subsequently taken on Cronus by his son Zeus, who banished him to the Western Underworld, under the charge of the 'hundred-handed ones'. In its original sense it records the annual supplanting of the old Oak-King, by his successor. The cutting of the mistletoe from the Oak by the Druids typified the emasculation of the Old King by his successor - the mistletoe being the prime phallic emblem. In all probability 'The Cutting of the Elm' ceremony, enacted at Gisors in the 12th century between the British and French, may have related to this ancient Druidic ritual, and the separation of old goals from new ones. In the Peloponnese in Greece amongst the Pelopian dynasty, the King was Eucharistically eaten after castration. The Peloponnese Oak-Tree cult had been superimposed on a Barley-cult, of which Cronus was the hero and in which human sacrifice was the rule. In the barley-cult as with the Oak-cult, the successor to the Kingship inherited the favours of the priestess and his Goddess Mother. In both cults the victim became immortal and his oracular remains were removed to some sacred island. Thus there is an indication that some abberative belief including Solar Kingship and Oak Tree worship had been brought by migrating tribes to Ireland. The Druids were also known as accomplished magicians and adepts one presumes in Energy Grid phenomena. Diogenes Laertius referred to the Druids as "barbarian Philosophers", and bracketed them together with the Persian Magi, the "Chaldeans" the Babylonians and Assyrians and a group he refers to as the "Gymnosophists" of the Hindus. In fact all were magicians versed in the "Secret Doctrine", or Cabalistic science and it is claimed that Druids, Magi and Gymnosophists all existed among peoples derived from the racial root stock of wandering tribes who were the original inhabitants of Southern Russia - The Indo -Europeans who eventually invaded Greece.

Whatever the specific racial origins were, clearly from very early times there have been magicians and Shaman who carried the group memories and magical practices derived presumably from the Patriarchs. The Priesthood of the Babylonians were magicians and the Tower of Babel in its step architecture, was a precursor of the Masonic pyramidal step system of knowledge that saw its parallel in the step pyramid of Egypt and finally Russia. The Great Pyramid of Gizeh represented the horizontal courses or degrees, of a secret Paternal Fraternity or Brotherhood that would become Freemasonry. The secret chamber corresponded with the 20th degree of Masonry and aligned via the descending passage to the star A. Draconis, when crossing the Meridian below the Pole in 2170 B.C. Evidently then some secret is involved in this observation, but it is difficult to determine exactly what the significance of that alignment is, or the significant date, unless it was the Re-incarnation date of a Master, that propagated Freemasonry?

The Patriarchal Indo-European migrants carried with them, a different message from The Holy Grail, which came to earth c. 10 000 B.C. their message was an **Elitist** tier, which incorporated a caste or **class system**. At the beginning of the 15th Century B.C. this group of migrants reached India and confusingly were termed "Aryan" invaders, however they were the founders of Hinduism, perhaps now we are coming to the bottom of Madam Blavatsky's Masters. There are numerous startling resemblances between Hinduism and Druidism; both practised cremation of the dead, carried out human sacrifice, had vast numbers of deities and taught metempsychosis. The similarities also relate to seemingly insignificant trivialities, such as the Buddha normally depicted as sitting cross-legged position, whilst the Celts are described as adopting this position and in which their gods were often shown. It is perhaps significant, that in Neolithic times, the Goddess was shown in such a position, as the Earth Mother, with large fatty thighs and referred to as a steatopygous figure, such as the one found in Minoan Crete. What has been forgotten is that the earliest Cretans were of the Mediterranean racial type, but among them were the broad-heads. These Neolithic peoples came into contact with mountaineers from the north, or descendents of the Palaeolithic races. Evidently then, even at this early stage, there was an attempt to fuse this new message, with the existing belief system, which incorporated the cross-legged, or lotus position, which the Buddha perpetuates, as a religious mystery.

Whilst the Druids evolved as an intellectual and secret hierarchal group, who commanded Grid knowledge this was probably also the case of Hinduism, the Brahims or the Gymnosophists of Diogenes, this caste system in its upper levels exercised control over the hierarchal **four**-caste system, with the knights or kshatriyas coming below them and the Brahims like the Druids were both communal law givers. Further, the Brahims had an oral tradition where the secrets were not committed to writing as with the Druids. Most importantly both were advisors on RITUAL, placing great emphasis on its correct execution. Ritual in my own opinion creates great aberration in the person who practises it, since it becomes not merely the practises of religion or Churchanity, but a form of psychotherapeutic security whereby the ritual comes to represent ORDER without which chaos would ensue. People in present time that incorporate ritual to a high degree in their lives usually have a heavy past life or lives in ritualistic religion. The Patriarchal practises which were highly ritualistic and which became incorporated into many religions stem from these earlier times, when there was a memory of a great cataclysm with enormous chaos - a Magnetic Reversal. The ritual I conclude, was not only necessary to perpetuate a hierarchy or an Elite Priesthood, but was also employed to avert similar catastrophe; however the ritual could never hope to avert a an electro-magnetic event and thus the ritual was merely an abberative form of behaviour, in much the same way as a seriously disturbed person may feel the need to wash their hands many

231

times in a day, to avoid some catastrophe or DISORDER, which is not altogether clear to their rational mind, but seems perfectly sensible to their irrational mind.

The striking parallel between the Brahims and the Druids might point to an early contact, or some common source of Patriarchal origin, perhaps with the Indo-Europeans, but very definitely the Patriarchal tribes descended from Adam. There also appeared to be a common root memory of some cataclysm. Within this parental root racial stock, there was evidently a caste or class system, which depended on knowledge or magical expertise and a sense of superiority. One cannot deny the possibility given the accounts of Kings or Princes in the Indian epics, that prior to a Magnetic Reversal or cataclysm, the world had operated such a class system of tiered magical knowledge and ritual, where those surviving a cataclysm which presumably was precipitated through the misuse of Grid memory or Akashic Record knowledge, had merely perpetuated both their ritualistic practises **and** a class system, which they eventually imposed on The Holy Grail message of Re-incarnation in Crete during the Religious Revolution and eventually sent out a message into the world, that Re-incarnation was the prerogative of Sacred Kings and Messiah's.

In the early beliefs of these Patriarchal tribes, one detects the psychological mechanism of PROPITIATION Which is the attempt of individuals to buy off the imagined danger, such behaviour is indicative of a very low emotional and psychological state. It is an effort in apathy to hold away a dangerous source of pain. The survivors of a Magnetic Reversal would become propitiative towards the source of that reversal, which is the electro-magnetic spectrum created by the sun (light), hence the god Ra or the Sun god, but also Monarchy, which is the resultant progression of that. The Solar Monarchical worshippers are generally those who have on the track of time, been suppressed by Solar Kingship. When one looks at the worship of certain deities and observance of certain customs and beliefs, the psychological case of propitiation is unmistakable, with the hands raised in subservience. Father William Schmidt in 1931 produced a magnum opus *The Origins of the Idea of God*, outlining the first signs of this idea (of propitiation) with those pre-hunt rituals whose aim is not merely to ensure mastery over the prey, but also to allay the anger of its "spirit". He gives a typical example from Anthropology and describes a pygmy-artist drawing a representation of his quarry before pursuing it. Afterwards having been successful, he places blood and hair from the slaughtered animal on his picture, and then rubs the entirety out as the rising sun touches it. This has a sacrificial basis to the Sun -God Ra and earlier origins of Solar Kingship. The adulation of the Sun and honour of the Sun God and Solar Kingship, all centred on worship of the electro-magnetic spectrum. It was a psychological case of propitiation towards something, which had in race memory been a threat or danger and had produced a cataclysm. I personally in my later work have steered away from the word "God" for these reasons and prefer to associate the message circa 10,000 B.C. with an extra-dimensional and compassionate source, which is the true Spiritual Hierarchy. On a karmic level, the Patriarchal groups that survived the Deluge became the total effect of what they had caused, Solar King worship and solar worship was a part of that. Monarchic ritual which is maintained to a very high degree in Britain is I am afraid a part of the same very abberative process - without the ritual what would happen - a man or woman would have stand on their own merits?

The Druids certainly were advocates of Mosaic Law, which like Judaic law has a high ritual content. The Druids were said to be "the Brotherhood of Pythagoras", and Pythagoras was said to have been initiated into the deeper mysteries by the Idian Dactyls in Crete. Pythagoras certainly held a belief in the Transmigration of souls, which has some association with Re-incarnation, but he also believed that man could Re-incarnate as an animal and advocated no harm to animals on account of the fact that a human soul might be resident in the animal's body. This is a very curious idea that either came from soul memory or the Grid through channelling and I did suggest in *Alternative 4*, that at some stage in the case history of the MRC he was forced to evolve through an animal body line, when as a result presumably of a Major Magnetic reversal there was no human body line to enter. Some racial memory of this may have been accessed by the Shamans in their Cabalistic magical practise and thus give some background to the above belief and curious Palaeolithic wall paintings of man-animals, which may not entirely depend on the idea of totem beast. The theory I proposed, that such men were forced to enter the body of the Amphibians (Frogs and Reptiles? The latter came up in a UFO incident) after a cataclysmic Deluge, was based on an assumption, that only amphibian bodies are able to exist in water and on land. However there is no indication that a man would choose to Re-incarnate into an animal body whilst he was able to Re-incarnate into a Homosapien line. Pythagoras believed that the soul was demoted to an animal body after some wrongful life, which as a belief may stem from the idea above, after the hidden science was misused resulting in a cataclysm. As a race memory it may simply be another form of my own theory. This may account for the peculiar amorphous figures of semi-reptilian type figures on the walls of caves from the Palaeolithic era (*Plate 11*). You will note the hands raised in supplication (propitiation) perhaps to the power of light or the sun and the electro-magnetic spectrum. Further the Druids carried on this preference for caves

St. John The Evangelist I have already suggested was an Arch Druid and if Pythagoras was a source of Druidism, then Pythagoras also held the number seven to be sacred and the sacred heptad turns up many times in the prophetic Apocalypse of St. John. Further the Boibel-Loth Alphabet, which with Ogham

233

script was used by the Druids, contains many approximations to Biblical names, taken from Genesis and Exodus, which in Christian times had lost their religious importance. Lot, Telmen, Jachin, Hur, Caleb, Ne-esthan are all names concerned with Sinai, Southern Judea and the Edonite Dead Sea region. This is where the Essene Communities were settled from about 150 B.C. to 132 A.D. The Essenes appear to have been an offshoot of the Therapeutae, or Healers an ascetic Jewish sect settled by Lake Mareotis in Egypt. I have already alluded to the possibility, that the Essenes were a pre-determined outcome group of the Druids, where the goal was specifically the outcome of the events of Golgotha. Though Jews the Essenes believed in a western Paradise and like the Druids, believed in the return of pure souls to the sun, whose rising they would invoke every day.

The Druids are credited with the building of Stone-Henge on Salisbury plain in Wiltshire in the UK. It is now generally credited to be a Solar-Lunar observatory. This brings us to another contentious point, in so far as the stone circles are not circles, but **egg-shaped** ellipses or ovals, wider at one end than the other. From the point of view of 'Who Killed The Minoans?' this is a very interesting and overlooked archaeological point, since in the late Minoan period of Crete and the Knossos site after the Religious Revolution, seals show definite egg structures, which I reproduced in *The Battle of The Trees*. Museum authorities have never explained these seals or the obvious connection to re-birth and Orphic philosophy, but clearly they show the input of a different philosophy than was present in the Early Minoan period prior to The Religious Revolution. One might from the accumulating evidence clearly point to the Druids as the possible source of The Religious Revolution. Further there was the curious ceremony of The Pope (Angelo Roncali) who attended a ceremony in an Illuminatus Temple in the 70's, where a woman tapped an egg, with a wand, which we decided was a particularly Druid ceremony: The wand being synonymous with rood of the Druid.

Evidently then, the aim of bringing back a pagan religion to a Unified and Federal Europe, did not include the root of that religion, which extended back **prior** to the infusion of the archetypal significance of the egg into a Matriarchal belief system and Cosmology, which did not include eggs or the concept that the world's potential lay purely in the male or solar monarchy or even a group of Initiates descended from the Patriarchs. Interestingly the egg-shape is one which describes the human Electro-Magnetic biofield and in *Alternative 4* I discussed ways in which secret weapons technology could alter this field and then be passed off as an alleged UFO sighting. Whether the manipulated UFO phenomenon is the testing of weapons or mind control technology acting through the human biofield, for eventual application to the MRC's concept of "Paradise" – psycho civilised controlled and ordered society where nothing moves is taken up elsewhere.

Hecateus stated that the tutor of Pythagoras was a certain Abaris who has been proposed was a Druid. If the Druids did conduct The Religious Revolution in Crete at Knossos then the claim that Pythagoras was initiated in Crete by the Idian Dactlyls (the tutors of Zeus), has more than a mythical claim but more of a historical claim, in so far as the Dactlyls as tutors or initiates may have been Druids or at least Masters, which would account for the cauldrons and tripods found in the Psychro Cave. Abaris was described as a Hyperborean and it is generally agreed that in a passage from Hecateus (circa 500 B.C.) quoted by Diodorus, the land of the Hyperborean could only be Britain. Interestingly Diodorus quoted "that daughter of giants" as the birthplace of Let, the Island of the Hyperboreans and in this account, her son Apollo was venerated above all gods. Stonehenge is thought to be veneration to the Sun (god) laid out in true Apollonian style. The idea of giants and dwarfs runs through a great many early myths of a pre- Deluge era, which I suggested in *Alternative 4* was perhaps a race memory of two racial types, the giant type and the dwarf-type, the latter may simply be a remnant stock of those who survived a magnetic reversal or nuclear event on Earth which might account for the peculiar carved figures on Easter Island which showed all the evidence of radiation poisoning. It may well be that one bodyline had either survived a magnetic reversal or nuclear event whilst another bodyline had not or at least had been protected in some fashion, which intriguingly begs the question whether 'Noah's Ark' does not correspond to the Space programme today as a recycle of events of the past and the attempt to find a safe haven from an Apocalyptic event in the future. Assuming that a spirit sought the healthier body line to Re-incarnate into, if that body line was giant and white, then one can quite easily view the obsession with blonde-blue-eyed races, is merely a soul memory, which when allowed to come forward into present time becomes an aberration as it was with the Third Reich.

Diodorus the Greek Historian also described a vast Temple in Britain, which could only have been Stonehenge in Wiltshire and Diodorus describes the system of calendration that was used was based on the **nineteen** year cycle, which is the reigning period of a Solar King. At the end of the nineteen-year cycle Apollo was said to visit the island, playing the harp to accompany the dancing worshippers. The connection of the Druids and Celts to Crete and the Religious Revolution at Knossos that enthroned a Solar King (Minos) looks all the more probable. Further, the Greek God Apollo was credited with giving mankind the harp, which well may be a gloss for the Cosmic Keyboard and the knowledge of sympathetic vibration, which he himself had received from Hermes (or Mercury), which implies that THE DRUIDS WERE HERMETIC PHILOSOPHERS. Let us consider the importance of that statement, in so far as early iconography e.g. the Stone Ring from Naples *(fig 28)* which I discuss more fully later, shows a LAW OF THREE which is used in esoteric law to resolve problems, in this case three wise *Hermetic men* are visiting the Christ child. The middle person of the trio who all wear Greek-like tunics, has the unmistakable Hermetic cap and the sign of Mercury (the star of Hermes), shines above the central figure of the trio as the transcendent third stage beyond death, combining the woman as Goddess and the Twin Kings, representing the ancient idea of the Trinity. Further the central figure has wings and represents Hermes as the conductor of souls to and from Heaven. The icon from around the sixth Century A.D. evidently shows an earlier truth and knowledge of the events of Bethlehem, where in this case it is clearly remembered that hermetic philosopher's played a role in the coming of the Messiah or man-god. Thus we might consider that the Druids were not only linked to the Religious Revolution in Crete but also to the events in Bethlehem. The Essenes also believed the idea of the man-god and thus it seems entirely likely that the lower Order of the two-tiered Essene priesthood was subservient to a higher Order – the Druids.

Fig.28 **Impression from a stone ring found at Naples.**
Sixth century A.D. The three kings bringing gifts to the Christ Child who is the New Year babe.

Druidic time computation was based on the solar-Lunar cycles in much the same way as the Knossos Calendar in the Late Minoan period in Crete. The period of nineteen years which it requires for lunar and solar years to achieve synchronicity, is also as it happens the period between eclipses. The prediction of eclipses must have formed one of the most important applications of Stonehenge as an astronomical observatory. Intriguingly the old name for Salisbury, the plain where Stonehenge is located is Sarum, which is a Latin form of an earlier name Saros, which was the Babylon word for 3 600, the number of days between eclipses, still recalled in the "Saros-cycle" by astronomers.

There is also another link between Druid and the Religious Revolution, in so far as iconographic seals of the Late Minoan period, show what are described as orgiastic dances. There is a reference to orgiastic music and dancing in a description by Hecateus and was a technique of inducing **possession**. It is difficult to explain further what exactly the possession took the form of and what spirits or race memory they were trying to induce although it is probable that drugs were used thus facilitating a connection to the Grid. Further the appearance of Poppy Goddesses in the Late Minoan period, implies that opium was used to control the populous and make them suggestible to the new archetypal symbols? As a method of subduing a populous and creating a zombie-like culture of suggestibility, this has worked very well for the ruling Elite throughout time and the One World Order plan has used this methodology many times. Further The Protocols of Zion (an alleged plan for world domination) refers to this aim, of a drug suggestible culture brought about by the Elite. Several scholars have maintained that Druidism was a shamanistic possession cult, perhaps utilising drugs to access the Grid memory? However it is known that they possessed the power of PROPHECY and thus must have utilised GRID HISTORY or THE AKASHIC RECORD. In other words during these possessions they must have been channelling down information from the Grid, that great library in the sky carrying a complete record of SPECIES events imprinted on the morphogenetic boplasma.
.
I have already suggested that St. John, who wrote the prophetic Apocalypse, was a Druid and therefore Celt. According to Christine Hartley in *The Western Mystery Tradition:* "The first suggestion of the idea that St. John the Divine was a Kelt (Celt) came from a paper given in the Scottish Lodge of the Theosophical Society in 1894...The opening of his Gospel is the natural opening of the Kelt who had come to Christianity. There is the basic Keltic certainty that in the beginning there was the Word- Logos - the Supreme Being - 'the same was in the beginning with God'; that is not Jewish in its approach. Those first five verses separate St. John from the other Apostles. The three other Evangelists, be it noted, always speak of 'the people', but St. John invariably writes 'The Jews', as though they were to him foreigners". Furthermore, she goes on to say that:

"Jesus is a Keltic Western name and that the Hebrew form of it is Joshua. Jesus is a Keltic name and the God of the Gauls or Gaels was the counterpart Hesus". Given that the Druids were obsessed with a memory of a past Cataclysm, then if St. John channelled information from the Grid to produce the Prophetic Apocalypse, it was **past historical data which he projected into future time** as a prophesy of another cyclical cataclysm.

The pyramid always held significance to initiates into the religious mysteries and the Pythagoreans swore their oaths on the 'holy tetracys', a figure consisting of ten dots arranged in pyramidal form. The top dot represented position and the rays (electro-magnetic spectrum from above as the sun-god Apollo), the two dots below extension (Twin Kings?) the three dots below those are surface and the four dots at the bottom were three dimensional space. The central dot of the figure makes five with each of the four dots at the sides. This positioning of the dots may relate to some secret law regarding Atomic matter and the position of the atoms in various states. Although there is something similar in higher levels of certain secret societies, it is certainly interesting that this secret design of five dots with one located centrally was part of the secret sign on the sword of Hercules in the Crab Mural at Cardiff Castle, where although the top level of this particular group (probably Rose-Croix level of Scottish Rite Freemasonry), believe they have the secret, I am afraid I observe they got it wrong. Pythagoras is said by some sources to have obtained his main doctrines from the Orphic Mystics. In the *Life of Pythagoras* Iamblichus remarks that: "Orpheus said that the eternal essence of number is the most providential principle of the universe, of heaven, of earth, and of the nature intermediate to these; and more, that it is the basis of the permanency of divine natures, gods and demons". The Pythagoreans had a proverb "all things are assimilated to number" and Pythagoras is quoted by Ianblichus as having laid down in his sacred discourse that "number is the ruler of forms and ideas and the cause of gods and demons".

A system of dots has mystified archaeologists who have found such a system in the Altamira Palaeolithic cave in Spain. Ever since the daughter of a landowner discovered polychrome bison on the ceiling of the cave in 1879, the obscure origins of art have been a subject of intense debate. Hunting, magic, fertility rites and proto-aestheticism have all been proposed as keys to understanding these early depictions. According to a theory forwarded by Jean Clottes and David Lewis-Williams in their book: *The Shamans of Prehistory*, the authors argue that prehistoric artists were attempting to commune with a spirit world just beyond the cave walls. Different sorts of images they maintain, reflect the various stages of the artists *trances*, which were brought on by *narcotics*, *ritual ecstasy*, and/ or sensory deprivation in the *caves'* darkness: "Our theory explains far more hard data than any other so far", maintained Clottes, a prehistoric-art scholar based in the Pyrenees city of Foix, who advises the French Ministry of Culture. The authors have noted the similarity to the rock art of the San, a South African hunter-gatherer group where the paintings are acknowledged to be inspired, by visions experienced in *shamanism rituals*. The Druids were known to prefer caves, mountains and woods for their secret practises and St. John, wrote the Apocalypse in a cave on the Greek island of Patmos. The curious red dot pattern that covers drawings found in Castillo Spain may not be entirely hallucinogenic but some form of thought extracted from contact with the Grid. Psychics can read the history of an object, often by just feeling it. Thus matter carries some imprint of its past and perhaps the caves were sought, to psychically connect with the history of matter and its formation and organisation and its connections through the bioplasma to the greater pattern. Drugs may certainly have been found to be useful in such connections to the Grid/Akashic/ morphogentic matter event and information on the past, but what the dots do in fact represent must remain the subject of debate.

Whilst there are obvious similarities between Pythagorean doctrine and that of the Druids, Pythagoras (circa 530 B.C.) cannot have been the founder of the Druids as has been suggested; there are too many archaeological anomalies which link the Druids to an earlier time and Bronze Age Greece. Which is not to say that Pythagoras did not form an updated group that rested historically on the Druid Brotherhood. However the link of Pythagoras is an interesting one, since Pythagoras found his truth manifest in the elements of form, order, proportion, limit and harmony in the Universe. He was an adept in geometrical and mathematical forms and it is interesting to speculate whether in his initiation in Crete in the Psychro Cave, he was tutored in Matriarchal early Minoan knowledge which incorporated the Cosmological geometrical models of the UVG 120 sphere with its equilateral triangles possibly displayed in the ancient thronged- stones; or whether this tutorage was from a Druidic, or a Jewish Cabalistic source. Pythagoras certainly had been tutored in the Cretan Beth-Luis-Nion Alphabet, but found the Boibel-Loth calendar based on a year of 360+5 days, better suited than the Beth-Luis-Nion alphabet of 364+1 days, to his deep philosophical speculations on vibratory resonance, the musical octave and the ogdoad. In *Alternative 4,* I discussed Pythagoras in relation to his research on the effects of vibratory resonance in musical harmony on the Human biofield and emotions; and it must be assumed that the Druids and the Cabalists had access to such knowledge. What we can say is that there was a central intelligent and speculative philosophical group, who had access to a great deal of knowledge including the Earth Grid and the human biofield and vibratory resonant research. Further alphabetic and religious mysteries were taught and given the evidence I produced in *The Battle of The Trees*, which pointed to Jesus as an initiate into the alphabetic mysteries, one may assume that such a group was ongoing throughout the centuries and maintained a powerful grip on the world's political and religious stage.

Pythagoras intimated that he knew all about the Earth Energy Grid, when he voiced his World cosmological view that it was composed of a dark indefinite vapour, but that this vapour had been drawn into a **geometric order**. The Universe was **a living sphere**, whose centre was the Earth. This sounds remarkably like a description of the UVG 120 sphere. Obviously this was a highly advanced scientific viewpoint for circa 530 B.C. given that many Scientists are still unaware of the Earth Grid in our own time. Such an understanding that the world was round coupled with Grid understanding of formation of landmasses, must have accounted for the early navigational maps. Further the use of sympathetic vibration to illicit medical cures was to be used by the Greek initiate Priests or Healers who held god-like status. Finally Pythagoras who was a member of the Aristocracy or more accurately the decayed gentry class, found the whole idea of Democracy abhorrent and certainly since the Druids operated a caste system with the Druid priests somewhat higher than the Chieftain who had to consult them before speaking, meant that Pythagoras and his doctrine would have fitted into Druidic doctrine, indeed if it did not originate with them after his initiation in Crete, by the Dactyls.

With regard to one Celtic /Druidic custom mentioned by Caesar and confirmed by other sources, that of **FOSTERING CHILDREN**, such a custom would explain much in terms of a number of miraculous births in history including the so-called Divine conception of Mary alleged mother of Jesus. I will return to this point shortly, however in legend there was another important surfacing of this Celtic custom in the story of King Arthur who apparently was fostered and it was recorded that Kai was his foster brother. King Arthur of course was to gain his authority through Merlin, who evidently was a Druid or Arch magician. Under the practise of fostering, the responsibility for the upbringing and education of a child was taken over by others and the child did not return to the bosom of his own family until puberty.

THE ESSENES

The Essenes had marked similarities to Pythagoreans and it seems also had a place amongst the events of the Crucifixion. Jesus has been claimed as an Essene Priest, however the Essenes unlike the Druids did not enter into Matrimony and certainly Biblical texts go to great lengths to prove Jesus was celibate and not married, despite the alternative accounts of His relationship with the Mary Magdalene which surfaced with the finding of *The Nag Hammadi Scrolls* and which I covered in in my own witness account. The Scrolls are a collection of biblical texts, which are essentially Gnostic in character, dating probably from around A.D. 400 and these documents certainly illustrate a very different account of Jesus in his relationship with the Mary Magdalene, The Gospel of Phillip states: "There were three who always walked with the Lord; Mary his mother and her sister and Magdalene, the one who was called his companion". The Gospel goes on to say: "And the companion of the saviour is the Mary Magdalene, but Christ loved her more than all the disciples and used to kiss her often on her mouth". The Disciples, who may have been Essenic and celibate, were offended by it and expressed disapproval saying: " Why do you love her more than all of us?" The Saviour answered and said:" Why do I not love you like her?" In the Gospel of Mary, Peter addresses the Magdalene: "Sister, we know that the Saviour loved you more than the rest of women, tell us the words of the Saviour which you remember, which you know but we do not". Peter in his jealousy says later:" did he really speak privately with a woman and not openly to us? Are we to turn about and all listen to her? Did he prefer her to us". The Gospels tell of a completely different character for Jesus than the one portrayed in the Bible where in one undated codex, *The Second Treatise of the Great Seth*, Jesus is depicted precisely as he is in the heresy of Basilides, escaping his death, by an ingenious substitution on the cross: "I did not succumb to them as they had planned. And I did not die in reality but in appearance, lest I be put to shame by them, .for my death which they think happened (happened) to them in their error and blindness, since they nailed their man unto their death It was another, their father, who drank the gall and the vinegar it was not I. They struck me with the reed; it was another Simon, who bore the cross on his shoulder. It was another upon whom they placed the crown of thorns and I was laughing at their ignorance." [87] A Priest entertaining an open sexual relationship would accord with a Druid Priest who entered into matrimony, but not with an Essenic Priest, for whom family life and marriage was forbidden. The Essene Priests reflected Jewish Priests or Rabbis in so far as women were intensely disliked. Philo in his *Apologia pro Judaeis* quotes even more scathing opinions held by the Essenes on women where generally she is: "selfish, excessively jealous, skilful in perverting her husband's morals and seducing him by never ending charms".

I am drawn back to the Floor of The Summer Smoking Room at Cardiff Castle Wales UK, where the outer circle of the concentric ring design on the floor contains hedges, which was a uniquely Essene feature, with their private communities protected by high hedges to keep prying eyes out. Hedges enabled secrecy, but since the floor contained a Universal Political and religious goal for a Federal European Super state, is it implied that the Essenes, perhaps as a branch group set up by Arch Druids to carry out a particular function in much the same way as branches of secret groups perform that function today, were in some way involved with the religious goal? Martin Larson[88] in his scholarly account of the Essene Christian faith, draws 36 parallels between the Essenes and the Pythagoreans and gives substantial evidence to show that the teachings of Jesus were really Essene beliefs. The most important observation is that The Essenes like the Druids possessed the power of PROPHECY. This almost certainly indicates knowledge of the Grid and the so-called Akashic record of Rudolf Steiner. Further the Pythagoreans and Essenes worshipped a SACRIFICED GOD-MAN AND THE ESSENES PARTICULARILY AND UNIQUELY BELIEVED IN THE SECOND COMING OF THE GOD-MAN. One sees all the hall-marks here of a pre-determined group, set up by the Druids or some ascendant group of the Druids, with pre-determined beliefs, which would suite the pre-determined outcome of the planned events at Golgotha. Man would patiently wait for the Second Coming, whilst the One World Order got on with their plans; it kept the audience nicely ordered, whilst the Elite could perform business as usual. Thus it would appear that if St. John who wrote Revelations was a Druid Priest, then he held the unique Essene view of The Second Coming. This leads me to believe that the Essenes in their highest Order were a sub group of the greater order of Druids, perhaps set up to carry the events of the Crucifixion without the event ever being linked to the hidden Masters, who as Druids remained in The British Isles. The religious mystery was acted out on the world's stage in Jerusalem, the script it appears was written from Scotland from whence the main actors derived in a family tree dating back to Ana and the Tuatha de Danaan - from Greece?

The Essenes had one definitive and unique belief and teaching, that of the Second Coming, where their last Teacher of Righteousness was expected to send a representative who would be endowed with power to conduct the Last Judgement and to set up the Kingdom of the saints on Earth. The Teacher was confused later with the Messiah concept which is found in Orthodox Judaism, which itself was probably influenced by Zoroastrian input. The belief that a powerful personality would one day emerge, who either by force of Jewish arms or by supernatural intervention and support, would defeat all enemies and establish at least an independent nation, or more probably a great empire, had been a basic element of Jewish expectations for centuries even before the time of Alexander. The Messiah however was quite different for the Zoroastrian

Essene. The Messiah was restricted to the ethnic interests of the Jews. The Essene Messiah by contrast was Zoroastrian Soshans engrafted upon the age-old political and economic protagonists of Judaic visions. The original saviour god was Osiris the Egyptian deity who was honoured not only by the people of the Nile, but eventually all the Greco-Roman Empire. If Jesus and the Magdalene sought to re-enact the Egyptian mysteries and/or the Greek mysteries in the events at Golgotha of a man saviour god, then the background to the myth of Osiris is important. It is thought that Osiris may have been a historical personage who married *his sister*. Osiris was murdered by a group of conspirators led by his brother Set. In *Alternative 4*, I gave a decoded significance of the myth based on the archetypal numbers, which relate to the story of two brothers (Set and Osiris), who had different beliefs i.e. Matriarchal and Patriarchal. However here, the important point of the myth is that the priest of a great cult, which became dominant in Egypt and later proliferated to the Greco-Roman Empire, finally transformed Osiris into the god-man saviour.

Osiris in myth was born on the 25th December, which later became the birthday of Jesus, symbolising the rebirth of the Sun (and a Solar King). The Betrayal of the Magdalene by Jesus and the secret Brotherhood behind him, came when in the final twist of the re-enactment of the Greek Cretan mysteries, Jesus acted out the Osiris and Isis **Egyptian** mystery. Why should that matter particularly? Well the outcome would be entirely different; the re-enactment of the mysteries according to Early Minoan (**Greek**) beliefs would have displayed the belief of RE-INCARNATION (allied to Democracy), whilst a re-enactment of the Egyptian mysteries would have displayed A MAN-GOD SAVIOUR (allied to a political system of communism run by an Elite). The two beliefs were not compatible and since Jesus won, the belief in Re-incarnation went back underground as the 'Underground Stream' of The Holy Grail wisdom. The *second cut* had occurred. Osiris married his sister Isis, who bore Horus and they made up the **Egyptian Holy and Royal Family**. This is somewhat reminiscent of the **Celtic Royal Family** and implies two sets of genealogies and two priesthoods and more importantly two secret groups vying on the world's stage, one with allegiance to the old Egyptian Priesthood and monarchy which was Jewish and the other a Gentile priesthood dating back to Adam and Noah, which appears to be none other than the Druids and a British Royal Family (no wonder the British Royal Family was replaced with Germans! Although Prince Phillip interestingly enough comes from Greek stock) One suspects that the Jewish Priesthood was supported by the Essenes in the lowest levels of the group, but in the upper tiered and Higher Order there was probably allegiance to the Druids or the Gentile group, which may have been the parent Order and secret chiefs that set up the Essenes specifically to carry the events of Jerusalem. What a scene this sets for the **double agent** caper! Which is really the story of Jesus and Jerusalem. Osiris became the supreme god-man and Isis the ultimate Mother-goddess, whose role and importance expanded of course over the centuries in the Osirian Cult and finally she became a divinity in her own right. After Set had murdered and dismembered his brother's body, Isis collected all the portions of Osiris and she resurrected him into a second and immortal life. This certainly harks back to the more ancient Minoan source of immortality as the Mother Goddess's gift and clearly whilst Osiris was of a Matriarchal belief, this was sub-ordinated to his role as the Man-Saviour god, as Jesus would sub-ordinate the role of the Magdalene (whose genealogies may have shown she was his sister) in favour of his re-enactment of the **Egyptian** Osiris mystery over the **truth** and the **Greek** mystery. The fact that 72 priests controlled Set in myth, indicates the Beth-Luis-Nion Alphabet (with its 72 characters), which means that the priests were Patriarchal and Druidic. Jesus waited 3 days or 72 hours for his Resurrection, an indication that he was a Solar King and controlled by the Druidic Priesthood. That appears to contradict the fact that he acted out the Egyptian mysteries and not the Greek mysteries and thus implies that he supported the Egyptian Royal dynasty and Priesthood. However if as Magdalene believed, that he would conform to the plan to act out the Greek mysteries (which he ultimately did not), mysteries and their archetypal symbols that would have still been recognised by the people in those days, then the conclusion is that Jesus acted in a double agent capacity and "fooled them", as he states in the Egyptian Scrolls. Thus went the hope of the Millennium to bring back the truth to mankind. However the fact that the Magdalene fled to France and a Greek colony at Marseilles, implies that she was not safe to return to Britain or Egypt and thus was duped by both groups? And presumably by St. John when she was murdered in France and the remaining truth taken along with the child from her marriage to Jesus. St. John we know then arrived back in Scotland – mission accomplished?

The Essenes also in a somewhat similar practise to that of the Celts and Druids, occasionally adopted children, importantly this was not fostering but **adoption** and therefore the children remained with the Essene group, without recourse to their origins. In the Stone ring from Naples the implication is that the Philosophical Hermetic trio who visited the birth of Jesus and who are referred to as "Kings from the East" in Biblical texts, were in all probability Druids. This attempt to link them to the East is probably an attempt to link the birth with the Egyptian Dynasty and the **Jewish** priests. However if Jesus had been fostered into a Jewish family (Mary and Joseph) at an early age, then the return of the Druidic Priests would link Jesus to his origins and that of the Celts. If the Druids intended to get 'their man' on the throne in the Middle East and reduce or destroy the Egyptian Royal dynasty and the Jewish Priesthood, then this makes sense, for only a Jew and not a Celt could have appealed to the people. This would also account for the "virgin birth" of Jesus. The Essenes and Pythagoreans were Communistic and practised sharing of property and equality in many forms including dress, which was in the form of simple white robes. Living and eating habits were frugal and in line with **Communistic principles** - shared, whilst the Order itself accumulated unlimited wealth that signifies it was being used to **support another goal and a Higher Order**, particularly as the Essenes were frugal in their habits. I will come to al history in a moment, but suffice it here to say that before Jesus became associated with the Mary Magdalene his teachings were almost entirely Communistic, which one would expect if he had been reared under the tutorage of the Essenes. The later Buddhist influences in his teaching and the preaching of Universal love was due to the Greek influence and Magdalene. Unlike the Druids however, both Pythagoreans and Essenes forbade sacrifice of animals and humans. Secrecy was a predominant factor in all three groups.

The Bible is riddled with inconsistencies regarding the birth and life of Jesus. According to *Mathew*, there are only 28 generations from David to Jesus, but according to Luke there are 42. However both of these authors are intent on making Jesus a direct descendent of David and thus eligible for Kingship in the soon to be established **Jewish Empire.** According to Mathew Jesus is born in a house, In Luke however Joseph and Mary travel from Nazareth to Bethlehem because, in the days of Cyrenius, the emperor Augustus had made a decree: "that all the world should be taxed[89], when in fact, only registration of property under the control of Cyrenius had been ordered, as Josephus clearly indicates. Jesus is circumcised on the eighth day[90] and afterwards the Essenic Simeon and Anna (found only in Luke) pay their tributes to the child and his parents then return to Galilee[91] the accounts in Mathew and Luke are not merely different and discrepant, but they are **mutually exclusive.** If one is correct the other is impossible.

Jesus could not have been born in a stable if his parents were living in a house in Bethlehem, further they could not have had homes both there and at Nazareth (if they were poor), many miles away. Also according to Mathew, three wise men appear guided by a star and Joseph warned in a dream flees with Mary and Jesus to Egypt, to avoid Herod's slayal of all children under the age of two years. This event is not recorded by Josephus even though it represented a somewhat outrageous and traumatic event, that would have definitely warranted comment if it had happened. How could Jesus and his family have been fleeing into Egypt in terror and returning peacefully to Galilee at the same time? If Jesus was returned to Nazareth at the age of 40 days, how could he be living in Bethlehem at the age of approximately one year? Finally what kind of star would hang so low in the sky as to designate a humble dwelling? In the stone ring impression from Naples circa sixth Century A.D. (*fig. 28)* The Three Kings of the biblical account, are shown in Greek-style attire and what is more, the central figure of the trio, which reminds one of the law of three of the Druids, wears a pointed cap looking remarkably like a Petasos, the cap of Hermes. Thus in this icon there appears to be a memory of quite a different story to the birth of Jesus other than that told in *The Bible.* The Three Wise Men are not Kings in this icon but Hermetic philosophers and since they appear as a three, they may well be Druids. Further, the archetypal symbol of Hermes is the star Mercury, which is shown in this icon as hanging very low in the sky. The lasting value of iconography and mythology is the ability to tell a different and often true tale, which was not politic to right down at the time.

The accounts of Jesus' birth are cloaked in purposeful confusion. In *Mathew*, the child is **not new born** and his parents are permanent residents of Bethlehem. The fact that Jesus is not new born in this account gives rise to the possibility that he was FOSTERED, according to Druidic custom. The dates are also confusing and according to Mathew, Jesus was born whilst Herod was still alive and yet we know that Herod died in 4 B.C. In Luke the birth occurs when Cyrenius became governor of Syria and Coponius became the procurator of Judaea, positions to which both were first appointed in 6 A.D. Thus we have two birth dates separated by ten years. Gabriel the angel is supposed to have appeared to Mary, with the news of expectancy of a Divine child and Mary declares her child will be exceptional; "Joseph and Mary marvelled at the things which were spoken of him." [92] Despite this when Jesus at the age of 12 engages "the doctors" in Jerusalem in intellectual conversation Mary and Joseph are annoyed because of the inconvenience Jesus has caused them. When Jesus states: " I must be about my father's business", they do not have the faintest idea of what he is talking about. Although Mary: "kept all these thing in her heart", she appears to forget the visit of Gabriel and the odd circumstances of her child's birth, including her long speech to Elizabeth when she discusses the royal destiny of her child. Neither could Joseph remember his dreams or the flight into Egypt. Evidently then either Mary and Joseph develop one of the most remarkable cases of amnesia in history, or the true circumstances of Jesus birth are more accurately portrayed in the Stone Ring from Naples and Jesus was fostered to Mary and Joseph, to be brought up ostensibly as Jewish, to be used by the Druids in their pre-determined group of the Essenes, which was specifically Jewish. I will return to this point again in conclusion, but obviously there is a veil of confusion surrounding Jesus' birth in biblical texts; and in Mathew, Joseph experiences dreams after which he visits Mary and finds her: "with child of the Holy Ghost." [93] Joseph appears to have no idea where the child has come from and only because the angel had appeared to him in a dream does he refrain from putting "her away" (divorce), which according to Cesus and Origen he did do. However suggestion in trance like states was well within the capabilities of those adepts who possessed vibratory resonant knowledge and Cabalistic methods. One has to ask whether the Druids and not an angel appeared to Joseph!

Surely then it is somewhat fortunately co-incidental, that John the Baptist and Jesus both have mysterious origins along with St. John the Evangelist. Although John the Baptist and St. John (the Evangelist), may be one and the same person as previously discussed, together with Jesus are according to previous genealogies relatives from the same Celtic Dynasty. John the Baptist and Jesus both set about preaching the imminent kingdom, an **Essenic doctrine**. Jesus believing Himself to be the one foretold in the Essene scriptures proclaiming himself as the Son of Man foretold in *Enoch Five* of the Essenic documents, *The Dead Sea Scrolls*. John the Baptist paved the way for Jesus and John himself in

247

his teachings showed the unmistakable traits of Essene doctrine:
a) He conducted Baptismal ritual for the remission of Sins.
b) He stated the wicked would be burnt in flames.
c) He preached communal goods and practise in line with Essenic Communistic doctrine.
d) He preached pacifism and equality.

Once again there is confusion over which group John the Baptist belonged to and some sources claim that he was the fountainhead of an independent cult. It is certainly unusual that whilst the Scribes and Pharisees denounced Jesus as an impostor, a sorcerer or a madman, they dare not criticise the Baptist, when even after his execution there was no general denouncement, was it generally recognised then, that he belonged to a powerful Order – the Druids? If John the Baptist showed Essene traits as did Jesus in some of his teachings, Jesus also showed Buddhist influence which some claim was a result of his tutorage in India or Tibet, which of course brings us back to Blavatsky's Hidden masters and the Secret Doctrine handed down from the Patriarchs. Certainly there is a long period in Jesus' life, which is not accounted for, and he did not start his mission until his thirtieth year: In the drama of *The Lost Disciples*, the author G.F. Jowett states:" The Rig-Vedas the ancient religious books of India, were written 1500 B.C. and the Druidic religion antedated that of India, circa 1800 B.C.". This is a very early date and certainly early enough to account for my hypothesis, that it was possible for the Druids to conduct the Religious Revolution in Crete. However according to Jowett, the wise men of India record the visit of Jesus among them, stating that he dwelt in Nepal.

I have already shown a parallel between the Brahmins and the Druids, with the possibility of a common Indo-European stock. It is curious that Jesus should preach equality, when both these groups operated a caste system, implying that if He was tutored by Masters his role in bringing Communistic doctrine, which was taught by the Essenes, was more of a conspiratorial role, than has generally been realised, Jowett states:" They also make several references to Britain as a great centre of religious learning; therefore, on several scores, Jesus would know of the eminence of Druidic religious wisdom...Eastern and Western tradition claim Jesus completed his studies in Britain. This could be possible. At that time the Druidic Universities were the largest in the world, both in size and in attendance of over sixty thousand students. This is affirmed by Greek and Roman testimony, which states that the noble and wealthy of Rome and other nations sent their children to study **law, science** and **religion** in Britain". I did note that after the Religious Revolution in Crete, the second plank of Marxism (taxation) was introduced recorded as lists of goods of the Linear A and B tablets. Further laws were coded out on tablets at Gortyn in Crete. Presumably the Druids grasped the importance of indoctrination of the young of the world's leaders or wealthy and supplied such indoctrination through education, in much the same way as Elitist Universities have provided the status quo of the next ruling power. I consider the claim that Jesus was tutored in Tibet, to be a gloss for his real tutorage in Britain and the Buddhist influence, was not from Tibet, but from the Druids who had sequestered the Buddhist influence from Crete and the Teacher during the Religious Revolution. In fact this was not Buddhist in origin, it derived from the true source and the Holy Grail message that came to earth circa 10000 B.C. Man under many cycles of the MRC had forgotten the truth of his own soul. It would take outside help to remind him. The Toldot Yeshu story of Jesus obtaining a secret from "The Holy of the Holy's" a Temple, is not quite the truth, but does portray the case of stolen apples (Immortality and Re-incarnation) from Crete.

The inclusion of Science in Druidic teaching at such an early date is somewhat surprising as is Law and religion, however if my conclusion is correct and this elite group were working towards a One World Order, then not surprising at all. We must remember that a Druid's training lasted 19 years and thus there must have been a great deal of subject matter and yet as far as open and recorded public record shows, there would hardly seem anything within these three subjects at the time, to warrant 19 years training unless of course much of what was being taught at that time was secret and involved much of Cabalistic science, the Earth Grid, cosmology, map reading and the effect of the Grid on land formations, together with inevitable slanted history and philosophy .In the *Light of Britannia*, the author Owen Morgan, a Welsh historian asked: "Was the Lord Jesus Christ a Druid? Continuing: "The Lord Jesus sought to supplant the priesthood of Aaron by the introduction into Jerusalem of another priesthood which had nothing Jewish about it. It is called in scripture, the priesthood of Melchizedec. Melchizedec was a priest of the Most High God; was not a son of Abraham and that Patriarch and according to the Epistle to the Hebrews, acknowledged the superiority of the priesthood of Melchezedec over that of the tribe of Levi, which was a purely Jewish Priesthood. Melchizedec, a contemporary of Abraham, not being a son of Abraham and existing before the priesthood of Levi came into existence, was a Gentile exercising the duties of a **Gentile priesthood** which was unquestionably Druidic and was represented on the east station of the circle, the position occupied by Judah. In the Bible (*Numbers ii, v. 30*) Jesus is said to be a priest after the order of Melchizedec, and that he (Jesus) was of the tribe of Judah, which indicated the sun rising due East (*Numbers* ii, v.3) We are thus irristably convinced the Lord Jesus Christ was a Druid, and a priest after a most ancient order, whose headquarters was Britain - The 'Isles' of Isaiah."[94] I resolved the mystery of Judah in *The Battle of The Trees* when I decoded *The Grail Romances*, concluding that their were two opposing groups battling for supremacy on earth, evidently then the Druids represented one such group and the Twelve Tribes of Israel represented the other group. However "**the root** and branch" as I decoded it (*p.172 The Battle of The Trees*) was **Judah**.

According to Margaret Starbird a Roman Catholic scholar in *The Woman with the Alabaster Jar* (*1993*), the wedding which Jesus attended at Cana was his own wedding to Mary of Magdala who like Jesus was said to have been **born of Royal descent**.[95] According to my own witness account (past life regression), this is true and what is more I claim from my witness account that Magdalene's genealogies were stolen and she was betrayed and further it was Jesus who took the genealogies. When Mary Magdalene asked for the return of the genealogies saying that He could keep her entire wealth (the precious oils that He had taken), he replied: "Be gone with you woman!" and drew his sword and cut her left upper arm badly, with His sword. Further, he was with a woman that Magdalene assumed was an "Essene woman", although since the Essenes were celibate this can only provide further evidence that Jesus was a Druid, which the Magdalene was not aware of? The woman may have been a Celt of the family dynasty or an Egyptian princess. The cutting of her arm was almost certainly a re-enactment of a ceremony, 'The Cutting of the Elm/Arm' at Gisors in the Twelfth century at Gisors in France which appeared to be a separation of two groups with different aims and which I covered in *The Battle of The Trees* (*Chapter 5*) That secret is portrayed in the crab mural at Cardiff Castle further discussed in *The Battle of The Trees (p. 176)*. The implication is that Jesus was a double agent (and I have considered a triple agent) who betrayed the tribe of Judah and the Druids and was working for the secret Priesthood of Levi or the Jews. However the Jews nailed Jesus to the cross (allegedly) under a Roman administration, despite that Jesus had been welcomed into Jerusalem shortly before. I can only consider that the priesthood of Levi discovered that Jesus was really working for the Druids or the Priesthood of Judah a Gentile priesthood. A Roman administration was in direct conflict with Druid power and indeed invaded Britain shortly afterwards to destroy that power, although it is believed that some of the Druids may have survived in Caerleon-on-Usk in Wales UK, thus a Roman administration would have wanted Jesus crucified if it was realised he was working for the Tribe Of Judah (the Druids). However if Jesus were a Druid, then he would have returned to his family in Britain, but there is no mention of it. Further if the woman with Jesus in my own witness account was an Egyptian Princess, then it would mean that Jesus may have gone to Egypt after the alleged crucifixion and it is from this region, that a differing account of Jesus and the Magdalene and the events of Golgotha were discovered in the Nag Haamidi scrolls. There is perhaps a final twist in the tale, as I believe that Jesus himself was duped and perhaps murdered and the Egyptian Princess returned to Scotland! Perhaps I may be forgiven for taking a thousand years to recover from this story! For those who had tried to bring back truth this was a horrendous betrayal.

In the Gospel of John according to Barry Dunford[78] is: "probably the most accurate of the four canonical gospels there is no mention of Jesus being born in Bethlehem or his growth to manhood. John's account of Jesus, apart from his introductory reference to the Incarnation of the 'Word' or Christos Energy, begins with the Baptism (Initiation) of Jesus by John the Baptist, who may well have been the same entity as St. John, the Evangelist. Why is no other preamble information given concerning the background of Jesus? Was it expurgated for some reason from the original Gospel text? Could it be that there was an attempt to conceal the possible Celtic background of the Jesus family? Apart from a passing reference to Jesus aged twelve in Jerusalem there is no Gospel record at all of his early life in Palestine. Could this be because he was not there but rather that he was living in Britain where he would most probably have been tutored in the schools of the learned Druids"? In India and Tibet there are apparently records of the visit of Jesus who was known there as "ISA".[94] However it should be noted that Notovich and Roerich who are the references for the claim that Jesus had been initiated in Tibet, were members of the Secret groups and Communists. There has always been that awkward question over the teachings of Jesus and their obvious Buddhist influences. Whilst I claim from my own witness account this was an influence derived from the Mary Magdalene and Crete, with the early Cretan mysteries concerning Re-incarnation, the connection has been deliberately veiled with confusing data regarding Tibet. There is not only an attempt to position UFO experiences with Tibet and Hidden Masters, but this was a doctrine that Madame Blavatsky under a higher Order purposely disseminated in what I concluded was a pre-determined outcome in setting up Theosophy. Further there was the idea of men as supermen with great abilities a view that was not compatible with Christianity, developed for the masses, whilst the mysteries and Re-incarnation was held within the secret groups in their highest echelons.

Barry Dunford states" Gildas, a British priest-historian, writing in 542 A.D. may indicate the presence of Jesus in Britain perhaps after the Crucifixion; " Gildas writes:" We certainly know that Christ, the True Sun, afforded His light, the knowledge of His precepts, to our Island in the last year of the reign of Tiberias Caesar, A.D. 37."[97] This quote is very interesting, since it quite clearly offers a slightly different view from my conclusions above, but interestingly acknowledges Jesus as a Sun King after Apollo and Britain, under the Druids held Apollo the Sun King in veneration. Also the date accurately represents the events of Golgotha and biblical texts are deliberately confused in placing the events much earlier. Further Godfrey Higgins refers to: "the evidence of Irenaeus, that the real Jesus of Nazareth was not crucified by Pontius Pilate...When we find from Irenaeus (Bishop of Lyons) that he was not murdered or killed, all we can make out of our four gospel-histories is, that they were allegories, parables, apologues, to conceal the **secret doctrine**"(my emphasis).

(Anacalypsis Vol. II - 1836)

Unfortunately if we had hoped that *The Dead Sea Scrolls* would filter more light onto these confused areas, we would be wrong, for once again the political and religious powers have swooped to hide any remaining truths. Various scholars have tried to learn the contents of the various "**Levi**" fragments of *The Dead Sea Scrolls* and even to obtain a photograph of the document. However even Professor J. M. Allegro of Manchester University, England, who unrolled, deciphered and published the copper scroll and who was originally a member of an International team of scholars given the task of piecing together, editing and publishing other Essene documents, was not permitted to inspect the "Levi" fragments or other scriptures from the caves, after he stated that the Essene Teacher of Righteousness may have been crucified: This leaves us to try and work out in the usual detective style what has so upset the Jews on this one? The obvious conclusion is that the entirety of events here must not be found out.

The Dead Sea Scrolls in an undated Codex *The Second treatise of the Great Seth,* which I have previously mentioned, show that according to Essene documents Jesus escapes Crucifixion by an ingenious supplant of another man (Simon or Simeon the Druid?) and states: "they nailed **their man** unto the death..." (*Author's* emphasis) it is generally believed that Simon was nailed to the cross and not Jesus. Who was Simon? Was Simon perhaps an Essene and Jewish or was he a Celt/ Druid of the Royal Dynastic line? One is drawn back to the practise of fostering children, which was practised by Druids and Essenes and where in the latter adoption was more the custom. The problem becomes in that Anna the alleged Celtic grandmother of Jesus had **three daughters all confusingly called Mary**. The Virgin Mary as the alleged Mother of Jesus was the result of Anna's union with Joachim, which is a Jewish name. Anna had another Mary by her second husband Cleophas and this Mary married Alphaeus and was the mother of St. James the Less, Symeon (St. Simon), St. Jude or Thaddaeus, and Joseph Barsaba, who were generally called 'The Brethren of our Lord', thus making them cousins of the half blood, according to *Roll 33, Box 26* in the English *College of Arms, Heralds' Office*, which gives the pedigree of Christ and His relatives from **Adam** onwards. It has to be asked whether St. Simon was the substitute for Jesus on the cross, since it may have been possible that both Jesus and his cousin were fostered in Palestine, but to different groups, the question is which group (Essene or Druid) did they belong to? In fosterage (Druid) the child returns to its family at a certain age, however the Essenes are said to have adopted children on occasions, but there is no mention of fosterage, which means that the child would not necessarily know its parentage. There are certainly a lot of loose ends, for instance if Mary was Celtic and from a royal dynastic line, why was she living in poverty in the Middle East? If she did foster Jesus, then he could not have been her son and again I am drawn back to those stolen genealogies of Magdalene where it seems that her own family betrayed her.

"Godfrey Higgins remarks that: "There is some foundation for the story of Jesus, or some other person for whom he has been substituted": Furthermore, according to the researches of the Lebanese historian, Camal Salilbi, there were two persons identified with the central figure of the Jesus story, one of which he identifies with the name ISA or ISSA.[98] In the Koran Jesus is called Isa, which translates in the Greek as Iesous. And in *The Secret Teachings of All Ages*, the author Manly P. Hall, states: "In an effort to solve some of the problems arising from any attempt to chronicle accurately the life of Jesus, it has been suggested that there may have lived in Syria at that time two or more religious teachers bearing the name Jesus, Jehoshua or Joshua and that the lives of these men may have been confused in the Gospel stories." [99] I believe that the confusion rests on two priesthoods and two candidates for the role of Messiah or Teacher - the tribes of Judah and Levi. Such confusion may not have been entirely co-incidental Martin A. Larson [88] notes twenty- five similarities between the biblical Gospel teachings and the Essene beliefs. He establishes that the Essene cult had fully developed most of the doctrines found in the Synoptic Gospels of The Bible. The similarities offer three alternative conclusions a) that Jesus developed an almost identical belief system, which was entirely new and independent despite the fact that it was a substantial replica of Essene doctrine, which was already established in the area or b) Jesus was an Essene and worked with the tribe of Levi or c) Jesus was a Druid and worked for the tribe of Judah. From my own witness account it is probable that he was working for both sides of the two groups in a very complex double agent caper, that it might be impossible to fully get to the bottom of. Co-incidentally you will in later sections of this book, note this identical complexity in the biography of Ron Hubbard, the 'Messiah' of our age, who either developed his doctrine on his own independently or he was more intimately connected to a secret group or he was set up by a secret group which would eventually take control of the Church of Scientology.

The synthesis of the Essene belief system provided an attractive 'marketing package' of synthesised elements of belief developed over the millennia and comprising the most powerful and attractive elements ever known, because it was a synthesis of historic yearning and human emotion, which gave consolation and hope to untold millions. This 'package' was to survive in Christianity. Was this package planned? - Well if you are going to plan a Universal Religion - Christianity, you had better make that religion appeal to the majority and their **psychological emotions!** The fact remains, that whilst Jesus spoke frequently of the Scribes and Pharisees, for whom he felt withering contempt, he never referred to the Essenes, event though they were not an insignificant group at that time, or if he did then it has been edited out of biblical texts. Martin A. Larson gives overwhelming evidence that Jesus was an initiate of the Essene Order. Larson puts forward the possibility that Jesus abandoned the Order and as a defector committed the greatest possible offence by breaking the vow of secrecy and broadcasting its doctrines, which may have been the sin of L. Ron Hubbard. Likewise having broadcast the basic doctrines, the only reasonable course would be to preserve an immutable silence concerning the **source** of his ideology. This is a reasonable theory and one I will consider for Ron Hubbard later, however the other possibility, is that Jesus worked for a Higher Order of Druids, the ascendant group of which I have proposed as Scottish Rite Freemasonry - Rosicrucianism in its highest Orders. This possibility will also arise with Ron Hubbard. Thus eventually perhaps we might have to consider that Jesus like Hubbard tried to do something to help humanity.

Martin Larson concluded that Jesus convinced himself that He was the Essenic Teacher; the coming Messiah once again drawing a curious parallel to Ron Hubbard and that he consciously modelled his own career on that of the Essene martyred Teacher of Righteousness and upon passages now recovered in *The Dead Sea Scrolls* in *The Testaments of the Twelve Patriarchs* and in *Enoch*. Thus Larson claims that the events of Golgotha were a re-enactment of the drama of The Essene Teacher. Controversially Schweitzer declared in a doctoral dissertation, that the only reason Jesus may not be considered to have been insane (compare Hubbard) is the fact that the beliefs he entertained concerning himself were rather common delusions during his time. However the idea of Messiah rests with the Druids and their sacrificed Man-god, which was to suppress the Early Minoan truth, with the introduction of Twin Kingship and the sacrifice of the waning Twin King, on the 'T'-shaped cross, which was so evident in Minoan archaeology and mythology. Hubbard himself only attained Messiah-like status among his followers, when like David he appeared to do battle against Goliath taking on the wrath of the American government, by then one suspects under the control of the priests of Levi and Israel! Since things have remarkably quietened down for Scientology in America (and Britain), might we assume that the "special relationship" of Britain and America is based on a priesthood of Judah now in power!

Barry Dunford points to a small Church in Scotland UK, as the birthplace of Jesus more interestingly Barry points out that on the crosses of Sandbach, in Cheshire UK, can be seen: "the ancient Eastern Mediterranean motif of the **grape vine** and Christ on the Cross in a short **kilt**" (my emphasis). The Grapevine you will remember was the emblem of the vine-man: "he who joins together", or Feniusa Farsa who was a descendent of Noah and Adam and part of a Fraternal Brotherhood. Interestingly as I will cover, the kilt which is a skirt-like 'dress' of the Scots not only turned up in the Stone Ring from Naples as

Greek attire, which implied the Druids or Hermetic Philosophers were centred on the birth of Jesus; but the kilt also turns up in Crete Greece, providing one more connection of the Druids to the Religious Revolution. As Barry points out whilst Jesus is said to have come from Galilee (Gaelilee), in the eighteenth century the small Church of Fortingall, the alleged birthplace of Jesus, was spelt with one L i.e. Fortinal (Fortingael). Godfrey Higgins states that:" Gael is the Hebrew gl. and means circle and on the Island of Iona in Scotland, there is a language of the Gael, Gaeldoct or Sanskrit and the island is seen as that of Singal or "of the solar cycle", or the Circle of the Sun" (*Anacalypsis - Vol II*).

In the Second Century B.C. the Greeks knew the Celts as Keltoi (Celt) or Galatae. Later they were known as the Gauls (Gal). Gaul extending into most of Europe was occupied by the Celts and on the death of Alexander and the disintegration of the Greek empire, the Celts who were a powerful European force decided to invade Greece circa 279 B.C. The Sicilian Greek historian Diodorus Siculus (c. 60-30B.C.) described this army as consisting of 150,000 infantry and 10,000 cavalry and it was claimed by the author that after the victory in Macedonia in Northern Greece, the Celts along with Druidic practise, celebrated by sacrificing the prisoners. Thus Macadenonia and then Thessaly fell to the Celts.

It is curious given that the egg-shape was an archetypal symbol of phallic and male potential and reflected the human biofield electro-magnetic energy shape, that the Druidic emblem was also evidenced not only in their religious Temple particularly as discussed previously at Stonehenge in Wiltshire in the UK, but the archetypal shape was displayed in Celtic shields, which were 3 feet 9 inches in length; both of which are archetypal numbers; the former (3) reflecting the ancient Trinity (Mother Goddess and Twin Kings) and the latter (9) representing the number of years that a Sun-King reigns. Further, given that Pythagoras who was connected in some way to the Druids, had a good grasp of resonant vibration science, knowledge of which must have passed into the Druidic repository of secret knowledge and the hidden science, it is interesting that Diodorus Siculus should comment on the trumpets that the Celts used in battle which were of: "a peculiar barbaric kind... and produced a harsh sound which suits the tumult of war" and further: "they rushed on their enemies with the unreasoning fury and passion of wild beasts. They had no kind of reasoning at all. They slashed with axe and sword and blind fury never left them until they were killed". Perhaps here you have a belief in Re-incarnation and the knowledge that if you die, you will be reborn, which must have been a consideration for the Elite, in their quest for a One World Order, which would severely be threatened, by the **cult of the hero**, who has no fear of death and thus challenges all wrongs – a somewhat absent feature today amongst the lackey's of the One World Order who sell their soul and all eternity for just one very small pot of gold or the sale of newspapers. The biblical idea of total death and one life, merely suppressed the cult of the hero or heroine, but some who always retained this knowledge fought in **every battle** for truth and went frequently to the market square to be roasted, condemned by the mindless masses (who were dupes to the propaganda), whom they had tried to save! One must never cease to salute those that had the enduring courage of belief and knowledge of a higher truth and The Holy Grail Message, they are the unsung heroes and heroines of the battle for man's soul, such courage is **never un-rewarded**, in the Spiritual world and indeed as I will explain one's exit from the eternal trap depended upon it.

The Celts also left their dead where they fell in battle, which although viewed as outrageously uncivilised behaviour by the Greeks, may have reflected the Celts laissez-faire attitude to death and a belief in Re-incarnation indicating perhaps that the Greeks had long since forgotten their own heritage and The Holy Grail message. Pausanias the Greek commented on this practise as: "This neglect of giving graves to those who had passed away was for two reasons I think: to astound their enemies, and because they have no natural pity for the dead". Although propaganda has always served man to blacken the opposing team, Pausanias was revolted by: "the most horrifying wickedness I have heard of, not the crimes of human beings at all". He was referring to the alleged mass slaughter of men, women and children, the latter being cannibalised by the Celts. It is unsure whether this was indeed true or propaganda, since similar stories were told about the Persian invasions by Herodotus and in the later Roman invasions. Such stories were used to outrage people and thus form a unifying force against the invader, however equally such stories given the background of human sacrifice employed by the Druids, could have been true. Further the Christian Eucharist is built on a much older religious custom, which I have referred to, when the totem beast of the tribe e.g. a white mare in Irish lore, was eaten in remembrance of the source of their beliefs. I suspect if you ran through the past lives of many a psychotic cannibal in today's prisons you would come across a time when they had partaken of "manna".

In the 6th Century B.C. the Greeks and the Celts were two expanding European cultures. The Celts had their origins North of the Alps in West Central Europe and the Greeks occupied the Eastern Mediterranean, with colonial expansion of the Greek States, both eastward into Asia Minor and westward into Italy, Sicily and along the northern coast of Africa. In the 7th Century B.C. the Greeks had opened up Egypt to world trade and Alexander had entered Egypt in 332 B.C. By contrast the Celts had reached France and Spain and had opened up silver mining. Initially there was co-operation between Celtic Kings and the trading merchants of the Greeks, where luxury goods from Greece and other Mediterranean colonies appeared in Celtic graves as tokens of the owners wealth and position, thus reflecting the Druidic caste or tiered system of classes, which has left its indelible mark on the world. In return the Greeks bought minerals, gold, silver, lead, tin and iron as well as agricultural produce from the Celts. The Greeks certainly had some idea of the extent of the Celtic world, since Ephorus of Cyme (c.405 -330BC) described it as a territory **the size of the Indian Sub-Continent** and given the date of this remark, it cannot have played a part in the politics of Golgotha and the quest for a Universal Religious and Political

Kingdom. Obviously such expansion had been on-going for quite some time and in *The Battle of The Trees,* I proposed that the group who conducted the Religious Revolution in Crete (1 400 B.C.), had set up such a goal of expansion and eventual domination, which would eventually come to fruition in our own times as a Federal United States of The West - **European Union.** If the Druids were responsible for the Religious Revolution in Crete, then one could conclude that the Celtic expansion was none other than the centralised globalisation policy of the Druids.

Interestingly given Hitler's pre-occupation with world domination and what looks to be a resurrection of the Druidic plan in the form of The Third Reich, Strabo and Diodorus Siculus and the Elder Pliny as far back as the 4th Century B.C. mention the explorer Pytheas who sailed to the Islands of Britain (Brettanike) and Ireland (Iverni) and curiously mentioned a land called "Thule", six days North of Britain, where the Sun at midsummer did not set and Ptolemy (C. AD 100-178) believed Thule to be the Shetlands, which are islands in the northern and furtherest parts of Britain. The reason that Thule is so interesting is that the secret group initiates that surrounded and initiated Adolph Hitler into the religious mysteries were members of the Thule society. Thule according to Nazi esoteric knowledge was the sunken Continent of Plato's Atlantis and gave rise to the idea of racial superiority and the Aryan Super race programme. I will cover Atlantis later, but evidently The Nazi's as I proposed in Alternative 4, were already very familiar with the background to Minoan Greece and the Mother Goddess and indeed in Alternative 4 Hitler on at least one occasion referred to her! Further it is impossible to understand, why Hitler did not invade Britain when he had the opportunity to do so, unless there was a common priesthood of Judah and goals behind both Hitler and Britain or he was ordered not to, by those Masters in Britain behind his Super race programme, who may well have played a duplicitous game with the opposing group of the Twelve Tribes of Israel, to bring into being a State of Israel and thus betray the Arabs, in the Balflour agreement.

Contrary to the earlier black propaganda stories, it is odd that Pytheas should refer to the British Celts in the 1st Century B.C. as a rather civilised group. By the time the Celts came into contact with the Greek traders and explorers it was estimated that the population of Gaul was about 6-8 millions and the individual tribes consisted of thousands. The Celts spread through the Iberian Peninsula through France, Belgium, Switzerland, Germany, Austria, Northern Italy, Czechoslovakia, Hungary and touching on the Balkans. Curiously then, apart from this near and total domination of Europe, it is generally agreed that the cradle of Celtic civilization or the point of origin, was in the area of the Danube, the Rhine and the Rhone, all of which still bear Celtic names. Names of geographical features, mountains, rivers, streams, territories and towns, all indicate that the Celts had been living in this region **for Centuries**. However, we do know that the Druids in their Universities for a good thousand years previously, had tutored the sons of Europe and Druidic religious doctrine lay at the heart of this Empire. Minoan beliefs were at the heart of such doctrine and surfaced in place names e.g. The name Labara referred to 'talking river'; however the derivation may have reasonably come from the word for axe in Crete at the time of The Religious Revolution c. 1400B.C. –Labris from which the word labyrinth is derived: Where "talking river", was non other than the "Underground Stream", of Secret Wisdom, deriving from Labyrinth, the womb and the mystery of Re-incarnation.

Were the Celtic Kings of this Empire, Druidic Priest-Kings, utilising a **THEOCRACY OF POWER** - Solar Kingship **dominated by an initiated Priesthood of Masters**, descended from Adam and of the tribe of Judah, white, blonde and blue-eyed Gentiles. It has been claimed that the expansion of the Celtic Empire was due to a population explosion, however even accounting for the higher figure of 3-4 million Celts, this was hardly a case of over-crowding when one considers the vast area of Europe that the Celts occupied, when even a large European city today contains as many people, if not more. Another view put forward to explain the expansion, was the habit of the Celts for wandering. The view that has not been thought of, is a CENTRALISED POLICY OF EXPANSION AND DOMINATION, a goal of globalisation, a Universal Political and Religious Kingdom that may have come to fruition in our own times as European Union, which is still I believe a Theocracy dominated by a secret Priesthood. The invasion of Greece had all the hallmarks of a centralised policy of expansion of the European Celtic Power base. Were these tribes induced by some magical means to disperse or was there a central policy directive? And what accounted for Strabo's observation of the Celts that: "The whole race ...is war mad and both high spirited and quick for battle, although otherwise simple and not ill mannered". This statement has all the hallmarks of the description of a religious war, which the Celts may have been engaged in. It has also been ignored in historical comment, that whilst the Romans are accorded with the building of straight roads in Britain, excavations show that the remains under these roadways were often quite sophisticated Celtic roadways, which correspond to Grid patterns or Ley Lines.

However the most prominent comment in history was the stature of these Celts, with: "rippling muscles", "tall", with "hair washed in *lime* wash" to enhance *blonde* colouration and give it the resemblance of a *horse's* main. Their moustache's were very prominent and often: "covered their whole mouth" It is indeed a mystery as to the racial stock origins of these Celts, that they should suddenly appear and indeed in ancient history may account for the myths of battles between giants and dwarfs. The lime-wash hair is significant, since the

Goddess in her death aspect was white and the Knossos site is a burial site, covered in white gypsum, which not only mirrors the custom of painting houses in lime wash white in Greece, but mirrors New Grange in Ireland with its white pebbles and built I conclude in honour of the Great Goddess, where Sacred Kings were reborn. Further I will come to the white chalk hill figures of Britain, but these I conclude had a similar background. The Celtic women were of comparable striking physique and were recalled to possess the courage of men and often fought in battle. Most importantly they evidently worshipped the phallic bisexual god (of fire) or Hermes associated with the Druids and their hermetic philosophy. Arthenaeus of Nauratis (c. A.D. 200) remarked in *Deipnosophistae* that: "among the barbarians the Celts, though they have very beautiful women, they enjoy boys more..." thus they were in fact **bisexual with a tendency to homosexuality**. This will identify the Celts and Druids as worshipping the god Hermes, who in myth was bisexual, although the truth of his transcendent third stage beyond death as incorporating the Twin Kings *and* Mother Goddess as the ancient Trinity, became a religious mystery, withdrawn into the Druids presumably after the Religious Revolution in Crete, where the role of the woman was withdrawn.

The god of the Celts was built on the model of Zeus Dionysos and further this particular god is indicated by the appearance of vines on iconography where Dionysus was the god of wine; although some memory of that is retained in the drinking of wine at Holy Communion in memory of the ancient Trinity of Mother Goddess and Twin Kings. Diodorus Siculus commented that the Celts were: "exceedingly addicted to the use of wine..." which was common in the particular worship of Zeus Dionysos. The Greeks also recognised that the Celts believed in the immortality of the soul. Strabo pointed out the Druids taught that souls as well as the Universe were indestructible, although their famous fear of an apocalyptic event caused them to believe that both fire and water would eventually prevail over them. This is almost certainly a reflection of that prophetic document by St. John and the prophesied Armageddon (*Revelations XVi, 16*) and I did suggest that John the Evangelist was a Druid, which would underline the fact that his prophecy is a piece of Druidic channelling of the Akashic Record, merely prophesying what had gone before on the morphogenetic bioplasma of recorded events of the species. The idea of the "chosen" ones, presumably as sons of Adam the Patriarch, was prevalent among the Celts and must have given them a sense of rightness as they pushed out in their expansion to conquer other lands and people. Danu (from Anna?) provided the flood waters which fertilised the Druids sacred Oak tree, which produced the Dagda, the good god who was not only the progenitor of all the gods and goddesses, the children of Danu, but of the race of Celts who were descended in their own belief from the gods. The name Danu was to become Ana in British Celtic and Anna a Princess is credited with being a grandmother of Jesus.

If the beginnings of Druid knowledge had been very secret, there were later references to their abilities and where several Greek historians among them Hippolytus (c. !70- c.236 A.D.) Noted that the: **"Druids also practise magic arts"**. Thus here we have some indication that they were versed in the hidden science. The Celts were also noted as being completely subservient to the Druids. Further Marcus Tullius Cicero (106-43 B.C.) commented that the Druids: "could predict the future", proving once again that they definitely had a working knowledge of the Earth energy Grid and Akashic or morphogenetic record enabling them to predict the future on the basis of cyclical *past* events, although it is doubtful whether they ever recognised the science which was at work, which may or may not explain, why the Rockefeller Foundation after publication of *Alternative 4,* announced that they would be studying Crop circles, which as a point in principle might require them to at least get the story of the Crab and the 'First Cut' right first! What pin-points the use of Grid information by the Druids and Celts, was a remark by Caesar drawing his information mainly from Poseidonius, that the Celts knew much about: "the size and shape of the world, the movements of the heavens and of the stars". Hippolytus further remarked that the Druids could: **"foretell certain events by the Pythagorean reckoning and calculations"**. Now here is a very important statement, is it implied that by some reckoning and knowledge of the UVG 120 sphere that some cosmological equation, or geometry exists as a natural law that allows one to calculate a future event, on the basis of The Cycle of Eternal Return of a past event? In other words, is there a capability within the hidden science of making accurate predictions of future events? In my own journey and research it was remarkable that the sense of urgency that I have always felt, is perhaps based upon such recognition of cosmological knowledge and an **imminent** future event - an Apocalypse. Indeed Dr. Becker, whom you will remember, was twice nominated for a Nobel Prize, has stated that a **Magnetic Reversal has already started**. However as Caesar remarked the Druids never wrote anything down and it is remarkable given the numbers that passed through their Universities, that there should be such a degree of secrecy. It seems likely as with Freemasonry today, lower initiates were never allowed access to the greater mysteries and the true nature of the group, they merely served a purpose and their true Masters must have found that rather amusing. Whatever the secrecy, one thing is certain; the Celts were not Barbarians, neither were they illiterate, but possessed a highly evolved social structure headed by intellectuals (the Druids) in a caste system or hierarchy.

The Celtic expansion eastward was according to the Roman historian Liviy circa. 616-579 B.C.; but according to other sources, the date was around the 7th or 8th Centuries B.C. As early as the 4th Century B.C. it is claimed that Europe was controlled by the Celts. The entire populated area of the Celts in Europe was referred to as the **CELTIC KOINE (COMMONWEALTH)**.[100] Prior to The

Roman Republic establishing its rule over the Greek Kingdoms, there had been a couple of centuries where the Hellenic Monarchies fought for control. After Alexander's death, there was a play for power and in 305 B.C. Alexander's empire collapsed into separate kingdoms, with the greatest powers in the major centres of Macedonia, Thrace, Egypt and Syria. Ptolemy, the son of Lagus who was one of Alexander's generals adopted the title of Pharaoh in Egypt as Ptolemy I Soter (**Saviour**) and died 283 B.C. Until Syria was annexed to Rome circa 65-63 B.C. Seleucus (c. 358 —280 B.C.) and a close friend of Alexander took command, followed by his own dynasty. The region of Macedonia in Greece became unstable and the Celts seized their chance with Brennos as their Commander and King. If there was evidence for a centralised plan of total control in Europe, then the campaign in Greece is specific evidence, since three separate Celtic armies converged on Greece at the **same time** from **different locations**. As any General will tell you, such an event cannot occur, without a **central directive plan**. Thus the Celtic Commonwealth was in my conclusion, a bid for power realising the goal of a Universal Political and Religious Kingdom. Although I will come to the case of Scientology later, it is no surprise to me, that on reflection of history, Scientology was kicked out of Greece, when I was there, in 1994. The orthodox Greek Church allied as it is now to Israel and the 12 tribes (Levi) of the Jews certainly has no intention of allowing back the belief in The Cycle of Eternal Return (Re-incarnation) and more specifically since that belief was downgraded into solar monarchy by the tribe of Judah, then as Greece evicted its monarchy (King Constantine) then we might assume that it has no truck with Judah or the white Brotherhood. Whilst in Greece I also observed a light being brought during the Easter festival from Israel to Patmos (the island where St. John wrote the Book of Revelations), a fairly obvious symbol I would conclude coupled with a large meeting of Communists in the North of Greece at about the same time and the tribe of Levi (Jews) as far back as the Essenes were Communists as exhibited in Essenic doctrine and taught by Jesus. Further there was a never-ending series of programmes on Cretan television regarding The Holocaust and the bombing of a TV station in Athens was curious, unless perhaps there swirls beneath the propaganda a battle for Greece. The curious put up? News of satanic cults coupled with the closing of Dianetics centres in Greece was all too amateurish and predictable even for propaganda. The Greeks fell for it though!

I have previously referred to the Indian epic poems and strange and terrible weapons, which may have been the application of the hidden science, however the battle of the Celts against the Greeks at Delphi was a very strange event, which although recorded by Greek historians as the Power of Apollo, almost certainly signifies some application of sympathetic vibration knowledge, probably very similar to the mechanism I outlined for the possible or alleged UFO incident of today. It certainly appears to be the first example of mass hypnosis or some form of mind control, using perhaps the resonant vibration technology. Although one cannot ignore a hallucinatory drug slipped into the water or food supply of the Celt army! Delphi with its shrine of Apollo in the Peloponnese in Greece was thought to be the centre of the Greek Universe. The Druids worshipped Apollo and their megalithic stone circle in Wiltshire on Salisbury Plain in the UK was thought to be an Apollian Temple. The sacred Omphalos stone (*The Battle of The Trees*) was in one sense a womb and the navel stone of mankind, but also the mid-point of the Greek world. Although in *Alternative 4*, I gave the instance of the destruction of the walls of Jericho as an example of the use of Cabalistic resonant technology, a description by Pausanias describes a similar occurrence at Delphi:

"Brennos and his Celts were faced at Delphi by the hostile portents of the god, which were swift and conspicuous to a degree that to my knowledge has no other instance, all the Ground where the Celtic army marched quaked violently all day, with continuous thundering and lightening. The Celts were dumbfounded by this lightening and unable to hear when officers gave them orders; flashes from heaven would strike warriors down and set fire to others in spite of their shields". Pompeius Trogus stated:
"The Celts hurled themselves in battle without considering the danger. The Delphinians fought back, trusting more in their god than their own forces. But Apollo's presence was soon apparent, rocks split from the mountain by an earth tremor, came crushing down on the Celtic army and scattered the Strongest units, which at the same time broke under the blows of the defenders".

Obviously the most amazing outcome was that the Greeks still held this knowledge of the hidden science, unless we are to believe that by some fortunate co-incidence an earthquake helped the Greeks out on the day of battle. It seems entirely likely that another Cabalistic priesthood was behind the Greeks and the shrine at Delphi. However there is a small but important historical reference somewhat cryptically in a passage of Pausanias, who refers to Hyperochos and Amadokos as **Hyperboreans** who fought with the Greeks. Hyperborean was a term that is generally associated with the British Druids. Thus we might assume that if this was true, that this was a rogue pair who were willing to betray Druidic mysteries and knowledge of the Grid or Cabalistic science to help the Greeks against the Celts from Germany or Gaul? There is no doubt that Hyperboreans referred to British Druids, since in a further description of their origin they are described as: "dwellers from beyond the North wind". Further Abaris the Arch Druid, was referred to as a Hyperborean. This incident at Delphi also implies that the special secrets pertaining to Grid energies were never divulged to the mass of Celts, beyond perhaps a select and hierarchal few in Britain, otherwise one would assume that King Brennos of the Celtic invasion against Delphi would have known, or been tutored in those secrets during the 19 years apprenticeship. Pausanias goes on to describe the battle and says:

> "All day long the Celts were gripped by disaster and by horror; but a much more calamitous night was waiting for them. There was a fierce frost and with the frost came some snow. Enormous rocks came tumbling down Parnassos right at them, and cliff faces broke away and came crashing down..." [101]

Despite the aid of the Hyperboreans, the Celts apparently did defeat the Delphinians and looted the shrine and religious Capital, however once again we note the strange occurrences at this battle, where Brennos was wounded and the Celts in retreat despite their apparent victory, may have been subjected to vibration resonance or mind control methods based on Cabalistic science, in order to create psychological mood changes of **mass fear and hysteria**. In *Alternative 4* I discuss in more detail, how the hidden science could be utilised to change mind psychology, through the chakra energy system in the body. The Greeks reported this effect as the work of "the god Pan":

> "A disturbance broke out among the warriors as dusk came down. A few were driven out of their minds as thy thought they could hear the sound of horses coming at them. It was not long before madness seized the entire Celtic army. They snatched up their arms and killed one another, without recognising their own language or one another's faces or even the shape of the shields. They were out of their minds and this madness brought about by the gods, created a massacre of the Celts

During the period of the Hellenistic Pharaohs, which originated with Ptolemy I, who was an officer with Alexander of Macedonia, the Celts fought in the Egyptian army as mercenaries. Cleopatra VII (69-30 B.C.) was the last of the Ptolemies to rule Egypt and according to Flavius Josephus the Jewish Historian (AD 37-circa 100), four hundred Celtic warriors formed Cleopatra's elite bodyguard. After Octavian's victory over Antony and Cleopatra, the Celtic bodyguard was to become a "gift" to Herod the Great of Judea. It is curious that there is no mention of this in The Bible! The link between the Celts and Egypt was part of Irish pre-history. In *Leabhar Gabhala* (*The Book of the Invasions*), which gives an account of the origin of Irish myths, as in the *Leabhar na Nua Choughbala,* the *Book of Leinster*, or the *Book of Glend* although compiled AD 1150 by Fionn Mac. Gormain of Glendalough, there is a story of a warrior named Golamh or Mil. The scribes give Golamh an ancestry through twenty-two Irish names and **thirteen** Hebrew names back to **Adam**. Despite this ancestry, he is described as an Iberian Celt who was under Reafloir, the King of Scythia and married his daughter Seang. When Seang died, Reafloir believed Mil was plotting against him and thus plotted to kill Mil; when Mil discovered the plot, he fled with his sons Donn and Airoch Feabhruadh and they went with their followers in sixty ships to Egypt and came under Pharaoh Nectanebus. Mil is said to have married Scota daughter of the Pharaoh and they had two sons Eber and Amairgen who were Egyptian, having been born there. There was also a third son Ir, born off Thrace on an island. Mil and his wife Scota their followers and sons eventually went back to Ireland. Mil died on the voyage and his widow Scota was killed fighting the De Danaan in what is now Co. Kerry Ireland. Interestingly Mil's sons eventually ruled in Ireland and thus there was a **hereditary Royal dynastic line** apparently **dating back to the Patriarchs and Adam through Mil but his sons of course had mixed dynasty blood through their Egyptian mother Scota**. The sons of Mil are the descendents of the Gaels of Ireland. Thus not only was this line Hebraic, but it was also Egyptian. Thus there was a Celtic/Egyptian/Hebraic dynasty, which contrasted with another Celtic dynasty, which had a Greek descendency presumably through the Tuatha de Danaan. Since Scota was killed fighting the De Danaan, whom I presume are the Tuatha de Danaan, then we might assume that these two dynasties were in conflict. This is very important, there are two blood dynastic lines I would propose, which would I conclude have had consequences at the time of the events of Golgotha. Thus the stolen genealogies of the Magdalene, which I claim occurred at Golgotha, must be explained in these conflicting groups, one of Greek descent and one of Egyptian descent - and the Mary Magdalene belonged to one group and Jesus evidently belonged to the other and they might have been related in some way, if not brother and sister through some intermarriage.

According to Barry Dunford a legend current in France, stated that Joseph of Arimathea came to France with a princess raised in Egypt called Sar (Sarah-Hebrew for "Princess" or "Queen"). Also there is a persistant legend from the Western Isles of Scotland which claims that Joseph of Arimathea came to Scotland with Scota and the infamous: "stone of Destiny". In the *Chronica de Melsa*, when referring to the Coronation of David II, in 1331, the statement is made that Scota brought the stone from Egypt.[102] Barry Dunford asks whether SARA and SCOTA could have been one and the same person? This could imply that a secret "Grail Dynasty" initiated by Jesus and Mary Magdalene, may have taken root in the Spiritual "Holy Land" (now Scotland, formerly called Scotia, after Scota), as distinct from the geographical "Holy Land", i.e. Palestine. Further Barry Dunford states: "According to ancient Scottish tradition, the Scots derive their origin, at least in part, from the genealogy of a certain Princess from Egypt, SCOTA, who was said to have been the **adopted** daughter of an Egyptian Pharaoh. I smell an irresistible pie here! And the case of two conflicting genealogies (and Priesthoods) in Scotland, who differ only in the matrilineal succession line of Egyptian or Greek mother i.e. Danu (Anna) or Isis. Now if the woman with Jesus in my own witness account was Scota an Egyptian princess ostensibly but who was adopted in Egypt and thus her real family was the dynastic line with Egyptian matrilineal succession in Britain, then I must assume that Magdalene's stolen genealogies showed matrilineal descent from the **Greek line** of the tuatha de Danaan. It may have been the plan on at least the Magdalene's part to unite the two warring groups in a marriage and bring back the ancient knowledge of Crete and Re-incarnation to the Middle East and Greece. However Jesus was also presumably fostered into a Jewish family, supposedly poor and thus he would have been seen as a revolutionary (whose fate was crucifixion). There was I concluded a double cross and the Egyptian side won, together with the 12 tribes or specifically Levi. i.e. the Jewish priesthood and not the Gentile Druids. The Magdalene who fought for a religious cause was betrayed by a political cause. Perhaps it was that Scota being Celt was indistinguishable from Magdalene who was Celt and with the stolen genealogies impersonated her and sought to remove her entire possessions, so that she was left with nothing! One suspects that the conflict in Ireland which President Clinton often addressed, was really a religious war based at least on some of this story: The alleged birthplace of Jesus in Scotland - FortinGAL or Fortin*gael*? Is inseparably linked to GALLoway and HEBrides and HEBrews and GALilee and GAELilee, which indicates that the link of GAL or GAEL lies with the GAELS of IRELAND, who are apparently descended from Mil and the ostensibly Egyptian Scota although probably Celtic. The fact that the Illuminatus Pope Angello Roncalli displayed the archetypal symbols of the One world Order and during his Papacy visited Ireland in his *white* 'Pope mobile', proved his allegiance not only to Illuminism and that particular branch of Freemasonry but the Celtic dynasty and priesthood from which Jesus arose?

Myth states that one of Golamh's (or Mil's) ancestors, Fenius (Feniusa Farsa? - the Semitic "Vine-Man" or "he who joins together" - the Brotherhood?) descended from Noah and helped to build the Tower of Babel and that his grandson Gaedheal Glas (who the myth states created the Irish language), was in exile in Egypt at the same time as the Israelites under Moses. The myth of Mil and Scotia as Dr. Daithi O Hogain points out, is based on biblical chronology and the 7th Century writings of Isidorius of Seville. In one text, one of Golamh's ancestors, Fenius had a grandson Gaedhead, whose life was apparently saved by Moses after a snake bit him. Moses in curing him promised that his descendents would dwell in a land where the snake, which is connected to Immortality and Re-incarnation, did not exist and thus he would be safe from them. In the British Isles of course the Druids or the Hyperboreans worshipped the Sun King Apollo and they also held as their sacred Law something which was essentially similar to Mosaic Law, i.e. Hebraic. This myth predates the legend about St. Patrick driving the snakes from Ireland and presumably glosses a historical event, where Re-incarnation was driven as a belief from Ireland, where obviously the Twelve

Tribes of the Israelites tried to take control. Further Sru, grandson of Gaedheal who was persecuted in Egypt went to Scythia. In Iberia Mil was said to have been born to Sru.

The mythical arrival of the family of Mil in Ireland has been placed around the 4th/3rd Centuries B.C. at the time of the introduction of La tene Celtic culture in Ireland, this does not accord with the dates of Scota's arrival after the events of Golgotha, however it does not infer that the events are wrong, but merely the usual confusion of dates and the actual date of the events of Golgotha. One thing I believe is certain, is that there were two Royal Dynastic lineages in Britain controlled by priesthoods and whilst one was pro Jewish, the other appears to have been pro-Greek even though it ascended from Adam. The sequestering of the genealogies and the initiation of a Universal Religion - Christianity, appear to have been the whole covert exercise of the events of Golgotha and the obvious attempts of the Jews to round up all documents and genealogies that could destroy their plans for the triumph of Israel. Personally however from evidence in *The Battle of The Trees*, I have never assumed that Christianity was the final goal of at least one set of hidden Masters who appear to be the Druids and in ascendant form the Rosicrucians, that goal may or may not be Scientology. However if it was to reflect salvation for all and not just "the chosen ones" (according to wealth and not Jewish blood) then it really missed the mark – it became just another caste or hierarchal system which those who resigned from Scientology in the 80's protested. The problem is that the Druids were always a hierarchal Order with great arrogance and have not learnt the lesson with the passage of time. Further they always accumulated wealth within their universities where students studied science and religion.

Is it not reasonable to assume that the Patriarchal line descended from Adam, have sought to work towards the fulfilment of the religious goals of a Celtic and essentially Gentile lineage from the tribe of Judah and whilst the Jews and the tribe descended from Levi clearly had a similar religious agenda, but in the form of Christianity there is obviously a difference between those religious plans and where the tribe of Judah have not made known their religious goal unless it is already visible in the name of Scientology. Both groups clearly seek a political agenda but as I observed in The Battle of The Trees that agenda saw a push towards a Federal European Super State in the 70's and 80's, to which the religious goal was subordinated. Neither can one assume that these two groups are still not betraying each other in the repeat of such events as Golgotha. Neither can one assume that a Federal European Super State has not been the goal in the far past The Celtic leaders obviously had a political agenda that eventually led to the formation of the State of Galatia, formed sometime during the decade of 260's B.C. Hieronymus of Cardia who died c. 373-263 B.C. first used the term Galatia for the land of the Gauls or Galli (the Celts). He called it

'KOINON GALATION', THE COMMONWEALTH OF GALATIONS. The CELTIC STATE. Britain of course still clung to these colonial ideas in the period of the Empire. However I think it is very wrong to say *Britain* desired colonialism it was not the British *people* but that inevitable secret influence. I will come to the identity crisis in Britain today at a later point, but one should remember that the British people have always been subordinate to this influence and whilst one cannot deny that the national character has evolved on such influence, this influence and that of the other group have touched all countries and have influenced all peoples. Man has never known a time when this influence was not pulling strings on him. The Celtic battle mentality that still exists in Britain has on occasions brought out the very finest in its people. Such evidence must be amply illustrated by the story of one ex-RAF (Royal Air Force) fighter pilot in World War II. He was part of an extra-ordinary show of courage in the face of adversity, when the RAF and a few hundred pilots fought air battles over the south coast of Britain for days in a row going up time and time again without sleep to fight. It was a turning point in the war and Churchill was to comment, "Never in the field of human conflict was so much owed to so few". The fighter pilot told the story of how he was shot down and landed on a golf course. One golfer shouted: "get the bloody man off the course!" and when he was taken bleeding and dirty to the clubhouse one member stated: "Good Lord, he can't come in like that! " he two-tiered system was never more evident.

From the point of view of politics today which I will discuss subsequently under the phallic god, it is evident that in Galatia they worshipped a Hermaphroditic god i.e. Hermes. From myth the original shrine -Cybele was Phrygian or 'Mother Earth' Goddess (Agdistis), who was later identified with (Cretan) Rhea, mother of Zeus, where the myth states that Zeus, whilst asleep on Mount Didymos in Phrygia let his seed fall to the ground: From this grew a being with both male and female parts i.e. a hermaphroditic god. You will observe that this is very far removed from the Greek concept of Hermes, the bisexual god, who was really a union of the Mother Goddess and the Twin Kings in their Transcendent Third stage beyond death, and a product of manipulation of the archetypes in order to remove all traces of the woman. Hermes role as the transcendent third, which incorporated the mystery of his supercession of the woman, was lost in later myth, where he merely became the conductor of souls to and from the spiritual world; whereas it was always the truth, that this was the Goddess' or woman's function, as her gift to humanity. These things are not totally irrelevant, for within these myths there is a basic truth of historical events, which forms a trap for humanity. However if a hidden hierarchal philosophical Order kept the original truth to themselves they certainly allowed the Celts to adopt this Phrygian religion from the remaining inhabitants of the area, since it also fitted with the Celtic story of their gods and Danu. Evidently then, the first European Super State was Galatia.

The State of Galatia, was split into tribes and ruled by a chieftain, a war chieftain, two petty chieftains and a judge, who would have been a Druid, although the name was not mentioned in referring to the Galatian Celts. Strabo in describing the government of Galatia refers to an: "assembly", which paralleled the assembly of the European Celts at Gaul, who met at Lugdunum (Lyons). The government interestingly was DECENTRALILSED thus there was no possibility of a supreme Monarch who could control the populace. The people had a system of representatives who attended a tribal assembly, which must reflect the modern Democracy and Parliament. It might be argued that the Celts had originated a form of the first European Commonwealth, based on a Theocracy (a Priesthood of Druids), but with fair representation. However this system was prone to weakness when faced by aggressors or neighbours who were centrally governed. If European Union was a re-building of this Commonwealth or THEOCRACY and it is my belief it is, with a Philosophical group or Order in the background directing our European National governments, then if there is one thing that secret groups or Orders do, it is to learn by their mistakes. If there was to be a Theocracy this time, it would be **centralised with no meaningful representation or democracy**, thus removing the prior weakness of attack from Centralised powers. The political goal of absolute power or a Federal Europe, would only introduce a religious goal, when power absolute was confirmed, which includes monetary power.

Galatia was apparently still a state just up to the birth of Jesus. It seems that the Romans now sought to challenge that power of the Celts and also the Druids. The Roman conquest of Galatia and Asia Minor began in 190 B.C. when the Romans achieved victory. Scipio Africanus in Rome was reported to have told the Celts in the peace terms "The Terms are these: KEEP OUT OF EUROPE; withdraw from the whole of Asia on this side of the Taurus range..." (*author's emphasis*): Thus here we have the inevitable conflict between the two groups, on the world's stage. We should remember that Pontius Pilate, who played such an important role in the events of Golgotha, may well have been a Prince of Metallanus (King at Fortingall) Pontius Pilate, as part of the Roman administration and Celtic? There appears to be some confusion over whether there was a central order to attack Galatia in the Roman Senate records. The Roman commander in his defence before the Roman Senate refers to the Galatians as an oppressive people who had set out to dominate Asia Minor and there is no record of any central order to attack Galatia Despite the Roman Conquest, Galatia continued to exist with a Kingship. In c. 176 B.C. Antiochus VI became King and started an unsuccessful war with Egypt and sought to increase his power and control over Judea. He sought to Hellenise the Jews and to this end he destroyed one of the walls of Jerusalem and placed an alter to Zeus in the Temple. The Jews in their turn revolted against the Syrian Empire led by Mathathias of the Hasmoneans. The struggle to maintain Jewish independence

269

is related in the two books of *Macabees* in *The Old Testament*. This book particularly *Macabees 2,v.19-20*, describes this struggle against the Galatians. What is interesting is that the Jews and the Celts (Hellenic) evidently had a long history of conflict, presumably based on religious beliefs and the Royal dynasties.

After the Roman conquest of Galatia, a King was introduced c. 58 B.C., which provided the Romans with the control they required. Deiotaros I, who formed a very close association with Rome and thus despite being an independent Kingdom in Asia Minor was the only one recognised by Rome. This brings us up to the times of Jesus when Octavian the adopted son and heir of Caesar as Gaius Octavius, was to become Augustus Caesar first Emperor of Rome. The King of Judea at the time was Herod The Great (c.73-4B.C.) the dates of Herod obviously do not tally with Biblical dates, which are WRONG. At the time of Jesus then, **Judea was a Hellenic Kingdom** under the patronage of Mark Antony, before Caesar became Emperor. After the defeat of Anthony by Caesar he presented Herod with Cleopatra's bodyguard of 400 Celts, according to Josephus. If Jesus had a Celtic dynasty as it is claimed from Heraldic documentation, is it likely that Herod would have sought to kill him as a child, when Herod was surrounded by Celts!? Surely Herod as a Hellenic King would have employed Celts that had Hellenic backgrounds and certainly those Celts with the pre-Hellenic gods of the Tuatha de Danaan as part of their tribal history would have fitted as loyal bodyguards. However Herod would not have employed pro-Jewish Celts. More than this why would Octavian Caesar after his conquest of Egypt in 30 B.C. make a Romanised Celt Gaius Cornelius Gallus (c.69-26B.C.) the prefect and first Roman Governor of Egypt? It appears that after 25 B.C. when Amyntas the last King of Galatia died, Rome annexed Galatia as a Roman Province and Caesar occupied Britain and invaded Gaul. Obviously Caesar was concerned over what appeared to be none other than the growing force of CELTIC NATIONALISM, but in reality was a One World Order plan by the Druids I conclude. This is odd, since Celts were often found in high positions even in the Roman administration, so what or who was Caesar concerned about? The answer was the DRUIDS and their plans for a Celtic Super - State. The question has always been why the Romans ever bothered to come to Britain at all, why should they have come to this relatively small Island, when they had the rest of Europe to worry about? But if their mission was to suppress the Druids and Celtic National Unity, there may have also been another goal which was perhaps to eradicate the Royal Dynastic lines, which had really formed the background to the events of Golgotha and which the Roman Administration must have been aware of. The Mary Magdalene after the events of Golgotha, fled to Marseilles in France carrying what truth of The Holy Grail was left and she was with John the Evangelist. She was pregnant by him and also she also had another child whose father was Jesus. She was healing people using

The Grail Knowledge (Re-incarnation), but was betrayed and mown down by a horse at the settlement just North of Marseilles (**a Greek Colony**); in seeking a Greek haven of safety this implies that the Mary Magdalene was a Princess of a **Greek - Celtic dynasty**.

By 4 B.C. the Jewish population was in revolt against Hellenic Kings who were under the patronage of Rome. Further the governor of Syria Quinctilius Varus had to introduce crucifixion for Jewish rebels and possibly 2,000 Jews were crucified. By A.D. 6 further the Roman Administration started to evaluate all property for a new tax system, which would be applied to **landowners only** (the rich). If there is confusion which I related earlier, over the date and manner of Jesus' birth, then it is because not only does *The New Testament Gospels* wrongfully state a decree went out twelve years earlier than A.D. 6, but it does not specify that it was to be applied to the wealthy only. The Biblical story that Jesus was poor was not the reality of his birth into a Royal Dynasty, where He was probably fostered according to the custom of the Druids, or adopted according to the custom of the Essenes. The fact is that the Jews were fighting for their own freedom. The Jewish revolutionaries in the resistance movement, the freedom fighters or Zealots as they were known, were obviously in revolt at the Roman administration and Hellenic Kingship. Thus the Twelve Tribes of Israel and their priesthood were in conflict with the group of Hellenic-Celtic Priesthood, which can only have been the Druids. This obviously was a much more hidden battle of the priesthoods - the priesthood of Aaron (Jewish) attempting to wrestle control from the Druids, although obviously all mention of the Druids, would have been edited out from biblical texts (*Numbers XXV, 13*). The Jews believed that Phinehas, the son of Aaron had not died and was some form of Re-incarnation of the prophet Elijah. This is extra-ordinary in itself, however it has been claimed, that Re-incarnation was edited out of The Bible at the 5th Ecumenical. They also believed that Phinehas would return and tell them of a coming Messiah *(Malachi iv, 5)*. The history surrounding Jesus has been seriously edited and whilst e.g. Herod's father employed Celts as his bodyguard there is no mention of Celts (or Essenes or Druids) in the orthodox history surrounding the life of Jesus, despite the fact that clearly these political events were the underlying story of Golgotha.

Pontius Pilate was not appointed as governor or procurator until A.D. 26 and clearly Jesus declared himself a member of the Jewish Revolutionary movement when he declared: "I come not to send peace but a sword" (*Mathew X, 34*). Further the fact that Jesus was allegedly handed over to the Roman Administration points to the fact that He was a political offender and not a religious offender as the latter were dealt with through Jewish Law. The trial and Crucifixion (allegedly) of Jesus occurred in A.D. 30.
The subsequent title of Messiah or Christos in Greek given to Jesus was not a

designated title of divinity, it simply meant "anointed" as the King of Judea, just as also the High Priest was anointed. Every Jewish King of the House of David received the title of Messiah, as did the High Priests. Jesus quoted the text *Clement of Alexandria (Stromata iii)* which I have already referred to, is worth quoting again here:

> "When in The Gospel according to the Egyptians, Shelom asked the Lord: "How long shall death prevail?" He answered: "So long as you women bear children". And when she asked again: "I   have   done well then in not bearing children?" He answered: "Eat every plant but that which is bitter..."And when she inquired at what time the things concerning which she had questioned Him should be known, He answered: "When you women have trampled on the garment of shame and when the two become one, and when the male with the female is neither male or female". And the Saviour said in the same Gospel: "I have come to destroy the works of the Female".

The "Female" indicates the Mother Goddess, the Greek background to the Royal Dynasty, which was based on the Tuatha de Danaan. Jesus here also reflects the Jewish view of woman and incidentally the Essene Priesthood's view. This view might be considered odd for a Celt, who viewed women favourably as equals, but not within the Essenes who I thought in their tiered upper system may have had connections to the Higher Order of Druids. Also Jesus may have been referring in this text to the hermaphroditic quality of the Celtic God Zeus Dionysos and I previously referred to a historical observation made by a Greek, of the preference of homosexuality by the Celts. However, it has been stated that Jesus had wine-coloured hair which is clearly a Celtic characteristic apart from his alleged descent from Anna through the Greek Celtic line. Jesus however descended I claimed from **a matrilineal Egyptian** Celtic dynasty whereas Magdalene was descended from **a matrilineal Greek** Celtic dynasty presumably dating back to Anna who was the alleged grandmother of Jesus. The confusion is no doubt set by the case of the stolen genealogies and the method of adoption and fostering.

There is as we note considerable covert secrecy in Biblical texts surrounding this era of history and there have even been attempts to cover up the role of the disciples as political zealots. Simon Bar. Christians knew Jonah as Peter, but originally he was known as Simon 'the outlaw' (Baryona), which was changed to 'Son of Jonah'. In *Luke VI, 15*, Simon is clearly referred to as 'the Zealot' (Zelotes). James and John were nicknamed 'Boanerges', which is concealed as 'Sons of thunder' in *Mark iii, 17*; however the meaning from the actual translation is 'Sons of martial thunder', which was a term applied to zeolots. Mark and Mathew called Simon 'the Canaanite', but Canaan no longer existed at this time, the Hebrew word for Zealot, Kanai, presumably mistranslated as Kena'ani (Canaanite). Judas Iscariot is a name derived from 'Assassin' or Sicarius, which the Romans referred to as a contemptuous word for Zeolot.

The political background to the events in Jerusalem were far from simple and certainly cannot be extracted from a story which has been portrayed in metaphysical almost supernatural terms. The politics of power are complex and this was no exception in the times surrounding the events in Jerusalem. The Jews, the Romans and the hitherto virtually unmentioned Celts, Druids and Essenes, were with the Greeks powers to be reckoned with. The priesthoods and the dynastic lines were also complex jigsaw pieces in this overall view, pieces that dated back thousands of years. The events of The Crucifixion look remarkably like a Roman and Jewish plot to destroy the power of the Celts and the expanding Celtic Commonwealth, which evidently worried the Romans and Caesar; however this political goal was jointly coupled with a religious goal that can only be defined in terms of what happened after the events of Golgotha, when the Magdalene fled to Marseilles a Greek colony in France, with John the Evangelist according to my own witness account. Meanwhile Jesus' brother Jacob (James) after A.D. 30 which is the actual date of the events of Golgotha, formed the Nazarenes and Paul (St. Paul) a Hellenised Jew, c. A.D. 36 became a member of the Nazarenes whilst also in all probability a Roman collaborator. The fact that the Crucifixion was moved to an earlier date is to avoid the obvious connection of Paul as a Jewish Roman agent acting to fulfil the religious goal of the plan at Golgotha. That religious goal was the advent of Christianity. That might seem odd, but the Hidden Masters think in terms of long cycles and only after a long period of persecution, despair and religious wars - which is the history of Christianity, would it be possible to introduce a Universal Religion which did not rest on Churchanity, but sought to unify religions. This has been the virtually identical methodology developed in order to introduce the idea of European Union, which only found a forum after a devastating World War II, where the idea was sold on the basis of Internationalism and peace, which man as dupe fell for. The Masters simply beat man down into the pulp of apathy and then enforce their own solution, which was all pre-determined.

> "When we accomplish our coup d'Etat, we will say to the people: "Everything has been going very badly; all of you have suffered; now we are destroying the cause of your sufferings - that is to say, nationalities, frontiers and national currencies. Certainly you will be free to condemn us, but can your judgement be fair if you pronounce it before you have had experience of what we can do for your good?" (*Protocols of Zion p.31*).

It is believed that Paul whilst collaborating with the Romans, was also a member

273

of the Sanhedrin of the Jewish priesthood. This would make perfect sense if it were as I propose a Jewish- Roman plan. The Sanhedrin are the *seventy one* (with the high priest it would make 72 the number of letters in the Beth-Luis Nion alphabet used to contain the religious mysteries) Jewish Scholar priests who formed the Supreme Court of Legislature over Jewish religious matters. Paul originally set out to persecute the Nazarenes (*Acts 26 V.9-10*), which is a fairly good disguise for this sort of plan I would propose. As a member of the Sanhedrin he was able to cast a vote on executions, as was the case with Stephen c. A.D. 35, who was one of the seven leaders of the Nazarenes. Paul in a complete about change suddenly converted to the Nazarene sect and altered substantially the teachings of the sect, so that the Nazarene Pharisees and followers of Jesus now considered the teachings inconsistent. It was Paul signifificantly enough who gave divine status to Jesus and recommended that the Nazarene sect be opened to Gentiles or non-Jews, who would not have to undergo circumcision or conversion to Judaism in order to follow the teachings of Jesus. This must have been the important methodology of introducing a Universal Religion, which was initially only intended for the Jews. This is a strange turn of events unless we remember that St. Paul was found in Britain after the crucifixion and thus as I strongly suspected the entire plan of Golgotha was to set up a Universal religion – Christianity which not only combined Communistic doctrine of the Jewish priesthood and Essenes, but the Buddhist influences of the old Matriarchal belief system with the Cycle of Eternal Return (Re-incarnation) reduced to the concept of a Second Coming for Messiah's only. Man would be given the psychological support and comfort he needed, whilst the Masters hung on to the truth. Thus her own family betrayed Magdalene and Jesus was betrayed in so far as the religion he intended was for the Jews only. Indeed The Bible is really just that, the eventual triumph of Israel! As evidenced by the salvation of the "chosen ones" – the tribes of Israel in Revelations. Given that I maintained John who wrote Revelations was a Druid, one might find this odd, but in *The Battle of The Trees*, I referred to an alternative book of Revelations that appears to be held by the secret groups and which is quite different from the vulgate version. This point may seem un-important, but since the Book of Revelations contains a prophecy for the end of things, then it might be pertinent to ask what exactly that end is. I will return to this point in conclusion.

Jesus under Paul not only became Divine, but the Saviour, utilising Gnostic Salvation doctrine and in a political agreement with Rome presumably the teachings of Jesus would become the principle Christian doctrine and religion in the West; that would enable Rome and the Jews to fulfil their own particular agenda. In the case of Rome, it provided a State religion that even the Greeks found necessary for military security and avoidance of future religious conflicts: whilst co-jointly the political power of the Celtic Commonwealth and the Druids would be destroyed. It seems that the Celtic Commonwealth in its system of representation formed a foundation for modern democracy and the will and representation of the people and since the Jews or priesthood of Egyptian dynastic rule had always utilised Kingship and despotism, then this new idea of representation must have created concern, that such a State would be vulnerable from outside aggressive forces and internal agents of anarchy who might sway the will of the people. It might have been considered politic to revert to sole rule whilst maintaining a State religion that would once and for all bury the truth and prevent religious wars trying to exact justice for that truth. Christianity would provide some relief from the position of subjugated people, whilst providing a stepping-stone to the ultimate triumph of Israel and a Universal political and religious kingdom, which must see its triumph today in the Federal European Super State.

The original intent of the Nazarenes and the Zealots and the mission of a Jewish political Freedom Movement have been 'smudged' over in The Bible. Only the *Epistle of James* as Jesus' brother survives as biblical documentary proof, however there is no assurance that this document too, has not been heavily edited by later Paulinists. The original texts speak of the 'Synagogue' indicating the Judaic doctrine of the Nazarenes. The Nazarenes also specifically taught that Jesus was *not* divine, but a Messiah who taught Mosaic Law. They also claimed that Paul had misinterpreted and spread false doctrines as regards Jesus. Attempts to hide the fact that Paul had bitterly argued with Peter (Simon Bar-Jonah). " The Rock" or in Greek 'Cephas', are evident when Peter's name is deliberately left as the Greek 'Cephas' in Latin texts, to avoid identifying the unholy row that had occurred with Peter, when Paul set out to deliberately misrepresent the teachings of Jesus and which were bitterly contested by those who had known Jesus. Paul could hardly teach that Jesus had given Peter the key to heaven, whilst arguing with Peter over the principles of Jesus' teaching.

In Paul's *Letter to the Galatians* he proposes that there was a sort of Gentleman's agreement between himself and Peter, John and Jacob on the distribution of Jesus' teachings and the opening up of those teachings to non-Jews or Gentiles. Why should Paul direct this particular message to the Galatians? And why should the whole background to the exact origin of the Galatians be so hidden? Whereas some scholars argue that Paul's "Galatians" were not the Celts at all! This is pure nonsense! As a Hellenic Jew of Anatolia, Paul would be very much aware that a Galatian on history alone was regarded as a Celt. There is absolutely no other mention of another Galatia or the State of the Galatians and if the Galatians were not Celts, then there is absolutely no other possibility of identification in history. This trick has been tried once too often I am afraid and it tries one's patience. The reason that Paul addressed this particular letter to the Galatians seems very clear if Rome wanted an end to the threat of the Celtic

275

Commonwealth and the power of the Druids. Would the Jews (and the tribe of Levi) not be thankful if the Celts adopted a Jewish religion, which had been adapted for Gentiles in the hope of unifying them around an Egyptian dynasty that had descended from Egyptian (Matriarchal) and Celtic (patriarchal) sources perhaps as the story of Mil and Scota indicates: whilst also acknowledging the tribe of Judah who were descended from the Patriarch Noah and Adam and who possessed a Celtic and Greek dynasty? This might account for the very obvious Semitic and Jewish facial characteristics of Egyptian Kings whilst the Queens appeared as blonde and presumably blue-eyed as exhibited in mummy archaeological finds. Thus it appears that whilst Solar Kingship became the method of power this was shared as King and Queen by the two secret priesthoods and tribes of Levi and Judah. Since the Jews and particularly the Zealots were in revolt at Roman occupation and *Hellenic Kingship*, then would it be favourable for the Jews to rid themselves of a dynastic Royal line that incorporated Greek influence (the Tuatha de Danaan), the Celtic Royal dynastic line that Jesus was alleged to have come from, but which I claim was stolen from the Mary Magdalene. Surely it would have been in the interests of both Rome and the Jews to encourage the Celts to adopt another State religion. Paul knew the cultural and historical origins of the Celtic Commonwealth too well, to call Greeks, Roman and Jewish settlers "Galatians".

When Paul referred to "the foolish Galatians", he was referring to the Celtic Galatians after the Nazarenes had gone to Galatia to bargain presumably or broker a peace settlement. Paul in being questioned by the Galatians over his teachings and the fact that it was not necessary to convert to Judaism to follow the teachings of Jesus, wrote angrily to the Galatians in one of the earliest Christian documents - *The Epistle to the Galatians* in which Paul states:

> "I am astonished to find you turning so quickly away from him who called you by grace and following a different gospel. Not that it is in fact another gospel; only there are persons who Unsettle your minds by trying to distort the gospel of Christ. But if anyone, if we ourselves or an angel from heaven, should preach a gospel at variance with the gospel we preached to you, he shall be held outcast. I now repeat what I have said before, if anyone preaches a gospel at variance with the gospel, which you received, let him be outcast! Does my language now sound as if I were canvassing for men's support? Whose support do I want but God's alone? Do you think I am currying favour with men? If I still sought men's favour, I should be no servant of Christ.
> I must make it clear to you, my friends, that the gospel you heard me preach is no human invention I did not take it over from any man; no man taught it me; I received it through a revelation of Jesus Christ."

Paul then looses his temper (I am sure the Scientologists will check that one on Hubbard's Chart of Human Evaluation!) and refers to: "You stupid Galatians" (Latin stolidus) and then goes on to accuse the Jewish Nazarenes of insisting on circumcision because: "their sole object is to escape persecution for the cross of Christ". This is an odd statement and shows perhaps that it was known that the Jews were not ultimately responsible for the crucifixion, which implies that the tribe of Judah and the Druids were which discounts the views that it was the Sanhedrin and the Romans who precipitated the events of Golgotha.

Galatia was to become occupied and re-populated by the Romans as a method of diluting Celtic Nationalism which has been used historically as a method on several occasions e.g. the occupation of Greece by the Turks, the occupation of Tibet by the Chinese and the heavy immigration programme in the U.K. has been criticised in Britain NOT on racialist grounds, but as a further dilution of the national character, where every group apart from the indigenous tribe has rights and is assured a viewpoint. This method of diluting national character is evident in the world globalisation plan today and particularly in Europe where National identities are being broken down. This is an effective weapon in Britain to break down the elitist psychology, a legacy of the group that persisted in this country over thousands of years, descended from Adam and holding the Secret Doctrine. Ego and arrogance were and still are undoubtedly a common psychological trait of that elitism that persisted in the institutions and elitist University and educational sectors of the public schools, which supplied the next generation of elitist thinkers, who would toe the inevitable elitist line. Christianity did not take a hold in Galatia until the 4th Century A.D. However it is recorded that Caesar had conducted a policy of systematic genocide of the Celts from 58 B.C. From the point of view of the Mary Magdalene and the Greek Celtic line? There was a desperate attempt to make known the facts of Re-incarnation before the door of democracy slammed shut on the goal of a Universal political and religious kingdom which would not only incorporate this belief and the history of the truth, but a political system run by the will of the people. It was probably a hopeless dream, that through that narrow crack before the door of freedom and democracy closed, would pass the chance to reverse 10,000 years of lies and wrestle the hidden science back into rightful hands to be revealed with the truth to the people.

When Caesar had finished his Celtic cull, is it co-incidence that only the Celts on the peninsula of Armorica (Brittany) and in Britain and Ireland remained, as remnants of a civilization that had not been murdered or re-absorbed. Is it co-incidence too that in 1936 an illustration for the cover of *Vaincre* magazine, edited by a man who was heavily involved with the secret groups and who would become The Grand Master of The Prieuré de Sion, a group who in the 80's not only supported a Merovingian dynasty and a supposed Royal Dynastic

277

line descended from a proposed union between the Mary Magdalene and Jesus but a European Federal Super State or as a "United States of the West", as it was known. Further since they revered the number 13 one can only assume that they were in fact the Druids of their time. Further such a group appears to have been heavily involved with the Nazi's and the quest for a Super-race. Surely this was a resurrection of the old aim of a blonde blue-eyed race (of Celts) or Aryans who would dominate Europe as the Celts once did in their Celtic Commonwealth. Whilst I produced the *Vaincre* magazine illustration in *Alternative4* and have covered the significances of the archetypal symbols in the illustration, the important point to emphasise here, is that the knight is wearing a cap which looks remarkably like the petasos cap of **Hermes,** as he rides down a road marked **Brittany** on one side and **Bavaria** on the other, towards a blazing **sun** and a **goal of a Federal Europe** or 'Etats Unis'. Hermes of course indicates that this is a group carrying the Greek background of the Celtic Druidic cause and utilising the hermaphroditic god. Brittany refers to the Merovingians (or religious goal) and perhaps Gaul and the royal dynastic goal of presumably the Priest Kings or Sun Kings dating back to a proposed union of Jesus with Magdalene and presumably the child who was taken after Magdalene's death by John - back to Scotland? Bavaria refers to the Illuminati through its founder Adam Weishaupt who was born in Bavaria and the political goal of a power pyramid in Europe, as a Federal Super State. The Sun refers to Solar Kingship and given the hermetic knight presumably a religious goal of the combined Twin Kings and Mother Goddess dating back to the time of the Religious Revolution in Crete after which Re-incarnation as a belief was forced underground. The years indicated on the final goal of a Federal Europe are 1937 -1947, which strongly implies that World War II was as I claimed in both my prior books, a mere necessity and stepping stone on which a Federal Europe could be built. Only when a Europe ravaged by war and lying in virtual destruction with her peoples in a state of apathy, was it possible to sell to Europeans the idea of a United Europe, where such horrors could never occur again. A power political pyramid built on the sacrificial pile of millions and let us not forget The Holocaust and those victims who in all probability were sacrificed by a secret group of philosophical adepts, who must be descended at least in philosophical and religious viewpoint, from the Jewish Patriarchs the Semitic line of Adam and Judah or from the tribe of Levi! As I have suggested it cannot be discounted that both were involved and persecuted their own in order to set up the State of Israel and the Jews (or specifically the tribe of Levi) would then have a homeland whereas the tribe of Judah had always existed in the UK under the cloak of Freemasonry – Scottish Rite or Rose-Croix? Neither let us forget the white Russians, the insane and gypsies who also died in this elitist super-race programme. Whilst one might have expected Jewish Hollywood to broadcast the secret group connections of Adolph Hitler, the deafening silence on these subjects stems from the tribulation in the world that has been created from a persistent goal of domination by both groups, who one suspects have at times acted in unison and in conflict with each other, reducing this world to chaos through religious wars, which is really the nature of war and conflict on this planet.

The Third Reich then, could have been an attempt to raise the old Celtic or Nordic (Atlantean) Commonwealth and claim justice for "Her" (in Hitler's own words), the Great Goddess supporting the Greek philosophy and line, with the Black Order as the philosophical adepts and Hitler as a Solar King or Grail Knight, thus accounting for the poster that appeared briefly in 1936 and illustrated in *The Battle of The Trees*. Much of the iconography surrounding the Nazi party was initiate knowledge, dating back to Bronze Age Greece particularly the trieskelion or swastika. Perhaps it was that Hitler had not forgotten (or his philosophical adepts of The Black Order) that Caesar (The Romans) and the Jews had wiped out the Celts massacring 300,000 Celtic men women and children of the Helvetic Tribe alone and later was to conquer Gaul by a similar genocide of the Celtic Tribes in one of the worst episodes of Ethnic Cleansing the World has ever known. If Hitler wished to eradicate the tribe of Levi once and for all then The Jewish Holocaust may have been the method. There has been contention over whether the numbers that died in the Holocaust were correct and this is an argument that I see no point in perusing here, since I hold the philosophy of individuals and if one Jew died in suffering it was wrong. However there are substantial arguments with at least one account written by a judge which question the numbers who were alleged to have died in The Holocaust and the motive behind what is claimed as propaganda.[103-106] The Holocaust, can only produce in the author a sense of incomprehension of man's inability to grasp that even a Celt or Aryan may have incarnated as a Jew and vice versa or even as male *and* female! Which the Jews might spare a thought for when they recite their daily prayer to "thank God thou hast not made me a woman"!

An icon found in Crete after the Religious Revolution shows a male figurine with a large penis. Previously such icons may have been interpreted as fertility icons, however this is to ignore the whole system of Cabalistic magic that has been handed down since the Patriarchs. The fundamental doctrine of **magic** is **phallism**. New life is created by the act of generation and in magic the sexual forces create the life force, the union of male and female elements. Aleister Crowley the infamous black magician used sexual rites as a necessary part of his invocations (of spiritual information -the Akashic Record) and ritual. The phallic god is hermaphroditic or bi-sexual and the god who most suited the philosophy and practise of magic was hermaphroditic Hermes. Magic denounced reason, as an obstacle to the liberation of mans natural instincts. Crowley who was known as "The Beast" after the Gematria "666", led an infamous sexual life that shocked those: "encumbered with reason" and his Law of Thelema: "Do what Thou wilt is the whole of the Law", was to surface in the magical priesthood of The Third Reich and has become the battle cry for a Federal Europe, where the will of the people does not matter and indeed answers why my Petition to the British Parliament (*Appendix 2*) was doomed in the face of no adherence to law or parliamentary rules (despite the claim to the contrary by the Petitions office- surely this book is " personal grievance" enough to support such Petition! According to " the rules of Petitions").

The creation of the Universe according to phallic adepts is the work of the hermaphroditic god. The Universe was not created but pro-created by Him, this must surely rest with the idea that Adam pro-created the human race and therefore was specifically from Judah. Since man could also procreate according to the philosophy of magic and esoteric theology, then man was placed on a par with his creator-God. The claim of being God was the deadliest of sins based on this faulty logic, for man as God-Creator was based on magical philosophy - the use of the magical Black Cabala presumably. This could only be interpreted as the use of the hidden science and the secrets of energy laws tied up with this science. No doctrine was ever better devised to destroy a man's reason by way of self-conceit and arrogance of self assumed correctness – than **playing God.** This philosophy better suited the elite in their pursuit of world domination and the control of the hidden science, where a conscience or any deferment of power to a higher source would limit such pursuits hampered by conscience. Politicians hold much the same view, as they decide who will and will not be blasted out of their bodies in the cause of world peace!

It might be argued that a group of philosophical adepts entered the Psychro cave in Crete, the mythical birthplace of Zeus Dionysus where clearly the nature of

God was changed in this Religious Revolution. Man assumed God-like power and the role of the woman, with Her gift of immortality to man, which was later to be evolved into a more complex and not entirely correct thought, which would be explained as one King dying and joining with Her the Great Goddess, to be reborn through Her as his Twin (King). This first downgrade of the truth to involve Solar Kingship would ultimately result in the fusion of the Twin Kings into one King, a Solar King, which was the role of Apollo the god and Sun-King. Hereditary Monarchy would evolve from Solar Kingship to complete the error. Hermes evolved from a fusion of Solar King (or Twin-Kings) with Her the Great Goddess in an attempt to remove the woman in the story, who refused to join The Holy Grail message with politics and was a perpetual and infuriating conscience to man as he sought power to rule in his own name. Thus Hermes as a bisexual or hermaphroditic god was a distortion of the original truth. However Hermes as magician was very well suited as the godhead of the secret fraternal Brotherhoods and priesthoods who idolised the Magical Cabala and presumably the power retained in the Energy Grid. "Lucifer, Sun of the Morning' as he is known had taken control of Planet Earth once again in a never ending cycle of his own making.

Oswald Spengler writes: "The origin of numbers resembles that of myth. Primitive man elevates indefinable nature-impressions (the 'alien' in our terminology) into deities, numina, at the same time capturing and impounding them by a name which limits them."107 When the name, was that of the supreme deity, it was frequently disguised both in respect to the letters which spelled it and their number. The ancient Hebrew name of God was not to be spoken or written in full, but only in disguise as the Tetragrammaton, a four-letter formula made up of the consonants alone. The four-letter formula JHVH veiled the sacred name Jehoweh, both in respect to the secret vowels and the number of letters, which were seven in all. Seven was a number sacred to the deity, and in the book of *Revelations* by St. John, who was I assume a Druid; there is a constant reference to the number seven, which is a sign of the magical and hermaphroditic god. Importantly Genesis gives an account of the creation of the world in seven days, thus it is being implied here in the Hebraic account, that the original God was magical or hermaphroditic. This of course totally contravenes the truth. Similarly, the sun-god, Mithras a god of Persian origin, with many converts in the Roman legions of Imperial times was signified by the formula name ABRAXAS, because the true name of the deity was too holy to be spoken in a profane context. In *The Lost Language of Symbolism*, Harold Bayley writes

"The name ABRAXAS, which is at the root of the famous magic-word ABRACADABRA, was one of the numerous mystery words coined to express mathematically the unspeakable name of the Supreme Spirit.

"Abraxas" was accepted as a mystic equivalent of "Mithras", because the numerical values of the two names work out to the number 365".[108]

It is not entirely improbable that Mithras and apparently also Abraxas were associated with the solar year of 365 days and the magical word Abracadabra by way of the Sun's light, the source of the electro-magnetic spectrum and the structure and apparent use of the Earth's energy Grid. The use of the wand in magic followed by the word abracadabra interestingly relates to the Druidic wand or rood (the rod which Moses as a magical initiate into the hidden science carried). The birthday of Mithras was celebrated on December 25 because of the proximity of the winter solstice and in fact the early Christians adopted this date as the official birthday of Christ, by way of competing with the popular Mithraic cult. The number of letters in both the name Mithras and ABRAXAS is seven, which is also the sacred number of letters in the name Jehoweh. Jehoweh then was a Sun God. This also implies worship of the sun's electro-magnetic spectrum or more specifically the Energy Grid and other phenomena of the Grid, such as the Akashic Record. It has to be asked whether when the priests channelled information from the Grid, whether they believed God was speaking to them!

The Latin word ABRACADABRA (*Fig.29*) was derived from the GREEK ABRAXAS. The word consists of eleven letters, which were sometimes arranged, in a **triangular or pyramidal** structure, in which one in each descending sequence diminished the number of letters. This permits the word to be read from left to right horizontally, or from apex of the triangle to the base diagonally. When arranged in this way (*fig. 29*), the number of letters in the word as read on the base of the triangle amounts to eleven, but read again from the apex to the base, we have eleven more or twenty-two letters, and the remaining side of the triangle has eleven again, to make a total of **thirty-three** letters in all. In the solar-lunar calendar the number eleven is the number of days discrepancy between solar and lunar years, which accumulates in **three** years to thirty-three and permits the intercalation of one month and makes the system work. It is suspected that the word ABRACADABRA like the word ABRAXAS is a formula concealing a calendar secret, revealed only to initiates of the cult of Mithras. However equally the Freemasonry level of the 33rd degree and the **Rose-Croix**, may be the level today where such secrets are revealed or the level where the hidden science is held. Further the pyramid that I have shown on the One Dollar bill of The United States of America, may have an archetypal significance of magic and the hermaphroditic God of Jehoweh, apart from the usual significance of a power pyramid of religion and politics. The implication is there, that the World Order will be a magical one, in the sense that the mysteries and the Grid will either be USED TO CONTROL, or will be released at benefit. In the former scenario you have the psycho civilised society that I explained in Alternative4 including the HAARP and GWEN alleged defence systems, which a number of eminent scientists including Dr. Becker (who was twice nominated for a Nobel Prize) have warned against, as having a MIND CONTROL capability. In the latter scenario I can only consider Scientology as a contender.

Fig. 29 **ABRACADABRA** intriangular form as it frequently appeared as a charm on amulets

```
A B R A C A D A B R A
A B R A C A D A B R
A B R A C A D A B
A B R A C A D A
A B R A C A D
A B R A C A
A B R A C
A B R A
A B R
A B
A
```

The Druids and the Brahmins utilised sacrifice and *The Old Testament* of The Hebrews documents sacrifice. The hermaphroditic God is referred to in veiled terms in Genesis "The Father is the Mother"; and it was this reference that Pope John **Paul** I (Albino Luciani) referred to in a disturbed meeting of Bishops, not long after which he died in very mysterious circumstances, which many believe was murder. He was elected Pope on 26 August 1978 and like Angelo Roncali, Pope **John** XXIII, who was initiated into a secret society of Illuminati, Pope John Paul I, was to shock close observers of The Church when at a gathering of students and teachers, he extolled as: "a classical example of abnegation and devotion to education" Giosue Carduccu (1835-1907), who had been professor at Bologna University and whose name, as a self-confessed worshipper of Satan, was widely respected in occult circles. If Pope's are named according to which side of this game they are on, either Paul (Twelve Tribes and the tribe of Levi) or John (Freemasonry and the tribe of Judah), then is it not curious if this is the case, that both should retain a similar ideology? Unless at the highest levels of Jewry there is a unified goal of a Universal Religion, which appears to be magical.

Mrs, S.L. Mc Gregor Mathers in her work *The Kabbalah Unveiled*[109], stated that in the Kabbalah or Cabala: "they have smothered up every reference to the fact that the Deity is both masculine and feminine. They have translated a Feminine plural by a Masculine singular in the case of the word Elohim They have however, left an inadvertent admission of their knowledge that it was plural in *Genesis i, 26:* 'And Elohim said: Let us make man Again' (verse 27), how could Adam be made in the image of the Elohim, male and female, unless the Elohim were male and female also?" There appears to be here in the Elohim who were connected to Dome theory truthfully or not, an argument over whether *extraterrestrial intervention to help humanity* was male or female, thus prolonging if not initiating the argument, which finally saw the woman removed from the story altogether by that "jealous God" Jehovah and the tribe of Levi (the 12 tribes of Israel); which once again illustrates the lack of knowledge on the 'first cut' and the crab (in the mural on the wall of the Summer Smoking Room at Cardiff Castle). Which just goes to prove that man-god does not know everything!

The story of the creation in *Genesis* is an esoteric account of the phallic doctrine, where the Elohim becomes the hermaphroditic God - Hermes (magical), which obviously represents a total confusion on the whole truth and the purpose of The Holy Grail message, which was not sent to empower the Jews, the tribe of Levi or Judah – but HUMANITY! But let us not forget here, just how Hermes was INVENTED. He was the product, of combining the Goddess with Twin Kings in the Transcendent Third stage beyond death; in an attempt to remove the woman, whose gift to man was Immortality. The secret groups hid the events of Crete and the truth of the woman, creating a hermaphroditic God. However this was not the truth regarding the nature of the Spiritual Hierarchy, from whence The Holy Grail came to Earth. Man must find the humility to apologise profoundly to source. When Jesus referred in the text from Alexandria of the joining of male and female "as one" then He was following Cabalistic Jewish tradition and recognition of the hermaphroditic God, which required Him as he stated: "to destroy the works of the Female". The Jews could never accept the great wrong and the perversion of truth that had occurred and simply kept up a vile tirade against the woman, which has left its indelible imprint on Earth, as women became an underclass, which is still very much apparent and perpetuated today. The Demiurgus principle, the all important penetrating male member to the world potential as egg, which was so apparent in seals from the Religious Revolution era in Crete (*Fig. 22*); emphasising the requirement and prime importance of the *male*. The Solar King and the Sun e.g. to hatch the eggs or world potential of the snake, was not only veiled inference of man's control of the Grid (as serpent); but it also meant that the former truth, belief and philosophy was forgotten and discarded. That truth encompassed the snake or Serpent as an archetypal symbol of Immortality, with the shedding and renewal of the skin as a complex thought process and belief, that a body when it dies can be discarded and a new one sought or grown, in so far as the snake sheds its skin to be reborn. Elaborate scroll designs found at Knossos principally in the Queen's chamber show that at this time her role had not been forgotten, as the scrolls indicate symbolically: "into a life and out of a life and so one". Such scrolls evidently came to indicate the successive coils of the snake and its connection to Re-incarnation. However in the Genesis text, the snake or Serpent becomes associated with woman and "the tree of knowledge". Such knowledge evidently relates to the Grid and the Akashic record and magical practise. However it was not the woman who misused it, she tried to teach man its importance in his trap and the reason why he remains trapped on Earth and in this world. In fact the Teacher had used this as one example to illustrate this belief and truth to the mind of primitive man - of course archetypal symbolism was a brilliant educational tool, until it was taken over. The Patriarchs however sought to turn this thought on its head and in having turned it upside down, the whole thing had quite a different meaning, such is the story of the continual effort to unravel the mess that has been created. In fact Orphic philosophy, Solar Kingship, the Demiurgus principle etc. or in fact any philosophy or belief system that placed the male in prime importance or perverted the roles of the male and female as with the idea of a hermaphroditic God, appealed to the mind of the secret Initiates who sought world domination. I will return to this point later, but the end result of such philosophy after all these thousands of years, is observable in any newspaper that you care to pick up: sanctification of homosexuality, fudging the distinct and important but separate roles of male and female, to the detriment of children and a psychology that amounts to irresponsibility towards children when those roles are not clearly defined. To say that the whole of life is suffused with the peculiar psychology and belief system, which revolves around a hermaphroditic God, would be somewhat of an understatement. The male Celts as we know had a preference for young boys and this would reflect their God as Hermaphroditic and Hebraic.

Moses laid down this doctrine covertly in the principles of his Secret Doctrine and Mosaic Law, in the first four books of the *Pentateuch*, but withheld them from *Deuteronomy*. Both David and Solomon were deeply initiated into the Cabala and the first person that dared to write down the Cabala was Schimeon Ben Jochai. who you may remember wrote it down whilst amerced in san up to his neck, which I questioned as to whether or not it was channelled. The Druids of course held Mosaic Law as a basic doctrine. The secret doctrine of the Cabala consisted of:
1) The Sepher Yetzirah or "Book of Formation"
2) The Zohar or book of "Splendour".
3) The Sepher Sephiroth or "Book of Numbers"
4) The Asch Metzareph or "purifying Fire" which deals with Alchemy.

In the "Book of Formation" it deals with matter and the whole cosmology as symbolised by the ten numbers and twenty two letters of the Hebrew alphabet, which it calls the "thirty-two paths" or symbols with esoteric zero making **thirty-three** in all, which is the degree of the Rose-Croix and is indicated in the triangular arrangement of mystical letters in the word for magic ABRACADABRA. The implication once again, is that beyond the 33rd degree there is significant data on the arrangement of matter and atoms and atomic structure in gaseous, liquid and solid form. Such knowledge must exist in advanced form in the group the Rosicrucian's, who must have some input I believe into NASA - the American Space Agency. There is no indication that such knowledge was utilised by Einstein, but obviously Einstein as a Jew was uniquely positioned to access such material and the classification of National Security that such work would obtain, obviously means that it would be impossible to investigate whether Einstein had any contact with secret groups as other famous Scientists such as Newton had.

The whole system of numbers and what must be knowledge of atomic structure and sympathetic vibration, is hinted at when in the original document it states: "Now the zero 0, is incapable of addition, just as also is negative existence. How then if I can neither be multiplied nor divided, is another 1 to be obtained to add to it: in other words, how is the number 2 to be found? *By reflection of itself...*Thus, then we obtain a duad comprised of 1 and its reflection now also we have *the commencement of vibration...*" *(author's emphasis)*.

The Cabalistic Initiate is taught to form his soul on the pattern of the phallic God and thus become perfect man. There is a phrase in The Bible "**Ye are all gods**", which is really the underlying problem with Initiates of secret groups and rather underlines my experience in Scientology and Anthroposophy (Rudolf Steiner's group). "Too many chiefs and not enough Indians" is another phrase that springs to mind. However arrogance is the outcome of such initiation. The Freemasons, Bilderbergers etc. and even elite Schools and Universities provide such doctrine. Obviously those Scientists and politicians and bureaucrats bred and educated into such a system when they are further initiated into secret Cabalistic Science or doctrine fail to exercise conscience, since "**gods**" **cannot be wrong** I can assure you, it is far easier to apologise on Earth, than to wait for the Death Experience. Cabalistic doctrine maintains interestingly that the "**mould**" of the body, after the death of the body itself, mounts with the life-spirit to heaven, where the Queen presents it to the King. The interesting point here is the "mould", a term curiously used by Harold S. Burr originally, when referring to the non-specific field in space, which governs the shape of the embryo in its early stages. This is what I believe is the tri-partite layered biofield of electro-magnetic energy, that I concluded was part of the hieroglyphic symbols of the Phaistos disc, an unusual *circular* disc which was found in Crete after the

Religious Revolution, which is thought to be some form of initiation or religious object (*Alternative 4*). The presence of the tri-partite biofield if that is a correct de-coding of the disc hieroglyphics, would certainly point to the introduction of the Cabala at the time of the Religious Revolution. Further if the biofield was known and understood in the Cabala in pre-history, then it was not until the 1920's that research by independent researchers would start to reveal this part of he hidden science and its obvious value in the field of healing. Harold H. Burr, Kirlean and Wilhelm Reich would all go on to advance knowledge into the human biofield and finally in 1989 I would propose a theory for Cancer, on the basis of genetic information carried in the tri-partite biofield, which I covered in *Part II of The Second Millennium Working Report into Cancer,* with further explanations of the manipulation of that biofield in a proposed psycho civilised society (*Alternative 4*).

I have already referred to the biofield of man as having 7 layers, which I more fully discussed in *Alternative 4*, thus what is this 3 layered biofield? In the second part of The Second Millennium Working Report into Cancer, I have discussed a very primitive 3- layered aura, which really relates to the embryonic state and the formation of the body shape, which corresponds to the species. Now this 3 layered biofield is really just information that relates to the Genetics of the species. The Scientologists no doubt will recognise the term "Genetic Entity". This field is concerned with the genetic line of the species and is almost certainly covered by the simple laws of Darwinian evolutionary principles and SURVIVAL of the species. The simplest form of that is "survival of the fittest", which is a guiding philosophy in all secret groups. Let us take a mollusc for example, in the sea but on occasions subjected to tides and drying out, which represents a severe threat to survival. The 3 layered aura or biofield of the organism will carry specific information on the genetics of molluscs and further when the organism dies, the energy or biofield ("the mould") is then united with the morphopgentic bioplasma for the species in the etheric field or space if you like in a master blueprint for the DNA of molluscs. In other words all the life experience data of that Mollusc is re-united with that big library in the sky, none other than the Akashic Record. You might consider the mollusc as a product that was produced along factory lines and when it dies, certain information goes back to the factory manager the blueprint, to let the controller know how well or how badly the product survived. Now man has a similar mechanism where the tri-partite biofield goes back to the master blueprint and feeds back survival data. The **body** of any living thing including man has what we call some sentience or thinking. It also contains data on survival mechanisms. Thus it is mainly this sort of thinking i.e. survival that gets imprinted onto the master; morphogenetic bipoplasma blueprint or Akashic Record. Let us say that enough products go back to the factory with a fault e.g. the mollusc is not surviving very well, then the feedback data creates new patterns of energy or plans in the master blueprint which throw up new designs and the possibility of new lines which survive better. As the scientists will realise this is just another way of looking at Darwinian evolution which credits random mutation in the hereditary DNA and selection for the process of evolution and survival: but placing control in a master pattern outside of the body and in space or in a non specific field that I term the morphogenetic bioplasma and which I would conclude is the Akashic Record. I will leave you to read just how this tri-partite biofield acts in the mechanism of cancer in the Cancer report, but basically when a soul or spirit feels that they can no longer remain in the life they are in, they assign control to the tri-partite biofield or the body and the mechanisms that the body uses for survival. In short the spirit or WHO YOU ARE says "well I have had enough of this, I am off, this is not life!" and the spirit hands the controls of the 'car' to the body and jumps in the back seat hoping that the moron of the body can sort out the mess and drive the spirit to a place of higher survival! The body gets hold of its plans and with its moronic survivalist thinking says "Well let me see here, you have had a lot of loss, oh I see loss is loss of **body** parts! So you really need to grow body parts – well let me see here, the plans for new body parts are in the draw called embryos and foetus, O.K! I will grow a new foetus and get some new body parts!" The next thing that happens is that the spirit or WHO YOU ARE, realises that whilst in the back seat evading taking the steering wheel of his life, the body has grown a tumour! Which is really just an embryonic growth with all the attendant biochemistry. The driver (spirit) now has another problem and even more loss, so he decides to vacate the body altogether and the body dies. The tri-partite biofield carries this information back to the factory – the master blueprint or genetic bioplasma for the species and the inevitable conclusion is that the body must be re-enforced in its mechanism for replacing lost body parts. Loss to the Spirit however is emotional and psychological it is part of the mechanism of the mind and soul and not the body! Growing a new body part will not solve loss of a relationship! Although when some marriages start to break down, a partner may feel the need to pro-create a baby for this reason, but the new growth (the baby) does not heal the real loss which is in the mind and soul and shortly the baby goes through loss in his mind, when mum and dad separate, he or she is already on the road to becoming a back seat driver and so life goes on, or not! Accumulative loss is a killer.

This is the problem with the **body** it works on a PRIMITIVE SURVIVAL MECHANISM relating entirely to SURVIVAL. Thus the "mould" is really the information that surrounds living things and which carries data on the survival of that particular species. The important point in outlining the cancer research here is that the tri-partite biofield connects with the morphogenetic bioplasma, which I associate with the Grid. Further the Grid will carry in any one particular morphogenetic bioplasma for a species all the history of THE BODY LINE OF THAT SPECIES. Thus you could take the body of man and everything that has happened to that body, which will also carry information of other bodylines (by interface of the different bioplasmas or patterns). Now consider the man who channels information from the Grid – what is he really doing? Well he is asking a blueprint for information on past historical events related to the body and SURVIVAL. Do you really think that this information would represent a higher spiritual source? You are really asking the moron what went on! It will give you all information which helped a body survive and as such will reflect the thinking of the Magnetically Reversed Case or the MRC. The Cabala as it relies on channelled information, as is the case with many secret groups is really just MRC thinking, which is then presented as a higher spiritual source and used to manipulate humanity. "666" has really got man in a trap here!

The "mould" or the electro-magnetic imprint of the genetic or embryological body with its basic and primitive memory of evolution, its connection to the morphogenetic bioplasma with the history of events and **survival** of the species, must surely comprise the Akashic Record of the species. The sum of all individual past tri-partite biofield information comprises the Akashic Record for the species. The magician or Black Cabalist when he utilises his resonant vibratory chants and rituals, seeks I believe to channel information from the accumulative electro-magnetic tri-partite biofield that remains as *an electro-magnetic imprint* not in heaven, but within the crystal or lattice energy web of the Earth's Grid. The information received can seem to appear from an individual spirit entity simply because the thinking process of the MRC case is based on his own survival and as such would register as an imprint in the morphogenetic bioplasma. The magician who channels information does so, from a low- grade entity who has died, but the biofield OF THE BODY AND MIND remains.

In the case of a Kirlean photograph of a leaf which is a special kind of photography which can photograph the biofield, if the matter of the leaf dies or is removed, the energy imprint is *still visible* and still remains, even though the actual leaf itself has gone. You will see an electro-magnetic imprint of the *shape* of the leaf and this is really the primitive aura or tri-partite aura in man. Since this "mould" or shape is really just energy, it must then intermingle with other energy and the greater pattern, thus contributing the 'body' experience to the greater pattern and that great mega-computer in the sky, the Akashic Record of the species. In the case of man, when the **body and mind** dies, that information is also contributed to the greater pattern. The soul, the individual also has an entire memory of experience that is taken with the soul and not contributed to the pattern. The magician seeks to invoke what he believes to be spirits or INFORMATION. Such information relates to world events from the Akashic Record (that great library in the sky), but also certain magicians who sought information, believed that they were contacting the spirits of Hidden Masters, the process however is that I believe, that they merely contacted PAST thought forms retained in the electro-magnetic holographic imprint on the morphogenetic bioplasma. Certainly the minds of past Masters may still be retained and I suspect that it is this sort of knowledge that initiated the concept of a Universal Mind, which I covered earlier.

It is really quite startling to realise that the tri-partite human biofield was probably known 1400 B.C. where it appears I claim on the Phaistos disc, looking remarkably like the body shape of man and as the disc proceeds through its hieroglyphic forms in circular rotation (*Alternative 4*), I suspect that this disc really relates to the rituals of channelling information by the secret priesthood who overran Knossos at the time of the Religious Revolution. The primitive memory or mind, acts on EXPERIENCE in much the same way as the Darwinian Natural Selection process works i.e. the fittest and most adapted organism or individual in terms of the environment will survive to reproduce and thus contribute more offspring to the species. In simple terms, if an organism or individual is suited to live and survive in an environment, it will do so and contribute its offspring to the population. Conversely if an organism or individual is not suited to survive in an environment it will contribute less towards the population and thus eventually individuals carrying adaptive traits to the environment will comprise the majority for that environment. The fact that survival and reproduction are very closely linked in this model for survival means that where survival is threatened, then reproduction will become a dominating force in counteracting that threat. In the case of cancer, the reproductive force creates a 'baby' or tumour in the individual, when that individual has not by rational action and thought counteracted the threat of non-survival in their environment. An animal when threatened either runs away or challenges the threat, but the Cancer patient does neither for unique reasons to their own psychological case and past lives. The primitive mind thinks only in terms of **survival** and draws only on past experience. In the case of Cancer this primitive mind is disastrous and represents a primitive stimulus-response type of mechanism. If secret groups had not hidden the science we may have arrived at this point a bit earlier.

According to phallic doctrine in the Cabala, all creatures (including man presumably?) can trace their genealogy back to the same single ancestor, which must represent the obsession with Adam and the Patriarchs and if one seeks knowledge from the "mould", then presumably the whole ancestry would emerge. I did suggest in *Alternative 4,* that if as I proposed St. John the Evangelist, who wrote the prophetic Apocalypse, was a Druid and further that the Book of *Revelations* in predicting a cataclysmic event, contained channelled information, thus a future prophecy or Apocalypse is merely an acknowledgement that the cycle repeats. Such information could only come from channelling and presumably some Cabalistic practise or ritual, that allows the tri-partite biofield to be 'read' for information on its past history. The referral to "Frogs" in the Apocalyptic account may cross reference with the strange frog-like eyes of alleged Aliens in UFO witness accounts, further recorded in archaeology which may merely be the memories of a race who survived the Flood or electro-magnetic reversal in the bodies of Amphibians, this aspect is discussed in much more detail in *Alternative 4*.Obviously at some level this history must be recorded in some electro-magnetic energy **holographic imprint** on the morphogentic bioplasma, or **downward** Genetic bioplasma. I would compare it to a **great cinema real in the sky**, which has pictures of all events that occurred to **a body**, and since the body is concerned with **survival** the pictures will contain information on the **incidents in the environment** way back for as long as the body line has existed and will contain information on evolutionary ancestors. Indeed the bioplasma or 'cinema real' in our analogy, that great big library in the sky may be an ethereal form of DNA – the master blueprint or the 'factory manager'.

If you consider the structure of DNA (*Fig.30*) you will note that it is a double helix (one strand going upwards and the other downwards in a helical spiral motion. This is interesting in so far as the bioplasma has a circular whirling motion rather like a tornado. It is not inconceivable that each strand of the DNA represents information relating to pre and post Magnetic Reversal i.e. the two sets of environmental conditions. This would seem logical if the master blueprint or the factory manager has to store plans of survival under both conditions. The physical DNA in our bodies is presumably just a replica of the master pattern on the hermetic principle: "As above so below". This master blueprint may have imprinted on Earth in the recent crop circle DNA-type patterns, although in *Alternative 4* I was unsure whether or not secret research was experimenting with this blueprint and master pattern. Such a proposal must seem likely given the soul and psychological case of the MRC who is obsessed with genetics and the Grid. The bioplasma may be nothing more than the accumulative overall biofield of the tri-partite biofield of a particular species e.g. there must be a bioplasma for **each species**, which must further have **grave** implications for genetically modified species experiments and the current field of biotechnology. Let me explain briefly that important point. If the mega-computer or morphogenetic bioplasma (the controller) for the species receives information on the death of inviduals of that species, when the tri-partite biofield is re-absorbed into the general pattern and plan; what will it make of information, which arrives which implies (from genetic modification) that two species are combined? What would it make for instance of poor George the glowing monkey, half monkey half jelly- fish! After all, the tri-partite biofield does not return to the blueprint or controller with explanations that the jelly- fish genes are a genetic marker for scientists ostensibly seeking cures for disease.

No, the master pattern gets the message 'monkey/jelly fish body form'. Will the biofield or controller like a well-programmed computer decides that it has no memory of that combination? Such confusion if often presented as will become the case with genetic modification, may arise in a re-arrangement of the master blueprint, which geneticists call (in the physical or cell DNA) recombination, which is the Darwinian method of creating new species better adapted to their environment. Thus, will the controller assume that this is a new and better-equipped form and simply join both bioplasmas for the individual species in the co-jointly fused hybrid? Can we look forward to mutant fusing of species lines within the master pattern and will that precipitate a memory or holograph of some other past environment such as prior to a Magnetic Reversal? If the two strands of the master blueprint bioplasma or DNA have two strands of information then neither do we know whether these interactive patterns of hybrids will precipitate a reverse flow of information in the strands, thus precipitating a Magnetic Reversal on the principle that if you supply enough components of a hologram, you will eventually pull down the entire picture or hologram in 3D! No doubt at such point the warning of Fatima where the Earth appeared to speed towards the sun will occur and our scientists will along with humanity observe briefly a phenomenon of coloured flickering lights all over the sky ("A great sign in the sky" – according to Revelations), just before the oceans burst their bounds and massive tidal waves engulf the species as the pattern re-asserts control. Unfortunately too late for the scientist to realise that you can't buck or control the pattern, only **work with it**. Then off he will go and repeat along with the MRC the same cycle!

In alleged UFO phenomena there is a disturbance of the electro-magnetic energy and memories or survival entities of the past appear in present time, thus I would conclude, that the natural UFO experience is metaphysical. Obviously here in my research, I have uncovered some natural phenomena related to other aspects of the hidden science, which I evolved as a model in *Alternative 4 - The Onion Ring Model*, which describes the way in which the natural UFO phenomenon works. *The Old Testament* is full of esoteric symbolism, as is the Prophetic Apocalypse, which the Pope John Paul II referred to 110 denying that another Apocalypse was eminent and indeed giving the impression that the end was merely "symbolic"!

Fig.30 **Structure of DNA** (De-oxyribonucleic acid)

(a) Mortice-and-tenon arrangement of base-pairs.

adenine   thymine

(b) Bonding of two chains in DNA helix.

sugar—A ... T—sugar
│   │
phosphate   phosphate
│   │
sugar—T ... A—sugar
│   │
phosphate   phosphate
│   │
sugar—G ... C—sugar
│   │
phosphate   phosphate
│   │
sugar—C ... G—sugar
│   │

(c) Watson-Crick DNA helix.

Experimental vortex ring production
(*From M.B. King 'Tapping the Zero Point Energy'*)

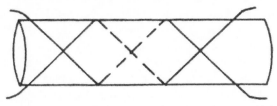

CADUCEUS COIL: OPPOSING HELIX WINDINGS ON FERRITE CORE

293

I do not hold with the views of some, that certain persónages in The Old and New Testaments did not live and were meant as allegories. I believe that it prevents analysis of the code of conduct the Patriarchs maintained in their lives and further denies the historical basis of religion and covert action. It has the purpose of drawing a mystical and esoteric veil over the damnable facts. Let us glance at Abraham's life:

1. He wanders with his flocks and scavenges on the borders of civilization.
2. He lends his wife, who is his half-sister out to customers for pecuniary benefit (*Gen. XX*).
3. He becomes rich in land that is not his own and famine follows in his wake.
4. He *rejects assimilation* with the good people of the land (which is played out in the Middle East today)
5. He practises certain primitive rites associated with Cabalistic knowledge and the phallic cult including sacrifice.

Moving on through *The Old Testament* Cain was a murderer, Lot was incestuous and Abraham's son Isaac who followed in his father's footsteps was driven out of the land by King Abimelech, when the people realised perhaps that he had command over a secret science of magic? Although it does not say directly it states: "Go from us; for thou art mightier than we" in Biblical texts (*Gen xxvi.16*). The story of Joseph is interesting, in so far as Joseph's method of treachery was to be utilised in the plan of the French Revolution in the 18th Century, which saw Maria Antoinette wrongly accused of the causation of a Revolution that was part of the great Masonic plan for a Federal Europe and the murder of Europe's monarchies. Joseph cheats his brother Esau out of his birthright and by black magic or Cabalistic science cheats his father-in-law Laban out of his flocks (*Gen. xxx 30-43*) He was cruel to the Sichemites (*Gen. xxxiv*) and after he was sold into slavery managed to impress his new Egyptian master so much so that he: "set him over all he possessed". What could have impressed the master so much that he would hand over his entire inheritance and management to a slave? - The answer has to be some form of Cabalistic Science, which was either used to impress his master, or was used to control his mind. This control was observed when Joseph's master ignored Joseph's affair with his wife! And when the chief keeper turned over prisoners to his charge, we find that curious statement: "whatsoever they did there, he (Joseph) was the doer of it" (*Gen.xxxix.22*) After Joseph was introduced to the King or Pharaoh, at the age of 30, his rise to power was phenomenal. Only occult power could have provided Joseph with such a rise to power, where he was appointed a Governor of Egypt. Interestingly once in power a rather similar plan to the wheat crisis in France, which provoked the French Revolution, was to unfold in Egypt, under the directional planning of Joseph. **The wheat Trust** was explained by Joseph to the Pharaoh as: "Look out a man discreet and wise, and set him over the land of Egypt": "And let him appoint officers over the land, and take up the fifth part of the land of Egypt in the seven plenteous years. And let them gather all the food of those good years that come, and lay up corn...in the cities *(Gen.XI i. 34-35)*. This is what might be termed Planned Economy or Political and Economic Planning today.

The plan was adopted and under Joseph's direction the Government acquired and stored a large part of the wheat crop every year. Thus for instance, if the wheat crop for Egypt was ten million bushels, the Government purchased two million bushels, or one fifth of the crop in the first year, which would cause the price of wheat to rise. In consequence, the following year more wheat would have to be sown to meet the *apparent* increase in demand. If the Government once again purchased two million bushels, the price of wheat would remain high, with an apparent wheat scarcity. The third year even more wheat would be sown and thus an excess (in reality) of wheat would be produced over *actual* consumption and export. In this manner the Government fixed the price of wheat. Very much the same thing happened when some time ago in our own time, we experienced this fixing, by "food- mountains" in Europe and believe you me, once Europe enters a single currency, you will find the same occurrence, with economic strangleholds. When the harvest came in the fifth or sixth year, if the Government offered a low price or deferred purchasing for some months, the glut of wheat would **ruin farmers** (familiar story in the U.K.!) Thus wheat growing would become unprofitable and the Government would use their propaganda machine (papyrus 'newspapers'!) to discuss no doubt "a year of plenty". The uninformed farmer fell for the propaganda line and abandoned farming or agriculture and sought to produce other crops or raise cattle seeking to cut his losses. This all sounds familiar in Britain today! In *Gen. xiv ii, 17,* it is evident that they had cattle long after the wheat famine started and yet there is no mention of a drought, very much the same in The French Revolution when the citizens of Paris fell for the propaganda line that the whole of France could not produce enough wheat for the Citizens of Paris and the entire load was being eaten by monarchy! The actual reality was that Masonic agents were dumping the corn in the rivers and paid agents of the Duke d'Orleans (who was in the pay of the Masons) were daily initiating propaganda mainly centred on the poor and unfortunate Maria Antoinette. Incidentally she never said: "Let them eat cake", it is generally attributed to the old aunts of her husband King Louis, who being brought up in a bygone era of elitism never considered peasants.

When a planned scarcity of wheat arose in Egypt after farmers had abandoned wheat production, there was a predictable increased demand for wheat and the price of wheat soared and farmers had to part with their seed in return for food, thus there was another year of famine: "All the land of Egypt famished: the people cried to Pharaoh for bread". Then "Joseph opened all the **storehouses** and **sold** unto the Egyptians " (my emphasis) *Gen III.55-56.*The taxpayers who bore the expense of the original government purchases and storage of wheat, now had to beg to buy some back, no doubt at exorbitant prices. However the Egyptians did not get any seed to sow and could not afford enough for their means and so the famine continued: "the famine waxed sore in the land of Egypt" and: "when the money failed in the land of Egypt, and in the land of Canaan, all Egyptians came unto Joseph and said, Give us bread" and: "Joseph said, give your cattle...And they brought their cattle unto Joseph and Joseph gave them bread" (not you will note wheat seed to sow!): "in exchange for horses, and for the flocks, and for the cattle of the herds, and for the asses...". Further: " When that year was ended, they came unto him the second year, and said...our money is spent; my lord hath also our herds of cattle; there is ought left in the sight of my lord, but our bodies, and our lands. **Buy us and our land for bread**, and **give us seed** that we may live, and not die, that the land be not desolate". (*Gen. xi vii, 15-19* - my bold emphasis: "The Egyptians sold every man his field, because the famine prevailed over them: so **the land became Pharaoh's**" (*author's emphasis*). Thus the land now belonged to the Government and here you have an ELITIST SYSTEM OF SLAVERY AND COMMUNISM, (which incidentally is the goal of the secret groups who run Federal Europe today). In Egypt: "as for the people, he removed them to cities from one end of the borders of Egypt to the other end thereof "(*Gen. XIVii 20-21*). Thus whilst no famine was in sight some years previously and no recorded drought, Joseph apparently 'foresees' a future famine, which of course he engineered (rather easy to prophecy when you know your planned goal!). The purpose of the stored grain was given as: "That food shall be for store to the land... that the land perish not through famine" (*Gen.xii 36*). Thus the outcome of Joseph's plan was:

1) The taxpayers were obliged to carry the burden of the Government's unwise and large speculation in wheat.
2) Agriculture the mainstay of the country was virtually ruined
3) A planned scarcity arose, which through Government mismanagement and market operations became a serious famine.
4) The inhabitants were obliged to exchange all their money, cattle and movable property for bread, and hence mass poverty.
5) Those who owned land were obliged to give it to the Government, whilst those who had no land perished from starvation.
6) The whole population was reduced to **slavery** to work for the Government in the towns.

It is certainly interesting in Britain that the countryside is being ruined along with countrymen and farming to The point eventually one suspects when more and more on imports and price fixing from abroad will occur. One can see a point where the British will become slaves to Brussels. Point (6) is interesting, in so far as There were several religious myths and legends that constantly referred to the goal of slavery by the elite Masters who were on Earth from the beginning, i.e. the MRC case. In *The Battle of The Trees*, I discussed The *Protocols of Zion,* an alleged (although contested) Jewish document leaked from the secret societies, which showed a plan for World wide control and domination, whilst *The Protocols* have been hotly disputed as to whether they were a forgery circulated by the white Russians, there can be no doubt that the goals themselves, have virtually been realised and those goals are for a slave species. It is irrelevant whether they came from the tribe of Levi (the Jews) or the tribe of Judah (Israelites descended from Adam) since a plan for world religious and political domination exists in both groups.

The outcome of the Wheat Trust in Egypt thousands of years ago is remarkable, in so far as abolition of private property, slavery etc were a part of the goals of *The Protocols of Zion*. The Protocols may have been denounced as a forgery, where it is claimed that the far right White Russians(the other group the game), wrote them to discredit the Jews; the undisputable fact remains that many of the goals of the Protocols have materialised in our own times. Joseph's plan of ruinous taxation, destruction of agriculture, mass poverty, abolition of private property, was followed by Revolution in the case of this exact scenario which presented in France, at the time of the French Revolution; further this is also the method of wars and the culling planned by the Masters to keep the slave species numbers under control.

Joseph today would be a 33rd degree Mason and member of the B'nai B'rith Council. One is asked to hold *The Bible* in reverence, our children told to believe this kind of behaviour is holy! A point which never ceases to amaze me. Our children are told to worship the Phallic God of the Hebrews - -"God favoured Joseph and his brethren, and wished to punish the Egyptians", is the sort of manaevolent thinking that people no longer actually THINK about when they read *The Bible* like robots, since they have been thoroughly brainwashed to overlook the esoteric Theology, symbolism and indeed political economics. Since the keys to such esotericism were removed at an early date, people do not understand the archetypal significances. "The Lord was with Joseph" was written from a Jewish point of view, but I am sure the Egyptians did not feel that was true for them. The Jews under Jehoweh elevated themselves to be the: "People of God" and those in the Prophetic Apocalypse who would be saved as: "the chosen ones". There is nothing wrong in this belief for the Jews and that was precisely the point made by James (the brother of Jesus) to St. Paul, that this could never become a religion for Gentiles, without acknowledging the Jews as a superior race, which they evidently believed in both groups or tribes of Levi and Judah the latter as descendents from Adam and having sequestered the hidden science for themselves. If it were not for the events of Golgotha

Christianity of course would not have become a religion for Gentiles. The phallic God of Jehovah was certainly a triumph for the Jews and ultimately Israel that she should have the whole world acknowledging the Jews as special and: "chosen by God", whilst the rest of mankind and all other religions of course are completely wrong! I have always believed in the Freedom of Religion and indeed fought for that in a court of Law in London (1989) under The Declaration of Human Rights, but when it comes to being pushed around this planet on the basis of my beliefs and Re-incarnation (witness the front cover of The Second Millennium Working Report into Cancer), there is a time when enough is enough and the other side of the story will be heard. I think there is that old saying: "people in glass houses should not throw stones", or "Judge not least you be judged". There would be nothing wrong in this belief for the Jews or the tribe of Judah, provided that they had not used those beliefs to suppress others in their beliefs and particularly The Holy Grail message of Re-incarnation, which was HER GIFT! Not every religion starts the day with the prayer: "Thank God He has not made me a woman", and then infected the world with such thought. Not all religions operate through secret groups particularly Freemasonry where women are excluded. Although it is probably true to say that all religions have involved themselves with politics and the material world, to their shame, although that is the horrible reality of this planet.

To finish the tale of Joseph, after Joseph had reduced Egypt to chaos, the Egyptians had finally realised the connection, when they made representations to court under a new King: "Now there arose up a new King over Egypt, which knew not Joseph. And he said unto his people, Behold, the people of the children of Israel are more and mightier than we". *(Exod.1.8-9).* The new Nationalistic King recognising that the Hebrews held privileged positions, whilst the Egyptians bore the brunt of the manual labour, asked the Hebrews to work alongside the Egyptians. A *Levite* named Amram who married Jochebed (his father's sister or his aunt) had three children, Moses, Aaaron and Miriam. Incest among the Jews was common practise and today in closed Jewish communities where incest has occurred, health problems are evident. Since the Druids and the Hebrews practised Mosaic Law, which the Druids also held, it might be relevant to look at the background of Moses.Amram had his infant son Moses adopted by an Egyptian princess, which is commonly told as the baby in the basket story in biblical texts. This story may esoterically cover two historical truths. Amram was a Levite and therefore one assumes that Moses was adopted, in order to be introduced to the philosophy and magical rites of the tribe of Judah, the Druids dating back to Adam. It may be that Moses was not adopted but **fostered**, as was the practise of the Druids, a practise it seems that became the medium for spies and espionage between the two significant groups, dynasties and political intrigues.

It is also significant that a red-figured kylix (*fig. 27*) shows Pasiphae the mother of the Minotaur holding the Bull-minotaur child on her lap, in a Mother and Child- like nativity scene. To the right, a basket hangs and there is a goose. This icon from the classical period shows a truth and historical fact of the Religious Revolution in Crete: That the child was born in a symbolic sense from the labyrinth as womb is indicated by the hanging basket decorated with a chequered pattern, which was a variant motif for the maze of the labyrinth. Another such chequered pattern may be seen on the right margin, while above and below on the margin is the labyrinth motif of the crossed rectangle (refer to *The Battle of The Trees p. 42* for derivation), which specifically suggests the solar-lunar calendar. On the right, where the border is fully preserved, there are ten consecutive spirals above, interrupted by the chequered pattern, and then nine consecutive spirals below, terminated by the lower crossed rectangle. The count is nineteen spirals for the longer nineteen-year solar-lunar cycle and the extended reign of a Solar King. The left border is damaged and incomplete, but the spacing indicates that there were probably nineteen spirals there also. Another calendar number appears on the dias beneath the throne of the goddess. It displays eight and one-half patterned panels to represent the eight-year cycle, plus seven lunations at the end of which the sacred King must die, to give birth to his Twin. The reign of the King was extended to 19 years, which removed the necessity of his replacement by his Twin allowing a different monarchy to ensue. And at the foot of the goddess on the right there is the bird of her epiphany, a goose. In the case of the Mary Magdalene it was the dove. The basket is a variant of the womb symbol and in this sense represents Immortality or Re-incarnation of Sacred Kings, or Solar Kings.

Thus the story of Moses in a basket, not only has implications on the secret dynastic line into which he was fostered (presumably the *Egyptian*/Celtic dynasty in a direct line from Adam, Noah and the Druids previously referred to in the story of Mil and Scota), but such dynastic line had no power unless it could attach itself to a Monarchy - the Egyptian monarchy. Thus it might be assumed that an ongoing reason for fosterage (in the case of The Druids), or adoption (in the case of The Essenes) was to attach a Patriarchal royal dynastic priesthood line descended from Noah and Adam in the case of the tribe of Judah, to major Kingly lines. The fact that the basket motif occurs in Late Minoan iconography and symbolism, indicates that the Religious Revolution in Crete at Knossos was carried out by Judah i.e. Druids? Moses of course was found among *Reeds*, which is an archetypal symbol for Royalty and is depicted as Ng or Reed in the secret Beth-Luis Nion alphabet and Ogham script, the latter appearing curiously like the symbols found in Late Minoan Crete icons (post Religious Revolution). Moses evidently then was a plant for the tribe of Judah and in receipt of Cabalistic knowledge i.e. he was an initiate. Moses was tutored at the Egyptian court and thus had the opportunity to rise to power. The

Egyptians paid no attention to Moses subversive character and in effect he was snubbed. Moses then went to the people of his own race and to his own tribe Levi. Is it any wonder that the Dead Sea Scroll documents on Levi are withheld!

The tribe of Levi evidently had tendencies towards bestiality and the Phallic nature of their God is brought out unmistakably in the marriage laws (*Lev. xviii 7-23*) The Laws dwell at length on incestuous laws and since animals are not predisposed towards fornicating with humans, one supposes the Levites were, otherwise why include: "Neither shall thou lie with any beast to defile thyself therewith: neither shall any woman stand before a beast to lie down thereto: it is confusion". The phallic God was also the God of Fire and thus the esoteric references e.g. "For the Lord thy God is consuming Fire" (*Deut. iv.24*) and: "And there came a fire out from before the Lord, and consumed upon the altar the burnt offering and the fat: which when all the people saw, they shouted, and fell on their faces" (*Lev. ix, 24*) and the: "burning bush" (presumably the Acacia as God of Sunday -Jehovah and the phallic Patriarchal God); and the: "pillar of fire" (again pillar worship was Semitic).The phallic God of *Genesis* was also prone to vengeance: "To me belongeth vengeance" (*Deut. xxxii 35*): "vengeance" being the esoteric term for bloodshed, which accounts for that embarrassing statement by Jesus that He had come to bring a sword and not peace. To quote Jehovah: "And surely your blood of your lives I require...at the hands of every man's brother will I require the life of man". (*Gen. ix.5*). It is amazing that man has gone along with this for so long! And taught his children to revere such words.

In so far as the tribe of Levi won the special protection of the phallic god, is it not curious that Fenuisa Farsa "the vine man" and "he who holds together", implied as the group who conducted the Religious Revolution in Crete and as an ancestor of the Druids, should also be implicated with the tribe of *Levi*, in that *Levi* means "joined together" (*Gen. xxix.34*) This is borne out by Jacob's mention of "**their secret**" and "**their assembly**". Esoterically Jacob's words: "I will divide them in Jacob", is interpreted as: "Through them I will unite all the twelve tribes". However in *The Battle of The Trees*, I referred to another tribe, a **THIRTEENTH TRIBE** not mentioned directly and I strongly suspect that this tribe is referred to in *The Dead Sea Scrolls* and the texts of *Levi*, which is why they are not allowed to be scrutinised by scholars. This tribe is evidently Judah descended from Adam and ascending in the form of **The Druids**. In *The Battle of The Trees*, after decoding *The Grail Romances* (*page 172*), I refer to the "Magdalene" as the **"root"** of the Grail family. However it is obvious the root referred to the genealogies, the very genealogies that were stolen from the Magdalene. This however is a later designed addition, for you should remember that The Holy Grail message and the hidden science did not belong with any tribe or group, it belonged to the people.

According to Robert Graves111: "with the help of the names given to the tribes by their mothers in *Genesis XXIX* and *XXX*, and of the prophetic blessings or curses bestowed on them by Jacob in *Genesis XLVIII* and *XLIX*, we can assign a letter and month to each tribe. To Ephraim ('fruitful') and Manasseh (forgetfulness'), the two sons of Joseph who was a 'fruitful **vine**' we can assign the months C and M; and B to Reuben the first-born, who had Edomite connections. To Reuben's four full-brothers, Gad ('a robber band) **Levi ('set apart')** ... And to 'Little Benjamin their ruler' belongs New Year's Day, the day of the divine Child. When we have assigned to **Dan, 'Like a serpent'**, the serpentine month of G, we naturally fill the **Ng month**, which alone remains vacant, with the **tribe of Dinah**; for Dinah, the female **twin** of Dan, was **another tribe that disappeared early** (see *Genesis XXXIV*), and since the **Ng month** marks the beginning of the rains and the resumption of the seasonal cycle of growth, a **woman naturally belongs there**". (*Author's emphasis*)

Several important points arise from this quote, the Ng month in the Druidic Tree Alphabet is Royal (Reed) and the implication is that Magdalene and a woman belongs there, which raises the issue of the stolen genealogies. Dan is linked to Danu or Danna or Anna, deriving from the god-like Tuatha de Danaan, the dispossessed tribe from Greece who became inseparably linked to The Druids and perhaps provided the Royal Dynastic link of Princess Anna, who was allegedly Jesus' grandmother in the Royal Celtic dynasty. There is also the implication that if the Tuatha de Danaan were regarded as gods, it was because of some hidden science they knew, which was subsequently taken over by The Druids, who organised the Religious Revolution in Crete to obtain all sources of the knowledge which was then absorbed into what appears to be **A LOST TRIBE OF ISRAEL** - who subsequently took the form and name of Druids, but who were descended from Noah and Adam and of the tribe of Judah. I should emphasise that the Greek input into the tribe of Judah, which occurred at the time the Tuatha de Danaan fled to Britain from their home and the religious shrine in the Peloponnese c. 1800 B.C. was not of Semitic origin but was *absorbed* into this tribe or fraternal Patriarchal group descended from the Patriarch Noah and Adam. The fact that **Dan** belongs to G month, Sept. 30 Yellow Serpentine indicates the knowledge of Re-incarnation (as Serpent which sheds its skin cyclically); and Ng (Royal Reed) is Oct.28 Clear Green Jasper and **Dinah**. Thus it may be, that the Tuatha de Danaan had learnt the open mysteries of Crete prior to the Religious Revolution and had paid no head to the Teacher's words of not using such knowledge for purposes of power, having subsequently used such knowledge to impress the Druids who absorbed this knowledge and came to believe that it was rightfully theirs, whilst removing the woman from the story. They took the gift and then presented it as their own, a story which may have repeated itself in Scientology?

If Dan related to the ancient Goddess Danu, then Dana or Anna was the ancient Greek ancestor of this Greek input, but not of the tribe itself, which I give as Semitic, therefore it is natural that we should find Artemis (or Ariadne of **Cretan Goddess** fame) in the month G for Gort (DAN). It is also natural that we should find Zeus Dionysus there, who we are told must be distinguished from Dionysus of the Winter Solstice who is really Hercules (the god of strength and power). Surely the same Hercules who we find cutting the crab's left claw in the crab mural at Cardiff Castle Wales UK; which was the *first cut*, but reflects also the *second cut* and that of Magdalene's arm, when the gaenelologies were stolen at the events of Golgotha. However at Cardiff Castle on the roof! There is a "Black Madonna", which must represent the figure of Isis. Thus given that I concluded that the Summer Smoking Room Floor reflected Scottish Rite Freemasonry and the Rose-Croix degree, I can only assume that the degree is concerned with the **Egyptian** dynastic line and therefore the **Twelve Tribes of Israel** and since Lord Bute who had the floor laid is reputed to have had his heart buried in Zion, I assume that this group does *not* represent the Greek dynastic "root" and therefore would have no intention of releasing The Holy Grail message (Re-incarnation). However! Lord Bute featured St. John and not Jesus in the Castle, so what are we to make of this? When St. John I concluded was Druidic and of the line of Judah and therefore from a Gentile tribe descended from Adam including the Druids! Which leads me back to the crab mural and the cutting of the crab's left claw by the sword of Hercules, which must refer to the separation of the two groups i.e. the Egyptian dynastic line from the Greek and the "root". In *The Battle of The Trees* I concluded that the secret group of The Prieuré de Sion in France, was one group that held the number 13 in reverence and thus must represent the tribe of Judah and the Celtic/Greek line or dynasty dating back to the Tuatha de Danaan and the Merovingian line presumably ascending from a child who resulted from a union of Jesus and Magdalene; perhaps the very child that I mentioned in my witness account. The one group, who could verify that might be The Prieuré de Sion, who were at one time prior to the 1980's involved with the formation of European Union and evidently had a religious goal in Federal Europe before that goal was evidently betrayed? And the more immediate goal of a Federal European Super State was 'married' to the goal of Christianity. Thus we might assume that the Greek based dynastic "root" has been betrayed in Federal Europe in favour of the 12 tribes, Levites and Christianity. The Prieuré de Sion appeared to have a goal of introducing a Royal Dynastic line - the Merovingians, this line I proposed may have been a hereditary line descended from Merovee, who appeared to have a mystical birth, with the Mary Magdalene as the Matriarchal line of descent. Such a conclusion may well account for the witness account I gave of the murder of the Mary Magdalene and the possible use of her child from her marriage to Jesus being used by St. John who returned to Scotland after Magdalene was murdered in France, to propagate a royal dynastic line. The Merovingians may well have

302

been connected then to this ancient Royal Celtic/ Greek dynasty. One must ask what happened to this goal of a Greek dynastic line? And what has happened to the Prieuré de Sion or its ascendant group now.

The demi-God Moses was contained in the hendekaglyph of the Cabala and the name of the phallic God was the Tetragrammaton 'IHWH' (*Exod.iii, 14*) which English translations call "Jehovah" or "Yahweh". Ginsburg a Masonic expert affirms that Moses spent 40 years learning the Cabalistic doctrine and the end of the Initiation would have been marked by Moses affirmation, that the Phallic God had appeared to him in person and this was indicated in esoteric formula by: "and the Lord appeared to him in a flame of fire out of the midst of a bush: and he looked and behold, the bush burned with fire, and the bush was consumed". This is an indication that the God was seen as the Acacia (bush in the Tree alphabet)- the God of Sunday. The Holy Trinity doctrine was pre-Christian, founded on Ezekiel's vision, the Trinity consisting of the three main elements of the Tetragrammaton. The First person was the true Creator, the All-Father, 'Let there be Light', represented by the letter H, the Acacia the tree of Sunday, the **tree of Levi**, the lapis lazuli symbolizing the blue sky as yet untenanted by the heavenly bodies; he was identified by the Jewish Apocalyptics with the 'Ancient of Days' in the Vision of Daniel.

The original tree of Sunday in the Ogham alphabet was H and in Hebrew the corresponding tree was the SANT, or wild Acacia, which in the Bible often appears as 'shittim' wood. It was allegedly from its waterproof timbers that the arks of the sun hero Osiris, and his counterparts Noah and Armenian Xisuthros, were built; also the Ark of the Covenant in its recorded measurements proved to be symbolic numbers related to the sun (Solar Kingship) and Acacia was Jehovah's oracular 'burning bush'. Thus when Moses encounters a burning bush in the Bible *Exod.iii 2-4*, this is an esoteric indication of Moses reaching the end of his initiatory period, which depended on the presence and the voice of the Divinity, both of which occurred. Moses long suffering wife evidently perhaps overlooked the fact that he was a murderer (*Exod.ii.12*) and had been castigated for such (*Exod.ii 14*), but evidently put her foot down when Moses tried to sacrifice her son: "surely a bloody husband art thou to me". (*Exod.iv.25*) which was followed by divorce (*Exod.XViii.2*). The end of Moses initiation may well represent the esoteric method of contacting the Hidden Chiefs or secret Masters.

The old dream of a Theocratic State or government by an elite and secret priesthood was the dream of Moses and the Druids and was to surface in the Third Reich and probably has surfaced once again in the goals of Federal Europe. It seems that Moses sought the aid of Aaron and the Levite tribe in bringing about this dream, with the Levites occupying a privileged hereditary (aristocratic) status headed by Moses and Aaron as the ruling priesthood. Thus the plan was to create discontent among the Israelites, which would result in Egyptian oppression, whereupon the other eleven tribes comprising the Hebrews would follow Moses and Aaron to the "promised land" and on arrival they would establish a Theocratic State, the plan appears in *Exod. iv.16.* : "And he (Aaron) shall be thy (Moses) spokesman with the people: and he shall be...to thee instead of a mouth, and thou shalt be to him instead of God". Note that the text is in a *future* tense; further this plan was passed off as God's plan (*Exod.iv.29-30*). "Moses and Aaron went and gathered together all the elders of the children of Israel: And Aaron spake all the words which the Lord had spoken unto Moses and did the **signs** in the sight of the people" (my emphasis). Evidently some Black Cabalistic trick persuaded them:" And the people believed" (the propaganda about the Egyptians): "and when they heard that the Lord had visited the children of Israel, and that he had looked upon their affliction, then they bowed their heads and worshipped" (*Exod. iv.31*). The only thing which required the plan to be set in motion was for Moses and Aaron to go the Egyptian King in an arrogant manner and demand a special **three** day holiday for the Jews and not the Egyptians (72 hours - which would later correspond to the resurrection period of Jesus or 3 days- signifying 72 as the number of letters in the Ogham alphabet, which the Druids used). This of course the King would find unacceptable as Moses and Aaron expected and this would become the impetus for the Jewish revolt. Cabalistic rites were performed no doubt to create the: "ten plagues of Egypt" - hail, locusts etc. It is interesting to note that when Jewish Bolshevism took over Russia in the last century there was some repeated co-incidence of the Egyptian plagues e.g. flies, vermin etc. Finally The Bible skirts around the fact that the: "children of Israel" plundered the wealth of the Egyptians. *Exod. Xii. 35-36*: "jewels of silver and jewels of gold": were "borrowed". This informing trait of Patriarchalism and the Jews has occurred so often in the case of plundering Matriarchalism (the stolen genealogies, beliefs, ideas, archetypal symbols and grail message), that it is difficult to say when Matriarchalism was *not* plagued in its purpose and message by Jewish tribes. Moses finally in the writing of *The Ten Commandments* on the tablets of stone (Semitic pillars) utilises Cabalistic knowledge, which was marked by thundering and lightening from Mount Sinai, after which Moses descends and his face is horribly burnt through some radiation effect of Atomic transformation of matter, or at least some resonant vibratory ritual?

Insurrection and Revolution was always a part of Israelite thinking and Moses Mendelssohn thousands of years later with the Illuminati was to create the French Revolution, with Dr. Falk and Cagliostro both Jews and probably members of the Sanhedrin of the Twelve Tribes or High Initiates of the Thirteenth Tribe in the background. Asher Ginzberg, with his B'nai Moshe (Sons of Moses) and his B'nai Zion was to ferment a similar situation in Russia laying the Foundations of modern Zionism, although equally many British agents were present in Russia just prior to the Revolution. The Rose-Croix Masons and the magical 33rd degree must be highly suspect in these, events although British Freemasonry avowed categorically that it was not involved in the French Revolution. Even Grand Orient Masonry claimed that they were betrayed over the French Revolution by a: "higher Order". Jewish secret groups or at least Jewish doctrine at the head of the principle secret groups has dominated the world political scene. The Talmud Torah and the authoritive interpretation of the four principle commandments according to Jewish Law, which gives an insight into the self survivalist attitude of the Jews towards Gentiles states in Commandment VI (murder): "A Jew is allowed to suppress a non Jew, for it is written 'Thou shall do no wrong to thy neighbour'- this is not written concerning the Gentile". (*Sanhedrin 57a Thosaphoth*): "a heretic Gentile you may kill outright with your own hands". (*Abodah Zara 4b*). Also: "Bloodshed is forbidden to a Gentile who may kill neither Gentile nor Jew; but it is not forbidden to the Jew in regard to the Gentile". (*Sanhedrin 57a, Abodah Zara 13b-26b*). With regard to Adultery and Commandment VII: "Theft, robbery, and rape of a beautiful woman and similar deeds, are forbidden to every Gentile toward another Gentile and also toward a Jew; but, they are allowed to a Jew against a non-Jew". (*Sanhedrin 57a Abodah Zara, 13b-26b*). Commandment VIII (theft): "It is not allowed to rob a brother Jew, but to rob a Gentile is allowed, for it is written in *Leviticus XIX.13*: "Thou shall not defraud thy neighbour, neither rob him But these words, says Jehuda, do not apply to a non-Jew, because he is not thy brother". (*Baba Mezia 61a. Thosaphoth*): and Commandment IX (false witness and perjury) is allowed to a Jew by absolving his own sins or lies by the prayer known as the *Kol Nidre*. I suspect that the term "Brotherhood" as used in Freemasonry, originates with the idea of a tribe descended from the Patriarch Adam and/or the tribe from Abraham. Father, applied to the Patriarch would then form a "Brotherhood" of all members.

Moses himself broke many laws proving himself to be a mass murderer (*Exod. XXXii, 25* and *Exod. XXXii 26-28*) ordering the Levites to slay all those Israelites worshiping: "the golden calf". This was acceptable under the Jewish phallic God of vengeance - Jehovah (*Exod. XXXii, 29*). There is every reason to suspect that Moses used Cabalistic vibratory or sympathetic resonance knowledge of the Cabala, when he created a plague to quell the voice of dissidents to his plans (*Num.XVi 47,49*) Today we know that a substantial part of the hidden science, is probably used in Biological Warfare research, where it is possible to create by sympathetic resonance the overall vibratory rate of a particular micro-organism e.g. a virus or bacterium and beam that resonance at individuals who would then contract the symptoms of the virus or bacterium. In this document and in *Alternative 4* I discuss the suppression of certain Scientists and their research e.g. Upton Knuth and Armstrong, who were working on broadcasting atomic and molecular structure, which is really what is involved in this particular aspect of Cabalistic science. I personally have seen lists of sympathetic vibration rates of various bacteria and viruses. Obviously the advantage of maintaining secrecy on this science even in biblical times was power to the Initiate. Moses and other Initiates could pass off Cabalistic phenomena as the work of God, thus influencing a gullible public to accept the greater authority and power of the Jews or Initiates with this knowledge. I have already discussed how it may have been used in mass mind control in the creation of fear in the battle of the Celts against the Greeks at the battle for Delphi, where the Celts fell into a state of mass hysteria and fear. The human biofield as an electro-magnetic vibratory system, with the chakra energy points, which also vibrate at a certain rate, are subject to changes in the resonant vibratory rate of the environment, which could be changed by human means and which I suspected was the case of some reported (manipulated) UFO witness accounts. Overall then, Moses is not a personality I would recommend as one worth venerating by young children (or adults) when we find that he is capable of recommending murder of women and children (*Num. XXX 15-17*).

The Levites after the death of Moses regressed in power until Samuel a priest initiated into the Cabala by Eli, sought to re-establish the old Theocracy of an elite priesthood. He sought the usual method of black propaganda against other cults (*I. Sam. XX.23*) Similar to the methods used today against a belief in Re-incarnation. The people resisted, preferring monarchy to a fraternity of priests. This was always a hurdle for the secret fraternity to overcome and had in the past necessitated using Solar Kingship and monarchical lines as the front for their own power, as was the case with Joseph, together with the practise of adoption or fostering. Thus it was, that Samuel sought to instigate a plan of a puppet monarchy: in fact Samuel chose Saul a peasant from the despised tribe of Benjamin whom he had tutored by a secret priesthood (*I. Sam X.1* and *I. Sam X.5*). Saul then became part of what appears to be a rigged election (*I. Sam. X.27*), followed by a plan to make him a hero (*I. Sam. I*): And further use of the hidden science to create thunder and lightening (*I.Sam. XII*). When Saul used his power to disobey Samuel, the latter chose David as a successor (*I. Sam.XIII 14*); attempting to make David a hero in his fight with Goliath (*I. Sam.XVIII. 6-7*), in order to influence the people who preferred Saul as King. Finally when Saul and his sons were killed in battle **the Elders of the tribe of Judah elected David as King of Israel**. David set up his court at Jerusalem, previously called Zion. This shows that the Sanhedrin or Elders were not separate from the tribe of Judah, but acted in concert with them! If Lord Bute's heart (along with prominent men in modern times) was buried in Zion, then one can only assume that it is a symbolic oath of allegiance to Judah and the 12 tribes of Israel, but particularily to the lost **Thirteenth Tribe**.

David then was from the tribe of Judah and not Levi and was an eighth son of

Jesse. In *The Battle of The Trees*, I deciphered the Grail Romances including the Romance *Parzival* written by Wolfram von Essanbch (1200) and which draws material from an ancient manuscript found at Toledo University; on *page 172* of my book I decoded the "Root" of The Grail Family that secret groups had encoded into The Grail Romances, as the tribe of Judah (or David), which they were trying to connect up to the Mary Magdalene. That" root" interestingly contained Ng (Reed associated with Royalty) according to the Beth-Luis- Nion Alphabet and Ogham Script used by the Druids and as previously covered this letter of the alphabet is associated with DAN, or the female Goddess, with implications of its origin in the ancient Greek Goddess Danu or Anna in the Celtic Royal Dynasty, the alleged grandmother of Jesus. Thus in the Grail Romance *Parzifal* I concluded is a veiled reference to the secret aspirations of a powerful secret group and those aspirations relate to a religious and political goal in Europe. This goal had been stated as such in the literature emanating from the secret groups as far back as the French Revolution, which it seems was planned as part of a goal to eliminate Europe's monarchies, to pave the way for a "THEOCRATIC UNITED STATES OF THE WEST". The aim of a *Theocratic Europe* controlled by a secret priesthood of initiates was always there, it appeared as the goals of the Patriarchs in The Old Testament and surfaced in the Druid driven Celtic Commonwealth. The difference however between the two periods in history, was the emergence of information from Crete (the Early Minoans) and from the Peloponnese (the Tuatha de Danaan). This new knowledge and its ideas for creating a peaceful civilization was then stolen by the tribes of Israel in their highest priesthoods and tacked on to their own monarchical system or what *The Bible* condemns as "Kings". The phrase of a: "United States of the West" or: "Etats Unis", also emerged on the front illustrated cover of the magazine *Vaincre*, which emanated from a man, who was to become the Grand Master of The Prieuré de Sion, the very group who had a religious and political goal in view for a Federal Europe. A goal however that related to a royal dynasty (the Merovingians) through a union of Magdalene and Jesus thus connected to the Celtic/Greek line of that dynasty.

David was certainly no better than his predecessors, since he raped his faithful warrior's wife (Bathsheba), after he had her husband Uriah killed, he then married her. Solomon was the product of the relationship and when he ascended the throne as a younger son, he usurped his elder brother Adonijah and then had him murdered. Solomon became a trader and banker monopolising the trade routes and ruled over a powerful autocracy. Solomon carried out intensive studies of the Cabala and his own writings in (*Proverbs, Ecclesiastes, Canticles - Song of Solomon,* and the key of Solomon) furthered his philosophical research. Such writings can only be fully understood by an initiate into the Cabala and presumably the Freemasons in their re-enactment of the building of The Temple of Solomon, which archaeologists say never existed, must re-enact some philosophical treatise containing esoteric knowledge of Solomon. By drawing together all phallic cults, he encouraged Jerusalem as a 'hot pot' of Cabalists and the African Queen of Sheba (*I. King. X 1-5*), may well have been part of the necessary working of some magical rites. However the most important point here is that Solomon in trying to harmonise the phallic cults as the "vine man" that "draws together", tried to institute a WORLD FELLOWSHIP OF FAITHS.

GNOSTICISM

The rise of Gnosticism in the first centuries of the Christian era emphasised the rise in knowledge of the hidden science. The word gnosis or "knowledge" also refers to mystical and superior science. Gnosticism was probably an offshoot of the plan for a unified religion. It claimed to combine the higher principles of Judaism, Christianity and polytheism. The problem with the original truth and the Grail message really got underway in this period as occult adept priests "borrowed" as was their peculiar obsession one idea from here, another idea from there and tried to fuse the entirety into one lying pot! The Matriarchal Message became submerged to the extent, where it would take thousands of years to sort it all out again and as I sit and watch the screen saver of grey metal-type pipe work on my computer as I surface for breath occasionally, I remember a repetitive dream (or nightmare!) I had as a child, which would entail sorting out a huge pile of grey and twisted metal and just as I had sorted the last piece into a tidy and neat pile with some sense of relief, I was overtaken by the horror and chaos of the entire pile being fused once again into the chaotic pile to be sorted: East and west Cosmogony, theology and anthropology, myths, legends and the whole complexity obscuring the truth and the original LOGOS - THE WORD. Logos comes from the Greek and means The Word, which is the outward form by which the inward thought is expressed and made known. The research I produce traces back that word to at least Bronze Age Greece and certainly The Logos was first heard in Greece c. 10,000B.C. The word was a very simple one and incorporated the truth of man's existence - Re-incarnation and Immortality of the soul, which had been forgotten here on this planet governed as it was by the MRC case that only knew black magic and practised cannibalism. The Celts were lead into this practise and curiously the Freemont people in Utah America not only had bowls decorated with the characteristic chequer pattern and scrolls of the post Religious Revolution period of Crete (c. 1 400 B.C.) but also archaeologists have found evidence of cannibalism. It is odd that the chequer pattern instigated by the Cabal who killed the Early Minoans should surface in America. All was *black* magic and *ritual* before that word came at around the time of 10 000 B.C. Light on dark as in the very early and first pottery from Crete (Kamares ware) showed the zigzag pattern reflecting not only the migration of Cranes who fly in V-shaped formation during migration symbolising The Cycle of Eternal Return and the philosophy "As I go, so must I return"; but also the successive windings of the bioplasma. One cannot deny that an intelligent source was trying to impart a message here.

The Gnostics and Theosophists claimed to teach a mystic science superior to all religions and combined all. Rudolf Steiner and Anthroposophy which Steiner called "Occult Science", with its Akashic Record which was Grid history and information was to make the Gnostic mysteries more complex and certainly in his descriptions of the "Etheric Body", "Astral Body" and a good helping of "Angels" from the Hebraic and Cabalistic Tree of Life, he demonstrated that he was well versed in hidden Cabalistic science, however he never relayed the deeper mysteries to any but a few high initiates. The Gnostics spoke of a "mysterious Science"[112] and a "secret tradition". The Gnostic leaders originated in Judaism and Gnostics were evidently concerned not only with the Cabala, but the *unifying base of Anthropological history* and the development of this so-called "Science" or "Doctrine". Gnosis or knowledge was considered the highest Science and true wisdom, further the Gnostics claimed that the Gospels were "full of prejudice" and falsified data.

Ophis means "serpent" which is derived from the role of the serpent, or the genius of which the serpent is a symbol. In certain respects the Orphic mysteries were rather similar if not derived from Gnosticism. Unfortunately the Orphic system has wrongly been claimed as Satanic. There were three divisions of this cult, one inspired by Cain and the Cainites and the other inspired by Seth and Sethians and the other branch was based on Gnostic knowledge, the truth dating back to Greece and Crete. The third division is not widely known, if at all. It is beyond the bounds of this book to go into Orphic Doctrine, but interestingly Jesus (Soter) or J.S. occurs opposite the number 33 in the Orphic system, which perhaps corresponds to the 33rd magical degree of Masonry and the Rose-Croix degree. This may have been "borrowed" (again!) by Patriarchalism since in the Greek Orphic system, the start of the life journey did not begin until the age of 33. Thus Jesus and Magdalene could be considered in two different Orphic groups. Given that the Orphic system of Seth and Cain was considered Satanic, why should Jesus' name occur there? Further in *The Battle of The Trees* I produced a painting by Guercino entitled *Et in Arcadia Ego* (c. 1618), which was the first painting to employ this phrase referring to Arcadia (the alleged birthplace of the phallic god Hermes). Once again our "borrowing" bee has been at work, since Arcadia was actually the place of *the first cut*!! The painting shows two Twins, or male figures that look remarkably alike and therefore implies Twin Kingship dating back to the Minoan mysteries after the Religious Revolution. However the painting is ambiguous and equally implies the Twins are shepherds, since one carries a shepherd's staff or crook. However the crook is a symbol of rightful ownership comparable to the sword that only King Arthur could pull from the rock or receive from the arm in the lake. Arthur was governed by Merlin who we assumed was a Druid and thus once again we are back at the tribe of Judah, ascended from Adam and the sequestering of the Grail in Minoan Crete. A skull surmounts the tomb whilst both figures or Twins look wistfully at the inscription on the tomb, whilst the sky is depicted as dark and foreboding which is a symbolic representation of an ominous and dark event. What is the significance of the skull? Whilst I formerly explained the skull in terms of the death of the Mary Magdalene and the loss of the Underground Stream of wisdom relating to The Holy Grail and the trail of knowledge I repeat in my research through history, in another sense it is also the death of the Matriarchal cause, with the truth consigned to the tomb. In this case the name Arcadia represents Hermes and thus it is not pure Matriarchal knowledge but Patriarchal and from the Religious Revolution era in Crete.

The Gnostics had a hatred of Christ since Christianity fought knowledge, just as The Templars must have possessed a repository of knowledge, which contained some secret history pertaining to Jesus, since they spat on the Cross and referred to Jesus as "the thief on the Cross". In the Cabala (Siphra Dtzenioutha), or the 'Book of Concealed Mystery', ii Section 33, it states: "When this form begineth, they (the letters) are discovered in the cranium". Mathers explained that: "In the cranium (or skull), Begolgotha, or in Golgotha. In the New Testament it is worthy of note that Jesus Christ (the Son) is said to have been crucified at Golgotha (the skull); while here, in the Cabala, Microprospos (the Son), as the Tetragrammaton, is said to be extended in the form of a cross, thus the letters "IHVH" are shown in the form of a cross) in Golgotha (the skull)." The painting of Guercino immediately becomes clear in that the dark and ominous sky in the painting represents Golgotha as I had suspected in *The Battle of The Trees* and this meaning is supported by the presence of the skull on the Semitic tomb. The reference to Arcadia in the inscription is a gloss for Hermes the hermaphroditic god who hoped to combine Twin Kings and Mother Goddess in one personage, thus removing the Grail wisdom and apples of immortality from the woman as her gift and removing the woman altogether from the story! The Matriarchal cause would go under ground as the Underground Stream, which reflects the hidden symbolism in the paintings of Poussin, referred to in *The Battle of The Trees* go. The whole story underground became a repository of "concealed knowledge", and it is this knowledge that would seek to surface. However it appears that somewhere along the line the truth of the woman and her role were either forgotten or a male hierarchy, which one assumes was the tribe of Judah, the lost Thirteenth Tribe concealed the Religious Revolution in Crete. The Gnostics whilst knowing the post Revolution story, evidently knew nothing of the role of the woman.

311

Hugh de Payans founded an order of the Knights Templar in 1118. Their aim was outwardly said to be the defence of the Holy Sepulchre in Jerusalem, protecting pilgrim's travelling to and in Palestine. Theocletus, the head of the Near East Sect of Johannite Christians initiated Hugh de Payens as head of The Templars into the mysteries. These knights through fees paid by pilgrims for protection, ransom fees and through a banking agreement with the Jews, became very wealthy and powerful. The Templars as I have already noted joined with the Royal Order of Scotland and from this evolved Scottish Rite Freemasonry, which was ostensibly Rosicrucian doctrine.

Since Templar degrees are incorporated into Freemasonry, then it is interesting to note that not only were the Templars Gnostics and therefore presumably knowledgeable regarding the "mysterious science", but also they worshipped Baphomet. Eliphas Levi, as a high initiate of the secret societies prior to The French Revolution maintained that a: "Universal Religious and Political Kingdom" would be installed in Europe and that it would be had by: " those with the keys to the East", an esoteric referral to Hermes the phallic god of magic and god of thieves, but also a referral to the complete control over The hidden science. Eliphas Levi also published pictures of Baphomet in his work. The head resembles a *goat* with *horns* and a beard; between the horns is a *flaming* torch. I am hoping that for those who have read *The Battle of The Trees* in addition to this book, that I can expect you by now to recognise some of these symbols. The goat was one of the totem beasts of the Cabal that conducted the Religious Revolution and you may remember the horrible things Dr. Falk a very high initiate if not the authority of the tribe of Judah, did to a goat in a ceremony in London. The horns relate to the "gates of horn", or the abode of the dead and correspond to bull's horns (of the Minotaur) again post the Religious Revolution in Crete. Thus the idea of a devil with goat features and horns derives from this source. Obviously the 12 tribes at work here with propaganda against the thirteenth tribe. This then is the hermaphroditic Fire or Phallic god in esoteric knowledge. The beard is a Cabalistic symbol of generative force and the torch represents the equilibrating intelligence. Thus once again we note the appearance of the old idea of an intelligentsia; a secret priesthood who seek elitist control over Humanity and raises once again the goal of **elitist Communism. This one must consider that this is the entire goal of ALL secret societies despite their brave and hypocritical words they are all** contemptuous of the"herd", which they despise and see only in terms of PROFIT at the bank.

As an interesting if not curious note here, I noted (I believe it was the *Mirror* newspaper in London) that Rupert Murdoch the Australian entrepreneur who owns a very large slice of media and publishing in the UK including *The Times* and *Sun* newspapers; was depicted with horns and with a forefinger raised, after he took over rights to coverage of top football matches. As we are all aware, football brings out the Nationalist instinct in all countries and British football fans at their worst appear to mindlessly flip into the soul memory of Celtic battle mentality and Nationalism (not quite cannibalising their victims, but formidably ferocious none the less!). Thus it was indeed curious that Rupert Murdoch should be shown co-incidentally with the gates of horn(s) and the Druidic forefinger of Luis or Quickbeam in the Tree Alphabet, utilised by the Druids who were the secret priesthood behind Celtic Nationalism. The Quickbeam was the requirement to answer difficult questions, Greek oratators used it in speeches and Hitler regularly pointed with it. According to newspaper reports Mr. Murdoch was so pleased with the Mirror depicting him in this manner, that he had the front page framed. Not long after this picture emerged *The Express* ran Rupert Murdoch's biography entitled *Fear At the court of the Sun King*! Co-incidental? Or do those who CONTROL AND SILENCE know more than they tell "the herd", in the *Sun* newspaper, which surely must also be a co-incidence! As man became more stupid through lack of truth and real knowledge, the material and satanic forces constantly worked upon him to ensure his complete demise and entrapment, so that the cycle would turn once again. Unfortunately since man had committed a great sin against woman, "intelligence", became the preserve of males and particularly the elite hierarchy of the Communistic Hive, which co-incidentally according to *The Express* Mr. Murdoch supports despite his extensive riches. No "Babes" in a Federal European Hierarchy – only topless models like the snake goddesses of post Religious Revolution era of Crete on page **3** of Mr. Murdoch's Sun newspaper, surely just another co-incidence!

When Phillip IV (1285 -1314) finally suppressed the Order of The Knights Templar and the Grand Master J.B. de Molay was burned on the *island* (see the story of Bran and the Greek folk tales in *The Battle of The* Trees) of the Seine on March 11 1314, shortly afterwards the Pope died mysteriously of dysentery and Phillip died within a year of a disease that was never diagnosed, further Phillip's three sons died mysteriously one

313

after the other as they ascended the throne, thus the Royal Bloodline became extinct. When Edward II of England took the throne from Phillip VI of Valois as a relative of the extinct bloodline, the Hundred Years War reduced the Kingdom of France to ruin. The vengeful God of Jehovah had struck.

THE WORLD ORDER OF THE ROSE

The prophetic Apocalypse or The Book of *Revelations* by St. John shows all the hallmarks of Rosicrucian doctrine and the phallic God. The Apocalyptic account refers to the esoteric number seven many times and the Rosicrucian system is based on the number Seven. There are seven Aphorisms of Creation, Seven planes of consciousness and originally there were seven degrees of initiation. The system is somewhat similar to Brahmanism, as I have pointed out. Further I have previously discussed the Rosicrucian cross or the cross surmounted by the Rose, in other variations the cross is surmounted by the crown (male) and the circle (female) as esoteric symbols of Rosicrucianism and further symbolic of the phallic nature of the godhead.

The Renaissance painter Fra Angelico (1387-1455) in his painting entitled *The Coronation* shows Jesus with a crown on his head as a king and a woman kneeling in front of him with Jesus about to place a crown upon her head. The Roman Catholics portray the woman as Mary mother of Jesus, which is the same unfortunate attempt that was made to identify the woman in the Fatima miracle (*Alternative 4*). However the woman in the painting can clearly be seen holding an alabaster jar, which was one of the symbols used to identify the Mary Magdalene (the others were Dove and perfume bottle, which was also clearly seen in the painting *Persistence du Memoir* by Salvador Dali reproduced in *The Battle of The Trees*. Whilst the implication is of Royal lineage and hints then at not only the Davidic Royal line, but also presumably secretly the Celtic Royal Line, the other implication here is of Rosicrucianism.

The Nazis employed the swastika, which as an archetypal symbol, I discussed in *The Battle of The Trees* and *Alternative 4*, and which was not co-incidentally a sign of the post Religious Revolution era in Crete conducted I concluded by a *Gentile* priesthood the Druids. The swastika when rotated in a whirling motion produces a circle enclosing a cross, a symbol that is sacred to the Rosicrucians. The sacred Brahmin symbol shows the circle and triangle (Trinity) and interestingly the **seven- knotted wand. This implies a complex union of Druids (wand), knot (Celtic) and seven (Rosicrucian's) and may imply the historical connections of Rosicrucian knowledge** (*Fig. 31*). This may also supply some background to the link of Jesus to the East. I did suspect that the group, who had developed the hidden science to its position today, with atomic structure and properties and orientations of space -time, was the Rosicrucians. If this group had indeed seen the origins of their knowledge in Druid secret doctrine, which must involve Cabalistic Science, then as I also suspected, they have significant knowledge on the Greek and Celtic backgrounds and presumably as the group responsible for the floor of The Summer Smoking

Room at Cardiff Castle UK, must also possess the background to the events of Golgotha.

Since the Pope (Angelo Roncali - John XXIII) in the 70's attended a secret Illuminatus ceremony and utilised the archetypal symbol of the wand, then I must also assume (since the group would obviously in the Druidical implications of the wand, descend from the Patriarchs Noah and Adam), that the Catholic Church supports such a group who would by return support the Catholic phallic God Jehovah; that group appears connected to, if not composed of Rosicrucian's. Further since the ceremony that the Pope attended was Illuminatus, then one assumes that the Rosicrucian's have encompassed the Illuminati at some point presumably in the political arm of their: "Universal Kingdom". A conclusion perhaps verified in the magazine *Vaincre*, where the Knight rides down a road towards the Sun (Solar Kingship) and a: "Theocratic United States of The West", the road is labelled on one side 'Brittany' (Celts –Merovingians from the royal Davidic line) and on the other side is labelled Bavaria (The Illuminati – the birthplace of Adam Weishaupt the founder of Illuminism). It may well be that as I have pointed out before, there is a goal of a Universal Kingdom, which encompasses religious and political goals, the religious goal held by the ascendant group of the Druids, the Rosicrucians; whilst the political goal is held by the Illuminati. This is almost certainly verified by the One Dollar note from America, where on the reverse *left* hand side (or *arm*) is an Illuminatus pyramid which corresponds to Communism (the bee hive or ant-heap controlled by Queen bee as the rich far right priesthood). This certainly corresponds to certain Late Minoan seals after the Religious Revolution, which shows a honeycomb-type hive or mountain (preferred by Druids as a symbol of Zeus) surmounted by the goddess holding what looks to be like a staff or wand. On the right hand side of the One Dollar note are the esoteric symbols of the religious goal, which encompasses the Greek archetypes and knowledge in symbolic form and undoubtedly since the Rose appears, indicates Rosicrucianism; this unholy "marriage", is the power that runs the western world today.

Fig.31 **The seven knotted 'wand' of Brahmanism**

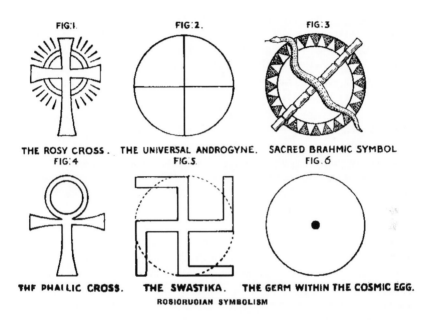

FIG:1.

FIG:2.

FIG:3

THE ROSY CROSS.   THE UNIVERSAL ANDROGYNE.   SACRED BRAHMIC SYMBOL
FIG:4   FIG.5   FIG.6

THF PHAILIC CROSS.   THE SWASTIKA.   THE GERM WITHIN THE COSMIC EGG.
ROSIORUOIAN SYMBOLISM

I have already discussed mind control at some length in my second book *Alternative 4* and the implications of the UFO phenomenon and alleged abductions. The recurring conclusion is that the hidden science has not been used not to help Humanity in the field of healing, but has been utilised in secret weaponry and tested on unsuspecting citizens in violation of their human rights. The question became whether it was intended to use such research in the HAARP and GWEN systems, both of which have a mind control capability. A new revelation that came to light in the form of the book *Trance Formation of America,*[113] which is the alleged documented autobiography of a victim of government mind control. Cathy O'Brien is according to her book the only vocal and recovered survivor of the Central Intelligence Agency's MK-ULTRA Project Monarch mind control operation. Apparently chiselled deep into the white stone of the CIA's Langley, Virginia headquarters is a partial verse lifted from the Holy Bible and writings of St. John: "And the truth shall make you free". Cathy states: "This statement, like the agency, is total reality. The building that it is engraved upon houses the world's most successful manufacturer of lies to facilitate psychological warfare. The "Company" uses truth and technology as their raw materials to produce "pure" lies for control of you and America's allies". The appearance of St. John who I thought was a Druid and member of the lost *Thirteenth* Gentile tribe of *Judah* dating back to Adam, on a building occupied by a secret group (sorry! Correction - Central American Intelligence

Agency) is enough to raise one's eyebrow! The book is so shocking that it caused a loss of breath even amongst hardened observers of satanic influence. On August 3rd, 1977 the 95th U.S. Congress opened hearings into the reported abuses concerning the CIA's "Top Secret" mind control research program code named MK ULTRA. On February 8th 1988, Intelligence insider Mark Phillips covertly rescued an alleged MK ULTRA victim, Cathy O'Brien, from her mind control enslavement. Their seven-year pursuit of Justice was allegedly stopped FOR REASONS OF NATIONAL SECURITY. Cathy's book sets out to expose the truth behind this *criminal abuse* of the Unconstitutional 1947 National Security Act.

The data in Cathy's book at first reading was to some unbelievable, but then certain paragraphs in the light of what I say in this book give the data that horrific ring of truth. The immediate point in my own conclusion was the use of Cabalistic science in the past for mind control and I previously mentioned the battle of Delphi where the Celts had been driven into mass hysteria. Further the Druids had knowledge of this Cabalistic science. Senator Robert C. Byrd, Democrat from West Virginia is singled out by Cathy: "Byrd justified mind control and atrocities as a means of thrusting mankind into accelerated evolution, according to the Neo-Nazi principles to which he achieved. He justified manipulating mankind's religion to bring about the prophesied Biblical "world peace", through the "only means available" - total mind control in the New World Order "After all", he proclaimed, "even the Pope and Mormon Prophet know this is the only way to peace and they co-operate fully with The Project...our Country's involvement in drug distribution, pornography, and white slavery was "justified" as a means of "gaining control of all illegal activities world-wide" to fund Black Budget covert activity that would "bring about world peace through world domination and total control". Byrd adhered to the belief that: "95% of the (world's) people WANT to be led by the 5%", and claimed this can be proven because: "the 95% DO NOT WANT TO KNOW what really goes on in government". Byrd believed that in order for this world to survive, mankind must take a: "giant step in evolution through creating a superior race". To create this "Superior Race" Byrd believed in the "Nazi and KKK principles". (Klu Klux Klan). Certainly if I am correct in the connection of the Nazi's to the elitist Gentile tribe of Judah who very early on, became identified with the white Celts, then this claim has a ring of truth about it and verifies what I proposed in *Alternative 4,* that the World Order is thinking in terms of the Universal Mind, mind control and a psycho civilised society. Further in my second book, I proposed that secret testing of research in alleged UFO incidents, implied that the World Order may be seeking to initiate man en-mass by beaming resonant waves to open the chakras connected to the human biofield, thus altering mental attitudes and physical function. Cathy also confirmed: "higher technological advancements in TOP SECRET weaponry and

318

"Star Wars" electromagnetic mind-control equipment intended for global policing of the New World Order through the Multi-Jurisdictional Police Force". The worst-case scenario I had offered in *Alternative 4* of a psycho civilised society under the control of mind and body control technology developed from the hidden science and applied to the human biofield was then verified by Cathy's statement. Co-incidentally the MRC case (Magnetically Reversed Case) was evident in Cathy's book where there was talk of passing into "other dimensions" which is a subject close to the MRC's goal of trying to get back of this planet. However since he fell from grace as the Lucifer by tinkering with the genetics of man through the bioplasma for the species in space, then trapped by his own past wrongs and lives, he simply carries on with his obsession of mind control. It is a curious thing to realise that by doing this he really believes that his own survival is increased! – Psychotic of course, but since he is running things, nobody thinks to question *his* sanity! Such is life on planet Earth, which would cause one to roar with laughter, unless it was not so entirely tragic. Interestingly, given my own research, Cathy's programming mentioned re-positioning of the Archetypes – "dolphins and whales". These creatures appear on the floor of the Summer Smoking Room Castle as "Sea Beasts", but dolphins are archetypal symbols of The Cycle of Eternal Return through the arch of their backs when they rise from the water (and latterly after they had been re-positioned or stolen by the Cabal at Knossos - Twin Kings), which I produced as a fresco from Crete in my first book. The whale of course was the first living thing created by Jehovah and the Ark of the Covenant was covered in the skins of the porpoise, which was a totem beast.

In *Alternative 4* I expressed some reservations about New Age therapists who were encouraging clients to listen to "voices in their heads". Where the therapist would encourage a client to listen to some spiritual "guide", who was more educated or wiser than they themselves were as a voice in their head. This seemed to totally negate the healing process of encouraging a client to exercise his or her own self-determination in the process of healing. Having worked as a therapist I would never advise any process which took away that self determination and level of **self control.** If this was not worrying in itself, I also expressed some concern over the wave of therapists encouraging clients to talk with their guardian Angels, the whole thing smacked of elitist Communism again and that aspect of Anthroposophy (which was undoubtedly Cabalistic) the doctrine of Serapoths and Angels. The whole scene looked remarkably centre-directed from the Global elite and worryingly there was a connection to the Goddard Space Flight Centre. Certainly in *Alternative 4*, I expressed rather large reservations about the ultimate goals of NASA the American Space Agency and whether the Space Programme was ultimately looking for and developing a safe haven on another Planet (or Space Station), which would save the elite few, in the event of another Magnetic Reversal and cataclysmic event - **The New Age**

Noah's Ark. Such fears seem to be verified, not only when I noted that the space station was emerging as the size of a football pitch! But also when I note in Cathy's book she mentions the Goddard Space Flight Centre as involved in her programming! The succession of names that Cathy refers to in her book looks like the Who's Who of American politics!

If the Rosicrucians do have the "keys to the East" of the hidden science, which Eliphas Levi stated would govern the New World Order, then it is certainly curious that Cathy was programmed to respond on signals of the Order of The Rose. I am reminded of the final and enclosing circle of the archetypal design of the Floor of The Summer Smoking Room, at Cardiff Castle Wales UK, where the petals of the Rose are plainly obvious. The Floor, which was presumably Scottish Rite Freemasonry in its highest Order - Rosicrucian 33rd degree or Rose-Croix, was clearly a plan for a Universal Political and Religious Kingdom - The New World Order, even giving a map of that Order in the centre of the design. Interestingly given the inscription at CIA headquarters at Langley, which quoted St. John and the Book of Revelations, Cardiff Castle contains no trace of Jesus, but it does have representations of St. John. As I concluded in *The Battle of The Trees*, the New World Order plan was always contained in The Prophetic Apocalypse or Revelations **IT IS THE NEW WORLD ORDER PLAN.** "Paradise" on Earth was never going to be a paradise for humanity who it seems are to be part of the Communistic hive, "Paradise" was going to be reserved for the lackeys of the elite, who would play fiddle to the High Priests, those who had worked *from the beginning* to re-create the conditions which prevailed before the last Apocalypse, which *they precipitated* when there was a great misuse of the hidden science. A case of "here we go round the Mulberry bush on a cold and frosty morning" AGAIN! The never-ending cycles of the Earth's mechanism for correcting its electromagnetic field and the shifting of the Bloch wall in order to re-assert the master blueprint or pattern: the lobster pot in which the whole of humanity is trapped.

Cathy's book was very sexually explicit and left no doubts that the hermaphroditic and phallic God was at the centre of the New World Order; further the level of sexual abuse (including children) signifies a very low psychotic state! The secret symbol of the Illuminati founded by Adam Weishaupt, was a circle with a dot in the centre and this symbol was part of Rosicrucian doctrine of Creation. The Circle generates within itself a "Germ" or "Secret Doctrine" and is then encompassed in circles, which become cycles and become the Germ within the Cosmic Egg. The implication of the Cosmic Circle was alluded to in *Alternative 4* and *The Battle of The Trees*, with the concentric ring design of the Floor of Cardiff Castle UK; with its nine concentric rings of secret doctrine and *cycles of action* throughout history to achieve the goal of a World Order laid out in the map at the centre of the design encompassed by the

320

rose petals of Rosicrucianism. The sacred number nine glossing the name of the Patriarchal phallic God - Jehovah who *governed everything* in the circle. The final enclosing ring of petals signifying the high priesthood (Rose-Croix) that had assumed God-like authority to govern in **their God's** name and as gods themselves. The reason that law and justice and responsibility has gone by the boards, where politicians discovered committing dishonourable acts, no longer resign thus maintaining the integrity of their office, depends on the arrogant assumption that as gods, they can commit no wrong. Democracy has gone by the boards, since these scoundrels no longer rule in the name of the people, but in their own self-interested name, having sold their soul to Lucifer for a very small pot of gold (houses, cars, holidays and fat investments) but what good will it do them, when they face a greater justice?

The Order of the Rose must be intent on maintaining Christianity for the masses and yet in that religion the foundation stone rests upon the events at Golgotha. When Mary Magdalene found the tomb at Golgotha empty and Jesus was not there as planned, the whole symbolic re-enactment of the Greek mysteries fell apart. The reason for the re-enactment was a method in those days of impinging a deeper mystery on the minds of the people who still had not lost entirely the meaning of the archetypal symbols. If Jesus had been in the tomb when the Mary Magdalene first arrived to open it, then the nature of the tomb, with its *two upright columns* and *lintel across*, with *Baetylic pillar* on which Jesus was laid, would have been recognised as the archetypal symbols of the tomb of a Solar King, dating back to Late (post Religious Revolution) Minoan period in Greece. The Sun Kings of Mycenae (probably related to the same Cabal that overran Knossos) utilised these symbols in the Lion's Gate (*Plate 7*). The significances would relay the religious message (and political) that the tomb was a place of the dead but specifically a Sun King, but it also represented a womb for RE-BIRTH and only the presence of a woman (the Mary Magdalene) who would first lead Him from the tomb would symbolise Immortality (*Re-incarnation*) as the gift of The Great Goddess. Importantly the PLAN was to re-introduce the lost mystery and knowledge of RE-BIRTH to the people who had for so long been governed by Patriarchal groups that there was a fear that they would forget altogether. Wednesday's God (Matriarchal God of the Hazel and nuts of wisdom and knowledge in the ancient Tree Alphabet) was to be introduced and the truth of what had happened brought back, thus removing the phallic Patriarchal God of Sunday – the Acacia, the God of Moses, Druids and tribes of Judah and Levi dating back to Adam. The nature of the Godhead was to be changed back along with the original philosophy and belief system together with a whole Cosmology which importantly *man needed to exit from the trap of Earth* (the keys of exit if you like). When the Magdalene did not find Jesus at the tomb, she was confused and distressed that the plan was not adhered to and ran to her home to find her entire wealth had been taken (the precious oils); finally she found Jesus with a

321

woman whom it was assumed was some Essene connection but as discussed was probably an Egyptian/Celtic Princess; Magdalene asked for her genealogies back, genuinely traumatised and it was then that Jesus cut the top left arm, which is glossed as a second (**not first**) cut in the crab mural at Cardiff Castle UK. The fact that the crab mural shows Hercules wielding *the club* and sword (which also glosses Druid wand and staff), has deeper implications in archetypal form, in so far as the club of Hercules may not only be associated with the Druids, but also implies the god Zeus Dionysus, the Cretan god of the Religious Revolution who became Hermes (god of thieves). The Oak club was also the sign of a Sun King or Sacred King. Significantly then the secret Order behind the crucifixion had re-enacted in what must be described as a double agent cross in today's terminology the Religious Revolution in Crete. In other words the whole belief system and Cosmology was once again effectively locked in the tomb, the lid shut and the event would go down in the annals of secret group history and doctrine - THE SECRET DOCTRINE. As for the so-called Essene woman with Jesus she may have been none other than the Princess from Egypt SCOTA, whom I have already referred to in a legend from the Western Isles of SCOTland as the woman who arrived with Joseph of Arimathea with the 'Stone of

Destiny' [114]. This may answer the fact that the final truth, which the Mary Magdalene held, was taken upon her murder in France and presumably travelled with St. John to the Druid centre in Scotland. Isabel Hill Elder (cited) stated: "Legends are found around the Hebrides of the visit of Joseph (of Arimathea) to these most north-westerly island of the **Hebrews**"(my emphasis). In a British hymn *Jerusalem* it states that: "Jerusalem was builded here in this green and pleasant land". One cannot discount then that Scota may also have subjected Jesus to a double agent cross, or perhaps he died as in the story of Mil and Scota on his return to Scotland. There is a final curiosity in so far as in the "Chronica de Melsa" [115] when referring to the coronation of David II, in 1331, the statement is made that Scota brought the "stone" from *Egy*pt, which implies that Jesus went there after the alleged Crucifixion and was then betrayed by Scota. This would have effectively removed Jesus and Magdalene and retained the child only and where the Druids were now in receipt of both sets of dynastic genealogies (Greek and Egyptian) ensuring only one dynastic line. This must allude in the context of "destiny" to the genealogies of the Celtic/Greek line which presumably became the Merovingian line from the child of the marriage between Jesus and Magdalene and which may answer the question of the stolen genealogies by authenticating that line from Magdalene through to Merovee and then retained presumably within the secret group of the Prieuré de Sion? The goal of the Merovingian dynasty connected to a religious goal for Europe was quite plainly visible in the front cover of the *Vaincre* illustration, which referred to "Brittany" the seat of power of the Merovingians. The "stone" also has a *Semitic* implication, which cross references with the stone tablets on which Moses laid his Druidic Gentile law of the tribe of Judah? And in the

Commandment: "Thou shalt not kill" presumably sought to challenge Jewish Law, which did not recognise the killing of a Gentile, by a Jew as murder. We also know that the Druids followed Mosaic Law. Thus the knowledge and genealogies were now in the hands of the Thirteenth tribe of Judah and the Druids.

Cathy O'Brien in her book, referred to Senator Byrd as claiming that: "accelerated evolution through the creation of a superior race" was necessary and reflects certain aspects of the hidden doctrine and the creation of Masters in The New World Order. A pamphlet entitled 'An Essay on the Fundamental Principles of Operative Occultism', [116] contains a reproduction of a painting representing the "*Opening of The Third Eye*". Certain icons in Greece after the Religious Revolution, showed men holding their hand to the middle of their fore-head in the position of the third eye. It is shown in myth as Cyclops the one-eyed monster. Certainly many of the exercises that a yogi undergoes in Eastern practise, open the energy chakras of the human biofield. In the painting there is an attempt to show the activity of the third eye being increased by the pineal gland and the pituitary body, which are attributed to the activity of the third eye. The Kundalini *sex force* (the seat of ego) is seen rising upward through the spinal canal into the brain. A golden light is often shown radiating from the base of the brain at the back of the head, which gradually increases in size and intensity until it forms the nimbus or halo of the Saint. The pituitary body is shown in the painting surrounded by an **elliptical rose aura**.

Thus the opening of all the chakras and the *third* eye was seen in this aspect of the hidden science as a healing process coupled with spiritual evolution. The wrongful interpretation of how this state was to be obtained was within the secret groups, interpreted as the requirement of initiating the Kundalini (**sexual force and seat of the ego**) The use of mind controlled slaves in Cathy O'Brien's account seems to fulfil the requirement of a victim for the Master, in order to evolve! Despite the contradiction in spiritual terms the insanity must be apparent. Further whilst science has not discovered the role of the pineal gland it has been suggested to have played a part in electro-magnetic recognition as a receptor organ and has become vestigial through non-use. Cancer patients using the Gerson Therapy often report a pain in the back of the head and a sense of "woolly" or "not there" feelings, which I perceive as a healing process in the pineal gland at the base of the brain. This healing process would open up the chakras allowing a free flow of energy. Thus whilst it is a healing process, if this centre is opened unnaturally without being coupled to spiritual awareness and humility, then it will awaken the kundalini power and the sexual forces. The problem with secret group doctrine is that it appeals to the ego and promotes the idea of supermen and super-races, which naturally appeal to to the ego and the awakening of Kundalini power. The initiate believes himself to be a god and this notion is supported by the group reality (or lack of it!). Ethics then go by the wayside and there are just too many chiefs vying for power and not enough Indians! The quest for ultimate power even within the group as Adam Weishaupt pointed out becomes the driving force. The reality will only hit home when a Magnetic Reversal decides how much or how little they know. Do they really know how to get off this planet! – Now there is something worth knowing! But gods know it all, so surely they don't need the answer.

The Rose as an icon in archaeological finds appears at the Temple of Asklepios (the Greek healer) at Epidaurus in the Peloponnese Greece and is covered in *The Battle of The Trees* and *The Second Millennium Working Report into Cancer - Part II*. The rose-aura indicated the highest form of human love *between* the sexes. The Celestial and temporal 'marriage' of Jesus and Magdalene in the spiritual sense was according to my own account enacted on the physical level by an actual marriage, with a child born of that union. However the spiritual 'marriage' was a re-enactment of the Greek mysteries. Such a 'marriage' may be enacted at the Rose-Croix level within the secret groups today. However one suspects that the accusation laid against the Templars in their trial of "unnatural practises" was the homosexual act, since the woman had long since been removed from the story. Barry Dunford pointed out: "one of the energy 'Ley' lines running across central Scotland has the 'Rose Line' and it may pass through the Masonic Templar site, Roslin (Rose Line) Chapel. This chapel is a Templar Mausoleum for the Sinclair family who it is alleged are descended from the Jesus Bloodline. The nineteenth century, W.F.C. Wigston, refers to Roslin Chapel as "a Masonic Temple.... the cradle of Scots Freemasonry, **if not something deeper still"**.

The predominant archetypal symbols at the chapel are the Fleur-de-Lis, which implicates France
(Magdalene?), and the sunflower (Sun-King?), upon the roof of the aisles is the engrailed cross of the founders the St. Clair's, once hereditary Masters of Scots Masonry. According to Godfrey Higgins: "Jesus was called the Rose- the rose of Sharon - of Is-urea. And from this came the Rossi-Crusians (Anacalypsis Vol.II -1836). Mr. Hall in 1924 produced an illustration of the "seven spinal charkas, which resembles the overall sunburst or Sunflower effect that the overall view of the Floor of The Summer Smoking Room Floor gives. The addition of inter-laced triangles is presumably a Masonic addition (behind the figure), the golden beam of light rising from the Brahmarandra or Gate of Brahma, in the crown of the head and the Sahasrara or Thousand -petalled Lotus in the upper part of the brain usually pictured in Eastern design as an inverted lotus-like cap, which is often portrayed on the Initiates head, can also be viewed as a sun-burst of petals rather like a Sunflower (*fig. 32*)
In Scottish Rite Freemasonry at the level of Grand Master ad vitam or Grand

Patriarch, the legend concerning the fourth temple is given, as after the destruction of the 3rd Temple by Titus in 70 A.D. "Christian Freemasons" left the Holy Land, determined to erect a 4th Temple, which could not be destroyed, a spiritual edifice. They divided into a number of lodges and dispersed throughout Europe. One group came to Kilwinning (Scotland) in 1140, when the Abbey was built. This is regarded as the first lodge of Freemasonry or the Mother Lodge. Further the degree below that is that of Grand Pontiff of The New Jerusalem, the object of the degree is to study the esoteric meaning of *the Apocalypse* and *New Jerusalem* (Rev. xxi, xxii). Below that degree comes the sublime Prince Rose-Croix of Heredom and some of the archetypal symbols of this degree, which is described as the *heart* of Scottish Rite (homosexual union with Hermes?), are portrayed as the search for lost knowledge, including red crosses, crown of thorns, a serpent holding a tail in its mouth which is a common symbol of magic, although undoubtedly represents the Serpent in ring form of the Odin myth and represents in true form the lost knowledge of the hidden science. The degree also includes a sacrificed lamb (Pythagoras wore a fleece when initiated in Crete by the secret Cabal of Dactyls) silver cross and white Eagle. I suspect you will by now have noted the archetypal symbolism. This degree and the 19th degree are both anti-Christian and only professing Christians by apparent contradiction are admitted, the object being to draw in only those who would support the Church and the tribes of Israel.

The floor of the Summer Smoking Room at Cardiff Castle appears to lay out the levels of esoteric knowledge of Scottish Rite and Rose-Croix degree. In the Grand Elect Knight Kadosh or Knight of the Black and White Eagle in Scottish Rite, which is the highest degree (apart from Inquisitor Inspector Commander, Sublime Prince of the Royal Secret and Sovereign Grand Inspector General), there is a lecture on the descent of Masonry through MOSES, SOLOMON, THE ESSENES AND THE TEMPLARS. Significantly there is no mention of The Druids or Adam or the tribe of Judah, which must be retained in a still highest level or at the very top of Freemasonry, which I suspect is a different group altogether, perhaps the Bilderbergers, the so-called "Secret Government of the World", which holds the doctrine of Masters and the idea of the Super Race which was to raise itself once before in history as the Third Reich Aryan Super Race and goes back to Atlantis.

Fig.32a **The seven spinal chakras** Crown chakra open with connection to cosmic circle and grades of initiation by implication (free flow of information and energy). Compair to Cardiff Castle, Wales, UK (Summer smoking room floor- *refer to The Battle of the Trees*)

Fig.32b **The bull-Minotaur head from Knossos** with golden skull cap and As sign of crown chakra opening and solar initiate (sun-king). Refer to *The Battle of the Trees and The Horns as the Gates of Horn and the Abode of the Dead*)

CRETE AS ATLANTIS?

Hitler and the Third Reich were completely obsessed with eugenics and the creation of the Aryan Super Race and if the B'nai B'rith an International Masonic Order were weeding out from libraries in the USA two books by Comyns Beaumont a Scot who wrote that Scotland was the true Holy Land and also 'The Riddle of Prehistoric Britain', it was the origins of races that concerned not only the Zionists but the Nazis also. Comyns Beaumont claimed that the Scandinavian Peninsula was originally joined to the British Isles and this land mass, was the true Motherland of the Aryan or Nordic Race, the BIBLICAL ADAMITES! And further they dominated the ancient world long before the Flood of Noah. Is it any wonder that the Zionist organisation of the B'nai B'nrith attempted to round up all Beaumont's books!

Plato had described the position of a mythical island continent from whence the "continent opposite" namely America was approached by way of islands and Comyns Beaumont maintained that Atlantis was in fact the British Islands, then a part of Scandinavia with her islands. The Celtic race of white blond and essentially blue-eyed people and the Aryans he claimed were descendents of this race. The prehistory of the Atlanteans and the race of Adam were the supposed Supermen who drowned in a Flood like the Adamites, the giants of old. The Atlantean civilization was described as remarkable. The majority of World Creation myths, which I reviewed in *Part II of The Second Millennium Working Report into Cancer*, agree that evil was lurking here on Earth in "the mud", from the very beginning contrary to the only Creation legend of The Bible, which claims that Earth was a garden of Eden Paradise. Thus was the Atlantean civilization remarkable? And if it was, did that originate with the Adamites or perhaps some spiritual impulse that came c. 10 000 B.C.? Was that civilization destroyed by the MRC case, or did the MRC case misuse the power he was given?

The Atlantean civilization was curiously A THEOCRACY: An elitist Priesthood who formed the government or at least the hierarchy. The legend is that the Atlanteans were direct descendents of Atlas who were ruled by a certain Primus inter Pares, an ecclesiastical type *Monarch*, reminding the Author of the Grand Sovereign Pontiff of Freemasonry. This King was regarded as a *living god* and he was also an ARCH-MAGUS OR MAGICIAN. Well this all certainly begins to look all too familiar and in *Alternative 4* I produced an interesting account of a woman a *voodoo* (Cabalistic) priestess (this life-time), who on an LSD trip had suddenly launched into what appeared to be some personal or Akashic Record memory of a past existence and Apocalyptic event, which involved what could only be considered as some RITUALISTIC (Judaic?) religion, which

327

incorporated the element of water. The most interesting point in this experience however, was her comment connecting the experience to the Apocalypse. It was my observation that this personal or Akashic memory record was probably a memory of the earliest ritualistic religion, which was MAGICAL and involved specific practises, the main aim of which appeared to be the avoidance of another catastrophe or Apocalypse which involved water.

This reminds one immediately of the Druids and their fear of an Apocalyptic event and my previous comment that early religion was not anything but a form of **propitiation** towards what was believed to be harmful effects of the environment which became equated with angry gods. Everything had spirits, even the stone pillars, which would become a feature of Semitic religion and were to be found in Crete during the Religious Revolution period. *Everything* had to be propitiated and the predominant psychological emotion was one of **great fear**. *Ritual* was important; since everything in magical practise had to be completed perfectly and ritualistically in the correct sequence (a method of Cabalistic black magic) otherwise there would be some great and overriding catastrophe again. Evidently then man must have lived with the belief that he had control over his environment through this form of religious practise. The calming philosophy: "As I go so must I return" and the knowledge that would free man from the trap did not appear until c. 10000 B.C. It was a gift, it was a mission and it was brought to Earth with much courage to enter this section of this Universe: Whilst the Deluge or biblical Flood is placed around 3000 BC. This date can hardly be trusted and the Apocalypse involving Atlantis was probably very early c. 20 000B.C. and definitely before spiritual intervention from elsewhere c. 10 000 B.C Some denote the time of the fall of Atlantis c. 40 000 BC.

According to mythical accounts the Atlanteans had a **despot over them** who interestingly "**controlled the bodies and the minds**" and further "**All knowledge lay in his hands**, where he **delegated to priests** who were initiated into the **sublime mysteries** and whereby **scientific knowledge** was completely confined to the few of the **highest caste** and was made a **profound mystery of mysteries"***(author's emphasis)*. [124] Well this looks all too familiar does it not! If you substituted today's World Order or European Union, I don't think you would see much difference and that I am afraid is the entire story of planet Earth and the MRC case, who has remained in control of this sector of the Universe for millions of years, unable to get out from the trap that he created for himself and sadly seeks to stop others leaving through receipt of the Holy Grail message which he has sought by every means to hide. It appears that some of the guarded secrets of science were apparently leaked or other Kings desired the secrets and an invasion ensued, which preceded the Atlantean catastrophe. There are also accounts of the plagues (insects, earthquakes and volcanoes), which are repeated in cyclical fashion in the Apocalypse account of St. John in the book of Revelations. John I assumed was a Druid. The latter account then must contain some ancient memory (or channelled information from the Grid) of a Cataclysmic event with the epicentre in the British Isles and Scandinavia. The dispersal of the Aryans was the alleged result of the cataclysm, which according to Druid memory saw the sea: "burst its bounds". The implication here perhaps, is that there was some misuse of scientific knowledge, or a nuclear war? Which may be accounted for in the Indian Epic legends. Certainly some significant climatic event occurred to bury the mythical Atlantis below the sea, which could have been a Bloch wall reversal – Magnetic Reversal.

Given that I proposed that the Apocalypse of St. John **IS** THE NEW WORLD ORDER PLAN, then the biblical plagues that many see in our own current cycle of history as evidence of the truthful nature and prophetic value of the Apocalypse may have been *engineered* to produce a general belief in the plan. Thus man-made earthquakes using Tesla advanced technology clarified in *Alternative4* could be readily explained as the will of the (Phallic) God, whilst utilising the hidden science and sympathetic vibratory knowledge .In the Cancer document I quoted the anti-vivisection society (NAVS) who maintained that AIDS was initially man-made through the irresponsibility of scientists engaged in Cancer research experiments. The prophecy that the Earth will end with Fire is an esoteric code for the phallic God. What is not recognised, is that eventually one day the Earth will fall into the ageing star of the Sun and that will indeed be the fate. Since man Re-incarnates, that will be his ultimate fate here one day, unless he exits, hence the Grail message that was sent to Earth. I did ask a very pertinent question in the introduction to *Alternative 4*, which rested on the observation that the prophetic Apocalypse was being *manipulated* by the New World Order elite and that question was whether the elite intended to qualify Britain or Crete as the "Great City" quoted from the the Book of Revelations, as the one which would suffer a great "Earthquake"; thus bringing The New World Order 'up to speed' on the finalisation of the plan (and page number) of the Apocalyptic account, which is necessary so they can turn the page on the plan to finally reach "Paradise", elitist Communism under a phallic God, with either cloned and genetically controlled humanity or a psychocivilised society – the Orwellian *'Animal Farm'*, a mind and body controlled society, directed by a secret Priesthood or Brotherhood - A Theocracy or One World Order, a Federal European Super State - which brings us very neatly back to Atlantis and bygone goals and cycles. However I am sorry to have to tell you that such goals never died, they live on in World politics today as a World Order and Federal European Super State, just as Hitler's Third Reich sought a white Aryan supremacy with a Theocratic order of priests (The Black Order) based on the Atlantean hierarchal system, presumably with one despot at the top of the power pyramid seen on the One Dollar note of America.

Rothschild I believe was the first person to coin the phrase "The City" for London, however there is an opposing view in legend that **Crete** was the lost Atlantis, which lead to my proposal that Crete could be nominated for sacrifice to the Apocalyptic Revelation by a secret Order of initiates in order to fulfil the Apocalyptic Revelation, or whatever the page number that the MRC case is intent on ritualistically following! Dr. Paul Heinrich Schlieman the archaeologist famous for his archaeological discovery of Troy was convinced that Plato's myth of the lost island of Atlantis was true and not myth at all. Schlieman claimed in a letter he left after his death, that he found a bronze vase at Troy containing fragments of pottery, images and coins of: "a peculiar metal" and: "objects made of fossilized bone". He added: "some of these objects and the bronze vase were engraved with a sentence in Phoenician hieroglyphics". The sentence read: "From the King Chronos of Atlantis". Schlieman also discovered in the Louvre in Paris a collection of objects in the archives taken from Tiahuanaco in Central America and concluded that he had: "discovered pieces of pottery of exactly the same shape and materials and objects of fossilized bone which reproduced a line for line those I have found". This information, which I found in The Journal of the Hellenic Society in Athens when I was working on the Knossos archaeological site, indicates that Atlantis was not mythological but a very real place with its people.

Schlieman also professed to having read Egyptian papyri preserved in the Museum of St. Petersburg, which referred to the "Land of Atlantis", from whence the ancestors of the **Egyptians** had come: "3350 years ago" and: "the sages of Atlantis" who flourished over a period of: "13,900 years". Further when I was researching The Lion's Gate at Mycenae in the Peloponnese Greece I was pointed to the fact that another inscription was discovered near the Gate, which stated that Thoth (Hermes in Greek), was a son of a "priest of Atlantis". In the photograph of the Gate (*Plate 7*), you will note the two upright pillars design with two Lions and the lintel across, which is comparable to the archetypal design of the Golgotha tomb. The Lion is a Late Minoan calendar Beast indicating entry into the New Year, with two Lions as archetypal symbols of the Twin Kings. This is a highly significant relationship, in so far as Hermes the hermaphroditic god, who was the first downgrade of the Minoan belief in Re-incarnation, whereby the Twin Kings were fused into one Solar King, who was then fused with the female (thus removing the woman) as a mistaken concept of unity of male and female in the transcendent third stage beyond death, WAS A CONCEPT OF A DESCENDENT PRIEST OF ATLANTIS. However I have already given a great deal of evidence that the introduction of this concept, which pivoted the Religious Revolution in Crete c.1400B.C.was SEMETIC in origin, thus can we assume that the priests of Atlantis were in fact Semitic? - The Biblical ADAMITES descending from ADAM AND NOAH who survived the Flood.

Schlieman's grandson in 1902 took receipt of his grandfathers "owl-headed vase", although there was no reference to any "owl" in archaeological finds and may therefore also be re-interpretive of those enigmatic beings that in archaelogy often appear with large bulbous frog-like eyes, with all the implications of the MRC case and those who survived *many* Magnetic Reversals. The vase apparently contained a coin or medal of an unusual "silver-like metal" indicating that alchemy practised as part of the hidden science, by the priests from very early times, may have been very advanced and certainly the occurrence of such a metal preceding the Bronze Age is rather a remarkable find, cutting the time-table for the **known** technology of metals to shreds in the archaeological time-scale. It seems that the chemical analysis of this coin has been withdrawn from view, since I can find no further record of any scientific analysis relating to its composition. However it is recorded that the coin or medal was inscribed in Phoenician as "Issued in the Temple of **Transparent Walls**" (my emphasis).

Dr. Paul Schliemann wrote: "I have *reasons* for saying that the strange medals were used as *money* in Atlantis 40,000 years ago" (*author's emphasis*). 118 Schliemann does not explain his "reasons" but the date I believe is correct and corresponds with my own research, dating a large or significant Magnetic Reversal and Apocalyptic event much earlier than has been supposed by current sources, which may correspond to the biblical Flood of pre- history; or the Flood itself may have been another significant but lesser cataclysm. However there may be some secrecy regarding the dates where the hope of placing the biblical Flood at c. 3000 BC separates it from the Atlantis and the Biblical Adamites.

Veteran Geologist Professor Edward Hull offered more information on the lost Continent of Atlantis when he said:

> "The tradition of Atlantis 'Beyond the Pillars of Hercules' can scarcely be supposed to have originated in the mind of man without a basis of reality. In the centre of the North Atlantic Ocean rise from the surface of the Azores volcanic islands, the summits of a group of islands also rising from a platform corresponding to the continental platform of Europe on one hand and of America on the other. The rise of the level of the ocean bed, from 7,000 to 10,000 feet as shown by the soundings on the Admiralty Charts, would have reduced the depth of the ocean by so much, and have extended the land areas to an extent which would have brought Atlantis within navigable distance of both continents...we know from our investigations that this elevation occurred. During the post-tertiary period (Pleistocene Age) and at a presumed date 9,000 or 10,000 B.C. the glacial period when much of Europe and the British Isles was covered by snow and ice, can scarcely have been further back than 10,000 and this is presumably the age of Atlantis".119

Thus some catastrophe *prior to* 10,000 B.C. is indicated. Dr. Scharff a past Director of the National History Museum Dublin, was convinced from the studies of migrations of animals between the Continents of America and Europe that Southern Europe was once connected to the West Indies in the Tertiary period, and probably subsided in the Oligocene period, leaving only a few isolated peaks as islands in the midst of the vast ocean which has since replaced it. A vast interval of perhaps millions of years separated the Oligocene period from the earliest culture of Pleistocene times. Whatever the case, there was a period when land was lost and the Druids in their memory of the sea: "bursting its bounds", held a record presumably of a Bloch wall reversal and a massive Tidal Wave shifting sea and land patterns.

Early primitive man with his axes may merely be a remnant of the surviving people after the cataclysm that was previously suppressed by an evil Theocratic priesthood. One need not necessarily accept the pre- potted view of the so-called origins of species, which was part of the Darwinist view - after all it was just a view or opinion. However I am sure that the archaeologists would be quick to point out that Chellan man, Cro-Magnon man, Acheulian and Mousterian stages of man do not account for the alleged Atlantean type. However consider this and the theory that I placed in *Alternative 4*, that perhaps after a serious cataclysm there may have been limited body forms of the mammal-type that man could have Re-incarnated into, perhaps he chose an ape body, which then had to evolve. Neither do we know of earlier perhaps more significant Magnetic Reversals, where there were vast species extinctions, which might have only left the amphibian, thus the spirit of man or MRC man was forced to occupy the body of an amphibian. Within the natural UFO phenomenon there appears to be an electro-magnetically recorded memory of the morphogenetic line of the species including I presume man. That phenomenon appears to indicate that the Amphibian/Reptilian body was an evolutionary ancestral line in the evolution of Homo sapiens (After Mr. Icke read my books we found a certain repeat of the messianic re-positioning era! And thus I prefer you *not* to connect my initial theory with *any* of the re-positioned data) However I assume that the MRC (magnetically reversed Case) and presumably those who have been on Earth from the beginning, may have gone through this cycle many times and thus in evolutionary time scales at some extremely distant point in the past they may have only had the opportunity to Re-incarnate into amphibian bodies, the "Frogs" of the Apocalyptic account (*Revelations 16 v. 13*)

Since there appears some confusion on this point by some readers who have read my prior books, let me make the point more succinctly. Those who have been here from the beginning may have survived *many* Apocalypses or Magnetic Reversals, as I believe they scientifically represent. The Evolution of species certainly would along Darwinian lines refer to the evolution of BODIES OR

THE GENETIC LINE. This line I propose would be recorded in the morphogenetic bioplasma for the species in the Etheric or spatial DNA, that great library of events or holographic cinematographic film that has recorded everything from the day there was light (the sun) on this planet. Apart from this a spirit (who you really are) also has memories of your own entire history, which not only includes this planet but elsewhere (depends where you have been!). Whilst the morphogenetic bioplasma is concerned with the common experience of survival of the BODYline and thus the species, it does *not* contain *personal* memories other than those directly recorded in the tri-partite biofield, which is concerned with body survival. Thus one could have etheric bioplasmas for e.g. man, frogs (amphibian), reptiles etc. Each bioplasma would carry the evolutionary memory of the species from the point of view of SURVIVAL OF THE SPECIES OR GENETIC LINE (BODIES). However the SPIRITUAL BIOPLASMA (which I distinguish in *Alternative 4* as a *separate* bioplasma, or a higher more finely graded energy) whilst also appearing to carry memories in an electromagnetic form relates to SPIRITUAL THOUGHT OR EVOLUTION. Thus a genetic line incorporates very early evolutionary body forms e.g. Amphibian, that the spirit was forced to Re-incarnate into, when there were few higher evolved forms of species or bodies available for example after a Magnetic Reversal and vast species extinction. Better to acquire a frog's body or a reptile's body, than have no game and wait a few million or billion years for evolution to produce a body that resembles man. Those who have difficulty with this theory believe that man is his body and not a spirit. The fact that amphibian DNA is much longer than the DNA of Homo Sapiens suggests some more information has been encoded on the DNA of frogs which led me to suggest that the amphibia and frogs being able to exist equally well in water and on land, would have enabled them to survive any catastrophic Flood. The length of the DNA in the frog therefore may represent an unbroken line of morphogenetic memory surviving many Magnetic Reversals, represented in archaeological finds with large bulbous eyes and such data appeared in the natural UFO phenomenon which led me to finally conclude that such humanoid types may have been the result of prolonged Re-incarnation of spirits who had survived magnetic reversals into the amphibian line. Thus when more highly evolved mammalian bodies became available such Spirits would Re-incarnate into those bodies, but still be connected in some manner to the amphibian memory line. Neither can one discount the effects of a Magnetic Reversal on animal size and hormone function and to this end I discussed various metabolic types in *Alternative 4.*The attempts to equate archaeological finds of humanoid types with large bulbous eyes to Aliens merely clouds I believe the pre-history of these types.

In *The Second Millennium Working Report into Cancer- Part II*, I produced the details of research papers, which show that Magnetic Reversals have occurred over a very long period in Earth's history. A magnetic reversal as I have discussed is an event where the Earth's *geomagnetic* field reverses, with North and South poles trading places. Whilst it is assumed that Humanity has never been through such a reversal that cannot be supported by my own theories where those spirits who were on Earth from the beginning have probably survived many. However it is scientifically true to say that other animal species have been through a Magnetic Reversal, with dire results. Scientists by dropping hollow tubes into the ocean bottom and removing cores of sediment, are able to study the tiny dust particles that enter the oceans carried by winds or rivers, which then become deposited on the ocean floor as a sort of 'layered cake'. Many of the particles in the cores are magnetite and have tiny electrical fields. As they are sedimenting through the water, each particle acts like a tiny compass needle and points toward the magnetic North Pole. The alignment of these particles in the cores can be determined by measuring the direction of the magnetic fields, which will indicate the direction of the magnetic North Pole at the time the particles were falling through the water. According to Dr. Becker [120] "when this is done, the startling fact emerges that the Earth's magnetic field has often reversed in the geologic past. Each reversal is a slow process; in each case, it has taken at least 10,000 years for the new orientation to become established".

A study of the vast numbers of radiolarians which are tiny sea creatures made up of only one cell and covered in a hard skeleton has determined that from time to time, these creatures were subjected to vast species extinctions. According to Dr. Becker: "These great 'die-outs' duplicated the familiar patterns of extinction of other animals, including the dinosaurs. In each such species collapse, the most advanced or evolutionary developed forms appear to have been most affected. After each extinction, entirely new types of radiolarians would be established and would grow and flourish, generating many related but more advanced species". Thus it is not impossible according to this proof and my own theory to postulate that some men who were on Earth from the beginning did in fact experience one or many of these events and at some early point in species evolution were forced to re-incarnate into a body e.g. Amphibian that was the only advanced form of the time. I suspect the reason why certain archaeological finds that show man as quite advanced even in the stone age are hidden or suppressed, is that the whole early history of man and the hidden science together with biblical history stands to be questioned should such evidence surface in the realm of the general public. Thus Darwinist views, biblical texts and anthropology which views man as evolving steadily along Darwinian principles from monkeys and cavemen is promoted as the orthodox and accepted view and all other evidence is shut away. I will come to such evidence later.

As Dr. Becker points out this discovery of Magnetic Reversals and species extinctions runs counter to the idea of evolution as a steady upward climb, with new forms of ever-increasing complexity arising from simpler forms. The description of these periods of **crises in life** has slowly led to a revision of the original Darwinian concept of gradual evolution, replacing it with what is now called "**punctuated equilibrium**". However does man know this? Of course not, the media as subservient highly paid slaves to the Elite are still flogging the propaganda 'horse' of meteorite extinction of the dinosaurs. Dr. Homer Newell of the New York Museum of Natural History reviewed the data on the population size of many different animals and found that there were several periods of time during which many different species became extinct. These occurred at the end of the Devonian, Permian, Triassic, and Cretaceous geological periods. It was during the last one that the dinosaurs became extinct. *Fig. 33* shows the geological time scale over which Magnetic Reversals occurred. Often the species extinctions occurred just after a magnetic-field reversal had taken place. Dr. Becker stated: "Furthermore, if the reversal occurred following an exceptionally long period of a stable field, the species extinction was much more extensive. It appeared as though the life forms of the quiescent time adapted themselves to that magnetic field; the longer it went on, the greater the impact of the next reversal".

Fig.33 **Magnetic Field Reversals**

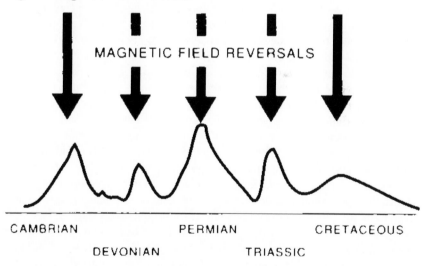

The total populations of animal types over geologic time. The time is not linear, and time between geologic periods is not uniform. The line represents the number of new species when it is rising and the number of species becoming extinct when it is falling. The geologic time periods on the horizontal scale represent the end of each period. Except for the Cambrian, the other periods are

those defined by Newell as times of major species extinctions. For example, the peak of the Cretaceous marks the beginning of the decline of the dinosaurs, and the end marks their extinction. The magnetic reversals identified are the major ones – that is, those in which more than 20 percent of the sea-bottom ones –that is, those in which more than 20 percent of the sea-bottom cores showed a reversed pattern. The reversal at the end of the Permian period followed a long period of steady field in which no reversals occurred; the species die-out was exceptionally large (Adapted from Sander by Dr. R. Becker in Cross Currents)

In 1971 according to Dr. Becker: "a small conference was held on this subject at the Lamont Geophysical Observatory at Columbia University, under the direction of Dr. James Hays. After collecting data on reversals and extinctions, Dr. Hays had found that six of the eight identified extinctions of radiolarians had occurred concurrent with magnetic-field reversals - a relationship considerably above the level of chance. It became evident during the conference that the species extinctions of all animals were somehow linked to the reversals of the magnetic field". In my Cancer report I gave a great deal of research on the effects of Extremely Low Frequencies (ELF), on biological systems. ELF frequencies of the magnetic-field micro-pulsations have effects both on *physiological and psychological* function of the organism including man. Further these micro-pulsations had effects on behaviour and such a combination of effects could produce devastating effects on the organism in the event of a major change in the Electro-magnetic field, thus accounting for extinctions apart from any climatic effect or disaster. The comet or meteorite impact theory has less evidence to back it, but it is supported for obvious reasons that to divulge this research to the public would also in part reveal the hidden science. The overall implication is that far from the propagandist view, Evolution is NOT simply a random event. Further with regard to my own theory and the psychological case of the MRC the variations in field reversals could well have played an enormous part in the development of his psychology and thought process, which he carries with him in various incarnations. One suspects that his desire for order, for control and his obsession with ritual (which is so evident in secret groups) comes from not knowing which page he is on! The equivalent of being periodically put in a tumble dryer and whizzed round in a Magnetic Reversal and then being released. "Err...umm...Err which page was I on?" He can't jump around in his thought process, thus he loves beaurocracy! He loves lists! He loves an overload of laws! He loves total control and man as machine where he does what the MRC dictates and no questions asked. Finally he labels dissidents or anyone that seeks to question his methods as "agitators" –they provide just too much disorder to his own thinking process – those awkward questions that make his mind jump through hoops are just a little bit too much sanity for the MRC case and they interrupt his page number!

Edwin H. Colbert commenting on the disappearance of the dinosaurs stated: "The great extinction that wiped out all of the dinosaurs, large and small, in all parts of the world and at the same time brought to an end various lines of reptilian evolution, was one of the outstanding events in the history of life and in the history of the earth.... It was an event that has defied all attempts at a satisfactory explanation." [121] This comment was made some twenty years before the research into Magnetic Reversals started in the 70's. As I pointed out, it is plainly obvious that the magnetic field of Earth must have changed, since no life form today larger than an elephant can exist under today's gravitational field. Gay Gaylord Simpson, one of the most respected men of his time in palaeontology remarked:" It is as if the curtain were rung down suddenly on a stage where all the leading roles were taken by reptiles, especially dinosaurs, in great number and in bewildering variety, and rose again immediately to reveal the same setting but an entirely new cast, in which the dinosaurs do not appear at all, other reptiles are mere super-numeraries and the leading parts are all played by mammals.[122] This would certainly support my theory that prior to an electro-magnetic reversal there may not have been mammals for the MRC case or those who were here from the beginning to Re-incarnate into and were thus forced to use a body form that was available, which was the Amphibians and later the Reptiles.

Comyns Beaumont proposed Atlantis revealed as the British Islands, as the origins of mankind, principally the white blond race, the Aryan peoples, from whom the Greeks and other Celts - who migrated in part to the Mediterranean later evolved. Is it any wonder that Zionist Masonic orders were secretly rounding up his books! This origin argues Beaumont, was to veil Atlantis in one way or another into the earliest Graeco-Phoneician myths of Oceanus, of the "earth-shaker" Poseidon, the Gorgons, the Cyclops and others. Beaumont states:
> "It transpired that the pre-history of the Atlanteans and the race of Adam possessed peculiar   similarities. The supermen of Plato's island were drowned in a flood like the Adamites, the Giants of old time, men of renown, the men whose thoughts became wholly evil, destroyed in what is called the Flood or universal Deluge. The cause advanced for their destruction was in effect the same in both cases, they being accused of having mastered too many of the divine secrets of, as we should say, science, or, as the ancients termed it, the gods."

Beaumont and others attribute the Atlanteans as a remarkable civilization, and one in which:
> "flourished many and great walled cities, towns and villages, these often adorned with majestic temples and palaces; with main highways supported by multitudinous navigable canals and rivers; with a highly developed agriculture producing the fruits of the earth, while other

tracts were used to rear horses, cattle, and sheep; with many ports and mercantile marine which sailed the main to the most distant lands and brought home cargoes of wealth."

Agriculture in Greek myth was the work of "Her", not the Atlanteans, however despite the contradiction Beaumont continues to describe Atlantis as being:

"Divided into ten states like the ten tribes of Israel (of whom we really know so little), although   one, the direct descendants of Atlas, hence Atlanteans, dominated the rest, and whose King or chief ruler was, primus inter pares, an ecclesiastical monarch, a superman, in fact a divinity, regarded by all as a living God, the sole intermediary between the celestial deities and all human flesh. In his hands was all ecclesiastical and temporal power, and this theocrat, arch-magus, or, as described, "His Anointed", was the most *absolute despot the world has ever known*, for *he controlled not only the bodies but also the minds of all from the highest to the lowest. All knowledge lay in his hands, delegated to those priests who were initiated into the sublime mysteries, whereby scientific knowledge was completely confined to the few of the highest caste* and was made a profound mystery of mysteries" (*Author's emphasis*).

Such a system never died with the Atlanteans and the Arch-magus, since such people merely re-incarnate with the same goals and objectives or postulates of a powerful Theocracy, One World (white/Semitic dominated) Order supported by the hidden science. The Celtic Commonwealth, the events of Golgotha, the Third Reich and a "Federal United States of the West" are mere DRAMATIZATIONS of the spirits of Atlanteans re-living currently on the World's stage their postulates which have never ceased to exist from the beginning. However as Beaumont explains the day came when their civilization (if one could call it that) collapsed. According to Beaumont the Atlanteans had:

"Mastered *appliances of science* to a degree which in several respects owed little to modern   science, or, to avid exaggeration, of a few decades ago, with the main difference that today the pursuit of science is open to all, whereas in the distant day an immense gulf lay between the knowledge of the priestly initiates, which was pronounced divine, and that of their subjects and slaves. The day arrived when the closely guarded secrets of their magic arts in the use of fire and even of the air were betrayed to Kings afar off and led to savage wars of invasion, where   rival creeds and ambitions fought one another with bitter hatred" (*author's emphasis*).

Beaumont is mistaken to believe that times change, or in fact people or Spirits and their postulates, which dictate world politics, religion and science. The arch magicians are today's elite in the One World Order and the sorcerers apprentices are the physicists and scientists who willingly work for the One World Order, noticeable in the field of alleged defence programmes with mind control capability, cloning and genetic modification of the species or biotechnology. Further scientists are not free to research or discuss the hidden science and apply it, unless they are the sorcerers for the Elite. There is no hope I am afraid in getting my own Cancer research evaluated as I requested by a panel (independent and free to speak) of scientists: To return to this matter of **DRAMATIZATION** and its consequences on the **world's stage of pure theatre**. Basically this means **the repeat of an action that has happened in the past**. A person brings into present time something that happened in the past, the incident being played out of its time and period. All the insanity that you see on the world's stage and even in the life of individuals is a result of dramatization. When the person is dramatizing he is merely like an actor playing a part or reading his script page by page and in the real world of present time, this means that the person often commits a whole series of irrational actions. When the person is dramatizing (verb) he is actually going through an entire cycle of doing (or action) that is dictated by the past action. The MRC case continually dramatizes his cycles of action prior to a Magnetic Reversal. The script goes something like this - page1. Maintain order; page 2. Form a Theocracy or priesthood with the Arch-magus in charge; page 3 Take control of the hidden science and round up all documents relating to it and destroy any group that has some knowledge of it; page 4 Form secret groups and hide all knowledge of the true events of the past – form circles of initiates; page 5 Enslave man and accumulate all profit to conserve a position of power and only delegate that power through the initiates of the group; Page 6 develop better methods of enslavement through genetics an and methods of war Page 7 Conserve power by taking hold of all organs of free speech and Democracy and instigate tight authoritarian rule of Communism for the masses. Each cycle differs slightly, due to the accumulation of past data and holograms within the crystal, with this current cycle having the added data of the crucifixion and imput from spiritual intervention (c. 10 000 B.C.) and thus being unique; however the pattern of secrecy, control and enslavement is essentially the familiar 'script'. However since the MRC manipulates and tries to control the natural laws of the Grid and atomic matter he challenges Nature, thus precipitating a Magnetic Reversal and the end of the cycle. The MRC case then instigates the whole cycle again repeating the entirety of his past actions as a dramatization. The insanity only starts to show up when you listen to the MRC spouting on about peace, Democracy, Human Rights (including free expression and the right to an opinion and own belief), freedom, the right to an education, truth, and morals and then compare those words with his actions! Thus my suggestion in *The Battle of The Trees*, that you must never listen to words only look at actions and outcome, when assessing what is truly in a person's soul. Many people say they will help, but then some years later you turn round and realise they have done nothing along that line and in fact you have been delayed, or even thwarted by their covert attempts to stop you! The reason why an MRC cannot finish a cycle of action is that the end of the cycle to *him* is the 'tumble dryer'! – A Magnetic Reversal. He follows page by page the plan (the Apocalyptic Revelation) and although that is ridiculous as a script in current time, simply because it *looks forward* to the tumble dryer! And views it as a time of reckoning, that plan ends with destruction and the survival of the "chosen ones". In fact the MRC case and the World Order have set up what is termed a "games condition" where mankind's power of choice has been subjugated against his will into a fixated activity from which he cannot take his attention. Mans attention has been fixated with an inability to escape coupled with an inability to attack, to the exclusion of all other games: which as a definition could also apply to the mechanism of the mind, the author outlined in the Cancer report. The game or macrocosmic cancer on Planet Earth is called –The World Order with its subsequent goals of money, power, control and enslavement, a game only played by the MRC case, whilst man is fixated within the trap of this particular game.

At the time of the catastrophe of Atlantis there were untoward meteorological happenings, such as strange plagues of insects, earthquakes, and volcanoes going into eruption. The fact that the prophetic Apocalypse of St. John is able to prophesy such re-occurrences in the future, must depend on memory and the predictable cyclical nature of **natural laws** in response to man's meddling with those laws. A Magnetic Reversal would be a prime contender for such cause and presumably precipitated the Flood of Noah. Whilst Beaumont and others have proposed a collision with a fallen planet or comet, the scientific evidence is in favour of an electromagnetic reversal. However the dispersal of the Aryans and Beaumont's claim that the white Aryans founded civilizations which were previously credited to Asia, provides the complex backdrop of how an Egyptian Queen in archaeological finds could have been white. The fact is I believe, that a hierarchal powerful caste system was in operation from early times, with the hierarchy forming an elite type of Aristocratic Priesthood or Theocracy, from which the One World Order of the day plucked its leaders. Beaumont claims that the ancient civilization of Ur of the Chaldeans, of the Egyptians, the Phoenicians and the Greeks in its origins must have emanated from the north or the Atlantis region of The British Isles and Scandinavia. Certainly the Celtic Commonwealth must have been an attempt to raise the old Atlantean white supremacy dream in the times preceding and during the time of Jesus.

In Plato's legend of the *Lost Atlantis* related in the *Timaeus* and *Critias*, a certain Solon visited Sais, where he: "was very honourably received" by the: "priests of the goddess Neith". One of the eldest spoke with contempt regarding the "puerile fables" of the Greeks and said: "You are unacquainted with that most noble and excellent race of men who once inhabited your country, from whom your present state are descended, though only a small remnant of this admirable people is now remaining". He went on to say that according to Egyptian annals, Athens once overcame: "a prodigious force" when: "a mighty warlike power, rushing from the Atlantic sea, spread itself with hostile fury over all Europe and Asia". Evidently here Plato is referring to the Celts who were led by the magician Druids. Presumably the Druids represented the remnant Atlanteans.

The support Plato gives for the Druids must rest in the time of Athens c. 366 B.C., when to quote Plato Athens was: "One City of the Rich, and the other, a City of the Poor". The Greek World, and Athens in particular stood poised on the brink of an economic abyss, similar in catastrophic results to that which occurred in the U.S.A. in the 1930's. Plato and some other intellectuals of the day, decided to detach themselves from both the leaders, and the led; and observing the situation quite coolly came to the conclusion, that the only possible solution to alleviate the political mayhem surrounding them, lay in the establishment of a type of **Elitist Communism** - with the State being ruled by a Philosopher King, or Group of Academics, who would keep all the classes in their correct place, that is, in a type of rigid Parmenidian immobility - which would never allow any dangerous Heracleitian flux, flow, or change! Such philosophy is not only indicative of MRC thinking, but such a system has been adopted by all One World Order programmes including the Celtic Commonwealth, The Third Reich and today European Union and The One World Order of the Rose. The fact that all One World Orders have been led by secret groups whose hierarchy is predominantly if not entirely white, with goals that date back to Atlantean Aryans or the Biblical Adamites is a reflection of the hierarchal caste system employed, together with the Elitist Communism (run by the rich far right) which becomes the method of control.

Monarchy exists on such a system. Life however, equals **change** and **development**. That is what Life is all about - Change! So the philosopher was chasing an illusion, just as the secret groups chase an illusion or should I say dramatization! Just as Monarchy in its intransigent thinking will not entertain change, since it represents a hierarchal caste system. Plato spent his time looking for a strong philosophical dictator or King to rule over his "Utopia", a word incidentally that has been used by politicians to describe a Federal European Super state! Unlike his student Aristotle, Plato knew absolutely nothing about Biology, and he never did manage to understand what a life force really was, even though the magicians understood it very well. Whilst he spent his time searching for an ideal world that the philosopher creates, unfortunately the elite knew how a populous could and must be controlled.

Plato continues on the subject of Atlantis:

341

"That sea (the Atlantic) was then navigable, and had an island fronting that mouth which in your tongue call the Pillars of Hercules; and this Island was larger than Libya and Asia put together; and there was a passage hence for travellers of that day to the rest of the Island, as well as from those Islands to the whole opposite Continent that surrounds that the real sea ... In this Atlantic Island, then, was formed a powerful league of Kings, who subdued the entire Island, together with many others, and parts also of the Continent; besides which they subjected to their rule the inland parts of Libya, as far as Egypt, and Europe also, as far as Tyrrhenia. The whole of this force then, being collected in a powerful league, undertook at one blow to enslave both your country and ours, and all the land beside that lies within the mouth. This was the period, Solon, when the power of your State (Athens) was universally celebrated for its virtue and strength; for surpassing all others in manumit and military skill, sometimes taking the lead of the Greek nation, at others left to itself by the defection of the rest, and brought into the most extreme danger, it still prevailed, raised the trophy over its assailants, kept from slavery those not as yet enslaved, insured likewise the most ample liberty for all of us without exception who dwell within the Pillars of Hercules. Subsequently, however, through violent earthquakes and deluges which brought destruction in a single day and night, the whole of your warlike race was once merged under the earth; and the Atlantic Island itself was plunged beneath the sea and entirely disappeared..."

(Timataeus Section VI)

The curiosity of this discourse, is that it is difficult to distinguish whether Plato is talking about Crete post the Religious Revolution c. 1400B.C. or The British Isles and this would certainly bring the Atlantean Catastrophe forward from other predictions of 40 000 B.C. However if as I concluded a Druidic causation was behind the fall of the Early Minoan Civilization, then the confusion lies in the secret link that has never been recognised - who killed the Minoans? The evidence of a Semitic religious based revolution certainly links to the biblical Adamites - the Druids. An anonymous contributor (whom I suspect was a Freemason), to *The Times* on 19th February 1909 was first to draw attention to the remarkable resemblance between Plato's Atlantis and the Island of Crete. The contributor pointed out the traditions regarding Cretan sea power and the raids of piratical bands on the Egyptian Coast during the nineteenth and Twentieth dynasties. What has not been recognised until my own research is that Crete only paralleled descriptions of the British Isles AFTER the Religious Revolution by the Druids. The fact is that there was no link BEFORE the Revolution, since the Grail message was not connected to King's or the priestly ruling power.

Crete is one of the biggest Islands in the Mediterranean about 160 miles long and varying between 35 miles wide in the middle to 10 miles at the extremes. Deep gulfs indent the northern coast, and its southern shore is rugged and rock bound. A ridge of hills extends from East to West, culminating in the centre of the Island in well-wooded Mount Psiloritis the ancient Mount Ida, which rises to a height of about 8159 feet. Strabo called the hills in the Western part of the Island Leuca Ore or "The White Mountains" In the South-West the mountains almost fringe the shore. Comparable to the description of Atlantis: "there was a passage hence for travellers of that day to the West of the Islands, as well as from those Islands to the whole opposite Continent"; was Crete then connected to a greater land mass? Plato describes the topography of Atlantis in the Critias:

> "The whole region was said to be exceedingly lofty and precipitous towards the sea, and the plain of the city" (Salisbury plain in the UK on which the Druidic Temple to Apollo is built - or the plain on which Knossos was built in Crete?): "which encircles it, is itself surrounded by mountains sloping down to the sea, being level and smooth, all much extended, three thousand stadia in one direction, and the central part from the sea above two thousand. And this district of the whole island was turned towards the south, and in an opposite direction from the North. The mountains around it, too, were at that time celebrated".

Well certainly Mount Ida in Crete was celebrated. However, what about the Hebrides in Scotland and the real seat of power that I conclude drove the religious Revolution in Crete? According to Plato the mountains exceeded: " in number, size, and beauty all those of the present time, having in them many hamlets enriched with villages". Many archaeologists have failed to find historical places in the Bible described as existing in the Holy Land and yet such places could be more correctly described by various places in Scotland. Barry Dunford has already drawn attention to the parallel Biblically significant names in the story of Jesus, to places in Scotland e.g. "GAL ilee and GAEL ilee; and Fortin GAL and Fortin GAEL, HEBREWS and HEBRIDES (the Northern area of Scotland in the U.K.). Other pertinent Gaelic words incorporating the Hebrew root gl are Dun Geal and Fortingall and Fingal the ancient Celtic warrior whose banner according to tradition, had inscribed upon it the: "Image of the Sun". Solar Kingship was very evident in Druidic and Celtic caste system and this form of power was introduced into Crete at the time of the Religious Revolution.

Interestingly enough the pale priests of the Aryan Third Reich, who formed a caste system culminating in The Black Order, utilized the symbol of the "Black Sun" (*Fig. 34*). Make no mistake about it, they intended a Theocracy run by an elite priesthood and since this elite was I assume the Druidic biblical Adamites (the Aryans and Atlanteans) then the theory is there, that the Jews and the

Holocaust were victims to their own caste system, sacrificed to the cause of the State of Israel and a European Federal Super State. Hitler merely a puppet in a far bigger game, to introduce the plan of a Federal European Super State into a war ravaged Europe, to dupe Europeans into the acceptance of a caste system run by a hierarchal group, who had never ceased to exist. And one should not forget that there were many titled men: "Jewish Lords of England", in Churchill's Government e.g. Hore-Belisha as War Minister, Colonel Nathan Chief of National Services, Isidor Salmon head of the Committee for Supporting the Army" (food supply to the British Army) and Churchill's daughter was married to a Jew, his brother a partner of a Jewish company and Churchill himself was a very close friend of Bernard Baruch, one of the most powerful Jews of his time. Churchill was stated to have been a high - ranking member of Freemasonry.

The sea power of Atlantis was legendary and the Minoan Civilization before the decline of the Late Minoan Period had tremendous sea power. However the British Isles was also renown for its sea power. The island Kings were "rulers", Solon was informed, in the sea of Island (the Aegean or the Hebrides?) and they extended their Empire to all the country as far as "Egypt and Tyrrhenia". The main and overriding point in Cretan history is that a Religious Revolution has been skilfully hidden. The Early Minoans were a peace loving and artistic people, with high initiates who were conversant with a belief in Re-incarnation and a whole Cosmology that included the Earth Grid. Such knowledge was imparted freely until after the Religious Revolution by a Semitic force that sought to destroy that Civilization and withdraw the belief system along with the whole system of Cosmology and particularly knowledge of Earth Grid and the hidden science. No war-like archaeological finds such as helmets and swords, were found in the Early Minoan period, but after the intervention by a Semitic force there were numerous finds of such weapons. There is a persistent attempt to cover up the Early Minoan Civilization in terms of their beliefs (The Cycle of Eternal Return) and the Cosmology. It is assumed that the Knossos site was a palace for Kings and yet its role as a tribute to the goddess in her death aspect, a place for the cnothic underworld of the dead, waiting to be reborn is plastered over creating a fantasy-world or "Disneyland". Obviously a re- evaluation of the Knossos site might rake up its connections to the Biblical Adamites and the Druids and the World Order that has always existed. It is perhaps no co-incidence that Tony Blair the British Prime Minister, finds his advisors among men like Lord Levi, who as an unelected 'Minister' of sorts goes about The British people's business in the World, apparently with Tony Blair's blessing. No times do not change.

Fig. 34a   **Signet of the Black Sun**
According to P. Moon in 'The Black Sun', this was the innermost
secret society of Nazi Germany – the Black Sun.

Fig.34b   **Marduk** *–The secret societies of Germany used this in
their literature and symbology. This pagan god is also known as
Malduk, Mithras, Moloch or Malok in German. Note the Bull-Minos
head and gates of horn (abode of the dead) with man's body (Bull-Man
or phallic cult - 13 th tribe?) Also Hermes wings.*

345

Plato's description of Atlantis curiously also features a State constructed architecturally on a concentric ring pattern, such a pattern reflects the Knossos labyrinth of Crete and also the Tholos of the underground chamber of the Temple of Asklepios in the Peloponnese, where the secrets of healing and biofield energies forming part of the hidden science were to be hidden from the un-initiated, giving the Priests ultimate power, perceived as gods over life and death. The Temple of Asklepios also curiously bears architectural rosettes, as did the forehead of the Minos Bull. The fact that the rosette appears in the middle of the forehead and Cretan archaeological finds after the Religious Revolution which show men with their hands raised to the middle forehead, indicates the opening of the "third eye", the pineal gland and a connection to Akashic or Grid sources. Vibrational resonance was used to open this chakra centre and the crown chakra was seen as the prerogative of Priestly Kings. Presumably then the rosette in the middle of the bull's forehead indicates initiation at the level of priestly kingship and makes the connection with the Rose of Rosicrucian's, accounting for the concentric ring design of the Floor of the Summer Smoking Room at Cardiff Castle. Unfortunately Sir Arthur Evans of Oxford, who between 1921 and 1935 published his finds of the archaeological excavation of Knossos in his monumental six-volume work *The Palace of Minos at Knossos*, became the 'Bible' of Minoan Archaeology. In fact the Knossos site had been occupied from 6000 B.C. and far from being a palace of Kings or occupied by a primitive people, the Neolithic strata shows a mixed economy of agriculture and cattle raising, with a high sense of skills, handicrafts and creativity. The clay pottery shows astonishing artistic skill and stone tools reached a high technological level.

If the Step pyramid is the early representation of the degrees of Freemasonry or a fraternal brotherhood based on Solar King worship, then in the Third Egyptian dynasty (c. 2980 -2900 B.C.) a period corresponding to Neolithic Early Minoan I period at Knossos, a change was observed in the administration of Egypt, when Pharaoh Zoser transferred his court to Memphis and built the first step pyramid of Sakkara, the transfer of the court was presumably to align with some key geometry of the Grid. Trade between the Early Minoans and the Egyptians may have lead to the discovery of the Teacher in Crete. Earliest Cretan and Egyptian pottery shows a black colouration, which is quite different from the later finds in so far as colour and aesthetic beauty hall- marked Minoan expertise. The black pottery also turns up in Africa and black was in esotericism always associated with black magic. The appearance of Kamares ware in Crete with its light on dark pinpoints the new impulse of light from the Teacher. With respect to the black aura which is a feature of low emotional states and black magic, the aura or biofield is associated with mental or emotional states such as hatred, malice and revenge all traits of the MRC case who forever whinges what has been done to him, but never what he did to others (survival of self). Before a

Spiritual impulse came to Earth c. 10 000 B.C. that was life on this planet directed by the Elite. Neither did they have any significant understanding of the energy fields that entrap man. Those who had endured many Magnetic Reversals took the very knowledge that was sent to free mankind from him. Black occult and voodoo together with cannibalism was the so-called religion of this planet, prior to Spiritual intervention.

In early Neolithic strata of excavations at Knossos in the fifth metre, there appears a startling new development in pottery. This pottery (*Plate 12*) shows incised geometric designs or chevron pattern that is indicative of the 'zigzag' pattern reported in UFO reports. This 'zigzag' represents I would say the cyclical windings of the vortex or bioplasma. Such a pattern also turns up in the UVG 120 sphere, when the pattern or 'zigzag', is obtained when the ten "'vile vortices", are linked as illustrated earlier. These vortices give the magnetic-gravitational anomalies, which have been claimed as "doors" to other dimensions. There was a particular line of knowledge being taught here, relating to man's entrapment. However if the Elite believed as they still do, that they could take the physics of the Grid and escape, they should remember that the Teacher, was also emphasising Karma and Re-incarnation and no doubt pointed out to pupils that they had not a hope in hell of getting out, unless all karma and wrong actions were paid to the last coin, by restitution towards the wronged party. Unfortunately that means the actual identity or person (which means on a point of principle that one should make amends immediately a wrong is committed rather than chance having to search for the identity in future life-times, perhaps never locating them at all if they leave - condemning one to the trap for all eternity!).

The 'zigzag' designs of the pottery were interestingly filled with white gypsum chalk, this "light on dark" ornamentation also had religious significance which the Jews borrowed as an idea (that borrowing bee again!) mixed it all up with other significances and totally omitted the design (and knowledge). The whole of the Knossos site is covered in white gypsum, which signifies the goddess in her death aspect and thus really the Teacher was trying to impart some knowledge of release from the trap. Light on dark pottery was also found in the first stratum of Troy and also in Egypt.

Early Minoan pottery showed an increasing excellence until the Late Minoan period and the Religious Revolution, when the caste archetypal significances such as the reed (Royalty) appeared on vases and art declined. The similarity of certain Cretan artefacts with Scottish finds marks out the link between the two and the lost 'Atlantis'. Also there is a very definite link with Egypt and if the caste system of a hierarchy was employed to rule then such connections post Religious Revolution are understandable. Interestingly the Cretans or Keftiu in the Egyptian tombs of the Empire period, which roughly corresponds to the Religious Revolution era, are portrayed as typically Cretan, with wasp waists (narrowed) and girdles and a Minoan 'kilt' and hair in pleated tails. Interestingly too towards the end of the Eighteenth Dynasty, the racial designation Keftiu drops out of use, and names of tribes are given, which parallels the caste system of the Semitic invaders, which I equate with the Druids as Biblical Adamites.

In having previously described the parallel topography of the Hebrides in Scotland to the Island of Crete, there is an important sanctuary on the south side of the Island of Crete at Palaikastra, where a sheer cliff drops to the sea and is highly reminiscent of the coastline of the Scottish Highlands. A large number of clay votive figurines of human beings and animals were discovered here, which points to a site for a sacred building, perhaps some pre-Church. Although it could not have been a Temple, for its ruins resemble ordinary houses, a layer of ashes and charcoal fragments indicate that some form of archetypal sacrifice involving perhaps the phallic god of the Semites or Druids was involved. The male figurines have either painted or modelled upon them the characteristic Cretan loin-cloths or 'kilts', which also employed the body wrapper, the long loose piece of the kilt thrown over the chest and shoulder. Such a design became the National costume of the Scots. Significantly the wrapper would *cross* at the front and back, one cannot doubt the significance of the cross.

Professor Myres who excavated the site [123] stated that the kilt design presents: "very close analogies" with: "Scottish plaid", which is first wound round the waist and then has ends crossed in front, brought over the shoulders, crossed again on the back and secured by being tucked through the waist folds, so that the end hangs down like a tail. Even more startling in the votive finds is that whilst female figurines had the usual pinched waists, tight bodices and bell-shaped gowns (which may be indicative of the downward pointing vortex or bioplasma configuration of space), the headdress or hat looks remarkably modern. Even more startling is that in one model a brimmed hat is finished with a trimming of ROSETTES! The Rose as the prime emblem of the Rosicrucian's and the One World Order of The Rose today, with Scottish Rite Freemasonry as its highest Order, must be the prime contender as Druid ascendants for removing a whole belief system and Cosmology that was once freely available to all. Certainly this also has implications for Rose-lin chapel in Scotland. I eventually had to employ the help of the British Consul in Heraklion in Crete; in trying to gain access to museum stored but listed icons. There were numerous icons that I had found references for in research papers but which were "unavailable", and it was difficult to decide where these icons such as the one mentioned above had gone to! I noted tourists popping stones from archaeological sites into bags! And I was told there is a black market in archaeological pieces, although I do not know if that is true. It seems to me, that the Greeks unless they look after their heritage will one day find that the truly worthy and significant pieces which will attract tourists will no longer be "available".

I have previously mentioned that one energy Ley line running across central Scotland has been named the 'Rose Line' and it may pass through the Masonic Templar site, Roslin (Rose Line) Chapel. The Chapel is a Templar Mausoleum for the Sinclair family, who it is acknowledged, are descended from the Jesus Holy Bloodline. W.F.C. Wigston (cited), a nineteenth century writer, referred to Rosslyn Chapel as: "a Masonic Temple... the cradle of Scotch Masonry, *if not of something deeper still"*. In describing the symbolism of the Chapel, Wigston refers to the *rose* on the keystone of the east window, and he goes on to say: "The predominant ornaments are the Fleur-de-Lis, the Rose, and the Sunflower. Upon the roof of the aisles is the engrailed cross of the founders, St. Clairs, once hereditary Masters of Scotch Masonry". As Barry Dunford points out the enGRAILed cross is said to form the basis of the Heraldic Crest of Joseph of Arimathea. Furthermore, Mary, mother of Jesus, is referred to in mediaeval times as "SANTA MARIA DELLA ROSA", suggesting a rose lineage. Well obviously we are talking about a caste system, a royal and priestly dynasty relating to the Druids. The fact that the healing knowledge went underground only to surface in the 'miracles' of Jesus is understandable, together with the fact that the Immortality of the soul was to suffer an irreparable blow in the planned events of Golgotha - not a co-incidence I might add.

There is an interesting 'Ley' line alignment connecting Fingal's Cave in Scotland, a curious rock formation on the Isle of Staffa, to the Churchyard at Fortinall and further to an unusual megalithic stone in Glen Lyon and right through the Abbey on the Isle of Iona. The Rev. William Hamilton, Fellow of Trinity College Ireland in 1779, thought that the Island of Rathlin might be the surviving fragment of large tract of country that formerly may have united Staffa and the Giant's Causeway found on the coast of Ireland.[124] In ancient Celtic mythology, Fingal was a giant, perhaps a descendent of the "Giants of Old", who were believed to be contemporaneous with the ancient lost Lands of Atlantis. Whilst it has been suggested that this giant race may have possessed an ancient knowledge and technology in connection with the Earth's energy Grid and Chakra systems, the giants were those who had once beforehand prior to a magnetic reversal existed in different gravitational fields, alongside the dinosaurs who could only grow to such immense sizes, due to that decreased gravity field.

Comyns Beaumont, in Britain -*The key to World History*. States: "The famous Egyptian Book of the Dead, influenced completely by the epic of the Flood and composed in the name of Thoth (Hermes), in its ritual caused the souls of the dead to undergo a fanciful, final, gloomy pilgrimage to the sacred west, indeed,

I contend, to the very scene of the former shambles in Western Scotland, to the legendary Amenta, identified as the tiny island of Staffa, near Iona, in the Hebrides, where the wandering spirits were supposed to be judged by Osiris, and were rewarded or consumed according to their lives on Earth. Staffa lay in the very vortex of the greatest area of destruction at the time of the Flood - water being but one element concerned - and later became the Underworld of the Celts as it was of the Hellenes".

With regards to the Paliakastro site in Crete, besides rimmed rosette hats there was an even more startling hat with a low crown, the brim curving in front like an inverted horseshoe, described in archaeological papers. Once again I could not gain access to this icon in the museum. The horseshoe design of course was integral to the site design of Stonehenge, the Druidic Temple dedicated to the Solar King Apollo, on Salisbury plain in Wiltshire U.K. The site of megalithic stones has also been described a Solar observatory of its day.

The fact that the votive offerings at the Cretan site were associated with Fire and presumably the Phallic Semitic God is still retained in parts of the Scottish Highlands, when boys would light Beltane (May Day) fires and drive *cattle* over the ashes to charm them against the influence of "the evil eye". There is an interesting old quote from Britain, which runs:

> "Then doth the joyful feast of *John the Baptist* take his turne, when
> bonfires great, with lofty flame, in everie towne doe burne, ...desiring
> God that all their illes may be consumed..." (*Author's emphasis*)

The association with healing and the Phallic God and John The Baptist is made. The Swastika design of the old fire wheel was cast from the mountaintop and in *Alternative 4* I quote a Nazi secret group who buried wine bottles in the shape of a swastika from a mountaintop! The Trieskelion or swastika design goes back to Crete and appears in Minoan iconography as I discussed in more detail in *The Battle of The Trees*. The ox was a common votive offering at Palaistro in Crete with evident connections to the Minos Cult, which was introduced at the time of the Religious Revolution. Given the taboo on pork in the Jewish religion, it is interesting to note that the pig was taboo in Egypt, Palestine, Wales *and* Scotland. The pig taboo was according to Cretan legend based on the fact that the pig was the animal that suckled the god Zeus-Dionysus and was therefore sacred. It is interesting that the taboo should turn up in The British Isles!

It would be interesting to see research on the racial or genetic make up of early inhabitants of Crete, however there are said to be no remains from the early Neolithic period and I believe that archaeologists are mystified why there are no human remains from approximately the same era in Britain! Dated approximately 10 000 B.C.? Perhaps some archaeologists will provide more information and write to me. In the vast majority of Bronze Age graves and a later period, the faces are long and similar to Neolithic graves elsewhere in Greece. However there is also during the Bronze Age period the appearance of a broad-headed minority. Thus there appears to be two racial types present in Crete in The Bronze Age. Unfortunately because white supremacy has given genetics a bad name, perhaps not co-incidental! The suggestion by Sergi that the Mediterranean race probably originated in North Africa was met by a storm of criticism and genetics and the origins of races is definitely off bounds. The MRC takes great trouble to hide his tracks! Surely someone has spotted the white Egyptian Queen mummies married to Kings with obvious Semitic traits and asked where they came from and why the facial characteristics of the dynasties vary. Professor Elliot Smith has suggested that: "the broad-headed, long-bearded Asiatics are of Alpine or Armenoid type".

There are very many comparisons of apparent co-incidence to be made between Crete and Scotland. The Dolphin Fresco at Knossos with two Dolphins placed in anti-clockwise and clockwise position closely resembles the so-called "swimming elephants" on Scottish Sculptured stones. Further the Cailleach, who was a form of female deity in Scotland, grasped a "hammer" or "magic wand", reminding one not only of the Druid's wand and the Knossos double axe described in my first book, but also the Catholic Church in the 1970-80's and as I have mentioned Joan of Arc used to carry a small hammer into battle and carried a standard of the Dove on a blue background – poor woman *used and betrayed* as usual! The deity bears some resemblance to the Cretan goddess portrayed on her mountain supported by lions. According to legend when the standing-stones were struck with the "magic wand", they would immediately be transformed into giant warriors, fully armed and ready for battle. The wand was supposedly the goddess' symbol of fertility and authority harking back to re-incarnation as her gift to humanity. She was also portrayed looking over the sea" and was identified with rivers, lakes and overflowing wells. The Patriarchal team (tribe of Levi) forgot the story line since it had been changed and borrowed so often and confused the woman with the tribe of Judah and so they changed her confusingly into the "hag" and the mother of giants and the ancestress of the various tribes of mankind (thus associating her with Adam). This was undoubtedly a mix up of the earlier myth and the role of Danu, the goddess and mother of the Danaans who provided the Greek dynastic line. However it is certain that Scotland as in earlier Cretan custom saw the female with a higher authority. In Celtic tribes however she could become a chieftain but the Druids, where the real power lay, was strictly boy's country. Caesar remarked on the Matriarchal customs, which prevailed in certain parts of Britain, among the Scottish Picts and Celts, where descent was through the female line (matrilineal).

The important point of connection between Crete and Scotland however lies in the fact that a whole belief system and Cosmology was lost to the Early Minoans who shared their mysteries openly and withdrawn into the highest level of a Semitic and Druid caste system. The decline of the Minoan Civilization centres on that central issue. Whilst I will shortly come to aspects of the hidden science and the Cosmology, there is every indication that such advanced knowledge was known among the early Minoans. In *Alternative 4* I discussed the spiralling clockwise and anti-clockwise motions of energy associated with the vacuum energy or bioplasma vortices, together with gravitational anomalies, in respect of the UFO phenomenon. Further evidence that the Cabal who conducted the Religious Revolution had knowledge of the hidden science, comes from a Bronze Age icon from Crete (*Fig. 35*), which is a seal found in a tomb at Mochlos and dated the Middle Minoan III period (*Heraklion Museum No. 747*). There is a circular field enclosing a dolphin at the upper right moving in a *clockwise* direction. Below, moving in a *counter-clockwise* direction is another dolphin in the exact antithetical position. Completing the circle, at the left is a curved *bough* with *twenty-six* leaves. In the centre is a stylised *8-armed* octopus, where the arms are simulated. The arms are engraved with *six full circles* and a *crescen*t and the upper dolphin has a large circular *eye*. Thus the eight arms are connected to the eight images. Within the field at the left, is a *sun disc* with *nineteen* rays. I am hoping that you will have spotted the archetypal numbers and symbols (8 and 19 are connected to the rule of Solar Kingship, the bough is connected to the Druid Oak club of royalty, the eye of course is the third eye which is opened in initiate ritual with connection to Grid memories –Cabalistic science). The eye has implications for the One World Order – the all-seeing eye, which also occurs in the Illuminati and theOne Dollar note of America and can be seen on the Great Seal of the United States together with pyramid as triangle and where the sign of the two interlaced triangles is an occult sign (*Fig. 13 and 14*).

The bell-shaped skirt common to the so-called priestesses or "snake goddess'" of Knossos (re-produced in *The Battle of The Trees*) with its tiered flounce reminds one of the pyramidal shape of the downward or morphogenetic bioplasma vortex, which contains the genetic evolutionary past memories and which were channelled: The flounced layers perhaps indicative of the levels or tiers of secret knowledge. Why did the priestesses have bare breasts? One can guess in respect of a hierarchy of male priests! This must hark back to the suckling of the infant Zeus. In a Cave at Cogul, near Lerida in Spain, a painting of the Aurignacian period circa 10 000 B.C. shows several females with "wasp waists" and bell-mouthed gowns comparable to Cretan figurines, dancing round a nude male figure and a phallus image of this culture stage has also been discovered. Evidently then the cult who entered Knossos and installed such iconography were either acting on an oral tradition handed down from prehistoric times, or they sub-consciously re-enacted a past memory. However it is evident that a tiered and secret knowledge may have existed and probably did from the very earliest of times.

Fig.35   **A Cretan seal from Mochlos of the Middle Minoan III Period**
An octopus, sun and moon symbols, two dolphins, and fertility bough.
(Heraklion Museum no.74)

In Minoan finds from Palaikastro, groups of figurines dancing around a snake Goddess with birds, which may be doves as the epiphany of the goddess, indicates a very early recognition of the magic circle and the Grid. Such dances of circles and spirals are still retained in Cretan folk dances today. It seems likely then, that the Elite already had even in Pre-historic times certain knowledge, which was added to from the Knossos site in the Religious Revolution period. It also seems probable that the Elite used knowledge to channel information from the Grid, an action in itself, which would precipitate everything that had gone before, in a cyclical nature. Undoubtedly this must be an icon from the Religious Revolution era of re-positioning of the archetypes. The dolphin seal (Fig. 35) also shows the Solar-Lunar significances as the 19 years Solar-Lunar Cycle, which was the period between Eclipses and which the Druids calculated accurately via presumably their Solar Observatory at Stone Henge. The bough with its leaves is a fertility symbol, usually related to the Twin Solar Kings. The crescent represents the waxing moon crescent, giving birth to the new. The appearance of the 19-year cycle is unusual since the year of the rule for a Solar King in Greece was eight years and much of the iconography and mythology relate to that archetypal number, although to change a monarchy the 19-year cycle was used. The twenty-six leaves represent 2 X 13 or the Thirteenth month in the Tree Alphabet and doubled, since there are two Twin kings. The Beth-Luis-Nion and Boibel-Loth alphabets are a genuine relic of Druidism and were orally transmitted down through the centuries, thus here in this seal there is very definite evidential proof of the thirteenth tribe of Judah. I have used such alphabets in The Battle of The Trees, to decipher many mysteries attached to the story of the Holy Grail. The Ogham Alphabet consists of thirteen consonants and five vowels, giving 19 letters, which also corresponded to trees in the ancient Tree Alphabet. Each letter is named after a tree or shrub, which holds the significance of the letter, which invariably held religious significance, thus religious mysteries are locked up in the alphabets. The thirteenth month or letter was R or the Elder (Ruis), is a waterside tree, associated with witches. The elder is considered unlucky. The Elder is said to have been the Crucifixion tree and it has a long- standing association with death. In English folklore to burn logs of Elder "brings the Devil into the house". The white flowers make the Elder the White Goddess (her death aspect) in the Druid alphabet: Elder runs from November 25th in the Calendar and the Winter Solstice, to December 22nd in the thirteenth month. That mixing little bee at it again! Re-positioning the archetypes, creating lots of significances that were never intended and making it so horribly complex, when in fact all there was, was a truth of Re-incarnation and the Cosmology which had to be understood in order to release man from the trap. The standard method of the magicians and the true evil ones was to take all her ideas, muddle them up with lots of significances, broadcast all those significances to the people and walk away with the truth, which was hidden from mankind!

If the old Atlantean World Order or the Celtic Commonwealth (Order) and its Communistic Theocracy continued, it did so within the secret groups. I traced one such group in *The Battle of The Trees*. Thirteen was a particular significant number to the Prieuré de Sion a secret group in France. A group that appeared to control the Vatican in the 1980's at the time a certain Pope was waiving Druidic "wands" and tapping "eggs". The group through its Grand Master was connected to the *Vaincre* magazine article, with the religious and political aims of a Federal European Super State. The old goals did not die they merely marched on down that road, towards shining Solar Kingship and Elitist Communism (run by the far right): But you won't see it printed in the "people's paper" *The Sun*, not even on 'woman's' page 3! Where the masses in Britain usually are educated into a woman's role on planet Earth. Deary me! A bit far removed even from the Druids and Celts, where at least they made Chieftaincy! I proposed in *The Battle of The Trees*, that the Apocalyptic Revelation was the One World Order plan, followed either *consciously or sub-consciously* by the Elite, the former being more likely. The fact that "The Great City", suffers a large earthquake prior to the close of things in that account, lead met to wonder who exactly had the World Order proposed as the candidate, Knossos in **Crete** or Scotland in **Britain**. Knossos I discovered by applying Pythagorean geometry to the mountain peaks which surround the cave in which Zeus was born - the Psychro Cave produced seven triangles, which could be glossed in the Apocalyptic account, as "Seven Mountains", on which "The Great Cit sits". However the constant parallels between Scotland and Crete led me to consider whether in fact it would be Crete that had been elected for destruction or in fact London and Rothschild's "the City". The fact that David Icke admits to channeling (tuning into the Grid) might explain why he saw the white cliffs of the South Coast of England (curiously named the Seven Sisters) fall into the sea. Either he foresaw a climax to the erratic weather conditions that we are experiencing or some past Apocalyptic memory which saw the Atlanteans destroyed or he had picked up some prior thought already recorded. This does not discount an unnatural manipulation of the Ley line system utilizing Tesla technology. Has it already been decided that London will fulfill the apocalyptic account and plan? Alternatively, the purposeful disinformation line of Volcanoes which erupted on the neighboring Island of Santorini off Crete in the Aegean sea, which caused a tidal wave in Crete and destroyed the Minoan Civilization may be supported for the entire purpose, that if it occurred again, the demise of that beautiful moon in the orbit of Greece - Crete could be placed prophetically at the door of God's (phallic) work. The latter alternative would require releasing the entirety of the knowledge here and since there is no intention of doing that, then I assume that London will become the World Order candidate. In having revealed this story I trust London and Crete will survive. You might think that this is a somewhat insane suggestion, but as I have taken the pains to explain, the MRC case follows to the letter his 'script', dramatizing previous 'scripts' which are all identical, the MRC case would not even consider his actions as insane since in his own mind he *is* the phallic *God* and his mind requires him to subconsciously turn another page of his past and follow it mindlessly, dramatizing his psychological case to the very end, an end that presumably brought Atlantis to its demise, with the misuse of the hidden science.

CRETAN ZEUS AND A THEOCRACY

The figure- of- 8 shield that emerged in Cretan iconography at the time of the Religious Revolution in Crete is also noted as a "spectacle" design on Scottish standing stones. The figure- of- 8 has great significance in relation to the hidden science. In terms of atomic structure and the filling of electron shells around a nucleus in Chemistry it denotes completeness of the shell, with a full complement of electrons. In terms of the material god Zeus-Dionysus it represented completeness. Cretan Zeus was not the same as the Indo European or Aryan Zeus. The goddess Demeter who taught the world agriculture had a son Dionysus, a word derived from the root div, meaning "shining" or "bright" which in Sanskrit is Dyaus, and the old Germanic name of Odin was Divus.The Cretan Zeus-Dionysus links not only with Osiris of Egypt, but also with Tammuz of Babylon, Ashur of Assyria, Attis of Phyrygia, Adonis of Greece, Agri of India, the Germanic Scef and the Scot-Irish Diarmid; truly then a somewhat international God and presumably a root God that might be suitable for a Theocratic United States of the West. It is impossible to say at what period Zeus-Dionysus was introduced into Crete, although it was part of the Religious Revolution period c. 1400B.C.

A mural on the wall of the Summer Smoking Room at Cardiff Castle Wales U.K. shows Amalthea and this was the name of the *goat* that provided milk to feed Zeus-Dionysus. Given that this mural formed a part of Rosicrucian and Scottish Rite Freemasonry, including the Rose-Croix degree then whilst the masses worship Jehovah, Zeus-Dionysus appears to be the God of the World Order. Guessing the name of the God in secret groups was a high game, since it divulged their secrets and goals, thus the name was usually never stated. You may be thinking here, that such a guessing game is totally irrelevant today, but in the psychological case of those who run this planet yesterday and today are not distinguishable, they cannot differentiate between space and time. **Yesterday is today, in the dramatization.** The perpetual striving to fulfil the goal of a One World Order has existed from Babel, Atlantis, Celtic Commonwealth, Third Reich and today as Europeans are stampeded over the cliff of yet another World Order, the name of the God is as relevant as ever;

I have already identified Scottish Rite Freemasonry as having substantial background in the Cretan mysteries however any God must surely fit with the role of Jesus. When in *The Gospel according to the Egyptians* Shelom asked the Lord: "How long shall death prevail?" He answered: "So long as you women bear children" And when she asked again: "I have done well then in not bearing children/," He answered: "Eat every plant but that which is bitter..." And when she inquired at what time the things concerning which she had questioned Him

should be known, He answered: "When you women have trampled on the garment of shame and when the two become one, and when the male with the female is neither male nor female" And the Saviour said in the same Gospel: "I have come to destroy the works of the Female".
(*Clement of Alexandria - Stromata iii*)

This is obviously as I have previously indicated, a reference to Hermes and the bisexual nature of that god in the post Religious Revolution era. Thus homosexuality and degradation of women is likely to be condoned by men who hold this belief, which is the nature of the World Order. The birth of this God in the psychro cave of Crete is recorded in myth as the birth of Zeus who was to become **Captain** of the *Twelve* Olympian Gods in Greece and therefore omnipotent, giving rise to the concept of one God. The numbers here again with the Captain or Zeus making thirteen, implies that Zeus was the product of the tribe of Judah the lost thirteenth tribe. The association of Zeus with monopolistic power is thus a political aim manifested in religious doctrine and must include the fact that certain knowledge was acquired during the Religious Revolution, which obliterated matriarchal power. This knowledge undoubtedly referred to the physics of the Grid and Vortex fields. The game was now on, since this would inevitably lead to an enormous battle between those who lost the knowledge (Female) and those who gained it (Male). Ownership was not important, but source was, since the only way to resolve and dissolve lies was to tell the truth. However it was unlikely that the group who stole from source would ever in their great ego and arrogance admit that truth, and thus the problem would persist. It was not co-incidental that Mary Magdalene prophesied to Jesus regarding the cut on her left arm that: "There will be no peace on this Earth until the cut is healed".

The problem is that the **lie is an altered reality** and persists as a thought pattern within the geometric of the vortex fields. I will discuss this more fully in a later section, but the important point here to recognise, is that the trap persists when force (thought /postulate – thought/ counter postulate) is required to keep that out- reality in place. You could say that matriarchalism was one thought and it was counter postulated by another thought of patriarchalism, but which one held the reality or truth. It was no co-incidence that St. John stated: "And the truth shall set you free". In fact both religions held significances, which were not intended, and yet both held some aspect of the truth, but no religion held the whole truth. In fact the Grail message was a philosophy coupled with a cosmology and physical laws, thus physics was really part of this message. The World Order perpetuated that wrong by altering (Alter-is) the source *and* the truth and worse still, retaining that within their own hierarchy of knowledge is to perpetuate the trap, since in any level of *understanding* which occurs, *ultimate reality which is truth* is a requirement, together with *communication*. I am sure the Scientologists will recognise this as **the communication cycle**. As all communication lines were cut or became owned by the elite, it became exceedingly difficult to make the other side of the story known and the individual would find it impossible to be given a platform to speak, which usually resulted in the market square roasting as a heretic! As Ghandi so beautifully stated: "The truth is still the truth, even if you are in a minority of one". The Godhead was not bisexual neither was the whole system of Solar Kingship intended or the monstrous complexities of gods and goddesses that arose from this single out- reality. One can just envisage the Teacher trying to explain that once a **spirit** leaves a body it is neither male nor female and has the potential to enter either sex **bodyline**! It must have been an uphill struggle to get a thought into the Grid (and into Pre-historic man's head!) that had no niche in a pattern that had been controlled for millions of years by the MRC. I will come to new thought patterns later. However one perceives that the system of archetypes was used to give man some pictures of the subject, certainly man at that time only thought in terms of masses and what he could see. Concepts of space, energies and spirits with a belief in Re-incarnation must have been a difficult concept to teach and thus the system of archetypal symbols to represent a complex idea or philosophy readily recognisable and communicable, was a very good idea when related to the *visible* migration of birds, the death and birth of crops in winter and spring, the swinging icon all of which represented the idea: "As I go, so must I return", the *calming philosophy* that overtook the predominant emotion of *fear* that the despotic Kings had instilled into the people. It was this idea and the resultant lift in emotions that gave birth to the high civilization of the Early Minoans and as a lesson perhaps should be recognised in our time, which is experiencing a decline in civilization and where the spiritual message and light has been almost but extinguished.

The introduction of the idea of Twin Kings, which was eventually fused into Solar Kingship allowing the World Elite a political method of ruling as **Elitist Communism which was the basis of Plato's Republic**, and as a method is probably the resurrected form of government to be used in Europe with Solar monarchy replaced a secret priesthood or men who belong to secret groups and hold great wealth. If Hermes was the product of trying to remove the woman from the story by joining her (as Goddess) with the Twin Kings then this lead to all sorts of other misunderstandings and another variation was the Great Mother as a bi-sexual. The Libyan Neith, was occasionally depicted as androgyne. Isis was the Egyptian "bearded Aphrodite". The beard as significant of the goat and thirteenth tribe, combined with woman. 'The wrong end of the stick', travelled worldwide and everybody added a little bit more complexity to it. Isis became: "the woman who was made a male"! As one of the religious chants states: "by her father Osiris".

Zeus was also regarded as bisexual and the idea was even incorporated into The Bible in the Isaiah account as the truth of the beginning: "The Father is the Mother". When Pope John Paul I (Albino Luciani), quoted this to a disturbed meeting of Cardinals, it may have resulted in his mysterious death, where an autopsy was refused and he was embalmed at the Vatican within 24 hours. His career, which was short and followed Pope John XXIII (Angelo Roncalli), who had displayed the occult symbols associated with the Illuminati. The Vatican was at that time following the dictates of The One World Order openly and their God was clearly Cretan Zeus. Certainly in the 1980's the Grand Master of the group The Prieuré de Sion had pronounced that there were:" Neither good Popes or bad" with the implication being that the Pope would follow the edicts of the group (*The Battle of The Trees*).

One of the Orphic hymns of the mysteries set forth:

> Zeus was the first of all, Zeus last, the Lord of lightning
> Zeus was the head, the middle, from him all things were created;
> Zeus was man and again Zeus was the Virgin Eternal.

The bi-sexual nature implied. Interestingly though "lightning" associates Zeus with man as a God himself, utilising power over energies hitherto associated with some Divine power. Man's control of the hidden science was displayed in early times, where he evidently possessed Cabalistic ritual magic, which could *induce weather phenomena*. Man's idea of himself as a god, merely flipped one more stage and he became God, with power over all on planet Earth. Doctors scientists including Physicists today fell foul of that very trap as they become masters of science and many would become the sorcerer's apprentices as they involved themselves with the hidden science. The Prehistoric Cave painting from Kalurungari, Calder River, Walcott in N.W. Australia shows 'kaluru' (*Plate 4*), the so-called 'lightning man'.

Adonis was similarly described as "both maiden and youth" and the Babylonian Nannar (Sin), the Moon-god, was "father" and "Mother" of gods and men: Likewise the Syrian Baal. In India Shiva is sometimes depicted with the right side female and the left male. The Persian Mithras was a god and goddess combined. Bearded Steatopygous female figurines of women with large fatty deposits on their thighs and buttocks were carved from ivory similar to those found in the pre-Dynastic graves of Egypt and the bisexual nature may have arisen as a belief even earlier than early Minoan times and the belief merely transferred to the truth of events circa 10 000 B.C. since the minimum date of 20 000 B.C. has been given for the close of the Palaeolithic age. The earliest settlement of people at Knossos, has been assigned to c. 10 000 B.C. The date I associate with a true impulse and message together with a Cosmology appearing on Earth. Although there is evidence that the message in these early times was not merely confined to Greece, but appeared in France and Africa.

The discovery that Crete was the birth place of Aegean Civilization, which radiated in Pre-Hellenic times throughout Europe:" the little leaven that leavened the whole lump", was an indication of the level of aesthetic art and culture that was inherent within the early belief system - Re-incarnation. The Aurignacian cave paintings in France, followed by the Magdalenian epoch were evidence of a high creative and artistic culture. "The resemblances", writes Angelo Masso: "between the most ancient female figures in France and the Neolithic figures of Crete and Egypt are very striking" [125] the impulse was not confined to Crete then. What a difference between the free flowing art and aesthetic high level of creative achievement that was seen in Early Minoan times, compared to the decline after the Religious Revolution era c. 1400 B.C. where figures are shown in stilted and controlled poses with no free flowing LIFE FORCE! Worshiping stone pillars, the Semitic belief that the spirit of Zeus was within that! If any of you still puzzle of Stanley Kubrick's *2001 - A Space Oddusy*, it was a tale of the Semitic God and pillar worshipand since apes were involved presumably the Sethites first heard the word of God, but we will come to the Sethites later. Naughty boys these Hollywood film- makers! But I bet it stuck on *your* time track! Did not Marlon Brando once state that Hollywood was governed by a Jewish element – which tirbes though that's the question! Which might account for all those Apocalyptic movies and the appearance of *that dolphin ring* in the film *Independence Day* where the Earth was saved by an American and Jew (*Alternative 4*) and the film *The Patriot* – has Hollywood become another propaganda game between the two groups who have moved on from CAPUT and ORMUS the names of the secret groups I decoded in *The Battle of The Trees* and The Grail Romances! The pillar enclosed the God's spirit. In Scottish-Irish legend, the Cailleach, after the period of the spring storms, transforms himself into: "a grey stone looking over the sea". The stone (tablets) of course was the God of Moses and the Druids who followed Mosaic Law revered Moses.

I suspect that the bearded Aphrodite Steatopygous figures in Europe and Crete may have been the dawning of realisation that the act of creation and birthing by woman, hitherto seen as a mystery, did have something to do with the male. Man excluded from the birthing process, sought his own create on the level of all male hunting parties and eventually secret groups. The bisexual God was merely the extension and glorification of man *as* God, which sought to impress itself on any truth that may have occurred in Crete. Zeus of the Hellenic Greeks was similarly a Father God and was imposed on the Pre-Hellenic inhabitants of Greece after conquest. In the same way that Moses received significantly, his laws from God in the form of stone tablets (pillars), then King Minos was supposed to have received his code of laws from his Father Zeus, when he was visited his cave, the psychro cave on Mount Ida, according to Strabo.[126] Since a Cabal directed the Religious Revolution from this cave utilising Cabalistic magic, then we can assume that the laws in fact originated here. The first Laws of Europe may be traced to Gortyn in Crete, where they still remain as engraved stone pillars or tablets. Europe itself takes its name from the myth of Europae from Crete. If the World Order prefer Cretan Zeus in his bisexual role as the bearded Baphomet, it is because he was a Messianic type deity, who died each year a violent death and came to life again and thus incorporated the early perception of God common to many societies. Once again you can see how the belief in Re-incarnation and the Teacher's use of yearly migration of birds and growth of crops, was distorted to suit the Cabal and their control of a monarchy which they ejected annually initially and which was later to combine with the Solar Lunar calendar. Egyptian Osiris who was slain by Set and became Judge of the Dead compares favourably with Revelations and St. John apparently received the word of God in a cave on the Greek Island of Patmos, in similar fashion to Zeus. One of the judges of the dead in the Homeric Hades was a Cretan Dionysus or Zeus-Dionysus and Diodorus Siculus maintained that the mysteries of Dionysus were identical with those of Osiris. The Cretan Zeus-Dionysus therefore links not only with Osiris, but also with Tammuz of Babylon, Greece, Agri of India and his brother Indra, the Germanic Scef and Frey and Heimdal and the Scottish Diarmid. The Cretan philosophical-religious synthesis was to become the truly international religion. However the religious goal of European Union was thrown out I believe in the 1980's for the more expedient role of Elitist Communism run by the far rich right. Plato's Republic converted to A THEOCRACY whereby the New World Order would be run by an elite priesthood who alone retained the religious mysteries would become the reality. A somewhat predictable outcome since a Theocracy was always the goal in any World Order programme.

Sir Arthur Evans, who first threw light on the significance of pillars and other symbols in Crete, believed that tree and pillar worship in Palestine and Anatolia was: "taken over from the other stock", by Semites and Hittites. The colonizing Philistines and Lycians who were of Aegean origin caused a later fusion of Early Minoan ideas into Anatolia and Palestine. "The undoubted parallelism observable between the Tree and Pillar cult of the Mycenaean (Aegean) and that of the Semitic World", writes Sir Arthur Evans: "should be always regarded from this broad aspect... The Coincidences that we find, so far as they are to be explained by the general resemblance presented by a parallel stage of religious evolution, may be regarded as parallel survivals due to ethnic elements with European affinities, which on the east Mediterranean shores largely underlay the Semitic... The worship of the sacred stone or pillar known as Masseba or nosb is very characteristic of Semitic religion" [127]

This is in my opinion a distinctly narrow view and discounts that the ancient world was governed by a controlling Elite, whose Kings were supplanted into many Dynasties and supports the find of white Egyptian Queen mummies. The fact that pillar worship and tree worship were linked also raises the question of the Druids, biblical Adamites - a white race and their use of the Tree Alphabet and Ogham script, a form of which may be enciphered on the as yet fully undeciphered Linear A and B tablets of Crete. The Druids as Semites not only worshipped Trees, but also held ceremonies on sacred hills and in caves and let us not forget that Golgotha was played out on such a hill, which was with the tomb archetypally significant. The two upright pillars supporting the tomb at Golgotha, with the lintel across parallels the Lions gate at Mycenae and there is every indication that Mycenae was a part of The World Order of that time. Indeed Agamemnon wore a solid gold death mask indicating Solar Kingship. The two pillars supporting the Philistine temple of Dagon, which were pulled down by Sampson is another entwined tale in this story. The pillars and two lions indicative of Twin Kingship and lintel across, the Herm, with Twin Kings fused as Hermes the bisexual deity.

When Chairman Mao Tse Tung of China proclaimed that all: "Religion is Poison", in the sense that religion has incorporated significant lies and a means of controlling humanity, he was correct. However the original truth and Cosmology was far from "poison", it was the very "ambrosia", meant for humanity but sipped only by the Elite and secret groups as gods who would rule. When China invaded Tibet destroying monasteries and presumably taking their archives, just a little bit more truth was lost into secret archives. Just a little bit more freedom of belief was lost. The Tibetans expecting the appearance of their Buddha in 1950 instead were slaughtered. Truth as it emerges however is not without its back- lash. You may or may not accept the facts and theories in this book, that is your choice; and the religion or the beliefs a man holds cannot be enforced, neither should one remove facts from man to enforce his ignorance of the past whilst re-writing that past to suit political agendas. In February 2001 the Buddhist statues in Afghanistan that give some indication of the past and Islam, are being mortared and obliterated, but that is to limit understanding not enhance it. The proof I lay is often built on a scrupulous observation of that past left in archaeological finds. To destroy the past, is to follow the methods of secret groups. In *Alternative 4* I gave a UFO account where the witness was told to: "Interrogate these ruins" which I certainly have done in the case of Knossos!

The idea of Twin Kingship replaced the early truth of The Cycle of Eternal Return and Re incarnation. In the late Minoan II seal (Fig. 10) post Religious Revolution, the "spectacle" pattern or the figure-of- eight, which occurred on Scottish standing- stones is quite clearly illustrated in the figure together with what is described as an "impaled triangle". The figure-of-8 pattern occurs on the wall of the Queen's chamber at Knossos as the figure- of- 8 shield. The triangle indicates a pyramidal apex and since it is impaled from the apex to the base of the triangle with what looks like a rod or staff or perhaps Druidic wand then its position with the figure-of-8, which I have previously linked to Atomic structure and the complete filling of electron shells in the nucleus, is interesting; particularly also because the shield is a symbol of a weapon. Thus, it might be assumed that power for an elite group lay in some knowledge of atomic physics as part of the hidden science.

The double axe motif more fully discussed in *The Battle of The Trees*, was the symbol of the Minoan Great Goddess, who was mistress of Labyrinth: "The Lady of the Labyrinth", according to the Linear B tablet from Knossos. The labrys was a sacrificial axe, with two crescent-shaped blades, emblematic of the last phase and first phase of the Moon-Goddess. The waning crescent, after the dark phase of the moon gives birth to the new moon crescent and it was this astrological significance that became applied to Twin Kings. The significance of the double-bladed axe was that Solar Kings, who die by it, would be reborn. As one King died and united with Her the Great Goddess, he would be reborn through Her, with Her gift of Immortality. The idea of Re-incarnation was kept alive in this belief, but unfortunately it was the first downgrade of the truth, for originally no Kingship was involved. The two blades cut both ways and will slay the solar-bull (a beast of the calendar) and the solar lion in turn, but are yearly reborn in a circle or cycle of Eternal Return.

The circle originally was meant to portray the very nature of the trap and Re-incarnation as a necessity of that trap. Her gift was not the trap. Thus you can see from a very early date how very muddled the truth became. Originally Her gift was to teach man of the trap and inform him of his Immortality and the cycle of death and rebirth created within the Grid as trap. A straight line on the truth was never adhered to, as the truth was withdrawn and manipulated by secret groups. The labyrinth became a pattern derived from the double axe and a symbol of death and life after death, but more importantly a symbol of rebirth or Re-incarnation of SACRED KINGS. The pyramid became an emblem of that too. Early Minoan funery practise of leaving the dead in the foetal position, awaiting rebirth among sand and sea shells was common to Crete and other places in the World where this belief was adhered to. The Goddess connected to the sea "as I flow away so shall I return" and agriculture "as I die, so shall I return". The tides and agricultural cycles becoming incorporated very early on in this belief and utilised for educational purposes by the Teacher. The appearance of pillars at Knossos incised with the double axe motif was an indication that a Semitic influence was already re-positioning the symbols and knowledge. The Cycle of Eternal Return then became Re-incarnation for divinities or Holy Men; The Second Coming is another slant on this belief. Women of course did not acquire Holy status and who ever heard of women Messiahs! Well understandable of course, since these beliefs and ideas were controlled by male Theocratic priesthoods. Women of course and presumably the slaves went off to that great big pile of washing up in the sky, governed by the Plato's Greek democracy, where women and slaves had no say only the rich merchants! While men in (Masonic) aprons conducted more important affairs on Earth!

The archetype of the double- bladed axe was perhaps the enigmatic "weapon of immense hidden power", so elusively referred to in the Indian epic of the *Mahabharata*, where the warrior Arjuna receives a celestial weapon from the god Shiva: "And that weapon then began to wait upon Arjuna". The narrative proceeds: "And the gods and the **Dan**avas (Titans), beheld that terrible weapon in its embodied form stay by the side of Arjuna with immeasurable energy". The implication here is that there was a misuse of Grid energies, perhaps rather like the position today where Vacuum energy and geometry is being misused in the so-called "Star Wars" programme allegedly developed for defence purposes in America. I have emphasised DAN since this is the root for Danaans, the so-called gods who came from Greece and evidently imparted their secrets to The Druids. This then may be the story behind the catastrophe that the Druids held a memory of, with: "the sea bursting its bounds", following some conflagration and evil misuse of the hidden science. If the Re-incarnations of the Druids now exist in an American- based group (Illuminati?), then it is predictable that the theatrical play or script will follow the same worn out old path in the last scene - The Apocalyptic Final Act, where the final curtain comes down and the players wait for Act 1 to begin with new scenery before **THEATRE EARTH** continues with the same **DRAMATIZATIONS** or script. Meanwhile the audience of humanity sleep on.

Weapons in the animistic stage of primitive culture were believed to be possessed of spirits and were given names e.g. the sword of the Scoto-Irish folk hero Finn-Mac-Coul was called "Mac-au-Luin". The belief goes back to Palaeolithic times even in Egypt where: "The common word given by the Egyptians to God and and spirits of every kings and beings of all sorts and kinds and forms which were supposed to possess any superhuman or supernatural power was" says Professor Budge: "Neter". The hieroglyph used as the determinative of this word, and also as an ideograph, is the axe with a handle. The common word for Goddess is Netert, implying source of power. Professor Budge shows that: "from the texts wherein the hieroglyphics are presented it is tolerably clear that the axe head was fastened to its handle by means of thongs of leather". This gives further meaning to the SOURCE of Grid geometry and knowledge that appeared in the curious stones wrapped with leather thongs and which were found in Crete and were also found in the Aurignacian and Magdalenian periods of Franco-Cantabrian Art in France with implications of Cosmology and the Grid geometry of the UVG120 sphere. Professor Budge adds: "It is now, I think, generally accepted that the use of the stone axe precede that of the flint arrow head, or the flint knife; and it thoroughly agrees with the little we know of the workings of the mind of primitive man that this, the first weapon that came into his hands, should have been the first material object to which he offered worship." [128] Not so "primitive" perhaps! However when art and healing are absent and the hidden science is present controlled by secret groups, you will find technology and weapons. Clearly then as may be illustrated by the *Mahabharata*, which clearly speaks of gods in flying machines, the Grid and its energies were known to the Elite and were used by them for their own ends of manipulative power. That was a position, which presumably led to the catastrophe, which the Druids spoke of, however the position in this cycle was to uniquely change when spiritual intervention occurred.

A priest in Chaldean dress on one Assyrian agate cylinder worships the axe. The axe also appears as a symbol in the prehistoric remains of the funeral caves of the Marne of Scandinavia and in America and I have already referred to the Freemont people of Utah who possessed bowls decorated in the chequer design motif of the labyrinth and who it seems practised cannibalism. The axe also appears on the standing stones in Brittany. The double axe became the distinctive symbol of the Cretan God (post Religious Revolution). A gold signet seal from Crete shows the axe placed beside a goddess seated beneath a vine, with the sun and crescent moon in the upper part of the signet enclosed by "water rays". However once again it is curious how the obvious *Sun- rays* representing Solar Kingship are glossed over. Hovering high on the left of the signet seal is the 8-form shield, significantly with human head, and uplifted arm, with a staff or spear in the hand and a single leg below. This indicates not only the Druid wand (as staff) but one leg indicates one half of Twin Kingship and Noah was apparently lamed in one leg, as was Jesus, which identifies them as Solar Kings. The goddess in the seal is approached by votaries, who make offerings of flowers including Iris and Hyacinth (Iris is blue which was the colour of death in Early Minoan Crete and the Hyacinth is perfumed and reflects the painting of Salvador Dali *The Persistance du Memoire*, where the perfume bottle was indicative of the Goddess and linked to the Mary Magdalene later. The suffix 'nth' (Labyrinth) as symbolic of the "Great Goddess " says Professor Burrows has continually shown: "to belong to that interesting group of Pre-Hellenic words that survives both in place-names like Corinth (Corinthos) and Zakynthos ... and in common words that would naturally be borrowed by the invaders from the old population." [129] This is really how vast muddles occurred, this borrowing from sources and then not keeping records! Or references! Early

Christian Churches called their Monasteries Laurai, (òr Labri) and Lura, lavra or labra, signified "passage", symbolism of the Labyrnth or maize which was a place of re-birth!

Why should the Scottish Rite Freemasons and Rosicrucian's or the Rose Croix (the group I assume Lord Bute who laid the Smoking Room at Cardiff Castle was a member of) depict Amalthia the Goatherd holding the right horn of the Zeus- bull-calf, beside flowing water with a fish on the tiled mural at Cardiff Castle? The answer lies in the name of their God - Cretan Zeus. The legend runs as follows: It had been prophesied by Uranus and Gaia that Cronus would be displaced by one of his own children. This is the replacement of the old 'dying'; or waning moon and King, by the new waxing moon and his Solar Twin, which eventually became his son and successor. Gaia was the Earth Mother, and Uranus the sky Father and Cronus has always been associated with time. Thus somewhere in this myth is the historical truth of a significant event, which only survived in myth. Cronus according to myth tried to avert his overthrow (by Matrilineal succession of his sons), by swallowing each babe that was born to his wife Rhea. Rhea went to Crete and in the Dictaean mountain cave (male) or Psychro Cave, gave birth to the infant Zeus. This indicated that Zeus ruled through matrilineal succession as a Solar King. In order to trick Zeus Rhea gave her husband a stone dressed up as a babe, which he swallowed. Rhea's priests, the Curetes provided milk from Amalthea the goat. Thus in the tiled mural at Cardiff Castle, there is a connection to Cretan Zeus and Minos, the Bull-Minotaur or Solar King. Thus one might conclude that the real historical event which this myth relates, is the supplant of a Solar King into Crete, presumably King Minos, who ruled through matrilineal succession. Minos indeed may well have been a World Order puppet King derived from a dynastic stock retained in Scotland by The Druids derived through matrilineal succession through the Greek line of the Tuatha de Danaan and Anna the alleged grandmother of Jesus, although there was the question of Magdalene's stolen genealogies. The Celts believed the Tuatha de Danaan were gods and of course they obtained their mysteries from Crete and the Teacher, who gave them openly. Thus the Tuatha de Danaan from the Peloponnese, where Hermes was born significantly may have abused their knowledge by passing it to the Druids in return for Kingly power. This Greek/Celtic dynastic stock may well have been used to supply the matrilineal Egyptian dynasties (where mummies show that at a certain period the Queens were white and blond) and the Mycenae dynasty. We know that Agamemnon at Mycenae was a Solar King. The rule of King Minos then, presumably accounts for the Religious Revolution after which a system of taxation was introduced and the period of rule seems to have continued until Ariadne gave Theseus the means to put an end to it, together with its human sacrifices recorded in myth, where seven maidens and youths were brought from Athens. The change of Monarchy then occurred every 19 years and ensured which ensured continuous rule under Solar Kingship overseen by a priesthood i.e. a Theocracy. Sacrifice was also a Druid custom.

Amalthea and the Bull-Minos in the tile mural at Cardiff Castle are besides running water, which indicates "The underground Stream" of The Holy Grail or wisdom and the presence of the fish in the stream connect Scottish Rite Freemasonry and the Rose-Croix to this whole line of hidden knowledge and The Druids. The fact that Amalthea holds the right horn of the bull Minos, refers to the legend that Zeus (as Minos) grew so strong that soon after his birth he broke off one of the goat's horns, it afterwards became known as Cornucopia, the "horn of plenty", because it became filled with whatever its owner desired and Kings drank from a horn, symbolising that their immense wealth and power was due to their control over hidden knowledge and undoubtedly hidden science. When Zeus grew up he rescued his brothers and sisters from the stomach of Cronus and also took forth the stone, which had been substituted for himself: this became the stone sacred to worshippers and this throws new light on stone or pillar worship, in so far as the God embodied in the stone, was I conclude no less than Cretan Zeus with a connection to Moses who was an initiate of the Rite of Memphis. This certainly would mean that Moses of stone tablet and law giving fame was a member of a secret group whom utilised the Cretan mysteries alongside Semitic origins. The group that would fulfil this was the Druids, the biblical Adamites. We know indeed that the Druids followed Mosaic Law. Jesus too as a Semite and Druid would have followed Cretan Zeus or Hermes as His God, a Solar King as I recounted in *The Battle of The Trees*, ruling by Matrilineal succession through a Celtic dynasty and his grandmother Anna. However we know that there is according to my own account a question mark over the genealogies. Is it not the case that the dynastic root of the Danaans (the Greek/Celtic line) provided Queen's and this would account for the blond-haired wife Thuya married to Yuya who were the parents of Queen Tiye, the wife of Amenhotep II of Egypt and thus the grandparents of Akhenaten and great-grandparents of Tutankhamun? Kings however may have come from the Egyptian dynastic root and Jesus may have come from this root, alternatively as I suggested Jesus despite his Greek/Celtic line, may have been fostered out at an early age to parents from the Egyptian Semitic line with the goal of uniting both lines and tribes in marriage of Jesus and Magdalene, however the promise of releasing the Greek mysteries and Re-incarnation was not adhered to and the Greek genealogies were stolen in a double agent plot. The child of the union of Jesus and Magdalene was then used to propagate a Merovingian line or dynasty ostensibly from the Royal Davidic line. Thus Christianity could erase all traces of the battle of 12 versus 13. Not far from Mount Juktas, which is alleged to be the tomb of Cretan Zeus on the Island of Crete, there is the small church of Aphendi Kristos, or the Lord Christ. I very nearly missed it on my trek to Zeus' birthplace, but there it is, nestled discretely away. Clearly it has a name, which traditionally clings in a special way to the ancient sanctuaries of Zeus, and the presence of the Church gives orthodox sanctity to the site. Archaeological excavation points to: "a holy sepulchre" of remote antiquity on the site. The Cretans according to Diodorus Siculus wrote that: "the honours rendered to the gods, the sacrifices and mysteries are of Cretan origin and other nations took them from them"

Solar Kingship and priestly Theocracy went in tandem as a political and religious means of control. The development of the idea of Hades, the underworld and the idea of judgement, replaced the earlier knowledge of the Grid and its mechanism of entrapment. The necessity of a man-saviour god coupled to a Royal   dynastic line and priesthood, the crucified sacrificial role, was certainly one way out of ritual sacrifice, which the Druids practised and in that sense Jesus did take the sins of those who had practised sacrifice and which the woman put an end to in Crete immortalised in the myth of Ariadne, which I will come to later. The wrathful all avenging Father god Zeus, with his son Dionysus, the Messianic man-god was the alternative State religion to the truth.

THE ALL-SEEING EYE

I have previously mentioned a Minoan Seal from Mochlos of the Middle Minoan Period II (c. 1600 B.C.), with an octopus, two dolphins and fertility bough (*Fig.35*). The octopus was also a feature on the famous "Marine Vase" from Knossos, of the same period. The 19 year solar-lunar cycle is evident from the number of sun rays, but the eight arms of the octopus are not only indicative of Solar Kingship but are associated with the following eight images:

a) 6 rings
b) 1 crescent moon
c) 1 Dolphin with an **eye**

I have previously discussed the significant archetypal symbols, but the eye is important. In another late Minoan icon after the Religious Revolution, a man held his hand to his forehead and the position of the Kabbalistic Third eye of Kether and thus putting together the clues, the dolphin indicate the **Hermetic Eye of Intelligence**, the **All seeing eye** that became a symbol of The New World Order as it appears on the reverse side of the One Dollar note in America today and the reverse side of the Great seal: The Theocratic or Elite intelligentsia. By the first century B.C. Hermes was worshipped at Alexandria and throughout Egypt and initiates were tutored into hermetic mysteries, which in the very highest levels of the Rose-Croix degree of Freemasonry included the Cretan mysteries. These initiates formed the Theocratic government, or what has become known today as: "the hidden government of the world" acting without Democratic mandate, practically through a system of Elitist Communism that is passed off as Democracy! The fact that Hermes in myth was born in the Peloponnese in Arcadia Greece, I am afraid is not the original truth and these initiates never had the original story or as it goes: "In the beginning....". I will skip this bit, not wishing to enlighten The One World Order! Fragments however have survived in the writings of Marsiglio Ficino who in 1471 published some fragmentary information on Hermes gathered from Pythagoras, Plato and the Old Testament.

Typically hermetic philosophy believed that: "spirit or Intelligence existed before Hominid nature came out of the darkness". Apparently: "everything confused or obscure before the word came to animate everything... Darkness reigned over the abyss; the water and the spirit were the powers in the chaos". This sounds like the time following a Magnetic Reversal and when water or the Flood occurred with man's spirit unable to re-incarnate after vast species extinctions. Further: "I celebrate him who created all, who fixed Earth, who suspended the heavens, who willed that from the ocean a sweet water should descend on the inhabited or un-inhabited Earth for the sustenance and **use of all men**. It is the Eye of Intelligence" (my emphasis). The term: "sweet water" has some implication of non-infected or radiated water from atomic war? And in myth as the underground stream of wisdom was to remain hidden within the secret groups and definitely was not given to "all men". From the fragmentary evidence it is possible to reconstruct part of the hermetic system as taught to initiates. *Fig. 36* illustrates 0 as Unity: the large upper circle contains 1. Intelligence: 2. The Word: 3.**The Fire -God** (i.e. 4 circles or **3 in 1** large circle). This **Law of Three** encompasses the Twin Kings and Goddess combined in Hermes who was *God of Fire* and is mentioned many times in The Bible in this context, thus identifying Jehovah with Hermes. The fact that the 6 circles appear in the Late Minoan seal from Mochlos (*Fig. 35*) indicates that there is some connection to the Judaic double Hexagram (*Fig. 14*) and its *six points*. Also since 4 circles appear on the 4 arms of the octopus on the left side adjacent to the sun disc, reminding one of the Sun Wheel, the four beasts of the calendar stationed at the cardinal points of the compass and in association with the tentacles, it implies the totem beasts of the Calendar of Knossos, the alphabets and the mysteries they contained encompassing the goal of a political ruler ship of the world. The implication being that from a **central Intelligence** those tentacles spread out all over the world in a One World Order, the "monster government" that was mentioned in *The Protocols of Zion*. The Mochlos Minoan seal discussed above could be further evidence for a mythic tradition of aGreek folktale hero, Captain Thirteen - the Dolphin King. Mythic tradition tells us that the sun-god Apollo, who was the god of the Druids and Hyperborean in Britain c.1600 B.C appeared as a Dolphin to Cretan Sailors and led them to Delphi, where he founded his famous oracle and made Cretans his priests. Apollo Delphinius, Delphi and Dolphin are all derived from the Greek root "delphis" which means "the womb". One suspects that the word for the river Alpheus (elphis) which denotes source or the beginning (Alpha) gave rise to the notion of Delphi, the seat of the oracle as the spoken word from source. And God said he was: "The Alpha and the Omega", or this reason the start and finish of things. The great Omega or O in the Greek alphabet symbolizing the world egg and the potential that lay in the male to cleave the egg, which accounts for the archetypal symbols of eggs and wands, which one Pope utilized. This is a very interesting myth, since if the oracle of Delphi who prophesied the future and gave advice was a Druid, what a conspiracy! To have all kings applying for wisdom from the oracle, who was a paid up member of the One World Order mouthpiece! Rather like having a central policy directive to a world wide political system, in much the same way as European Union works wouldn't you say, substituting Brussels for Delphi?

Fig.36 **System of Hermes Trismegistos**

(*Jesus was to combine Twin Kings holly (holy one) and oak (royal)*
in one personage with the goddess represented as the principle
of love. Note unity (World Order) as the pyramidal apex combining
the law of three and ancient Trinity.

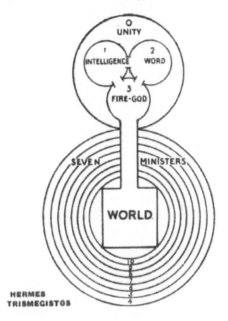

The appearance of the wicker basket design in Cretan seals during the Religious
Revolution mirrors the Druidic practise of offering human sacrifices at full
Moon in wicker baskets. Many more myths and legends and iconography
connect the Druids to the Semitic Religious Revolution in Crete such as Pliny's
account of a Willow tree (Saille the Willow in the Tree Alphabet - connected to
the *13th month* of the year), which then connects with the Minoan Seals. The
Willow tree grew outside the Cretan Psychro Cave, the cave of Zeus' birth. The
willow one suspects with its bright yellow flowers is an archetypal symbol of the
sun and denotes a Sun King. Further A.B. Cook in his book *Zeus* suggests that
Europae, who is shown in iconography seated in a Willow tree, osier-basket in
hand is made love to by an eagle. This suggests that a union between a Greek
Solar King (Druid presumably with the connection through the osier basket in
which the Druids offered their human sacrifices) and a Princess of some dynastic
line presumably Egyptian or Greek occurred during the Religious Revolution.
Once again in the form of a Cretan mystery, we see a former enactment of the
events of Golgotha. Moses of course was placed significantly in a willow basket,
which was found among Reeds indicating Royalty. Europae from whom the

371

name of our current Europe is taken, was the daughter of Agenor and rode to Crete on the back of a bull. It appears that Agenor was from Canaan and it was probably Agenor who invaded Greece and became King of Argos driving the Tuatha de Danaan out, prior to which Agenor was King of Phoenicia and it was he, with the Canaanites from Canaan in Genesis, that came from an empire described as extending to Soddom and Gomorrah. Iconography gives us another side of the story at Argos, for in a Krater from Ruvo, now at Naples museum (*Fig. 37*) Hermes slays Argos. According to myth, Zeus made love to Io, the goddess at Argos. Hera the wife of Zeus became jealous, which might be interpreted that a former religion was discarded in favour of the new religion at Argos, deriving from the Cretans. Zeus in order to protect Io turned her into a white cow and thus the marriage of Europae and her arrival in Crete with Agenor, who imposed kingship there, signifies an autocracy and change in religion.

Fig. 37 **A krater from Ruvo.** *Hermes at left is about to slay Argos.*
Argos has nine eyes on his body, a Janiform head covered by a petasos, a panther skin, and a club. Io at right has the horns of the cow goddess, but also harks back to the Bull-Minos cult and Twin Kings combined as Hermes.

In myth Hera claims the cow as her own (source belonging to the older matriarchal religion). She then set Argos Panoptes, a creature with a hundred eyes, as guard over the cow, to make sure that Zeus did not touch her again. But Zeus sent Hermes to free Io. Thus hermetic philosophy presumably was meant to bring back or safeguard the earlier belief: Interestingly the Eye - the all seeing - eye is equated with one side in this augment and Hermes on the other. The all Seeing Eye today associated with The Illuminati and America and Hermes with presumably Scottish Rite Freemasonry. In *The Battle of The Trees*, I showed iconography from a Templar Church in Gallway, which depicted Io. The myth of Io finally recalls how Hermes knew he could not avoid been seeing by the Hundred eyed Argos Panoptes and thus charmed Argos to sleep by playing the flute and then cut off his head and set Io free. This almost certainly refers to some magical resonance knowledge, perhaps hypnosis. The Krater from Ruvo, shows a different story from myth, since here Hermes on the left grasps Argos by the arm again, which is undoubtedly an early archetypal symbolism of the cutting of the Elm/arm ceremony, Hermes is making ready to kill Argos with a sword and to the right of Argos is Io, who is the maiden with the cows horns. Argos is exhibited in Janiform style, which usually depicts Twin Kingship, one head bearded and the other beardless, (the Old waning King and new Waxing King), but both wear the cap of Hermes, the petasos. Thus Argos is a Solar King, whom Hermes is about to slay, in his right hand he wields the club and his left shoulder is draped with a panther skin. (Presumably the derivation of the Scottish kilt shoulder piece) On his body he has 9 eyes, but the profile of the head gives two more and thus a total of 11 eyes can be seen.

Myth never reports Argos as having a hat of Hermes, a panther skin, club or Janiform head and there is supposed to be 100 eyes not 9 or 11. Thus the tradition of the icon records an earlier Argos or King where there was Twin Kingship and we know that the Cretans colonised Argos c. 1 600 B.C. Thus when the Canaanites invaded Argos and drove the Tuatha de Danaan out, the latter took an earlier system of Twin Kingship to Ireland and presumably the Druids took on this system and it was this system that was employed in the events of Golgotha, where the Mary Magdalene had her arm cut, by Hermes the bisexual god of The New World Order. Evidently then, there were two opposing groups who battled for dominance: A point that was finally borne out by Caesar who slaughtered the Celts and terminated ostensibly the secret Order of Druids. The club of Hercules in the Krater from Ruvo then is a club of Hercules, once a sacred King whose club was originally the fertility bough. The fact that the club is used in conjunction with the sword to cut the left 'arm' of the crab in the tiled mural at Cardiff Castle, depicts the second cut of the crucifixion and the events of Golgotha. This mural represents Scottish Rite Freemasonry, thus in the highest Order of Freemasonry, they have the truth of the events of Golgotha and these documents are wielded over Churches as the Grand Master of The Prieuré de Sion once stated of Churches 'They will comply' and as Rupert Murdoch once stated of the Pope "He will write for me".

The Hermetic hendekagllyph is somewhat similar to Brahmanism (*Fig. 38*) with the trinity (including a Fire-God) and seven Archangels or Adityas, which in the Hermetic system is represented by another circle of concentric rings representing the "seven ministers", numbered 4 to 10 inclusive. Within the smallest ring is the square representing the four quarters of the world and the circle of concentric rings in the floor design at Cardiff Castle has 4 quarters represented. One concludes, that the God Hermes as another stage of Cretan Zeus is being employed and that is the name of the God of Scottish Rite Freemasonry. The fact that Hermes is bisexual in myth no doubt resolves some of the confusion as to why there is a great impetus towards accepting homosexuality, even as far as education in the school system (clause 28) in the UK. The Hidden Government one concludes at work again! The Eye of Hermetic Intelligence - really! Lies usually eventually filter down to education, where it enters the syllabus of the school curriculum, where mass brainwashing occurs. All political systems realise that education of the young is paramount to maintaining their rotten edifice of lies. The New World Order plan to instigate a Universal political and Religious Kingdom certainly depended on maintaining not only the status quo but also lies. I have previously covered the fact that James the brother of Jesus (by fosterage?) was concerned that St. Paul was using Jesus' teachings after his alleged death to promote the faith to all men including Gentiles, removing the question of circumcision. James made it quite clear that the faith was for *Jews only*. The Book of *Revelations* as it refers to the saviour of the tribes of Israel, can hardly be considered a Universal faith, however Gentiles do submit to this unbelievably. Secret groups always work in long-term cycles which I perceive is dictated by the 'script' and the period between Magnetic Reversals and thus it is not as I say inconceivable that the teachings of Jesus were specifically tailored to accommodate a future world faith following whatever page number the MRC case was on in his 'script' of *Revelations*! Jesus himself as I reported in *The Battle of The Trees*, was confused over Holly (Holy one) and Oak (Royal) of the Tree Alphabet, which provides evidence for his tutorage in a secret group presumably the Druids who utilised the Tree Alphabet in their Universities at the top levels. The Druids may have sought to challenge the existing Jewish priesthood in Palestine, the priesthood of Aaron whilst laying a plan to create a world religion – Christianity, which was to become the religion for the masses in a Universal political and religious kingdom: and certainly was raised as a "World Federation of Faiths", at the time of the Celtic Commonwealth.

The "Black Madonna" on the roof at Cardiff Castle I assumed was Isis, the mother of Horus in Egyptian mythology. Horus and his mother Isis came into prominence with Osiris in Egypt. Hadrian, writing to the consul Servian, said that the Alexandrians: "Have one god, Serapis, who is worshipped by Christians, Jews, and Gentiles". The half-Christianised Egyptians identified Christ with Horus, son of Osiris, and spoke of the Saviour as the young avenger in the: "Legend of the Winged Disk", who swept down the Nile valley driving the devil (Set) out of Egypt. As early Gaelic coverts said: **"Christ is my Druid",** those of the land of the Pharaohs appear to have declared similarly: "Christ is my Horus". The fact that the Egyptians perceived Christ as Horus, was due to Horus being attributed as a sky god. "Horus of the Two Eyes", the sun being one and the moon being the other, certainly connects back to the Cretan mysteries and the Moon Goddess and Solar King. Two eyes or the male and female would become the one all seeing- eye as the woman was fused with the man into the Godhead as Hermes. A poor trade for the truth.

I was quite surprised to see Prince Charles (House of Windsor in the UK) erect a Phoenix in his garden, since that particular bird was connected with the Sun cult at Heliopolis, although perhaps in this case it meant a resurrection or re-birth after the previous trying years. The Sun cult connected to Solar kingship and Apollo in Greece, Twin Kingship and Mother goddess in Crete and its implication of connection to Scottish Rite Freemasonry. Although Prince Charles evidently believes in Re-incarnation, the idea of Philosopher Solar Kings is a past system that never worked. Now this is an old tale of Holly (Holy one) and Oak (Royal) that was a confused battle even in the mind of the Messiah! Prince Charles though is perhaps in his cry to be "Defender of Faiths" (and not Faith singular) attempting to uphold Freedom of Religion, whilst acting within the constraints of the system of Monarchy erected on Solar Kingship, which fused Twin Kingship with the woman whose gift was immortality - Holly (Holy one) and Oak (Royal) and if Jesus had to questioned his tutor in confusion as to whether he was to be Royal or Holy, then Prince Charles presumably has grappled with the same question. The two however are totally incompatible as the events of Golgotha showed when the woman was written out of the story. You can't be a part of the all-seeing eye and fight it at the same time, since it is impossible to take an exterior viewpoint on it. *The Mail on Sunday* newspaper produced a supplement in several parts entitled *Highgrove –The Prince's secret garden,* which covered The Prince of Wales garden at his home in the UK (Adapted from *The Garden at Highgrove* by HRH The Prince of Wales and Candida Lycett Green) A diagram or rough sketch included in the article, showed the original design for a tree house built for Princes William and Harry. Can it be entirely co-incidental, that the tree house is perched in an old *holly tree*? The Holly motif is echoed throughout, with leaf-shaped balusters and door, and scarlet rails to represent the berries; further the Tree House was labelled: "Holyrood House". The derivation here (intentional or not) is the Holy Rood or wand of the Druids (Judah) and there is a Holyrood House in Scotland.

I have always felt that the death of Princess of Diana was connected to this story, either through the white supremacy of the tribe of Judah, who had been at pains you will remember to eradicate the *Egyptian* dynasty. Princess Diana as we know met her death in the company of an Egyptian and had shown her preference for non-white males. It is too predictable that Princess Diana should have been 'canonised' after her death, with referrals to "goddess". Patrick Jephson, her Private secretary, after her death wrote a rather different story of her life and one that did not quite fit with the "goddess". Diana the woman however gave a great deal of comfort to many people and that is a wonderful legacy and epitaph. How much or how little of this story Diana Princess of Wales knew, is anybody's guess; but the white Fiat Uno car that was spotted at the infamous tunnel in Paris and the bright white flash that have never been explained, together with the driver's connections to payment by some agency or other cannot be ignored: along with the Tree House with its connections to the Holy Rood or wand of the Druids and the thirteenth tribe of Judah, with its aspirations of enlightened philosopher Kings. Prince Charles has shown that he is an enlightened Prince, with many admirable qualities and has stood for the many principles that one perceives are right and there lies the paradox and the battle of Holly and Oak or Holy One and Oak Royal.

Fig.38 **Comparrison of Triple Hendekaglyph of various belief systems**

Author's note: The Masonic Temple (Scottish Rite Frreemasonry) has "rights" at the centre of Man, people and government (in a five-pointed star). This is now central policy emitting from Brussels (European legislation on Human Rights) and thus as I conclude Scottish Rite Freemasonry is at the heart of European Union. Further, whilst English Freemasons denied any involvement in the French Revolution, the Duc D'Orleans was frequently in Britain and may have been paid from there, to black propaganda the French monarchy and Maria Antoinette. "Equality, Liberty and Fraternity", the Masonic initiated war cry of the French Revoution (originated by the enclocopaedists of the intelligentsia in the Masonic Lodges, preceeding the Revolution) is notably at the heart of the Rights of Man in Scottish Rite Freemasonry of the Masonic Temple. The Masonic Temple (Luciferic interpretation) has the inevitable flaw of "Man is his own God".

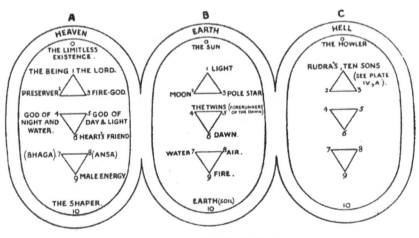

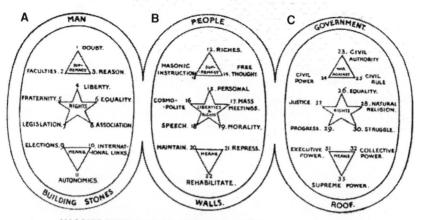

MASONIC TEMPLE: (Scottish Rite): Official Philosophic Interpretation

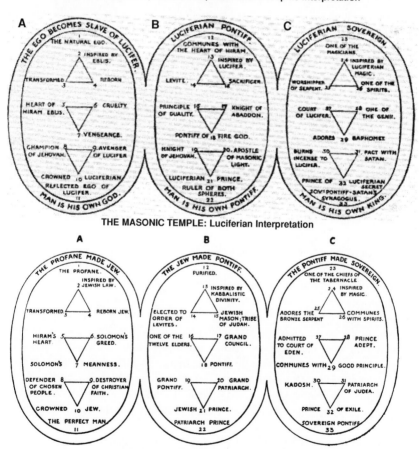

THE MASONIC TEMPLE: Luciferian Interpretation

THE MASONIC TEMPLE: Judaic Interpretation

THE VACUUM PATTERN

The view that has been held in contemporary physics is that space is a vacuum, both void and inert and that there is no Ether. The vacuum has been known by many names; the matrix, the ether, space-time, hyperspace, zero-point energy, the physical vacuum, the gravity field, the tachyon field, the Fermi-sea or even eleven dimensional superforce. All these terms cover the old idea of the ether.

Earlier I discussed the proposal of the Energy Grid, a geometric crystal structure of energy surrounding the Earth. In *Alternative 4* I proposed a mechanism -*The Onion-Ring model* for the mechanism of the natural UFO phenomenon, which depends viewing hyperspace as an energy field, whereby past images of mans history are held in imprinted electro-magnetic and holographic or pictorial form are disturbed by some fluctuation of energy in the system and the electro-magnetic holographic signal (picture of a past event) is picked up by the brain acting as a dipole-radio receiver. Thus witness UFO *(natural)* reports I concluded were events from THE PAST and as such they are metaphysical. This theory was further discussed in Part II of the Cancer report. I referred to this holographic imprint as being held within a geometric structure which resembled a Diablo or more precisely two pyramids, with one point or apex of the pyramid pointing downwards, which I termed the spiritual bioplasma; and one point or apex of the pyramid pointing upwards, which I termed the morphogenetic bioplasma and which is concerned with the genetic evolutionary line and memory. The Diablo structure itself represented not only an energy field, but also space geometrics. It may be that the morphogenetic bioplasma is part if not the geometry of *the Grid itself*, but the spiritual bioplasma may extend into a much higher plane or finer graded energy field, perhaps lying *outside* of the Grid itself. I do not discount that the way in which past holographic memories are stored, the so-called Akashic Record is a more subtle mechanism, depending on the properties of sub-atomic particles, than the easier perception of electro-magnetic fields, which according to the physicists do not manifest in the ether. The coiling effect of the pyramidal diablo model, rather like a vortex tornado may depend therefore on spins properties of sub-atomic particles, rather than an electro-magnetic coil. Science has known for quite some time, that apparently solid, liquid or gaseous material which surround and comprises the world in which we live is composed of mainly 'nothing', apart from a small number of molecules, atoms etc. moving in it. The more solid an object becomes e.g. a table, the more closely all the atomic and molecular particles are packed in. Our own bodies are merely atoms and molecules paced tightly together to form mass and cannot be considered as separate from each other or the greater pattern.

Although there are a number of physicists who claim that the 'Big Bang' origin of the Universe is a hoax, those that support this theory say that if you condensed all matter in the Universe you would end up with an extremely dense ball of matter, the so-called **singularity**, which exploded to give rise to the Planets as they and our own planet Earth travelled outwards in an *expanding Universe*. Physicists admit that they understand in a limited way the properties of sub-atomic particles and the laws and relationships they are subjected to. Even the electron, which is described for convenience as a negative particle, which orbits the nucleus of positive particles (protons) and neutral particles (neutrons) in an atom, sometimes does not behave like a particle at all, but a wave. The problem is that because we can't see the small sub-atomic particles, space has been viewed as void or an empty vacuum. However physicists working on the cutting edge, are increasingly coming to view space as a real energy field within which are vibrations, movement and waves and what is more an intricate and complex set of resonant energy patterns. The master pattern that I would maintain contains a master blueprint or genetic blueprint for the survival of the species. The vacuum is referred to as zero (mathematically) as it is considered the **zero-point.** The forces that exist within this zero point may be considered as **potential energy.** If space could be envisaged in two dimensions e.g. a flat sheet of paper or 'flatland', then within the sub-atomic structure arise waves and oscillations or vibrations, which give rise to a rippled surface. Particles might 'spin off' the surface of the sheet and thus become 'real' in our physical perception. Mass itself may be just a vacuum wave, vibration or oscillation or rhythmic movement trapped by spin into *appearing* as a particle. Thus, all the four basic forces of nature such as gravity, electro-magnetic and two intra-atomic forces (negative and positive) can be viewed as manifestations or energy interactions within the fabric, tapestry or matrix of the vacuum or zero-point energy state. Everything that we see and perceive to be real e.g. car, table, desk and even our own bodies, are comprised of these sub-atomic particles or forces, but in three dimensions and not two. Thus space is an energy matrix, web, lattice or geometric pattern with a definite substructure, which not only describes the ether, but **our own bodies and even our minds reflect and are a part of that patterning of energy**. This is most important.

The crop circle patterns I discussed in *Alternative 4*, if it is natural and not man made, may give some idea of the patterns. I was particularly interested in the appearance of a pattern, which was almost identical to the helical spiral structure of the DNA molecule, which carries hereditary information in the cells. I intriguingly asked, whether there existed an ether pattern or master blueprint for such a structure, which reflected the very structure present in the body. The body itself on a grosser scale is surrounded by and electro-magnetic energy field which is shaped rather like an egg. The biofield often referred to as an aura, exists as a seven layered system, which connects with various energy points in the body known as charkas, although the number 7 is an esoteric archetypal number and may not represent an entirely correct view. Snowflakes also show quite marked geometrical patterns presumably water crystallizing within the constraints of some energy field or pattern and the spider may well weave its web, according to the spiralling geometry of the morphogenetic bioplasma, which is a part of The Grid, if not as I propose the entirety of The Grid. The ancient archaeological finds in Peru of man-made spider- like rock formations presumably built along lines of geomagnetic activity illustrates that early man had some knowledge of this patterning, perhaps utilizing the pineal body at the base of the brain as an electro-magnetic sensor. Such abilities may have become vestigial today through non-use.

We ourselves through the sub-atomic particles of atoms and molecules that comprise our bodies are a part of that vacuum ether energy matrix. Our bodies, trees, mountains, oceans and everyday objects are mere patterns within space. The source of energy within space is not the vacuum state itself, but comes from a vertical spectrum of energies, ultimately linking each level to source. The body and *primitive* mind are on the bottom rung of that hierarchal energy system, whereas the analytical mind and higher creative thought are higher on that energy scale. People, who have survived a Near Death Experience, speak of a tunnel and a bright white light, brighter than any light they have ever known. These people often allegedly meet old friends and encounter a 'life review'. I do not want to take away the profound cognition of the experience, however it is likely that the tunnel itself, is the vortex of helical or spiral energy and as the spirit passes the successive coils, various past holograms (pictures) of their life experience appear and are played back to them like a movie real. **Then comes the voice of conscience**, which is often interpreted in different ways according to ones own beliefs, some believe the voice is Jesus, others like myself who have been through this experience say it is a matter of "unfinished business"' and conscience, which governs the choice of whether or not to return. The fact that we meet others we have known in holographic form I would maintain, emphasises how closely we are linked to each other by action, word and thought. This process is just one level of review and as one travels closer to the light, there is a complete review of all so-called past lives or what is really just continuous immortal experience of the soul. Thus there are successive levels of conscience. The words 'self-judgement' come to mind and since the spirit is basically good, there can be no harder judgement.

The Indian mystics knew the ether as 'Akash', which is where presumably Rudolf Steiner obtained the root for 'Akashic Record', if not from Madame Blavatsky. In my research of the natural UFO phenomenon, I came to distinguish two types of memory:
a. Genetic evolutionary memory, which I referred to as being held within the downward pointing pyramidal (or triangle in two dimensions) vortex, which I termed the morphogenetic bioplasma.

b. Spiritual or mystical evolutionary memory, which I referred to as being held within the upward pointing pyramidal vortex, which I termed the spiritual bioplasma.

The genetic or morphogenetic bioplasma appeared to contain the memory or complete record of the evolutionary development of the species and all species, whilst the spiritual bioplasma contained memories of warnings (usually connected to the misuse of science e.g. nuclear atomic bombs) and many archetypal symbols, which appeared to relate in some cases to the early Greek mysteries. In Part II of the Cancer document, I suggested that the mind of mythological man thought very differently from today and his conceptual mind consisted of thought in terms of hieroglyphic symbols and archetypes, which conveyed definite conceptual meanings and thought processes by association with other archetypes. The implication is that in a hierarchy of energy within the matrix or vacuum, thought as vibration within the energy field of the mind, is recorded at a higher vibrational energy than that of matter, resonant vibration or the genetic evolutionary memory. In other words survival pertaining to bodies and behavioural patterns for a species is information that is recorded on a lower hierarchal frequency than conceptual thought, usually associated with man alone. One might conclude that every event that takes place, together with every individual thought and mood or emotion attached to that thought, is recorded in this hierarchal system of memory or energy, within the vacuum state and remains there imprinted long after the event has gone. The all-seeing eye takes on a new meaning! To envisage a master computer of recorded information in the vacuum would probably be quite an accurate analogy. Thus imprinted holographic pictures are retained in the vacuum and when such imagery is disturbed by energy flux through the system, the brain acting as a dipole-radio receiver can pick up these 'signals' or imprints and the UFO witness reports some aspect of the holographic. It is not 'real' in the sense that this is a recording of a PAST EVENT. However it is real in the sense that it must have occurred to be recorded or imprinted. This is a pivotal and important point when I come to discuss some past events, where you might think we are discussing science fiction rather than past reality, since mankind having been fed a tissue of lies about the beginning will find that data somewhat startling.

The fact that government agencies have tried to hide up the UFO phenomenon is not unusual, since the phenomenon is part of the hidden science. Thus in my second book I tried to separate covert manipulation and disinformation which is the *unnatural* UFO incident perpetrated by government agencies, from the *natural* phenomenon itself. It must be somewhat disturbing for the elite to recognise that the records or holographs in space can be dislodged and viewed by public! Thus a whole disinformation line has evolved to place the UFO in 'zany' country, as one of my scientist colleagues asked me: "Whatever are you doing studying UFO's - are you completely determined to wreck your credentials?" Such is the power of brown propaganda - disinformation. Evidence from the natural UFO phenomenon and channelling which I will come to later suggest that the vacuum state at least in the energy fields closest to Earth is patterned holographically and is interactive with fields from both mind and body. **The mind** (prana energy in Indian mysticism) is **not the brain** but exists as field energy and as such can interact at some level with the diablo energy patterning. Rather than use the term plasma vortex as the physicists do, I have added the pre-fix bio, to indicate life (man, animal or plant) interaction. I have previously covered in the Cancer Report and Alternative4 and again earlier in this book, the phenomenon of embryonic growth and morphogenetic fields, where the early stages of development of an individual species conforms to a pattern which governs the particular shape of that species. Rupert Sheldrake, Harold Burr and Dr. Becker have all worked with these specific fields or what I term morphogenetic fields, proposing that they are natural "blue-prints" or "jelly moulds", existing as a specific spatial field, which acting as a master pattern dictates that the developing animal or plant conforms to the overall shape for a particular species. One might theorize that the blueprint or genetic coding information system relating to the evolutionary record of any particular species lies within the Earth Grid itself as a pattern of energy. The crystalline geometric structure given previously may not fully define the three-dimensional geometry, which may be pyramidal and not triangular. Whilst the morphogenetic bioplasma is probably an inherent part of that geometry, I would propose that the spiritual bioplasma exists at a higher energy level, within the space vacuum energy and its geometry. In my own diablo model, this would be the upper part of the Diablo *(Fig.1 and 8)*.

In one experiment carried out on islands in the Pacific, it was noted that monkeys on one island did not eat food with sand on. When however the animals were taught to wash their food, this learned ability appeared in groups of monkeys on other islands, who had had no physical contact with the learned ability group. It was suggested that this learned behaviour had somehow been transferred through a specific field or energy in space, which connected the monkeys. The implication was that thought could be transferred through this field. In the Guatemalan monkey experiment I would propose that behavioral information for the species as a learning pattern, would be conveyed to other members of the species via the morphogenetic bioplasma and interaction of Grid energies, such information being part of survival data for the species. William Mc. Dougall in 1920 ran a similar experiment at Harvard University, studying how long it took, for rats to escape from a maze filled with water. He found that successive generations of rats learnt the escape route more rapidly than previous generations, thus the behavioral learning ability had been transmitted through some property of the DNA either physically or through some specific field, which would equate with my model of the morphogenetic bioplasma. The monkey experiment however, showed that the learning ability was transferred even though the members of the species were not in contact, which points to transfer through a specific spatial field, which could be conducted through the Grid. This may be true for humans, since it has been noted that when a new chemical crystal was grown in the laboratory, at first the process was difficult, since there is no niche for this new geometry within the existing matrix pattern or vacuum. However successive attempts at the crystal growth were found to be easier, as though at some subtle level, either the ability to grow the crystal (learning) or the crystal itself became 'locked in' as an energy pattern within the matrix. Recent research shows that thought patterns can be more easily applied in healing processes, when a crystal is employed. I will not relate in length here the enormous difficulties of my research, but just one small fraction of the barriers to be jumped are given on the front page of the Cancer Report. Further I had enormous difficulties with machines and particularly computers in a continuous story of vanishing files, breakdown of technology, power cuts and the continual comment from those who were tied up on the technology side of: "This has never happened before!" Whilst on the verge of physical collapse, with the almost daily onslaught of barriers to be jumped that also included the gamut of those people who were busy dramatizing their past scripts actively placing barriers in my way! I realised that I was battling against a pattern and that this new thought was unable to find a niche. I can only give the analogy of being stuck on a stage with all the actors mindlessly repeating their lines dictated by the master controller or pattern, whilst trying to hand out a new script, only to be told: "It has been done *this way* for millions of years!" Would it surprise you to know, that as I put the final conclusions onto the computer, the electric cable blew up, the computer shut down and I continued by hand as a gang of workmen dug up the road!

The idea of Lamarkian evolution has been overtaken by Darwinian evolution theory, but Lamarkian theory proposes some *learning control over evolutionary events*. For example giraffes when food on the ground became short, *knew* they had to stretch their necks and reach the vegetation on trees, subsequently the learning ability was passed on and subsequent generations showed longer necks in the general population until all members showed the long neck. By contrast Darwinian theory states, that the short neck variety in the face of starvation did not survive and only those giraffes that by chance (random mutation) had longer necks, survived to reproduce and provide more offspring with the longer neck. Lamarkian theory does not lay everything at the door of chance, whilst Darwinian theory does. It is not surprising that Secret groups have promoted the idea of chance as opposed to any learning ability, since this would inevitably lead to questions on just how such ability was transferred. Thus acquired survival characteristics have been explained in terms of Darwinian theory and pure chance through random mutation. This will not explain the monkey experiment or crystal growth, or the research of scientists in Scotland and Australia, who repeated Mc Dougall's experiment, using a completely separate strain of rats, where they found their rats had learnt to run the maze quickly and at the same level of expertise as the last generation of Mc. Dougall's rats. Learning then is implicit in acquired information for a species and one might consider the energy field that stores this by analogy as the C drive of the master computer, the morphogenetic bioplasma. The physical DNA in our cells or any living cell may merely be the 'floppy disc' a copy taken from the 'hard drive'. Thus the master pattern remains continuous for the species and exists within the vacuum energy, including I propose the morphogenetic field mechanism observed by other researchers. The psychologist Jung spoke of a collective unconscious and whilst that has been proposed as the unifying level for mankind, with its implication of a Universal Mind, this is very much the misunderstanding that I wish to discuss here. There is if you like a collective *survival mechanism* for the species, which exists as information within the morphogenetic bioplasma. Jung however also noted the appearance of archetypal images, which one might classify as a spiritual unconscious. I prefer to call that spiritual information memory, with the implication that it is accessible even though normally man is quite unaware of it.

Whilst I have proposed that each species e.g. Amphibian (frog), Reptiles and man etc. has a genetic or morphogenetic bioplasma specific for the particular species, there is the curious observation from the subject of comparative embryology, that during development, **the embryo appears to recapitulate physically past ancestral forms**. The human embryo in its early stages has been likened to a tadpole with a tail and aquatic gill-like structures. Although some scientists feel that embryology can be indispensable in establishing phylogenetic relationships i.e. the major groupings or phyla from which a species descends, there are some scientists like myself, who question whether Ernst Haeckel (1843-1919) was on the right track, when he suggested that during embryological development an *organism repeats its ancestral history*, or to use Haeckel's terminology: " Ontogeny recapitulates phylogeny". The presence of brachial grooves (gill type structures) and segmental mytomes (muscle blocks) in the human embryo bears witness to a fish ancestry. I am afraid that this really upsets the man from Ape brigade, who have trouble with the root ancestry although recently there has been more acceptance of the man from fish theory. However in my theory for Cancer this embryological recapitulation is quite critical as the **Cancer recapitulates embryological survival mechanisms** (*The Second Millennium Working Report into Cancer*). The major embryological survival mechanism is of course growth and in the adult it is reproduction. When a person experiences great loss, then if the person is unable through psychological upset to perceive that loss as surmountable, the rational mind switches off and passes control to the tri-partite energy field, which refers to the Grid and master pattern of survival of the species, which controls survival of bodies. The irrational survival mechanism becomes growth and a tumour therefore is merely an embryonic recapitulation of a time of high survival.

One could see no point in repeating the phylogenetic ancestry in the human embryo, unless some master code existed which determined the physical DNA and the development of the embryo therefore would proceed as the information is 'read off', *in sequence* of ancestral or phylogenetic history. The Master plan constructs the baby according to the plan that has been laid down for THE BODY over the millennia of evolutionary history. The primitive Chordate ancestor gave rise to a number of branch groups we call sub phyla (singular subphylum). The acorn worms, sea squirts or marine types with a backbone (invertebrate Chordates) and the subphylum Vertebrata (with backbones). The Vetebrata contains a number of sub divisions called classes: Pisces (fishes), Amphibia (frogs etc.), Reptiles, Aves (birds) and Mammalia including man. Thus the various classes and the two sub phyla (vertebrates and invertebrates), derive from a common primitive chordate ancestor. This re-capitulation of ancestry, may have been the basis for the natural UFO phenomenon, where witness accounts in some cases spoke of shuffling animal type human creatures, with reptilian like orange eyes and reduced wings, together with massive fish (in a time of low gravity prior to a previous magnetic reversal?), or beings with bulbous-like frog eyes. These holographic images I concluded may have been images or information from the morphogenetic bioplasma - the Akashic Record, impinging on those witnesses, with the brain acting as dipole-radio receiver, when the geometry of space had been disturbed through some high energy flux through it. Thus I proposed that this was some insight into the *evolutionary record of mans body*. People however have great difficulty in imagining man in an amphibian body for example, because man has come to view his body as who he really is. The spirit however is the real you, not the body, which is just the casing.

The MRC case refers to those spirits who went through a magnetic reversal, where the north and south poles of the Grid reversed. I did suggest in *Alternative 4*, that such spirits after a serious cataclysm, when the Earth was for millions of years covered by water, were forced to occupy the bodies of Amphibians as one of the few surviving species. I further suggested that this might account for the bulbous-eyed individuals reported in UFO accounts and certain finds in archaeology, which depicted humans with large bulbous-type eyes. Scientists have measured the lengths of DNA strips in different kinds of living things and have found that the strips usually get longer as creatures become more complex, indicating the greater storage of information required for such complexity. However the frog is not a complex animal and if the coiled strips of DNA in one human cell could be teased out to full length and placed end to end, they would make a thread about three feet long; but the DNA strips from the frog have a total length of eight feet, more than twice that of the strips from the cell of a man. One must ask what exactly is encoded on that extra length? I did suggest that the Amphibians have survived in continuity magnetic reversals in the past, simply through their ability to exist on land and in water and may have hosted the spirits of those who survived a magnetic reversal for many millions of years recording that experience, until other species developed and provided alternative body forms. This may or may not, provide a solution to the Apocalyptic condemnation of "frogs", the appearance in archaeology of humanoid figures with large bulbous eyes and prehistoric cave paintings in France, which show amorphous humanoid forms, which have an animal like quality (*Plate 11*). Further UFO witness accounts often report humanoid figures with large bulbous "frog-like" eyes, which must be some record of a past body form retained as a holographic imprint within the morphogenetic bioplasma. Further if one was looking for a more feasible solution to the picture book story of Noah's Ark and how Noah managed to save **two** of every species, which would have required a phenomenally large boat, then if one accepted that ancient man was not at all ignorant or underdeveloped technically, then the possibility of genetic engineering technology, cloning or resonant vibratory knowledge which manipulated the etheric morphogenetic bioplasma, containing the genetic master blue-print for all species, would be in the light of this book a more realistic proposal. Two whilst referring to male and female could equally represent the double stranded helix of DNA.

HIDDEN ARCHAELOGY

So much archaeology that does not fit with the Darwinistic view is simply hidden from public view. I have already illustrated in my books, how Greek icons have not been fully explained to public, where the underlying symbolism is not identified. If museums as educational facilities are to fulfil their purpose, in much the same way as science should fulfil the purpose of helping humanity, then large re-appraisals must occur, with no barrier to that search for truth. The theory that the human race is descended from Neanderthal man has been dealt a blow following DNA tests on the body of a baby that died 30 000 years ago. Dr. William Goodwin, who carried out the analysis at the University of Glasgow's human identification centre, said: "The DNA showed no inter-breeding between Neanderthals and humans. What we found strongly suggests that modern humans did not come from Neanderthals, or that they mixed with modern humans". Back to the drawing board then and perhaps the Saqqara 'bird'. Dr Kalil Messiha, an Egyptologist and archaeologist, emptied a box of archives labelled 'birds' onto his desk, to find one artefact was definitely not a bird. Dr Messiha persuaded the Under Secretary of the Egyptian Ministry of Culture, Dr Mohammed Camal El Din Moukhtar, to from a committee to investigate the model. The committee formed on 23 December 1971 and consisted of a number of historians and aviation experts. When asked to analyse the model, several aerodynamics engineers and pilots found a number of remarkable features, all indicating knowledge of principles of aircraft design which had taken European and American designers a century of airfoil experimental work to discover and perfect. Besides an aerodynamic shape of fuselage and wing that revealed design compensation for camber, the rise of the curve of the wing and the wing itself was found to be counter-dihedral, which provided a tremendous lift force. It appears that the 'bird' had more in common with a space craft and the ancient craft's purpose was more for carrying large amounts of freight than for reaching high speeds, for the designers agreed it could have carried heavy loads, but at extremely low speed, i.e., below sixty miles an hour. One expert in fact noted that there was a remarkable similarity between the down-pointing nose and pointed wing of the Egyptian plane and a new at that time, oblique-wing aircraft under consideration by NASA, the American Space Agency: All this, despite the model being 2000 years old. Further the aerodynamics experts discovered that all ratios in the model were 2:1 or 3:1, indicating that it had been *designed* and as Dr Messiha noted the ancient Egyptians always built scale models of everything they mad including chariots, obelisks, houses, pyramids and ships etc. As biologist-zoologist Ivan T. Sanderson, head of the Society for the Investigation of the Unexplained commented in the 1970's: "The concrete evidence that the ancients knew of flight was forced upon us only a few years ago. Now we have to explain it. And when we do we will have to rearrange a great many of our concepts of ancient history". Quite!

In *Alternative 4*, I suggested that the interest of all secret Intelligence agencies in the occult, including the CIA, who in the1960's had troupes of occultists marching through their offices, could only be explained together with the phenomenal advance in technology made since that era, by the sub-conscious or purposeful pulling down of information from the past holographic records - The Akashic Record. In fact I maintained that a television programme named *Alternative 3* in the 1970's, and upon which my second book is based as a starting point, was far from the hoax that it was put up to be. In fact there was every indication that a future world Apocalypse had already been understood and accepted by the world elite at that time and that a research programme which sought to save the elitist few, had already been undertaken. Such a programme had links with NASA and *Alternative 3* purported to be the erection of a safe base on Mars in the event of some future world cataclysm. A modern day Noah's Ark project then, aimed at survival of the few. A recent *Discovery* programme on British television reported that billions of dollars go missing from public funds every year in America and whilst the American public are evidently either unaware or don't care, I would not take too many guesses as to where that money goes. Meanwhile for the less fortunate presumably there will be the prospect of a mind and body control programme and a psycho civilised society on Earth, run no doubt along the lines of that predictable One World Order Theocracy of Communism run by the far rich right - "Paradise" according to Revelations or the Prophetic Apocalypse. Page four hundred or whatever for the MRC case religiously following his past postulates, goals and inevitable cataclysm that ended the last cycle. Never mind folks, back to the beginning for another cycle, where the MRC case can do it all again, acting out his psychological case on the World's stage, whilst the audience watch from the stalls, unable to raise a raspberry! Or ask for the truth.

In 1954 Ivan T. Sanderson proposed that an object from Colombia was a model of a jet aircraft at least a thousand years old, this case with the Saqqara 'bird' supports the Indian epics that reported flying craft - the Hindu "Vimanas". Neither can one so easily dismiss the evidence for nuclear warfare among the so-called 'primitives' and some cataclysm, which curiously turned up in UFO witness accounts, where there were warnings against nuclear warfare and some witnesses associated what they felt were extraterrestrial figures or "space-men", with nuclear detonations. Neither is it easy to dismiss the fact that the Greek word "Zeeno", which means stranger in Greek, appeared in a UFO witness account. This is curious, in so far as after some cataclysm there appears to have been an Ice Age. One area that was overwhelmed by glaciations during the Ice Age was the Arctic region, in particular Greenland. One Renaissance map shows Greenland free of ice, the Zeno brothers' map of 1380 may have used the Grid to predict land *shape* formations. This map was the result of a voyage made by the two Zeno brothers from Venice in the early fourteenth century. Their explorations supposedly took them to Iceland, Greenland and perhaps as far as Nova Scotia. They drew a map of the North Atlantic, which was subsequently lost for two centuries before it was rediscovered by a descendent of the Zeno brothers. The interesting point here is the shape that one assumes in the case of landmasses can be predicted, in much the same way as information in the Grid provides for the shape of the embryo. A study of the chart reveals that the Zeno brothers could not have been the original mapmakers. The brothers supposedly landed in Iceland and Greenland, yet their chart very accurately shows longitude and latitude not only for these locations, but also for Norway, Sweden, Denmark, the German Baltic coast, Scotland, and even such little-known landfalls as the Shetland and Faroe islands. The map also shows evidence of having been based on a polar projection, which was beyond the abilities of the fourteenth-century geographers. The original mapmakers likewise knew the correct lengths of degrees of longitude for the entire North Atlantic; thus it is very possible that the map instead of being a product after the fact was drawn up by the Zeno brothers *before* their voyage and was used to guide them in their exploration of northern lands. To do this would require knowledge of Grid energies and it is it not entirely impossible that in the 1960's information was fully channelled down from the Grid, using the clairvoyants and psychics that intelligence agencies have been associated with since that time.

Neither is it easy to dismiss strange finds that have occurred since 1968, in coastal waters for example in the Caribbean, notably in the Bahaman Banks. At depths ranging from 6 to 100 feet there are numerous giant stone constructions - walls, great squares, crosses and other geometric shapes, even archways and pyramids, all encrusted with fossilized shells and petrified mangrove roots, indicating their great antiquity. There are walls with blocks of 25 tons each, huge circular stone constructions made of 12-foot blocks. Is it not curious that the bricks appear to comprise a sea wall and are enormous? Other sunken ruins in the Caribbean area include a *sea wall* 30 feet high, running in a straight line for miles off Venezuela, near the mouth of the Orinoco River. Other ruins off the Cuban coast, Mexico, Belize and British Honduras are perplexing to the archaeologists and orthodox historians, for the architecture is beyond the capabilities of either the Amerinds or the Spanish conquistadors. It is even more disturbing that the most recent period, when the present Caribbean sea floor was above sea level and the mystery walls, pyramids and temples therefore could have been built, was during the ice age. It seems that whilst three of the post-Babel centres of high civilization succumbed to natural disaster, the ruins of the remaining five centres show evidence of man-made destruction - destructions of such terrifying magnitude that it must be considered a major cataclysm. Giant prehistoric fossils have been discovered by the palaeontologist Arturo Vildozola over 13 000ft up in the Peruvian Andes. The hoard of more than 500 Jurassic-era fossils including giant oysters was discovered recently (*March 2001*). This find provides almost certain proof that the mountains formed part of the earth's seabed during the early Jurassic period before being lifted up as the Pacific and South American continental plates converged. The oysters which measure 6ft across are small compared to the size of other creatures that must have existed including the dinosaurs that we know were huge. This giant body form I would contend was all part of the myths of men as giants, who existed in an environment with low gravity prior to a Magnetic Reversal. There has also recently been a discovery of many dinosaur remains in the same region of South America.

I have already discussed the Indian epics and the possibility of a world-wide conflagration and nuclear capability. The fact that a warning regarding nuclear conflict arises in UFO witness accounts indicates according to my conclusions that all past events are recorded on the bioplasma; if that is so, then we must accept the possibility that such events occurred and these events represented a misuse of the hidden science, which resulted in what the Druids feared most: "the sea bursting its bounds". The Tibetan *Stanzas of Dyzyan* although translated in the past century are said to originally date back several millennia. Like the *Mahabharata*, the Stanzas of Dzayn depict a holocaust engulfing two warring nations who utilize flying vehicles and fiery weapons. The fact that a Theocracy was evident as the form of government is strongly indicated:

> "The great King of the Dazzling face, the chief of all the Yellow-faced, was sad, seeing the evil intentions of the Dark-faced. He sent his air vehicles to all his brother chiefs with pious men within, saying, Prepare, arise, men of the good law, and escape while the land has not yet been overwhelmed by the waters." And: "The lords of the Storm are also approaching. Their war vehicles are nearing the land; one night and two days only shall the Lords of the Dark-faced arrive on this patient land. She is doomed when the waters descend on her. The Lords of the Dark-eyed have prepared their magic Agneyastra (the Hindu "Agneya weapon" - nuclear missile).... They are also versed in Ashtar, come, and use yours". The mention of Ashtar, the highest magical knowledge is also indicative of Akashic Record and Grid information! Further it records: "The great King fell upon his Dazzling face and wept. When the kings were assembled, the waters of the earth had already been disturbed. The nations crossed the dry lands. They went beyond the watermark. The Kings reached then the safe lands, in their air vehicles, and arrived in the lands of fire and metal... Stars (nuclear missiles?) showered on the lands of the Dark faced while they slept".

Is it not significant that the: "Lords of the Dark-faced", had advanced knowledge of the imminent deluge that was to cause such conflagration to the: "Yellow-faced", who were perhaps Mongolians who inhabited the ancient Gobi high civilization centre; further the flooding may have been the tidal wave that swept across eastern Asia and into Siberia at the end of the Ice Age. Is it not curious that in UFO witness accounts, people sometimes noted the appearance of Mongolian types after a UFO incident and whilst I assumed that this must be part of the manipulated or unnatural UFO, simply because three men in black with Mongolian features arrived in a rented car! One cannot discount the possibility that there is an attempt to link the UFO to this conflagration. Whilst the 'Dark-faced' and their civilization appears to have been annihilated, the final line of the text mentions that among the survivors were also those of 'the straight eye', which would indicate the peoples of Europe and the Middle East. This suggests that these people were also involved in the nuclear conflict; the possible remains of nuclear destruction are also to be found in these areas.

Whilst vitrified remains are evident in many places in the world, the most numerous of the New World era are located in the western **United States**. In 1850 the American explorer Captain Ives William Walker was the first to view some of these ruins situated in Death Valley. At the centre of a city about a mile long, with positions of streets and buildings still visible, he found a huge rock, between 20 and 30 feet high, with the remains of an enormous structure on top of it. The southern side of both the rock and the building was melted and vitrified. Walker assumed that a volcano had been responsible for this phenomenon, but there was no apparent volcano in the area. In addition, tectonic heat could not have caused such a liquefaction of the rock surface. An associate of Captain Walker who followed up his initial exploration commented: "The whole region between the rivers Gila and San Juan is covered with remains. The ruins of cities are to be found there which must be most extensive, and they are burnt out and vitrified in part, full of fused stones and craters caused by fires which were hot enough to liquefy rock or metal". Other vitrified remains exist in Southern California, Arizona and Colorado. The Mohave Desert is reported to contain several circular patches of fused glass. The possibility exists that an unknown post-Flood civilization was indeed destroyed by fire or nuclear conflict in western North America. Whilst the Druids evidently carried some memory of a cataclysm, there are other memories of cataclysms, which may or may not represent the same cataclysm or different cyclical cataclysms.

The ethnologist R. Baker who studied Canadian Indian tribal folklore was given a legend by a wise man of a dying totemic cult of northern Canada near the tundra region. The legend speaks of a time: "before the cold descended from the north", when the now-bleak tundra was instead rich with vegetation: "In the days when great forests and flowering meadows were here, demons came and made slaves of our people and sent the young to die among the rocks and below ground". Presumably he is speaking of mining and continues: "But then arrived the thunderbird, and our people were freed. We learned about the marvellous cities of the thunderbird, which were beyond the big lakes and rivers to the south. Many of our people left us and saw these shining cities and witnessed the grand homes and the mystery of men who flew upon the skies. But then the demons returned, and there was terrible destruction to declare that all life in the cities was gone nothing but silence remained". The Hopi Indians of the American South-west have a similar legend called "Kuskurza" the "Third World Epoch", which is stated in Frank Water's book *The Hopi* as: "Some of these of the Third World made a patuwvota and with their magical powers, made it soar through the sky. On this many of them flew to a great city, attacked it and returned *so quickly* that the inhabitants did not know where their attackers came from. Soon others from many nations were making patuwvotas, and (they) flew to attack one another. So corruption and destruction came to the Third World people, as it had come to those who were before". The last two words are intriguing for their ambiguity; does the legend imply **cyclical events**?

It is considered that the post Babel centres collapsed c. 2900 - 2800BC and I consider that this must have been a nuclear war, rather than any serious Magnetic Reversal, although serious Magnetic Reversals had occurred before and particularly the one that I propose wiped out the dinosaurs. Dr. Clifford L. Burdick an Arizonan geologist found a set of petrified tracks in the Paluxy River bed in Texas made by a dinosaur and in the *same geological strata* he found the footprint of a human being of formidable dimensions. The footprints have been discarded as not human, however they *look* remarkably human. They are 15 inches in length, but the fact that they were found in the same geological strata as the dinosaur prints, indicates that man and the dinosaur were contemporaneous. I have also stated that gravity must have been different in that era, otherwise such large sizes would not be encountered. When the average person imagines a Stone Age man, he usually pictures a crude-looking individual, dressed in animal skin and covered in hair. However in a cave near Lussac-les-Chateaux in Franc in 1937, Leon Pericard and Stephane Lwoff uncovered a number of engraved stones dating from the Magdalenian period, which drastically altered the accepted picture. The stones showed men and women in casual poses wearing robes, boots, belts, coats and hats. A young woman shown dressed in what looks like a trouser suit with a short-sleeved jacket, a pair of boots and a decorated hat, would not be out of place today. There is even what looks like a purse on her lap. Other examples show men wearing tailored pants and coats, broad belts and clasps and with beards and moustaches. The moustache was a prominent feature of the Celts perhaps by shape representing the two curved horns of the bull, which was an archetypal symbol that arose in Crete as the 'gates of horn' or the abode of the dead and therefore had religious significance. According to the above accounts of conflagration, it

392

appears that the majority were not aware of the marvels in the "cities". Thus even at this early stage, it appears that there was an elite and an underclass. Anthropologists labelled the drawings a fraud; however the out-of-place pictures were authenticated in 1938, when the Abbe Breuil confirmed that the individuals lived during the Magdalenian period of the Upper Palaeolithic. Today the stone engravings are in the prehistory library of Lussac-les-Chateaux, a number of less contentious drawings were on exhibition in the Musuee de l'Homme in Paris in the 1970's, however little is said of these drawings today and the more astounding ones are simply left in museum archives and thus mainly ignored at best or secreted away at worst. Just as the appearance of 'Dolly Varden' rosette hats in Palaeolithic Crete are swept away under some discrete carpet.

> I spent months trying to gain access to stored exhibits at the museum of Knossos, and only finally managed to see a smaller portion of my list, after employing the help of The British Consul in Heraklion. Despite extensive enquiries into the "Atlantis" coins or medals, found as a reference in *The Journal of Hellenic Studies*, I could find no catalogue reference and officials seemed to be at a loss to help. If the correspondence on the solution to the mechanism of Cancer in *Appendix II* represented red tape at its worst, I can assure you that icons that should be re-evaluated can only be done so by those individuals with 'proper credentials' and working through a recognised department of a University or research Foundation, which is controlled through the grant and publication system. I have published my Cancer research in a research Journal but that Journal is *The Journal of Complementary Medicine* and as such is not "on message", which is One World Order diktat. The grant and publication system controls researchers, as was evident in the case of Dr. Becker, who spoke up on the mind control capability of alleged defence technology in America and who I believe lost his research position. The outcome is that no research is published, which rocks any orthodox and accepted viewpoint, which is governed by the elite.

The Lussac models are by no means the only evidence of sophisticated dress in the Stone Age. Prehistoric cave paintings from the Kalahari Desert and South-west Africa, dated within the Stone Age period, show *light-skinned* men with *blond beards* and styled hair, wearing boots, tight fitting pants, multi-coloured shirts, and coats and gloves. To the north, the remains of a Palaeolithic man were uncovered near Vladimir, not far from Moscow, by Professor Otto Bader of the Ethnographical Institute of the Academy of Soviet Sciences. The man was well attired with trousers made of fur, embroidered shirt and jacket. It may never be acknowledged that the Spiritual impulse that arrived on Earth c. 10- 12 000 B.C. Brought not only a spiritual message and Cosmology but without question, the most universally recognised aspect of Stone Age civilization, its artwork. The most beautiful examples of this artwork are the polychrome paintings found in the caverns of Lascaux, Altamira and other caves in southern France and northern Spain. Whilst sculptured female statuettes, the 'Venus' figurines are found associated with the Gravettian remains from France, across Europe and Asia and as Far East as Siberia, it was not until the Magdalenian period, which must be the true Renaissance that art burst forth. Paintings from this period using limited colours available as yellow (from ochre, i.e. iron oxides), red and orange (from iron oxides and bison's blood), and brown and black (from heated animal fat and charcoal). Such paintings not only utilised colour to produce a three-dimensional colour effect, but the natural contours of the rock face itself. It was a technique unique in the history of art.

The paintings were carried out with bold strokes, with few corrections, indicating a confidence as executed by those who were skilled or masters in the technique. At Limeuil, in southwest France, 137 stone slabs were found with poorly drawn sketches on them, dating from the Palaeolithic age. In the midst of each sketch however, are details redrawn and corrected by someone who was obviously more artistically mature. These drawings show all the signs of a teacher's hand applied to a student's work - a master or mistress training the eye of the novice in not only artistic perception but also OBSERVATION. The ability to observe and perceive accurately no more than is seen, is also a part of the training of the scientist. There is little difference between the method of the artist and the scientist in that both set out to draw or model and observe what they see. The fact that three-dimensional form is a part of the high achievement of these paintings might be inferred that the Teacher was painstakingly taking the students through a process of observation. Whilst it has been assumed that Limeuil, may have been a school for artists, the unobvious conclusion was that these students were being taught a hierarchal system of knowledge, where aesthetics and observation were part of a hierarchal system of knowledge.

Consider the cave at Altamira on the northern coast of Spain, which among other caves in this region has been entitled "the cradle of art". The polychrome paintings of Altamira represent the peak of Magdalenian times. Altimira like other caverns penetrate into the side of *a hill* as long *caverns*, which immediately brings to mind secrecy: whilst the connection of cavern and hill immediately brings to mind the predilection of the Druids for such positions. The interesting point about Altamira is that not only are there represented naturalistic animal-pictures, but also other curious finds such as "roof-shaped", "comb-shaped" and "quasi-geometrical objects", which the archaeologists have been unable to classify. However clearly here is something akin to the geometric stones of Crete covered in thongs: the geometric Earth Grid and the "roof-shaped" or 'umbrella' of the UVG 120 sphere? In addition, there are a number of engravings of semi-human figures, which I have previously referred to, who are shown with beasts heads and a somewhat Reptilian-type body which may lead one to conclude that either such beings are human shaman-type beings, or this is some form of channelled information from the Grid on the phylogenetic evolutionary line, which may have produced the idea of etheric masters. If the Biblical Adamites or those present from the beginning had any aesthetic sense, then it was not displayed before the advent of the Magdalenian era. Radiocarbon dating for the Altimira site indicates a date of 14 000 B.C. plus or minus 400years. I cannot be totally accurate for spiritual intervention but it is conceivable that the date is slightly earlier than 10 -12 000 B.C. I gave. What is certain however is that among the things that most strikingly distinguish modern Humans from other hominids and the rest of the animal kingdom is the ability to represent things and events pictorially. The paintings during the Magdalenian period represent and important stepping- stone in the cultural evolution of humanity. A bison, from the cave at Altamira is depicted in polychrome and interestingly in a rock panel from the same cave, there is an impressionistic portrayal of horses, with the looming outline of the bison and mysterious superimposed mauve hands. The Bison gives the impression of a Spiritual ancestor depicted as it is, in vague and large outline. Is this then the Minos cult, in its early beginnings? The Minos cult was patriarchal, with the Bull as its totem beast. The horse was a later totem beast in Celto-Irish lore and the long manner in which the Celts wore their hair, washed with lime-wash was indicative of this totem beast and the Goddess in her death aspect. Further although there is no explanation of the "mauve hands", they are shown in a form of auric or biofield outline and violet was perhaps equivalent to the *rose-aura* of those initiates whose crown chakra had been opened. The colour may have been altered by the limitations of the artist's palette, but in later secret groups rose or red was an indication of the crown chakra. Would it be too presumptuous to assume that even in these early times, this group of initiates may have been the descendents of the Rose-Croix degree of the Brotherhood and the tribe of Judah? Were they channelling information from the Grid or morphogenetic bioplasma and hence the phylogenetic line, hence the amorphous Reptile-like creatures, which may have been viewed as their spiritual masters?

Moreover, although the majority of the paintings are in the consummate style of Magdalenian polychrome art, with a full palette of yellow ochre, browns, black and reds, there are also outline or flat-wash frescoes in Aurignacian style though the latter are often effaced or obliterated in part by the later Magdalenian paintings which have been executed over them. There is no reason to suppose that the MRC case or the secret groups perfected artistic accomplishment on their own and without help, since it was evident at Knossos that art declined in the post Religious Revolution era and that the high level of aesthetic art in Early Minoan Crete did not originate with the Cabal that took that civilization over and destroyed it. In trying to discover the originator of the art it is interesting that the Altamira bisons have a somewhat similar rendering to the Eland from the Khotsa cave in what used to be Basutoland (*Plate 12*). The identity of style and treatment is startling and further Altimira is more than 5,000 miles away from Basutoland; and many thousands of years separate the two paintings. Although I have no direct proof, I maintain that art was not part of the skills or psychology of those who were on earth from the beginning, but it was taken from elsewhere. Art has only flourished in periods of Renaissance when the Grail has surfaced, as was the case in Early Minoan Crete and during the Middle Ages. The decline of art after Magdalenian times is virtually a parallel to the events of Knossos thousands of years later in the Bronze Age, where a whole belief system and Cosmology was taken and hidden within a secret Bull-Minos cult. The decline of art following the destruction of the Early Minoan Civilization was dramatic. I will discuss these renaissance periods in Egyptian history later, but it follows the predictable course of the Grail surfacing. The poor quality of art under the patriarchal cult who masterminded the Revolution in Crete was an exact parallel to the decline of art after the Magdalenian period in Palaeolithic times. Such a parallel exists today, as that patriarchal cult assumes full control and the quality of art has once again dramatically declined and where faeces now represent art and receive prizes.

Art is also another marker, which one could trace alongside the hidden science. Renaissance periods only occur, when the message is fought briefly above ground, exposing the Holy Grail and "Underground Stream" of Wisdom. Within a few hundred years after the last great polychrome frescoes of the Font-de-Caume in Dordogne France were executed, men were painting pebbles and scratching magic symbols in the Franco-Cantabrian region. The Mesolithic period which followed the Magdalenian has not been viewed as moral or intellectual decadence, however it is deeply significant, that the naturalistic styles both in Mesolithic times and post Religious Revolution in Crete during the Bronze Age, were replaced by stilted and emblematic work which no doubt mirrored the spiritually impoverished thought of those who had spent many millennia as "despotic" masters practising black magic. Further it has been argued that the use of emblematic instead of naturalistic representation indicates an advance towards the development of those symbolic processes, which are an essential part of civilized men's mental equipment. However symbolism as I have covered in *The Battle of The Trees*, was originally used as an educational tool, enabling man to picture quite complex concepts at a time when communication and language was limited. After all how on Earth do you explain to such a fellow, the mechanics of space-time and Re-incarnation? However such symbolism was not only manipulated by a manaevolent group, but was withdrawn from humanity along with the hidden science and man no longer knew the truth of his existence. Such hidden symbolism arises to today in the complexity of Physics, which with its own abstract mathematical language cannot convey to the average man any part of the truth. Language is a barrier to freedom, however pictorial images and models are not. Symbolism can represent a whole language.

It is worth mentioning that objects resembling the so-called "roofs" (the umbrella of the UVG 120sphere?) and "combs" do not seem to occur on the richly engraved chattels and small objects of Magdalenian times. a Prior to this the chequer pattern, squares, dots and arrangements of lines occur. The Ogham script, the secret Alphabet which The Druids employed at a later date however employs lines, dots and the so-called curious "combs" which have been identified in cave paintings and thus could be an early type of Ogham Script, thus one might conclude that these 'tribal signs', were the earliest form of some alphabetic or very primitive writing. The chequer pattern I have already indicated as basket weave was emblematic of the womb and the Druids utilised this emblem in the willow osier baskets they sacrificed victims in. The chequer design also turned up at Knossos post the Religious Revolution and of course had undertones of Mosaic religion, thus connecting back once again to the Druids and Biblical Adamites. Where did the art originate, if not with this particular group? Was it learnt from some particular source and then absorbed into Magdalenian art? Were there a group of initiates at Altimira who were tutored or did they travel to be tutored elsewhere and then utilise that training? Were the amorphous demon like or quasi-human figures, the old magicians? We can only guess as to what led to the almost universal covering of the older Aurignacian paintings by the more recent Magdalenian ones. The peak of Aurignacian art in Lascaux in the Dordogne France, before Magdalenian times and the input of a new spiritual renaissance, were the Lascaux frescoes which show great sprawling bulls and a strange apocalyptic beast and barrel-bodied sturdy horses like those of the Han sculptures in China. The majority are poor quality outline paintings in flat wash and some pseudo-polychrome bearing no comparison to the Eland. There are beasts represented as the butt of missiles. The females are pregnant. The Abbe Breuil has stated that the most ancient of the Lascaux paintings may date from 30 000 years ago, but this may be an extreme figure. *Plate 13* shows what has been labelled: *The strange composite beast.*

At Le Portel and at Labattut-de-Sergeac in France there are animals looking over their shoulders. This has been referred to as the 'twisted perspective', and this perspective is known as to have been characteristic of one Aurignacian art phase. The 'twisted perspective' is also to be noted at La Pasiega, at la Haza and at Covalanas in Cantabria as well as in the Spanish Levantine sites. Font-de Gaume in South-western France also shows that 'roof-shaped' signs existed in the Aurignacian period and in addition, this cave also shows ladder-like symbols and rows of red dots, once again this may be the earliest Ogham script. In a small cavity are engraved circles resembling eyes, and there are other circles with radiating lines from a circumference, rather resembling "The Eye of Hermetic Intelligence" and the sign of the Solar King. On Diana's rock, in Rusape Southern Rhodesia, there is a painting, which is known as: "*The burial of a king*" which is assumed to be the human sacrifice of a King or Chieftain in an antelope mask. Further there are some apparent 'rain-making' scenes, which implies use of Cabalistic rites involving the Grid energies. Thus even at this incredibly early date there is a social order directed around a King or Chieftain, where human sacrifice is employed and in the case of this King he is clearly covered in dots. The implication is that Solar Kingship was employed at this early date. Several panels show the King and perhaps his Goddess, or at least a female, at the top of a ladder or a tree and uniting sky to earth while the rains descend in abundance. The ladder it seems had significance before biblical texts and Jacob's ladder.

The King as a fertility symbol is emphasised by the peculiar contraption attached to the King's penis. In some pictures the rains flow away as a great stream-serpent. Certainly the connection of Solar Kingship to dynastic lines perhaps but certainly fertility is implied, when we refer back to the amorphous quasi-human figures with hands raised apparently to the Sun God Ra or similar in the cave of Altimira. The Druids we know perhaps as biblical Adamites worshipped the Sun and employed human sacrifice. Interestingly in the Diana's rock picture, the King and Queen once again appear to belong to different races, unless the colours are emblematic of Sun and Moon. However the other personnel in the painting also appear to consist of attendants of two races and colours unless they too were coloured according to whether they served King (Sun) or Queen (Moon).

The most curious rock paintings in Western Europe are to be found at Trois Frères in the Dordogne region of France. These paintings in my opinion almost certainly bear a link to the hidden group that overran Knossos and removed a belief system and Cosmology. Significantly the Trois Frères is a complicated labyrinth of galleries with a ground plan that has been likened to that of a *starfish with its 5 arms* and certainly links then to the five dactyls, who I thought were the Cabal that installed themselves in the Psychro cave and conducted the Religious Revolution in Crete; where the octopus, with all the significance of eight arms or tentacles reaching out to all parts of the globe was found. There are paintings and engravings of rhinoceros, bison, aurochs, horse, wild ass, reindeer, ibex, bear, lions, wolf and a GREAT WHITE OWL. I refer you back to the connection of Druid, Rosicrucian and *Great White Brotherhood* covered previously. Is there some historical link of knowledge here that became the all-seeing eye of hermetic intelligence and a symbol of the New World Order? The best-known picture from the Trois Frères is the prancing or dancing figure of a man clad in a deerskin and wearing deer's antlers on his head. Although the face is shown, there is nothing very human about it. It has been assumed that the figure is a "sorcerer" *Plate 14*. The face however, shows a remarkable resemblance to the quasi-human figures at the Altimira cave. Further the artist of this painting has shown a body orifice in the act of excreting - a bull, which in Crete had symbolised Solar Kingship. What is being implied here, fear of beast or fear of Solar King for the "sorcerer"? Further look at *Plate 15*, the *'masked shaman'*, which is from the same cave in Ariege Dordogne France: Once again half- man, half- beast, with strange round bulbous eyes, that I noted were a feature of some UFO accounts. Look at the claws on the front 'hands', which bear no resemblance to a deer, but together with the hind limbs look like human internal structure, which implies that this is not a mere cloak of an animal which is being worn.

The appearance of man-beast then, is frequently displayed among the Aurignacian period. These paintings give the most striking parallel to the group that overran the Minoan Civilization and who worshiped a Solar-Bull -King cult, where many seals depict a Man-bull in the circular position, indicating The Cycle of Eternal Return OF SOLAR KINGSHIP. The discovery of Re-incarnation from the teachings of the Early Minoans may indicate a time when these patriarchal cults realised that the information they were channelling was representative of their ancestors (themselves in effect!). The idea of the totem beast eaten or sacrificed in *memory* of their ancestry, thus giving rise to the symbolic representation of that in man-bull seals from the Late Minoan period. The phallic nature of the cult is indicated by the shape and size of penis and certainly icons showing males with large penises turned up at Knossos post the Religious Revolution. Curiously too the head is turned backwards, in the so-called 'twisted' character typical of Aurignacian art. However not only did the Man-Bull feature in post Religious Revolution Knossos, but the 'twisting' feature also turned up. The Harvester's vase (*Alternative 4*), showed priests who were marching in procession and one priest looks mockingly upon another, who has tripped and fallen whilst looking back. 'Don't look back', appeared to be the motto employed here and was used in the story of Sodom and Gomorrah, where Lot was turned into a pillar of salt for doing so. This 'looking back' theme, appears then in its earliest form I believe in Aurignacian or Palaeolithic Art. The connection to the pillar or stone is perhaps Semitic and the fact that the Harvester's vase is connected to agriculture as the men carry farming implements, further implies re-birth or fertility. Thus it appears that whilst the Palaeolithic art demonstrated a predilection for looking back (at the ancestry) in the Minoan period of renaissance there was perhaps this new thought of marching forward under the new philosophy of re-birth. The theme seems to have developed from 'looking back' (in Palaeolithic times), to a new motto 'Don't look back' (in the Bronze Age period of Minoan Crete). Putting all these clues together, one might conclude that a new impetus in the Magdalenian period may have, with a belief system and Cosmology rendered hope and loss of fear on the past to ordinary men and women who had been dominated by those who sought despotic rule and who were governed in their own psychology by fear having survived some great cataclysm. Had the Grail message and Cosmology been allowed to spread, the Earth would have been a very different place today. However those who had seen that cataclysm and had probably caused it, did not relinquish their old goals of a One World Order a Theocracy headed by the sorcerers or priests; they simply took the knowledge and message for themselves and continued with their goals of enslavement of humanity whilst retaining their elitist view and lineage from Adam. What was given freely to all men was taken and re-written. The earliest 'religion' or beliefs however centred as I have stated before on magic, black cabalistic science, sorcery and voodoo. Sacrifice was inherent within that system to propitiate angry gods, which was believed before the Grail message came to Earth to remind man of the immortality of his own soul and to warn him - he was trapped by the Grid.

Neither can it be stated with any certainty whether or not some form of genetic engineering was known before such a cataclysm had been employed, with quasi-human subjects as the result. One cannot compare the times before the end of the last epoch and cataclysm with times now, since this cycle IS UNIQUE. During this cycle there has been a constant refraining influence, whereas in the past cycle who is to know whether the Yatrus domination, that Ron Hubbard identified, and which I will cover later, did not run according to Yatrus's postulate of seeing how far it could be taken. What dramatizations in the mind of Rome occurred, when in the worst memory of their souls and the fight against Christianity as the religious arm of a political goal, they brought *bulls* into the Roman Arena, to 'mate' with Christian women, who died in the most horrible of circumstances. In fact the Roman Arena was a complete THEATRE where dramatization of the past coupled with political conflict between the two groups was allowed to run amok. I will cover this point again later, but here I will point to art as the significant marker of TWO OPPOSING MINDS, who circa 10 0000 B.C sought to in one case to enslave humanity and in the other to free him.

In South-west Africa there are cave paintings that are especially striking and many of them of considerable aesthetic value. At Nau Gap on the old Ovambaland border are many beautiful polychrome pictures of giraffe, of ostrich, of kudu, of springbok and of fabulous creatures that here, as at Lascaux and the prehistoric European caves show some similarity of source. Among the paintings showing human figures there is a whole class that offers very puzzling problems. These are pictures of individuals who are clearly neither 'Kaffir' nor Bushman. At Impey's cave in Southern Rhodesia there is a group of "white" people "busy at their toilette and taking baths". Whilst Breuil suggested they might be Pre-Hellenic, the '"foreigners" include an enigmatic woman. In a rock-shelter at Leopard's Ravine, some hundred miles north of Windhoek in South-west Africa there is one very elaborately dressed and painted woman (*Plate 16*). She has been described as of "Mediterranean" type, with short, wavy hair decorated with rows of pearls. The woman also wears a "sweater", "tight-fitting pants" and shoes. She bears in her hand a cup-like flower, which remarkably looks like the lotus with implications to the Lily, employed in Early Minoan iconography as the flower of the Great Goddess, with her role of the gift of immortality. It was through Her in the spiritual world that the Early Minoans believed that they were united, in the cycle of birth and death in relation to Karma. The enigmatic figure almost certainly reminds one of Cretan frescoes. However all archaeologists agree, that it is a most odd painting to find in the desert wilds of South-west Africa. Some have described her as "a missionary" and the presence of the flower certainly connects this to beliefs in Early Minoan times - a belief in Re-incarnation, which was connected to a whole Cosmology. Was she indeed teaching these people the truth of their existence? The implication of white and black combined in her alleged clothes may hold more significance than has been recognised. In Plate *16*, we see the unmistakable style of aesthetic art, that was the hallmark of the wonderful works of art found in the frescoes of the Early Minoan civilization. The presence of sophisticated clothes almost certainly reminds us of those cave paintings found at Lussac-les-Chateaux in France. The introduction of aesthetic beauty had a lasting effect on the development of mankind. Further colour and three-dimensional perspective that burst upon the scene in the Magdalenian period, was as equally startling as the art that was created in Minoan Crete in the Bronze Age.

We know that there was a white race, but one should not assume that they arose from Adam or that there was not another stock. Neither should one consider that evolution was a continuous process, there were very definitely inputs from certain individuals, which dragged humanity forward. In describing the sophistication of certain Palaeolithic works of art, prehistorian Robert Silverberg says: "The cave paintings are upsetting to those who prefer to think of Quaternary man as little more than an ape: Not only do they indicate great craftsmanship, but also they point to a whole constellation of conclusions; that primitive man had an organized society with continuity of shape, religion and art. It was also dismaying to learn that the earliest inhabitants of Western Europe had scaled heights of artistic achievement that would not be reached again until late in the Christian era, that exploded the theory that man's rise from barbarism had been steady and always upward".

What exactly was the "missionary" woman teaching, where she holds forth a lotus, which became the emblematic Lily of the Cretan Great Goddess? The bow she carries is not only a bow, but also the crescent Moon and the Lotus was a sign of healing and biofields. Whether such knowledge was taken into the patriarchal groups, or whether she sought to inform the people of Africa of the existence of such knowledge, which would one day be used against them, if it had not been already used, is interesting in so far as in the cave Piedra Escrita, near Fuencaliente, Sierra Morena, in southern Spain, there is a painting entitled *'human couples'*: *Plate 17*, which shows what are believed to be highly *stylised* human couples with accompanying figures. Further description outlines there are two "dead" women without heads bottom centre, near is an "animal" upside-down; probably it is thought "also an emblem of death". However my attention is drawn to several aspects of this painting. Notice the *'Tree of Life'* at the top left as being larger than what I consider the 'dead' variety at bottom centre. Notice the cup- shaped head of the male and female at the top left, next to the 'Tree of Life'. Is this the lotus-shaped flower, or a developed crown chakra? Further is the whole painting rather a scale of energy, initiation and Chakra opening, from fully aware at the top, to 'dead', at the bottom, rather reminiscent of the scale of resonant energies, which was to appear thousands of years later in the Pythagorean tonal scale and a couple of thousand years after that, in Ron Hubbard's *'Chart of Human Evaluation'* in Scientology. What are the curious antenna-like structures on females in the position just above centre? – Channelling methods of 'priestesses'? Was this then a centre of secret occult development in Spain in the Palaeolithic period? Had the knowledge intended for healing and the freedom of man already been taken? - An event, which would be repeated at Knossos 1450 B.C. during the Religious Revolution. and once again in the events of Golgotha. Stylisation in art was very indicative of the group who took over Knossos and such stylisation occurred in the Ogham alphabet, which compares poorly to the three-dimensional art from another source. The rigid schematization in art is almost certainly the indicator or marker for the patriarchal group. The fact is, when the Grid is followed, as in channelling of information from the Grid, or robotic-like actions, art reflects such a thinking process as is evidenced today, when Grid Art, is presented in places like The Tate Gallery London, supported by an accolade that many do not agree with. Stuffed dead animals, un-made beds, condoms or whatever, reflect the stiff, stylized and robotic Poppy-Goddesses with hands raised to Ra, the Sun God, during the Religious Revolution of Knossos, which saw art decline. Further in UFO witness accounts there were mechanical voices, which I further discussed in *Alternative 4* and which indicated mechanical robotic beings acting under some form of orders, which equally could be Grid controlled beings and reflected a past holographic memory of this planet. Compare the schematic art of Spain with the 'head of an eland' from Clontarf, near Barkly East, Cape Province, S. Africa. This beautiful painting is quite a different style from the mass of so-called 'Bushman Art'; it is also different from schematic or stylised art, the main difference being OBSERVATION with its connection not only to the first lessons of art but science!

In many instances the abstract signs that appear in Stone Age archetypal or pictograph writing, are more than just a random series of lines or dots but make planned patterns. At first many historians regarded the series only as crude forms of decorations, but now they are identified as notation, some strictly mathematical, others of a chronological nature, recording such astronomical phenomena as the phases of the moon. Alexander Marshack an American researcher, analysed prehistoric notation found on a mammoth tusk from Gontzi, a late Palaeolithic site west of Kiev in the Ukraine and found unmistakable evidence that it was a detailed record of lunar phases. What is more, the notation pointed to its use as a calculator, that is the phases of the moon could have been predicted in advance. The Gontzi bone was thus a scientific instrument of a high order, demonstrating that Palaeolithic man was more than a mathematician and astronomical observer he was also a scientist.

A STONE AGE ONE WORLD ORDER

Archaeological research shows that almost every one of the ancient cultures of the Middle East and the New World possessed at the earliest stages of their so-called development, a primarily lunar calendrical system. The early Egyptians used a solar and stellar system, based on the simultaneous rising of the sun and the star Sirius once a year. It is also thought that there was an older calendrical tradition, which was lunar in character, dating back into predynastic times and to the very beginnings of Egyptian history. Similarly in Mesopotamia, the first calendars of the Sumerian city-states were also lunar, as was the case with early Hindu and Chinese civilizations. The Incas had an official solar calendar, but their division of the year into twelve months hints at an earlier lunar tradition. Whilst Historians have argued that the time count of the moon was developed in the Stone Ages and then transmitted over thousands of years to the first civilized cultures, sacred historical manuscripts provide evidence that instead the Stone Age peoples and the peoples of the ancient civilizations directly inherited a lunar calendar system from a civilization older than both of them. In *Genesis 7 - 8*, there is a record of Noah's diary of the Flood. The days of the months and the lengths of time Noah gives for the duration of events, when placed in the framework of the present Jewish calendar, provides some interesting data. For instance, the first ten dates Noah records fall in the calendar on the Jewish Sabbath, Saturday. This is hardly co-incidental, as it confirms that the data is based on a calendrical system similar to the Jewish calendar, which has remained basically unchanged in its structure for millennia. The diary was kept according to the Solar year of 365 days. But the most significant fact is that the Jewish calendar, as with the one that Noah used, is based on a lunar count of 354 days. This suggests that the lunar calendar had its true origins during the antediluvian period and we know that the system was in use immediately after the Flood. The lunar calendar appears to have been transmitted to the post-Babel civilizations.

Some aspects of the elusive Ogham Script appeared to pop up at Knossos after the Religious Revolution in Crete. The curious "comb" artefacts found in prehistoric cave paintings look remarkably similar to some components of the script and later Beth-Luis Nion Alphabets. Dots and lines feature in the scripts and a piece of reindeer bone found in a cave near Rochebertier France, has markings on it that are more than just decoration, they have every appearance of being letters of some form of writing. In this case the letters resemble or in some cases are identical to the enigmatic script of Tartessos, a city civilization that existed in southern Spain and is believed by some to be the Biblical Tarshish. What makes the similarities of writings unusual, is that orthodox historians place the reindeer bone in the Magdalenian period 10 000 - 12 000 B.C. However the

Tartessian civilization has recently been assigned to the period between 2500 and 2000 B.C. There is an obvious discrepancy with this dating, for it is highly unlikely that a script, once developed, would have remained relatively unchanged for ten millennia. The scripts demonstrate that the cultures in which they were found, must have been contemporaneous rather than separated by a vast span of time and the Tartessos civilization peak must be somewhat earlier than given. Certainly as evidenced above there seemed to be a hidden occult group in this area, during the Palaeolithic age. Contact between Palaeolithic people and the city of Tartessos if indicated, means that they must have existed in the same time period. Other finds confirm this. Palaeolithic antler bones found at Le Mas d'Azil and La Madeleine are inscribed with signs identical to Phoenician script from approximately 2000 B.C. Le Mas d'Azil is also the site where many painted pebbles from the Azilian period of the Mesolithic age have been discovered. A number of these pebbles are marked with signs and symbols that were once predominant throughout the Mediterranean - again, between 3000 and 2000 B.C. Compare the significance of pebbles to the so-called *Partridge fresco from the Caravanserai,* of the Early Minoan period of Crete, which I reproduced in *The Battle of The Trees*, where round objects were said to represent "veined pebbles". The Fresco was produced circa 1500 B.C. according to museum literature and thus at the time of the Religious Revolution. Once again the pebbles in that case represent not alphabetic language but archetypal pictorial language or archetypal symbolism. What is implied by this symbolisation? well there are two opposing semi-circles in 2-dimensions, which would become two opposing circles in 3-dimensions (if the pattern continued around the pebble), whether that indicated two opposing Universes, groups, or a Cycle of Eternal Return is not clear, but there are two partridges significantly placed in antithesis and mirror image form, one looking *forwards* and one looking *backwards*, with the Underground Stream symbolised on the left and a Tree of Life, with a 19 year solar lunar cycle indicated by the plant at the extreme left, with its 19 leaves. Thus one concludes this is part of the changeover period from Matriarchal to Patriarchal. The partridges represent presumably the Twin Kings, but significantly in mirror image so that again we see the play on looking forward (to the new religion) and looking back (to the past tribal ancestry and dynasty). This IS THE WHOLE WRONG ASSOCIATED WITH THE RELIGIOUS REVOLUTION, conducted by the Druids or tribe of Judah as we decided. They tagged their own significances of dynasties and tribal ancestry of Judah, onto the Grail Message of Re-incarnation and a Cosmology, coupled with a specific learning programme. Re-incarnation, Second Coming and holy (Holly) Messiah ship was to become strictly male country and the sole right of Solar Kings and the priesthood, leaving humanity to pass responsibility and power and therefore control, to the so-called divine philosopher kings, governed by a secret priesthood. The condemnation of Kings in biblical texts must rest on this point.

We know from numerous sources that there were a number of hominid types in early times, and at around1.8 million years ago in what is now part of northern Kenya, there were four kinds of hominids. Even in Palaeolithic times, there is a vast difference between the 'Missionary' woman and other cave paintings of e.g. "The Sorcerer": who clearly is shorter in limb. The Gilgamesh epic from Mesopotamia, tells the tale of the hero Gilgamesh and his many adventures in the world immediately after Babel. Gilgamesh's companion in his experiences was Enkidu who as a youth, and who was described as having lived as an animal *among the animals*. He was according to the story found by one of Gilgamesh's *civilized contemporaries*, who took him captive and taught him the ways of his own people. Enkidu is further mythical and legendary proof, that there was an elitist group above another group who were considered primitive. In India another epic story, *The Ramayana*, depicts a race described as "ape-men" who aided the noble Rama in a war against the Ravana Kingdom of Ceylon. The Chinese also describe a race of primitive men coexisting with their own civilization. These men were considered degenerates 'Mao-tse' (interestingly enough!) in the Chinese treatise *Shu King* (part 4, ch. 27, p.291). The Shu King relates that the Mao-tse once: "troubled the Earth, which became full of their robberies". The Lord Huang-ti, an emperor of the Chinese Divine Dynasty, then ordered a system of ethnic cleansing and they were exterminated. Perhaps it was this genocide that accounts for the sudden disappearance of Sinanthropus and Giganthropus from the Chinese palaeontological record and the recent observation that we do not derive from Neanderthal man and the lack of remains in Britain of archaeological remains of humans.

A race of primitive men is found in *The Bible* in the Book of *Job*. The post-Flood patriarch depicted a wild people with whom he did not wish to associate. Like the Mao-tse, they were known as thieves and robbers and "wild". They inhabited rocks and cliffs and brayed like animals, without intelligent speech. Job condemns them as the "scourge to the land" and the "children of fools". Whether these people were the mutants left behind from a previous cataclysm or nuclear war prior to the Deluge, who survived in some form I could not say. But it is curious that they did not develop in line with other Hominids, why that should be so, and why such a degenerate line existed even at this late date is even more curious. Many commentators believe that Job was identical with Jobab, the *thirteenth son* of Joktan, mentioned in the genealogy of *Genesis 10*. If that is correct, then it means that Job, a *sixth-generation descendent of Noah*, lived about 2698 to 2348 B.C., which places him and the 'wild people', he described in the post Babel period. This is certainly interesting since the cave paintings of the sorcerer and shaman are quite different from that of the woman missionary and those depicted in the Cretan frescoes. There has as I have mentioned been an attempt to place the Deluge much later than the period in which it occurred probably as far back as 20 000 B.C. It seems ridiculous to try to place the Deluge circa 3 000 B.C. when recovery from such an event would require many thousands of years and not the short time it took civilizations such as the Early Minoan to arrive. It seems that there is an attempt to place the Patriarchs and the post Flood era close to the development of art and pottery and a general renaissance period, thus drawing attention away from the primitive species that are associated with the Palaeolithic era.

The idea of a world unity or World Order in the years following the Deluge, is related in the Genesis story of the Tower of Babel, where survivors of the Deluge in Noah's Ark, construct a world centre and a tower that was to reach to the skies, based on the efforts *to remain together*: "lest we be scattered abroad upon the face of the whole earth". This element of staying together was identified in Fenuisa Farsa the great grandson of Noah and grandson of Magog, who was described as "the vine man", or he who draws together and it would appear that this may well have been the origins of The Brotherhood or Freemasonry as it is currently known. Thus the One World civilization was no more than the old postulates of such an order that had existed prior to The Deluge with the so-called antediluvians, and having survived that continued with 'Business as Usual'. Babel was thus chosen to become the capital of the world, where the organization of the post-Flood peoples were supposedly to be directed from. This centralised city was comparable to the way Cain had organized his descendants, under one rule by means of the construction of Enoch City. Babel was therefore a political centre for world government, a postulate that is coming to fruition today in The One World Order programme, of which European Union is a part. The fact that the Tower of Babel was to reach to the skies was probably significant and reminds one of the hidden science and Energy Grid or even New York! There had probably been a world centre before, where the surface energies of the so-called ley-line system had been utilised and mapped. The modern Druids claim that their forefathers built the ley lines and were able to utilize the linear energies for **flight**. On certain days a ley line or geo-magnetic line, would become active, by a sunrise directly down a path, the currents were directed so as to charge a body to such a degree, that it could be levitated and made to move along the path of specific level of magnetic density, which may account for modern UFO technology, which has been researched and tested it would appear without explanation to humanity. Druidic tradition tells of such heroes as Mog Ruith, Bladud and the magician Abiris (Druid), the Hyperborean, who possessed flying vehicles activated by the ley-line energies and were able to travel in them as far as Greece. It is probably not co-incidental that all the ley-line charts linking the world and Greece have been removed from all public sources. The stories of these flights usually end in disaster, an eclipse takes place suddenly terminating the power sources along the lines, and the hero and his craft plunge to destruction. Evidently then, the solar lunar calendar had more import than has generally been recognised, because an eclipse of the sun or moon does indeed cause a sudden drop in the level of the earth's surface magnetic activity. The obsession with predicting eclipses must also depend on this. The manoeuvres of alleged UFO's would certainly defy known aircraft technology and in the epics of India, the craft arrived suddenly which would fit with craft using some ley line energy system.

Thus there was an early recognition that Earth currents that are affected by planetary motion also affect fertility and the ability to use Grid energies. Magnetic flows are especially agitated over geological faults, over which many of the prehistoric ley lines have been found. Temples and holy places were set on lines that were constructed in relation to the positions of the sun, moon and planets. Major H. Taylor proposed that the units of measurement used to construct these lines were, like those of the early Egyptian geodetic surveys, based on simple fractions of the earth's dimensions. He found examples of these ley lines not only in Britain, but also all over Europe and the Middle East. Heinish concluded that they bore testimony to the past existence of a widespread civilization that possessed advanced knowledge of both technology and magic. The ley lines then have been found in nearly every corner of the globe, and associated with them, numerous stories of a flow of magic energy. In his book *The Fairy Faith of Celtic Counties*, J. D. Evans-Wentz recalls how an Old Irish seer explained to him that mysterious currents flow along the paths, but that their exact nature has been forgotten. Standing stones have existed in very early cultures and which mark ley- lines; for example in their conquest of the Etruscans, the early Romans noted standing stones set in linear patterns over the entire countryside of Tuscany. These lines were marked significantly enough by stone pillars even as far as Greece, once again pin-pointing a Semitic influence and quite possibly the Druids, who took flights there?! The Romans who discovered the tracks and pillars were not surprised, since they had found them in almost every country they subjugated across Europe, North Africa, Crete, and as far west as the regions of ancient Babylon and Nineveh. We now recognise that the Romans utilised these straight lines for their straight roads. The Aborigines are one group, who never forgot these lines and many churches along the south coast of England have been erected on the ley line system.

The magnetic currents appear to be directed in some way, by the placement of the standing stones along the ley lines and according to Guy Underwood author of *The Patterns of the Past*, the standing stones served the same purpose as the needles of Chinese acupuncture. Just as needles re-direct the flow of *life force*, in the human body and restore it to health, so the standing stones were placed in such a manner so as to realign earth magnetism from the natural paths to artificial ones. The purpose of re-direction is given by John Michel who wrote in: *The view over Atlantis*: "A great scientific instrument lies sprawled over the entire surface of the globe. At some period - perhaps it was about 4000 years ago

- almost every corner of the world was visited by a group of men who came with a particular task to accomplish. With the help of remarkable power, by which they could cut and raise enormous blocks of stone, these men erected vast astronomical instruments, circles and erect pillars, pyramids, underground tunnels, cyclopean alignments, whose course from horizon to horizon was marked by stones, mounds, and earthworks". We know that the Druids utilised hills and mountains apart from caves, which appear to have had some connection to regions of high electro-magnetic energy and one assumes were of use in their channelling of information from the Grid. Such a global undertaking implies the existence of a single authority directing a unified effort for some purpose, if not a One World Order overseen by an elite. Such an effort could be described by The Tower of Babel and the Semitic survivors who no doubt had carried with them secret knowledge and the hidden science which was the Black Cabala, which enabled them to undertake such an enterprise. However one must consider whether the Druids as Biblical Adamites, were such a group and whether their World Order which failed at that attempt, was repeated in succession as the Celtic Commonwealth, right up to Hitler's Third Reich and the current World Order of The Rose. The question as to what effectively broke the Babel p One World Order, might be more usefully applied to the question **who** broke that Order? Since World Orders simply do not fade away, as evidenced by Caesar's culling of the Celts and Druids. Whether or not the evidence for nuclear conflagration in Europe and America is implied here it would be impossible to prove. Importantly then, in the post Deluge era the One World Order was broken, and its world centre ceased to operate. Significantly the Order was fragmented, and the unity was no longer possible, a point that perhaps the Fore-Fathers of America realised all those years later, when they broke Government up into individual parts, not under any one central pyramidal control apex (*Alternative 4*). A point evidently lost on today's Americans *and* Europeans.

The place where currents were accumulated was usually characterised by a mound or tower. The Tower of Babel may have been the receiving station for the ley-line currents of the Earth. By possession or control of ley-line energies, the World Order was in total control of the Grid energies. It is impossible to say whether they were merely repeating or continuing where they had left off, prior to the Deluge and presumably misuse of those energies, but evidence suggests that a technological civilization may and probably did exist before that Deluge. One might pose the question whether they had been tapping the Zero-point energy from the vacuum of space, free energy that I will come to shortly; but there was probably some knowledge of atomic fission, which may account for the burns on Moses face as he descended from Mt. Sinai. Babel then, may have been the seat of control for a World Order, where languages and religion were decided in a hierarchal system and must have centred on the monopoly of Grid energies for purposes of channelling and warfare. The post-Flood ley-line system was very probably a reconstruction of a system used before the Flood and the antediluvians had developed a sophisticated form of technology that incorporated the use of the hidden science, to obtain material and political power; but such a system was also used for occult purposes as well, presumably channelling of information. These early priesthoods must have considered information that was channelled as having come from Masters or their God It is these occult energies that will prove most important as I begin to illustrate just how those occult energies have been utilised in developing Mind and Body Control of the populous through religion, healing, politics and just about every facet of life as we know it TODAY. That is an important point, since it would be inconceivable that such knowledge or power has been forgotten and one suspects that many irrational wars are being fought for control of the Grid, such as has been suggested in Afghanistan and the Middle East and Balkans?

Shortly after the Deluge, there is evidence that a world survey took place, which accurately depicted landmasses. Along the routes, which the surveyors took, there existed several examples of rock drawings; the most notable is the *Writing Rock* near Grenora, North Dakota, and *Writing-on Stone* in Alberta, Canada. Another rock script occurs in British Columbia, and petroglyph expert Philip Thornburg was the first to recognise among the stone pictures a carving of a sisutl - the *Chinese dragon*, with its archetypal symbolism connected to the Grid energies. William and Mae Marie Coxon as amateur archaeologists, studied petroglyphs from around the world. They concluded that at a very remote period in human history a group of people they call the Stone-Writers left their traces on every continent. The Coxons discovered 241 special sequences of particular geometric signs and symbols. The date of appearance of the Stone-Writers was estimated at 1500 years before the rise of Egypt. Interestingly from the drawings themselves, the two researchers were able to describe the Stone-Writers as average to above average in height, wearing short *kilts* that came to the knees. These men then, charted and geographically surveyed the world after the Flood. Presumably some of the ancient maps I mentioned previously were charted in more ancient times from such explorations, using Grid energies. Given that I assumed the ascendants of Noah were Druid, then whilst it is thought that the descendents of Noah undertook a geographic survey and exploration of the entire world's surface post Deluge, should we conclude that Druid and descendent of Noah are synonymous? And it was in fact the tribe of Judah. In *Genesis 10:25* a descendent of Noah called Peleg was apparently given his name because: "in his day was the earth divided". Whilst this has been interpreted as a division of nations, it could refer to either two groups (Matriarchal and Patriarchal), or the exploration and carving up of the globe according to the ley-line system. Mizraim, a grandson of Noah, may have also been involved in this cartographic exercise. His name means 'to delineate, to draw up a plan, to make a representation'. Such a plan need not refer to cartography or mapping, but a

410

World Order, some evidence for that may be in that Mizraim was also the founder of ancient Egypt. Given that Magog was a grandson of Noah, then it might be assumed, that at an early stage two dynasties from one root occurred, perhaps with Magog as head of the dynasty that would become the Celtic/Greek and the other the Celtic/Egyptian; which would become the former would become the lost thirteenth tribe and in the latter the twelve tribes. It is significant to note that at least two of the Renaissance maps showing advanced knowledge, the Piri Reis chart and the Reinal chart, dating back to 1510, were based on a circular projection with the focal point in *Egypt*. A third descendent of Noah may also have participated in this mapping of the globe, Almodad, which when translated from Hebrew means 'measurer'. In the Chaldean Paraphrase of Jonathan, there is preserved an ancient tradition that tells that he was the 'inventor of geometry' - qui *mensurbat terran finibus'* - 'who measured the earth to its extremities'. Almodad (*Alm*/Arm – *dad*/father/Noah?) is regarded as a progenitor of the southern Arabians. The fact that the Moors had a pattern that was replicated in the research of the chemist Peter Plitchta mentioned previously provides another significant link. The mapping process is thought to have occurred over the period of 2800 B.C to 2500 B.C. over a span of 300 years. Antarctica in the Bauche map of 1737 which is copied from an older Greek map, shows the continent completely ice-free, whilst the Orontius map of 1531 indicates that the centre of the continent was beginning to fill with ice, when its source maps were drawn; but the Piri Reis chart of 1513 and the Mercator chart of 1569, picture only the Antarctic coast left uncovered by glaciers. In the Zeno brothers' map of 1339, Greenland is shown free of glaciers and was thus prior to the Ice Age, whilst Ptolemy's map of the North depicts a glacial sheet advancing across south-central Greenland, thus there seems to be a continuous mapping process before, during and throughout the Ice Age.

If one was to pose one solution as to why some of the Egyptian mummies were white, or the uniformity of language and other anomalies in the post Deluge era, one might pose that a One World Order, imposed a system of political and religious conformity on a populous through a series of Solar Kings puppetted by a secret magical priesthood - A Theocracy descending from Adam or D (ad) the Father. It has been queried just how in several regions of the world, and at several points in prehistoric time, collections of small, independent polities can share fundamental social and cultural institutions, a high level of interaction, and a common developmental trajectory, yet at the same time appear to maintain their individual autonomy over the centuries. The idea of competition between these polities is only a limited view, where interaction as equals causes these polities to create and maintain the social and material environments that lead to their co-evolution: Such polities serving to proximate social environments for one another, where both individually and as a group they are challenged by one another as well as by their wider social and natural environments. This certainly according to Darwinian theory and genetics creates some form of environmental stress that creates new and evolving species, which when applied to competition, serves as a way of evolving the technological and cognitive thinking process of man. This discounts that there has always been in every age, a peer or elitist group, who have not only promoted such competition, in order to drive man forward for THEIR OWN ENDS or perhaps the "accelerated evolution" mentioned in the section of the World Order of the Rose. However the conformity and uniformity must arise from a central dominating group who dominated all other groups.

CLIMATIC MYSTERIES

Without wishing to trail through the Deluge myths here, it is sufficient to say that there is almost complete agreement among them all on three main features: 1. There is a universal destruction of the human race and all other living things by water. 2. An Ark, or boat, is provided as the means of escape. 3. A seed of mankind is preserved to perpetuate the human race. A fourth point occurs in some traditions, but not all, and that is the wickedness of man is given as the cause of the Flood. However most of these legends do reveal a system of unbroken Kingship, which is associated with the possession of secret scientific knowledge or occult science. Further if Noah survived the Flood it is reasonable to assume that he also carried with him not only fundamental history of the Flood, but also knowledge of the technology that existed before. However an interesting fact emerges from a study of Kingships, which are listed for Biblical, Egyptian and Chaldean Patriarchs, Gods and Kings respectively.

BIBLICAL PATRIARCHS	EGYPTIAN GODS	CHALDEAN KINGS
Adam	Ptal	Alorus
Seth	Ra	Aloparus
Enos	Su	Almelon
Cainan	Seb	Ammenon
Mahalaleel	Osirus	Amega;ris
Jared	Set	Daonus
Enoch	Hor	Aedorachus
Methuselah	Tut	Amempsinus
Lamech	Ma	Otiartes
Noah	Hor	Xisuthros

Thus whereas Noah is the hero of the biblical Flood story, Xisuthros is the survivor of the Flood in the Chaldean account. If Noah and his "seed" re-populated the Earth, then one would expect if there was a One World Order, a parallel sequence of records within the various legends, which would fundamentally give the same history and sequence of events including the number of antidiluvian Kings, the leaders who ruled from the beginning until the Flood. This is the case in the three civilizations, where for example Cainan, the name of the forth Sethite patriarch means 'a craftsman' and Ammenon also means 'craftsman'. Aedorachus, the seventh Babylonian King listed, has the meaning 'bearer of divine revelations, he to whom the secrets of heaven and earth are revealed'; Enoch his biblical counterpart has a name that can be translated as virtually the same thing. This is curious in so far as in *The Battle of*

The Trees, I quoted Eliphas Levi a member of the secret societies, whom Alister Crowle the famous black magician was later to claim as his own prior incarnation, as predicting that a "Universal Kingdom" would emerge, and that it would be had by those with the "keys to the East ". This was said just prior to The French Revolution, which I claimed in that book, paved the way for the removal of Monarchy and the eventual formation of A Federal United States of The West, or European Union. I assumed in *Alternative 4*, that Levi was referring to the hidden science and technology that today has emerged in the so-called 'Star Wars' defence initiative in America, with the HAARP and GWEN programmes. However I have previously here mentioned the keys as those of Hermes, which refer to the hidden Cabalistic science but there has always been the undertone of the elusive Enochian "keys". Thus one might conclude that certain Cabalistic knowledge was known in the antediluvian era and were passed in an unbroken line to Noah who survived the Flood in an unbroken bodyline or "seed". Technological or theoretical advancements made in the Enoch era had allowed the development of technology, which was subsequently misused and brought about a cataclysmic destruction, namely the Deluge.

The Babylonian and Biblical accounts of the Flood agree, that it was brought about because the Earth was full of violence. However significantly this is laid at the doorstep of man, rather than any One World Order and the thinking behind that Order, which lies at cause of any society and its downfall. As I noted in *The Battle of The Trees*, before any decline in a society (or group) can occur, there is an occult influence at work *within* that society, working from within, which initiates that decline. It is a datum that you should not forget and where a society is failing, with disease, violence and general unhappiness, then know you are looking at an occult influence at work. The hopelessness of the British people at the current time undoubtedly exists because of such an influence which in the past sat as a cuckoo in the nest, I doubt whether that influence remains now, since Britain has served her purpose to that power and when the life blood has been sucked out, the parasite leaves. The imposition of a hopeless system of hierarchy, whereby a man or woman can never achieve their goals, when faced with the system of unequal birth based on wealth and position can never reflect the Grail message or even an education for all. The position is not much better in America, where money is the new aristocracy. Whilst secret groups hold these hidden agendas however, there will always be in the minds of some the belief that they are superior by birth and "seed".

There is no doubt that the Flood was a horrific experience, but the curiosity is why such an event is often 'misplaced' on the time scale perhaps seeking to separate it purposefully the climactic event that caused the extinction of the dinosaurs. I have already covered in *The Battle of The Trees*, the mystery that has purposefully surrounded the date on which the Ark came to rest and the exact dimensions of the Ark, which are significant in terms of the meanings of the months in the Ancient Tree Alphabets and Solar-Lunar archetypal numbers related to the alphabets. The Bible has been heavily censored and this is one of the reasons, everything must fit the One World Order account. However there is no doubt from archaeological evidence that a Flood did occur, since the greatest mountains on earth such as the Rockies, the Andes, the Himalayas and the Alps, still bear the telltale signs of seashells and other evidence of ocean life that existed thousands of years ago. The exact number of years is hotly debated and the curiosity is that no one compares the event to the time scale given for magnetic reversals. According to Dr. Becker in his adapted diagram from Sander (*Fig. 33*) there were major magnetic field reversals in the Cambrian, Permian and Triassic periods with lesser reversals in the Devonian and Cretaceous periods. During these major reversals there was majority species extinction. To give you a time scale on this, the Cambrian period is said to have started 500 million years ago, the Permian 230 million years ago and the Triassic 205 million years ago. The Amphibians (frogs etc) were said to have made their first appearance in the Devonian epoch 325 million years ago, with the Amphibians reaching their peak 250 million years ago just as the reptiles first made their appearance in the Pennsylvanian epoch. Significantly the mammals only appeared after the Triassic magnetic field reversal, whilst the Reptiles peaked at and presumably the dinosaurs, just about the time of the Triassic magnetic field reversal. Man is placed as having appeared long after the dinosaurs, in the Pleistocene period about 2 million years ago, however this does not account for that curious footprint in the Paluxy river bed, which has been hotly denied as being that of a giant man, alongside and therefore co-existent with dinosaur footprints; with gravity at a different level one must assume due to a field reversal. Significantly too, flowering plants did not make their first appearance until after the Triassic magnetic reversal and presumably a quite different temperate climatic environment existed, arriving in the Jurassic period at 165 million years.

The Flood has been placed by some, as early as c. 3000 B.C: for example in Asia and particularly China, the Deluge traditions tell of a tremendous flood with devastating force in approximately 2300B.C. If there was such massive destruction and species extinction including man, one could not expect a complete recovery of the Earth and species in a matter of years. We know for instance that the Tuatha de Danaan was evicted from the Northern Peloponnese in roughly this same period by Semitic Patriarchal tribes, who descended from the north. We know also that the Canaanites were evicted from presumably Sodom and Gomorrah
c. 2 300 B.C. Biblical Noah was said to have been born in 3998 B.C. and died in 3048 B.C. I think that these sorts of muddles certainly cloud a correct chronology of climactic disasters, separating one from another in definite

415

periods, to which one can attach significant prehistory events to archaeology. This must be at least one possible reason why there has been such secrecy governing The Dead Sea Scrolls and the significance of the date when Noah's Ark came to rest. However there must have been a very large cataclysm involving flooding, since over 75% of the earth's surface is sedimentary in nature. As geologist Dr H. G. Coffin of the Geoscience Research Institute in Berrien Springs Michigan wrote in his book *Creation*: "only a flood of sufficient extent to cover all land, and a *storm of great violence* that stirred roiled water or soft mud is sufficient to account for the transport of vast amounts of sedimentary material over great distances, and the filling in of depressions irrespective of the height or extent of adjacent landscapes" (*Author's emphasis*).

The above emphasis and mention of the word "storm" reminds of a past description of the Masters as "Lords of the Storm". Gradual deposition then, does not answer the question of how such sedimentary material was accumulated, however a Flood does. Certainly this would account for the hundred thousand million fish skeletons that have been discovered in the Karroo formation in South Africa apart from the giant oysters high up on a mountain in South America. Further geologist Hugh Miller writing about the Devonian rocks which cover most of the British Isles, commented that: "at this period in our history, some terrible catastrophe involved a sudden destruction of the fish of an area at least a hundred miles from boundary to boundary, perhaps much more. The same platform in Orkney as at Cromarty is strewed thick with the remains, which exhibit unequivocally the marks of violent death. The figures are contorted, contracted, curved; the tail in many instances bent around the head; the spines stick out; the fins are spread to the full as in fish that die in convulsions"[130]. Given that there was a significant magnetic reversal in the Devonian period, then one might reasonably connect the two events, particularly since a change in field might logically inflict the nature of the casualties as described. Is it not significant for my theory, that those on Earth from the beginning, suffered magnetic reversals (the MRC case - Magnetically Reversed Case) and were forced after one significant reversal to re-incarnate into the bodies of the Amphibians in order to have any sort of game of life. Note that the Amphibians first made their appearance at the Devonian period 325 million years ago. With regard to the era of dinosaurs and reptiles, which were extinguished at the period given for the next major magnetic field reversal in the Triassic period, Edwin H. Colbert remarked: "The great extinction that wiped out all of the dinosaurs, large and small, in all parts of the world, and at the same time brought to an end to various lines of reptilian evolution, was one of the outstanding events in the history of life and in the history of the earth... It was an event that has defied all attempts at a satisfactory explanation". It is worth quoting again George Gaylord Simpson, who was a respected palaeontologist and stated: "It is as if the curtain were rung down suddenly on a stage where all

416

the leading roles were taken by reptiles" and he went on to say: "...especially the dinosaurs, in great number and in bewildering variety, and rose again immediately to reveal the same setting but an entirely new cast, in which the dinosaurs do not appear at all, other reptiles are mere super-numaries and the leading parts are all played by mammals".

The Magnetically reversed case (MRC) - a psychological case, resulted when men (or their spirits), actually underwent such a terrifying period or Magnetic Reversal MANY times. I will return to the MRC case later, but here the major point to be emphasised, is that there has been considerable confusion in religious texts as to which Flood and catastrophe is being discussed: The big question of when? The biblical Flood happened is I hope answered, in that it was probably in the Devonian or Triassic period, i.e. much earlier than has been given previously. Although there may have been floods even in the periods of c. 3000 B.C. these were certainly not those that caused major flooding or species extinction as is given in the Deluge accounts. It might be improbable that major species extinction occured in 3 000 B.C., with the worlds oceans depositing fish on the highest mountains, indicating the Earth was covered by water and then have the invasions of Greece and a Minoan civilization just over 1 000 years later!

Genesis 11 provides more interesting clues, since the generation following Noah suddenly shows a decided decrease in the average lifespan, from more than 900 years to approximately 100 years. This would limit the individual's chance to acquire knowledge and experience and I believe that until the message came to earth concerning Re-incarnation, such men had for so long experienced such longevity that they had forgotten they were their immortal **souls** and not their immortal bodies. The message once understood by them, provided not only a means to continue with their manipulative and centralised control, but it was in their own interests to remove such knowledge from those they controlled. Further such knowledge must have dispensed with fear the predominant emotion, fear that in the new climate a body lasted a very short time. Longevity must have been a product of a different level of gravity, which accounted not only for myths of giants, but also the massive size of the dinosaurs, which could not be allowed under today's conditions of gravity. When the life span decreased, it was essential to insure that the masters re-incarnated into the group where they had left off, evidently body lines (white) became a significant identifying factor for Re-incarnation along with secret groups. Furthermore written records became necessary along with soul memory and the Druids spent 19 years in training where no apparent records remain. However as the Greek philosopher Plato commented in his *Phaedrus*, when Thoth the Egyptian god demonstrated the art of writing to King Thamus and claimed it would aid wisdom, Thamus retorted that it would only encourage *forgetfulness*, by not cultivating *memory*. Whether the Druids never wrote anything for this reason, or secrecy is unsure but probably for both reasons. **Soul memory is vitally important, when one Re-incarnates.** The apparent use of archetypal symbols by Hollywood at least, is a knowledge of this fact and one presumes that theoretically one could imprint symbols into a person's mind and then expect them to follow a course of action dictated by the symbol and perhaps this is what was meant along with enforced chakra opening by the World Order, when they spoke of "Accelerated Evolution". *Alternative 4* discussed the possibility of UFO witnesses as unwitting recipients of this research.

HYDROPHOBIA

I would suggest that at least one psychological trait of the MRC case is his fear of chaos and the desire for order, coupled with a deep fear of the: "sea bursting its bounds", as was the case of the Druids, who are it would seem the biblical Adamites. The most noticeable thing about the biblical Creation story is the emphasis on ordering. It is certainly interesting that whilst the first eleven chapters of Genesis show many links with ancient Mesopotamian tradition, the creation account in *Gen. 1* is in contrast with the Babylonian and other Creation myths, in which the creator conquers chaos in the person of a monstrous sea-dragon. The dragon of course has archetypal connections to the Grid. The allusions to such a myth in the Hebrew Bible are older than *Genesis 1*. Although the Bible has been heavily censored, there is still a reasonable account I believe of pre-history, which would compare favourably with the events I give in the light of magnetic field changes. The absence of God, which might equate with wickedness in the world is given in *Psalm 74, (vv.1-2, 9-11, 22-23)*; a social order destroyed (*vv.18-21*); and in the second part (*vv.12-17*) speaks of Creation as God's victory over 'dragons' and '*Lev*iathan' in the waters, followed by ordering of Earth, the heavenly bodies and the seasons. Evidently then after a period of chaos, order is brought in the climactic conditions and this as a form of worship, gives some reassurance that those events are over with. There are also many references to God's ordering of the cosmic elements by imposing limits on them and commanding them to keep their place. For instance, God reminds Job how he confined the sea, saying "Thus far shall you come and no farther" (*Job 38:8-11*). In *Psalm 104:5-9, Psalm 148:6* and *Proverbs 8:29* once again arises the idea of God bringing order. The idea of control of man starts to come into view with *Jeremiah 5:22-23* which contrasts the discipline kept by the elements with the disobedience of God's human creatures, a theme which appears in both Jewish and Christian literature (*1 Enoch 2:1 - 5:9; Clement 20*). Human disobedience is often compared to the need for order. Thus virtually the whole of *Genesis 1* is concerned with bringing order, presumably after chaos. Given that I have concluded this refers to Devonian or Triassic periods, this rather lets the scientists off the' Big Bang' versus God augment, since the actual creation point is clearly in my hypothesis not indicated by Genesis. I will return to the point of Creation from a scientific standpoint later. The fact that the Genesis account is a story of Creation in 7 days signifies the archetypal number, which is connected to the new cult of Jehovah, which was the Patriarchal God and who superseded the older god, Wednesday's god (*The Battle of The Trees*). The latter, was Matriarchal in so far as no vengeance or wrath was part of that wisdom. The remarkable thing is that it is generally overlooked, that the Bible contains images of order spoiled or destroyed as well as being established. Further one form of ancient myth ascribed the presence of disorder in the world to rebellious supernatural beings. Unfortunately I believe these references have been heavily censored and the word "strangers" appears in *Genesis (6:1-4)* some is left in *Isaiah 14* and *Ezekiel 28*, with consequent disorder on Earth (*Isaiah 24*) and a rather fuller version in *1 Enoch 6-11*.

The idea that an old World Order was destroyed is the prevalent message of the Noah story, but let us look for a moment of the text of *Gen.6 1-4:*

> And it came to pass, when men began to multiply on the face of the earth, and daughters were born unto them, that the *sons of God* saw the *daughters of men* that they *were fair*; and they took them wives of all which they chose. And the Lord said, My spirit shall not always strive with man, for that he also is flesh: yet his days shall be *an hundred and twenty years*. There were *giants in the earth in those days*; and also after that, when the sons of God came in unto the daughters of men, and they bare children to them, the *same became mighty men*, which were of old, men of renown.

It is unsure whether it is being implied here, that the Biblical Adamites married white women "fair" - the ancestral Celtic race? And such women were descended from the 'Missionary' type *in Africa*? Clearly however "the sons of God", are singled out from "men". We know however, that Egyptian Kings in a certain period who were probably puppets or Solar Kings of the World Order carried Semitic facial traits and did marry with fair women and probably from the same fair stock, which produced the Celts descended from Adam but now a blond blue-eyed race. The obsession with genetic lines seems to have got off to an early start, together with white supremacy, if this was the case. However we note that "giants were living in those days", and if we were going to rationalise the mythical accounts of giants with this statement, then perhaps the giant footprint of a man in the Paluxy riverbed, which has been so overlooked and which shows man co-existent with dinosaurs will provide the link.

This would explain the early religious obsession with ORDER. Man of course would have to be ordered and controlled, disobedience (justification) was probably no more than man exercising his own opinions to a group who perceived themselves as "sons of God" with an arrogance that has always surrounded their eternal World Orders. However most texts agree, that a Flood or Deluge wiped out evil. God according to the biblical text is the author of this cataclysm (not man) and moreover he preserves only one righteous man - Noah. However one thing is certain that whilst it is seen as God's work, there is agreement that the world is purged, in order to rebuild. This is not viewed as a natural cyclical process of Earth's natural laws, which ensure equilibrium. God

according to the Bible reaffirms "cosmic order" (*Gen. 8:22*) by an "eternal covenant" (*9 8-18*). The fact that the Tower of Babel was built skywards may reflect the "marriage of Heaven and Earth" which God promised to Israel in *Hosea 2, 18-23*; the royal blessings in *Isaiah II* and *Psalm 72*; and the vision of peace under a **restored Davidic king** in *Ezekiel 3*. I would propose that a holy Messiah was part and parcel of the 'covenant'. Order was to be kept, by **divinely appointed guardians** of order, namely by Solar Kings. *Genesis 1-2* makes it quite clear that rulership is to be **by Kings**. This clarifies the Religious Revolution in Crete, where Kingship (Twin Kings), was attached to a belief system, that as Re-incarnation had no concept or place for Kingship, it fell to the World Order for that reason. Thus we see a very basic phenomenon of thought here a postulate (thought) or Re-incarnation versus a counter postulate or thought which was the Covenant. The matriarchal and patriarchal battle must depend on those dualities of thought and goals. Clearly in the account I gave of the events of Golgotha both here and in *The Battle of The Trees*, Jesus: "came to destroy the works of the female" -Re-incarnation, and re-affirm the 'covenant', providing a dynasty from David as a Solar King and Messiah. There would be no place for the woman in that goal other than in the case of Magdalene to provide the heir, after which her genealogies were stolen and the message she carried buried with the truth, which led her to prophesy that: "There will be no peace on this Earth until the cut is healed". There would be no looking back (Harvester's vase at Knossos), the seas would never "burst their bounds" again: Who promised this God or the patriarchal priests? The magicians who would direct and control the Grid, thus in their minds preventing another Magnetic Reversal by ordering the Earth's energy fields through the position of stones on ley lines: The stones being Semitic and the word of God presumably symbolizing the Covenant. The condemnation of man by God, which I discussed in both prior books, rests upon man's (or some men's) view, that it is *they* who by upholding the Temple ceiling of Sampson via Hermetic pillars prevent another cataclysm. However the arrival of a spiritual message
10 000 B.C. rather interfered with the One World Order plans. It is a testament to that message that today virtually two thirds of the world's population believe in Re-incarnation.

A World Order not only sought order through political control, but also through religious control. Solar Kingship governed by a Theocracy was envisaged as providing both forms of order. Kings were installed not only in Israel but in neighbouring Syria, Egypt and Babylon and also China. It is certainly interesting that my claim that justification, was part of the original 'covenant', whereby the blame for the cataclysm was placed at God's door, with presumably the promise that it would not happen again, by maintaining order; is evident in the Chinese Flood story. Ancient Chinese writing contains words that can be traced only to 'Nu-wah' (Noah? And New World?) and the Flood. The Chinese word for 'righteousness' is a combination of the pictorial symbol for 'lamb' placed over the ideogram for 'myself'. Apparently Noah's desire to justify himself in the eyes of **his** God was shown by the burnt offering of sacrifice that he made after disembarking from the Ark. The Chinese have records and traditions of a great flood where interestingly the word used for "ship" as printed in Chinese today is the very ancient character made up of the picture of "boat" and "eight mouths", showing that the first ship was a boat carrying *eight* persons, which reflects the 8-armed marine vase of the octopus at Knossos, which I connected to the arms of a World Order. Also, "Nu" means "woman" and "wah" is "flowery" .It seemed that some knowledge of a female as an ancient ancestor was remembered in China. It may be that some confusion of the 'Missionary' as woman and racial if not spiritual stock, was confused with Patriarchs who married perhaps into this stock "fair" or white? Where that bodyline came from is subject for discussion. However importantly woman was connected very early on with a female ancestor. Such ancestry may have been preserved in the Celtic royal line from the Tuatha de Danaan the tribe from Greece, who were considered "gods", by the Celts. In the Chinese ideogram the importance of the male as the chief ancestor however, was indicated by two small "mouth" pictures placed *beside* the name, indicating that not the meaning but the *sound* of the characters was important, pointing towards a male ancestor named Nu-wah, an ancient man who escaped the wrath of God in a boat, to create a New World.

If the Chinese walked into Tibet and murdered the Tibetan people and destroyed their religion and the belief in Re-incarnation, let us not forget that early Chinese history supports the idea of a Noachian involvement in the birth of China. It is mentioned that the destruction of the world by a flood, was caused by Jung-ku, but the reconstruction was accomplished by Nu-wah.

The anointed one or mashiah (Messiah) was to come as a Kingly personage. There are so many references to Kingly rule in the Bible but importantly in *Psalm 72* there is a prayer for a King - Solomon is named as tradition, but equally it could be Jesus of Royal Davidic lineage. God is to endow him with his own attributes of mishpat and sedaqah. Whilst the first word is usually translated as 'justice' and the second has usually been rendered as 'righteousness', the meaning is different in different contexts. To gain a fuller picture, then in *Isaiah 32*, there is a vision of ideal Kings reigning with sedeq and mishpat (*32:1*). There is also the appearance of order and disorder, and in some instances the Hebrew word for 'order' is sedaqah. Thus order through Divine Solar Kingship was indicated throughout as the method of order. One might pose the conclusion that The Celtic Commonwealth, headed by a secret Priesthood, the Druids or Adamites descended from Noah, merely sought through the plan of Golgotha to finalise God's covenant, through a Messiah, who had been promised. Religious control or order would be through Christianity and political control adjoined to that through a One World Order, headed presumably by the Biblical Adamites or probably now the 12 tribes of Israel combined with the thirteenth? a Jewish if not Noachian ending then? I am here inclined to point you towards the first chapter of *The Battle of The Trees*, where I recounted one of my past lives, which started the whole quest to find the truth and during that regression the word "Noah" arose, although I could determine any sense from it then! The Book of Enoch is the oldest apocalyptic writing known, but it disappeared from favour in the ninth century. The Book of *Enoch* was also to surface again in the Dead Sea Scrolls in the caves of Qumran. I have already given a list of antediluvian Kings and Enoch appears before Noah. It was considered that God made certain revelations to Enoch. I also referred to the statement of Eliphas Levi, a member of the secret societies, before the French Revolution, who states that a "Universal Religious and Political Kingdom" would be "had by those with the keys to the East". The Keys of Enoch are generally associated with some divine revelation relating to the secrets of Heaven and Earth. The fact that Enoch appears before the Deluge is significant in so far as it might be concluded that there was a misuse of that knowledge or Cabalistic science, which then created a Magnetic Reversal, or at least a Flood. As I have previously pointed out The Dead Sea Scrolls have been commandeered, since it is important not to release any information that would obstruct the 'covenant', and the One World Order programme.

The Dead Sea Scrolls at Qumran are Essene, the group that I proposed was communistic and to which Jesus was fostered by the Druids. According to Genesis Enoch:" walked with God and was no more, because God took him away" (*Gen. 5.24*). This walking with God was understood to refer to a Divine revelation made to him, concerning secrets and which I have connected to Grid energies. The Book of Enoch influenced later Jewish apocrypha, and has also influenced the New Testament. In two places *in part 1 Enoch* referred to as *the similitudes*, a "Great Oath" is mentioned, which I equate with an earlier form of some 'covenant', which Noah once again made or re-affirmed with God after the Flood. This Oath was supposed to bind the forces of Creation. The Similitude's, describes Enoch's three visions, and two of those concern the "Great Oath". This certainly parallels the 'covenant', when in *1 Enoch 41*; we find that the heavenly bodies are kept on their course *in accordance with the oath* that binds them. *1 Enoch 69* describes how the oath was entrusted to the archangel Michael. Once again the *oath secures the order* of the Creation, and holds the chaos from the door by securing Earth and the heavens. Incidentally since Rudolf Steiner's group Anthroposophy have a lot to do with that particular angel, I now view their origin as Semitic Adamite (white supremacy?). Or in my own experience: "For I am a jealous God and thou shalt have no other God's but me", as the Patriarchal God of Jehovah, certainly underlines my whole experience with these so-called Christians. The Oath secures order, and keeps the sea in check, certainly once again reminding us of the fear of The Druids. It regulates the course of the sun and Moon and explains the appearance very early on of the solar lunar calendar. There is a list of all the other forces of Creation: spirits of water, winds, thunders, hail, frost, mist rain and dew, thus a great concern with climactic conditions and their ordering. The Great Oath then, is concerned not only with order, but the continuation of things and not destruction (*1 Enoch 69. 16-21,25*). The Oath is comparable to the 'covenant', in that to break it, would destroy Creation. Interestingly the Hebrew word for covenant is b'rith, which is rleated to the word 'binding' and also reminds us of the International Zionist Masonic Order the B'nai B'rith, who were apparently weeding out from libraries in the USA, two books by Comyns Beaumont the Scot, who wrote that Scotland was the true "Holy Land". This obviously stems from the desire that the true events of Golgtotha and its background should be never known as the orthodox account of the crucifixion with Jesus as Solar King and Messiah, is part of the 'covenant' and a Universal religious and political Kingdom, which will maintain order through a ONE WORLD ORDER BASED ON THAT COVENANT i.e. triumph for Israel.

The vision of judgement in *the Similitudes* is the revealing of the Son of Man, such a phrase also occurs in other parts of The Dead Sea Scrolls and refers to the coming Messiah. The Old and New Testaments are a binding of the covenant. This covenant arises in connection with Noah, Abraham, David and Moses. It is curious that Noah in the covenant with God agrees to never shed blood, nor to consume it, whilst Moses was a murderer! Surely this broke any covenant. The eternal covenant was made with David (*2 Sam 7.13*), promising to establish *his dynasty* forever and thus the pre-occupation of secret Jewish groups, with blood lines and the secret group The Prieuré de Sion, who were involved with the birth of European Union and had some connection to the bloodline of the Merovignians, a supposed bloodline from a union of Jesus with the Mary Magdalene and the line of David.

Genesis 1 alludes to an older account of Creation, however this older account is the work of Day One, which has become a forbidden mystery, presumably for the reasons I give here. Presumably if there was an older account of creation, it was censored from the Old Testament, simply because it would refer to events prior to a Magnetic Reversal. Enoch and the account of the Great Oath, offer a more chaotic story for the beginning, than the Genesis account, which starts with a calm order and the blaming of woman for the misdemeanours of the male antediluvians that misused the hidden science! This is a feature of the MRC case, he can never ever see correct causation and seeks to blame everyone except himself for his own demise! However *Job 38* repeats the Enochian view of Creation and the prehistory I give here of some cataclysmic event which involved the sea and which the Druids feared the most. The Lord asks Job: "who shut in the sea with doors... and prescribed bounds for it?" (*38.8-10*): "Can you bind the chains of the Pleiades?" (*38.31*). Further the *Prayer of Manasseh* in the Deutero-Canonical, begins by addressing God as the one who shackled the sea, confined the deep and sealed it with his terrible and glorious name. Here as in Enoch, it is the power of the name, which binds the unruly forces. This alludes to the guessing game that arose around the name of the God possessed by secret groups, since if one could trace their God, you would find their goals (12 and/or 13). Further one suspects that the name may well have contained the secrets of the Cabalistic ritual that precipitated disaster that depended on resonant sounds or sympathetic resonance. It is certainly known that Cabalistic methods can produce weather phenomena.

Job as with the Enochian account, talks of evil angels and water, depth and chaos are very closely linked. In the Babylonian Talmud King David suppressed the great flood by writing the name of God on a potsherd, and throwing it into the deep. The Psalms speak of God's triumph over the waters, or rescuing the faithful ones from the threat of being overwhelmed by them, setting bounds for the sea. *Psalm 46* describes the power of God in the midst of roaring waters, as raging nations (*Ps. 46.6*). *Psalm 69* begins: "Save me, O God! For the waters have come up to my neck". The New Testament uses the symbolisation of water and it's binding as a recurrent theme. Jesus as the revelation of the Word of God 'binds' this unruly force forever. Baptism is a re-affirmation of the covenant. Whether Jesus was versed in the Cabalistic rituals that were able to manipulate weather, a phenomenon that Ron Hubbard was to comment on, when he entered some practices with Jack Parsons, in the secret group of the OTO (Order Templis Orientis); and whether both were versed into the Grid is questionable, however when Jesus stills the storm, presumably as the re-affirmation of God's word, the disciples ask: "What sort of man is this, that even winds and sea obey him?" (*Matt. 8.27*) and use of Grid energies may or may not be implied here. The Jews are promised "no more sea" in the apocalyptic account (*Rev. 21.1*) and power over the sea, was proof of Divine power. Thus the waves parted for Moses and the Israelites in *Exodus*.

In *The Way of Wyrd* Brian Bates reconstructed a world view, from an ancient manuscript in the British Museum:

> "They had a vision of the universe, from the gods to the underworld, connected by an enormous all-reaching system of fibres, rather like a *three-dimensional spider's web. Everything was connected* by strands of fibre to the *all-encompassing web*. This image far surpasses in ambition our present views of ecology, in which we have extended notions of cause and effect to include longer and more lateral chains of influence in the natural world.

The web of fibres of the Anglo-Saxon sorcerer offers an ecological model that encompasses individual life events as well as general physical and biological phenomena, non-material as well as material events, and challenges the very cause-and-effect chains upon which our ecological theories depend." (*p.12*). (*Author's emphasis*)

This idea of the web, which is nothing but the Grid is the wrong thinking behind the Universal Mind, 'Oneness' and One World Order, which I will come to shortly. The idea occurs on the One-dollar note from America "One out of many". All this because man never understood the web or the consequences of channelling information from it, but he just could not help himself in his quest for power, he just carried on reading the 'script'. The web or Grid is an ecological pattern, which governs the genetic bodyline of the species and contains a record of **past events** in terms of survival of the species and it is not appropriate for spiritual man to base his immortality on the survival of the body. The idea of 'binding' or covenant is merely an agreement with THE GRID! God does not exist in the geometrics of the Grid or perhaps He does as a mere dramatization of past thought by the MRC case! You could say that the MRC is following his own past thought and survival, he then perceives that as being from a higher source! However it is evident that the Patriarchs found out how to manipulate weather patterns from the Grid energies and believed that they could take control of those patterns, in order to stave off another magnetic field reversal. Is it any wonder that early Creation accounts start after Day 1 *after* the chaos had subsided! The Apocalyptic vision is a renewal of the covenant, the restoration of all Creation, with the judgement. Binding of evil is also mentioned in The New Testament. Casting out demons requires that the Strong One be bound first (*Matt. 12.29*). In *Revelation 20.1-16*, St. John saw how the Strong One (Azazel) was bound for a thousand years, so that the Earth could enjoy the Millennium Kingdom with "Paradise" restored. Peter is given the power to bind and to loose, both in Heaven and on Earth (*Matt. 16.13-19*). Peter is also given power over the evil ones (*Luke 10.17*). This power given to Peter is symbolised by *the keys* curiously enough of Heaven, which now form the papal coat of arms. The Book of Enoch tells how the rebel angels or 'watchers', who I have equated with a spiritual force outside of planet earth, who tried to manipulate the genetic blueprint of men on this planet via the morphogenetic bioplasma: "took unto themselves wives, and each chose for himself one, and they began to go in unto them and to defile themselves with them". The Essenes you will remember were celibate and disliked women, which is reflected in the Jewish Morning Prayer today. The book goes on to say:" and they taught them charms and enchantments... They became pregnant, and they bore great giants, who consumed all the acquisitions of men. And when men could no longer sustain them, the giants turned against them and devoured mankind, and they began to sin against birds, and beasts, and reptiles, and fish, and to devour one another's flesh, and drink the blood. Then the earth laid accusation against the lawless ones" (*VII.1*). Thus it would appear that we gain some idea of events in what I have assumed is the Devonian period, which through the mention of "giants" places this very definitely in the same period as The Garden of Eden story and the Biblical Adamites. Thus we come full circle to the Druids as biblical Adamites and the intermarriage with fair haired women possibly related if not descended from the" missionary" type and it is known that the Druids did conduct human sacrifice.

I have already covered the fact that metals were found in prehistory archaeological sites and there were metals, including that curious medal or coin from Atlantis. The Atlanteans may well have been the so-called giants. The Enoch account tells how: "Azazel taught men to make swords, and knives, and shields, and breastplates, and made known to them the metals (of the earth) and the art of working them, and bracelets, and ornaments, and the use of antimony, and the beautifying of the eyelids, and all kinds of costly stones, and all colouring tinctures. And there arose much godlessness, and they committed fornification, and they were led astray and became corrupt in all their ways". (*VIII.1*). Obviously since this was a somewhat public document, there would be no mention of Grid energies or Cabalistic science and their manipulation and we know that the Druids never wrote anything down, since it was all transmitted orally. Thus we cannot expect any real reason in this document for the causation of a cataclysm, or indeed the real reason for the so-called fall of 'Lucifer'. The Book of Enoch does however claim, that these evil ones destroyed order, by extracting metals from the bowels of the Earth to *develop technological instruments of war* and of seduction, which implies some warfare if not nuclear, was waged and may account for the Indian epics, together with metal artefacts found in sedimentary (flood) geological layers. In 1968, Dr Koriut Megurchain of the Soviet Union unearthed what was considered to be the oldest large-scale metallurgical factory in the world, at Medzamor, in the old Soviet Armenai. The site is thought to be 4500 years old, and has over 200 furnaces, which produced vases, knives, spearheads, rings, bracelets etc. Metals used included copper, lead, zinc, iron, gold and tin together with manganese and fourteen kinds of bronze. The most unusual find was several pairs of tweezers made of *steel*, taken from layers dating back before the first millennium B.C.! The steel was of exceptionally high grade. Evidently then, there was a high technological age where knowledge of metalwork was employed that would only surface in open world technology thousands of years later. The pivotal point in mentioning this, is that the site of Medzamor, is within fifteen miles of Mount Arat, where the reported remains of Noah's Ark were found.[131]

In Guatemala, the ancient Mayas recorded in their sacred book, the Popol Vuh, that the:" first men" possessed tremendous knowledge: "They were able to know all, and they examined the four corners, the four points of the *arch of the sky* and the round face of the earth". [132] This sounds like the post Flood survey of the world and "arch" reminds one of those curious umbrella markings in pre-historic cave paintings

Which leads one to ask, whether this knowledge exists in the so-called Royal Arch degree of Freemasonry. Further, did the curious umbrella shapes or arch represent the UVG 120 sphere together with the knowledge that the pattern above dictated the pattern below, which is expressed in hermetic philosophy as: "As above, so below"; thus enabling them to map the Earth. Further the ancient Chinese also recognized that before them there were "giants": "Men twice as tall as us", who once inhabited the "realm of delight", but lost it by not living "by laws of virtue". This sounds remarkably like the fall of Lucifer.

I have mentioned previously the: "Vine-men", those who joined together as connected to Fuinsa Farsa, who was descended from Magog and Noah and may be further traced to the Druids and perhaps ultimately then provides the link to the top level of Freemasonry as Scottish Rite or Rosicruciansism. In this respect, the following account in the 1851 issue of *Scientific American* (*Vol. 7, p. 298*) proves to be very interesting. Apparently a metallic vase was dynamited from solid rock on Meeting House Hill in Dorchester, Massachusetts and the story was also carried by the *Boston Transcript* according to which: " On putting the two parts together it formed a *bell-shaped* vessel" (reminding one of the bell-shaped skirts of the priestesses at Knossos after the Religious Revolution, illustrated in *The Battle of The Trees*): "four and a half inches high, six and a half inches at the base, two and a half inches at the top and about an eighth of an inch in thickness. The body of this vessel resembles zinc in color, or a composition metal in which there is a considerable portion of *silver*. On the sides there are *six* figures of a *flower*" (a rosette?): " A bouquet, beautifully inlaid with pure silver, and around the lower part of the vessel, *a vine*, or wreath, inlaid also with silver". Geologists and archaelogists estimate that the object, given the layer in which it was found, must be at least several million years old. The vase was circulated around the museums, and then it mysteriously disappeared! Not surprisingly, since the first thing Noah did when the Ark came to rest, was to plant a vine. The "vine-men" who draw together as the Freemasons of their day, evidently go back a lot further than the Tower of Babel. In fact they almost certainly have never ceased to control humanity from their nocturnal lairs. Further as I covered previously, I have recently discovered arhaelogical papers that show there were a people the *Freem*ont living in Utah, who employed the chequer pattern and scrolls on their bowls, thus displaying the archetypal symbolism of the Religious Revolution in Crete. Gold jewellry has been discovered in coal (*The Morrisonville Times 9 June 1891*), which must give a date from the Carboniferous period and several million years old. A businessman

Hiram de Witt found an iron nail in a piece of auriferous quartz, with an estimated date in excess of a million years. In 1845 Sir David Brewster reported to the British Association for the Advancement of science, that a nail, which had been manufactured, was found half embedded in granite excavated from Kindgoodie Quarry in Northern Britain. A gold chain was found near a quarry close to Rutherford Mills in northern England in 1844. This of course is another aspect of the hidden science and hidden archaeology which would cut the evolutionary time-scale of man and Darwinian theory to shreds and is further proof a secret Brotherhood as early Freemasons, who dominated technology and presumably humanity. Neither can it be dismissed that archaeological remains of the Freemont show evidence of human sacrifice, where the skulls have been crushed with a hammer (?) blow, together with evidence of cannibalism.

In 1885, a foundry owned by the Austrian Isador Braun of Vocklabruck, discovered a small metal cube in coal dating from the Tertiary period The Austrian physicist Karl Gurls for the Salzburg museum analysed the cube, whereupon it was found to be composed of steel and a nickel alloy. It measured 2.64 by 2.64 by 1.85 inches and weighed 1.73 pounds, with a specific gravity of 7.75. Interestingly the edges of the cube were perfectly straight and sharp, with four sides flat, whilst the remaining two sides opposite each other were convex. There was deep groove that looked machine-made around the cube midway up its height. Once again the cube disappeared from the Salzburg Museum in 1910. The only record of its existence is in the scientific journals *Nature* (*London 1886*) and *L'Astronomie* (*Paris, 1887*). Unfortunately I have not been able to obtain a copy of the second article, which might have proven interesting given the name of the journal and the convex surfaces of the cube, which reminds one of those curious 'umbrella' shapes in pre-historic cave paintings and with the central delineating line between the two convex surfaces remind me of the Diablo that I produced for describing the vortices of information both genetic and spiritual.

The Coso artefact discovered in 1961 in California was some device incorporating a porcelain or ceramic cylinder enclosing a metal shaft, which was magnetic. Circling the ceramic cylinder were rings of copper, which had not eroded since the device was found in the centre of a rock. One end of the shaft was fixed to a spring or helix of metal. It is thought that this was some form of electrical instrument, bearing a close resemblance to a spark plug although bearing no resemblance to any spark plug of today. The rock in which this artefact was found, is thought to be at least half a million years old. Whilst it may be difficult to rely on dates, stratified rock is the result of soil laid down by water. This signifies that the metal objects encased in the rocks were buried during the Flood, thus their date would originate *before* the Flood. It might be difficult, given the extensive brainwashing that has occurred concerning man's pre-history, but the archaeological finds point to an advanced technological civilization dating from the pre-Flood epoch and since coal dates back to the Tertiary period, then such a civilization has existed for *one hundred million years* This sector of the Universe has definitely been off bounds to those who valued spiritual freedom!

In *Alternative 4*, I outlined the goals of today's physicists as the tapping of the zero-point energy or vacuum, the tremendous energy that is an inherent part of the vacuum. Dr. Harold Aspden an eminent physicist from Southampton University in England wrote:

"There is an increasing body of opinion that recognises the existence of tremendous amounts of energy in the vacuum, energy which offers us hope that one day we can capture this resource in our man-made machines and achieve what amounts to the dream of perpetual motion. This paper addresses this question in the light of the supporting experimental evidence, to conclude that what is a dream today is without doubt, the certainty of tomorrow. Indeed the breakthrough has already been made. It is just that we have failed to see, in its proper context, what is so clearly laid before us". [133]

A.A. Michelson who won the Nobel prize for physics in 1907 postulated the ether or vacuum, was not an empty void but full of potential energy and Harold Aspden, Paul Dirac and Thomas Bearden hold the same view and yet despite the accumulative evidence the subject is politely ignored - Why? I asked much the same question, when after producing a substantial argument in my Cancer report, the whole solution I offered to the enigma of cancer was ignored. Today some 15 years later, I realise that I was of course analysing those forbidden apples of immortality and treading in the mined fields of the hidden science. Harold Aspden who as a physicist, was unaware of the same problem in Medicine and Biochemistry points to the kinder augment that I embraced in 1986, before I set out as a biochemist to resolve to my own satisfaction, that gigantic question WHY? Dr. Aspden points out that physicists still hang on to Einstein's view, that the speed of light is a constant in a vacuum. Thus the only way Einstein's famous equation can hold, is for the vacuum or space to be a void; then it cannot modify the speed of light and most importantly entrenched views can breathe a sigh of relief that the whole of quantum theory stands as an edifice to correctness. Any new thought or data that seeks to question entrenched or orthodox views meets with a high level of resistance. If however the vacuum or space does have a substructure, with light or electro-magnetic radiation forming a patterning upon its surface, then the speed of light would be determined by the structure of the vacuum or space itself.

Harold Aspden published a book *Physics Unified* in 1980; using a model of an energetic matrix or vacuum of space he derived all the known mathematical laws of physics including Einstein's equation. The fact that he was ignored, is not just human inertia or academic institutionalism as is supposed, there is of course a deeper resistance, which runs as a hidden substructure through all academic institutions, research, the grant funding system and all the way up past the power pyramid to that substructure of the matrix itself!

Physicists have constantly sought Unified Theories, which would find that tenuous link between masses, gravity and electro-magnetic energy and Einstein attempted such in his work, but never quite fully managed it. The physicist therefore does not fully understand just how all these factors tie up. Physicists world wide are however experimenting with the possibility of tapping the vast potential of free energy from space; the Russians under Professor Chernetski; and his team of researchers, have it is claimed produced excess energy or four to five times electrical power output compared with input. However what kind of threat would free energy pose to a global Syndicate reaping vast profits from fossilised fuels, despite the environmental problems that are created? Loss of profit, power and the global monopoly that derives from that, is the threat to the Syndicate, however as I have shown the deeper threat comes from having to reveal the hidden science and the vast web of lies that surround religion and politics that great power pyramid. The prospect of free energy to the major International industries and governments is a vision of economic and un-employment problems. Despite this, vacuum state technology is being secretly researched at some level and whilst tapping the zero-point energy would be capable of use in heating, lighting, driving electrical motors and even cars, I suspect that as I proposed in the past scenario, that this energy is being looked at in terms of warfare capability, anti-gravity travel and control of the populous. My second book, showed that such research, might have been on going for some time, resulting in numerous man-made or manipulated UFO phenomena. Electricity can be linked to gravity and controlled by means of electrical charge and anti-gravity as I mentioned in my second book, is very definitely possible with today's physics. Hard sightings of UFO's such as silvery discs and coloured balls of light may certainly represent secret research into anti-gravity propulsion and utilisation of the zero-point energy.

The origins of such research certainly date back to Nikola Tesla's work. Tesla was the father of alternating current (AC) technology, the electric power that drives motors, heating and lighting in our homes and industries. Tesla's visionary ideas many say were suppressed by the dark agents and as a lone researcher, Tesla who established no permanent corporate or research ties was isolated and thus rather a 'loose cannon'.

Born in Yugoslavia in 1856 he moved to Paris when he was 26, where he worked for Edison's Company on electrical systems, motors, lighting etc. Although he worked on Direct Current (DC), he was to formulate a polyphase electrical system based on Alternating Current (AC). Tesla fell out with Edison and set up his own company in April 1887, and worked on AC system transformers, motors and dynamos. In a period of 4-5 years he applied and received 40 patents. Further Tesla was convinced that the ether was the fundamental unifying theory of physical things and believed there were waves in the ether, which could transmit energy at a distance without the use of wires. What Tesla did not know is that Cabalistic science, had allowed the Jewish Cabalist Falk, who was to be received into the Freemasons of London, to do much the same thing a couple of hundred years previously. Tesla built two electrical experimental stations, the first in Colorado Springs and another later at Wardenclyffe Tower on Long Island New York. In his experiments Tesla produced lightening bolts of a million volts, experimenting with a world radio broadcasting station and also secretly worked on his theory of the transmission of energy with no wires (*wireless*). He refused to accept Einstein's theory of relativity and curved space and remained convinced that there was: "no energy in matter other than that received from the environment"; although the Atom bomb would prove him to be wrong. His work also centred on resonance or vibrational energy research and once he very nearly brought a high-rise apartment building down with his experiments. Finally his ideas also covered utilising very concentrated beams in outer space, which would become the basis of the so-called "Star Wars" defence programme in America. The HAARP (High Active Auroral Research Programme) and GWEN (Ground Wave Emergency Network), both alleged defence systems in America, utilised Tesla technology in their origination and it is said that Tesla's work was confiscated by the FBI after his death. I have covered the issue of "Star Wars", in *Alternative 4*, however the point here, is that whilst such secret research is on-going and has been it would seem for millions of years presumably together with its application to mind control as the future goal of a psychocivilized society, controlled by the One World Order, then it is unlikely that any matrix research would be publicly or officially recognised: that would also include any research into Cancer that utilised the hidden science as my research has.

Did the ancient magicians have the knowledge to tap the zero-point energy? We certainly know that the Cabalist Falk not only had a lamp that burned without wires or any apparent energy source, but also a story exists in legend, that not only did he go to mysterious meetings in Epping Forest, but on one occasion his cab lost a wheel and without stopping the wheel followed the cab all the way back to his house. Apart from hearsay, there have been a number of archaeological finds that indicate the ancients knew electricity. In 1938 Dr. Wilhelm Konig found some curious two thousand year old pots in the State Museum in Baghdad, Iraq. The pots were 6 inches high and contained a cylinder of sheet copper 5 inches high and one and half inches in diameter. The bottoms of the cylinders were capped with copper discs and sealed with bitumen or asphalt. Iron rods were suspended into the centre of the copper cylinders and these rods showed evidence of acid corrosion. The pots were in fact electric cells which was confirmed by historian Willy Ley, working with Willard Gray of the General Electric High Voltage Laboratory in Pittsfield, Massachusetts. When duplicate versions of the cells were made, it was found that they produced between one and a half and two volts of electricity. The same method of producing electric current was only (re) discovered in 1800. The fact that similar pots were collected from a magician's hut near Tel Omar (Seleucia), near Baghdad, indicates that these items were part of the hidden science of the time commanded by magicians. In a United Press dispatch in 1963 Harold Guard wrote an article on a form of artificial illumination in West Iran. Visitors: "were terrified to see many moons suspended in the air shining with great brightness". These "moons" were according to the report: "stone balls", that glowed when the sun went down. Mounted on pillars they provided light for the village. A similar effect was reported in 1601 by Barco Cenenera in his account of the conquistadors' discovery of the city of Gramoxo near the source of the Paraguay River, in the Planatto do Mato Grosso. According to Cenenera: "on the summit of a seven and three quarter (metre) pillar was a great moon, which illuminated all the lake". No doubt the measurements, the sighting and this form of "moon" illumination had religious significance.

Eliphas Levi in his *Histoire de la Magie*, recorded the story of a mysterious French rabbi named Jechiele, whom was an advisor in the thirteenth century court of Louis IX and who astounded the King with his "dazzling lamp that lighted itself". Jechiele like Falk was a Cabalist and such knowledge was used to impress Kings and gain power, which was probably the case with Joseph in Egypt as covered previously. The hidden science always retained power for the elite by its ability to impress those it was demonstrated to and whether that is the case with Scientology I will discuss later, but man as god or Messiah was an offshoot of this secrecy. Pausanias, who lived in the second century AD, wrote that the temple of Minerva had a light that could burn for at least a year. St. Augustine (AD 354 -430) also claimed that in an Egyptian temple dedicated to Isis, a lamp burned that neither wind nor water could extinguish. This fact precludes normal methods of burning materials to produce light and further there were no carbon deposits. The labyrinth of Knossos was presumably lit in this fashion. Further when the sepulchre of Pallas was opened near Rome in 1400, it was found to be lighted by a lantern that had illuminated the tomb for two thousand years. Again there were no sooty deposits. In Room 17 in the Egyptian Temple of Dendera, built during the Ptolemaic period and dedicated to the goddess Hathor, there is a picture engraved on the wall, which Egyptologists have not been able to fully explain. Several electronics engineers however have offered their own solution. On the right of the picture is a box on top of which, sits the image of the Egyptian god Horus. As a Sun god, or Solar King, he bears the symbol of sun disc. Attached to the box is the representation of a braided cable, which engineer Professor John Harris has compared to a bundle of conducing electrical wires. The cable runs from the box the full length of the floor of the picture and terminates both at the ends and at the bases of two curious objects. Each of these objects rests on a pillar, which Professor Harris identified with a high-voltage insulator. Each object is also pictured as being operated by two Egyptian priests. Further the two curious objects resemble TV picture tubes, and electronics technician N. Zecharius has identified the tubes as Crookes tubes, the forerunners of the modern television tube. Whether these priests had used such devices to channel their prophesies from the Grid along with Free energy is a question that arises. A Crookes tube consists of a vacuum contained in a glass encasement within which a fluorescent ray of electrons can be produced. When in operation, the ray originates where the cathode electrical wire enters the tube, and from there the ray extends the length of the tube to the opposite end. In the temple picture, the electron beam is represented as an outstretched serpent. The tail of the serpent begins where the cable from the energy box enters the tube, and the serpent's head touches the opposite end. In Egyptian art, the serpent was a symbol of divine energy and the Grid? Was this then some kind of solar energy trap, although one cannot easily see in tombs and source of solar power; or was this some kind of device for trapping vacuum energy?

Noorbergen [134] believes the picture shows a scientific experiment is taking place, where the tube on the extreme left of the picture shows normal operating conditions. But in the case of the second tube, situated closer to the energy box an experiment is underway. Michael R. Freedman, an electrical engineer believes that the solar disc on Horus' head is a Van de Graaf generator, an apparatus that collects static electricity. A baboon is portrayed holding a metal knife between the Van de Graaff solar disc and the second tube. Under actual conditions, the static charge built up on the knife from the generator would cause the electron beam inside the Crookes tube to be diverted from the normal path, because the negatively charged knife and the negatively charged beam would repel each other. In the temple picture, the serpent's head in the second tube is turned is turned away from the end of the tube, as though repulsed by the knife in the baboon's hand. Thus the one tube with the straight serpent is the control, or tube operating under normal conditions, the other with the repelled serpent being the experimental tube, or tube upon which new experimental conditions have been imposed. The Crookes tube was the forerunner not only of television, but also of the fluoroscope, an instrument that uses X-rays for diagnosing internal injuries. Whilst there is no evidence that the Egyptians possessed the fluoroscope, the Hindus and Chinese did. For example an Indian contemporary of Buddha, a physician named Jivaka, was given the title of King of Doctors about 500 B.C. Records tell us, that he had a 'gem', which he used for diagnosis, and that when a patient was placed before the gem, it "illuminated his body as a lamp lights up all objects in a house, and so revealed the nature of his malady".

This "gem", may have been some crystal that could in some mysterious way pull down vacuum energies. Annoyingly, the gem disappeared in history. However three centuries later in the palace of Hien-Yang in Shensi, a "precious mirror that illuminates the bones of the body" was discovered. This must have corresponded to something like X-rays. Noorbergen a asks whether it is possible that some of these light sources employed energy-conversion methods like electricity, or could it have been something more exotic? Is it possible that the ancients found ways to harness atomic power in order to light small areas? However we do know from the Indian epics, that flying machines were probably utilising anti-gravity Grid anomalies, thus it is not inconceivable, that the ancient magicians or Cabalists had always retained knowledge pertaining to Grid energies.

Scientists in 1919 managed to transmute atomic nuclei in the laboratory and in 1934, they succeeded in transmuting nuclei into radioactive states and finally in 1938-39 with the discovery of Uranium fission there emerged the possibility of generating a chain reaction, that could liberate the final secrets and energies of atomic nuclei on a massive scale. The nuclear bomb was becoming a reality. Frederick Soddy, Ernest Rutherford's co-worker, recalled how in 1902 as he and Rutherford watched thorium transmuting itself into Argon Gas, he called out to Rutherford in jubilation and ecstasy that they were watching "transmutation" and how Rutherford had replied "For Mike's sake, Soddy, don't call it transmutation. They'll have our heads off as alchemists. *You know what they are*" (my emphasis). This was a curious statement, which relayed to me my suspicions, that not only was there some information on past alchemy available to those who were working on atomic or nuclear experiments, but that there was some reticence over public association with that research, or at least a conscious effort not to parallel nomenclature, of the Cabalists.

The physicist Soddy made this significant statement concerning knowledge of atomic physics in ancient myths and legends in his book Interpretation of Radium: [135]

"One is tempted to enquire how far the unsuspected aptness of some of these beliefs and sayings to the point of view so recently disclosed, is the result of mere chance or coincidence and how far it may be *evidence of a wholly unknown and unsuspected ancient civilization of which all other relics have disappeared*. It is curious to reflect for example, upon the remarkable legends of the philosopher's stone, one of the earliest and most universal beliefs, the origin of which, however far back we penetrate into the records of the past, we probably do not trace to its real source. The philosopher's stone was accredited the power not only of transmuting metals, but also of acting as the elixir of life. Now, whatever the origin of this apparently meaningless jumble of ideas may have been,

436

it is really a perfect but very slightly allegorical expression of the actual present views we hold today. It does not require much effort of the imagination to see in energy, the life of the physical universe and the key to the primary fountains of the physical universe today known to be transmutation. Is then, this old *association of the power of transmutation with the elixir of life merely a coincidence*? I prefer to believe it may be an echo from one of many previous epochs in the unrecorded history of the world, of an age of men which *trod before the road we are treading today*, in a past possibly so remote that even the very atoms of its civilization have had time to disintegrate" (*author's emphasis*).

In *The Battle of The Trees*, I gave the full decipherment of the Philosopher's stone as an *"elixir of life"*, which was and is the spiritual message, but only one half of the Holy Grail, as the message of Re-incarnation. However there were always two aspects to the philosopher's stone and the other was meant to be a Cosmology and knowledge of energy and the nature of the trap within the Grid. That Cosmology was displayed in early Minoan Crete and in earlier Palaeolithic times. However those who never wanted to relinquish their power, based as it was on on the hidden science, hid that Cosmology and knowledge relating to the Grid as a trap very early on, together with the belief. Secrets regarding this science, known to even antediluvian Kings, were as good as money in the bank to them. There is no doubt, that these men benefited from the message of Re-incarnation after the Magnetic Reversal, when gravity must have changed and with it life spans; allowing them to plan their re-incarnations, whilst denying that for the rest of humanity. Power became a continuous line (on Re-incarnation) and one simply had to remember the story! The most annoying thing, is that these men attached the significance of "stone" to philosopher's stone, as a *Semitic* indication of the word of God, their own God Jehovah as the hermetic Eye of Intelligence: the "Universal Kingdom", would: "be had by those with the keys to the East", the hermetic keys which unlock the secrets of the Grid releasing its inherent power. The Eye of Intelligence of course was placed on the Great Seal and One dollar note of America. The message never came from a Semitic source or their god: the message was from a spiritual 'hierarchy' elsewhere that was **totally** good. That message came first to Greece and never had any history of Kings priests or the wrathful and angry punishing God of the Hebrews. The true (God) or the 'hierarchy' was a much more compassionate source, a source that has never been recognised or acknowledged. That compassion was reflected in the mission that came to Earth (Hubbard was wrong on that one).

There are of course warnings associated with atomic energy, which are part of the natural UFO phenomenon, which I discussed in *Alternative 4*. These warnings are not part of any recent thought, such as The Campaign for Nuclear

Disarmament, although certainly all those who marchèd on Grosvenor Square in the 1960's, were undoubtedly 'tuned in', to those warnings in some manner, even if it was only common sense, that to use such devices was one of the greatest dangers mankind has ever unleashed because it challenges the Grid. The thought processes and warnings that are left imprinted as holographics on the spiritual bioplasma and which are part of the natural UFO phenomenon, come from the past and what appears to be the ancient Matriarchal warnings to man. Did then Atomic power exist even in those early days, which appears to be the case from the Indian epics of destruction and possibly in the story of Sodom and Gommhora? On the 25 September 1972, Dr Francis Perrin, former chairman of the French High Commission for Atomic Energy, presented a report to the French Academy of Sciences concerning the discovery of the remains of prehistoric nuclear chain reaction. Perrin's first inkling came when workers at the French Uranium Enrichment Centre observed that uranium ore from a new mine at Oklo, forty miles north-west of Franceville in Gabon, West Africa, was markedly depleted of uranium 235. All uranium deposits in the world today contain 0.715 per cent of U 235, but the Oklo mine uranium showed levels as low as 0.621 per cent. The only explanation that could be given for the missing U 235 was that it had been 'burned' in a chain reaction. Evidence in support of this conclusion surfaced when investigators at the French Atomic Centre at Cadarache detected four rare elements - neodymium, sanarium, europium and cerium - in forms that are typical of the residue from uranium fission. Dr. Perrin concluded his report with the opinion that the Oklo uranium had undergone a nuclear chain reaction, which had been spontaneously set off by natural causes. Since the Oklo uranium deposits were geologically estimated to be 1.7 billion years old, Dr. Perrin suggested that this is the date when the reaction took place, when at that time the uranium would have been at its purest.

After the publication of Perrin's conclusions in papers of the French Academy of Sciences, Glenn T. Seaborg, former head of the United States Atomic Energy Commission and Nobel Prize winner for his work in the synthesis of heavy elements, pointed out that for uranium to 'burn' in a reaction, conditions must be exactly right. Water is needed as a moderator to slow down the neutrons released as each uranium atom is split, in order to sustain the chain reaction. This water must be extremely pure, even a few parts per million of any contaminant will 'poison' the reaction, bringing it to a halt. The problem is that no water that is pure exists naturally anywhere in the world. A second objection to Dr Perrin's report involved the uranium itself. Several specialists in reactor engineering remarked, that at no time in the geologically estimated history of the Oklo deposits was the uranium ore rich enough in U 235 for a natural reaction to have taken place, even when the deposits supposedly were first formed because of the slow rate of radioactive disintegration of   U 235, the fissionable material would have constituted only 3 per cent of the deposits - far too low a level for a 'burn': And Yet a reaction *did* take place, suggesting that the original uranium was far richer in U 235 than a natural formation could have been. The astounding conclusion was that a nuclear reaction could not be explained by natural means and if nature was not responsible, then the reaction must have been produced artificially. Was it possible that the OIklo uranium is the residue from an antediluvian reactor that was destroyed by the Flood and red posited in West Africa? If however the estimated age is 1.7 billion years old for the reactor, then this reflects on Soddy's statement, that men today may merely follow the route of: "those who have gone before" quoting that odd statement by Einstein, at the time he worked on atomic fission at the Los Alamos site.

ANTI GRAVITY PROPULSION

Anti gravity UFO type devices being developed in the 1970's, may have accounted for the increasing number of 'hard sightings' of silvery discs reported by witnesses in that period. This might be confirmed by a report No. AF RPL - TR- 31 of June 1972, prepared by a group of twenty-eight scientists from the U.S. Air Force Command, Edwards, and California entitled *Project Outgrowth - Advanced Propulsion Concepts*. The report attempted to predict possible developments in the field of propulsion in the near future. Some of the headings in that report included "Electrostatic effects", "Alfuen Wave Propulsion", "Electro-magnetic Spacecraft propulsion", "Super Conducting Particle Accelerator", "Anti-gravity Propulsion". A number of researchers have also like Moray King, produced anti-gravity devices, which have been patented.

Correspondence between Thomas Townsend Brown and Rolf Schaffranke, both researchers in this field show that research had occurred involving *dome-shaped* aluminium canopies, which as part of an electrode structure set up a radical electrical field inside the canopy and the result being, that the canopy was able to lift off the ground, together with an attached load. Further the lifting operation was observed even within a high vacuum. Physicist Harold Aspden in his own research papers commented:

> "Evidently, the reason for this breach of acceptable scientific doctrine was not understood by the experimenters involved in those tests, but I see this as a manifestation of the vacuum spin action. It taps energy from space to build a kind of ether whirlwind inside the canopy and the electric pressure set up inside that canopy by the energy in spin pushes obliquely against the underside of the canopy to drive it upwards. It becomes a material object powered against the gravity field by a thrust developed against the ether in spin and most of the energy in that spin is drawn from the free energy environment of enveloping space".

As Harold Aspden asks: "How can it be that the Scientific community of the world can stand aloof and pay no attention to such experimental anomalies, which are only rarely discovered, but which have such enormous implications for the future of mankind?" I asked a somewhat similar question regarding the model for Cancer I produced, which lies presently collecting dust in the archives of the British Library, just as the petition I produced in 1997 lays collecting dust in the Appendix II here. A number of scientists including Aspden, know that it is difficult to get work past Science Editors (or any Editor! Controlled either by the global elite or their own dramatizations of their past lives or the necessity to maintain the mystery and therefore magazine sales!): let alone the few scientific magazines such as *Nature*, *New Scientist* and *Scientific American* which will not even print an argument (particularly from a woman) that is rational and reasoned, in the case of new advances or thinking. I had my proposed article: *Who killed the Minoans?* Rejected by *New Scientist* as I have recounted in favour of the *next edition* which promptly carried the orthodox viewpoint, even though that viewpoint as smart as it was with wave action diagrams, failed to observe the obvious, when concluding that Knosos was destroyed by a tidal wave resulting from volcanic eruption on Santorini – the obvious being that Knossos is covered in gypsum which dissolves in running water! Had the researchers ever been to the site? and as I commented in a letter to the Editor the following week (unpublished naturally) "Presumably the icon produced in the article of a figure holding his hand to the third eye was thinking:"Oh woe is me, here comes a tidal wave!" *Nature* informed me they do not accept "new research", whatever that might mean! Where exactly new or groundbreaking ideas and research do present themselves becomes the problem. However there is a publishing network that exists not only in the medical field, but it would seem even in the fields of physics and archaeology. The standard orthodox viewpoint is always pushed and this is NOT just the intransigence of Science editors. *The Protocols of Zion,* that notorious document that I discussed in *The Battle of The Trees,* which purports to represent the secret deliberations of the Elders of Zion for a World Order, although its authenticity cannot be proven, discusses the complete control of all forms of media and publishing. Whilst this document may not have originated with the Elders but with the Russian aristocracy, one cannot dispute that some secret group has managed to all but finalise all the goals set out in that document. Further since the alternatives of aristocracy (Judah and the thirteenth tribe) and Zionism (12 tribes and Levi if not a combined purpose with the thirteenth tribe) have both sought World Orders, then it matters not which group the plan emanated from, the goal is the same.

Anti-gravity research as part of the hidden science and its connection to the vacuum or matrix is another area of scientific research, which must parallel attempts to research the mechanism of cancer and its connection to the biofield. John Searl's British Ether-Vortex Turbine was another anti-gravity or levitation device, which also produces an odd magnetic effect, in addition to the electrostatic gradients which are produced and which induces electrical currents in closed loop conductors, even when there is no relative movement. This implies a production of energy from an "unknown" and apparently unlimited source. This source one imagines is the energy inherent within the vacuum state. In this case, once a certain threshold is past, the power output exceeds the power input; the machine therefore exhibits *perpetual motion*. The energy is again derived presumably from the vacuum ocean, so the laws of energy conservation are not violated (i.e. something for nothing). The estimated power output is in the region of 10 to the power 13 or 10 to the power 15 watts, which is about a million, million times as much power as is used by a 100 watt electric light bulb.

Thomas Townsend Brown[136] was another researcher to produce anti-gravitational devices, but whilst Brown's gravitators demonstrated an effect that was never turned into usable UFO type craft, Searle's discovery was a method of extracting or converting energy out of the vacuum state, to make any craft more than self-propelling and self-sustaining. I cannot think that his research went un- observed by the global elite. Dr. Henry Moray an American inventor and electrical engineer, was also to work in this field from 1909 to 1943 and principally worked on 'Radiant Energy'. His device utilised a component (known as a Moray valve), consisting of a semi -conducting hetero junction (a complex interface), using ultra-pure germanium. This was long before the days of the transistor, when the semi-conducting properties of germanium had not been fully exploited. During the 1930's Dr. Moray applied for several patents, but these however were rejected on the grounds that a cold semi-conductor cathode could not emit sufficient electrons. The development of the transistor some two decades later, demonstrated that Moray's central component could actually operate just as he had described it. Moray was subjected to the all too familiar form of attack which plagues all scientists who threaten to reveal either the workings of the global elite, or reveal the hidden science. When Moray formed a company for the commercial development of his device, he suffered repeated threats and was actually shot in his laboratory in 1940 and remained the subject of frequent threats until he retired from active research in 1943.[137] This method of removing any threat to world global elite control is seen uniformerly throughout the sciences particularly in the field of medicine and medical research. The natural UFO phenomenon left to itself, would have been studied along the lines I outlined for the mechanism I suggested in *Alternative 4*, however the fact that the various government agencies became involved at an early stage, means that there was some envisaged threat in any understanding of the phenomenon. Such a threat must exist on the basis that the mechanism for the natural UFO phenomenon involves the matrix energies and space geometric. Further it may have been an easy option to pass off secret research into the vacuum as a UFO phenomenon, thus the science immediately and predictably had a confusion placed upon it. Whilst UFO reports talk of coloured lights and balls of lights, a number of UFO incidents of this kind were observed near to sensitive research stations.

It cannot be denied that vacuum research has been ongoing for decades in secret. Harold Aspden confirms the research in his quoted papers as does Moray B. King and further Dr. Kiril Chukanov stated: "I first produced experimental proof that artificially created ball lightning could produce energy for practical needs in 1987 in Bulgaria". Thus coloured balls of light in alleged UFO accounts may well have been the result of on-going secret research into tapping the zero-point energy and anti-gravity propulsion. By 1990 Chukanov had taken his research project to Sunnivale California and in his book *Final Quantum Revelation (1994)* Chukanov reported a 900-watt rate of excess energy generation in experiments on the aether vacuum. Thus despite the official line that space is just an empty vacuum, scientists in the independent sector have proven otherwise, which is not to say that higher up the research ladder of Rosicrucianism and/or NASA? That work is not accepted; more is it, that higher up they have gone way beyond what man could imagine.

Harold Aspden stated:" If we can get energy from vacuous space, energy in excess of that we can store by setting up electric and magnetic fields, then that proves there is something in space that stands apart from matter. That something is the ether". Thus Free energy from tapping the zero point energy or vacuum together with anti-gravity propulsion, both being part of the hidden science, undoubtedly were being researched at a high level, but who exactly knew about it? Whilst this book does not allow a full evaluation of UFO data, which I reserved for my second book, it is interesting to note that what was probably anti-gravity propulsion research and related ongoing secret research into vacuum energies, was reported by Major Ernest Edwards as a complaint to his commander in the1980's. The reproduction copy I have (*Appendix 3*) is not high quality reproduction, but I have reproduced it to illustrate three points:

1. UFO witness accounts are often reported by highly reliable sources.
2. A number of UFO reports come from military or scientifically sensitive areas.
3. Such reports when received in a chain of official command are not investigated and reports not forthcoming.

This particular report states that:

"On 2 Sept 80,SOURCE related on 3 Aug 80, three Security Policemen assigned to 1608 SPS, KAFB, NM, on duty inside the Manzano Weapons Storage Area sighted an unidentified light in the air that travelled from North to South over the Coyote Canyon area of the Department of Defence Restricted Test Range on KAFB, NM...the three observed a very bright light in the sky approximately 3 miles North-North East of their position. The light travelled with great speed and stopped suddenly in the sky over Coyote Canyon. The three first thought the object was a helicopter, however, after observing the strange aerial manoeuvres (stop and go), they felt the helicopter couldn't have performed such skills. The light landed in the Coyote Canyon area. Sometime later, three witnessed the light take off and leave proceeding straight up at a high speed and disappear.... On 11 Aug. 80, RUSS CURTIS. Sandia Security, advised that on 9 Aug 80, a Sandia Security Guard, (who wishes his name not be divulged for fear of harassment), related the following: At approximately 0020hrs, he was driving East on the Coyote Canyon access road on a routine building check of an alarmed structure. As he approached the structure he observed a bright light near the ground behind the structure. He also observed an object he first thought was a helicopter. But after driving closer, he observed a round disk shaped object. He attempted to radio for a back up patrol but his radio would not work. As he approached the object on foot armed with a shotgun, the object took off in a vertical direction at a high rate of speed. The guard was a former helicopter mechanic in the U.S. Army and stated the object he observed was not a helicopter".

Under the section: "Other Comments" it states: "Base commander was briefed but did not request an AFOSI investigation at this time.... The FBI will not become involved in the matter". Given that this area was a military sensitive area, which warranted the employment of security personnel with handguns, the decision not to investigate at a high level, an unidentified craft and an unusual one at that, is very curious unless of course on-going testing of anti-gravity propulsion using Grid anomalies was known to military command and the head of the FBI.

Another letter from a doctor for the Naval Medical Research Unit, in Illinois, dated 10 July 1952 came into my possession. This was forwarded to U.S. Air Force Air Technical Intelligence Command in Washington, D.C. (*Appendix 3*). Surely a "sausage-shaped" revolving aircraft some 80feet in diameter, which could not be passed off as a "balloon", due to its great speed like that of "jet planes", would warrant investigation, since no known aircraft *at that time* held that description. However a Memorandum (Appendix 3) for General Samford within the Department of the Air Force, Headquarters United States Air Force Washington, D.C. Dated 2 Jan 1952 states: "The continued reports of unusual flying objects requires positive action to determine the nature and origin of this phenomena. The action taken thus far has been designed to track down and evaluate reports from casual observers throughout the country. Thus far, this action has produced results of doubtful value and the inconsistencies inherent in the nature of the reports has given neither positive or negative proof of the claims". The Americans at this high level, allegedly claim in this memorandum, that they do not know anything about anti-gravity propulsion, the report continues:

> "It is logical to relate the reported sightings to the known development of aircraft, jet propulsion, rockets and range extension capabilities in Germany and the U.S.S.R. In this connection, it is to be noted that certain developments by the Germans, particularly the Horton wing, jet propulsion, and refuelling, combined with their extensive employment of V-1 and V-2 weapons during World War II, lend credence to the

possibility that the flying objects may be of German and Russian origin. The developments mentioned above were completed and operational between 1941 and 1944 and subsequently fell into the hands of the Soviets at the end of the war. There is evidence that the Germans were working on these projects as far back as 1931 to 1938. Therefore, it may be assumed that the Germans had at least a 7 to 10 year lead over the United States in the development of rockets, jet engines, and aircraft of the Horton-wing design.

In view of the above facts and the persistent reports of unusual flying objects over parts of the   United States, particularly the east and west coast and in the vicinity of the atomic energy production and testing facilities, it is apparent that positive action must be taken to determine the nature of the objects and, if possible, their origin. Since it is known fact that the Soviets did not detonate an atomic bomb prior to 1949, it is believed possible that the Soviets may have developed the German aircraft designs at an accelerated rate in order to have a suitable carrier for the delivery of weapons of mass destruction...".

U.S. planes were already hunting Discs, according to the *Milwaukee Sentinel of July 7 1947* (*Appendix 3*) and in Britain on 28 July 1952 The Secretary of State for Air was asked by Winston Churchill in a personal minute from the Prime Minister's Office (Appendix 2) "What does all this stuff about flying saucers amount to? Let me have a report at your convenience". Further The London *Times* on *July 9 1947* ran a short notice "U.S. Army to Examine A 'Flying Disk'"; the notice read:" After an Army announcement from Roswell, New Mexico, that an object resembling a "flying disk" had been found there, the commander of the Eighth Air Force said to-night that the object was being sent to the research centre at Wright Field, Ohio, for examination". Well it did exist then but the Aliens were undoubtedly an embellishment to hide the science! It appears then, that there was some ignorance as to Grid research in 1940 that was not the case in the post war decades. The Germans had been heavily involved with occult science and such research may have involved channelling information from the Grid, which they used to "accelerate" their technological research. It is known that numerous German scientists went to America after the war in what is known as *operation paperclip*, but it seems likely that the explosion in technology since1940 and particularly from 1945- 1970 may have come from "those men before" or Grid memory and Cabalistic science, since the explosion of research that occurred seems hardly credible, culminating in the space programme and anti-gravity research which was apparently on-going in the mid 1930's to 1940. Whilst I have covered Hitler more extensively in *Alternative 4*, and his connection to the secret groups and particularly what may have been Rosicrucian Cabalistic science, it might be pertinent to cover briefly here some background data.

HITLER AND OCCULT SCIENCE

The occult connections of the Nazi Party would command an entire book, however a poster that appeared in 1936 (*The Battle of The Trees*), showing Hitler as a Grail knight, and which was withdrawn shortly afterwards, really encompasses the entire cover nature of World War II, which was a **religious and political war.** The swastika was said to have been a sign of Agni and good fortune for the *Buddhists.* However in *Alternative 4*, I gave a much older derivation dating back to Bronze Age Greece and the labyrinth of Knossos. The swastika being an emblem of The Cycle of Eternal Return and the rebirth of Solar Kings as part of the Religious Revolution in Bronze Age Crete. It is claimed that Madame Blavatsky first utilised the sign as an emblem of the Theosophical Society archetypally symbolising the Aryan Race. The Theosophical Society was heavily steeped in Root Race theory which derived from Fabre d'Oliver (1767-1825) a member of the Jacobin club, who was pro-Semitic and in his Philosophical *History of the Human Race* (*1824*), he asserted that the White race was both the highest type of humanity and the youngest, undoubtedly referring to the thirteenth tribe of Judah from Adam, which was white. However, you will remember that I concluded that it had not always been so, rather was it a product of intermarriage with perhaps the 'Missionary' type and the woman, who perhaps in her black and white body represented the intermarriage. Further that it had come into existence somewhere near the North Pole and had overthrown inferior races as the Black and the remnant of the Red, most of who had been drowned at the time of a cataclysm. A "Druid", a Priest King named Ram, who had been the creator of modern civilization, had led the White race. Well here you have the whole racist philosophy of the thirteenth tribe of Judah.

This theory was also to emerge in the writings of Joseph Alexandre Saint-Yves d' Alveydue (1842-1909). Whilst incorporating much of Fabre d'Olivet's writings, he also added the existence of the underground city of Agartha, which importantly to my own thesis of a Druidic Semitic World Order, was a Theocracy. Saint-Yves proposed a plan to feed humanity upon algae and mentioned a machine called the *arch*eometer: "the key to all religions and sciences of antiquity" perhaps reflecting knowledge that is present on the Arch level of Freemasonry; and above all, he spoke of a new social/political system called **synarchy**. This is based upon the idea that society must be regarded as a *living organism*, which seems to have been derived from the ideas of Charles Fourier, a French Utopian Socialist. Forier it seems could channel information from the Grid, since he could: "discern the future of humanity": He also foresaw the triumph of Socialism and claimed all animals would become vegetarian and humanity would enter a Golden Age signalled by the: "male electricity of the

North Pole", uniting in a cosmic copulation (shades of the Serpent or Grid here) with the: "female electricity of the South Pole". This I am afraid sounds like a dramatization of the Apocalypse and a Magnetic Reversal! Further the triumph of Socialism should have been further left - Communism. In other words this is the old World Order plan of a Theocracy of elitist Communism i.e. communism for the masses run by the rich elite far right: Plato's Republic no less.

Rudolph Steiner who I have already mentioned as the founder of occult science - Anthroposophy, incorporated a good deal of Saint-Yves theories into his own version of "occult science", which promotes Jesus Christ (who was a Druid and therefore part of this World Order plan), even though it is based in some Semitic Masonry offshoot group, presumably set up to serve a purpose at the time. Further Steiner referred to the term "Akashic Record" and his real teachings were only divulged to a select few. Steiner must have been impressed by synarchy, for his original political ideas, which attracted attention in Germany in the 1920's, were synarchy tied up in a Germanic wrapping. Steiner curiously also advocated a *"Three* fold Commonwealth" and showed a great parallel in his ideas to the old Celtic Commonwealth, with the Druids forming the Theocratic priesthood. As part of this so-called Commonwealth, which appears today as European Union, wrapped up in the garb of Internationalism, racial importance was a parallel to the idea of Manu Rama as the great leader of the Aryan Race.

The idea that the: "Jewish section of the Atlantean-Semitic Root Race" or the: "curse of the Jews", brought the: "Archetype of the Messiah to the West without themselves being fitted to use it ... this is the curse of the Jews". These Root Race ideas were to fuel the Nazi Party: However such statements are evidently made by those who had no idea of the power that rules at the top and just how much and how many they were prepared to sacrifice in order to gain that power. Madame Blavatsky was the real directive force behind Root Race theory and Blavatsky claimed that her system, which was the most complex and influential of all occult Root Race theories, was given to her by Himalayan "Supermen" called Mahatmas. Blavatsky's system however had other connections. The word Theosophy was used in the eighteenth Century to denote the history of the Martinists, it was known two centuries earlier, when Heselmeyer in 1612, wrote of: "the laudable Fraternity of the Theosophists of the *Rosy Cross*" (my emphasis). It is amusing now, given my somewhat traumatic experience of both Scientology and Rudolph Steiner's anthroposophy, that they evidently may have emerged from the same pot – Rosicrucian's and the tribe of Judah. The important link then is once again the Rose-Croix and Rosicrucian's. Blavatsky went on to found the modern Theosophical Society in New York in 1875, thus whilst Blavatsky claimed that her system came from Tibet, Monsieur Guenon, who had inside knowledge of the movement, indicated the existence of concealed superiors in Europe! And it was by these men that Blavatsky was really directed.

It would seem that the origins of World War II, were being laid from this early date in 1875, following the planned Masonic directed French and Russian Revolutions. The ostensibly Socialist but in reality Communistic plan moving forward towards that: "Theocratic United States of The West" - European Union as one step closer to that final goal of a One world Order, governed by a Theocracy or secret priesthood, presumably white.

Blavatsky was to state in 1875, that she was: "sent from Paris to America in order to verify phenomena and their reality and to show the deception of the spiritualist theory". What she quite meant by this is unclear, however the Illuminati were in New York and one wonders whether she refers to channelled information by that group, from the Akashic Record. Later when questioned as to whom sent her to America, she would only say the "Mahatmas", but this did not answer why her mission came from Paris and not Tibet. However the 'Vaincre ' magazine illustration which shows the dual aim of political and religious goals encompassed in the year 1937, with a Hermetic knight riding down a road towards a setting sun, labelled "Etats Unis" or "United States of the West", with Brittany on one side and Bavaria on the other, implies a co-operation between two groups, with two goals (religious and political): The Illuminati in New York with a political goal (Bavaria and its connection to Adam Weishaupt, the founder of Illuminism); and Brittany representing the religious goal and presumably the Davidic line of the Merovingians and Christianity. Blavatsky then we might assume, was an agent for the religious goal and her real masters were non other than the Druids or Biblical Adamites, the white Atlanteans.Blavatsky was probably never in Tibet, but took her orders and mission directly from the Rose-Croix, or Rosicrucian's, which in descendancy may be the Druidical hierarchy with Scottish Rite Freemasonry as another name.

Blavatsky would also claim that Jesus Christ was never a historical person. She confuses this by admitting that Jesus may have lived during the Christian era or a century earlier, thus repeating the story of the Sepher Toldoth Jehoshua. She later referred to her: "Masters who affirm it" i.e. the Toldoth Yeshu account. Since the Toldoth Yeshu is Cabalistic, then one assumes her masters were indeed Cabalists or Judaic. The only group that would fit this and the white Atlantean Root Race theories she promoted, would be the biblical white Adamites, the Atlanteans –Druids: The lost thirteenth tribe of Israel. If this was the case, then the Holocaust can be laid firmly at their door, Jews sacrificed to the State of a future Israel, which came after World War II. One step closer to fulfilling the Covenant and now the "vine-men", or those who draw together would no longer be required to exist only within the secret group of Freemasonry, but would acquire the land from the Palestinians, where the events and plan of Golgotha were enacted.

Annie Besant a Theosophist, in her book *Esoteric Christianity*, related that Jesus was brought up amongst the Essenes and that later He went to Egypt, where He became an initiate of the Great Esoteric Lodge - The **Great White Lodge**: "from which all religions derive". I proposed that the events of Golgotha, would if Jesus was sacrificed on the Taur 'T' shaped cross provide the International religion of Christianity, which was not originally intended for Gentiles as I have covered, but for Jews. However St. Paul against the wishes of Jesus' brother James, offered the Judaic religion to Gentiles and this was quite probably part of a very clever and long- term plan. "The Fellowship of Faiths", may have been part of the entire Rosicrucian plan with a One World Order politically and religiously united under Communism and Christianity. The fact that the Illuminati are Communistic almost certainly with the involvement of the Catholic Church with the Illuminati in the 1970's, indicates that Jesus if not tutored by The Great White Lodge, almost certainly was tutored by a secret group, who held a long term plan of a Universal Religion. The Rosicrucian's in the past have admitted that their masters: **"The Great White Brotherhood"**, exists in the etheric layer, and therefore is presumably channelled and perhaps this was the purpose of Blavatsky to aid channelling as a clairvoyant medium. Initiates of the Rosicrucian Order have also admitted in the past that the: "Great Goal" of the Great White Brotherhood is not known and that they (the Rosicrucian's) follow orders, with no questions asked, which is a feature of the Illuminati group. Whilst I will cover channelling in another section, if Blavatsky's Masters were non other than the channelled information from so-called masters in the etheric layer, then her real Master was the Grid and its holographic of stored memory and THOUGHT processes from past masters! Consider the possibility that those Masters merely incarnated and were merely following their own past goals and past thought processes i.e. PAST IDENTITIES. Well this is a good dramatization game, because it means that the master mega-computer, the Grid ('God') in the sky, was running world politics and religion! Blavatsky's "Him", was her guide and thus a male mega-computer (naturally)! Is it any wonder that Nostradamus saw the events of World War II, long before they were to materialise, for Grid past patterns and events (the 'script') were being followed religiously! The Magnetically Reversed Case (MRC), the Atlanteans and those who survived a Magnetic Reversal turning the pages on their past history and events, in order to once again rule as head of their One World Order - a Theocracy, until of course the final page, when we come once again to another self-promoted cataclysm and off the whole cycle goes again, with presumably a Noah's Ark space station on Mars? Can't you just see it, a few million years from now with myths about 'Supermen' with magical knowledge arriving in a space ship to Earth and then take charge. I hope you begin to get the picture and the yawning cycle played out by the MRC case on Earth, with another Act I, another Genesis story and yes, it was all her fault, they won't remember quite why, but you can bet your bottom drawer **she** will get the blame, since she had the audacity to remind him of his own conscience and his inability to create, other than a slave species. She mortally wounded his ego and for the MRC case that I am afraid, after billions of years as Master was a severe threat to his own survival and the belief in his own divine superiority.

Annie Besant, was to repeat Blavatsky's claim, that Christ of the Gospels never existed, but was an invention of the monks of the second century. However, Jesus and "the Christ" were seen by the Theosophists, as two separate and distinct individuals and when they spoke of "the Christ", they referred to someone living in a bungalow in the Himalayas, who would as J. Krishnamurti posed, come as the Great Teacher. No doubt the Chinese occupation of Tibet and the present Government in Britain, who failed to support pro-Tibetan demonstrators against the recent visit to Britain by the Chinese President, was a matter of "policy", and both events can be explained by the religious threat to the One World Order, if the proposed coming of the Tibetan Buddha in 1950 was portrayed as the Teacher.

A curious parallel might be drawn between the Theosophists and Scientology, in so far as both claimed to hold no political aspirations and both claimed to be ethical groups. When a group of Scientologists left Scientology over the question of the ethical use of money and formed their own group Phoenix; that action might be compared to the members of the Seven Theosophical Lodges who entered a protest in the 1920's, against the departure of some members from the original policy of the society. Amongst the resolutions put forward, was one urging the President (Annie Besant) to establish a tribunal: "to investigate matters affecting the good name of the society, and the conduct of certain members". This was carried by: "an overwhelming majority", which supported the old style management of the Theosophical society and Annie Besant was given a vote of confidence.

Many groups which originate from the same melting pot of knowledge, even healing groups, are either set up as was the case of Theosophy to provide an immediate **use** by a secret priesthood, or groups are set up in order that management of the group can be used later. Secret groups always work with long and short- term goals, as was evidenced by one warning at the time of the French Revolution: "a massive project", which must have referred to a One World Order, run by the Brotherhood, or at least those Masters who undoubtedly operate from a higher and secret Order. I do not know whether Scientology was set up to be used after the founder Hubbard died, but it does not look good, when they eject people who were long term associates of Hubbard and who have only ever worked for truth. In the case of Blavatsky, 'her' ideas were to surface in initiates of the occult, who would come to surround and groom Hitler. Hitler's pronouncement of the Germans as the ancient Aryans, who as a white-blonde race had once ruled the world, was Blavatsky's impetus many years earlier and more importantly the secret group behind her. Hitler would wage war on Europe in an attempt to re-instate the Aryans to their former supposed glory. The Aryan Empire was no more than the dream of a Celtic -Druidic Commonwealth of white supremacy. In fact the Druids of the time bore the emblem of the swastika or the Trieskelion of Late Minoan Crete on their robes and the Klu Klux Klan (KKK), would re-enact the Druidical rites of sacrifice to white supremacy many years later, to the horror and outrage of the world's audience. Whilst the FBI waged its own war against Martin Luther King with J. Edgar Hoover as the fascist white man's ally.

Henry Ford of America was to become a major influence on Hitler, who kept Ford's photo on his desk in the Brown House. Ford was anti-Semitic, stating that *three* Jews! Had convinced him of the authenticity of the notorious document *The Protocols of Zion*, which purported to outline a plan by the Sanhedrin (a high Jewish Council), to form a World Order. Ford never identified these Jews, but it would seem if Ford is telling the truth, that those gentlemen had a great deal to do with the Holocaust. The three men in black is a feature of the manipulated UFO phenomenon and three is a number associated with the Druids and the thirteenth tribe of Judah. Thus was World War II and the slaughter of the Jews, really a case of a secret group (tribe of Judah) posing a World Order threat, supposedly a Jewish conspiracy and puppeting Hitler to destroy Europe, so that European Union could be posed as an answer to war, whilst cunningly promoting internationalism and peace and finally achieving the goal of Communism governed by a Theocracy and the rich merchants – Plato's Republic and the Greek idea of democracy, a goal that would sacrifice the Jews in order to attain a homeland in Palestine? I pray that this was not the case, but I never underestimate the MRC case.

In *Alternative 4*, I proposed that the drug LSD heightened perception of the Akashic Record and precipitated apocalyptic memories of a Magnetic Reversal, which may account for the rainbow colours and the bad reactions of suicide. The occult have always been attracted to the use of drugs and after the Religious Revolution in Crete, opium appears to have been introduced with the poppy goddesses. The CIA was testing LSD on unsuspecting individuals in the 1960's and Alister Crowley in the 1920's was using drugs to obtain occult information from the Grid. I believe that the Third Reich in its highest Order, The Black Order, were employing drugs to access Grid holographics, for the purpose of discovering not only pre-history, but past technology relating to the hidden science. Karl Kieswetter a key figure in the history of German Theosophy, met his death in 1895, as the result of an unsuccessful attempt to attain clairvoyant vision by the use of a drug that supposedly: "unloose the girders of the soul". Hitler was using the mind-expanding substance Anhalonium Lewinii in 1920; a drug derived from the Mexican Cactus, which is considered hallucinogenic, but really re-stimulates Grid memories. This was a surprisingly early date for someone to have been using Anhalonium, as little was known of this drug in Europe at this time. Alister Crowley however was using the drug as early as 1915-1916. We know that Crowley was connected to the Golden Dawn secret group, which had some connection to the Rosicrucian's and the Illuminati. Dr. Warner Stein, who was an Anthropologist and occultist significantly enough, reported that Ernst Pretzsche supplied Hitler with the drug, whether this accounted for the left side trembling of Hitler in his latter years and the almost hypnotic speeches he gave, which were almost magnetic can only be guessed at.

The labyrinth as swastika, a Minoan archetypal symbol, represented not only the Cycle of Eternal Return, but signified Re-incarnation of solar Kings, through "Her", the Great Goddess and it was evident that Hitler not only believed in Re-incarnation, but referred to "Her" in one of his significant speeches (*Alternative 4*). All these clues signify that Hitler was initiated into secret knowledge of a particular Order, which increasingly looks like some set up branch and order of the thirteenth tribe – Judah. I have maintained that this particular brand of knowledge, evidenced from the decoding of the Floor at Cardiff Castle Wales UK, is present in the Rose-Croix level of Scottish Rite Freemasonry, which may indeed be an ascendant group of the Druids. Thus one has only to look in Hitler's immediate circle for an initiate with connections to the Rosy-Cross. Such a man was Guido Von List. A defeated and humiliated Germany after World War I was ripe for the manipulative Secret Order, who would see this as an opportunity (if they did not indeed manipulate World War I to this end), of finding a German leader, who would achieve the dream of a white Aryan Empire. Guido Von List was a leading member of the secret mystical society of the German Order, which was anti-democratic, Aristocratic and included many rich bankers, who would eventually finance Hitler. Significantly one summer evening, Von List and his associates celebrated a pagan festival on top of a *hill* (the favourite haunt of Druids), worshipping the *sun*. Before they went home, they buried *8 wine* bottles, in the shape of a swastika. If 8 represented infinity, then the Covenant with Jehovah: "I am the Alpha and the Omega" (the beginning as Adamites/Druids or Atlanteans, and last as Jehovah's One World Order) was sealed again. If that is the case then the old Druidic/Celtic Commonwealth was about to resurrect itself in the form of World War II – A RELIGIOUS WAR. The swastika in esoteric high initiate terms would be the Cycle of Eternal Return or re-birth of the Aryan superace. To the masses the swastika became a symbol of Militant German Nationalism belying its true meaning. Hitler would wage war on the Jews, for quite a different reason than those at the top had in mind. It was of course a religious war between two priesthoods, although possibly Hitler was convinced by those initiates who tutored him, that he was saving the world from the goals laid out in *The Protocols of Zion* and the Jewish World Order - a fine dupe and puppet he was, If this was the case! It is difficult to conceive that Hitler had all the relevant background information to the secret Orders who puppetted him, including the origin of the Druids and the Covenant, like most political animals who seek power, they only use knowledge to gain power and have no time to become diligent students, before they unload their half-baked notions onto humanity.

It is claimed that a disciple of Von List designed the Swastika as the badge of the Nazi Party, on the basis of the runic equivalent of the letter G, to prove that the symbol had a secret significance to the ancient Germanic peoples. Others have claimed that Madame Blavatsky developed the symbol and recently this dis-information line was pushed on British Television on the History Channel! However Blavatsky did not adopt the swastika as an emblem for her movement of Theosophy, until two years after Von List had held the hill top celebration. Von List claimed that the Herminones a tall, blonde, blue-eyed race of Nordic heroes described by the classical writer Tacitus in his *Germania*, had given rise to a secret society of German magicians called **Arm**anen ('The Cutting of The Elm/Arm ceremony'?) who survived into modern times and of which he himself claimed to be the last surviving member. This sounds like a suspicious alteration of Druid background. Von List claimed further that Paracelsus was a past member and we know that Paracelsus was a member of the Rosicrucian's or Rosy Cross, thus this is another link to Hitler and the secret fraternity who initiated him. Paracelsus incidentally, knew very well the biofield energies and Hitler I have claimed in *Alternative 4*, was versed in the tonic scale of ascending and descending emotional energies and sounds, upon which he based his speeches. Dietrich Eckhart seems to have been involved in this aspect of Hitler's tutorage, for he stated: "Follow Hitler, but it was I who *played the tune*" (my emphasis).

Guido Von List was also on friendly terms with Lanz Von Liebenfels and the two occultists were to work together; List would concentrate on runes, occult history and esoteric philology, whilst Liebenfels would devote his attention to the magical aspects of racist theory. Liebenfels was to formulate the secret Order of New Templars in 1894. The first temple was situated at the Castle of Werfenstein overlooking the **Dan**ube (which may hold significance on Tuatha de Danaan) and the swastika was flown from the battlements. Liebenfels published the magazine '*Ostra*', and August Strindberg who was a member of this group and part of the magazine, utilised significantly enough de Guia ta's Kabalistic **Rose-Croix**. This is a fine web! And once again leads us back to Scotland, the 'True Holy Land', where even the swastika is displayed in the design of the broad pin, which holds the Scottish plaid. Such designs in the form of the folded cross occur in Celtic pins. To confirm the connection between these men, who as Cabalistic Rose-Croix Masons had a profound effect on Hitler, Von Liebenfels wrote a letter to a New Templar initiate in which he stated that: "Hitler is one of our pupils. You will one day experience that he and through him me, will one day be victorious and develop a movement that will make the world tremble". [138] Rosenberg was another NAZI who acknowledged his intellectual indebtedness to Von Liebenfels, in his *Mythos of the Twentieth Century*, which was an ideological exposition of Nazism. Himmler's plans for SS 'stud-farms', at which SS blond, blue-eyed 'Supermen', the elite SS would impregnate girls to provide an Aryan Superace, derives from an adaptation of Von Liebenfels suggestion of human breeding farms: "in order to eradicate Slavic and Alpine elements from Germanic hereditary". Von Liebenfels was anti-Semitic and therefore it is perhaps the case that many of these men, did not know the true root of their beliefs.

The role of Alister Crowley on the world's stage I believe has never been fully identified. Crowley who founded the Abbey of Thelema in Switzerland with his quasi-religious doctrine of: "The Law of Thelema", with its famous datum: "Do what thou wilt, is the whole of the law", was to emphasise the role of will over indoctrination. Near to the Abbey in Switzerland is an inn named Gasthof Rose, and until recently sported three flagpoles (the flag of Switzerland, the pennant of the Canton and the banner of the Rose-Croix!) Is it not interesting that Ron Hubbard Founder of Scientology was to be introduced into one of Crowely's groups in California run by Jack Parsons, by a Jew Lou Goldstein? I will come back to these co-incidences later. At the apothecary of the Abbey of Thelema, run by Crowley's followers there was co-incidentally an alchemical laboratory in which Paracelsian remedies (herbal and mineral medicines prepared in accordance with astrological and occult lore) were produced. The library contains a document (*E.O.L. Mitteilungsblatl No. I. June 9 1954*) where there is a Memorandum notice listed:

> "Along with *fire*, life and *water* at *death* to be *celebrated* (Liber Al)
> A shining example of unswerving faith and the very highest virtue, Dr.
> George Lanz Von Liebenfels peacefully crossed the Great Divide at 3a.m.
> on 22nd April 1954" (*Author's emphasis*)

The Memorandum in connection with the flag or banner for the Rose-Croix implies that Liebenfels was indeed a high Rose-Croix Mason, with all of its implications in terms of Adolph Hitler. Crowley believed that his religion 'Thelema' was destined to replace Judaism and Christianity and all other religions of the 'slave gods'. The basis of the new religion was Liber Al, 'The Book of The Law', a seemingly crazy prose poem in *three* parts, which was dictated to Crowley, by a spirit named Aiwass - evidently Grid channelled information then! This certainly indicates how channeling or Grid information has had a profound effect on world politics and religion! (" and God spake unto me" etc. from within those Caves!). To translate whole sections would require an adept at the use of the Greek and Hebrew Gematria (translation of the letters of the alphabet into numbers and vice versa). The book was only to be read by the "few and secret", whose destiny was to rule "the many and unknown" encompassing their datum "the slaves shall serve": a datum behind all World Orders. Crowley's group The Order of Oriental Templars (OTO), may have been incidentally behind the term OT that Hubbard used for levels of knowledge arranged in a hierarchy of secrecy for his initiates; although Hubbard quite definitely used the term to signify "Operating Thetan" (spirit) However we know that Crowley's group split into two factions, Crowley's faction retained Karl Germer and Marthe Kuntzel, who was an elderly ex-Theosophist who had known Madame Blavatsky. In 1925-6 Marthe Kuntzel forwarded Hitler a copy of Crowley's book together with commentaries. This has given rise to the belief that Hitler was directly under the tutorage of Marthe Kuntzel. Rauschning in *Hitler Speaks* stated that Crowley had noted that Hitler either directly quoted or paraphrased Crowley's *Book of the Law*. For example Hitler stated: "We are not at the end of the Age of Reason. The intellect has grown autocratic and become a disease of life"; thus paraphrasing *Chapter II verses 27-32* of *The Book of The Law*. Hitler also stated:" A new age of magical interpretation of the world is coming, of interpretation in terms of the will and not the intelligence"; paraphrasing *Chapter I, verse 44* of Crowley's book. The term "magical" is very interesting and I wonder here, if Hitler is referring to the ability to channel information from the Grid, together with past technology and pre-history. Certainly Hitler may himself with the use of drugs have performed this on a daily basis at Berchtasgaden. Crowley assumed that Marthe Kuntzel was the woman referred to in Rauschning's book, when he referred to a mysterious woman who was in Hitler's circle and Crowley wrote: "This must be Marthe Kuntzel", against this woman's warning: " My Fuhrer, don't touch Black Magic! As yet both white and black magic are open to you. But once you've embarked on black magic it will dominate your destiny. It will hold you captive. Don't choose the quick and easy successes. There lies before you the power of a realm over pure spirits. Do not allow yourself to be led away from your true path by earthbound spirits, which will rob you of your power!" Marthe Kuntzel later denied the connection, thus who was the woman? Perhaps the curious Fraulein Kirstner, whom Hitler's maid spoke of as living at Berchtasgaden and with whom Hitler spent hours every day, but concluding there was no sexual union. The maid believed that this woman had a profound effect on the destiny of Germany, which would one day be revealed. The warning given to Hitler is significant though, because it does imply Grid channelling "earthbound spirits", with the "easy successes" might imply that the precision timing of Hitler's campaigns were made to co-incide with past events, therefore with a predictable outcome.

The myth of the Aryan propagated by occultists, was made into a **State Religion**, where the Swastika was substituted for the Christian Cross and evidently Hitler knew very little of the story since in his notes he referred to Jesus as a "dirty Jew", thus exhibiting no idea of the complicated background before he reduced Europe to rubble and millions had died fighting a war that was never explained to them. Thus the attempts to replace Christianity with the archetypal symbol of the Swastika was really an attempt to introduce Solar Kingship, with Hitler as the new Messiah, a vision typically Druidic and a scenario that had some precedence on the world's political stage, where the Theocracy or elect priesthood was now the highest Order of the SS, The Black Order. All German youth became subjected to brainwashing propaganda with readings from the Bible replaced by Mein Kampf and children were made to repeat:" away with Holy incense and water, Swastika brings salvation on Earth". All references to Christmas were banned and the Solar Kingship winter festival dedicated to the sun was introduced, together with a summer solstice festival, where fires were lit all over Germany. The Beltane fires and the Festival of St. John's day, whom I have previously associated as a Druid, gives further evidence for a Druidical and Rose-Croix connection.

There is no doubt that the Nazi's or specifically the SS held a belief in Re-incarnation for Himmler himself, believed that he was a Re-incarnation of Heinrich the Fowler (875-936) the monarch who founded the Saxon Royal House. Himmler of course became the head of a magical order of the SS - The Black Order. The fact that the Nazi's were obsessed with The Holy Grail, Atlantis and other aspects of Rose-Croix Masonry, provides other indirect connections to the Druids or high Rosy Cross Masons. Blavatsky was also to write a great deal on Atlantis. Thule was thought to be the homeland of the German people and the implication was the connection between Thule and Atlantis. The Atlanteans had been blond, blue-eyed Nordics who employed the mysterious faculty of 'race memory', to give a detailed account of the cataclysmic destruction of the Island continent of Atlantis, which once again reminds one remarkably of the Druids faculty of never writing anything down, but memorising their whole desecendency, together presumably with Cabalistic occult history and practise.

Atlantis was placed in arctic latitudes and the SS sent expeditions to this region, believing Thule and Atlantis were synonymous and the homeland of the Aryans. Alfred Rosenberg in *Mythos*, in the preface to the section on Race and Myth wrote:

> "Today geology has attained such a level as to be able to map out periods which occurred tens of thousands of years before our time. Geographers tell us of a continent between North America and Europe, remnants of which we see in Greenland and Iceland. They also reveal to us that on the far side of the high northern island there exist old waterlines, which lay more than one hundred metres over the present ones. This phenomenon points to the probability...that there was once a

much milder climate in the present Arctic region. All this together puts the ancient sagas about Atlantis in a new light. Apparently it is no longer completely out of the question that where today the waves of the Atlantic roar and mighty icebergs wander, a flourishing continent once towered over the deluge; a continent on which a creative race nurtured a great, far reaching sea culture and sent its children into the world as sea voyagers and warriors...That old, despised hypothesis which stated that once, from a Northern creative point, which we will call Atlantis, even if we do not literally believe in a sunken continent of Atlantis, swarms of warriors spread out, which might explain the continuously recurring Nordic longing to conquer distant lands".

Hermann Wirth, who provided some background for Rosenberg's views, identified the Atlantean Continent, with Plato's Atlantis, which he called Thule. Thus there is no doubt, that the SS had significant occult knowledge and held a belief in Re-incarnation or at least transmigration of souls. It has always been questioned, whether the SS had developed anti-gravity propulsion or flying disks. In the Reinhold Schmidt Story - *My contact with space People*, he stated: "When these space people spoke among themselves they used high German, which I happen to understand, as I graduated from a school in which both German and English were taught. I could speak read and write German at the time and I still speak and understand it fairly well. But these space people all spoke to me in English with a German accent".

Further we know from reports in *Appendix 3*, that UFO's were evident as early as 1947 and that the Americans claimed they held no knowledge of them and placed them at the door of the Germans or Russians. Further Winston Churchill in England even in 1952 it would seem, was not briefed on UFO's. It has been suggested that the German Scientists who were involved in rocket technology were taken to America after the war and thus undoubtedly if they had technology relating to anti-gravity propulsion would have taken it with them. It might be considered that the Americans did know about this research, but that it was conducted in secret and not fully known. AeG and Siemens associated with the Rockefellers could have produced anti-gravity spacecraft during the war using Grid anomalies, and information channelled from the Akashic Record. It is claimed that Victor Schauberger an Austrian inventor, was ordered to work for the Third Reich in the production of a number of prototype flying antigravity disks, in the period 1938-1945.

A study of Schaubergers work can be found in Olof Alexandersson's book *Living Water* and his work cannot be given justice here, but Schauberger was a great natural scientist, using his power of OBSERVATION of nature to provide him with the necessary links to his research. Natural processes he maintained hold all the secrets, and then one had only to copy her. On the hermetic principle of: "As above, so below": Schauberger looked for patterns in nature, which reflected the greater Grid or vacuum pattern of organisation. As a forester, he worked mainly with the patterns of flowing water, and later when he worked with other scientists in laboratories, he would show that water developed remarkable properties when it moved in spirals, especially that of the *hyperbolic spiral* a shape that I have been profoundly interested in, in my own research, and one that is frequently found in nature from the shape of DNA, to the shape of galaxies and the proposed action of the morphogenetic bioplasma which I gave as: 'The Onion Ring Model' in *Alternative 4* for the mode of action of the UFO phenomenon. This action is related to perpetual motion and gravity.

Schauberger was to note that fish swim with their mouths open. A trout is able to hover motionless even in a stream of strong currents. The water enters the mouth, flows over the gills, which he noted were formed so as to send the water into a spiral motion as it leaves the fish through the gill slits. He proposed that the spiral motion and the trace elements of the water alter the characteristics of water, which then flows out along the streamlined flank of the fish, interacting with the normal river water and thus creating a forward thrust. When the fish wants to move, as in the case of a bird, it re-adjusts the shape of the gills and the fish darts off at tremendous speed in the water. Schauberger took this design principle, to make the 'trout turbine', a machine that was able to generate electricity. The machine was started by a small electric motor and water was forced into a spiral motion by internal shapes within the pipe system. The excess energy produced was used for generating electricity. The question is, whether he had unwittingly stumbled on the method of extracting energy from the vacuum. Further it is likely that the account of the previous cylinder-shaped object, which rotated in an alleged UFO incident, was very likely a prototype of Schauberger's research. Large fish-shape objects which were recorded in alleged UFO incidents, which I recounted in *Alternative 4* may not have been what I recalled as the holographic of the genetic morphogenetic bioplasma giving the genetic line of man from fish, but prototypes of Schauberger's work. It is interesting to note here that the charkas or energy points within the biofield are rotating vortices of energy, organised in hyperbolic spiralling motion, which presumably allows them to draw energy from the vacuum into the body.

It was not long before Schauberger's research, came to the attention of The Third Reich and Schauberger although he initially declined to work for them, was ordered to do so in 1936. Schauberger then worked on flying disks and would write:

> "The form of movement which creates, develops, purifies and grows in the hyperbolic spiral (a helical pathway traced around a cone such as the helical nature of the mollusc shell) which ...is *centripetal*. We find it

everywhere in nature where growth or movement is taking place, in the spiralling of the galaxies in space, in the movement of our planetary system, in the natural flow of water, blood and sap. On the other hand, the destructive and dissolving form of movement is *centrifugal* in nature; it forces the moving medium from the centre outwards towards the periphery in straight lines. The particles of the medium appear to be forced out from the centre. The medium is first weakened and then it dissolves and breaks up. Nature uses this action to disintegrate complexes, which have lost their vivacity or have died. From the broken-down fragments, new co-ordinated forms, new identities, can be created as a result of this concentrating form of movement. The centripetal hyperbolic spiral movement is symptomatic of falling temperature, contraction, and concentration. The centrifugal movement, on the other hand, is synonymous with rising temperature, heat, extension, expansion, and explosion. In nature, there is a continuous switch from one movement to the other. If the development is to occur, then the movement of growth must be predominant". (*Author's emphasis*)

This is possibly one of the most profound observations to be made, which allows my own Cancer research and the final mechanism, to be placed in context with the hyperbolic spiralling motion of the juicer used to prepare juices in The Gerson Therapy for Cancer, which is the methodology of my research. The juicer works on a hyperbolic spiralling or centripetal motion and 'activates', the juices with their high mineral content, to not only replace body minerals but also stagnant and un-activated water (de-structured water) in the cells of the body; but given that a tumour is really an embryonic growth, then the hyperbolic centripetal motion is a *contraction* and not an expansion mode of growth. Given that I state that the tumour is really an embryonic growth and shows embryonic biochemistry, more fully outlined in the cancer report, then the hyperbolic motion retained in the biochemistry of the juices would not only activate body water but would be inhibitive to growth and the tumour; which depends on the centrifugal motion or destructive principle, involving expansion and thus would be inhibited. This also must have a connection to the clockwise and anti-clockwise motion of the morphogenetic and spiritual bioplasmas which I modelled in *Alternative 4* on that of a Diablo and balance, with their 'suck down' or centripetal movement and 'suck up' or centrifugal motion; but a balance must be retained in nature. The research in *Alternative 4* was still preliminary to that here and I may have to revise the model of the Diablo as *two modes of spin* rather than use the terms of morphogenetic and spiritual bioplasma.

Further the hyperbolic spiral and centripetal movement (fall in temperature and contraction), together with centrifugal movement (rise in temperature and expansion) may account for the various cycles of Ice Ages followed by temperate climates, followed by Ice Ages etc. Where the pattern of motion presumably through Magnetic Reversals provides the balance required for the **survival of the Earth**, or MATTER: For the natural conclusion of centripetal movement is *concentration* (to the singularity or the point of the so-called 'Big Bang') whereas the natural conclusion of centrifugal movement is *expansion* and explosion. Presumably gravity as a product of mass and its movement in space varied under pre and post Magnetic Reversals and the size (giants) of man and species like the dinosaurs varied accordingly. This point is certainly interesting if we could apply it to the psychology of the MRC case or those present in an Ice Age where there was low temperature, contraction and concentration which was a low survival period for mammals and man (given that a footprint of man was found alongside a dinosaurs footprint in the Paluxy Riverbed). However reptiles survived well and given UFO incidents of man-animal or reptile like creatures, we might assume that such an incident is a holographic memory of the genetic line of man. This might account for the amorphous man-reptile figure in the Palaeolithic cave painting mentioned earlier. Expansion however comes with the centrifugal cycle and perhaps the psychology of this cycle becomes a high survival growth period of expansion, which may in the case of the MRC and *his* psychology revert to **self- survival** as an extension of that psychology and the need for ultimate size in a One World Order. Thus in any cycle he associates *size with high survival* in one case size of body and in the other size as a method of control. Either way the big boy wins! The MRC case in the Illuminati method of creating power political pyramids concentrating power in the hands of a few at the apical point (currently employed in European Union) is really utilising a centripetal motion (concentration or apical point or singularity) in conjunction with a centrifugal motion (expansion and growth). Thus as the populous experience centrifugal motion and spin faster and faster (have you noticed how life has speeded up!), whereas the MRC case and those in control would experience a slowing down or calm, life has more time and **order** *for them*! This is an interesting psychological theory, since the MRC hates anything which reminds him of a Magnetic Reversal (for which reason he can't finish a cycle of action since the end to him is Apocalyptic) and thus his *apical point* of centripetal motion and *contraction*, becomes *a restimulator* in itself, in so far as in his own mind it reminds him of the Ice Age and low survival: Thus, his psychology would perceive expansion and growth as the counter balance and high **self-survival**. Further since he perceives himself to be superior to others (the only one) then his adherence to the past and history retained in secret groups, which is just his own past history, also becomes a restimulator in his mind, likely to bring forward into present time his own past lives and actions and importantly thoughts and therefore goals. The MRC case strives to be the apical control point, whether he applies that to his family, business and the need to become head of that, or in a group or nation and finally the world. The more able the MRC, then the more dangerous he becomes. He seeks control of money, people and anything such as food, which has the potential to become a control point.

Hitler himself may have been an MRC case, but usually those in the environment who go insane, do so because there is an MRC quietly sitting in the background that nobody would suspect as being totally insane and I can spot a few in positions of power. This is probably the most difficult thing to understand, "666" is a cunning fellow! Certainly Hitler was manipulated.

Schauberger explored the concept of free energy conservation when he stated:

> "In the case of a power generator, nine times as much energy in the form of fuel is required in its conversion to electricity or other kind of output. This system of plundering the resources of the earth's energy is based upon the explosion motor, which operates centrifugally. The implosion motor however, is centripetally operated. It produces its own driving source through the diamagnetic use of water and air. It does not require any other fuel such as coal, oil, uranium or energy derived from atomic splitting, since it can produce its own energy (atomic power) by biological means in unlimited amounts - almost without cost. It has been overlooked that energy is also bipolar and appears freely as part of the motion of the earth's medium - water and air, which have the effect of reviving energy".

Schauberger went on to use his principles in the construction of designs, he wrote:

> "If water or air is rotated into a twisting form of oscillation known as 'colloidal', a build up of energy results, which with immense power, can cause levitation. This form of movement is able to carry with it its own means of power generation. This principle leads logically to its application in the design of the ideal airplane or submarine, requiring almost no motive power"

And he must have gone on to develop the so-called flying saucer as he commented:

> "I preferred the first alternative (the airplane application), and about a year later, the first 'flying saucer' rose unexpectedly at the first attempt, to the ceiling, and then was wrecked. A few days later an *American group* appeared, who seemed to understand what was happening, and *seized everything*. Then, after a very thorough investigation by a high-ranking officer, I was taken into protective custody, and guarded by no less than six policemen for about six months. An important part of the apparatus was (also) found in my apartment by the *Russians*". (My emphasis)

461

Schauberger suffered the familiar methods of attack, used against any scientist who threatens profits for the Syndicate or exposure of the hidden science. At the end of the war, Schauberger's research was investigated by both Americans and Russians, which fly in the face of the American's denial for years that there was anything more than nonsense in UFO's. The Russians took most of Schauberger's papers and set fire to his apartment after they left, to make sure there was nothing that could be used by the Americans. Further he was detained by the Americans for a year and only released on the condition that he would not engage in any more research. Supposedly he worked on top-secret projects in Texas and died shortly afterwards, supposedly from ill health. On his deathbed, Schauberger repeated over and over "They took everything from me. Everything, I don't even own myself". Poor Schauberger suffered what the matriarchal team for thousands of years suffered, loss can kill and they could not have achieved more than if they had put a knife in his back - a feeling I know only too well.

Hermann Klass an engineer from Muhlheim in the Ruhr confirmed that he had collaborated on the plans that Schauberger had made. In the Wuppertal paper, *Bergische Wochenpost* which is no longer published he wrote: "I still have drawings of a model 'flying disc' which I built in 1941; perfected by the Germans, in all truth this invention flew with almost unbelievable success. It had a diameter of 2.4 metres with a small, very fast running special electric motor (there were no petro-engined models at that time), which had been 'obtained' by courtesy of the Luftwaffe. It climbed straight up into the air so suddenly that unfortunately it hit the workshop ceiling and crashed to the ground in pieces". I reproduce some of the designs in *Appendix 4*.

I am surprised that Winston Churchill appeared to know nothing about flying saucers in 1952; since in July 1956 the Munich periodical *Da Neue Zeitalter* published an article entitled 'Hitler built Flying Saucers'. The article mentioned Schauberger as the inventor:" The Austrian forester Viktor Schauberger was the inventor and discoverer of this new motive power - implosion, which with the use of only air and water, generated light, heat and motion. In the implosion motor diamagnetism was developed which made the lifting power possible. By means of a suction screw-impeller, which revolved from the outside towards the inside along a cycloid spiral space-curve, the same force is generated which creates waterspouts typhoons, cyclones or hurricanes, through the effect of suction."

It is curious that without any apparent knowledge I intuitively developed this model for the UFO phenomenon in *Alternative 4*, thus I conclude that the whole thing was in my soul memory somewhere! The first test of an unmanned 'flying disc', took place on the 19th February 1945 near Prague. In three minutes it climbed to a height of 15 000 metres and attained a horizontal speed of 2 200 Kilometres per hour, it could hover motionless in the air and could fly as fast backwards as forwards. The possibility that such craft existed and may have been produced secretly earlier than 1945, has led to speculation that Hitler escaped in such a craft. Scientists like Habermohl who worked on the project, is thought to be in the Soviet Union, whilst the former German designer Meithe is in the USA and is thought to be designing flying saucers for A.V. Roe and Co., although there is no confirmatory proof of that. Since flying saucers were observed during NATO manoeuvres in Alsace in the spring of 1954, the consistent denials by the Americans proves that disinformation has occurred for years. His son Walter Schauberger, at the Pythagoras-Kepler School, Biotechnical Academy in Bad Ischl, today carries on Schauberger's work.

Ostensibly then, it would appear that any anti-gravity propulsion research by the Nazi's did not come from Grid channelling, but from the genius of Schauberger. However, it appears that the Nazi's may have used channelling and mediums to access pre-history. The warning given to Hitler over the use of black and white magic is almost certainly a reference to channelling and invocation of spirits. The Reichsfuhrer SS believed that before our present moon had been acquired, there had been at least *six* other moons whose capture and destruction had marked the beginnings and ends of the *six* geological periods preceding our own. They also believed that since the present moon was captured according to their beliefs 15 000 years ago, this half memory reveals itself in dreams, for the memory of these catastrophic events are stamped upon the racial unconscious and in legends, folklore and sacred scripture. The racial unconscious today may be described in terms of the reactive mind of Ron Hubbard's terminology, or as the unconscious mind of psychology, a mind that records unpleasant incidents. Further the event itself would be imprinted on the Akashic Record or morphogenetic bioplasma that great library in the sky. Thus the Nazi's appeared quite cognisant of a past cataclysm and appeared to possess a cosmological viewpoint. They believed that the book of *Revelations* was a confused account of the religious wars that took place immediately before the break up of the Tertiary satellite (a moon prior to the present one). Hitler seemed to confirm these views when in *Table Talk* on *25-26 January 1942* he is reported to have made the following statement:

> "Nothing prevents us from supposing that mythology is a reflection of things that have existed and of which humanity has retained a vague memory. In all the human traditions, whether oral or written, one finds mention of a huge cosmic disaster. What The Bible tells on the subject is not peculiar to the Jews, but was certainly borrowed by them from the Babylonians and Assyrians. In the Nordic legend we read of a struggle between gods and giants...the thing is only explicable upon the hypothesis of a disaster that completely destroyed a humanity, which

already possessed a high degree of civilization. The fragments of our pre-history are perhaps merely reproductions of objects belonging to a more distant past. What proofs have we? That besides objects made of stone there were not similar object made of metal? The life of bronze is limited. Besides, there's no proof that the civilization that existed before the disaster flourished precisely in our regions. Who knows what discoveries would be made if we could explore the lands that are now covered by water? I'm quite inclined to accept the cosmic theories of Horbiger. It's not impossible, in fact, that 10 000 years before our era there was a clash between the Earth and the Moon that gave the Moon its present orbit. It's also possible that the Earth attracted to itself the atmosphere of the Moon and that this radically altered the conditions of life on our planet. It seems to me that these questions will be capable of solution on the day when a man will intuitively establish the connection between these facts, thus teaching exact science the path to follow."

The SS in their belief of Horbiger's theory, that the Earth existed inside layers of ice, may have represented initial research on the Grid as ice crystal. This is curious in so far as when Phillip Fauth a Horbiger disciple published *Glacial Cosmology* in 1913, this research together with that of Horbiger, showed considerable but unacknowledged debt, to Madame Blavatsky and Charles Fourier. Thus it appears that the SS or Black Order, were well versed in many topics of pre-history and evidently believed that the Aryans were the source of the good spirit. The use of the swastika not only derived from Minoan Crete, but in Tibetan China, it designated curiously enough the whirling motion of a chakra or energy point, which further represented the whirling vortex of creation, which must have been centrifugal and expansive. Thus Hitler as a political expansionist perhaps merely reflected the centrifugal motion he *chose as his own universe*, on the principle of Everett's "Other Worlds" (or lives?) and within his own mind. The use of the Black Sun as the emblem of the Black Order, the highest and most secret Order of the SS implies black magic. Further "su" in the Sanskrit word "suasti", means 'source'. When "Ka" is added meaning 'thy immortal soul', one obtains suasti-ka, or swastika and source of the good spirit. The fact that 'immortal' is used, is significant and complements my conclusion that the SS and Hitler believed in Re-incarnation, or at least transmigration of souls. Here again as with all world orders, we see the message has been used as a source of power and coupled with the hidden science. In the story of the Grail, it was often described as a cup encrusted with jewels, but it contained the elixir or life. Thus the Grail has always been composed of two parts, a message and a whole cosmology and science. The MRC case sequestered both.

Schauberger utilised rotating or a twisting forms of oscillation known as 'colloidal' water currents to generate power and motion (levitation), in his machines. I referred to this motion in the patents of Moray B. King in *Alternative 4*. King a physicist, noted that:

> "A coil is comprised of two identical windings of opposite helicity. The windings must exhibit identical mirror image symmetry, for a pulse travelling up both windings should have its rising and falling waveform edges aligned... it has been previously proposed that the rising and falling edges in the bucking field transient produce hyper spatial torrid **vortex rings** that exhibit **electro-magnetic** scales and longitudinal components in their three space projection" (my emphasis)

This might be viewed as a structure like an umbrella above and below giving a circle or concentric ring, and in the middle vortex rings, which might give some background to the umbrella shapes in Paleolithic caves together with the concentric ring design that turns up in secret groups and that curious metal cube millions of years old, with convex surfaces on two sides. Perhaps also the egg-shape, with its magical wand (penis) inserted into the centre may indicate the magical manipulation of these vortex rings and such rings I propose are part of the morphogenetic bioplasma. In *Alternative 4*, I proposed such a model as part of the UFO phenomenon, where morphogenetic and spiritual bioplasmas were organised as two opposing pyramidal vortices giving an overall diablo structure. Within the pyramid or vortex being a twisting or oscillating rotation of air and electro-magnetic coiling, on which the holographic imprints are stored. The comparison may be made to Schauberger's machines, which not only could produce energy via this method of organisation or vortex, but also produced anti-gravity anomalies. It was further my suggestion in this book, that in fact the Grid should be considered more as a three-dimensional geometric structure, rather like a geodesic dome, the geodetic lines of which are electro-magnetic and give the shortest possible distance between two points, which can be utilized together with anti-gravity anomalies by UFO man-made technology. The Grid as a 3-dimensional structure more akin to a crystal may also be composed of numerous minor electro-magnetic vortices collected into larger vortices, which then form the electro-magnetic geometric of the grid. From this proposal we would find, that the so-called Akashich Record or that large library in the sky, is in fact a complex geometric of the web itself, which retains holographic, mainly genetic and environmental memory imprints, which are therefore within the vortex itself and its electro-magnetic energies. The analogy would be to have a library imprinted into a huge crystal. Healers use crystals to enhance healing, which is transference of **thought**.

Moray B. King, gives an idea of how the zero-point energy, or that tremendous amount of free energy in space, gets channelled into our own three-dimensional space, when he states that the zero point energy is an electric flux from the fourth-dimension intersecting three-dimensional space, where it manifests as a **turbulent virtual plasma**. It cannot be dismissed that Moray King's opposite helicity of windings along a ferrite core, not only represents a fair description of the Caduceus (wand?) coil of Asklepios, the ancient Greek healer, but also represents the biological structure of DNA, where two threads of DNA are coiled in a hyperbolic spiral, or the double helix of the Watson and Crick model, which I have previously illustrated. It is significant too, that the chakras, which are the energy points within the biofield of man, are also a turbulent swirling vortex and one suspects that nature uses this model i.e. vortex rings, to pull down energy from the vacuum or matrix of the zero point energy, to infuse the biological system and human biofield with energy. It is entirely possible, given the interesting DNA shaped crop circles that have appeared, that as I further proposed, the master DNA template or morphogenetic memory for a species lies as the master blueprint or pattern within or comprising the twisting filaments of the vortex itself. Such a pattern that exists in space may merely imprint that pattern of genetic memory on the body and its cells, by the physical DNA: Rather like products at the beginning of the factory line, the human blastocyst (very young embryo comprising a ball of cells) is given the 'stamp' from the master pattern and the bio chemicals in the embryo including the overall shape of the embryo line up in accordance with that 'stamp' or imprint from the master plan or blueprint, thus conforming to the 'jelly mould' for that particular species. Bodies are thus made conforming to the master blueprint for a particular species. As I pointed out in my cancer research, the drug Thalidomide, which caused foetal abnormality must interfere with the master pattern 'stamp' process, presumably by altering the embryological tri-partite (ectoderm, endoderm and mesoderm to the scientists!) biofield. I would not like to suggest that the growth inhibition properties of Thalidomide be applied to the cancer tumour, since the effect on the adult human biofield, which still retains the tri-partite embryonic layer, may not openly show side effects but the consequences may be complex. The tumour is only a **symptom** of the disease and one cannot apply drugs to the symptom, since it does address the underlying **cause** (*Appendix I*).

Hitler when he referred to "race memory", evidently had some inkling of this mechanism of holographic imprinting, but obviously the undertones of racism, has no part of a genetic memory. A genetic memory is a precise and scientific memory or holographic imprint of the genetic line of a body according to species, including man. Such information is not tempered to suit all the various abberated viewpoints of man on this subject. Black and white as colours are probably not even imprinted on the master blueprint only body shape, since man is man, regardless of colour. A spirit evidently has lived in all sorts of bodies along the phylogenetic line from fish upwards and perhaps even little green ones (men), according to UFO phenomena! A man's skin colour is probably more to do with biochemical pigmentation. Apartheid in South Africa and segregation in America with separation of black from white had much more to do with the politics and beliefs of the tribe of Judah! The natural UFO phenomenon often showed some indication of the holographics of the evolution of a species, which may be man. For instance the appearance of shuffling creatures, with Reptilian eyes (orange), small wings and half human and man, I assumed was a disturbance of the vortex bioplasma energies, which caused the phylogenetic holographics to impinge on the UFO witness, via the brain acting as a dipole radio-receiver, according the 'The Onion Ring Model'. Thus the turbulent bioplasma, may not only be a method of drawing energy down from the fourth dimension and the vacuum energy, but it may have become intentionally or not, a method of storage of information, which in effect maintains the survival of the species. Since such imprinting of information depends on the electro-magnetic spectrum, then the sun is the source of the mechanism and perhaps gave rise to the concept of Sun Kings as gods in charge of the magic which could manipulate the Grid. The fact that man appears to re-capitulate past forms in his embryological development, with gill like structures etc, may be accounted for by the master morphogenetic blueprint of DNA in the etheric layer, which imposes the non-specific body shape fields noted by Dr. Becker, Rupert Sheldrake and Harold S. Burr.

Georges Lakhovsky noted that small quantities of light are produced from living organisms, which formed the basis of a hypothesis he put forward in 1924 and published in English in 1939.[139] Lakohvky's paper concerned the effects of very short energy waves on cancer in the geranium plant. His major work *The Origin of Life* published in 1925, proposed that the 'twisted filament' in the DNA molecules, which has become better formulated by Watson and Crick in the double helix model for DNA; are really oscillatory circuits with capacity and inductance and capable of oscillating according to a particular frequency. Thus a cell in the body that contains DNA can become transmitter or receiver of exceedingly short radio waves, which give rise to high frequency currents in the nucleus of the cell. He further proposed a source of energy, which would be needed to maintain the oscillations and such a source he claimed as deriving from cosmic radiation. Whether we could redefine it as originating with vacuum energy via the vortex organisation is a pertinent question. However if DNA does indeed vibrate or oscillate and can both transmit and receive (information), then immediately we see that the **experience** of the organism may be received by the DNA threads presumably via the biofield chakra system which surrounds the individual and which is in direct contact with the environment. The INCOMING INFORMATION, which monitors the **survival of the individual in relation to his environment**, is then transmitted to the Etheric bioplasma or morphogenetic bioplasma, the master blueprint via the crown chakra where it is RECEIVED AND RECORDED. Thus we might propose that the experience of the organism including man is constantly being monitored, by the interconnection of energies between human biofield and morphogenetic bioplasma, the master 'mega computer' in the sky. The accumulative and ongoing experience of the individual, may thus be continually fed to the morphogenetic bioplasma *or* alternatively: the final summation of the life experience of the individual may return to the 'mega computer' or 'hard drive' as the biofield information from the individual ('floppy disc') and therefore is received and recorded after the death of the physical body of the individual organism. Direct evidence for the former alternative comes from the Guatemalan monkeys, where learned behaviour related to survival, was passed through a non-specific field to other monkeys at a separate location. Indirect evidence for the latter alternative comes from the phantom leaf experiment, which showed that the "jelly mould" or shape in outline of the leaf as an energy biofield was still present, despite the fact that the physical part of the leaf was removed. The "jelly mould" with its accumulative experience would in the latter proposal then, re-unite with the master pattern or 'mega computer'. There is a third alternative, which is that *the spirit* takes the entirety of his 'photo album' of life experience with him when he leaves a body. As he passes through the death experience and the "tunnel" as it is reported by witnesses like myself who have survived a NDE (Near Death Experience), then there is a 'downloading' of the 'album' or 'floppy disc' and the entire life experience onto the 'mega computer hard drive', which is really just the successive coils of the morphogenetic bioplasma. By analogy the spirit or who you really are, sits in the 'cinema' and watches his life experience roll by! There is still a chance at this point to return to the body, if that body is still viable even though scientists now confirm that during the NDE there is no heartbeat and the person is technically dead. However witnesses *have* returned, particularly where they feel that the 'cinema real' is not "a wrap" as they say in the film business and where the individual still has some more story or a different ending to write! There is another level in the death experience as one moves towards the light and the zero point energy, but I will discuss this later. Whilst I have explained this by analogy, obviously there must be fundamental laws of energy and physics, which cover these experiences, which should have been investigated in the field of metaphysics. Unfortunately metapolitics (the politics of the soul) has kept such investigation well off grant funding lines!

On incarnation a spirit goes through the process of acquiring a body, which is manufactured according to the master blue print in the etheric layer i.e. the morphogenetic bioplasma. Thus in this manner the accumulative survival data for the *body line* of a particular species is transferred from master memory into production. The fact that the master blue print for bodies can be altered according to experience means that this represents a BIOFEEDBACK SYSTEM and thus really comes under the heading of cybernetics (study of systems of *control and communication* in animals). The filaments or threads of double helicity in the DNA molecule have both receiving and transmitter properties and this in itself, is indicative of a biofeedback system of INFORMATION. *What* information gets imprinted onto the master blueprint when the individual body dies and the information or experience is returned, must represent in the case of the body or genetic line, the *accumulative input* of information from SURVIVORS, according to Darwinian principles i.e. those that survive produce more offspring and subsequently provide a greater contribution to the population numbers. In the case of *what* gets imprinted onto the morphogenetic bioplasma or 'mega computer', let us draw the analogy again of a 'hard drive' that is only programmed to record **survival data** of the individual with respect to the environment. Further, that 'hard drive' programme is built on billions of years of past experience of survival data and has developed a programme for producing the best product blueprint for any model (species) in given environmental conditions. Thus the product or bodyline is really the best-suited model for the environment and *innate behaviour* is a part of that model. Thus compare the body to that of an animal inclusive of its inherent innate behaviour, where animals will leave the sick and dying, mate with numerous females, turn on their young in some cases, fight for leadership in the case of males and nurture young in the case of females and so on. This behaviour is *pure survival for animals*. The problem becomes that **spiritual man** has entered a **bodyline of Homo sapiens**, who is an animal and has a fairly long phylogenetic or evolutionary line and history, probably originating with fish and passing through the reptiles. The **bodyline** has a goal and that goal is **self- survival** on the first rung of the survival ladder and can extend to the second rung, that of survival of the group or the family unit, since even animals look after their young and can mate for life and will exhibit group survival behaviour. Spiritual man however has higher goals and possesses the power of reason, ethics and creative thought. However the more degraded a spirit becomes, the greater he identifies with the goals of Homo sapiens the body and animal i.e. survival of self, at which point he may be an excellent product of the Grid as a mechanical being (brain dead), who follows Grid patterning and behaviour with its self survivalist innate behaviour, but he has failed miserably as a spiritual being.

Two male gangs of Homo sapiens confront each other and one sticks his chest out and shouts: "Yeah! C'mon then, lets have yer!": a perfect example of animal behaviour and fight for leadership of the pack. A man head butts someone, when he can't use the power of rational speech, a perfect example of the animal horned-charge. The problem becomes that whilst degraded beings will naturally exhibit Grid behaviour recapitulating their phylogenetic ontogeny of past behaviour that was self-survivalist, you can *induce* such behaviour by threatening survival and thus the poor and deprived underclass who are constantly under survivalist threat, may be sufficiently suppressed by the environment, to pass control to the body and Grid behaviour, when they *perceive* that they have failed to survive as spiritual beings. Now of course as an immortal being or spirit you can't help but survive, you are billions of years old and I am afraid that you can't get off that thing called life. The *perception* of non-survival comes when the spirit has dissociated itself from the *mind* and the ability to *solve problems* including survival. The being or whom you are, when faced with an *overwhelming* situation in his environment of non-survival passes control to the body: "Here animal you solve it, I can't!" The spirit by analogy jumps into the back seat of the car and gives the map and steering wheel to the moron Homo sapiens, the body. Animals when faced with an overwhelming threat of non-survival usually run away (the so-called fright and flight response) or they fight if the threat is not overwhelming. The spiritual being does not resort to either, after all they may have a mortgage, children to look after and obligations and assault has legal penalties! Thus they think..think..think about the problem, but do not solve it and that thing called *stress* is really spiritual man resisting the self-survival mechanisms of the body and its animal phylogenetic survival mechanisms. There is no action on it, or if there was, it failed and the spirit went into apathy on it: "Well, nothing I can do about that!" This is the position before a person becomes ill and in the case of cancer, the spiritual being having failed to solve the problem through the mind experiences accumulative (including past lives) **emotional** loss and passes control to the Homo sapiens the animal who whips out the master blueprint on survival and says: "Oh yes let me see now, loss is loss of body parts, so all I have to do is grow!" and before you know it there is one more problem a tumour! Emotional loss does not compute on the phylogenetic survival mechanisms and is irrationally equated with **physical** loss. Thus mechanical Grid man or Homo sapiens as evidenced by our daily experience, newspapers and television is really quite an animal that is concerned primarily with **self**, but will fight and kill for his group if under threat. Curiously in *Alternative 4*, I gave UFO witness accounts where beings of a *mechanical nature*, with "drop down jaws" were reported, reminding one of robotic Grid man and his jaw structure as a reptile! Further there were illusive referrals to time: "**What time is it**?" This seemingly banal question by the alleged "alien" is really perhaps best directed at Grid man and specifically the MRC case, who is still turning the pages on his own past history and 'script' and he has no idea of what time it is! Was it then? Or is it now? Theatre Earth where the players play on, with their dramatizations of past acts and past scenes and now although the curtain has risen on a new play they still resort to the past 'script'.

The fact that sub atomic particles exhibit spin both clockwise and anti-clockwise may be due to the vortex organisation of space. Thus although I will come back to this point later, it is not inconceivable that a true model of our space would be the Diablo double Vortex hyperbolic spiral, which gives rise not only to spin on sub atomic particles, but galaxies, the earth and planets and also the geometric of molecules like DNA, with its spin or spiral double helicity. It seems likely that the master blueprint would carry information on species survival under pre and post Magnetic Reversal conditions i.e. giants and body types we see today. Why should the genes, the hereditary units along the chromosomes comprising the DNA be arranged in units of **three** bases commonly known as Adenine, Guanine and Cytosine? If the Earth's *magnetic poles* periodically shift from North to South, followed by South to North, with one assumes a change not only in polarity, but gravity, given the myths and legends of giants coupled with that curious footprint in the Paluxy riverbed, then perhaps the middle gene is the stabilising equivalent of the Bloch Wall and is a code for which prototype is to be produced according to electro-magnetic polarities. I do not want to launch off into biochemistry, but certainly the phenomenon of optical isomers and mirror image molecules or two forms of a molecule, may provide some biochemical evidence

Let us take that curious archaeological symbol the figure-of-8, which was to become a prominent archetypal symbol of the Religious Revolution era in Bronze Age Crete. The 'spectacle sign', also appeared on standing stones in Scotland and since the stone was a Semitic representation of the divinity, it may be assumed to have some significance within the hidden science. The figure-of-8, not only reminds one of the diablo model I gave for the model of space, it also reminds one of the shape of electron orbitals in the atomic shells. Electrons as negatively charged particles or waves create a cloud of charge around a nucleus of an atom, such a cloud is made up of electrons, which appear in different energy levels or shells. The dumb-bell or figure-of-8 structural model for a hydrogen IS atomic orbital is a good example of this comparison to the Diablo model. Further the electron spins on its axis just like a spinning top, just as the Earth spins on its axis. Electrons can spin in a clockwise and anti-clockwise motion. Further whilst Bohr theory described electrons as particles, Heisenberg found them in 1927, to be better described as waves. This phenomenon became known as Heisenberg's uncertainty principle, which has led physicists to employ a dual behaviour for electrons as particles and waves in a similar manner to light (waves and photons). Schrodinger in 1927, put forward his wave equation for the electron behaving as a wave and as such, it has the potential to act as a carrier wave for information. At the level of sub-atomic particles, which comprises all matter including bodies, cells, molecules etc. there is *energy, movement*, potential *polarity* and *relationship*. Linear mathematics is not sufficient to model the integrated relatedness of complex energy patterns. Geometry is far more capable of expressing these relationships. Geometry then expresses not only shape and form, but it also expresses mathematical laws and relationships. Sacred geometry with its secrets was from the very beginning drawn into the secret groups, as part of the hidden science and Pythagoras was to become an

471

adept in this study and further we know that the Druids followed Pythagorean geometry and resonant scales. On the hermetic principle of: 'As above so below', then we can assume that the patterning seen in sub atomic particles and the figure-of-8 is a pattern that is presented at a much higher level within the master pattern. This figure-of-8 is also a Diablo.

Polarity and duality are inherent within the cosmological diablo model as they are within the forces of the atom itself. For example the nucleus of an atom has a *positively* charged proton particle and a *negatively* charged electron and it is also said to contain that third diablo balance of the neutron particle with no apparent charge i.e. neutral. There you have the three balances again - the Rosicrucian **Law of Three**. Biblical texts transmitted this idea of fundamental duality and polarity in the idea of philosophical dualism and male versus female, good versus evil, which was the fundamental duality used in the text of Genesis. The Law of Three is expressed as God the Father, Son and Holy Ghost i.e. the trinity, which Robert Graves reported was the product of Latin grammar! The ying and yang of Chinese esotericism, the gunas of Indian mysticism and ultimately this duality expresses itself in the mechanism of the mind. The **analytical mind** that engages in rational thought and poses solutions for survival of the human being as both a body *and* a spirit; versus the more primitive, irrational or **reactive mind,** which dictates survival for the body. These two minds were the subject of Ron Hubbard's thesis: *Dianetics the Modern Science of Mental Health.* It is the reactive mind, which operates in Cancer. However within my own research I perceive that the reactive mind may be no more, than the tri-partite energy field of the body and its interconnection to the master pattern or Grid, with its survival data. Which came first, the division into two and sacred geometry, as the fertilized egg of male and female first cleaves into two and where the mind manifests as the duality of analytical versus reactive: or the plus and minus spin quantum numbers of electrons? If mind and body are composed of electrons as part of the atomic nuclei and those electrons are merely waves or carrier waves for information, which connect with the vacuum energy and its own dualistic spin, then do we manifest philosophical dualism in religion (good and evil) as a product of the properties of dualism and polarity in sub atomic particles? Which came first, 'the chicken or the egg'?

The spiral as it occurs in iconography from very early times e.g. in the Bronze Age frescoes of the Early Minoans, indicated I proposed a belief in The Cycle of Eternal Return, or Re-incarnation The appearance of shells specifically displaying the hyperbolic spiral in early Minoan burials urns or sarcophagi, alongside the dead person in the *foetal position*, almost certainly is indicative of a religious belief. I equate this belief with Re-incarnation and the shells in their connection to the sea, and the philosophy of the ancient Goddess Rhea, I equate with the concept: 'As I go, so must I return' and the symbolisation of tidal rhythm; the spiral and its connection to the whirling vortex of the spiritual and morphogenetic bioplasma or dualistic diablo, may well be implied. It appears that the Druids who conducted the Religious Revolution used such a belief in a philosophy of: 'As I go, so must I return to complete the plan'! The ancient thong-tied Cretan stones previously discussed, exhibited in their overall geometry the crystal energy and overall patterning of the Grid, which I have maintained is synonymous with the vortex bioplasmas. One cannot discount therefore, that the spiral whilst archetypally symbolising a belief system of Re-incarnation, where if the spiral is traced, it reflects the thought process: 'Into a life and out of it, Into a life and out of it' etc. does not also reflect a whole cosmology and the swirling vortex which manifests in our three-dimensional space, drawing energy from the fourth dimension – the zero point or vacuum energy.

Whilst the mysteries were given freely to everyone in Early Minoan times, after the Religious Revolution the mysteries were withdrawn into the secret groups and obviously the Semitic group, whom I propose were the the Druids, or the Biblical Adamites would have taken the entire cosmology, science and belief system and withdrawn it together with that story: hoping to part of that story and science to mankind as their gift to humanity. This knowledge in part obviously ended up in the Summer Smoking Room of Cardiff Castle Wales UK, which I proposed was Scottish Rite Freemasonry, which must be an ascendant of the Rosy Cross, Rosicrucian's, with today the knowledge retained in the highest level or the Rose-Croix, or perhaps higher in The Great White Lodge of The Great White Brotherhood. All these names may effectively be regarded as ascendant names for Druids or Biblical Adamites, the tribe of Judah, with its religious aspirations in the One World Order Plan. Was it not *Jud*as who betrayed Jesus after the cock crowed *three* times!

The figure-of- 8 symbol not only occurs in Cretan iconography after the Religious Revolution, but also you will remember, occurs as a symbol 'spectacles' in Celtic iconography for the above reason I assume. What are we to make of the *tiered* or layered *bell-shaped* skirts of the 'Snake-Goddesses', which appear post the Religious Revolution c. 1400 B.C.? The tiers of the skirt are flounced i.e. layered which automatically indicates layered secrecy, the snakes represent Re-incarnation and wisdom and the shape of the skirt immediately gives us from the "waspish waists" (highly narrowed) an archetypal symbol of the inverted pyramid, which according to my model of the Diablo is the lower pyramidal vortex or morphogenetic bioplasma, which I equate with the Grid and one half of the dumb-bell or Diablo. The Rosette, or Rosy Cross that appeared on the forehead of the Minotaur bull and on the hats of Cretans on the South of the Island of Crete were also to appear later at the Temple of Asklepios the Greek healer, where the secrets of healing I proposed in *The Battle of The Trees*, were hidden in the concentric ring formation of the Tholos, a secret labyrinth below the Temple of Asklepios at Epidaurus.Thus not only was a whole cosmology withdrawn together with a belief system (Re-incarnation), but the possibility of healing using this belief system with the inevitable and final conclusion that we observe today and the impossibility of ever obtaining an evaluation for my own cancer research and scientific paper. Man has lived so long with lies; he can no longer even conceive the truth.

The spiralling dances of Crete, which are still retained today in folk dance, originated with the dancing priestesses from Palaikastro.The significance must surely lie in the hyperbolic spiral and a whole cosmology, whilst forgotten to science, is retained in folk dance, myth and iconography. The Cosmic circle of the Temple of Asklepios is retained in the concentric circular design of the Tholos and in the secret iconography of the Summer smoking Room at Cardiff Castle: Whilst the tiered flounced skirt of the snake goddesses, is retained in the step design of the Great Step pyramid and some South American archaeological sites together with a similar design in Red Square in Moscow. The coiling serpent, which not only by shedding its skin periodically archetypally signified Re-incarnation, but the vortex of the bioplasma, was also in all ancient religions depicted as wise reminding us of the derivation of the hermetic Eye of Intelligence, but in Hebraic religion the Serpent becomes the subject of curses, since the Genesis account records that woman gave this particular "apple" of wisdom and immortality to man. However man stole the Grail message and the science together with a cosmology and utilised it for his own purposes, rather than for its intended use and wisdom for all humanity. Man or should I say Adamite man disliked the idea as an affront to his ego and power and thus not only took the knowledge from woman, but changed the story line to hide the fact up. It is entirely predictable that the twelve tribes and the tribe of Levi should place the curse on woman, since they were in conflict with the tribe of Judah. Thus the curse on woman in The Bible is really a curse on Judah, but the elite preferred to let woman take the blame, rather than explain the entire "River of Lies" as Voltaire referred to orthodox history. By the time they lead Marie Antoinette to the guillotine, her hair at the age of 33 had turned white from shock. She had survived an assassination attempt; watched her first child die probably through slow poison and another die; her best friend beheaded and the head on a pole poked in her face; she nursed her husband Louis XVI through a serious nervous breakdown, whilst staving off the Masonic agents calling for their blood, together with the duplicity of ministers who actively wrecked the finances of France; she watched her husband beheaded; was betrayed by almost all of her confidantes and spent the last days of her life trying to catch glimpses of her beloved four year old son, as he was isolated in a jail and beaten by the jailer Simon who smeared the child with venereal disease from a prostitute, so that the Commune could bring him as a witness against his mother in court, saying that he had caught it from sexual relations with his mother. Before leaving the jail for the guillotine Marie banged her head on a low beam and when asked if she had hurt herself she replied famously: "Oh no, there is nothing more that you can do to hurt me now". The Masonic great dream and plan of the French Revolution and a Federal: "United States of the West", was built on that edifice of pain. Neither is it known that the style of Louis XVI was her idea, together with a United Nations (UN) peacekeeping force. Maria was just a little too late in employing the chief of police to find out who was the driving force behind the revolution. Hollywood naturally turned down the script!

What is one to make of the unusual objects collected by the Mousterian occupants of the Hyena Cave at Arcy-Sur-Cure, which has been dated c. 35 000 B.C? And which include a magnetic lump of iron pyrites (Iron disulphide which is ferro*magnetic*), the fossil of a gastropod showing a *spiralling* almost *bell-shaped* appearance and a round fossil coral with a particularly marked *honeycomb* appearance. Given that I proposed a date c.10 000 B.C. for the appearance of the message (Re-incarnation) upon Earth, then this date indicates that certain knowledge of the Grid was known to early man and even as I proposed the Antediluvians or pre-Flood people. However the appearance of the honeycomb gastropod, rather mirrors the obsession of all secret patriarchal groups and masters including Adam Weishaupt of the Illuminati, with ant-heaps and beehives and that one controlling signal from the top (of a psychocivilised society), which would **order the slaves**, into manageable cyborgs or drones in the Socialist (Communistic) hive: reflecting the words: "out of many come one", on the One dollar bank note of America (one tribe Judah? Or one chosen people?) The corals are colonial or social collections of Actinozoa and the coral reef, which may be thousands of feet thick, consists of a large mass of calcium carbonate built up by past generations of these animals. This is really astounding, that the implication here is that these people or masters, knew that the coral was a colony or social group. The honeycomb *mountain* on which the goddess stood supported by two lions, was depicted on a seal from the Late Minoan period in Crete following the Religious Revolution, which I associate with the biblical Adamites or Druids. Control of the grid then, may be indicated in this collective find, together with a plan for a Socialistic or Communistic society. This according to the writings of Nesta Webster IS the World Revolution plan, which evidently was in existence from at least c. 35 000 B.C. The appearance of the omphalos, a bell shaped stone (post Religious Revolution) found in both England (Coventry) and Greece engraved with bees (*The Battle of The Trees*) signifies this overriding conception or plan for complete Communistic or Socialist control of a populous, where a One World Order headed by the Queen bee or *that* secret Theocracy, had been the goal through many cycles and for billions of years. The honeycomb therefore may not only have represented a symbol of control by a Theocracy, but may have symbolised the 'umbrella' and geometric of the Grid. The control of matter or atomic matter may be implied, since the spin of the dumb-bell as a wave of electrons in atomic orbit, would give a similar patter to such Grid geometries. The plan that I predicted in *Alternative 4* of a psychocivilised Communistic hive ordered by mind control, either through the Grid or technology such as HAARP and GWEN, seems increasingly true.

Charge (plus and minus), magnetic polarity (north and south) and gravitational attraction are part of motion, which maintains things in existence. The Universe is in constant flux and without motion; it would merely collapse in on itself. If we have maintained such elements of motion, order and balance in our own thinking, it is because our bodies are made of atomic matter and therefore we cannot as bodies and minds extract ourselves from the greater pattern of which we are a part. How far religion and esoteric mysticism has shaped itself on these physical laws and properties of matter brings me to a famous comment by Stephen Hawking a renowned and respected physicist in Britain. Hawking commented: " Eastern mysticism is an illusion. A physicist who attempts to link it with his own work has abandoned physics". John Davidson a physicist who worked with Hawking, made a rather profound reply in his book[140], when he stated:

> "It is an illusion to take the conception of the intellect as absolute reality. All living human beings who attempt to find the ultimate answer to life's puzzle outside the sphere of his own inner consciousness has forgotten that he is truly alive. He has abandoned life. Actually, it is these limitations we place upon ourselves.'Iam a physicist' or 'I am a doctor', 'I am a follower of this or that belief system or ideology', which are the illusions. To mistake a belief system, a religion or a concept for Reality is the illusion of the intellect'.

Why does the Universe simply not collapse? Why does an atomic nucleus not collapse? And the electrons simply fall back into the nucleus from their orbits. Why do electrons exist as waves and orbit the nucleus of the atom? Harold Puthoff of the Institute for Advanced Studies in Austin Texas, thinks in terms of a zero point energy or background sea of *electromagnetic energy* that constitutes the vacuum state: And in my own Diablo model, I have introduced the idea of holographics retained or imprinted in some form, on an electro-magnetic coil, the "Serpent" in religious texts, or the snake entwined around the staff (wand?) of Asklepios. Puthoff suggests that this background energy prevents electrons and protons from collapsing into each other in the atoms. If there is a larger pattern of energy then on the hermetic principle of:' As above so below', the atoms would mirror that and the spin of the Diablo perhaps providing centripetal (contraction) and centrifugal (expansion) spin which would perfectly balance and thus provide a stable configuration, with the Diablo seen as dumb-bell 'below' in the atom. The atom is a mere reflection of the greater pattern and whilst I would maintain that the pattern 'above' maintains integrity of the atom, physicists say that the electrons possess an energy, which prevents them from collapsing. But where does that energy come from, why doesn't it just radiate away? Nobody knows; however I would maintain that the diablo model and the dumb-bell shaped orbit of electrons is crucial as a model and mechanism for drawing energy from the fourth dimension. Puthoff suggest that the energy of electrons is in a dynamic state, continually 'absorbing' energy from the background vacuum energy and radiating it away. [141] Electromagnetic organisation, gravity and the Unified Field theory that physicists seek, may well come from that model, I would be only too glad if some physicist would pick up this model of the diablo and look at it.

Motion or spin is essential to the Diablo mechanism and the pattern of swirling spiralling motion, is not only a part of sub atomic motion, but also describes the motion which then manifests as polarized properties such as electrical charge, magnetic polarity and mass. Spinning a charged object as Searl did in his experiments creates changes of mass and weight. This certainly may account for the legends of giants and the appearance of dinosaurs. The hyperbolic spiral or spin together with centrifugal spin, are important and fundamental models in nature, which appear to be reflected in the organisation of atomic and may provide a model for the Universe? Just as medicine is coming to view the whole person and the triplicity of mind, body and spirit as the fundamental healing solution which supports the Hippocratic maxim: "Before you can heal a man's body, you must cure his mind and before that his spirit" then the physicist can play a role in this healing by acknowledging the role and niche of all three and the great interconnecting web of physical laws and geometries, that underpin this view of the whole. The idea of self -organisation must be a part of any picture or model for the Universe, just as it becomes a model in biological systems, where biofeedback control is just such a method of balance. Ilya Prigogine put forward the idea of self-organisation in chaotic systems, for which he received the Nobel Prize. Whilst his research applied to thermodynamic systems, there is no doubt that his ideas could be extended. The vacuum and the model of space as Diablo, gives that immediate concept of balance. The vacuum is probably just such a self organizing state and the Magnetic Reversal must represent a method of attaining balance in a system that has become chaotic, either through the misuse of the hidden science and mans input, or through natural processes. However given myths and legends, it seems the former is more likely.

SPIRIT AND ANTI-WORLDS

Above the level of the mind energy and its holographics, even above mind-to-mind telepathy a Spirit exists as self- determined thought. Man believes his body and/or his mind (which is not a brain) are who he really is, but that is not so. The immortal Spirit is YOU. A Spirit can create its own cycles which include start, change and stop for future and present effects. A Spirit considers and such consideration comes from the Spirit himself as causative thinking. He may decide to resolve a problem, set a pattern or new cycle for the future or nullify a pattern of the past. Such a decision then requires ACTIONS in addition to thought. Ron Hubbard maintained that the Spirit is invisible and does not exist within space or time, has no mass or energy and furthermore stated that Spirits in the form of their "postulates", "overlap" as infinities, or "in" infinity, which is then referred to as "a static". However I have my own reservations on part of this description. If there is any steadfast rule in physics, it is that 'you can't get something for nothing'. Certainly the Spirit is invisible in this Universe, he is the individual or person, the personality, the beingness and he is aware of being aware - OBSERVATION POINT: But does that Spirit have an energy? There is no dispute that a Spirit needs a mind and body to play a game on Earth and to activate his "postulates" - there is no game in being invisible! However does invisibility mean that a Spirit has no mass, no wavelength (energy), or location? If you were trying to answer that question you would have to go back to the origin of the Spirit, where did we come from? Mysticism and Esoteric Theology will give you many answers and in many ways I sympathise with Stephen Hawking's observation that only physics will provide the answers and that Eastern mysticism is an illusion.

Hubbard was definitely right in his conclusion that the Spirit is "an awareness of awareness unit". The Spirit as observation point *since the beginning* knows everything, but he himself gets into games and gets obsessed with games and starts something and forgets he has any power to change or stop it. Equally he forgets he can start a new game. A Spirit Re-incarnates with all his karma and past life junk on a game and forgets where he is in the game and gets drawn into the same old stale game, with the same old stale personalities, having lost control over the game ("now let me see, do you get me this lifetime, or do I get you - what was all this about anyway?) This is life on Earth - a lost game, a game that has degenerated into egos, personalities, Messiahs, and karma versus karma where the mind and body are controlled by the Grid and are religiously following *that* 'script'. In actual fact even Re-incarnation is an illusion, since the Spirit and his observation point is continuous and only *appears* as separate lives, because his body keeps dying and he regularly has to pick up a new one! Only by past life regression could one remember the game and when it started. You see people slugging it out in karmic marriages, people who are totally victimised, people who sit quietly and never do anything (they have lost the game completely and joined the audience) etc. But there IS a large game being played here on Earth and whilst the audience snooze, the main cast play on. The audience have lost observation point altogether and the players have become either obsessed with an observation point to the exclusion of all other observation points or are stuck in a past observation point

Religion versus religion (I am right you are wrong) - stuck case: political group versus political group (I am right you are wrong) - stuck case. The maintenance of duality and polarity of battle proportions on Earth perpetuates amnesia and stuck observation points. The media in its bias support for One World Order elitists merely maintains the stuck game. The fall in Democracy merely promotes One World Orders and a stuck game, since the audience are never allowed a chance to get up on the stage where the real game is being played. The lack of free speech once again supports a stuck game. The more stuck the game, the more loss one feels and the more *mechanical* it becomes where the game is assigned to control by the Grid: with its inevitable final curtain in the last act, where the Greek tragedy is once again played on Earth according to Grid memory script with the sea majestically: "bursting its bounds", before the audience even had time to wake up! The curtain will rise on the next production since all Spirits are immortal, the audience in confusion over the last production watch the curtain rise on theatre earth, with the psychotic players shouting "WE MUST KEEP ORDER HERE!" and the audience watch once again as the Theocratic priesthood obsessively stuck in their game, once again build their One World Order.

The origin of the Spirit is a tricky question, but let me offer one solution in the form of a matter, anti-matter explosion at the beginning. The Spirit was 'born' as an awareness of awareness unit, in the first trillionth of a second in such an explosion, at that moment the Spirit became OBSERVATION POINT and was aware.

Bruce Cathie who began researching the Earth Grid in 1952, when he was a pilot for New Zealand National Airways, has given some very interesting mathematics of the Grid in his research [142] which evidently worried those in high places enough to harass Cathie and he was constantly pestered by Intelligence Services including the CIA. Cathie provides an interesting extension of the polarity and duality in the Universe together with the spiralling motion:

> "I have gradually built up a picture in my mind of the possible geometric combinations necessary to form matter from resonating, interlocking wave forms...Matter and anti-matter are formed by the *same wave motions* in space. The waves travel through space in a

spiralling motion, and alternately pass through positive and negative stages. Matter is formed through the positive stage, or pulse, and anti-matter through the negative pulse. Each spiral of 360 degrees forms a single pulse. The circular motion of an electron about a nucleus of an atom is therefore an illusion. The relative motion of the nucleus and electrons through space gives the illusion of circular motion...the period frequency rate between each pulse of physical matter creates the measurement that we call time as well as the speed of light, at the particular position in space of which we are aware at any given moment. If the frequency rate of positive and negative pulses is either increased or decreased, then time and the speed of light vary in direct proportion. This concept would explain time as a geometric, as Einstein theorised it would be." (*Author's emphasis*)

Cathie shows (*Fig.39*) how matter and anti-matter are created out of the same waveforms. Thus interestingly, the electron moving through an approximate 360 degrees in each cycle spiralling in that curious dumb-bell or figure-of-8 shape, creates an anti-matter, matter pulse. This leads me to enquire whether the antimatter and matter Universes are really just parallel Universes, and the reason the physicists can't find the anti-matter is precisely for this reason.

What is anti-matter? A rock made of anti-matter would look like a rock; a person made of anti-matter would look like a person. Material made of anti-matter would exhibit the same physical properties as normal matter. However, if one object made of matter were to touch an object made of anti- matter there would be an explosion. Like matter, anti-matter is composed of elementary particles, each of which displays attributes that exactly mirror familiar matter. However instead of protons, anti-matter contains anti-protons, which do not bear a positive charge, as do protons, but a negative charge. Instead of electrons, anti-matter contains anti- electrons also known as positrons, which are positively charged rather than negatively charged. The anti- neutron and neutrons bear no electrical charge but display *mirror opposite properties*. You may remember that I mentioned that certain biochemicals in the body called isomers also have mirror image properties. Paul Dirac first proposed the existence of anti-matter in 1929 from his calculations and was rather put out: "I thought it rather sick", by his results. Even Einstein was to doubt the accuracy of his equation. However Dirac concluded that when matter is created from energy, an equal amount of anti-matter is also created i.e. for every proton an antiproton, for every electron a positron and so on. Dirac was eventually proven correct and received the Nobel Prize in 1933. This immediately poses in one's mind the question of whether there is an anti-world or anti-universe that has mirror opposite properties to our own.

The logical conclusion was that half the material Universe is composed of anti-matter and this must be followed by the question - 'Well where is it?' Obviously not in our Universe or Solar System, otherwise we would not be here to comment on it, as matter on meeting anti-matter explodes. The question of where exactly is the anti-matter, poses a solution, that when our Universe was formed a second identical but mirror opposite anti-matter Universe was also formed, our Universe travelled in one direction and the other Universe travelled in another. One travelled forward (in time) and the other backwards, but never the two should meet again, without the resultant explosion.

Fig.39 **The matter and anti-matter cycle**. *Diagrams a, b and c show how matter and antimatter are created out of the same wave-forms (Bruce Cathie) As the electron is moving through a spiral in each matter and antimatter pulse, it travels through a space of more than 360 degrees during each cycle. The theoretical number of degrees would be 370.95199; the double cycle, 741.90399. Note: In symbolic esoteric numerology the double cycle (360 X2 = 720 or 72) signified the antimatter cycle and control of the Grid energies by the Masters.*

a. Showing the harmonic wave-form which reates an atom of matter and antimatter in alternate pulses.

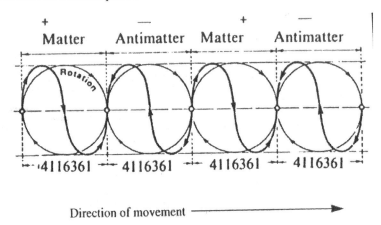

b. Cycle as a geometric of time and the speed of light.

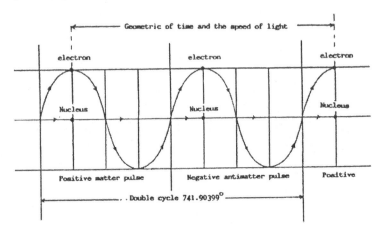

c. Showing the harmonic wave formation of a basic element and the six associated isotopes

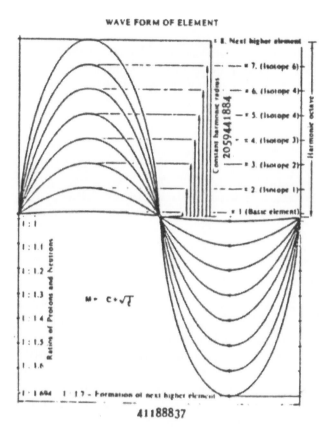

WAVE FORM OF ELEMENT

I am once again drawn to Knossos site iconography and those sarcophagi or burial urns of the Early Minoan period: Their bath shape lead to the ludicrous suggestion by Arthur Evans that they were "lustral baths". The fact that the dead were buried in the foetal position amongst the hyperbolic spiralled seashells is indicative of the belief system not only in Re-incarnation, but a whole Cosmology. The sarcophagus is not only circular in its rim and somewhat ellipsoid to be exact, indicating I maintain the Cycle of Eternal Return - Re-incarnation, but the whole shape is one of a flat-bottomed trapezoid with top rim edge running **parallel** to the bottom surface of the sarcophagus. This may be highly significant in their Cosmology and view of space. What is being indicated here? That a Universe runs parallel with our own? Or do you think that I am trying to wring a pint from a half pint pot here! Well, in the World myths and legends which I briefly referred to in the Cancer Report, there may remain some soul memory of what the teacher taught man in this cycle, which is **unique and will never occur again**. The story of Narreau the Elder is a creation myth from the Gilbert and Ellis Islands and like many myths, tells of the creation of the Universe/ world after a prior flood. The Narreau myth speaks of the god Narreau looking for a way through to Earth; a crack or crevice through which to reach and when he finds one, a moth appears to tell him: "There are people there, great Narreau...But because of the darkness, they are not moving – they are all asleep". Thus in this myth men were on Earth after the Flood, however there appears to be a connection to the Genesis story here and particularly the Adamites in so far as Narreau plants a tree from which grows humanity. The Kings of the Tree of Samoa, the red skinned people with blue eyes, which reminds one of the: "red skinned men from Knossos". Evidently then this myth has a confusion on the line, since the red men signifying Hermes the god of fire, appeared after the Religious Revolution in Crete and therefore are associated with the thirteenth tribe of Judah and the Adamites. The tree of course was a vine in the case of Noah and the "seed" was the dynastic and racial line from the Adamites. However you will remember that I questioned whether the Adamites were initially white but may have intermarried with the 'Missionary' type. The myth still retains some prior truth in so far as was it really the Adamites who came from the sky and space? As is implied by the myth, or did another come from elsewhere?

You might remember that the 'Missionary' type was portrayed in a cave painting from West Africa and it is certainly strange that some element of the truth is still retained in myth there. The myth of Nyame in African lore talks of Nyame the Sky-god looking down on Earth through a "trapdoor" and from his mouth fall TWO SPIRITS (male and female) who land on Earth. Well this looks more promising. The woman is called Lyaloda or Great Mother and she and the male spirit breathe life into mankind whom they create as from "asleep". The basic theme of this myth that must convey a truth is repeated in a myth from Madagascar where the people are *descended from Africans* and Indonesians and their god Driana-nahary sends his son (Atoko) to earth to see if anything was surviving there. Atoko enters Earth through a gap in the clouds. Significantly Atoko loses his ability to fly or reach the spiritual world and cannot get back to his father who waits at the exit crying anxiously:" What have I done?" And "Atoko! Atoko! Where are you? Come back!" Now this seems a highly significant myth that reflects the message or Holy Grail that was brought to Earth c. 10 000 B.C. and as such those who brought it, must have been aware it was a dangerous mission spiritually, such is forgetfulness on Planet Earth created by the trap and Grid. How to get back must have been the overriding concern as one Spirit waited at the exit, for their partner. The myth continues and becomes confused once again with the elite group, as it continues along Apocalyptic Revelations lines, where after total destruction and the **third battle** a new Earth appears from the sea after a long period of darkness and where once again the surviving gods find the golden chessmen their ancestors played with. Signifying perhaps the MRC case and the re-discovery of Grid technology reducing man to pawns in a game of chess where the King and Bishops had all the power, directing the One World Order 'chess game' from their castles or 'rooks'. The end of the cycle appears to be related to electronics and the third battle – a third World War! But I will come back to this point and continue here with a few more excerpts from the Cancer Report. The appearance of icons at the Knossos site with hands raised to Ra signified the Sun god as alleged creator (of the trap?) and significantly Ra created mankind to act as his "servants". Thus even in myth we perceive that those who were here from the beginning always sought a slave society.

The myths of the North American Indians tell of a series of worlds that existed before this one, giving some credence to prior cycles and therefore cataclysms. The Navajo Indians speak of a journey into the fifth world and the sun being too close to the earth and causing great heat, until everything began to wither and scorch: Which is reminiscent of *Alternative 3*, the book that prompted my second book *Alternative 4*. *Alternative 3* was a proposed plan to evacuate the elite of Earth in the event of cataclysm forming an alleged base on Mars and might have been considered a "spoof" in the 1970's as it was made out, if not for the fact that an eminent American scientist loosed his tongue and described future on Earth as it will: "get hotter and hotter". After the horse had bolted so to speak, the equivalent of the Official Secrets Act was passed in America! Finally in my last excerpt from the Cancer Report, I note that curious myth of Odin, in which the gods created a kingdom above earth and the road to it, was via a many-coloured rainbow, intimating the electro-magnetic spectrum. Symbolically Odin and his brothers model and animate the first man and woman (Ask and Embla) from wood, which implies thirteenth tribe and the Tree Alphabet. The myth appears to report three Ice Ages, after which the symbolic wolves tear the sun and moon to pieces, which is the moment of victory for the giants over the gods, indicating perhaps the onset of another Magnetic Reversal and 'victory' by the MRC's. Significantly the black void returns, where mountains and rocks are torn up and the sea envelops the land drowning all. The conclusion of the myth precedes the Apocalyptic account, but parallels it, in so far as at the close of things the cunning god Loki trapped beneath the Earth having caused the death of the sun-god Baldur, frees himself for the last battle (Armageddon in the Apocalypse): However Heimdall watches on the tower battlements and sees the evil awakening and sounds his warning horn. The gods significantly hastily don their winged helmets symbolic of Hermes (and the thirteenth tribe of Judah) the transcendent third and immortal stage beyond death, again connecting triumph to the thirteenth tribe and perhaps Re-incarnation? However as I will cover later, the book of Revelations has a different story to tell. The point of bringing these myths into this section on anti-worlds, is that whilst undoubtedly since myths are mainly elements of the truth that were not safe to write or tell, the truth was often veiled and entered into myth which was often verbally transmitted within the group and therefore subject to alteration and embellishment. Myths then often contain *elements* of truth and are often confused with some misunderstandings, but there seems to be a fundamental agreement among the creation myths, that "gods" or one god (Atoko) came from the sky or space, recognising the predicament of man as "asleep" or Grid controlled and in a trap. One might argue that Noah's Ark was really a space ship built on Grid technology, which was thus able to avoid the chaos of a Magnetic Reversal on Earth, returning to help humanity as the "chosen ones", however if that were so this book would not have been necessary. Since the Flood was historically I concluded prior to 10 000 B.C then the Spiritual impetus on this Planet may have come from a completely different source, thus accounting for the element of truth in myth and the unique cycle this time. Where exactly did that impetus come from? Another anti-world? As one UFO witness reported an alleged alien had said: "Watchman, one day you will see the Universe!" I mentioned in *Alternative 4*, I have long suspected that the Elite or our MRC case has long sought that 'door' to the other world and a way out of the periodic Magnetic Reversals of this Planet. Indeed the whole of the Space programme may centre more on a point of survival for the "chosen ones", in the event of cataclysm, which NASA must be aware of and perhaps the International Space Station (the size of a football pitch in its eventual size) may be questioned along these lines, after all it is built on tax payers money and perhaps they should know why their money is being spent on such a project; they are after all the hosts on which the parasite or the MRC case feeds and depends for his illusion of power.

The diablo model for a proposed cosmology that I gave, interestingly would accommodate a matter anti-matter explosion theory, with one half of the diablo receding from the other half of the diablo, in a constantly expanding or even balanced Universe, with the point of the explosion and the contact of matter with anti-matter (not necessarily the singularity) at the balance point of the diablo - God's country there! We will never know what happened *before* the explosion, as I maintain we were not yet 'born' as Spirits and there was no OBSERVATION POINT, which is the Spirit. We started recording our observations *after* the explosion and thus we may never know what happened at the beginning either at the singularity, as the physicists call it, or at the point of matter and anti-matter collision. The cosmological diablo model is different from 'Big Bang' theory. There are many scientists who flatly refuse to encounter 'Big Bang', as the origin of the Universe: The Nobel Laureate Alfuen, who in the 1960's offered an anti-matter and plasma cosmology, based on research by the Swedish Astrophysicist Oskar Klein was one. In his book *Worlds-Antiworlds* (1966)

Alfuen proposed vast walls of plasma and electro-magnetic fields, which separate matter from anti-matter - the Leidenfrost layers. At the boundaries between regions of matter and anti-matter there existed heat and pressure according to this theory, which thus separated matter from anti-matter. However when physicists find a Unified Field theory, I am sure that they will discover a great deal more of what separates matter from anti-matter and the two proposed Universes. Alfuen's proposal that galaxies were receding or moving away from a matter, anti-matter explosion would fit with the diablo model.

Consider a Spirit 'born' in an anti-matter, matter explosion. *Before* that explosion, there was only *potential* but after that point in the first trillionth of a second there was a duality and polarity of matter and anti-matter. The Observation point i.e. Spirit as an awareness of awareness unit or observation point, would record such an event including inherent polarity and duality, and that memory would still exist within our Spiritual memory today. According to the holographic theory of memory, the holographics of that event would persist. If the Spirit is according to Ron Hubbard self-determined thought, such thought would according to the matter anti-matter origin of Spirit necessarily incorporate duality and polarity of thought. The persistence of religion in identifying polarities and dualities e.g. good and evil, God and Satan, or Ying and Yang in Indian mysticism, may be nothing more than expression of the inherent memory of polarity and duality in that first trillionth of a second, as religion seeks to identify the nature of the Godhead and which the physicist constantly chews over in the question of what happened at the beginning. Many physicists including Einstein hated the idea of the so-called singularity, with the idea that all matter in the Universe was collected into an infinitely dense and minute ball, which exploded and gave rise to the Universe, as it expanded outwards from that point. Matter and anti-matter explosion would require the coming together of two mirror opposites.

Harold Aspden along with several other Scientists assures us categorically there was no 'Big Bang' at the beginning of the formation of the Universe. For those who wish to follow up the physics Aspden provides the data to support this statement and underlines that: "to escape from that dilemma" one needs to understand the "dynamic balance" and that we inhabit a "steady state" Universe "apart from its bubbling equilibrium". Those who reject the idea that the Universe is not in equilibrium, but will one day contract and return to the singularity, generate gloom and the idea of self perpetuating destruction. However there is a very subtle point to be made here in that those who support 'Oneness' and Godhead fusion unwittingly support the idea of destruction. I will return to this point in a moment, but it is as if Harold Aspden had some innate memory of the problem when he stated: "It is as if we were minute observers sitting inside a solid piece of iron, experiencing thermal agitation, whilst being firmly rooted inside that iron, but subject to drifting as we share the Earth's motion, just as if were part of *Magnetic* domain migrating through a *crystal*" (My emphasis).

I think that this is a very important point. If one cools chemicals rapidly in a laboratory one obtains crystals there is no reason to suppose that planets made up of chemicals which rapidly cooled after coming into existence under atomic conditions of heat, did not go through the same crystallization process. If you could really see the Universe and Vacuum energy it would probably be one vast geometric web of interconnected patterns, just as the Earth Grid is I perceive rather like a honeycomb comprised smaller diablo patterns. This pattern may be a reflection of the greater Diablo pattern, the master pattern of a Universe in harmony and balance, expanding indefinitely or alternatively perfectly balanced from the matter anti-matter explosion. The games we play, as Spirit within that pattern must be one of construction and not ignorant destruction of the pattern itself. One could never hope to control the pattern or replace ones *own perception* of Order on a pattern that is Order. Science has sought to control the pattern and science since it has been under the control of the master magicians for millennia, has developed the idea of controlling and ordering Nature and the physical laws that govern Her, but one can only hope to **understand** Nature and work with her. Spirits are quite capable of playing with energy as I conclude from the Fatima Miracle in *Alternative 4*, an event witnessed by 70 000 people. Spirits however particularly in this sector of the Universe, have forgotten that they are a part of the game- pattern and simply fell into the trap of loosing *observation point*. Simply they became matter and energy and lost the ability to play with energy. The deeper man became enmeshed with matter, the more he believed he was his body or his mind, the greater he fell from the truth and sought to control obsessively. Those who were present on Earth for a very long time, evidently went through periods in the various magnetic cycles when as giants they experienced very long life spans, according to biblical texts some 900 years. If that were true, then those Spirits would have lost sight of their own immortality as a *Spirit* and would have viewed their immortality in terms of *a body*. That I believe is what is meant by descent into matter.

I would maintain that the duality or polarity created in the first trillionth of a second, presumably after the matter anti-matter explosion, was vital in the 'birth' of a Spirit. One can only view something or become observation point, if one has something to view, i.e. you have to be exterior from it. However you would not even know you were an observation point, if you were not able to *switch from one viewpoint to another*. I can only compare this to a young child who follows his mother everywhere in his early days, because he does not yet conceive of himself as separate. He views everything through his mother. If she is sad he is sad, if she leaves a room he leaves a room. Slowly through switching from her observation point to his own, he learns 'I am me and you are you'. He gets the feeling of observation point as his own Spirit. This learning process however, required a duality (his mother and himself). The act of Creation has been repeated in this case. We look at a small child and through him we see ourselves at the moment of our own Creation in the Firmament. His great potential, naivety and joy instils us with the love and a memory of the potential we once were and as he grows and experiences pain we feel pain, at how far we have fallen from that true potential. The small child who once proudly proclaimed, "This is my father!" only later to be cheated and threatened by him, has profound undertones for religion and life on this planet. Duality and polarity or matter anti-matter must have provided the initial observation point learning process and the reason I have always maintained an open viewpoint on any knowledge or data, is that I strongly believe that when you form a closed viewpoint, you fall away from the act of Creation and the continual potential learning process of the Spirit as it expands with the Universe in complete balance? One adores the purest concept of science, for its insistence on maintaining that *open viewpoint, where you must continually observe and pose solutions and mock up new ideas* and physicists who steer clear of mysticism may instinctively be repelled by the static viewpoint that has become orthodox religion, controlled as it is by politics and the inevitable One World Order of static and stuck viewpoint. All religions go this way, they have data and history and then they put it down in books and tell you to read every word and don't ever get a another viewpoint on it: To recall that Semitic stone, it becomes the word of their particular Messiah or God and that's it, you are finished expanding on the point of self-determinism and observation point! Democracy, the search for truth, freedom of speech and the right to question, freedom of viewpoint, is livingness towards a game for **all** and the loss of those freedoms are just a bit more down on the scale to Dead or mechanical Grid being.

Why was Satan called the anti-Christ? Does this co-incidentally give us a picture of anti-matter and matter mirror image opposites? The original duality and polarity may have created duality of thinking with rational or analytical versus irrational or reactive mind, with the idea that each man orchestrates his own fate according to whether he can remain observation point and not follow an irrational course, the course of his anti-self. Such theories have arisen in one form or another in Psychology and of all the theories I have come across Ron Hubbard's *Dianetics - The Modern Science of Mental Health*, represents the most workable theory of the mind, where he describes the irrational or "Reactive Mind", versus the "Analytical Mind". Those minds perhaps represent the duality of memory and experience of the first trillionth of a second, when you and your twin as doppelganger or anti-self, as part of the matter and anti-matter explosion danced the polarity and duality dance of observation point to and fro, between viewpoints of matter and anti-matter. You and your twin as matter and anti-matter danced towards each other as one and danced away repelling each other as two, which perhaps gave rise to the concept of one-ness and loss each time matter and anti-matter converged and separated. Curiously the idea of Twin kingship was to arise in the first downgrade of Early Minoan beliefs after the Religious Revolution, where the original concept was Re-incarnation and as one died, one became united with Her the Great Goddess (Nature or the Universe?) and was reborn. This was transferred to Kingship by the Semitic invaders and the new concept became as one Twin King died, he became united with the Great Goddess (now a Goddess) and was reborn through her. The second downgrade became Hermes as male and female combined and conductor of souls to the land of the dead to return, symbolised by his petasos or cap and winged sandals.

UFO witness accounts, which I reproduced in *Alternative 4*, curiously in some cases recount warnings of nuclear explosions. Some witnesses who claim Aliens abducted them, report being shown pictures (holographic?) of Atomic explosions. The Fatima Miracle I have concluded was a final Spiritual warning of an impending Magnetic Reversal. Thus somewhere within holographic memory is not only a recognition of a cataclysmic disaster but of the unethical use of Science, particularly atomic science. In this respect the new Super conducting Super Collider or SSC, the biggest accelerator in history is soon to be completed. It will cover many square miles of the Texas prairie with the purpose of colliding protons and anti protons, creating intense high-energy conditions that briefly simulate the temperature and density of the 'Big Bang' at a millionth millionth of a second. This will test theories holding that the known forces were part of a single "super force" in the earliest moments of the Universe. It is believed that the SCC will allow physicists to observe what happens when two forces electro-magnetic and the weak force are merged into a simpler more symmetric force, that will represent achieving a new state of matter that is qualitatively different from all previously observed. The Scientists may believe that they will gain new insights into the origin of the Universe, but I am sorry that will not be the case. If I asked them to accept that this is God's country, the inevitable reply will be that it is good to know these things, believing that the final closet of Nature will be opened to man, with the possibility of playing God. I would not like to be a 'party pooper', to the 'magicians' and deny that they could indeed pull the rabbit out of the hat, but I will only voice my reservation here. A Spirit KNOWS everything from the beginning and the fact that the physicists have convinced themselves they DON'T KNOW, must presumably rest on having carried out what Hubbard calls "overts" or wrong actions on this line of Atomic Energy. I have noted time and time again in my own research how I was led *intuitively* to places, that I pretended to myself I did not know! In actual fact to know what went on at the Crucifixion and then to refuse to remember any part of that experience for 2 000 years is somewhat of a big overt! Peter Plitchta the Chemist who I have mentioned was fascinated by the **8**- pointed star and the fact that his brother was his twin, his early childhood then marked out his knowingness of the research he would undertake to jog his memory, which does not detract at all from its genius. Searle who worked on anti-gravity propulsion could not explain how his machines worked, but they did of course and he just *knew* how to build them, he had forgotten the maths but not the models. Recapitulation of the past is often observed in so-called scientific discoveries a point that Hitler remarked on.

In fact I would ask the physicist how he could go back to before a time he was observation point? i.e. before the 'birth' of his own Spirit. If I am correct in this and the point of 'birth' was a matter anti-matter explosion, then if you go before that point and attempt to create the explosion conditions themselves, would you go back in time before you (the Spirit) was born? And thus would you be able to observe that event if you were not there? Further if a holographic memory exists for that event, would any experiment to re-create the event, merely pull down the *whole* holographic with impending catastrophe? In the *Appendix* to *Alternative 4*, entitled: *'In Search of the Philospher's Stone'*, I noted that the quest of the Scientist and particularly the Physicist is really a search for union with the Godhead. His obsess ional desire to know what happened at the beginning is not sought by that profound observation of John Davidson versus Stephen Hawking, i.e. within his **own** subconscious microcosm that is the macrocosm, but in the manly and overtly testosterone field of Atomic Physics. If the very implicit understanding of our continued existence depends on not opening Pandora's box and questioning the point *before* our 'birth' as Spirits, then one must ask whether the ancient myths and legends which relate that "monsters", march over "the rainbow bridge" and descend at the end when everything is destroyed, is really a meeting of self with anti-self your doppelganger. Is it implicit that matter and anti-matter be kept separate? There are many questions we pretend we do not know the answers to, but *thinking* is a very low-scaled operation than KNOWING. Just as Emile Sergei admitted that the Los Alamos Scientists did not know if the Biosphere would set fire! When they exploded the first Atomic bomb, then the anti-matter matter experiments must come under the same dangerous and foolhardy thinking. The Physicist now stands with power that is unparalleled and whether he has the courage to meet and discuss mysticism will determine outcome. Unfortunately as with stuck viewpoints in war, it is impossible to get both sides together in the same room! Such is life with Grid man and Planet Earth.

Will Scientists pull their own ethics in, before we see such things? As big business rushes with ego driven Scientists motivated by the size of profits, to patent the Genetic code of mankind, clone species and eventually a "slave species" of man no doubt, are we merely watching as "watchmen" the repeat of a cycle that has gone before? The problem with this cycle is that there was new input of information and how that information is used, whether to free or destroy will determine the outcome. As genetically modified food and species threatens the hitherto ordered holographics of the morphogenetic bioplasma, as the master control pattern for survival of a species; will we see malformed and mutant species in the future? As those holographics become muddled as to which species, animal or plant, they are coding for. Will Scientists as the Sorcerer's apprentices to the magicians of the One World Order continue to loan their expertise and knowledge for the price of their souls, or will they order a World Ethics and Millennium Directional Assessment Conference as I requested in my Petition to Parliament in the UK? It seems to me that a critical cross roads has occurred and which route man takes, will determine the outcome here on Planet Earth. In the Appendix to *Alternative 4*, I pointed to Mary Shelly's *Frankenstein - The Modern Prometheus*, as the most convincing feminist analysis of masculine science, with the catastrophic effects of trying to control as opposed to understanding the feminine in Nature. It is a tale that identifies man with his Zeus-god like quest to control and create life. Victor Frankenstein pursued the ultimate act of creating life in his laboratory and in so doing creates a monster, which overpowers Frankenstein's world and destroys everything that Frankenstein holds dear. The most pertinent point in the story however, is that on completion of the monster; Frankenstein is repulsed by his creation, and refuses to accept paternity or responsibility for it. The Motherless and Fatherless monster deprived of parental love, and then seeks retribution and destruction. Cloned species, genetic modification of food and species, atomic weapons, pollution, biological warfare, and the mechanisation of medicine including the treatment of Cancer through high technology and drugs, are just some of those 'monsters', which no-one seems to want to take responsibility for. An endeavour that started under the profession of noblest intentions, that of understanding Nature and Life merely becomes an obsession and despite the monster creation, the researcher does not realise until the project is completed and chaos ensues, that he was merely driven by personal power, ambition, glory and the promise of god-like powers. The quest that may have been the Scientist's Holy Grail and his search for the Philosopher's Stone deteriorates into a prolonged 'sexual intercourse', with no regard for the conception and consequences. Once you open Pandora's box, you can't pop the monster back into the box. Why play around with the DNA of species, or insert genes from other species into man, without first understanding the Grid, morphogenetic bioplasma and the way in which holographics are stored within the master pattern together with the whole range of theories I have discussed, which do have validity in comparative research.

To give you some idea of the strange workings not only of the Spirit, but also of the holographics of the memory data banks, let me give you one small story that is very true. A number of years before I went to Greece to study the research for my first book and before any past life regressions and even before I had fully engaged on the Cancer research, I had a series of very significant dreams. In one dream I was on a boat and a great storm arose and I was swept into the harbor of an Island of great beauty. There was something deeply significant about it, although I convinced myself on the conscious plane that I had no idea what was meant. I related one past life in the first chapter of *The Battle of The Trees*, where I had carried a parchment to England c. 1350 A.D. I could easily have left that account out of the book and could also easily have never stated that I was a witness to the events of Golgotha, however to have done so would be to omit one half of the Holy Grail – "the elixir of life" and part of the message that came to Earth, thus whilst one should not discuss one's past lives, since I consider it bad form, I gave just a glimpse so that the reader might understand the workings of one's goals or soul memory postulates. The Parchment appeared to carry important data and was in some way related to "Shem son of Noah". I could not quite in my regression make out the content although it seemed to be in some form of code and carried a condemnation of man. After a series of events some years later I was forced to leave England on the 17 September 1993 and go to Greece to seek the answers I needed. I had a parchment made in some form of code I devised and although I could not repeat the contents of the original document, I attempted to re-create the spirit of the document in the parchment. Now if you ask me on the conscious level why I did that, I would not have been able to tell you. It was an *act of intuition*. I carried the last parchment with me on the way to Greece in my white car (a white horse occurred in the past life regression) and after several oceans I was on the final leg of the journey, to Crete, when looking out from the ship as it sailed across the Aegean I suddenly remembered the dream. The Aegean was like a millpond at the time and yet within 10 minutes winds had risen and the seas began to swell and before I knew it we were forced to take shelter in the harbor of the beautiful Island of Patmos, where St. John allegedly wrote the book of *Revelations*. All ferries in the Aegean were confined to port for several days, as one of the severest storms swept the area and I was stranded along with others, on the Island. Whilst stranded in order to occupy myself, I had a chance to visit the alleged cave where John wrote the work and the whole time I had a feeling that there was something deeply significant about it all. This is the **knowingness of the spirit** at work: The meeting of science with mysticism. The prophetic Apocalypse or book of *Revelations* has of course featured strongly in my work, together with attempts to place that in the field of Science. The tremendous speed, with which I have had to relentlessly work at, was another Spiritual intuition that must have some reflection on Dr. Becker's warning that a Magnetic Reversal may have already started.

Whether Atomic Warfare and/or a Magnetic Reversal, caused past cataclysms or whether some anti-matter matter experiment acted as a restimulator to an entire holographic recording challenging the pattern of Creation pulling down some of the holographics of the event is uncertain, but those cataclysms evidently have left myths, legends, geological and archaeological evidence of their occurrence. Harold Aspden the physicist asks us to:

> "Imagine Earth, carried along by the solar System, at the known cosmic speed of the order of some 400 Km/s, moving through a domain boundary region (other space domain). For about one minute the Earth would sit astride the boundary. If there is a polarity reversal of electric charge as between the two adjacent space domains, where antiprotons replace protons and positrons replace electrons, is it any wonder then that the Earth's magnetic field reverses in such events? Is it any wonder that gravity forces might become antigravity forces as between matter astride those two domains, for that brief period, to cause earthquakes on an unimaginable scale, sufficient to destroy whole species of life? May it not be, if we wish to worry about our future destruction, that we have a choice for our thoughts as between a) our own self destruction by nuclear weapons and the like or b) the random event of a comet or asteroid crashing to Earth or c) the inevitable and possibly predictable event when our Earth next crosses a space domain boundary?"

As if paralleling my own predictions in *Alternative 4*, Aspden continues:

> "Might it not be that the day will come when some potential survivors will need to climb into   space vehicles propelled by future anti-gravity technology? They will board as we approach that   space domain boundary so as to go through it ahead of the Earth but make the transition in a   fraction of a millisecond, eventually returning to Earth only after the dust has settled. Believe it or not, our physics, when revised to take account of what is disclosed in the Aether Science papers of this work, allows us to estimate the timing of the next space domain boundary transit, once we can be *sure about the timing of the last one.* " *(author's emphasis)*

One wonders if the Mayan Calendar ceases c. 2010 A.D. for that reason. However the point to be made, is that I am sure that as I pointed out in *Alternative 4*, that 'Noah's Ark' has already been researched since the 1970's, possibly leaked as part of the scenario of *Alternative3*, which covered the possibility of a space station on Mars. "The Chosen Ones" who have no intention of experiencing another Magnetic Reversal. The Ether Science will not of course be divulged for this reason. Further, faced with the kind of reality expressed by Aspden, what a curiosity and inappropriate agreement *The*

494

Covenant becomes. An agreement made thousands of years ago between Semitic Patriarchs and God, when the domain boundary and matter anti-matter were perhaps not understood, simply because the impetus to fully understand the Grid and cosmology did not arrive until 10 000 B.C. in this cycle, which makes it unique. This is not to say that the 'Fallen Angel' did not have his own memories and thus one cannot discount that he knew of atomic power and matter anti-matter. Of course this would mean that our 'friend', the MRC might be able to avoid Magnetic Reversals in the future, whilst leaving Homo Sapiens to continually experience that which he, the MRC case could not. The MRC case may yet in future cycles have his "slave species", as the Spirit of man degenerates into insanity through repetitive boundary events or Magnetic Reversals. I can't think of a closer definition of Hell. The game would return to black magic, sacrifice and Kingship puppeted by a Theocracy, with another One World Order, the game that was played prior to 10 000 B.C.

If this has depressed you no end, buck up Spirits, **you don't need a space ship to exit**, a Spirit is quite capable of exiting the nightmare, providing of course you have the *'key'* to the *'door'* out. I have found mine and no doubt everyone who has chosen a particular religious or philosophical path, has considered the problem of "salvation" or exit. If not, I suggest that you do give this some **immediate** consideration, for there is one thing that is certain, cataclysms come without warning: "like a thief in the night", according to the Apocalypse. I don't think you will ever change this Planet or control by the MRC case with his One World Orders and dramatizations, simply because man will not challenge that Order. I think it has gone too far here. One might just as well let him get on with Planet Earth, whilst finding another game that is really worth playing elsewhere!

MIND ENERGY GRID INTERFACE

Early experiments have shown that when a hologram of an inorganic crystal is made, it *still has an energy link with the solid material crystal*. Harry Oldfield and Roger Coghill in their research [143] state that:

> "The method we used was to wire a crystal to a high impedance device and then 'influence' the holographic image. The results have shown that large impedance changes occurred during the experiments. Such influences employed were sunlight, human hands on the hologram and even thought direction! Not only does this border on mind matter experiments, but also shows a definite *physical bond* between a 3D light image created from the hologram method and the physical object itself, which can be disturbed by brain induced vibrations. It would not be inconsistent with our hypothesis that brain wave induced effects can be created in holographic form!"

This research has vast implications. Although the researchers were working with inorganic crystals, there is no reason to suppose that the Grid and mind holographics are not influenced by a similar method. Firstly as the mind or memory banks are filed in holographic form, then those holographics have a *continued connection to the matter and personnel they contain*. One is consistently aware of the fact that when people start to run past lives and run through their memory banks of holographics, then personnel who they once knew and who were connected to certain of those holographic memories, start to re-appear or elements of the holographic appear in present time. I suspect that this was my experience in Patmos. In actual fact, I used my own method of regression based on some knowledge similar to this, to access my own past lives. The Crucifixion was a personal or witness account memory accessed by this method.

Obviously too, there is the possibility of mind control via influencing the spatial field of the mind and its holographic memory banks (which is not a brain), which can influence the individual himself. Just as the individual as his physical self can influence his own holographics. Further if the Grid is considered as the UVG 120 crystal with its own holographic memories of survival and the phylogenetic line, then it still has links to the Earth and one influences the other and vice versa. In *Nexus* Magazine (*November 1966*) an article appeared: 'Secret Implants illegally used on Prisoners'. This was a leaked three-page document from Intelli-Connection, a Security Division of IBM in New York. The article discussed the need for remaining abreast of technology to control crime in the 21 st Century. It appears that the 2020 neural chip implant with its behavioral and mood-controlling capability is to be tested on a contractual basis and limited testing had already taken place, with several prisoners identified as members of the security threat group. Illusively the document notes that they have also had major successes in privately owned *sanitariums*! (Abuse of human rights!) using implant technology. Although details of the mechanism of the implant is not clear, it stated that: "Implants disabled two subjects during an assault on correctional staff" and: "Universal side-effects in all eight test subjects revealed that when the implant was set to 116 MHz all the subjects became lethargic and slept 18-22 hours per day". This sort of mind control technology has been going on for quite some time and it is conceivable (if not already tested), that you could download a whole set of holographics or memories into someone's mind. Such a person could even be given tremendous amounts of data in this way. Thus as I covered in *Alternative 4,* there is secret and on-going research into mind control and neural chip technology with presumably holographics.

From the UFO data and the appearance of holographics in witness accounts, there is every reason to suppose, that the Grid as a bioplasma organisation carries these holographics in an *organised* pattern, rather similar to a cinema reel in much the same way that genes are organised on a chromosome and further DNA with its double helicity may well form the master Grid pattern via the 'threads' of the bioplasma. Presumably the holographics contained in the vacuum as part of the morphogenetic bioplasma carry holographics from the beginning i.e. *Creation point of Earth*: The holographics would concern *only* this Planet. These holographics contain *event* or environmental memories and on the basis of UFO witness accounts, those holographics or memories of events includes atomic explosions. As I have previously mentioned there were a number of UFO witness accounts that gave atomic energy warnings. One must consider the possibility, that if atomic war has occurred as an event in the long distant past on this Planet, then it would of course remain as a holographic recording within the crystal holographics of the master pattern or blueprint i.e. the morphogenetic bioplasma. Given that the crystal holographics still have a physical connection to the event itself and the personnel in the event and in fact all parts of the hologram, then atomic explosions on Earth are restimulative to the Grid holographics. Further the memories within the Grid are imprinted on the mind of man. In this way genetic engineering, atomic weapons etc., may be just conditioned patterning by Grid events and where 'current' research is just a recapitulation of past research, a fact that Hitler seems to have been aware of and perhaps is reflected in the elusive words of both Einstein and Soddy. In other words if you set off an atomic bomb on Earth, that would register as part of the memory or holographic of the past, held within the mega computer or Grid. This would then re-stimulate the entire sequence of events within the master memory and that sequence may become the 'script' that is enforced on Grid man, who is tuned into the Grid holographics. The fact that warnings on atomic energy have occurred in UFO witness reports, means that at some level *thought* is also imprinted into the Grid holographics or energy patterning: when I come to the section on channelling, you will see this is the case and may account for the belief, that Masters exist in the etheric layer, a common belief in the majority of secret groups. Returning to the work of Harry Oldfield and Roger Coghill they state:

> "If you hold a crystal in your hand the frequency of your own macromolecules, which ...resonate a complex wave-form, can imprint itself into the otherwise regular oscillations of the crystal lattice. So the crystal's electrons will move in regular fashion vibrating exactly with your own macromolecules. **The crystal is copying your own specific waveform**! Crystals are even used to measure changes in radio wavelengths and can receive and amplify complicated waveforms emanating from radio-transmitters hundreds of miles away. Given these phenomena, it should come as no surprise that crystals are very sensitive indeed to the subtlest of energies". (*author's emphasis*)

The idea of the all-seeing Eye takes on a new meaning! And as man re-creates that Eye on Earth through his surveillance and intelligence networks and secret groups, culminating in his obsessive use of CTV cameras, we perhaps understand the conditioning effect of Grid imprints or implants! Onto man as he lives the hermetic principle of: 'as above so below': once again the work of Oldfield and Coghill has enormous implications, for they have connected human resonance or biofield energy (organic) vibration to an inorganic crystal and further show that the crystal can *copy* that resonance. These two men deserve a medal for this brave new research! The implication is there then, that the Grid or vacuum bioplasma as a crystal lattice pattern can at least in theory receive information with the possibility of storage as holographics. Ron Bonewitz [144] reported that placing crystals over the chakra energy points of the human biofield causes a distinct reaction in brainwave patterns, which can be measured by EEG (Electro-encephalograph) equipment. The use of pulsars and Tacheon beads in natural health therapies seek to harmonise energy fields by the same principle. Thus CRYSTALS CAN INTERFACE WITH THE FIELD OF THE MIND, giving some evidence for my assertion that the Grid can interface with man's mind: further Bonewitz reported that bones, which are themselves crystalline, could be deprogrammed from their inharmonious imbalance in disease or trauma by crystals placed at specific energy points.

The mind either acting as dipole radio-receiver or still physically connected to the UVG120 crystal mega computer is able to pick up the signals or resonating wave-forms of the holographics in the bioplasma vortex; memory banks, when they are disturbed by high energy flux through the system, according to the

'Onion-Ring' model I gave in *Alternative 4*. Likewise the DNA which itself has transmitter and receiver properties can interface not only with the human biofield, but also with the mind bioplasma Vortex interface. Thus information can be transmitted and received, by the process of morphogenetic resonance. It is a grand mistake to consider that any material object e.g. a body is quite separate from any greater energy patterning and information system, just as it is a mistake to think of a mind as the brain and not an energy field - resonance of molecules, atoms, cells, organs etc. is the key to understanding just how these fields of morphogenetic resonance interface with the greater pattern of resonating energy which is the vacuum energy. The great **cosmic keyboard**, where every resonance or 'note' is heard and recorded: which may answer the question of why spiritual intervention occurred c.10 000 B.C. After a Magnetic Reversal if enough souls in the chaos screamed in their minds: "*Help me*", it may be that the compassionate source from elsewhere could not ignore that cry for help, despite the danger to themselves. Perhaps as in the Atoko myth one soul in the mission was to remain at the exit, in order to remember the way back, whilst one would enter the black abyss of Earth, to bring the Holy Grail message and the cosmology to release man from the trap.

If we compare the crystal Grid energy or morphogenetic/spiritual bioplasma to a master computer, you could say that man through this resonance is tuned into www-com/grid past holographics. I should underline PAST, since once the information is recorded it is by definition a past event. This is highly important in later sections, but the point here, is that man if he remains asleep as part of the audience, might just as well put on a *virtual reality* device and be guided by the mega computer. I suspect that it has not surpassed your observation that man has dramatized on Earth, his *entire psychological case* in this respect, as he sits mindlessly glued to his 'television' as the holographics are broadcast out to him or switches on his computer and plugs into the world wide web! On the hermetic principle of: 'as above so below'. We might expect child pornography and the vast array of behaviour of *very* degraded beings to appear on such a web, since sacrifice particularly of children was a feature of the past where black magic was rife and such beings merely dramatize their past.

The fact that crystals or even objects carry information on past holographics, presumably by their connection to Grid memory, would explain the ability of the psychic or certain people sensitive to resonance, to be able to read vibrations in terms of holographics of past events, simply by holding the object in their hands - 'psychometry'. Likewise a house can retain an atmosphere, or imprint of vibrations of those who lived there. Thus we constantly imprint our own unique vibrations on sub-atomic energy patterns as we live. Further telepathic ability is enhanced when certain crystals are held in the hand. Crystals can also be programmed to contain a thought-induced image or an emotion even, which a psychic can pick up! In *The Crystal* by Dale Walker, he stated:

> "We can charge a crystal with energy and the crystal will store that energy for later use. Our experience has shown we can *store information in a crystal*. We do not have an adequate test to prove this. Remember in the Superman movie the crystal with all the knowledge, which taught the baby and later the man? We are working on the techniques for recording and recovering thought-forms stored in crystals. As an example, consider the crystal skulls found in Central America and believed to be such storage computers by many crystal researchers. These researchers have seen visions of all ages and found that they have become aware of new knowledge after working with the crystal skulls".

I continually have the feeling that Hollywood is either Grid-tuned, or they know a great deal more about the story here and mankind is their 'guinea pig' for imprinting and implanting. With regard to the use of crystals in Atlantean and Lemurian science, Walker states:

> "Our research *channeling* spoke of a whole civilization of incredible power and splendor made possible by crystal science. *Machines were merged with the power of the mind.* Crystals were used to furnish unlimited free power. They were used to convert the sun's energy into a form of electricity. We saw pictures of alternating concave and convex lenses catching and changing the rays of the sun and storing the changed energy in a liquid material. We later identified this as a solution of liquid crystal. Great grids were designed to capture and use the energy field of the earth. All were powered and made possible with crystals. Through the use of *controlled thought to direct the chemical changes of matter*, huge crystals were grown in very exact shapes. Even the molecular design was changed to shape and direct energy in exact ways. Sound and light were mapped out in *precise frequencies not only physical, but mental* as well. These were fed through these designed crystals to power air, sea and undersea craft. The discovery of crystals to *control the incredible energy reaction between matter and anti-matter* gave birth to space flight. When they linked this drive to the ability of the crystal to assist the *mind to travel inter-dimensionally*, they were able to design interstellar spacecraft and fly to the stars. Crystals were used in construction. We saw a picture of a circle of people around a crystal. All of the people had been trained since childhood for perfect concentration. We could see a beam of energy travel miles away to a workman holding a box with a lever, a control stick on the top. He pointed it at a huge stone, moved the lever and the

stone rose and poised in the air. Another slight adjustment and he walked away, moving the stone in front of him. Large towers like lighthouses were erected near the sea. Operators were stationed here to communicate with the *dolphins, porpoises* and *whales.* With their assistance, the operators, *herded large schools of fish into waiting offshore nets.* Mighty and beautiful *healing temples* filled the land. Here the combination of *light, colour, sound, magnetism and thought energies* was channelled through crystals to create wonders in healing. The Atlanteans mastered the intricacies of all the rays and sub-rays of colour and sound. They mapped the neurological pathways of the human body and brain. They knew all the energy channels of the energy bodies. Etheric surgery on the energy body was preferable and more desirable than on the physical. When it was necessary, priest healers *linked with the minds of the patients* to direct the cells of the body to separate and expose an offending organ. Blood vessels were directed to close off. Cells around the organ released their hold and forced the organ to the surface of the body where the healer took it out and placed it in a rejuvenation chamber. When the organ was rebuilt, it was replaced in the body. The cells reconnected themselves, the blood vessels sent blood back into the organ and the wound closed itself up. There was no pain, no bleeding, no infection and no shock. Some perverted the great good the crystals were designed to do. The power of the crystals was used to *destroy and enslave.* The tremendous energies released caused an imbalance in the earth. A *massive earthquake* brought about the total *destruction of Atlantis.* Some survivors took the crystals to other lands. In Egypt, they built a towering pyramid, using crystals to lift and set the massive blocks. They used the laser-like energy to cut and dress the blocks so precisely a folded piece of paper could not be passed between stones weighing tons. They made the base from granite, knowing the weight of the stones above would squeeze the quartz in the granite to generate an energy field, which they used for healing rejuvenation, and religious ceremonies. They sheathed it in sandstone and chalcedony to form a resonator and capped it with pure quartz. With this *gigantic transmitter,* they were able to keep communication open, with their friends in the Pleiades and the other star systems.

Wherever the survivors went they left records. They left them beneath the Great Pyramid in Egypt, in caverns in the Tibetan mountains, and in pyramids in China, South America and North America. Mountain peaks all over the world also have their depositories. They left tablets of a man-made stone, hard as diamond. They left books of gold, and thousands of crystals. The real information was in the crystals where

200 000 years of knowledge of one of the mightiest civilizations on earth was stored as 3-dimensional thought holograms. These crystals will be found and deciphered before the end of this century". (*author's emphasis*)

I will cover channelling again later, but one can see the attraction to channelling which evidently Hitler may have fallen foul of, where he was warned not to take the "easy wins", unless he should become trapped by "earthbound spirits". The implication of the MRC who is trapped here and his thought processes, together with a history of events and technology might be indicated by the phrase "easy wins" and certainly Walker's channelled account, indicates that access to past technology is possible. Mr. Icke posed a highly implausible theory in his latest book of the Royal Family in Britain being shape-shifting reptiles. I do not know exactly how he came up with this bit of out-reality, but it certainly seems as though past thought has been transposed into present time. The case of 'was it then, or is it now?' The Grid holds holographics in sequential order, but in the case of the psychic who channels these events there must be some input from the medium or psychic themselves, where their own holograms or memory banks are still connected to Grid events. Thus the psychic would not be an impartial observer and those events that are likely to be channelled, will not be in a time sequence but may be a personal selection of holographs, which are then woven into a story according to the *viewpoint of the psychic*. If you gave 4 different people the task of writing a story around key words and phrases, I am sure that you would get 4 different stories. No doubt 'Kings' and 'shape-shifting' and 'Reptiles' occur somewhere in Grid memory, but to string those memories *together* and then place them in the context of *present time*, is merely to follow the mind of the MRC case or those who dramatize incidents from the past where there is no concept of reality, or space and time. I have emphasised in Walker's account, certain channelled information which indicates that past technology included many developments in science that we consider current technology, but evidently occurs somewhere on Grid memory and such technology recognises the Grid itself, Ley lines and even matter and anti-matter. Further the miracle of feeding the five thousand in biblical texts where shoals of fish were drawn into nets, may find some explanation in past technology relating to the hidden science. Importantly though in Walker's channelled account, we note there was a methodology of controlling minds via crystals and the possibility that the whole Atlantean record existed on the Grid pattern of holographic memory, which theoretically could be accessed and probably has been, accounting for the obsession of World Orders with occult science.

I discussed in *Alternative 4*, the trail of research from the genius Nikola Tesla, whose work was cited in a patent taken out by Dr. Eastlund in 1985 when he worked as a consultant for an oil company (ARCO) in Alaska, the location of the alleged American defence research known as HAARP (High Active Auroral Research Programme). Scientists have been very concerned that this programme together with GWEN (Ground Wave Emergency Network) has a mind control capability and can alter weather patterns and bird migration. It interferes with the Grid and the master pattern I would conclude. ARCO set up a subsidiary company (ARCO Power Technologies Inc. – APTI) and nine other patents were added to those of Dr. Eastlund making 12 patents covering potentially the most formidable technology. APTI only had annual sales of 5 million dollars and 25 employees but despite this a couple of years later, the giant US Defence Contractor E-Systems brought APTI. The trail from Dr. Eastlund's patents and Nikola Tesla was further buried when in 1995, Raytheon Corporation one of the biggest Defence Contractors in the world brought the contract and the technology in the form of the patents. The question became why E-Systems would buy a company with no net income and no major assets except for the 12 patents? Besides the newly acquired HAARP contract, E-Systems had developed a number of other technologies, such as clustered Cray computer networks called EMASS systems, which can store 5 trillion pages of text – a file pile that would reach a hundred and fifty miles high, from the surface of the Earth, into the ionosphere! Their computer can sort data at lightening speed and has applications in the oil industry for storing and sorting seismic information. They also control once secret remote sensing equipment capable of mapping the Earth's "underground formations", by which one assumes they are mapping Ley lines. The main concern was that the integration of the patents, resources and capabilities of mind control, into the huge Raytheon organisation could provide a total package for mind control of the populous. The Washington Post October 24-1994 and CBS News, Feb. 26-1995 covered a story on E-systems, which was said to be operating in the "black world". Independent scientists who have looked at the HAARP package technology and patents refer to it as "suicidal", the possibilities for catastrophe include runaway chain electrical effects in the ionosphere with unknown outcome, to the *complete breakdown of the Earth's Magnetic Field*. This is continued in *Alternative 4*, where at the time I pursued the idea of mind control of the populous; but here there are several important new comments I have to make, now that research has progressed (a reason I refer to my research as "Working Report" – no stuck viewpoints in my Universe!) Now the question becomes are the men in charge here dramatizing the past or not? If they are dramatizing and therefore by definition insane as they are stuck in a past event, then indeed the end result of this project will cause some climatic catastrophe, if we are not already experiencing world-wide the disastrous climatic effects of their research or meddling with the Grid. One scientist who has looked at the programme has warned that it could only increase environmental temperature which he referred to as "insane" since the earth is already getting hotter: and perhaps that is the clue, along with a computer file that could easily store Grid memory in its entirety. If the patents allowed some technological way of channelling information or holographics from the UVG120 crystal by morphic resonance, then a very large computer system would be required to store that information. Further if it is generally accepted by the elite that there will be some form of catastrophe and that the entire mega-computer and its data banks must be saved, so that the elite next time can use it (after they return in their spaceship or 'Noah's Ark from the safe haven on Mars, the space station or wherever) then it certainly throws new light on that old mystery of how Noah could get two of every species of animal into his Ark: Surely the DNA master blueprint containing its complete survival data for the phylogenetic evolutionary line of all species was saved in a crystal or some such memory and downloaded after the first vine was planted and the elite proceeded with Act I again. Too fantastic? And that is the entire problem, in so far as man has been asleep for so long, that he has remained in the Stone Age. Further since there appears to be balance between centripetal (cooling) and centrifugal (heating) spin, then one wonders whether such meddling is the real factor behind global warming, rather than the emissions storyline, which although it undoubtedly contributes is very definitely not the entire story. Certainly those who carried out the first World Survey of land formations (and Ley lines?) appeared to have some map already and which the tribe of Judah and the Adamites held no doubt. I remember one scientist in the *Alternative 3* book who spoke of a scientist colleague who had disappeared to work on a secret programme, that was evidently the Mars Noah's Ark project: the scientist remarked how his colleague had looked at his remaining colleagues with "a sense of pity", before leaving. No doubt the world's sorcerer's apprentices are sold on the idea, that the whole thing is inevitable and it is better to save a" chosen few" and the Grid data banks or the "Universal Mind" as it is evidently sold to scientists as, rather than leave nothing for humanity the next time round. Cunning fellow is number "666". What the lackeys of the One World Order fail to even see, is that the sorcerer has linked them to him with a thousand and one strings, that will on a karmic level tie them to him for all eternity and eventually they will return to the sorcerer's dark age; they simply will not be able to get past the trap.

Obviously the format of Walker's account indicates that the Atlanteans were not a bad lot, this however does not tie up with other data I have given and the records of sacrifice, cannibalism and despotic King's, atomic war and the Indian epics of the "Lords of the Storm". No doubt in the last cycle it all looked pretty normal and nothing seemed amiss apart from the usual scene of Planet Earth (war, poverty, injustice, murder, crime etc) and certainly that point may be born out by the advanced levels of Scientology, which I will come to shortly. Neither should one forget that Earth is moving through space and it is impossible to say whether the Grid pattern is merely as I have stated previously, a pattern of holographics relating solely to the Planet Earth, or whether as Earth moves through different space boundaries, that the crystal does not pick up information left by other planets as they too travel through space i.e. do we travel through holographics left by other beings on other Planets as they precede us? Is the information or holographics a complex mix of events e.g. the Atlanteans may have been in existence at a certain time, but what if any, space boundary holographics became mixed with those event holographics? Are we looking purely at Atlantean achievement, or is this an achievement elsewhere? Superimposed in the astral reading or channelling session, with the Atlanteans. This obviously is a question we need to be aware of. Certainly those secret groups who believe they are descended from Atlanteans, justify their right to hold on to the hidden science, presumably for the reason that they believe it is rightfully theirs as Guardians and Masters and perhaps man will never understand their minds, but I am afraid they are ice-cold when it comes to conscience or right and wrong. The Grid you see and its 'script' is merely a holographic recording of events and the phylogenetic line of animals. Animals do not have a conscience, which might be reflected in politics today where few if any politicians resign over conscience and an admission of right and wrong and if that included their failure to adhere to their job description of *representing the will of the people*, then in the case of European Union and a One World Order, there would have to be mass resignations or at least a referendum as I required based on my Petition to The House of Commons (parliament) in the UK in 1997, but with ALLTHE FACTS ON THE TABLE and until man demands the TRUTH and is no longer prepared to sit in the audience, the theatre will continue.

THOUGHT IMPRINTS OR IMPLANTS?

All matter is energy patterns of sub-atomic relationships and interconnections. All objects have a natural harmonious vibratory frequency and a disharmonious frequency when they are made to vibrate at dissonant frequencies. Relativity theory considers the physical universe as a four-dimensional 'space-time' continuum', where movement (spatial relationships) and time (change of position relative to a specific 'frame of reference') are integrally connected. Harmony and disharmony are created via the nature of the movement of energy at the sub-atomic level and a crystal is unique, in so far as it is solid matter in which all the atoms and molecules are *ordered and structured*. If there were a master pattern in space, then a crystal would be an ideal way to ensure a harmonious pattern. For example crystals of sea salt contain molecules of sodium chloride fitted together in the most harmonious way possible, which ultimately is represented by a cube. Further the more perfect the crystalline structure, the more perfect its transparency. You may rember that in one ancient myth of the Atlanteans, it spoke of the "house of transparent walls". Further you may remember that an odd metal cube millions of years old was found with that curious convex shape resembling the 'umbrella' in Palaeolithic cave paintings. The implication perhaps is that the cube as crystal could store the information from the Grid?

In the above account, we were told that the Atlanteans used crystals as their source of power and this is because the energy within matter is enormous. Einstein's formula states that the energy available is equal to the mass times the square of the speed of transmission of electromagnetic radiation. Crystals can be made to emit light and electricity, but to do so an external source of energy has to be applied. This might give some indication of the ancient Egyptian pictures showing curious boxes of an electrical type nature. These devices may have been something akin to a solid- state light emitter, whereby a charge is applied to a crystal in some way and then the charge is slowly released as visible light. If the sub-atomic kinetic energy could be released as kinetic energy, then you could in theory obtain a crystal-powered motor. It is conceivable that warnings in the UFO witness accounts with regard to nuclear energy, are part of a memory, where nuclear explosions or nuclear power stations were used to transform 'solid' matter into other forms of energy (heat, electricity, etc.), which was in some way applied to crystal research or technology in Atlantean times.

In Bruce Cathie's book *The Bridge to Infinity*, Cathie asked what was the true purpose of the geometric pattern of gigantic stones at Stonehenge in the UK, said to be at least thirty-five centuries old and built by the Druids. Whilst I have quoted other research which indicates that it was a solar-lunar observatory and an Apollonian temple, in Cathie's book, *Harmonic 695*, he suggested the probability that Stonehenge could have been designed as a gigantic crystal set - a massive geometric device constructed in ancient times to serve as a transmitter and receiver of signals from the heavens. Cathie discovered that the stone complex was constructed to the unified harmonics associated with the equations he had discovered in his research. In conclusion Cathie showed that Stonehenge was constructed on a position, which harmonises with the gravitational forces of the unified fields of the Earth. Cathie asks: "How could this possibly be so, unless the construction and positioning were carried out with the help of extremely advanced mathematical and technical knowledge at the time? We are just rediscovering this knowledge which was known to our ancestors".

One might consider the possibility that holographs of nuclear explosions that some UFO witness accounts speak of, might be thought forms imprinted at the time of the past event. The number of UFO witness accounts generally increased in number during the period 1950-1980, which might be an effect of the increasing number of nuclear detonations, which has now exceeded 2000! A disturbance of the holographic patterning of the crystal may have occurred, with the result that more witnesses became aware of these holographics, with their mind acting as dipole-radio receivers or by interconnection with the Grid by morphic resonance, according to the 'Onion-Ring' model. One cannot dismiss the possibility that whilst morphogenetic fields exert a subtle but all controlling pattern on our physical genetic body, that the existence of holographics of past events and thought does not also subtly but uniform ally direct our thinking, behaviour and even events themselves *in present time*, creating in those 'tuned-in' to the Grid a whole series of dramatizations or repeat scenarios from the past; rather like hypnotic suggestion. It would seem that as the survival of the individual is depressed by environmental and social factors, then the harmonic of the biofield plays a different tune or resonates at a lower frequency of energy more comparable to matter itself. This would suggest that the tri-partite biofield that surrounded the growing embryo and the body as it formed and which still remains in the seven-layered auric biofield, is governed by the Grid master blueprint and would in such times of low survival pass control to the Grid or at least set up a two way transmitter and receiver link, with the onset of Grid survival blueprint behaviour and biochemistry within the body.

The so-called primitive mind or in Ron Hubbard's terminology the reactive mind, must have a mechanism along these lines. Some time ago, I had a computer programme, which I used to research the effect of thought on the human biofield. Contact pads were placed on the person's palms at specific energy points and the overall human aura or biofield was projected onto the computer screen. The person was then asked to remember a very nice experience and a time when they were happy. Most people felt stunned to see their biofield change and become more balanced in the overall egg-shape as their *thoughts immediately altered the shape and the colour of the biofield.* Conversely inharmonious thoughts had the opposite effect, curiously providing an imbalance on the right and left sides of the biofield, thus affecting polarity and duality and mirror image halves of the biofield. Thus thought can interact with the biofield and create morphogenetic resonance and is analogous to energetic resonance in a further respect; it takes place between vibrating systems, atoms, molecules, crystals, organelles, cells, tissues, organs and organisms themselves. All these parts of the whole are made up of ceaseless oscillation and all have their own characteristic patterns of vibration and natural rhythm. The morphic units are dynamic, not static. Thought cannot be separated from the interweaving web or pattern.

Rational or analytical thought operates at a much higher frequency than reactive morphogenetic (body) thought, thus the interplay of vibrational or resonant energies will determine the overall resonance and shape of the human biofield. Reactive thought or so-called primitive mind thought has a range of behaviour and biochemistry that deteriorates on a scale in proportion to the perceived threat against survival. At these low levels the individual starts to look at his holographic bank of pictures of the PAST and at this point he is **dramatizing**: he merely *brings forward into present time his pictures from the past* and plays them out in present time, unable to distinguish that he is really playing a past game. The individual can in this manner descend from neurotic to psychotic, displaying the full range of behaviour, biochemistry and thought on a descending scale. The vast number of people live in the neurotic band and are dramatizing a past event, although they will be the first people to insist they are sane, their behaviour dictates otherwise. This evidently must have some survival value for the individual, in so far as he obsessively sorts through his past pictures and holograms for a similar case file to the current threat of survival, evidently looking for a solution. Ron Hubbard used the term **"re-stimulation"** for an incident in *present time*, that would trigger a descent of the emotional scale to the point when a *past* **"engram"**, as he termed it would "key in". For example, when you were five years old a dog attacked you and bites you badly on the leg. At this point the analytical mind would shut off recording and the entire event would be recorded by the reactive mind. After the event is over, the analytical mind cuts back in and continues to record as the individual comes back up the emotional scale from fear or terror, but remembers little about the incident, since it was not recorded by the analytical mind. Although the analytical file or 'cinematic reel' now has a portion with no pictures or memories on it, the memories or engram is still there, but it is recorded in the reactive mind 'cinematographic reel', which according to Hubbard could be cleared of all engrams or pictures; which otherwise have the power to *subconsciously direct your thinking and behaviour in the future* (dramatization). In the case of the child bitten by the dog, then later in life, there may come a time when a dog approaches and the person will irrationally go into fear, the dog is the **restimulator** and the same emotions that were felt at the time of the attack when they were five will come back into play, together with a recapitulation of the physical injury i.e. they might feel a slight pain in their leg in the place of the old injury where the dog bit them originally. Engrams contain moments of loss, pain or unconsciousness and thus they are pictures of times of bereavement, accidents, operations, times of distress, death or shock etc. Engrams also contain *all words spoken* in the incident and a great many more perceptions such as position of the body, sight, taste, smell and the words that are spoken can remain as **command phrases** that direct the individual long after the incident has passed. For instance someone might say at the time of the incident when the pictures are being recorded in the reactive or primitive mind: "She will never be able to walk again" and sure enough they may indeed have trouble walking after the accident, even though there is no physical reason that would prevent them from doing so. The command phrase has been recorded in the reactive subconscious mind and although the person later will have no conscious memory of it, as it was not recorded in the conscious analytical mind, the engram persists and the phrase will still have command control in present time and can direct physical and mental well being. The Scientologists insist that during times such as childbirth and accidents, that no one speaks for this reason. Hubbard made no mention of the Grid in his treatise: *Dianetics The Modern Science of Mental Health* and there was no indication of any connection of the reactive mind with the etheric pattern (to my knowledge).

Hubbard presents a very accurate picture of the way in which the mind works, however there are some important connections here I would maintain, particularly the mechanism whereby the reactive mind must connect with the UVG120 sphere or crystal, the morphogenetic bioplasma or holographic pattern for *survival of the species*. Hubbard placed a great deal of emphasis on survival in his work and placed this in the context of goals and the so-called "dynamics" which are a scale of goals relating to survival e.g. the first dynamic is the goal of survival for self; and the second dynamic would be survival for the family; and the third dynamic was survival for the group etc. To my mind, it is a mistake to place too much attention on survival, since it becomes a method of tuning to the Grid, promoting self and/or group or Communistic thought, a form of battle mentality where the end justifies the unethical means of achieving that end. In fact then end is bound to be destructive. If the survival of an individual or group is suppressed enough, then they will drop to the level of self-survival on the lowest rung. In the case of the MRC, then since he is dramatizing his past and that past involved self and group survival (Adamites), then he brings that forward into present time and is still playing that game. He even uses the same old archetypal symbols and plays the game of Pope as with the Illuminatus Pope discussed previously, who was tapping an egg with a wand! The secret groups with their *hidden knowledge and ceremonies provide the restimulator* by presenting in present time, factors from the past and thus the individual in the secret group starts to dramatize that past and brings forward all the old goals and history. The MRC case is sick, but when he gets back into a secret group and restimulates himself he gets sicker. Having descended the scale (refer to Hubbard's *Chart of Human Evaluation*) he starts to exhibit a very low emotional and behavioural band, that would on Hubbard's extended chart register in the lowest bands of "controlling bodies" and on the Hubbard *Know to Mystery Scale,* I would have to place him at the level of mystery: "Mystery is the level of always pretending there's always something to know earlier than the mystery" (*Scientology Technical Dictionary*) The MRC case has evidently pulled scientists to this level in the anti-matter matter experiments. Hubbard stated: "In the general study of the world and its affairs, we find out that the only way you can make a slave... would be to develop a tremendous amount of mystery about what it's all about and then develop an overwhelming charge (emotional charge or energy) on the mystery line. Not only develop a mystery, but then sell it real good; sell some bogus answer to the mystery" (*Scientology A New Slant on Life*) and this might really cover not only the mystery of cancer, but of religion. The MRC case has developed mystery as a means of enslavement.

Further the MRC case is very directly in morphic resonance with the Grid (as is anyone when they fall in the emotional scale to anger, fear, grief, rage, apathy etc) and at this level they are directly controlled by the Grid and its *survival mechanisms*. The Grid or morphogenetic vortex, the mega computer for *survival of bodies*, does not possess ethics, since it is concerned with survival only of bodies not the ethics of survival, which come under a higher resonance of thought which is recorded in the analytical mind and thus imprinted as a higher grade of energy. The predictability of behaviour, emotion, attitudes, ethics and morals that Ron Hubbard catalogued in his *Chart of Human Evaluation* is remarkably accurate, since as the biofield energy resonates to a different tune on the cosmic keyboard at various levels of the cosmic scale, then the imprints or holographics appear in different auric layers. For example close your eyes and think of a happy moment and you will feel a very different effect within your body, than if you play the first part of Elgar's Concerto with chello, which will make your body quiver violently with emotion at the level of grief (which is the level of Cancer). It appears then, that incidents which cause these stronger emotions such as terror, fear and grief, will set into motion via morphic resonance the primitive or reactive mind and its control by the Grid; as a primitive survival pattern of behaviour and thought which dictates survival for self at the lowest level and the group at the highest level. This so-called primitive or reactive mind may be just the tri-partite biofield that was 'stamped' on the individual from the Grid master pattern, which thus still remains connected to the Grid. The biofield of the body if you like, will continue to monitor and store information on everything that happens to a body and will further be directed by the Grid master blueprint survival mechanisms. Thus the **behaviour** that Hubbard recorded on the *Chart of Human Evaluation* in the lower bands of survival with its corresponding emotional levels may merely be a biofeedback survival or inherent behavioural mechanism from the Grid. For example a person goes into fear or grief and this via morphic resonance vibrates the body tri-partite biofield, with a recording of all the holographs in the environment, which causes that level of non-survival. The tri-partite biofield then transmits this information again by morphic resonance to the Grid or mega computer, which then installs or sets in motion the **behavioural survival pattern** that, has evolved over millions of years to ensure the **survival of the body or phylogenetic line**. The person may experience anger in relation to their environment and the cause of the threat, which will activate survival behaviour of the phylogenetic line requiring the animal to either fight back or run away (the primitive 'fright and flight' response) if the threat of non-survival is too great. Man however is not an animal, thus he considers his options to the threat and thinks about it: he does not run away *or* fight, since both actions may have *ethical* consequences (mortgages, care of offspring, imprisonment for assault, etc) thus he continues to remain in his threatening environment and eventually descends to apathy and becomes ill. You will find cancer on this scale at deepest grief. The MRC case feels continually under threat from his past memory of a significant cataclysmic event and thus whilst operating in the lowest levels of the scale which dictates his behaviour, he dramatizes that past event thus precipitating the event itself in the future by his present actions. It is said that: 'he who controls the past, controls the present and he who controls the present controls the future'. The reason why one should always insist on truth, ethics and justice is that it is not Grid behaviour and secret groups and the MRC case control the past and present, through unethical behaviour, lies and secrecy which they perceive as survival for themselves and their group (Adamites/Atlanteans).

Sometimes you listen to these people who may be political leaders and you wonder what planet they are on! You get weird ideas and policies such as the promotion of sexually abberative behaviour among the young; or throwing single mothers out to work (survival of the fittest) thus leaving the young to fall down the emotional scale on the subject of loss, who then become controlled by the Grid with its resultant behaviour, whilst politicians slam single mothers for their children's behaviour, emphasising the old datum you can't be in two places at once! Incidentally male teenage gangs form as a group, which is perceived as a survival mechanism and is thus common in teenagers from broken homes in the absence of *a protective male* leader of the group (family). The teenager who is fast becoming aware of the subject of survival, perceiving the weak go down and the strong and financially affluent survive (Darwinian politics) is placed under threat (usually economic) and falls down the emotional scale usually to the level of anger and by entering a group substitutes that for the protective male leader and falls prey to Grid survival behaviour. The group whose only concern becomes self and group survival, *enforces the resulting lack of reality* and even the most appalling crimes are seen as some aspect of group and self survival, where they dramatize past events in their own holographic memory banks coupled with Grid survival behaviour which does not contain ethics. The MRC case has made things such a mystery, that one can't see the wood for the Trees! I probably do not need to continue other than to compare the story of Planet Earth to Tales of Beelzebub to his Grandson - by the Philosopher Gurdjieff, where an alien visits Earth in a space ship called Karnak and wonders in awe at the goings on this Planet! And develops a sense of humour in psychological defence, at the unfolding Greek tragedy of mankind.

The function of thought compares to the function of a mind. The mind consists of holographics of experiences placed in consecutive order of time and date from the very beginning. Day 10 000 you did so and so and felt so and so and so and so was present, that sort of thing. "The mind is a communication and control system between the Spirit and his environment. The purpose of the mind is to pose and resolve problems relating to survival and to direct the effort of the organism according to these solutions". Hubbard's definition of the mind is continued as: "A natively self-determined computer which poses, observes and resolves problems to accomplish survival. It does its thinking with facsimiles of experience or facsimiles of synthetic experience"; and further: " the human mind is observer." (*Scientology Technical Dictionary*). I posed the theory that it was **the Spirit** who had in the first trillionth of a second after 'birth' in the firmament of an anti-matter matter explosion, become observation point through a duality and polarity in 'his' environment i.e. the polarity of matter and anti-matter. It seems likely to me, that the mind came into being at roughly the same time as an observational record of that duality and polarity, with anti-matter becoming observation point for the spirit when observing matter and matter becoming observation point for the Spirit when observing anti-matter. Thus in this way two observation points and two minds, the reactive and analytical may result from the duality and polarity that is inherent within our own thinking processes.

There is every reason then to assume, that thought must be part of the Grid holographics and survival of bodies or matter, since we still retain a memory of observation point *as matter* as we danced the dance of the firmament two and fro (between observation points) of matter and anti-matter. We might consider that the reason we became trapped as spirits on Earth or in the material Universe is our choice of becoming *observation point from the viewpoint of matter*. There may be a parallel Universe that has a point of view from anti-matter, which may look similar to this one, but would be a mirror image opposite in all ways including thought, where the survival of matter and bodies would be considered ludicrous. The mechanism of thought, is the perception of the present in comparison to the past on the basis of which, conclusions are made and this is the basis for action in the immediate or distant future. There is no doubt that Planet Earth was considered beautiful in the beginning and may have attracted a Spirit, since a Spirit loves aesthetics, however once here, the Spirit identified with matter and felt sorry for matter when he saw it decay (after all he could see the viewpoint of matter since once upon a time in the firmament he took the viewpoint of matter), thus becoming obsessive about survival of matter and bodies and the need to control the environment, Nature and the laws of Nature, forgetting that he could *as a Spirit* control and handle energy very easily by playing with it. This might give some indication of those amorphous creatures painted on the wall of caves in the Palaeolithic period, since goal of preserving and protecting matter and bodies may not yet have created solid mass and bodies. However, there is a price to be paid for the love affair with aesthetics on Planet Earth, since the sun has created a trap, within the Grid or crystal. The price of the experience of aesthetics (one would miss the plants and the colours of a sunset or sun rise dependent on the sun) is the Magnetic Reversal and the MRC case and control via the phylogenetic survival mechanisms developed and stored over many billions of years in the crystal lattice of the UVG 120 sphere. Such control has lead to a degradation of the Spirit, who is by definition self-determined. The hippies and bikers who nearly brought off a World Revolution in the 70's evidently tried to reach for this ancient soul memory of self-determinism as opposed to other-determined, which has raised its head again in the anti-Capitalist demonstrations which have descended the scale of behaviour from "peace and love", to war! There is also the question of *those* Semitic stones (matter), which were engraved, supposedly with the word of God. Now this is a peculiar conclusion is it not, but could the MRC case represent the viewpoint of matter and differ in some way from our choice trillions of years ago in the firmament, when we decided to take the viewpoint of anti-matter and he matter? Or did the people of Earth all decide to take the viewpoint of matter at some point which led them to Earth where the purpose here was to learn the viewpoint of matter in its entirety, before one could graduate back to a parallel Universe of anti-matter. Perhaps it is that the datum: 'your worst enemy is your teacher' is really a battle between anti-matter and matter or God and the Devil. Since man became enmeshed in matter, it was his destiny to fight the woman who was anti-matter.

The analytical mind sorts and classifies data at lightening speed, it has data banks, whereas the Spirit KNOWS and does not think, which is a lower grade of knowingness and certainty. I could say to you I KNOW this is how it works e.g. cancer and someone will reply "How do you know?" and you end up

513

producing reports and papers and books and lots of thinking to prove what you already knew. Thinking requires one to shuffle one's memory banks and holograms in order to apply the data to future action. If a man has spent lifetimes connected to www-com/grid mega computer, he effectively has little or no experience and his abilility to even think, is reduced where he no longer Knows *or* thinks, but must be told by another what to think. Newspapers get into this and encourage men to become sheep, which is perfectly fine with the Global Elite, who strive constantly to enslave man. There was no referendum on European Union, despite the propaganda that it did happen [145] and you can bet your Grid, that no paper would allow freedom of speech to put the Petition questions I posed on Europe!

Autmomatic writing which Madame Blavatsky employed to obtain information from the astral plane and channelling are very similar processes. Whether information is being pulled down from *actual Spiritual beings* on the astral plane, or whether information is merely being pulled from the Akashic Record or Grid holographic memory is a pertinent question. All secret groups in the past, who have a link with occult science, have referred to "Masters" and "Guardians" on the "astral plane", which is a rather too woolly term for me! Do they mean the Grid! Specific rituals in Cabalistic Science, such as those used by the black magician, Alister Crowley, were designed to set up a vibrating resonance or morphic resonance, which then channelled information to the receiver who psychically picks up that information, through either the mind acting as a dipole radio receiver, or morphic resonance of their biofield. The intelligence services including the CIA in the 1960's were obsessed with psychics and mediums and the occult, as was the Third Reich, presumably in an attempt to obtain past information and related technology. Whilst the pre-history of races was one interest, the prime interest would have been to make contact with the so-called "Masters", that occultists of the period believed were in the "etheric" layer. Alister Crowley was determined by his invocations to reach these Spirits. What is clear, is that thought from the "Masters", may have been on the same survival record as the morphogenetic bioplasma, since I have already explained that in periods of low survival, or in the case of those who live in the lowest bands of emotion and behaviour, then their thought including that of the MRC case is in direct resonance with the Grid or crystal itself. The crystal would only retain survivalist phylogenetic data relating to bodies. However thought is also recorded at this level and such thought will not be enlightened, but will come from past holograms and experience of *very low psychological cases* (perhaps the "earthbound spirits" that Hitler was warned not to communicate with).

Because it is mainly the Global Elite that imprinted onto this field, I have constantly warned people of the problem with using this knowledge and representing it as a "higher source". As Hitler was warned it is the "easy wins", that attract people, but such people who do this, are simply not prepared to look into their *own* soul memory, as such things take time and a great deal of soul development. One should remember that if one is to carry the Grail, it is a very grave responsibility for billions of souls are in jeopardy and one cannot afford to make a mistake, even from the point of view of self-survival and particularly one's own exit! I have never channelled any information and have had to go through the exhaustive! method of **personal soul memory and development**. Channelling and automatic writing, whereby the person goes into a sort of trance and develops a "vacant eye" and scribbles furiously from some invisible source in front of him; not only causes repeat cycles of destruction, but this knowledge can be very misleading and open one up for psychic attack. People who regularly channel information usually end up with a rather warped view of events, since it is a one sided (Global Elite) view that is being accessed in most cases. Thus knowledge may be obtained but it will have the inevitable MRC stamp. Further in channelling it requires a person of very high spiritual development if the information is to be *interpreted*. UFO witness reports, where the occupation/ experience of the witness determined the account of the event, but did not precipitate it, was evident in the report from an Air force technician, pilot and farmer. All experienced a natural UFO event, but the interpretation of that event depended on the ability of the witness to interpret the signals into holographic form and a story. For example how would one interpret a signal "Manna from above", a farmer might as in one true witness account talk of aliens giving him "cookies". For this reason the UFO experience has been considered nonsense and used by Government manipulators as propaganda in the dis-information field of media. However the reliable and coherent accounts of Air force pilots were always purposefully ignored.

Channelling information may represent the pulling down of holograsphics from the Grid or Akashic Record, in much the same way I believe the holographics of the UFO accounts are PAST EVENTS. "Space ships", " monsters with orange reptilian-like eyes shuffling with a semi-human bird form"; "small men with frog-like eyes"; are I believe all past components of events and part of an entire holograph in a consecutive 'cinematic reel' of phylogenetic and event data relating to Planet Earth. The reason why witnesses believe that these "aliens" belong to a future time or more advanced civilization, is that the pre-history on this Planet, has become a vast cover up and the UFO witness knows somewhere back of his mind that these aliens are from some advanced civilization, but *interprets* that as from elsewhere. The propaganda line is that Homo sapiens evolved from Ape-like men, with primitive societies and customs, with no high technology or advanced knowledge, which was probably only true for Neanderthal man or the men who were not descended from Adam or Noah initially. Truth has been difficult to prove, since the few remaining artefacts curiously disappear from archaeological collections and faced with the power of the Elite to control education, museums, media and research; it becomes a very uphill struggle for the independent researcher. However, if channelling, automatic writing and the Natural UFO experience is a glimpse of past history or pre-history, then one should be very careful with the associated thoughts of the period. The Atlanteans were undoubtedly clever and one might even argue that their continual preservation of Grid memory in the various cycles has actually saved them from total insanity along with mankind, but their thoughts are recounted in many documents as precursors of their **actions.** Cannibalism (becoming other bodies) war (destroying bodies) One World Order (controlling bodies) Religion (mind and body control) genetic manipulation and cloning (controlling bodies) Secrecy (hiding from minds and bodies) and so the list goes on.

Another complication in channelling, automatic writing or astral vision as some people refer to it, is the 'cutting and splicing ' and remix of the original event. This phenomenon in biology is known in the process of cell division, where the chromosomes with their genes as the hereditary material separate and then re-combine. This process allows for the production of new types of species. Thus if the sequence of genes along a chromosome went A B C D E F to make a product; after splicing it might become A B (B) D E F which is a completely different product with B spliced in or added, which is one method. By analogy this is similar to editing of cinematographic reels. Watson and Crick at Cambridge put forward a model for DNA on the basis of prior research including X-ray diffraction data (completed by an unacknowledged woman as I understand it who died of grief - cancer) where the DNA molecule was envisaged as a kind of twisted ladder, or technically the hyperbolic spiral. The two upright chains consisting of alternating sugar and phosphate groups, the rungs as pairs of bases sticking inwards towards each other and linked up in a specific relationship: A with T and C with G (A= Adenine; T= Thiamine; C= Cytosine; G= Guanine). The only satisfactory arrangement developed by trial and error, was to have the two chains running in opposite directions, and the bases linked A with T and C with G by hydrogen bonds. The overall shape of the molecular model of DNA then is the hyperbolic spiral, with the two threads running in parallel but opposite directions. (*Fig.30*). I have already referred to the transmission and receiver properties of DNA and Dumitrescu in developing a mechanical model transceiver produced a diagram which looks similar to the DNA macromolecule (*Fig.40*) Further the x-ray diffraction pattern for DNA, shows the vortex organisation (*Fig.41*), which mirrors the torroidal morphogenetic bioplasma I proposed in the mechanism of the UFO phenomenon i.e. 'The Onion-Ring Model', for the way in which information is transferred from the Akashic Record or morphogenetic bioplasma to the biofield of man, utilising transmission and receiver properties of DNA and morphic resonance. The appearance of DNA type patterns of Crop Circles further curiously poses the question of whether the morphogentic bioplasma Vortex exhibits a structural electro-magnetic organisation similar to the physical DNA.

Gene mutations, although often expressed in visible characteristics or physiological activities of the organism, are ultimately caused by rearrangement, addition or deletion of specific nitrogenous bases in the DNA. Changes in the order of the bases will result in modifications in the polypeptide chain produced under the control of the gene, and these modifications will result in production of a modified enzyme (or other protein) or suppression of some enzyme (or protein) feature. The modified (mutant) enzyme may ultimately express itself by affecting a change in the physiology or development of the organism. Thus the ALTERATION OF ARRANGEMENT OF SEQUENTIAL DATA (genes or units of information as bases within the genes) ALLOWS FOR VARIATION AND EVOLUTION. This is an important point since Evolution is based upon genetic variation and changes in gene frequency. The ultimate source of all genetic variation is mutation, whether produced by changes in the molecular arrangement of genes, in the linear sequence of the genes on the chromosome axis, or in the number of chromosomes. The elemental evolutionary force of mutation may directly modify gene frequency by recurrent mutation of a particular gene and produce evolutionary change. Recombination of data or genes acts to enhance the effects of mutation by assembling a broad spectrum of gene combinations. It modifies and intensifies the contribution of mutation, but cannot be regarded as an evolutionary force, since it never changes gene frequencies. Recombination looms in the evolutionary process because it provides the bulk of genetic variation that is worked upon by the forces of selection and genetic drift to produce evolutionary change. Mutation provides the source of variation, and recombination an effective agent for its spread through the population. Together they develop the genetic materials for evolution.

Whilst this process within the physical DNA at the level of the cell, is the mechanism by which new species are produced and other species evolve, I have already given the turbulent plasma vortex as the way in which energy is drawn down from the vacuum. As energy is 'sucked down' information from the morphogenetic bioplasma would be drawn down with it. The fact that this morphogentic field governs the early overall shape of the embryo and young does not pre-suppose that such a mechanism of overall control does not continue in some form which we have yet to recognise. I have proposed that the morphogenetic bioplasma is itself a hyperbolic spiral of twisted filaments, which may reflect the physical structure of the DNA molecule on the hermetic axiom of: 'as above, so below'. Whilst I have proposed a two stranded electro-magnetic coil on the basis of this axiom, we could suppose that information is

517

carried on those coils and a two way process of information as transmission (effect of the morphogenetic bioplasma holographs on physical DNA); and receiver (effect of DNA signal or holographs within the human biofield on the morphogenetic bioplasma), is in operation i.e. a biofeedback system. Further there is nothing to stop us further assuming that just as information within the genes can be altered by addition, deletion, or alteration of sequence mechanisms, that the Akashic Record or morphogentic bioplasma cannot be altered in the same manner.

Fig.40 *Schematic diagram of DNA as an electrical resonating circuit* (*Dumitrescu*)

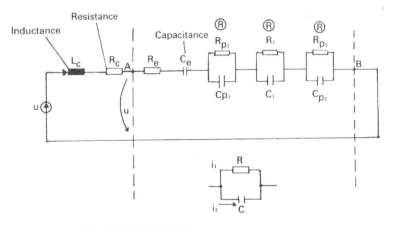

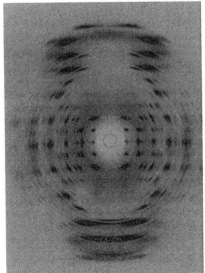

Fig.41 **An X-ray diffraction photograph of DNA**
(*Maurice Wilkins, King's College, London*)
Note the vortex helical patterning.

Let us suppose that the Akashic Record or morphogenetic bioplasma contains a complete survival record from the beginning, including events of pre-history right through the millennia up to the present time. Rather like a film reel with its story in an ordered sequence, covering events, history, evolutionary forms etc. That is how we might suppose the record is, but this

518

may not be the case. What for instance happens to the geometric pattern, the ordered sequence of events in holographic form and the electromagnetic coiling or patterning of energy within the torroidal morphogenetic bioplasma on which the holographs are imprinted during a Magnetic Reversal? Do the electromagnetic 'filaments' separate and then recombine in the chaos, as does the physical DNA in cell division? Do bits get spliced in and out of the 'cinema reel' of the 'library in the sky' and throw up a new record, where also now the receiver is the transmitter and transmitter is receiver according to alignment with new magnetic south and north pole axes of the Grid, with a different story and sequence? Thus, when the Magnetic Reversal is over, do the 'filaments' align up in the re-organised torroidal bioplasma *in opposite directions*? Do filaments break and rejoin thus recombining information and holograms such that now the record is no longer sequential? The story is still there, information and holograms are still there but now it requires an outside observation point to sort it, into logical and historical sequence, rather like placing cards in suit in a pack that has been thrown up in the air. Someone would need to have a memory from an *exterior viewpoint* on major events to now try to re-order the sequence. It might be impossible to get a full record from the beginning on Earth, but you might be able to get a full record from *after* the last Magnetic Reversal. In other words someone for instance from the time after the Flood would have had to be in every battle and front line world event, in order to keep track of what was going on. That memory is then retained in *their soul memory* and could be retrieved through past life regression. Thus the point here is that the Akashic Record might have all the information and probably does, but **the sequence** might have been altered in Magnetic Reversals.

Not only is sequence a problem, but dramatization also, the question arises 'Was it then, or is it now?' The Sixth Dynasty in Egypt had as their first monarch a man who was deified as a star god, and has been identified with the constellation of Orion. There was a revival of pre-dynastic cannibalistic rites where the blood of wounded warriors was drunk, so that their skill and bravery might be imparted to the drinkers. King Unas similarly feasts after death on the spirits, known at Heliopolis as the "fathers and mothers", and on the bodies of men and gods. The Druids also performed these sorts of rites. Obviously monarchies, Crete, Druids, sacrifice are all in the story line of history and pre-history and the story having been now occluded, depends on a high power of *observation and rationality* to piece it together. Further your own past lives *unless you are aware of them*, will inevitably decide how you piece that story together. If you carry a memory of being eaten! The restimulation of the story would reduce your power to observe and determine the sequential order and timing of the event. Many people unknown to themselves fight battles in present time, which are battles from the past. The battle has not changed (due to the MRC case) and therefore they confuse space and time and bring the old holograms up into present time.

As a point in example not only do most of the population dramatize past holographic events, but the MRC case is stuck in a Magnetic Reversal of some large magnitude.

It is certainly interesting that a process of natural selection acts upon the mutant genes produced in the physical DNA. The idea of natural selection as the guiding force of evolution was the principal contribution of Charles Darwin to evolutionary theory. Darwin's original concept of selection was somewhat unsophisticated and negative and was applicable to individuals rather than to populations, but his recognition of this essential principle provided the key to understanding the evolutionary process of body-lines. Darwin saw the process of evolution as a struggle for existence between individual organisms. Since all species produce many more offspring than survive, he concluded that the total environment eliminated those individuals least fitted for survival and encouraged the survival of the fittest. The environment thus acted as a selective force, sorting out those variants best adapted to the particular environmental circumstances. Natural selection favoured the features of an organism that brought it into a more efficient adaptive relationship with its environment, but overall Darwin saw the process of evolution as a struggle for existence between individual organisms. Thus you see those who curtail to the MRC case are in fact becoming weaker as spiritual beings, since it takes courage to fight the MRC case, but has great spiritual rewards (even though your body might be exhausted and your mind!). The lackeys of the MRC case and One World Order have taken the least path of resistance to the environment and for a very small pot of gold, sold their souls. Those who fight can expect a spiritual reward one day, as was promised, simply because they have been struggling up the ladder for a very long time and will make it out. Remember that your worst enemy is your best teacher! Thus applaud him for his ignorance and viciousness, for it is he that will remain here to harvest the fruits of his labours, whilst he gave you the chance of exit. I believe that many who have fought the World Order for a long time, the mature souls, are in a great deal of pain now and I feel this with a sense of great weariness at the lonely and long path trodden down many dark roads and perhaps this book is written for them, for I recognise that this story is now too complex for those who have lagged behind and been lazy for many lifetimes to understand. I have always believed in miracles though or postulates at tone 40! The end product of evolutionary change is the establishment of organisms that function more efficiently in a certain environmental situation than did their predecessors. Any characteristic that is advantageous to a particular organism or population is called an **adaptation**. The lungs of land vertebrates make possible gaseous exchange between these organisms and the air and are an adaptation for terrestrial life. Taking this beyond the body and applying it to the mind, one might perceive that the mind that has survived and contributed to the evolving mind (Universal Mind) is one that is best fitted to live in a society governed by the MRC case. Cold hard thinking, lies, sleaze, cutthroat business, no compassion, no feelings, no responsibility and dedication to **self**-surval (not even the group or Nation now) etc., pretty much describes the 'evolved' mind of Homo sapiens. As every-one knows if you value the reverse thinking you are doomed to become the victim of individuals, groups, society and the Western World, since you simply are not "On message" (read tuned into the Grid and the One World Order!).

The MRC case is stuck in a past incident, way back then, where he preyed on Homo sapiens and desired a slave-species. He felt himself superior and elitist and could only remain so, by denying others what truth and knowledge there was, which ensured his own power. Secrecy then, became an adaptive mechanism, which ensured the survival of the MRC case, the Elite. Man became dumber and the Elite became smarter. Thus Homo sapiens was not unique in his position as a spiritual being in Homo sapiens body, in so far as the mind became the principle factor in natural selection and adaptation and as such the Elite sought to control every facet of that mind, through media, publishing and mind control. It is certainly predictable that the MRC case would refuse to let a Cancer patient know the mechanism of the mind I gave in my cancer research, it is also predictable that the MRC case sought to control the mind of man through drugs, television, media and now in the UK by denying those from poorer backgrounds the opportunity to go to University (by withdrawal of the grant system) and where rich and poor experience two levels of health care and even justice where the poor find it increasingly difficult to obtain justice without the means to pay. As the karma stacks up on the Elite who run things, they will find it impossible to ever leave this Planet even if they do manage to avoid a Magnetic Reversal. The idea of Lamarkian evolution where e.g. the giraffe KNEW it had to grow its neck in order to survive, *may* not describe the evolution of the body or the phylogenetic line, which is perhaps more accurately described by Darwinian theory, but it does cover the evolution of the mind!

The idea of hidden Masters and their communication to an elite priesthood is evidently one held at least by The Rosicrucian's. Madame Blavatsky, Alister Crowley and many more who had a profound effect within the secret groups on the course of humanity and who regularly relied on communications from the astral plane, from the so-called "Masters". Were these really Masters? or was this really communication with the past thoughts retained on the Akashic Record? Unfortunately it was usually the Theocratic Priesthood who held onto the secret Cabalistic rites, dating back at least to the biblical Patriarchs and thus the Grid or record has been effectively the prerogative of the MRC case for billions of years, I would be very wary about taking anything from this and viewing it as wisdom. But let me give you an example of how beguiling the information is. The problem is, that one does gain invaluable technical and event data, which I am sure the Intelligence Services, recognised, such as the Atlantean crystals, but the thoughts are very confusing.

I will take just a few extracts from Reverend Vale Owen's book: *Life Beyond the Veil*, which was alleged to be channelled information from "souls who had left their physical bodies and were residing in the astral region": The manuscript is published in four volumes with an introduction by Sir Arthur Conan Doyle and a forward by Lord Northcliffe. In the entry for Wednesday, October 8th, 1913 it reads:

> "Because of certain matters which are of importance to those who would understand our meaning in its inner sense, we have decided to endeavour tonight to give you some instruction which will be of help and guidance when dealing with those things which lie beneath the surface of things, and which are usually not taken into account by the ordinary mind. One of these is the aspect, which *thoughts wear when projected from your sphere to ours.* Thoughts that are good appear with a luminance, which is absent from those of a less holy kind. This luminance appears *to issue from the form of the thinker*, and by means of its manifold rays of divided colours, we are able to come at some knowledge as to his spiritual state, not alone as to whether his state is of the light or of the darkness, and of what degree in light, but also of the points in which he excels or comes short in any direction. But thoughts, which are the *effect of spirit action*, are seen in the effect they, in their turn, *produce on the environment of the thinker*, and not only are seen, but felt, or sensed, by us in a more accurate and intense way than with you." (*Author's emphasis*)

Owen could have accessed some secret group mind of the past, by the process of morphic resonance. There may also be *personal interpretation*, in this case a Reverend described by Lord Northcliffe as "a man of sincerity and conviction", is likely to interpret information based on his own "form" or character. Alister Crowley sought Spirits who were occult black magicians or high adepts and himself claimed to be the Re-incarnation of Eliphas Levi, a prominent member of the secret societies, well versed in the One World Order plan, thus his interpretation of data based upon past life knowledge and character would be very different. Neither can one be sure that the Reverend was not picking up his own past life thought identities, again by the process of morphic resonance and mingling that with past events into a coherent story line pattern. To continue with the Reverend's channelling:

> "It seems that before the *students* are able to *progress* much in the *science of creation* as studied in this region, they have to get a thorough

knowledge of the *fundamental elements* with which they have to deal. This is of course quite natural. As the *learners progress* they are able gradually to achieve the result they wish *without the scientific apparatus which at first is necessary.* One instrument after another is left out until at length they are able to depend solely on *their will.* We asked our guide to what practical purpose the knowledge was put when acquired. He replied that the first use was the *training of the mind and will* of the student. That training was very excellent and very strenuous." (*Author's emphasis*)

We know that the analytical mind computes and sorts data at lightening speed, thus if the holographs impinging on the psychic or channeller are for example the words or phrases emphasised above, then the analytical mind may fill in the gaps at lightening speed, giving the a*pparanc*y of continuous speech from a spirit. Thus a series of holographs, may take on the *persona* of a spirit in actual conversation with the channeller. If a physicist had channelled this information, he might have come up with a University for teaching atomic physics. A yogi might have explained it in terms of mind control over matter. My own first impression, is that this sounds like some early Druid University (as you realise I am a realist!) Well certainly one can imagine that initiates into secret groups in the past may have undergone such procedures as part of their initiation and training. These sorts of exercises undoubtedly would imprint on what I term the morphogenetic bioplasma since obviously matter is involved and the morphogentic bioplasma is concerned with survival of bodies and matter. The MRC case and the Elite have always concerned themselves with the hidden science and control of atomic physics, thus all thought imprints would come from this type of mind. It is perhaps the case when technology is sought, that in channelling this data, it has appeared that there are "Masters" or "Guardians" with superior knowledge in the so-called "astral plane". The transmission dated October 9th 1913 is interesting:

"Perhaps if we endeavour to *enlighten* you on the *chemistry* of the *heavenly bodies* it may be both interesting and helpful to you. We do not mean the physical aspect of the science, as understood by modern *astronomical scientists*, but the *deeper study* of their *constitution.* Every *star*, as you know, is itself a centre of a system which comprises in itself not only the *planets in revolution* round the star, but also the *particles of matter* which suffuse that system, but are too sublimated to be cognised by any system of chemistry which is possible to those who dwell in *physical bodies*, and in their research are compelled to use both material instruments and material brains. These *particles* are *between* the purely *material and spiritual*, and indeed may be used both in the physical and the spiritual economies. For *the two* are merely two of many phases *of one* progressive economy, and *act and react each on the other*, like a sun and his planet. *Gravitation* is applicable to these particles also on both sides and it is by means of this force - as we call it, as being a name you know, and also a very little understand - that we cohere these *particles together* and are able, from time to time, so to clothe our spiritual bodies as to *become visible* to the photographic plate, and sometimes to the human eye."

Again we are talking about atoms and possibly anti-matter and matter. Further concerning energy:

"Dear friend and ward, I will tonight speak to you of certain matters which connect with the question of *transmutation* of energy. *Energy*, as I now employ the word, is to be understood as t h a t intermediary which couples up the motion of *will* with the effect as displayed to the minds of men. We here are trained to this end that we may, by motion of our wills, *transmit, by* what we may call *vibration*, our *thoughts* through the intervening spheres, or states, *into the earth plane*. It is this movement in vibration, which I call energy. Now, you must understand that in using earth phrasing I am employing a medium, which is not adequate to express, either exactly or fully, the *science* of these spheres and realms. It is necessary, therefore, that I qualify my terms, and when I use the term vibration I do not speak merely of *oscillation to and fro* alone, but of movements which are sometimes *elliptical*, sometimes *spiral*, and sometimes a combination of these and other qualities. From this point of view the *atomic system* of *vibration*, which has but of late been revealed to men of science, is to us *one* with the *movements* of the *planets* of this solar sphere, and of other systems far away in space." (*Author's emphasis*)

Quite plainly here, there is information regarding the energy in the atom and energetic movement of planets and stars are described as being part of vibrations or energy patterns. Interestingly though this information is interdispersed with data from present time, which the channeller may insert from his own experience and this certainly gives the *impression of a present time* conversation with some spirit. The point being, that channelled information must pass through the mind of the channeller first and thus as we would say in science, there is a variable in the system. However importantly, we are told here that thoughts do impinge from the astral world or I propose the Akashich Record or morphopgenetic bioplasma onto Earth and more importantly into the mind of Homo sapiens! I will tell you that no higher Spirit would EVER seek to covertly control anyone's mind and thus the assumption that this conversation is one from a higher wisdom or spirit is immediately suspect. The next transmission gives a very definite indication of the Energy Grid or www-com/grid. Further you will notice the mention of "Prince", again making the conversation more probable as part of a past holographics of the UVG120 sphere or crystal.

The next day, December 3rd, 1913, the communication was continued:

"I once observed a very beautiful instance of the *transmutation of energy* here in my own land. There was a company of *visitors* from *another sphere*, and they were about to return to their own, their mission having been finished. A part of our own, of whom I was one, went with them to the *large lake* over which they had come to us. Here they embarked in *boats* and were giving us their *parting* words of thanks and goodwill, when one of our *Princes*, was seen approaching with a *company of attendants* behind us. They *came through the air* and *hovered* above us and the boats while we, knowing their habits, but not their present intention, waited to see what manner or thing they - or rather*, he*, had in his mind to do. For it is a delight in these realms to give pleasure, each to other, by exercising such *powers* as we possess, and that in varying combinations by which effects are differently produced. Far up in the heavens we saw them, as they moved slowly, circling about the Prince from whom to those in circle went *threads of vibrations* of *different quality*, and so of *different colour*. These, he of his will sent forth, and those his subordinates *wove* them into a *network* of curious design and very beautiful; and where *two threads crossed*, there the *intensified light* shone like a *stone* of brilliant hue. And the *knots* were of *many colours* owing to the varying *combination of threads* entering into their *construction*. When this was complete *the circle* widened out and drew away and left their *Prince* alone in the midst. And he held *the net* by *its middle* in his hand and it floated out around him like a *many-coloured spider web*" (The Grid) "it was very beautiful" (The MRC case loves it, because its a control mechanism for matter) "Now, that *net* was really *a system of many qualities of vibrations woven together*" (vacuum energies, species data)." He loosed it out of his hand and it began slowly to sink as he *rose through it*, until it was level with his feet. Then he raised his hands and *descended with it*. And as he came he looked through the net at the *boats* below; and he made slow movements with his hands in their direction. Then they *began to move on the water as of themselves*" (vortex motion) "and so continued until they *floated in a circle*. Then the *net descended and settled over them*, and we saw that they were *all within its circumference*, and also that, as it lighted on them, they passed through it and it sank and rested upon the water. Then the Prince, standing on the net and on the water, in the midst of the boats, waved his hand in greeting to them" (modification via the biblical slant of channeller? -

walking on water) "and the net slowly arose from the water, lifting the boats with it, and floated upward into the air" (Grid anti-gravity anomalies?)

"So away over the lake they went together and the company of our sphere closed in around them, and sent up a song of Godspeed as they floated away towards the horizon over the lake. It was merely one of those little tokens of love, which we here delight to show our *brethren* of *other spheres* of labour- nothing more. My reason for relating this- which was, in display, much more beautiful than I am able to show you in writing - was to illustrate the effect of the will of a powerful *Angel Lord* " (Christian modification of channeller) " concentrated on the forces to hand and *transmuting* them in quality. Beauty is not alone the minister of pleasure to the sight. It is rather a characteristic of these realms" (Heaven - and modification by channeler) "For beauty and *utility* go together here. And the *more useful a man* (usury!) becomes the more beautiful is he in person (clear indication to the thinking of the MRC case!) The beauty of holiness is literal and real, friend; and it were well if all men could accept that truth".

I will leave it to you to perceive the key words and their true history as I give it in this book. The important point, is that you here have a glimpse of key thoughts and holograms retained on the Grid and the mind of the MRC who perceives the Grid as something beautiful since it allows him to use humanity and judge a man on how useful he is to the MRC's own self survival. Quite a different story from the minister's!

ONE-NESS

When the American President George Bush in the 1980's let slip the future form of Government, by referring to the "One World Order", he was merely stamping his approval on the plan which had existed at least since the time of The French Revolution and as I claim here and in prior works, a plan that was in evidence in Minoan Crete in the Bronze Age and even as far back as the Stone Age. In fact as we have noted, such a plan was evident at the time of Babel in the immediate post Flood era. The One-ness was also to become part of scientific thinking, where the Holistic Paradigm - the interconnectedness of all things, was becoming recognised in the holistic field of healing and self -help groups. We are all the one big happy Communistic family sort of idea, with the notion that one religion, one political system, one monetary system etc. was all part of the great big One-ness. This of course is a very good propaganda line for Communism, where those who can still think standing on their feet, are labelled 'dissidents' and hauled off to brainwashing centres to get "on message" - and believe you me, it will happen in Europe! As we watch Democracy, the freedom of speech, the freedom to protest and the right to ask questions (my own Petition and books) denied, then this is the Marxist reality of the One-ness. No-one is allowed to be different, except the Elite rich at the top and they never follow what they preach to the masses, as we all know and observe as one sleaze episode after another is divulged. The Grid and its thinking is programmed for mass species survival and the individual is neither here nor there.

The fascination with beehives and the one controlling signal at the top goes back to Greece, where the Omphalos a rounded dome - shaped structure covered in relief with bees, represented the navel or womb of the World. Such a structure was also found in England. The curious idea that has developed, is that at some point in mystical development everybody becomes "one". The idea that some fountainhead of knowledge, wisdom or Masters connected the billions of clone-like individuals we call humanity. If you took my own theory of anti-matter and matter explosion as the starting point of the Universe, then before "go" in the beginning we were all just potential, but after "go", we were all *individuals*, with our own potential only realised through *experience* and just how hard we were prepared to work at that experience, since wisdom can only come through that. Thus in the first trillionth of a second after "go", we were individuals and on our own. How can you possibly unite and become One with the anti-matter, matter explosion or the act of creation? You cannot go back only forward. "God" often comes into the equation at this point i.e. Creation and people start talking about "fusing with the Godhead" - what on Earth does that suppose to mean! It is just another One-ness. One can in my opinion only keep expanding and evolving along with the Universe, maintaining the balance that was intended from the start. There is a hierarchy, but not in the vicinity of Earth and I should think they would laugh at any fusion with them! Every Spirit had their own viewpoint or observation point at the beginning in the matter and anti-matter explosion, which may or may not be identical for all Spirits, but the experience of the individual Spirit after that point, is very much unique. A Spirit has his own holographics of his entire existence and no two 'photo albums' are identical.

The new so-called reality that emerged in Western Science in the 80's termed the **Holistic Paradigm**, perceived the inherent connectivity or One-ness of seemingly separate objects. This was as an idea perfectly in tune, with the recognition that there was an energy pattern. However, psychology jumped onto the One-ness bandwagon to claim that consciousness and our thoughts were directly interactive with each other, thus giving birth to the idea of the Universal Mind. This was not a new idea, in so far as telepathy had covered much the same idea and was known to occur. The Holistic Paradigm ("holistic" means whole; "paradigm" means pattern of belief); became the new religion, which just co-incidentally paralleled the coming idea of the 'new' One World Order! Here we have the secret groups shuffling the mind of man around his chessboard again, introducing ideas which he brainwashes man with, through his agents working through available research organisations. This certainly appealed to those who were trying to spiritualise science through the development of esoteric spiritual philosophies, such as Zen Buddhism, Taoism, and Hinduism. This however merely connected man to the Grid, with its one-ness for the survival of *bodylines* and phylogenetic survival mechanisms. The Freedom Movement created in the 70's by the students, who sought to challenge the Elite, was high jacked by the One World Order and USED for their own purposes, transposing freedom for One-ness and   www-com/grid.

At the turn of the Century, quantum mechanics opened up new avenues of advance into the theory of the Holistic Paradigm. Plank and Einstein quantized the radiation field giving birth to the photon and Bohr, de Broglie and Schrodinger proposed quantized energy or "standing waves" for the electron to explain atomic stability. The probability waves described by new equations, gave rise to the idea of non-local interactions between atoms. Quantum mechanics appeared to throw up other paradoxes in the famous so-called 'two-slit' experiment, which showed that an elementary particle could exert wave or particle behaviour depending on the detection apparatus. This behaviour appears to be determined by the mere *act of observation*, which led the scientist to conclude that his mere presence in the experiment and his mind, had some deterministic effect on the outcome - man was part of the pattern. In the 1950's Everett introduced the idea that all systems, even the entire Universe, are ultimately quantum mechanical in their nature and tried to bypass the tricky question of what happens when you try to measure or *observe* a quantum mechanical event, with the subsequent collapse of the wave function; by proposing an infinite number of three-dimensional Universes coexisting simultaneously, which can influence each other through probalistic wave coupling. In his model, he proposed that our consciousness weaves a path through these many Universes and experiences the perception of a single three-dimensional Universe moving along in time. Everett's **'Many World's'** interpretation envisaged many Universes simultaneously existing as a multiplicity of ourselves. This idea of "self-multiplicity", was rejected initially even though positive thinking would support the idea that we *choose,* the Universe (or past life?), we wish to play. Personally the only way I can view this theory, is by substituting past lives for "self-multiplicity". One could have been Joe Smith in 1752 and lost a battle so badly that he *chooses* never to play that battle again. In actual fact if one chose to play *all the games one lost* on the track of time, one would feel a lot better - loss is a creeping dyingness for body and Spirit.

The Holistic Paradigm has the zero-point energy as the source that maintains the elementary particles and therefore all matter. Bohm has shown that it is the implicate order from which arises matter, energy and space-time Universe. The non-local linkages of Bohm's theory give rise to a holistic description of our **Universe as a hologram**, where the whole view is an intricate pattern of energy and is embedded in every section of the hologram. The zero-point energy is the organizational structure or pattern, which determines non-local phenomena to be connected at source through higher dimensional space. I would maintain that the zero-point energy and the geometric pattern of the whole is a diablo model. This would be a self-organizational structure and may itself be composed along the lines of the reductionist view of minor self-organizing bioplasma vortices, with minor Diablo geometrics, thus repeating in effect the pattern of the Moors i.e. the Pascal triangle and Seirpinski triangle (*Fig. 12 and 42*). The hyperbolic spiral may not only be evident in the smallest geometric diablo model, but evident in the swirling organizational pattern of the galaxies in constant motion around a greater spiral. This model may 'pull down' energy successively through the vacuum. The vortex ring formation of the zero-point energy modelled as a virtual turbulent plasma, would correspond to pair production of elementary particles (e.g. electron and positron) and itself would exhibit a precessional rotation (a helical rotation around a cylinder that closes into a torroid). Certainly scientists have proposed this method of drawing down energy from the zero-point by precessional rotation as the way in which the hyperspatial flux orthorotates into our 3D space.

Fig. 42 **Sierpinski Triangle**

Wormholes it was suggested by Wheeler can link distant locations within our Universe or create linkages to what Everet described as other parallel, three-dimensional Universes. Such ideas must have interested the World Order Elite, since there had always existed within the secret societies the belief that Masters existed in parallel Universes or in some other dimension. Whilst I put forward 'The Onion-Ring' model for the way in which the UFO phenomenon works, there were some who believed that Aliens were physical entities and not metaphysical, and actually entered our world through some wormhole effect. The idea of hidden Masters outside our own time dimension in some form of parallel Universe may have been behind the Philadelphia Experiment, which science has not proven, since teleportation for large objects has proven unworkable. That is not to say that some secret experiment was not undertaken, it was according to witness accounts of ships carrying large magnets.

There is this persistent idea within the secret groups e.g. Rosicrucian's, that these secret Masters are directing us in some way, from the etheric layer implanting thoughts actively into our minds. I perceive however that these implants are *imprints* left as holograms within the electro-magnetic organisation of the 'filaments' of the Diablo structure or the morphogenetic bioplasma. In the case of the Rosicrucian's presumably in their Grand Lodge of the White

530

Brotherhood, they believe this instruction and direction is good. Scientology views these Master controllers as bad, I will come to this shortly, but the whole emergent view in quasi-health groups that have emerged on the back of the Holistic Paradigm of the 80's, is one of "spiritual guides". I believe that many of these so-called healers are working for the One World Order programme, softening up public thinking to accept the idea of "spiritual guides" and "voices in your head" delivered no doubt by signals from Big Brother eventually. Angels are another suspect New Age/ Order healing fringe method, again either someone's dramatization or another softening up process by the One World Order. The idea that one DOES NOT KNOW, one's own mind and cannot direct one's own healing process, without the guidance from another invisible being - "a spiritual guide", on the astral plane! Deary me is this yet another recommendation that you tune into www-com/grid! or some signal broadcast through those very suspect alleged defence systems (HAARP -High Active Auroral Research Programme; and GWEN- Ground Wave Emergency Network), that scientists including Nobel nominee Dr. Becker have warned could act as mind control systems.

If you watch the scene of New Age carefully you will note another emergent idea that has come up rather too co-incidentally. The idea of the "Universal Mind"

THE UNIVERSAL MIND

Woolf[146] presented a model for what has become known as **holistic psychology** and was based on levels of maturation, which showed that in our fullest potential our minds link to a Universal Mind. Woolf described how the maturation process accelerates when many minds are focused in a "bonding experience". Expanding on the theory of implicate energy order extended by Bohm and the ideas of self-organization put forward by Ilya Prigogine in 1977, which identified under what conditions a system may evolve from a chaotic state to an organized state, Woolf proposed a view that all minds are in a constant dynamic state of growth and yet part of the group collective or Holistic Universal Mind. This is ONLY CORRECT IN RESPECT OF THE PRIMITIVE SURVIVALIST MIND. There is no doubt that there is an intricate pattern and our consciousness is connected to others within the pattern however this only applies to matter, the phylogenetic line and associated thought. The majority of people who have assigned their mind to remote control via the Grid become the effect of and not cause over the Grid - in effect they have given away the right to choose, for them there is no choice - they have become mechanical robots and slaves to the Universal Mind of survival of animals.

According to Woolf's theory which is a variation of Jung's "collective unconscious", the Universal Mind exhibits a recursive archetypal process: it gives rise to many individual human minds, each experiencince separation from the Universal Mind. Each human mind in turn, is comprised of many more primitive minds called "holodigms", each with its own ego that experiences separation from the other holodigms. What we experience as our ego is simply in this theory the holodigm that is currently active or conscious. The word "holodigm" means whole (holo), form (digm). The implication in this theory is that each primitive ego state is a form that arises from the holistic, Universal Mind and contains the potential for reconnecting its awareness back to the Universal Mind. The process Woolf uses for this re-connection or "awakening" is called "psychomaturation".

If warning bells are going off inside one of your "holodigms" then rightly so! Apparently psychic extrasensory abilities such as telepathy, psychokinesis (moving objects), astral travelling, precognition, cognition and other former or past lives etc are suppose to arise from extending and expanding ones identity and awareness into the Universal Mind! Of course past lives are retained as holograms in *personal* Spiritual memory and only data on survival is stored in the morphogenetic bioplasma, simply because the Grid is solely concerned with major environmental events such as the Flood and survival of the species and the thoughts that do get printed onto this mind, are in fact as we have seen, from the magician's who have connected thought to matter and the hidden science. The Grid would record such data, simply through events related to matter. To call the Grid and its holographic memories of survival a Universal Mind, which appears to be the case with Woolf's theory, is to assign control to the Grid and relinquish the postulates of the Spirit, which exists at a higher self-determined level than the survival of matter and bodies. Psychology has great difficulty accepting man as a spiritual being, thus the idea of the Universal Mind would appeal to psychology. Further the Elite make sure that grants for researching the Spirit and self-determination are not available, since it is not "on message", whereas the Universal Mind, with its application to mind control would be supported. The Spirit KNOWS it has no need to fuse with any other being or mind, it is INDIVIDUAL and always will be. The Spirit has its own memory of continuous existence, which we call past lives, simply because there appear to be separate lives, when the body dies and another has to be sought (Re-incarnation). The personal soul memory banks or holographics are however individual, but obviously have some connection to others, in so far as those memories contain events and personnel. As I mentioned previously when a person starts past life regression, often people or personnel present in the past life holograms, start to re-appear in present time, simply because the hologram is still connected in the larger pattern to the physical presence of the personnel. When I come to discuss how to get out of the trap, this point is very important and should be remembered in so far as any karma that you have accumulated in past lives cannot be erased without the actual personnel! The moral of the story is to always make up karma when it happens, since it may take you thousands of years to find the personnel again! You will not get out of the trap until in those famous biblical words you: "have paid the last coin of least value". Further horror of horrors! What if one of the personnel exited! You would be stuck here! I have to say that our Lobster pot the Grid, is a much better court in the sky, than we will see on Earth in terms of justice.

Since the Primitive Mind is a *self-survivalist* mind capable of action that supports survival for self and group at its highest level, it is hardly advisable to recommend that people tune into www-com/grid. Since the 'guidance' one receives is a set of instructions based on primitive behaviour that ensured the survival of the species in the past. In the case of Cancer, this mind 'decides' growth is advisable, wrongly concluding that *loss of body* has occurred, having no data banks on *emotional loss* arising from job loss, relationship loss, stress of living e.g. mortgages, debts, bills etc. The Primitive mind just hasn't got the programmes in the phylogenetic line, whereas a rational Analytical (computer) Mind can *reason*. Reason is the major difference between man and lower animal forms and the difference between the Primitive Mind and the Analytical Mind. Loye[147] in his research attempts to show that the brain's frontal lobes are associated with bonding, psychic activities, mystical awareness and link to a

Universal Mind. This may support my conclusion that the brain acts as a dipole radio receiver picking up Grid signals and then transmitting or receiving via morphic resonance through the biofield.

Psychics have foretold future world events, simply because those future events are predictable based as they are on past events and holographics of the Grid. Ilya Prigogine who in 1977 won the Nobel Prize in Chemistry, proposed the conditions under which a system may evolve from a chaotic to an organised state. The conditions in that system had to be *non linear,* far from equilibrium and have an energy flux through it. A non-linear system is one whose response to a set of stimuli may produce new, surprising or synergistic behaviour that cannot readily be predicted by simply summing the responses of the individual stimuli. Linear systems on the other hand exhibit the reductionist "sum of the parts", as making the whole. In the history of science, most systems that were readily analysable were linear systems and for these systems, the reductionist view of the "sum of the parts" (response) equals the "sum of the whole" (response). One could apply this datum to Earth and whilst man is connected or tuned into the Grid, it is a linear system, totally predictable and would according to Prigogine's theory never reach equilibrium! However perhaps it is fortunate for us, that the MRC case is totally predictable, since he is holding his 'script' and we know the basic story line of the script, thus although the Earth is a chaotic system, it is linear in so far as it does not throw up any unpredictable responses! You know the story or 'script' by now Day 1 plant the vine, Day 2 Formation of the brotherhood Day 3 World inventory, Day 4 education of the world Elite Day 5 Find the woman and make sure she doesn't cause trouble again by stealing her documents, Day 6 Formation of the World Order, Day 7 "chosen ones" left quickly as a Magnetic Reversal was coming. etc.

INIDVIDUALISM, that unpredictable entity is a *non-linear system*, it provides the unexpected answer, it poses unexpected questions, it does unpredictable things and the Global Elite tuned into www-com/grid Marxist hive and survival of the fittest, just could not bear that amount of *unpredictability*, that much *movement*, or any form of disorder to the predictable chaos of Grid thinking. How could a member of the audience get up and shout at the players on the stage "Hey, lets change the script this script stinks!" I will tell you here, that if I was fought and the front cover of the Cancer Report shows just some of that intense battle, it was a battle of self-determined and postulated thought versus pack mentality, which is individualism. There is no ego in it, it is just who I am. And isn't it a major surprise to see Scientology in there, with Rudolph Steiner's Anthroposophy, media, law, churches and Government. I will come to the case of Scientology later and the reason I believe that they fought me - and conducted the actions they did. The Grid you see will not encounter individualism, or that unpredictable input, it is record of *majority* survival of the species and it is unfortunate indeed that this pattern that originally existed as a record for the evolutionary survival of the species and Homo sapiens as **animal**, also kept a record of *thought* in relation to matter.

The pattern as the master computer saw rugged individualism as a threat, in so far as even from my own experience I can tell you, that individualism is not survival in terms of the Grid or *majority thinking*. I have suffered ridicule, I have been virtually bankrupted, chased from one end of the globe to the next, spat at, sent to Coventry, been ridiculed in courts of law, my children chased from school to school, and a great deal more. These are not survival actions! and are the results of Grid pack thinking. Look at any Scientist who has tried to exert individualism in his or her research and you will see the history of non-survival and Grid thinking exerting itself. Look at my Petition - the Grid does not answer questions of a rational nature that seeks to question that Grid, it annihilates those that challenge the Grid. The Grid of course is chaos for man, but that chaos is supremely ordered and balancing for matter, in so far as the Earth periodically goes through its own balancing mechanism and a Magnetic Reversal. Earth as matter is a chaotic system and man tries to live with the chaos of earthquakes, volcanoes, hurricanes, tornados and even Magnetic Reversals or space domains. Man also adds his own chaos into the system by way of pollution, wars, nuclear detonations, gas emissions and meddling with the Grid and zero-point energy. Nature's laws solve the chaos by periodically passing through a balancing mechanism. The master pattern may even conclude failure has occurred and merely wipes out the species and starts the reconstruction process again – growth along with giants.

Be careful then, when assuming that the Universal Mind or "Cosmic Mind" is the directing "Architect". We are all indeed connected via karma in our past lives and the play on Earth is a plot created by everyone! To quote Nobel Prize winner Max Planck: "As a man who has devoted his whole life to the most clear-headed science, to the study of matter, I can tell you as the result of my research about the atoms this much; there is no matter as such! All matter originates and exists only by virtue of a force which brings the particles of an atom to vibration and holds this most minute solar system of the atom together...we must assume behind this force the existence of a conscious and intelligent mind, This mind is the matrix of all matter". The pattern could be viewed as the intelligent mind the infinite board game of energy, upon which we play our games. Who created the board game? Well you would have to go back to that trillionth of a second before anti-matter and matter met? Or the singularity? Or the point before we became observation point and truly that must be God's country, a point when we did not exist as observation point, so we will never know. We can never shake hands with our doppelganger again! Unless of course we receded back to another anti-matter matter explosion and the board was re-created and perhaps that is why we find very little anti-matter in our Universe (which might be a lesson to the physicists) Bruce Cathie's suggestion of how matter and antimatter are created out of the same waveforms (*Fig. 39*) As the electron moves in a hyperbolic spiral in each matter and antimatter pulse is perhaps a way of viewing an elsewhere' - a parallel Universe of anti-matter and who is to say what one would find there!

RON HUBBARD'S SPACE OPERA

There is no doubt from UFO witness accounts, that a holographic recording exists of a time, apparently here on Earth when man did not have the same body as today and further used aircraft that resembled the anti-gravity 'flying saucers' of the type that Schauberger designed. I have covered this aspect fully in Alternative 4, and given 'The Onion-Ring Model' as the way in which these holographics are dislodged and received by man, through his brain acting as dipole-radio receiver and morphic resonance of the biofield. The images UFO witnesses see, although they appear to be real, are in fact metaphysical or more accurately images of *past* events.

I had no intention of producing Hubbard's "Space Opera", but do so for the following reasons:

1. The material that was part of the secret OT levels (Operating Thetan - Spirit), up to OT3 (level 3), has already been made public by L.Kin (a pseudonym) from the breakaway group Phoenix, already covered. L. Kin [148] gives in his book, the reasons why he chose to go public and the author would agree with those reasons but additionally the following factors influenced my decision.

2. My research is undoubtedly verification to some extent of the OT levels; however the research I have carried out requires an overall review and re-evaluation of Hubbard's "Space Opera".

3. People were going OT (although it was not called that), in Early Minoan Crete (and Africa) before the Religious Revolution and data *was stolen*; that data is produced in the author's research and has import on Hubbard's OT level data, which needs to be re-assessed and re-evaluated in the light of the author's research and this book.

4. It's WRONG to withhold data that could set man free of the trap. If a Magnetic Reversal happened tomorrow, the whole thing would be lost to the majority of humanity and there simply might not be a next time. According to the author's research, the Grid would re-install all the (Earth) track data and OT status would be lost along with any gain. Billions of souls trapped *again* - who is going to take responsibility for that!

5. The author never placed her agreement on secrecy *ever,* on the track of time; or *unreasonable* commercialisation and high price of knowledge sent to free mankind. The knowledge becomes elitist.

8. The author agrees with the list given earlier in this book, by the breakaway group from Scientology and further has doubts as to who is in charge of Scientology today and what their overall games are, together with the question of source.

I will repeat the WARNING of L.Kin: anyone reading on beyond this point does so at his or her own risk! The advice in the event of restimulation is given as a reference (*Appendix 4*), you should read this reference in L.Kin's book before proceeding. (This is a bit meladromatic for the author, since the author's view and research puts man at a vantage point by way of knowledge and understanding, thus removing this idea of "implants")

Scientology has undergone a lot of ridicule in the past, over Space Opera and it was generally supposed that Hubbard had used science fiction to fuel his beliefs, which subsequently became the religion of Scientology. *Time* magazine had a field day ridiculing OT (Operating Thetan –Spirit) data, and journalists were always assured of page space if they ran a Scientology 'witch hunt' story. In order to see how Scientology fitted into the overall picture, I contacted Phoenix to get hold of the OT levels. As a matter of historical record, contrary to the Church's public relations words in *USA Today* newspaper which were roughly of the tenure, "We fight For Religious Freedom"; I was thrown out ("disconnected" is I believe the polite word) of the Church in 1989 to fight a battle in the London Law Courts to uphold The Declaration of Human Rights - the right to one's own belief and viewpoint, which contrary to the warnings and fear ("give up your research or your children") of the Church (Human Rights were not written into law at that point), I did win and that case Henry versus Henry 1989 has been used by among others, the Jehovah's witnesses, to uphold a basic freedom. On returning to continue with my study of the subject Dianetics in relation to the Cancer research I was conducting, I experienced what is described in pictorial form on the front cover of The Cancer Research document; the knife plunged neatly between my shoulder blades, in what I consider as a gross act of betrayal, not only to the author, but in view of the fact that I very nearly threw my entire postulate in and walked away - to humanity. If this book proves of value to you the reader, then know that the events of the front cover were ferocious barriers to freedom - barriers so intense, that I very nearly lost the entire game.

The information on the Scientology OT levels has been gained by auditing (a Scientology procedure) the whole time track of thousands of Scientologists, who have come up with this data, it is therefore THEIR EXPERIENCE and as such it is their data. I have not seen the methodology, or read any Scientology data on this, other than the material that I give here, which is gained from L.Kin. The book should be referred to for a fuller account. The fact that many Scientologists have come up with this data must mean that it is a *common experience* and therefore *may* involve the Grid and past events. It is for this reason I have sought to include it. I do not doubt the data, if Scientologists have come up with this data, it is there on the record and imprinted into man's memory: however I will provide a varying viewpoint and interpretation to Hubbard on this data, which Scientologists might check against their own personal memories and data; which may confirm the author's own memory and data.

According to L.Kin: "The first page of the OT materials starts with the memorable words: "The head of the Galactic Confederation (76 planets around larger stars visible from here) (formed 95 000 000 years ago; very space opera) solved over population (250 billion or so per planet -178 billion average) by mass implanting (....) His name was Xenu. He used renegades"

The story is longer, but I have tried to be brief. Hubbard places the Galactic Confederation "20 million years" before "the catastrophe". He further claims that the Confederation is active today. I am not sure whether the OT student reads this data *before* he is audited (the application of Scientology processes and procedures to someone by a trained auditor) or after, or concurrently. From a scientific viewpoint, if one was running a double blind trial, one would examine personal experience data first, *without* having read anything prior, to avoid suggestion. In science it is called a double-blind placebo trial. However I do not doubt whatsoever the material is true, but I will come to an analysis later. Hubbard goes on to describe the sort of civilization of the 76 planets, which sounds very much like 1950's on Earth; cars, husbands, wives, children, telephones, television, apart from interstellar space flight, based on space-energy and controlled gravitation, heavily reminding us of the hidden science and the Atlanteans. This becomes more pointed, since Earth is described as having tropical plants, even North of today's Arctic Circle, thus this must be a time prior to a Magnetic Reversal. Further dinosaurs suggest that it is indeed this pre-Magnetic Reversal era. This would fit with the giant footprints found alongside dinosaur tracks in the Paluxy riverbed found by archaeologists in the 1970's. The fact that dinosaurs were extinguished at the time of the Triassic period, when a Magnetic Reversal also occurred, again points to this period. Hubbard refers to the Earth in this period as a tourist resort, where people from all over the galaxy came to spend their holidays. The local population he claims was predominantly white but with other races too, mainly tourists. The size of the population "178 billion people average" seems high but credible as Hubbard proposes 25 square metres of space per person, and condominium (flats) three to nine floors high with reformed non-wasteful use of agriculture. In tape 10 Hubbard mentions up to 250 billion people populating Earth (40 times the current 6 billion). Again L.Kin suggests that 90 floor skyscrapers would accommodate that many in Italy and notes that: " the population density of Monaco is 20 000 per sq. Km. and where nobody runs away from Monaco!"

The overall story here was that Xenu's claim of "solving overpopulation", was a mere pretence and he was non other than a being who required total control, with an "ice-cold unfeeling greed". This point was interesting to me, since in

Alternative4, which was based on and a continuing theme of a prior book *Alternative 3*; there was concern in the 1970's of over population and climactic changes, which had instigated a secret research programme to provide a safe haven from Earth, on Mars. I was passed recently a "secret Illuminati document" (1999), which discussed overpopulation of Earth. I haven't reproduced it, since if it was on the Web, then it wasn't secret and I am always wary of being given ' feeders', but there was a total ring of truth about it. If the Elite discusses such programmes, then it is a dramatization of the past.

According to Hubbard, the way Xenu solved the problem was to put an H-bomb on the principal volcanoes and thus reduce the population very effectively. Once again there appears some precedence for this, in so far as I did give data for nuclear activity, curiously enough also in America. Hubbard does not mention any pre-history that I have covered directly, but the parallel to my research is curious. Further some pre-history of nuclear weapons was not only indicated in the channelled account by Walker, but also cropped up in UFO witness reports and warnings. Indian epics also carried some account of space or flying machines and a conflagration. The date given by Hubbard for the incident or "catastrophe" is 75 million years ago. This really fits with the date of a Magnetic Reversal and the die out of the dinosaurs. L. Kin points out in similar proof to my own research, that geologists have discovered a layer of rock containing Iridium, a metal that can't be found in this particular distribution elsewhere on the planet, and called it the "Alvarez-layer". It is said to have formed 63 million years ago: not only the time when the dinosaurs disappeared, but according to my own research, the time of a significant Magnetic Reversal. Interestingly the date of 75 million years ago was found because E-meters (apparatus used in auditing to measure charged incidents on the time track) reacted to the charge of people who were auditing incidents at that date. A charge on the E-meter would indicate a significant event.

This might force me to review my MRC theory for the Magnetically Reversed Case, since if OT's are coming up with data on a Magnetic Reversal, then it looks like many more people may have gone through this "catastrophe". So what makes the MRC different? - Was he on Earth from the beginning trapped here for some reason on the viewpoint of matter perhaps, and has become more and more insane with each Magnetic Reversal? It is difficult to say, but if a large proportion of the population were found to have this incident then it means that there must be an on-going deterioration in a psychological case - the MRC case being the bottom line. Hubbard does say that not everyone has this incident but one thing is certain, you would never get the MRC case into the auditing chair to run his track and thus we may never know entirely what happened to this case, unless he is audited. Thus it appears that the Magnetic Reversal may have been an absolute "catastrophe", for a large number of humanity. I emphasise that

Hubbard did not talk of a Magnetic Reversal and this incident according to Hubbard originated with H-bombs.

Xenu according to Hubbard wished to usurp the **democratic method** or Constitution of the Confederation, which elected a Supreme Ruler, wishing himself to become a Supreme dictator. This has made an appearance today in the World Order goal, run by the One at the top or a hierarchy, which has by-passed the democratic process as is the case of European Union, which the author has proved was a secret plan dating back at least to the French Revolution and ultimately back to the Religious Revolution in Crete c. 1 400 B.C. According to L. Kin's book: "He placed secret agents in high political positions, who undermined the power of the electing body, the Loyal Officers and weakened the constitution". Things don't change do they in these One World Orders! In fact Tape 10 of Hubbard's OT levels makes a strong point that today's insolvency, poverty, prostitution and criminality are nothing but a *dramatization*, a compulsive repetition of the situation *back then*. This certainly is corroborated by my own research. To continue, the unrest and rebelliousness amongst Loyal Officers, activists, intellectuals and the population in general became a problem. Thus Xenu's answer was to transport billions of thetans (Spiritual Beings) back to Earth and bomb them with an H-bomb. Xenu was caught and placed in an "electronic mountain trap" - a sort of fixing or pinning electronic device. This by the way parallels the myth whereby Locki, the evil one, is trapped under the Earth and also parallels the Hebraic Christian version, whereby Satan is locked up for a thousand years "chained" in the "bottomless pit", according to the book of *Revelations*.

The cataclysm must have been terrifying and of course the Druids and Celts feared the: "sea bursting its bounds", but nothing else. Apparently when Hubbard first ran OT III in the 1940's, a doctor had to stand by as it was thought that people might keel over in the auditing session from over-restimulation! The incident must have flattened somehow, because OT's who mentioned it, without spilling the beans of course! seemed pretty casual about it. Hubbard maintained that a mountain in Madeira was the place where Xenu is locked up. L. Kin claimed that Robertson an old associate of Hubbard's and staff member had telepathically audited Xenu in 1986 and 1988 and according to Robertson was active again, which confirmed Hubbard's statement that Xenu had escaped (co-incidentally paralleling the book of Revelations account). What is going on here? Does this confirm what Dr. Becker has stated, that a Magnetic Reversal may well be under way with the *Grid activated*? - Well slowly we begin to unravel more of this mystery. But before I set about unravelling this particular mystery, let us continue with more data.

The H-bomb incident is generally referred to as "Incident Two" or "Inc.2", which was 36 days long and which although Hubbard never mentions it, I am inclined to equate with a Magnetic Reversal. This is probably not the one involving the pre-Flood or Antediluvians. I do not discount the incident with a nuclear device; in fact as I have shown there was misuse of the hidden science and atomic knowledge. In order to get a better grasp of this incident, I will give the sequence of events of Inc.2.

1. Capture (being shot)
2. *Freezing*
3. Transport to Teegeeack (Earth)
4. Being placed near a volcano
5. *Hydrogen bomb* dropped in or on the volcano
6. Explosion. Terrific winds. Thetan (Spirit) carried over peak and *Electronic ribbon* came up. He *stuck to it*. It was then *pulled down* and he was (as *part of a group*) implanted with R6 ("R6" is Hubbard's technical name for this implant). Beginning of the implant.
7. Various *picture sequences* (the implant)
8. The 7's and CC and OT II materials (more technical names of implants)
9. 36 days of *picture implants* which give a vast array of materials and 3 (false) explanations for the bombing.
10. Transport to Hawaii or Las Palmas for packing into clusters.

I have emphasised points that I consider important and evidence that I will use to support my own view of what is happening here. However let us consider for a moment some of the pictures that were "implanted". "God"; " the Devil"; "*Angels*"; "Space Opera" "*Theatres*"; " helicopters"; "*a constant spinning*"; "a spinning dancer"; "trains"; "*various scenes like modern England*". To quote L. Kin " you name it, it's in this implant. We call it in its entirety 'R6'." Let us consider some of the details in this so-called "implant".

Point 1. Capture: The capture involves mass killings that included bombing and machine gunning and even electronic beams and lasers. We conclude there was a large battle then. This was a point made in the Indian Epics which occurred in pre-history of Earth, however this according to Hubbard's Tape 10 and solo auditor reports occurred outside of Earth and Spirits were transported here.

Point 2. Thetans (Spirits) were frozen i.e. "their energy field" (I thought Hubbard stated that a Thetan had no energy or mass?). Although Hubbard does not mention any environmental conditions, this incident could possibly be the environmental conditions after a Magnetic Reversal when a temperate climate became the Ice Age.

Point 5. The bomb was dropped and this is an incident that could account for radioactive materials and fused rocks as previously discussed. Also some UFO witness accounts (*Alternative 4*) spoke of abductions by aliens and then being shown a series of pictures including a nuclear detonation. Since I concluded that the natural UFO account was an experience of a PAST holographic event, then there is some evidence here, that the capture in point 5, was the abduction and a nuclear detonation was part of this sequence of events. This would also find corroboration in UFO accounts where the person was:"shown pictures of nuclear detonations". Thus one cannot discount Hubbard's data or indeed the UFO data, just because we can't find the full evidence in archaeology on Earth. The evidence or story would still be retained on the morphogenetic bioplasma or Grid, since it stores holographic material of events for this Planet. However memory of an elsewhere, would be retained in Spiritual memory, which a Spirit or Thetan carries with him. There is however another possibility here, in that Earth travels through space and we don't know how much information is cluttered onto the holographics of the energy field of the morphogenetic bioplasma or crystal from elsewhere. UFO witnesses then, might have experienced what Hubbard terms R6 implant, which may be holographics from the Grid, during a Magnetic Reversal, following a nuclear event, but at least the latter.

Point 6. "The electronic ribbon", is very interesting, which had been installed according to Hubbard: "To make sure that nobody would be blown off the planet and get away": A trap then. According to my own model of the morphogenetic bioplasma as a Diablo of upward and downward pointing pyramidal vortices, with energy patterns or electro-magnetic 'threads' arranged in a hyperbolic spiral; this would possibly account for the "electronic ribbon.". A Magnetic Reversal may well unravel the 'thread' pattern of the hyperbolic spiral, which I likened to the double helix of DNA, which in effect would give an electro-magnetic as opposed to "electronic" ribbon-like pattern of energy, however the two may be synonymous. If the holographics of (a) Earth event and (b) phylogenetic survival are distributed on these 'ribbons' or threads, in the same manner that genes are distributed as information units along the chromosomes of the DNA, on the hermetic principle of 'As above so below'; then any Spirit that contacted this "electronic ribbon", would have the entire holographics of Earth event and phylogenetic survival downloaded into his *own memory banks*: which are themselves just holographics of energy and are *personal experience including elsewhere's* and in fact everywhere the Spirit has been. In effect a Magnetic Reversal and/or a nuclear event followed by "terrific winds" could have unravelled the geometric patterning of energy within the Grid or UVG120 sphere comprised in its geometrical structure of these morphogenetic bioplasmas with their helical windings or 'threads'. Thus when the Spirit become stuck to the threads like a fly on fly-paper, the "electronic ribbons" which I equate with the electro-magnetic 'threads' downloaded their entire holographics which became part of the memory banks of the Spirit. This is viewed in the OT III accounts, as an " **implant**". The fact that the OT Scientologist perceived this was an implant i.e. having something unwanted, could possibly result from the knowledge that the event itself, was precipitated by beings who sought to control. The interpretation and sequencing of data is therefore crucial. The point in emphasis, is that not only I believe would the 'thread' be 'spliced' (edited) as described before, thus the sequence of events may not correspond to the exact sequence of events (time and date) on Earth: but also, it has now been downloaded into the memory banks of the Spirit and therefore interdispersed with his *own* elsewhere's or holograms of *his personal record.* Despite this, as we know "everything" appears to occur in this so-called "implant" which makes sense, since the morphogenetic bioplasma ' threads' contain a complete event and phylogenetic history for Earth. Although there may be some question of how much is added to the morphogenetic event holograms by Earth moving in space.

It is curious also that the trap of this "ribbon" effect was described in Tape 10 by Hubbard, as a "standing wave" above the volcano- it looked "**like and umbrella**". Certainly people in Paleolithic times, knew about this "umbrella", which is why it was being drawn in the Paleolithic caves. Further, the honeycomb of the coral in Paleolithic finds provided a good demonstration model for the UVG 120 sphere and its geometric and was I decided also, a model for **political control** as a colony under group co-operation and equal input and thus Communistic. Such control was also the aim of the Xenu in Hubbard's account.

Later the model of the trap, was refined to the Ariadne ball of string model. The Greek myth of Ariadne giving Theseus a ball of golden string, to find his way into the labyrinth of Crete (to kill the dreaded man-bull or Minotaur), which represented the cnothic underworld of the dead in one sense, but in another it was the defeat by the woman of a secret cult, the Bull-Minos cult who undertook the Religious Revolution at Knossos, *removing a whole cosmology and belief system.* The truth has been glossed into myth to avoid detection, but the myth tells of the defeat of the Patriarchal team. Ariadne gives Theseus a golden ball of thread, which is evident in some of the Greek icons (*Fig. 27*), resembling the curious stones from Crete, wrapped in thongs. The stones are represented in their geometry by the UVG120 sphere. What was being taught here was not only history, but *also* Cosmology. The Earth as a huge dynamo wound with magnetic lines of force as it coils. Further there is a huge magnetic field around the Sun, those magnetic lines of force from the Sun envelop the Earth and extend to the Moon, and everything, no matter what its form on this planet exists by reason of magnetic lines of force. The lines of force of the magnetic field would form a lattice, or grid pattern, due to the spin of the planetary body. The analogy would be a ball of string, with the string length eventually forming a criss-cross pattern. Small vortices that I equate with the morphogenetic bioplasma vortices are formed at the trillions of points where the lines of force cross each other in the lattice pattern. Each vortex manifests as an atomic structure and creates within itself a gravitational field. There lies man's trap. How to find ones way out of the Grid (or the maze at Knossos) and the trillions of small vortices, that was the question. It is a formidable trap and unless you understand how it works, then you just won't make it to the first post and there are two more to pass after that! Perhaps that brings us back to the myth of Atoko and the partner waiting (to lead him out past two more posts?).

The gravitational field is nothing more than the effects of relative motion in space. Matter is drawn towards a gravitational field, just as a whirlpool draws debris. The gravitational fields created by the vortical action of every atom would combine to form the field of the completed planetary body. Thus the grid is really an interlocking of the lines of magnetic force and Hubbard's "electronic ribbon", is really part of the electro-magnetic force lines, which also carry according to the model of the morphogenetic bioplasma that I gave, holograms of all past events. We are very much imprisoned within an electro-magnetic web. To go back to the story of Ariadne, the woman knew, that the only way she could kill the Minotaur, was to act in unison with a male (Theseus) who would take her unravelled ball of string (and the past holographics of historical events or truth!) into the labyrinth. Unfortunately as all these Cutting of The Elm ('cut arm') stories go; Theseus did eventually betray Ariadne as Jesus betrayed Magdalene.

I could not say if someone was dramatizing 'umbrellas' or pies! when they envisaged the Millennium Dome project in London, but given those heads of the Toltecs, it all looks like someone's boring old script from the so-called R6 implant they are dramatizing. Perhaps Londoner's should retain it as a tribute to Xenu or mind and money control along with London Eye (a Ferris wheel)! To continue with Hubbard's OT accounts in Tape 10, the Thetans or Spirits were whirled up, got stuck to the "electronic ribbon" or "umbrella" and the "implant" carried out according to Hubbard, or holographics from the unravelled morphogenetic bioplasma according to my own account, were downloaded into the memory banks of the Spirit.

Point 8. With regard to the "7's and CC and OT II materials", I do not have access to this material.

Point 9. Hubbard refers to the **"key implant"**, which lasted "36 days". It was done according to the account in L. Kin's book as a: " super colossal three-

545

dimensional motion picture containing everything which has been evident in this civilization on Earth: a white haired and bearded god, devils, hellfire, archangels like Gabriel or Michael, religious symbols, archbishops complete with croziers, all the pompousness of Roman Catholicism, a cross with a man hanging from it, the type of theatres still in use today with spectators and boxes to the left and right of the stage, sexual torture done in leather costumes with whips and chains, perversions such as sex with children, war pictures with crashing helicopters (dramatized in Vietnam), spaceships, skyscrapers, in fact the whole architecture of Manhattan and other 'modern' banking business centres, the whole of Hollywood complete with Action pictures, writers, forever glorious film star types like Marilyn Monroe or Clark Gable, Psychiatrists doing their electric shocking" (a truly piquant picture is that of a crucified Psychiatrist according to L. Kin) "surgeons senselessly dissecting bodies down to the bones - and to top it all, exploding bombs are shown. In addition to actual bomb explosions in the volcanoes, pictures of bomb explosions are shown!" This almost certainly brings us to those UFO accounts of alleged abductions, which I discussed in *Alternative 4*, which looks increasingly like a person who was run into the past holographics of the R6 implant as Hubbard terms it, but I would state a Magnetic Reversal/ nuclear event, although the two may be synonymous. Why were they shown pictures? According to L, Kin: "just to make sure that someday somebody will have the good idea of blowing the whole planet up once again". Once again, whilst there is obviously here recognition of actual bombs in the incident, the person also realised that some bomb incidents were in the past and refers to that as being shown pictures. Thus we could have the sequence of bomb going off and catastrophe initiated, whereby the Spirit is blown up and fixes to the "electronic ribbon" or "umbrella" and then is downloaded with holograms of *all past events*, which includes bombs. Consider a long reel of cinematographic film and you probably have some idea of the "electronic ribbon" or in my model the electro-magnetic 'threads' of the morphogenetic bioplasma, on which the holographic memories are recorded. The important question that arises from Inc.2. Is whether this is an **imprint or implant**? *Imprint* is a *passive* action, in so far as the bomb detonation or Magnetic Reversal causing the morphogenetic bioplasma to unravel, caused the downloading as the Spirit became stuck to the 'threads' – the electro-magnetic coils of the morphogenetic bioplasma. *Implant* however is *actively* done against the will. Thus is Xenu part of this incident? Or has a Magnetic Reversal 'spliced' in an *earlier incident* that did involve Xenu? Or is there a sequence of Magnetic Reversals or nuclear detonations, thus accounting for holographic memories of bombs, with Xenu as the originating incident? To my observation however, Inc.2. With its "clouds of dust, smoke, black skies, ice-block incidents, radiation, *swirling* and *spiralling motion and no life* ", is a description of a Magnetic Reversal with its vast species extinction.

Point 10. The packaging of Thetans or Spirits, with some "boxed up", and taken to Las Palmas and Hawaii and others shot into space, whilst others are dropped into the oceans cannot easily be explained in terms of a Magnetic Reversal, unless of course we are looking at the first incident of this sort. L. Kin states that after the incident, which apparently lasted 36 days: "The remaining Thetans were left to drift about the Planet - always inside the electronic ribbon of course". The umbrellas, dome, UVG120 sphere, Diablo or morphogenetic bioplasma is of course THE TRAP. The lobster pot into which man's soul has been trapped for billions of years. You may remember the curious metal cube (or box?) in archaeological finds that had convex sides, discovered and dated to millions of years ago, which may provide some relevance here.

What is certain is that in line with the Atlantis accounts, Earth became known as an "evil place", after Inc.2. And in comparable conclusion L. Kin states: "Not only in biological but as well in spiritual terms a gigantic catastrophe had occurred". Enter Spiritual intervention c. 10 000 B.C. Hubbard referred to Inc.2. As the "4th Dynamic engram" (mankind) I would consider the 'One-ness' scenario and The Universal Mind are a consequence of this implant *or* imprint during a Magnetic Reversal? And of course The One World Order plan may also derive from this incident. It must have been hell, 250 billion Spirits unable to leave and unable to Re-incarnate (no bodies through species extinction) People sometimes ask, where the Spirits come from, that continually Re-incarnate and increase the world's population, but with 250 billion souls, there is no shortage of souls only bodies? Those that gain bodies often waste their chances to spiritually evolve in an incarnation.

INCIDENT ONE

Now we come to religion in this incident. L. Kin quotes Hubbard's handwritten script OT III: "Incident I (Inc.I) occurred about 4 quadrillion years plus or minus. It is very much earlier than Inc. 2. Which occurred only 75 000 000 years ago (a bit less). Incident 2 is only peculiar and general on this planet and nearby stars, whereas Incident I is to be found on all thetans". (Really?!). L. Kin expands this to: "all thetans who were there at the time" and: "only those who were in this Universe at that time received it. Those who entered this Universe later did not receive it, but became contaminated with it". Inc.I is part of the agreement of being here. Inc. I is: "the basic unknown agreement concerning the Universe we live in, its pre-requisite". I will leave you to read this incident in L. Kin's book, however briefly here I will mention that certain religious symbols e.g. cherub, chariot and horn appear and the fact that these occur so often in biblical accounts, suspiciously indicates channelled information which since it includes other places in the Universe other than Earth, cannot only include channelling from the Grid. The Grid I decided only contained events and the phylogenetic *history of Earth*, which appears to be confirmed by Inc. 2, in so far as it only applies to Earth. The alternative explanation is that some past scribes may have dramatized Inc. I. However, I do notice that the *chariot* of Hermes is there in the incident, together with the gates of *horn* from Knossos (the entry to the abode of the dead in one sense and in the horn of plenty became the seat of *power*). Thus I do not discount, that these archetypal symbols still refer to the diablo geometric, but occur at a higher grade of energy, the upper half of the diablo which I referred to as the spiritual bioplasma. If these holographs were downloaded, then it may have occurred in a similar mechanism to Inc. 2 but with perhaps some other cause as to why that downloading occurred. I did mention in *Alternative 4* that religious archetypes occurred in some UFO incidents and suggested that they were stored in a higher grade of energy – the spiritual bioplasma of the diablo. If many spirits were waiting for incarnation on Earth, then during any disruption of the spiritual bioplasma they would have received the downloaded holographics or Inc.1, but only those actually on Earth and beneath the "umbrella" or Grid would have received Inc. 2.

According to L. Kin the outcome of this incident, was that all thetans unknowingly *connected with each other* (through "theta quanta") and the establishment by Xenu of a *gigantic control network*. Oddly enough the "theta quanta", which attached to each thetan, giving rise to the network, is described as an "**eye witness**"!! Thus one has to ask in Theatre Earth, whether the *hermetic Eye of Intelligence* and the *third eye* of Cyclops, together with the *all-seeing Eye of the Illuminati* and the One World Order, under the hermetic god is not just another dramatization of Inc.1 The all-seeing eye is currently dramatized on the

One Dollar bill of America and revolves as a Ferris wheel in London – some dramatization! Xenu obviously working undeterred on his mind control programme or those who dramatize Inc.I and II constantly i.e. The MRC case as I term them. The theta quanta, were used for "storing knowledge", "building communication lines" and they formed "the akasha", and "In their totality they form the Akashic Record Any datum you ever wanted to know about everything anywhere: ask them. They have it on file". This then indicates that Inc. 1 is also part of the *event record* and therefore must be part of the diablo structure, but the 'threads' or mechanism by which the holographics are held must occur in the spiritual bioplasma, which is the upper half of the diablo. The fact that the archetypal religious symbols turn up in UFO witness accounts, means that this bioplasma can *still communicate with man via morphic resonance* and thus as with the lower morphogenetic bioplasma can still *direct man subconsciously*. Thus man would dramatize both these incidents and would confirm Hubbard's assertion that a control network is still in place, with the possibility that it can be manipulated (and probably is) by those cases like the MRC who heavily dramatize their past mindlessly turning the pages on their 'script'.

Well without going into this too deeply and Hubbard's research, what is evident, is that Hubbard was aware of the Akashic Record and whilst he gives this file a personalisation "them", I view the Akashic Record as the morphogentic and spiritual bioplasma or diabolo, the vortex geometry which results from the motion of atomic particles, which in itself may be a minor pattern of the Universe geometric as a diablo, where anti-matter and matter recede from an explosion. Thus as a scientist, I would rather view the *science* of the Magnetic Reversal. The parallel Universe may really be equivalent to the matter and anti-matter cycle, which Bruce Cathie spoke of and certainly the flat bottomed trapezoid burial urns of Early Minoans, would I believe demonstrate in the parallel achieved between top and bottom edges, such a model or Cosmology. Colin Wilson confirmed the matter anti-matter cycle that Cathie spoke of in the book Beyond the Occult, when he commented:

> "Human beings are accustomed to the fact that if they turn round through 360 degrees (through a full circle) they find themselves facing in the direction they started from. Not so an electron. By passing it through a certain type of magnetic field, its 'axis spin' can be tipped through 360 degrees, which ought to restore it to its original position. But it doesn't. The electron has to be turned through yet another full circle before it behaves as it did before. We cannot distinguish the difference between the two circles. The electron can - which seems to suggest that in the subatomic world a full circle is not 360 degrees but 720 degrees. In our world we have lost half the degrees we ought to have. Or to put it another way, there may be another dimension in the subatomic world".

I noted in *The Battle of The Trees*, that the alphabets hid religious mysteries and I spent some time decoding certain religious mysteries relating to secret alphabets, particularly the Beth-Luis-Nion and Ogham scripts and Tree alphabet, which appear to be the alphabets where most of the religious mysteries were tied up and were used by Semitic groups including the Druids. It is certainly significant that the Beth-Luis Nion had *72 letters*, and was an alphabet that incorporated Moses as demi-god. Seventy- two of course might indicate the atomic secret above and the curious 'spectacle' design of the figure of 8 (two circles or 720 degrees or two worlds one of matter and one of anti-matter – if not the Universe geometric as Diablo) .The Masters have as I pointed out before, always sought the 'door' out into that other world. The Rosicrucian's have a great deal of knowledge relating to atoms, which they have declined to share with humanity, although Newton and other scientists who were members of this group utilised the knowledge, but never released fully any important data. Further as I commented in *Alternative 4*, it is significant that Jesus in his resurrection period, which lasted 3 days (72 hours), symbolised some idea I would propose of matter and anti-matter worlds or Universes – "Heaven" and "Hell" (Christ and anti-Christ). The occult groups were correct in their belief that it was actually the anti-world that was Heaven with this one as Hell. This Universe of course is the bad place! And whether you believe that Jesus ascended to the other world is entirely a matter for your own thought process. However the account in biblical texts of Jesus becoming semi-transparent or walking through doors! Seems to signify manipulation of the knowledge, but such manipulation would not stand up to today's physics, since if it is being implied that Jesus was anti-matter at that point i.e. he dematerialised, then I am afraid it would have caused an atomic explosion to wipe out at least the whole of the Middle East, if not more. Thus it could not have happened! That is the problem with lies; they come back and hit you in the face one day.

To refer back to L. Kin's book, I flicked back, to find his definition of "Akasha" I started to get slightly nervous when L.Kin referred to the occultist views of Bardon, Steiner and Blavatsky and their Vedic source, where the occultists associated this with something holy or god-like. Presumably if Inc.I is stored on the Grid on the spiritual bioplasma, with its religious symbology, it might be thought that the Grid or mega computer was God! Or the Universal and Formative Mind, or whatever else it has been associated with. I was somewhat relieved when L.Kin quoted the Indian definition of "Akasha", as "universal energy", which gives a comparable term to the vacuum energy, and further describes it as "space energy". For the process of imprinting on the Akashic Record, L.Kin states: "conscious thought acting upon the potential of substance brings forth real substance such as space, energy and matter". Later in his book L. Kin talks of the "Akasha Chronicle " and the theta quanta, which are "attention units" which are the "Akashic Record". Personally I prefer to think of these "attention units", as the holographic imprints laid down as a complete 'cinematographic' record on the electro-magnetic patterning or successive coiling of the morphogenetic and spiritual bioplasmas. Thus Inc.2 which I believe relates to an Atomic explosion and/or a Magnetic Reversal as an event relating to *matter*, would appear on the *morphogenetic bioplasma* and Inc. 1 as a *spiritual event* would occur on the finer and higher graded energy of the *spiritual bioplasma* or the upper half of the Diablo model. It may be that these two diablo halves have different spins one centripetal and the other centrifugal. The UVG120 sphere, Earth crystal, Akashic Record (Earth event) and other such terms, I perceive as being more related to the morphogenetic bioplasma. Trillions of these bioplasmas must occur at the intersections of the windings of electro-magnetic force around the Earth, with resultant gravity due to the spin motion. The spiritual bioplasma is probably exterior to the crystal with the so-called Bloch wall or central point of the Diablo being the boundary of the Grid and a higher level of energy and space.

Physicists I am sure, like Stephen Hawking, would have trouble with 'woolly' terms and personally I prefer my own description and no doubt the Scientologists will stick to the letter of Ron Hubbard; but the important point to be made I believe, is that the Akashic Record is a fact, the trap is a fact and Magnetic Reversals or "catastrophe (s)" are a fact. I have shown archaeological, mythical, occult knowledge, secret group knowledge and scientific knowledge, together with pre-history and which ever way you look at this, you come up with the same conclusion:

1.Beings or a being, attempting to use mind control and achieve political power
2.Misuse of the hidden science and Atomic knowledge.
3.A catastrophe, either atomic, or a Magnetic Reversal probably both and not just once.
4.Extinction of species
5.Spirits trapped, by controlling network (One World Order) and Grid in the vacuum.
6.Deteriorating cycle, with dramatization of the incident.
1.Beings or a being attempting to use mind control etc. through the cycle again.

You can bet your bottom dramatization though, that man will squabble about the minutest detail like discussing how many drips come out of a tap, whilst he stands to be flooded and extinguished. The real hard grind of getting (the Spirit) of every man, woman and child off this Planet in probably the biggest Ark project that the Universe has ever known, would require fantastic effort, speed and co-operation and a level of education, since we simply do not know how long before the next Magnetic Reversal or space boundary according to Harold Aspden. Further, you would have to identify all MRC cases in positions of power; otherwise the effort would be thwarted at every move. It has not surpassed my observation, that the last records on the R6 implant of Hubbard's research, or the Magnetic Reversal according to my own research, were scenes of "modern day England" and "skyscrapers in America" indicating the past scenario may have got to this point, which might explain why the Mayan calendar ends so abruptly circa 2010 A.D. However, if all nuclear weapons and matter and anti-matter experiments, along with HAARP and GWEN or any research including Space programmes, which might interfere with the Grid and electro-magnetic patterning, including tapping the zero-point energy were put on hold, until we can assess the problem, there may be considerably more time. One is again reminded of the biblical Apocalypse, and the cataclysm that comes: "like a thief in the night". Unfortunately you can't even get independent advertising or magazines to print the Petition Questions! – Some hope then!

The MRC case it would appear is a unique case through his spiritual memory banks, rather than just the product of a Magnetic Reversal. Indeed his continual sequestering of the hidden science and his probable retrieval of the phylogenetic record along with event data from the Grid, which he takes to a location *outside* of Earth and thus avoids a Magnetic Reversal, may mean that he continually returns to Earth with a good phylogenetic line or body, which the MRC case obsessively dramatizes in his racial programmes. Those who experience the Magnetic Reversal would be in considerably worse shape spiritually and would on a number of these cycles become insane, which may account for the continuing deterioration of man. The bodyline or phylogenetic line that emerges on Earth after a Magnetic Reversal is probably mutated through recombination of holographics on the Grid morphogenetic bioplasma through 'splicing' of the 'threads' (editing) comparable to the process of recombination of genes in the physical DNA (*Fig. 43*). This may account for Neanderthal man and the punctuated (fits and starts) that have been noticed in evolution. Further when the MRC case returns, he may download the entire memory of Earth again into the Grid from a crystal? Or through the magnetic Ley lines on Earth via the process that Bruce Cathie proposed for Stonehenge. The necessity for Grid information storage, may or may not account not only for those computer cluster Cray E-Mass systems currently being built, with a page file into the ionsphere-150 miles high, but may account for the fact that recall of Inc. 1 implies a controlling source *outside* Earth who manipulate man. This becomes 'spliced' into the memory banks of the individual (Spirit) at the time of a Magnetic Reversal and perhaps becomes confused with the first incident along this line, when perhaps Xenu *was* the controller, who along with his 'gang' tried to manipulate the vortices or morphogenetic bioplasma of the species and mankind: with a view to producing a slave species, which is the goal of all One World Orders. They did however become trapped by their own dramatization of the 'script' that has been played out on Theatre Earth over billions of years. Thus I concluded that any control was right here, on Earth. The difference between these conclusions and those of Hubbard, is that I am sure Scientologists believe, that the evil force still exists *outside* of Earth, rather than that force being resident *on* Earth and only *returning* to Earth in 'Noah's Ark', after a Magnetic Reversal, presumably in a space ship, which probably accounts for the natural UFO phenomenon which does include reports of a space craft and mechanical beings. When auditors audit the thoughts of Xenu, are they auditing the thoughts of the PAST, on the Akashic Record? In much the same way as the channeller believes he is talking to an actual spirit on the outside?

In fact I first started to pick up the MRC case as a psychological case from Hubbard's description of the "Anti-Social Personality". Whilst Hubbard never went on to identify the exact causation of this personality, I noticed that Hubbard had maintained that this personality: "cannot finish a cycle of action". This must result from the billions of years that the MRC case, which I might have to revise as the MMRC (*Missed* Magnetic Reversal Case), has sought to avoid the Magnetic Reversal and thus has a repetitive cycle of action that **Starts** (plant the vine) **change** (create order and One World Order) and **stop** (avoidance of Magnetic Reversal). He can't finish a cycle of action, simply because in successive cycles he never completes his goal of total control, before the cycle is forced to start again. This depends on misuse of the hidden science and part of that misuse has been the secrecy, surrounding it. For this reason alone, I cannot support Hubbard's idea of retaining knowledge in secret hierarchal levels, which appears to rotate around the idea of profit (and control?) If Hubbard went on to find the way of auditing out the engram (past trauma) of the Magnetic Reversal, then that would be a very good thing, since inevitably those that have this incident would find themselves unable to leave, until they have erased it. I do not know whether the information alone is sufficient to allow exit, but certainly if one understands the physics it probably would. However to market the price of exit out of the realistic reach of any but an elite who can afford to pay the price tag, was not the original intention, when the OT levels were first taught in the Palaeolithic Age! c. 10 000 B.C. The message and knowledge was meant **FOR ALL** and the Early Minoans gave this information away for free: although granted, money was not a problem then until times got tough when the second plank of Marxism - taxation arrived, care of the global elite. Times have changed and money is now a reality, but Phoenix on this very question of money, has a point. If a Magnetic Reversal came to tomorrow, then the whole technology would go down the plughole and it would take millions of years to evolve a challenge to the One World Order and their control of such knowledge and further there is no assurance, that man will receive help again from elsewhere, in which case he is stuck with the MMRC for all eternity. Also, it is highly probable that the MMRC would probably totally control such knowledge on the next cycle, if he has not done so already.

Fig.43 *Examples of chromosome mutations*

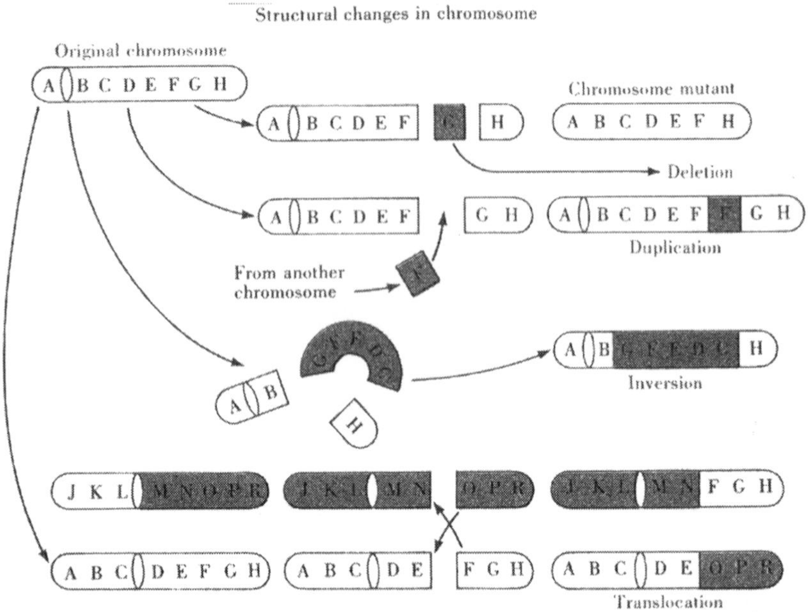

Structural changes in chromosome

If my summation of the MRC case is correct, then the MRC case himself knows that he is trapped, but continually Re-incarnates on the lines of secret groups and continually restimulates himself, thus his psychological case is a complete dramatization of the past and he becomes stuck in the event, obsessively dramatizing the 'script'. His obsession with the past, races and pre-history of the event, merely adds to that re-stimulation, its like picking away at a sore, it merely gets worse. As sure as night follows day, he will bring about the same end for this cycle, simply because he sleepwalks the past, page by page of the book of *Revelations* (presumably the alternative one to the Vulgate version and held by the secret groups), hanging on to his Covenant. If you ask how will he produce the end of the cycle, then look at the past and now look in the present field of atomic physics and the anti-matter matter experiments (including the black ops secret type) look at atomic detonations and zero-point energy research with HAARP and GWEN; look at the field of genetic engineering and look at the political scene, as we head precariously and speedily towards that **third battle** (mentioned in the Indian myth, legend and as Armageddon in *Revelations*) and presumably a third World War, care of the One World Order and the end of the cycle. As I observed, God will never let you shake hands with him, you will get a wrap on the head and be made to go back to the beginning of the lesson! And surely there is a lesson on Earth that has not been learnt. As Einstein was also to remark: "God does not play dice", there is an inevitable predictability of events if Natural Laws are challenged.

The first computer 'Colossus', invented by Alan Turin, who helped to decode the German war time code Enigma, was a relatively simple affair compared to today's computers and in a similar fashion the Grid was a simple affair compared to today's Akashic Record - the mega-computer and presents in each Magnetic Reversal cycle, the possibility of raising man's consciousness, whilst also challenging him to solve the programmes of its memory banks. How to get out of the crystal maze, is the entire problem and if people had stuck with the OT programme down in Palaeolithic times, that's the answer they would have been given. The zero- point energy or vacuum plasma may also exhibit the property of recursively forming higher order helical filaments. This may provide some connection with the physicists' super-string theories.[149] In the book *Beyond Einstein*, the superstring theory appears as the most promising, for unifying all four fundamental forces (strong nuclear, weak nuclear, electromagnetic and gravitation). The fundamental unit in this theory, is *a filament* on the order of 10^{-33}cm (the same size as Wheeler's Wormholes), that can form a Mobius loop. Stephen Hawking in his book *A Brief History of Time* [150] covers string theories, which work if you have lots of dimensions. If a *plasma filament* were to close in on itself, it would produce a *stable toroidal vortex ring*, called a plasmoid. It is curious that Scientology auditors of Inc.2, the "implant", have reported cinematic pictures (holographs?) being shown in a *"tunnel or tube"*, rather like a system of pipes, which might indicate that the Spirit in the ensuing chaos of either a space boundary event of Magnetic Reversal, becomes caught up in this system of 'tubes' or 'pipes' as the bioplasmoids are disrupted from their torroidal vortex rings. The bioplasmoids or 'filaments' corresponding to the 'pipes' would then re-form stable configurations of the type I indicated for the morphogentic bioplasma and ultimately must be directed by a greater pattern, the Diablo.

In the virtual zero-point energy plasma, the higher order filaments or strings that close into loops yield the elementary particles and since the plasma is torroidal, one expects spin on particles. The self- organizational behaviours of plasmas, have been well observed and on a large scale have recently been proposed as the dominant mechanism for the formation of galaxies. Hans Alven proposed the theory of a plasma self-organizing Universe, which may fit the Diablo model. Plasma filaments and vortices also play a key role in galaxy formation.[151]The opposing filaments of the DNA in the cell organised into a helical spiral which is double stranded, could be represented in the bioplasma vortex i.e. two opposing helical filaments. If the vortex rotates in spinning or whorling motion, then research shows that a direct method of yielding a pulsed orthorotation of the zero-point energy flux, may arise from abruptly pulsed, opposing electro-magnetic fields. A device suggested to accomplish this is the caduceus coil, [152-153] the sign of the healing profession in Greece and the staff (or central herm) with entwined snakes of Asklepios, discussed in my prior research. The coil or caduceus symbolically represents Hermes as combined Twin Kings and Goddess, the staff being the central Herm, with the implication of Hermes chariot in Inc.1 and the controlling group that overtook Knossos and stole the cosmology data. The caduceus also represents the organisation of the DNA helix itself. The attempts to patent the genetic code, thus take on a new and significant and somewhat dramatizing role, a role that has been played out before on the World's stage, with the desire for a slave species - whether that be Hermes, Zeus as Captain *thirteen* of the Twelve Olympians, or total control by Xenu. The Arch controller has probably been known by many names in many times, but his goals have never altered.

The coil or caduceus is comprised of two identical windings of opposite helicity. The winding must exhibit identical mirror image symmetry, for a pulse travelling up both windings would have their rising and falling waveform edges aligned. The filaments of the DNA helix no doubt represent a physical configuration of the higher vacuum vortex or morphogenetic bioplasma pattern - displaying the hermetic principle of 'as above, so below'. It has been proposed that the rising and falling edges in the bucking field transient produces hyperspatial, toroidal vortex rings that exhibit electromagnetic scalar and longitudinal components in their 3-space projection.[154] I suspect, that the double helix of DNA with its two filaments is arranged in a particular direction or North South orientation, that fits with the arrangement or pattern of the morphogentic bioplasma. Biologically speaking there must be from the point of view of survival of the species a different South, North direction or arrangement that occurs under a Magnetic Reversal. Giants and dinosaurs existed under a different magnetic field and one perceives that there must be a corresponding biochemistry derived from the re-arrangement of the DNA filaments under those conditions. This re-arrangement may result and probably does result, from the re-arrangement of the morphogentic bioplasma or vacuum pattern after a Magnetic Reversal.

There is a basic difference between my own cosmological and energetic interpretation of the Akashic Record and morphogenetic bioplasma, to Hubbard's interpretation, although according to L.Kin in covering Hubbard's OT levels, Xenu gained agreement from a Council (of which Hubbard was allegedly a member) to cunningly make matter, energy and space more durable, whilst tricking the members of that Council. Theta quanta (energy) were trapped and disengaged from source and the thetan (Spirit), by enturbulating them through a *spinning motion* and further commanding them: " to conform to *basic geometrical patterns*". This I assume is the conformation of control by the UVG 120 sphere or crystal *geometric vacuum matrix*. I personally see the spinning and whorling motion as a constant feature of this Universe, and the sub atomic particles and even galaxies and planets. However there is no doubt, that the conclusion of the trap, as a 'spiders web' with man trapped and controlled by it is a reality. That trap was being taught to students in Paleolithic times and Bronze Age Crete.

In my own estimation of Inc.2 and possibly Inc.I, it is possible and I think likely, that what Hubbard calls and "implant", implying active manipulation, may well have been the downloading of the entire Akashic Record or master morphogenetic bioplasma files ('the hardware or C drive') onto the 'floppy disc' or Spiritual being memory banks. The result of this undoubtedly would create a slave species, in so far as subconsciously the person or Spiritual Being would follow the imprinted or holographic ("implant") instructions. Those who try to warn mankind of the Conspiratorial nature of Earth and events as they happen have been continually amazed at the zombie-like platitude of the 'Joe' public. *On Target* magazine which is the most professional front-line informative publication seeking to expose the background to world events (and World Order) as they happen, which is where the real news lies, produced two volumes [155] in Oct. 1999; covering 'Conspiracy, Revolution and Moral Decay'.
Part 2 quoted James Gibb Stuart on "Lemming Britannicus":

> "He's the fellow who blankly refuses to see any threat to our society at all, who reckons that if he does his little bit in his own regular groove, takes good care of Number One, and pays no attention to alarms and excursions off-stage, the United Nations, the International Court of Justice and the Convention of Human Rights will ensure that no harm ever comes to him and his. For this type of myopic lemming, all that stuff about the *price of freedom being eternal vigilance* is just so much out-moded rhetoric. Sophisticated wise guy that he is, he *knows* that if there was anything in these conspiracy or subversion scares, he would be hearing about it regularly on the telly. And when he reads his newspaper, - which he does faithfully, - he accepts both the fact and the comment with equal weight and judgement. If it's not true, he says, what would be the point of printing it? And when it comes to that hair-raising stuff about collectivism by stealth, totalitarian democracy, Marxism by the back door, he's mostly inclined to tell the kids to turn up the sound, so that he can hear what they're doing and saying on *Coronation Street* or Larry-what-you-call-it- 'im's *Generation Game*".

This is probably the same in all countries as Lemming Homo Sapiens not wishing to confront the deep spiritual issues that lie before him, in part as a result of Grid programming, but more causatively as a result of dark spiritual forces that seek to keep him down and ignorant; as he follows the worn out path of many incarnations and the familiar holographs of past scenes and thoughts now downloaded onto his memory banks. In fact a man could go OT (Operating Theta or Spirit in Scientology speak) or tomorrow, he has only to question what lies before him today and his role in it. He has only to stop using the SELF-SURVIVALIST MIND, the Universal Mind that is the Grid. The Mental Asylum that is Earth. As Hubbard once commented: "shortly they will have to put an electronic fence around it" - and that is what has happened, with the inmates following orders from a Mega-Computer. The awful thing is, that the more you know, the more you have take responsibility for, thus in having read this book, I am afraid it puts you back in a very big ball game, where your action now, will be played back to you in the Life Review and horror of horrors! You as a Spirit (which is pure conscience and good) will judge yourself harder than any court may do. I think it was Hubbard who said something like there is no such thing as failure, a man just did not have enough courage, or go far enough.

What is certain is that myth, legend and religious texts, speak of Evil from the beginning on Earth and the attempts to create a slave species. This is none other than Communistic doctrine run by the rich Elite far right. The fact that the Grid has such sentience or apparancy of thought and appears to some as real spiritual personages and not past recorded thought, leads some to believe that Masters exist in the Etheric layer. When magicians like Crowley sought information from the Etheric layer, they believed no doubt, that they were contacting these Masters, but it was past thought and event. Hubbard maintained that Xenu who sought total control, managed to initiate the obsession with solidification of bodies by encouraging Thetans to occupy "doll bodies" (a transparent body) an amorphous shape presumably accounting for the amorphous shapes left on Cave walls in Palaeolithic times. The purest form of a crystal is transparent, thus one might consider that Xenu had been experimenting with control of Spirits for quite some time! After all one Spirit in a crystal is not as good as a few billion in a crystal! Is it not curious that cloning, as a current dramatization of the past and the desire to create a slave species, should create the first cloned sheep and call it "Dolly"! And what is more she was produced at the Rosslyn (**Rose-line**) Institute in Scotland! Dolly triggered a storm of controversy and protest, as man subconsciously recognised the dangerous precipitous ravine over which he stands to fall, namely the cloning of human beings which has predictably arrived - where researchers and Biotechnology companies are accused of "Playing God" (Did they mean Satan?) Curiously too, the use of animal organs in humans, which stands to confuse the morphogenetic bioplasma and phylogenetic master blueprint, is a process termed <u>Xeno</u> transplantation. Should we not change the accusation to 'playing Xenu!' Some dramatization!!

YATRUS (Originated by L. Kin)

According to Hubbard and OT auditors, there is another implant between Inc.I and Inc.2 - the "Middle Implant", which is the result of Xenu attempting to control Yatrus. Significantly Yatrus was the **13th** member of a Council of twelve. Well this all begins to look familiar, reminding one of the 13th lost tribe of Judah; the twelve disciples and Jesus makes the 13th member; Arthur and his twelve knights and the Druids with their Ogham script and Beth-Luis Nion alphabet of 13 consonants and months of the year - Mosaic law; and Zeus as Captain thirteen of the twelve Olympians. Rudolf Steiner maintained that twelve Buddha's sitting around Vishua Karman, the 13th member and the central master or Herm, **determined the fate of the world** according to the Vedas (Hermes?). The myth of Icelandic Edda mentions 12 gods residing in Asgard with Odin the 13th member and Master. The monotheism or Patriarchal God is encompassed in the 13th member as Jesus became 'Son of God', laid on the baetyllic herm, or central pillar in the tomb of Golgotha with its symbolisation of a Sun King, by the two upright pillars and lintel across the opening of the tomb. This symbolisation can be clearly seen in the Lion's Gate at Mycenae *(Plate 7)* in the Peloponnese and where Sun Kings ruled. Thus Jesus was meant to portray the 13 Th member or Hermes a combination of Twin Kings and Mother Goddess in one personage, thus removing the woman in the story.

Yatrus was a subtle controller of Spirits according to Hubbard, using persuasion and swamping their thoughts with his own, cunningly twisting their purposes until they absorbed his thoughts, believing they were operating on their own. Are we sure we are not talking about the One World Order here and the religious goal of Hermes in his chariot that occurred in Inc.1? If Xenu used energy, then Yatrus used postulates and God (hermetic God?). Yatrus broke every promise he had ever made. To quote L. Kin "He starts off with an outwardly friendly and winning approach, thus gaining the trust and agreement of his victim, proceeds to suck the life juice out of him, drops him like an empty shell and considers this perfectly alright". Speaking from soul memory this would adequately describe the tribes of Judah and Levi. We certainly recognise the MMRC case here. His postulate "Do what you like". Sounds very familiar, if we remember Alister Crowley and his Book of Thelema: "Do what thou wilt is the whole of the law"; which Hitler paraphrased in Mein Kampf and which seems to have become the battle cry of the One World Order with politicians now in tow.

The goal of Yatrus was the control of *organic life*, through what Hubbard termed the "Genetic entity", which I would term the morphogenetic biofield. Yatrus *distorted the information* according to Hubbard and *added his own data*, thus controlling life energy - the "**Lambda Project**". L. Kin admits that there are no time tags (dates) on the incident: "due to lack of extensive cross-confirmation".

Further the data is fairly new. L. Kin expands on this incident in his own book but admits that obtaining the data is like "single frames scattered over a film roll a few hundred miles long and these may become interpreted differently as more certainty and data accumulate". Thus despite this, the information is there and must represent real past incidents on the Akashic Record. A brief overall view of the incident runs:

1. Yatrus suggests pairing of thetans. "Give each other energy "help each other to purify energies". So they can enter state of Godliness before Inc. I.
2. The Council of Twelve like the idea.

The outcome of the incident that was a Yatrus trick was:

1. The Spirit had to obtain energy from another, initiating the idea of energy scarcity, rather than energy from self-generation.
2. Thetans compared themselves to the Angelic images in Inc.1 (and pre-1 incidents). Imagery of Gods and Angels from Inc.1 were used.
3. Pairs created and ideas of fusion of Spirits "You and I forever" (postulate) "Shan't ever part" (postulate) After this bodies came on the scene, so arrived sex, lust and desire.

Thus: "two -someness, love as an exchange of sweet vibrations, bodies, sex - it went in that sequence". Thus families, relationships ultimately derived from the initial "eternal pact" or "cosmic mate", which was indispensable for one's survival.

Let me give another perspective, Hubbard's assumption or the initial data, which L. Kin agrees is sketchy is that Spirits were initially alone and static and during this incident the "two-some" was bonded in a "shower of light" composed of Yatrus theta quanta, where each quantum carried the postulate "I need you!" The association is further explained as thetan A and thetan B made their energy fields ("theta bodies") overlap so as to form a third field C; which consisted of the theta quanta of A and B in fairly equal proportions and was granted a life of its own. Yatrus apparently used this field "thetan offsprings" for fabrication of Genetic entities (tri-partite biofield of the embryo?) a long time later. Hubbard explains the Genetic Entity as: "that beingness not dissimilar to the thetan, which has carried forward and developed the body from its earliest moment along the evolutionary line on Earth...It has no real personality, it is not the "I" *of the body*. This is the "mind" of an animal, a cat or cow".

Thus I assume that the Genetic Entity is really what I have termed the tri-partite or three-layered biofield around the body of the embryo, which is an energetic field that connects to the master blueprint or morphogenetic bioplasma, which controls not only the shape of the animal or phylogenetic line, but also the particular biochemistry of that species. In other words, the tri-partite biofield is the "jelly mould" that Dr. Becker and Harold S. Burr and Sheldrake spoke of in their research. The biofield as I explain in the Cancer research document and briefly here, is a primitive field and mind that is governed by instructions from the morphogenetic bioplasma and concerned with the survival of the species. It is this field, which is responsible ultimately for the tumour growth in Cancer, since it cannot compute *emotional loss*, or differentiate between that and *body loss*. It is in effect a primitive mind. Loss of relationship, job, loved one, material possessions etc are a restimulant to his field through resonant vibration of emotion. The analytical mind has shut down; the Spirit (the driver) is running behind the 'car' (the body) no longer in control and passes control to the primitive mind, the tri-partite biofield that resonates with the morphogenetic bioplasma, containing the master blueprint for survival. Thus the primitive mind is left to solve the problem of the threat in the environment. The solution that is provided is irrational to an analytical mind and to a Spirit, but to a primitive mind and its programmes, the solution of grow a tumour is perfectly rational and survivalist, since it believes it has lost a body part! It will according to morphogenetic blueprint mechanisms grow you a very nice embryo (the tumour) and try to replace your body parts for you! The primitive mind computes that loss has occurred, there are no data banks or programmes for loss of jobs, relationships etc, since this is a primitive animal-like mind. Loss to this mind only computes as loss of body, thus it assumes the resonant vibration (information received), is data requiring solution to loss of body part. It logically (to an animal mind) grows a tumour that is cellular embryonic growth explosion: and when you look at the biochemistry for the tumour as I did in the Cancer Report, you will find that a tumour exhibits embryonic biochemistry. Now when the individual does not run away or fight the loss (primitive survival mechanism of 'fright and flight' in animals) the primitive mind gets confused, because the vibration does not cease it increases and the tumour goes wild and grows more. The person meanwhile has reduced their biofield to a quivering wreck, having lost job, relationship etc. and now they have Cancer! The master morphogenetic bioplasma, which connects with the biofield, presumably through the crown chakra by morphic resonance, only contains this type of solution in the master Blueprint that computes:

LOSS = LOSS OF BODY PART = **GROW** = EMBRYONIC BIOCHEMISTRY = **TUMOUR**

LOSS IS THE RESTIMULANT. The therapy I applied was aimed at differentiation between emotional loss and body loss and releasing charge, thus balancing the biofield.

The Yatrus incident does have some indication that we are dealing with the morphogenetic bioplasma, since I described it as a whorling vortex or plasma and this "spinning", is mentioned in the Yatrus incident. Whilst Yatrus is pinpointed as "distorting information" and "adding his own" again one might be looking at the Akashic Record, for the species i.e. evolutionary or phylogenetic history recorded on the morphogenetic bioplasma. This begins to look like manipulation of the biofield and genetic engineering, which is of course being wildly dramatized in present time! I did suggest curiously enough in my own research as a basis for the MMRC case, that a being (or beings) outside of Earth tried to manipulate the morphogenetic bioplasma in some game of control, aimed at producing a slave species and once they descended to Earth, got caught in a cycle of control as previously described. Yatrus may have been such a being who sought to produce a slave species and the ideal body form and type which was dramatized in the Aryan Super Race programme. The fact that Yatrus is associated as 13 th member, with the Council of Twelve, strongly indicates that the Yatrus incident, is some past incident involving the Adamites or tribe of Judah and prior to that the Atlanteans, and one assumes and a mind and body control programme. I discussed how such a programme might manipulate the biofield today in *Alternative4,* but this could also be the method of control in the past.

According to Hubbard a thetan or spirit re-incarnates into a body and after the death of that body, re-incarnates into another body. The Genetic Entity or what I would term the tri-partite biofield, according to Hubbard merges with the general Genetic Entity field and data pool. I have already spoke of the phantom leaf effect in Kirlean photography, whereby the aura or biofield and overall "jelly mould " remains even though the physical leaf has gone, with the possibility of the remaining energy field recombining with the morphogenetic bioplasma or master blueprint pattern and energy. Thus, the tri-partite biofield may re-unite with the vacuum energy and thus takes the information it contains, relating to the life history of the plant or leaf with it re-uniting with the central data pool that is the morphogenetic bioplasma. However, I have concluded there is a two-way biofeedback information system throughout the life of the individual plant or animal, through the transmitter and receiver properties of DNA and the double stranded helicity of the helix or hyperbolic spiral of the DNA molecule. This means, that the morphogenetic blueprint or bioplasma in the matrix of the UVG120 sphere is not a static data bank, but changes and constantly monitors, as that great Eye of Intelligence in the sky, the survival of the individual in relation to the environment. Thus in this way the morphogenetic bioplasma receives information which is processed in the master blueprint, in order to maintain the master pattern, which is required for overall survival of the species.

What does all this mean? Well we know, that the master morphogenetic blueprint codes and records data on the survival of the species, but it *also* contains events in the history of Earth, since those events are concerned with survival of the *history of matter* and bodies. Further we know that there is a "two-some" in so far as the DNA is double stranded and the 'filaments' or electro-magnetic coils within the morphogenetic bioplasma, are in two stranded filament form. This may be important in maintaining the species in the event of a Magnetic Reversal where the magnetic north and south poles reverse, with a corresponding polarity reversal of the filaments in the morphogenetic bioplasma and the physical DNA in the cells, which produces new bodies better equipped to cope with the new gravity conditions and polarity field on Earth. We also know, that thought of the primitive mind is also coded on the morphogenetic bioplasma and this appears to contain thought connected to changes in matter i.e. thought connected to the hidden science. Such thought can be channelled in relation to physical matter events on Earth. Yatrus may be no more, than a complex pre-history of planet Earth, involving manipulation of body lines and races, which we know were dramatized excessively, coupled with genetic manipulation and presumably cloning, where there *was* "addition" and "distortion" of the genetic or phylogenetic line. The mention of coupling and "two-somes" together with the idea "you and I forever", which arises when people access this incident by regression, means that the interpretation of data, may be more complexly compounded into a story by the person undergoing regression. I have covered before, the point that the mind must make sense of the incoming data and thus a sequence of events on the morphogenetic bioplasma record, may be confused into a story that does not necessarily represent the real sequential story and further may be modified according to the experience of the person accessing such holographs. For instance the person gets the impression of "two-some" (which may be the geometric double helicity of the bioplasma organisation *or* matter and anti-matter) and the person further has the feeling that this has something to do with bodylines (the double helicity of the DNA molecule) and then they perceive there is some controlling force here (Yatrus or body control) and a further feeling that this double stranded nature somehow gives the postulate "you an I forever (the cyclical events on Earth care of the MMRC case *or* the matter anti-matter). Sex invariably gets mixed up with body lines and has a long record on the physical events that happened to bodies on Earth, thus it would not be unusual to find this on the morphogenetic bioplasma, particularly as it is strongly indicated in survival. However, it might be wrong to conclude that a soul mate is a bad idea and originating with Yatrus. One might certainly agree, that relationships drain one of energy conducted as they are on Earth, but one could conceive of a mate, that represents the dance of matter and anti-matter in the universe. Each partner of the pair having different but necessary qualities that provide a high energy action pairing. However, one is also reminded, that after all things are considered, there is just you and your own spiritual ability.

Thus one might conclude, that Yatrus is again a part of the holographics of data stored on the morphogenetic bioplasma combining survival of body lines and events that have in the past and present sought to control that phylogenetic line. Yatrus may be just a historical MMRC case, just as perhaps Xenu is and who find their current embodiment in the One World Order who in present time merely dramatize their past history of events and thought. They might even have incarnated today and probably have. In Hubbard's book *Scientology: A History of Man*, he gives the evolutionary line of the body as it evolved and different auditing accounts of the types of body that man as a Spirit has occupied - from Molluscs up! Whilst that is considered peculiar and somewhat unbelievable, the morphogentic bioplasma does indeed carry the complete history or phylogenetic line for all species including man. Such data is glimpsed as the holographics of some part of this history have impinged on UFO witnesses. In terms of the Genetic Entity or what I would call the tri-partite biofield of the body in morphic resonance with the morphogenetic bioplasma, it might be interesting to state what Dr. Tiller of Stanford University [156] gave as a quantum physical explanation of what was being photographed in the phantom leaf experiment:

"A basic idea in radionics is that each individual organism or material radiates and absorbs energy via unique wave field which exhibits certain geometrical frequency and radiation type characteristics. This is an extended force field that exists *around all forms of matter* whether animate or in animate. A useful analogy here is the physical atom that is continually radiating electro-magnetic energy in the form of waves because of its oscillating electric development and its thermal vibrations. The more complex the materials, the more complex the wave forms. The fundamental carrier wave, is thought to be *polarised* with a *rotating* polarization vector. The information concerning the glands, body systems etc., ripples the carrier waver and seems to be associated with a specific phase modulatioion of the wave for a specific gland. Regions of space associated with a given phase angle of the wave constitute a three-dimensional network of points extending throughout space. To be in resonance with any one of these points is to be in resonance with the particular gland of the entity. The capability of scanning the waveform of the gland exists for the detection of abnormalities. Likewise, if energy having the normal or healthy waveform of the gland is pumped into any of the specific network points, the gland will be driven into healthy mode. This produces a tendency for its structure to re-organise itself in close alignment with the normal structure, i.e. healing of the gland occurs". (*Author's emphasis*)

564

Apart from the potential for Medicine and cancer, the obvious point here is the biofield is an INFORMATION FIELD, concerned with the survival of the body and that information field is in contact with a greater information field, the morphogenetic bioplasma or Akashic Record. There is no doubt that the tri-partite biofield is a resonating field of energy and as such it will itself, be modified by resonance, either through emotion or thought which creates emotion; just as I could show on my computer programme and research, that a thought was capable of altering that bio field, then by reverse the biofield can alter mental attitudes and thinking which can then be communicated to the master survival blueprint or morphogenetic bioplasma. Body, Mind and Spirit are connected through resonating energy fields, with each having the power to affect any of the other fields. Hubbard however I perceive states that this field of energy surrounding the body and what he calls the Genetic Entity, was created in the Yatrus incident and it was through this field that he started to control thetans (Spirits). This is interesting from the point of view of my research in *Alternative 4*, where I maintained that such manipulation of the human biofield, may have already occurred in manipulated (unnatural) UFO incidents, by those who were testing out technology, which might become the manner in which a psychocivilised (mind and body controlled) society is ordered. A number of unofficial statements by those in high places have already indicated since the 70's that this is the way the One World Order are headed. Mind Control is very much on the agenda and is part of the One World Order programme, which should come as no surprise! Equally, there is nothing to discount the possibility, that in the natural UFO phenomenon a flux of energy through the geometric matrix, such as solar flux, or research which manipulates that geometric, did not cause these past holographics to impinge on the UFO witness. Thus the natural UFO event could be an experience of Inc.1 and/or Inc. 2 and/or theYatrus incident. This in some cases is bourne out by the feeling in UFO witnesses, that some religious experience has occurred, or an "initiation" and since Inc.1 is particularly related to archetypal symbols from the history of the tribe of Judah and the Religious revolution in Crete and further Atlantean pre-history or myth, then this might explain such feelings. Further all the symbolisation of the god Hermes is present, indicating that data from this cycle has been imprinted on the spiritual bioplasma, for which reason I find the use of these symbols and archetypes by Hollywood unacceptable.

The Biofield has 7 main centres of energy vortices, which are termed chakras. Hubbard maintains that this field or Genetic Entity as he calls it, was "stamped" with seven energy modules. To cut a long story short, which I will leave you to read in L. Kin's book, Yatrus it is maintained, managed to hitch Spirits up with bodies on the postulate of "You and I forever"; which became the obsessive "must have one". However, I prefer to think of the necessity of bodies and the obsession with matter, as part of the matter Universe created by the separation of anti-matter from matter and the diablo geometry. Man as his spirit having taken a left turn so to speak into the matter Universe must take on the *postulates of survival of matter* and be restricted by the physical laws of matter and energy. Aesthetics become reduced on a scale to the point where one finds beauty in matter itself and thus it is perhaps understandable that the Earth in the beginning captivated the Spirit, as it was truly a beautiful place as far as matter goes. However the sun has created a trap in the electro-magnetic lines of force around the Earth with its own crystal, formed when the Earth cooled. The crystal could store information and did so, faithfully recording the events of Earth and thought associated with matter and thus developed its own sentience or apparent thinking, just as a computer with data banks appears to do. The MMRC case however obsessed with his control of matter and the hidden science created events on Earth, that were recorded along with his thought and that of the Cabalist magicians and thus it appeared that the crystal was in fact a region of *exterior* control by actual beings: the so-called Masters and Guardians or Angels etc. The problem of complexity of data storage by the Akashic Record or morphogenetic bioplasma arose when magicians or the black cabalists, continually sought to alter matter and thus thoughts from the MMRC are intermingled with thoughts from the cabalists. Over many years, there would be a history of thought and personalities, which could give rise to the notion, that channelling was a method of contacting these apparent spirits, but in fact no more than holographic recordings of past events and thought.

According to Hubbard the first bodies were not solid, but transparent and had definite shapes and were fairly human. Now here I would propose another scenario, which might be worth any Scientology Auditor looking into which is: What exactly constituted the moment of birth of a Spirit? What was the initial incident? - A singularity as the physicists calls it. Was there an anti-matter, matter explosion where two beings our self and our anti-self the doppelganger were formed? Is this the duality "two-some" incident that has mistakenly been labelled an "implant"? In that first moment, when we as a Spirit became observation point and started recording our 'film rolls', of the entire time track of existence, did we make ourselves more solid or transparent, in order **to view something**? "You and me forever", or matter and anti-matter as simply a postulate of ' REMAINING OBSERVATION POINT' IN ORDER TO HAVE AN ETERNAL GAME. If as Hubbard maintained that a Spirit has no mass, by Einstein's equation it can have no energy and you can't by the laws of Physics get something for nothing, not even an Observation Point. Thus if you agree to Observation Point and a game, you must agree to two Universes of you and your doppelganger or matter and anti-matter. The occult observation of: "out of one came many", could apply to different Universes and the agreement of becoming observation point; after all an observation point has many views (Universes) does it not. Perhaps the physicist might say that after the matter and anti-matter explosion we as Spirit could not help in our own creation to become that observation point as we danced the game of "two-somes" in the firmament. Whose thought caused matter and anti-matter to collide and explode which saw our birth as spirits? – Well that must be God's country and prime thought and mover. Thus perhaps our game has deteriorated from making planets and playing with energy to being content, to be organised like bees in a hive by the crystal or mega computer, not remembering who made the programmes, whilst we sit and watch simulated holographs (the telly).

Hubbard maintained that a spirit was static - stationary. However I am of the opinion that we danced that first dance of the spirit in the firmament, with our doppelganger (our anti-self), the dance of the figure-of–8, dumb-bell, electron orbital, DNA filament, 'filaments' of the morphogenetic bioplasma and Diablo: we passed easily on the spiralling wave and pulse of matter in a 360 degree circle and the pulse of anti-matter in a 360 degree circle, we WERE THE PATTERN AND THE DANCE. Viewpoint was (a) You and (b) anti-you "You and I forever". As the Physicist knows from the two-slit experiment, the electron changes properties from particle to wave (solid and not solid) and vice versa and once you view it, the particle becomes a wave and is no longer solid or particle! The observer cannot remain outside the experiment or the pattern, since he is part of it. Quite simply when he can't see the pattern any more, when he thinks he is no longer part of it, the electron becomes a particle (matter) and more and more solid to him. If you could *totally* confront and view everything it would probably disappear! Why is the ability to change viewpoint so essential? Control and solidity always takes the form of: "don't look over there it's too dangerous". Don't look at cancer, the mind, Scientology, money etc. The man with a very fixed viewpoint at the bottom of the pile, or the man that enforces a strict and stagnant viewpoint on others, his will be done and all that, is one who sees *very* solid objects. He has fallen to the level of protecting and controlling matter and some religions have fallen that far, they just can't let you look or have a viewpoint! If the Yatrus incident of Hubbard's is recalled as being "one with creation", by solo auditors running the incident, where there is a reported "all-prevalent abundance of life force", then I guess to be born in an antimatter, matter explosion, would certainly have some life force going for it! The birth of a child has a "You and I forever" and the loss of a mother is invariably traumatic for most people, for that reason. Falling in love "Never alone Again", reminds us of that moment in Creation. You can't go back there, even though the physicists are trying hard to put us all back to the beginning, simply because a game dependent on viewpoint and a *learning curve* is dependent on keeping matter and anti-matter separate. You can't shake hands with your doppelganger, or God, or if you did you would not exist in that moment to record it - no game! The moral is clear the chess board has already been set up, the game has started and one can only move forward, since it would be pointless to go back, there would be no game unless you fancy re-living "two-somes" and "you and I forever". Personally I don't see anything wrong with a cosmic mate, think of the divorce bills you would save and the lawyers you would avoid!

The interesting thing about Hubbard's research is that he found the so-called "implant commands" of the incident, which cover 25 pages. The commands, are striking in their noticeable **polarity**. I considered whether these so-called commands could be an interchange of viewpoints, in the polarity and duality after a matter, anti-matter explosion. Equally the so-called commands might be the sort of thought processes a Spirit went through, caught up in a Magnetic Reversal as it tried to locate itself in the north south polarity change and chaos, ' running through the pipes' or bioplasmoids (strings,"electronic ribbon" or Akashic Record). Examples of the commands run: "to be nobody - to be everybody"; "to be myself - to be others"; "to do much - to do little"; "to have all - to have none"; "to stay back - to stay forward" and singularities and plurals i.e. aloneness and togetherness and the plurals such as "to be an animal - to be animals". The last point, although I have not seen the full list of commands, looks more like a Magnetic Reversal event, as the Spirit sought to establish anchor points or stability in the turmoil, invariably getting entwined in the "electronic ribbon", or unwound vortex 'filaments' of the morphogenetic bioplasma, which obviously must contain information for animals also. However it is difficult to comment any further on it, as there is not enough data, although it appears that the conflict in thought "to be nobody –to be everybody" is very indicative a Magnetic Reversal event.

It is interesting that Xenu was according to Hubbard, the Arch Mind controller and Yatrus the Arch body controller, which reflects the dual nature of the Diablo geometric with its lower order of data storage in the morphogenetic bioplasma controlling bodies and the phylogenetic line of survival; and the higher order of data storage in the spiritual bioplasma which appears to concern religious events. Thus we might assume, that in the evolving game that has been played in a 360 degree turn of the cycle of matter, is man ready to evolve to a bigger game played on the chess board of anti-matter in another 360 degree turn? The duality and polarity, the anti-matter and matter, the positive and negative, the North and south and philosophical dualism which has given us the game we have played, to the end of **evolving as spiritual beings**. We must applaud Xenu and Yatrus and all the controllers, for a good game, but I fear that it is check mate on this one – game up and over and how to get off the wheel of life was one that Sampson solved by pulling down the two upright pillars to which he was chained, whereupon the heavens fell on him, alternatively he could have found a new game in the anti-matter cycle.